The Crossroads of Competition Law and Energy Regulation

Laura Rimšaitė

The Crossroads of Competition Law and Energy Regulation

Springer

Laura Rimšaitė
Legal System Research Department
Law Institute of the Lithuanian Centre for
Social Sciences
Vilnius, Lithuania

ISBN 978-3-031-73237-9 ISBN 978-3-031-73238-6 (eBook)
https://doi.org/10.1007/978-3-031-73238-6

This Springer imprint is published by the registered company Springer Nature Switzerland AG
The registered company address is: Gewerbestrasse 11, 6330 Cham, Switzerland

Contents

Acronyms

ACER	Agency for Cooperation of Energy Regulators
CBAM	Carbon Border Adjustment Mechanism
CFD	Contract for Difference
CHP	Combined Heat and Power
CJEU	The Court of Justice of the European Union
CO_2	Carbon dioxide
EBRD	European Bank for Reconstruction and Development
EC	European Community
EIB	European Investment Bank
ENTSOE	European Network of Transmission System Operators for Electricity
ENTSOG	European Network of Transmission System Operators for Gas
ERGEG	European Regulators' Group for Electricity and Gas
ESA	Euratom Supply Agency
EU ETS	European Union Emission Trading System
EU	European Union
EUR	The euro
Euratom	European Atomic Energy Agency
GATT	General Agreement on Tariffs and Trade
GBER	General Block Exemption Regulation
GW	Gigawatts
HBER	Horizontal Block Exemption Regulation
IAEA	International Atomic Energy Agency
ISO	Independent System Operator
ITO	Independent Transmission Operator
LNG	Liquefied Natural Gas
M&A	Mergers and Acquisitions
MAP	Minimum advertised price
MW	Megawatts
OECD	Organisation for Cooperation and Development
OPEC	Organisation of Petroleum Exporting Countries
OU	Ownership Unbundling

PCI	Project of Common Interest
R&D	Research and Development
RPM	Retail Price Maintenance
RRF	Recovery and Resilience Facility
SDR	Special Drawing Rights
SGEI	Services of General Economic Interest
TEN-E	Trans-European Energy Networks
TFEU	Treaty on the Functioning of the European Union
UK	The United Kingdom
US	The United States of America
USD	United States Dollar
VBER	Vertical Block Exemption Regulation
WTO	World Trade Organisation

Chapter 1
Introduction to the Crossroads of Competition and Energy Regulation

Abstract The convergence of competition law and energy regulation holds enormous significance in an era marked by rapid changes in the global energy sector and a more competitive economic environment. At this juncture, there is a convergence of economic processes, environmental demands, and legal institutions, resulting in a critical point of intersection. This book thoroughly analyses the intricate intersection between competitiveness and energy regulation. This text explores the intricate relationship between these two domains, which have a substantial impact on worldwide energy generation, consumption, and administration. The book explores the regulatory framework that spans both the competition and energy sectors, providing insights into market power and the balance of the regulatory environment. For residential, industrial, and transportation sectors, fossil fuels play a crucial role as essential energy sources, enabling convenience and progress often overlooked. Societies face complex challenges related to market dynamics, environmental concerns, and geopolitical circumstances as they strive to obtain sustainable, secure, and affordable energy sources. The quest for balance has led to the development of competition law and energy regulation as vital elements in upholding fair and competitive markets, as well as guaranteeing access to reliable energy supplies while promoting environmental sustainability.

In a time, characterised by a swiftly changing worldwide energy landscape and a more competitive economic climate, the convergence of competition law and energy regulation has significant importance. This juncture represents a critical point where economic dynamics, environmental necessities, and legal structures collide. This book undertakes an extensive examination of the complex convergence between competition and energy regulation. It delves into the complicated interplay between these two spheres, which significantly influence global energy production, use, and management.

The book investigates the regulatory landscape, which encompasses both the competition and energy sectors, shedding light on market power and the regulatory environment's equilibrium. Energy is unquestionably the fundamental driving force behind contemporary civilization. Fossil fuel serves as a vital energy source for residential, industrial, and transportation sectors, facilitating ease and advancements

L. Rimšaitė, *The Crossroads of Competition Law and Energy Regulation*,
https://doi.org/10.1007/978-3-031-73238-6_1

that are frequently overlooked. As societies endeavour to achieve sustainable, safe, and cost-effective energy supplies, they encounter intricate obstacles pertaining to market dynamics, environmental considerations, and geopolitical factors. The pursuit of equilibrium has resulted in the emergence of competition law and energy regulation as crucial components in maintaining equitable and competitive markets, as well as ensuring the availability of dependable energy sources while fostering environmental sustainability.

The energy sector is currently undergoing a significant and far-reaching evolution. The transition from conventional fossil fuels to sustainable energy sources, the progress made in energy storage and distribution technologies, and the increasing focus on reducing carbon emissions necessitate a reassessment of established energy methodologies. The alterations are fundamentally transforming the energy sector, leading to the emergence of novel stakeholders, innovative technology, and regulatory complexities. Central to this change is a fundamental inquiry: How can we guarantee that the energy sector progresses in a manner that is not solely economically efficient but also socially and environmentally conscientious? Competition law and energy regulation jointly aim to address this fundamental inquiry.

In light of the global movement towards a low-carbon future, it is imperative to foster innovation in clean energy technologies while simultaneously ensuring the presence of competitive markets. This necessitates the careful alignment of policies. State intervention and subsidies can have an impact on market dynamics and raise concerns regarding fair competition and the long-term sustainability of the market, particularly in relation to state support for specific energy technologies. Market liberalisation is a regulatory approach that aims to promote investments, improve efficiency, and enhance consumer benefits by fostering competition in the market. The integration of renewable energy sources is facilitated by placing a strong emphasis on competition within the renewable energy markets. This method not only facilitates the advancement of innovation but also contributes to cost reductions, thereby accelerating the transition towards sustainable energy.

Cross-border cooperation plays a crucial role in facilitating regional collaboration among regulatory authorities, thereby fostering cross-border energy trade, facilitating resource sharing, and promoting market integration. The attainment of an ideal equilibrium is of utmost importance in guaranteeing the preservation of a harmonious distribution of interests. The achievement of a balanced and mutually beneficial relationship between competitive markets and a reliable energy supply requires the successful execution of policy coordination and regulatory alignment. By prioritising consumer interests and concurrently advocating for sustainable energy practises, energy consumers are empowered within a dynamic energy landscape. The promotion of cross-sectoral collaboration plays a significant role in bridging the gap between competition law, energy regulation, and environmental policy, ultimately supporting a comprehensive approach to energy governance.

Competition law, alternatively referred to as antitrust law in certain jurisdictions, has conventionally been assigned the responsibility of curbing monopolistic conduct and upholding equitable competition. It seeks to foster competitive markets by prohibiting anti-competitive practises, monopolistic behaviour, and unfair market dominance. The fundamental tenets of this framework encompass the prohibition of anti-competitive agreements, the misuse of dominant positions, and mergers that have detrimental effects on competition. These concepts are presently being implemented within the complex dynamics of the energy industry. The concept indicated above promotes consumer well-being, innovation, and facilitates efficient resource allocation. Conversely, energy regulation assumes the roles of safeguarding energy security, promoting environmental stewardship, and ensuring consumer protection at the opposite end of the crossroads. The regulatory framework establishes the guidelines and criteria that regulate energy markets, effectively managing the competing interests of energy stakeholders, including generators, distributors, consumers, and environmental concerns. The primary responsibility of energy regulators is to ensure the efficient operation of energy markets, with a focus on delivering dependable services to customers while mitigating adverse external effects.

The intersection of competition law and energy regulation in the ever-evolving energy business is a critical point that significantly impacts the direction of energy markets. The convergence of these prominent spheres signifies a complex and transformative point at which the objectives of promoting fair competition and ensuring a reliable and environmentally friendly energy supply align. Market power in the energy sector has the potential to result in the consolidation of control among a small number of entities, which may have the effect of impeding competition and limiting consumer choice. The task of simultaneously addressing market dominance and promoting energy security presents a substantial challenge.

The process of navigating the crossroads is a complex endeavour that requires careful consideration and strategic decision-making. The dynamic evolution of energy markets and regulatory frameworks gives rise to a convergence of competition law and energy regulation, offering a range of potential benefits and obstacles. What are the best strategies for utilising competition legislation to mitigate anti-competitive behaviours within a sector that exhibits natural monopolies and intricate supplier chains? What strategies may energy regulators employ to achieve a harmonious equilibrium between the principles of market liberalisation and environmental sustainability? These are some of the numerous inquiries that necessitate meticulous examination and inventive resolutions.

The convergence of competition and energy regulation poses several problems and opportunities for shaping the direction of energy markets. To achieve a sustainable and competitive energy landscape, it is crucial for policymakers, regulators, and stakeholders to adeptly navigate this critical point by formulating a clearly articulated vision and promoting cooperative initiatives. The implementation of this approach is of utmost importance in the establishment of a robust, effective, and customer-oriented energy industry.

In the subsequent chapters, this book delves into the inquiries of this convergence, clarifying the possibility for change by integrating competition and energy regulation in the pursuit of a sustainable energy future. Every chapter of this book explores a distinct aspect of the complex junction under study, including scholarly perspectives, analytical evaluations. This book offers a thorough examination of various aspects that shape the future of the energy business, ranging from the effects of mergers in the energy sector on competition to the complexities associated with cross-border energy cooperation.

1.1 Organisation and Content of the Book

This book provides a thorough examination of the suitability of competition legislation in the energy sector and its impact on the achievement of market completion and liberalisation inside the internal market. Legal theory has engaged in a more focused analysis of certain problematic aspects within the institutes of energy and competition. Nonetheless, it is deficient in its ability to offer a comprehensive structure that effectively incorporates obligations for corporations.

The first part of this book explores the historical progression of regulatory frameworks in the energy industry, highlighting the necessity of market liberalisation. This study also examines the interaction between provisions in energy legislation and the requirements imposed by competition law. This analysis aims to explore the issues surrounding the relationship between the Euratom Treaty and the Treaty on the Functioning of the European Union (TFEU).

The subsequent part will examine the concept of prohibited agreements, the exploitation of dominant positions, and their ramifications for the process of liberalising the energy market. A comprehensive examination was conducted to thoroughly analyse the subject matter of this relationship, encompassing a study of the practices and legal precedents of the Commission. The aim of this study was to ascertain the distinct forms of abusive conduct linked to positions of power within the energy sector. An evaluation was conducted to analyse the impact of long-term energy supply contracts, along with supplementary limitations, on the formation of a competitive domestic market.

The following section focuses on the effect of different concentrations on the level of competitiveness in the market. This research examines mergers and acquisitions in the energy sector, assessing their possible impact on market competitiveness. Furthermore, this part delves into crucial Commission rulings as well as other relevant publications. The association between the divestiture procedures used by companies in order to comply with energy regulations and merger regulations enforced by competition law is assessed.

The next section examines State aid, with a special focus on its application in the energy business, by analysing specific cases. The inquiry has principally examined the impact of State aid on the creation of a strong and competitive domestic market. The evaluation of many categories of State aid demonstrated their impact on market competitiveness and the balance between business and consumer interests. This section delves deeper into the modernization of state aid and assesses the impact of current legislation on the energy market.

Following section analyses the scrutiny of general economic interest services and their implications regarding State aid regulations, alongside special and exclusive privileges. Within the convoluted landscape of the energy industry, the intricate interplay between exclusive and special rights, in conjunction with services of general economic interest (SGEIs), serves as a prime example of the delicate equilibrium between market forces and the well-being of the public. The allocation of exclusive rights, which are frequently awarded for critical energy services within certain geographical areas, and the provision of special rights, which confer advantages to specific participants in the market, are significant. The challenge of striking a balance between energy liberalisation and competition principles and the need for energy security, universal access, and sustainability is especially apparent inside the European Union.

The last section offers an initial analysis of the worldwide outlook regarding the application of competition principles and legislation. The necessity of regulating international competition law arises from the existence of trade challenges and the imperative of ensuring equitable market competition. The important aspects include the absence of specific laws and the limited applicability of existing World Trade Organisation (WTO) pursuant to competition law. Moreover, it is crucial to address the prevailing shortcomings in energy industry regulation. The establishment of pricing mechanisms by oil-producing countries might have detrimental consequences for consumers due to the presence of market concentration and the emergence of cartels. Countries that engage in exploitative practices within their oil-producing sectors exert a negative influence on other countries. This section also aims to critically examine the capacity of the WTO to develop and implement regulations concerning international competition law.

The range of research methodologies are utilised to find and thoroughly explore the issues being studied. The systematic analytic approach makes it possible to conduct a thorough evaluation of various occurrences, whether in isolation or as a whole. The examination of competition institutions in the energy industry has been conducted in a thorough manner, encompassing an analysis of both competition law rules and practical aspects.

The systematic analytical approach was used to analyse the many characteristics associated with the enforcement of competition law requirements in the energy business. This analysis revealed various concerns with interrelationships. The aforementioned technique allowed for a full review of the issue at hand as well as the examination of several strategies to effectively resolve the current situation. The comparative historical method was used in the study to evaluate and compare key occurrences during different periods of historical development. This research resulted in a deep understanding of the historical underpinnings of legal governance in the energy business. The historical evolution of energy law and its impact on the regulatory system were thoroughly examined and evaluated.

The document analysis approach is used to evaluate legal documents, international legal acts, case law from the European Union's Court of Justice (CJEU), and Commission decisions on energy sector regulation. The application of this methodology was critical in interpreting the content of numerous papers, illuminating the intricacies of legal regulation, and identifying potential conflicts in legislation in the energy industry.

Given the persistent advancements made towards achieving decarbonization goals and the ongoing execution of infrastructure initiatives, there is a need for a comprehensive analysis to completely explore the interaction of the competition and energy regulation. Therefore, in order to propose a solution, a thorough investigation has been conducted, the results of which have the potential to improve legal governance and align the interests of enterprises and consumers.

The outcomes of this study will offer significant perspectives for policymakers and organisations engaged in the execution of energy-related policies. Moreover, these findings will have substantial consequences for the progression of energy law as a scholarly field and its tangible implementation in the legal profession. This research endeavour aims to offer significant contributions towards the improvement of the existing legislative framework, with the ultimate goal of attaining a balanced and mutually beneficial relationship between business interests, consumers, and other pertinent stakeholders.

Part I
The Energy Sector Regulation: The European Union Perspective

Chapter 2
European Energy Market Evolution

Abstract Liberalisation and market integration entail the reduction of government restrictions and trade obstacles to foster economic openness, as well as the merging of domestic markets with the global economy. The start of the 1990s unified European energy market project was a notable achievement. The aim of this initiative was to eradicate monopolistic structures and develop a competitive energy landscape. To promote market liberalisation, the division of energy corporations into separate businesses, and the unfettered transfer of energy between different jurisdictions, a set of directives and rules were put into effect. The result was the creation of a deeply interconnected energy system in Europe, which enabled the spread of competition and options for consumers. In the early twenty-first century, the energy sector faced an urgent requirement to prioritise sustainability. The consequences of climate change, growing concerns about resource exhaustion, and the quest for cleaner energy alternatives have accelerated the shift towards renewable sources. Wind, solar, and hydropower are renewable energy sources that have become more important in the energy sector. The European Union has set ambitious goals to reduce carbon emissions and promote the shift to sustainable energy systems.

2.1 Introduction

The progression of the European energy market has been a noteworthy trajectory over the course of history, characterised by significant changes in energy sources, market frameworks, and regulatory models. As we find ourselves on the cusp of a forthcoming period characterised by the reduction of carbon emissions, advancements in technology, and a focus on environmental responsibility, it is both enlightening and motivating to reflect upon the journey that has led us to this point. The present introduction chapter establishes the foundation for our research into the development of the European energy market, offering background information, rationale, and a preview of the influential factors involved.

The European energy market, in its present form, possesses extensive historical origins that span several centuries. Since the inception of localised energy generation

L. Rimšaitė, *The Crossroads of Competition Law and Energy Regulation*,
https://doi.org/10.1007/978-3-031-73238-6_2

and distribution, the energy sector has undergone continuous adaptation to cater to the evolving demands of society. This evolution has led to the development of expansive transnational networks. Coal, which played a pivotal role in driving the industrial revolution, was subsequently supplanted by oil and natural gas during the twentieth century. The aforementioned transitions not only resulted in changes to the composition of energy sources but also played a significant role in influencing geopolitical dynamics and economic frameworks.

The latter half of the twentieth century marked the emergence of the European Union (EU) and its aspiration for a cohesive Europe. The establishment of the European Coal and Steel Community (ECSC) in 1951 demonstrated that energy had become a crucial component of this overarching goal.[1] It occurred in the aftermath of World War II, with the primary aim of instituting regulatory measures within the coal and steel industries. The signing of the Treaty of Paris by Belgium, Italy, Luxembourg, France, the Netherlands, and West Germany facilitated the establishment of this reality. The aforementioned international organisation played a crucial role in commencing the process of integration that finally resulted in the formation of the European Union.

This landmark initiative served as a foundation for fostering further collaboration within the energy domain. The years that followed witnessed the formation of the European Atomic Energy Community (EURATOM)[2] in 1957 and the progressive evolution of the domestic energy market. The Euratom Treaty addresses the matter of Community regulation in the sector and outlines the primary energy policy goals that Member States have pledged to uphold. While the European Union did not possess exclusive jurisdiction over the energy sector, it was delegated to the discretion of individual Member States. Nevertheless, it was not until the implementation of the Lisbon Treaty that a distinct segment specifically addressing energy policy was established.

Nearly half a century later, energy matter was incorporated into the Treaty on the Functioning of the European Union (TFEU),[3] encompassing the imperative of ensuring energy supply security and granting Member States the autonomy to determine their preferred energy mix.[4] The inclusion of such a provision was of significant importance in order to safeguard the autonomous rights of the individual States. During that period, there existed vertically integrated energy companies with monopolistic control in the Member States. These companies possessed significant authority to influence price determination through state involvement, thereby compelling them to offer services in the public's best interest.

The concept of liberalisation and market integration refers to the process of reducing government regulations and barriers to trade in order to promote economic

[1] Treaty establishing the European Coal and Steel Community, ECSC Treaty.

[2] Consolidated version of the Treaty establishing the European Atomic Energy Community. *OJ C 327*.

[3] Consolidated version of the Treaty on the Functioning of the European Union. *OJ C 326*.

[4] Szabo (2016).

openness and the integration of domestic markets with the global economy. The initiation of the single European energy market project in the 1990s marked a significant milestone. The objective of liberalisation efforts was to eliminate monopolistic structures and establish a competitive energy landscape. In order to facilitate market liberalisation, the separation of energy corporations into distinct entities, and the unrestricted movement of energy between different jurisdictions, a series of directives and laws were implemented. The outcome entailed the establishment of a highly integrated energy system inside Europe, which facilitated the proliferation of competition and consumer choice.

At the beginning of the twenty-first century, the energy sector encountered a pressing need to prioritise sustainability. The acceleration of the transition towards renewable sources has been driven by the implications of climate change, increasing apprehensions over resource depletion, and the pursuit of cleaner energy choices. Renewable energy sources such as wind, solar, and hydropower have gained significant prominence in the energy sector, with the European Union establishing ambitious objectives to mitigate carbon emissions and facilitate the transition towards sustainable energy systems.

In the present time, we are situated at a critical juncture characterised by a convergence of both difficulties and favourable circumstances. The European Green Deal, which was announced in 2019, represents the European Union's dedication to achieving the status of the first climate-neutral continent globally by the year 2050.[5] The envisioned future entails the attainment of energy sources that are not solely environmentally friendly but also possess the qualities of long-term viability, reliability, and cost-effectiveness. This goal requires a significant overhaul of the energy industry, encompassing aspects such as digitalization, decentralised production, creative finance, and consumer empowerment.

This chapter aims to examine the legal requirements that must be met in order to construct the internal market, as specified in the basic legislation of the European Union. Additionally, it will explore the obstacles and controversies that arise during the implementation of these criteria.

2.2 European Coal and Steel Community Treaty

The European Coal and Steel Community was established in 1951 with the signing of the Treaty of Paris, marking the inception of a supranational entity.[6] The aforementioned endeavour represents a noteworthy achievement in the advancement of European unity and cooperation following the conclusion of World War II. The

[5]Communication from the Commission to the European Parliament, the European Council, the European Economic and Social Committee and the Committee of the Regions. The European Green Deal. COM/2019/640 final.

[6]Treaty establishing the European Coal and Steel Community, ECSC Treaty.

European Coal and Steel Community played a crucial role in the founding of the European Union and laid the groundwork for further economic and political cooperation among European nations.

The primary aim of the European Coal and Steel Community was to promote the harmonisation and consolidation of the coal and steel industries among its member states. The European Coal and Steel Community was created by six founding member states, namely Belgium, France, Germany, Italy, Luxembourg, and the Netherlands. The fundamental principle behind this integration was to centralise the manufacturing and distribution of coal and steel, two essential resources for industrial production and defence. The objective was to promote economic recovery and establish stability in the post-war period.

The European Coal and Steel Community pursued distinct goals and stood out in a number of significant ways. The principal aim of the European Coal and Steel Community was to develop a harmonised market for coal and steel among its member states. This involved the elimination of barriers to trade and the promotion of an unhindered flow of commodities and resources within the community. To achieve these goals the suppression of the trade barriers, limitation of discriminatory practice and control of the state subsidies were implemented. The European Coal and Steel Community exhibited a supranational character, indicating the existence of organisations vested with independent decision-making power, distinct from the governments of its constituent nations. The strategy adopted during that particular age with regards to international cooperation and integration was distinguished by its innovative nature.

The accomplishments of the European Coal and Steel Community in promoting economic cooperation and harmonious relations among its member states acted as a stimulus for subsequent efforts towards European integration. The events listed above played a crucial role in paving the way for the signing of the Treaties of Rome in 1957. These treaties laid the groundwork for the creation of the European Economic Community and the European Atomic Energy Community (Euratom).[7] The accords described earlier experienced a series of developmental and transformative stages, ultimately leading to the formation of the present-day European Union. This phenomenon transpired as a result of the adoption of the following treaties, most notably the Maastricht Treaty in 1992 and the Treaty of Lisbon in 2009.

The European Coal and Steel Community foreseen four institutions: The High Authority, a Common Assembly, a Special Council and the Court of Justice which were predecessors of the European Commission, European Parliament, the Council of the European Union and the European Court of Justice.

The executive body of the European Coal and Steel Community was the High Authority, which had the primary responsibility of overseeing the integration process and managing the common market. The body consisted of delegates from each

[7] Consolidated version of the Treaty establishing the European Atomic Energy Community. *OJ C 327, 26.10.2012.*

participating country who wielded considerable authority on topics pertaining to coal and steel. The act of consolidating resources played a pivotal role within the framework of the European Coal and Steel Community. The process entailed the amalgamation of coal and steel production quotas, enabling member nations to collectively use and synchronise their resources to effectively regulate output levels. The primary aim of price control within the framework of the European Coal and Steel Community was to achieve price stability in the coal and steel sectors. This purpose was pursued in order to address the negative consequences arising from rivalry among member states while also fostering fair pricing practices for both consumers and industry. The European Coal and Steel Community developed a Social Fund with the objective of providing support to workers through adaptation and retraining processes in sectors that have been impacted by structural changes resulting from the integration process. The High Authority was enabled to issue several legal instruments, the binding Decisions, the Recommendations whereas the implementation particularities were left open for the member states to decide and the Opinions which were not legally binding.

The Common Assembly served as the antecedent of the European Parliament, consisting of delegates from the national parliaments of the Member States. The High Authority was subject to supervisory power. The direct election of members did not occur until the Treaties of Rome were implemented. The purpose of the Assembly is to provide a counterbalancing force, offer guidance, and have the authority to dismiss the High Authority.

The Special Council of Ministers, which served as a predecessor to the Council of the European Union, consisted of government representatives.[8] The primary objective of the study was to achieve harmonisation between the activities of the High Authority and those of national governments. The subjects pertaining to coal and steel were specifically allocated to the High Authority, with the Council possessing the ability to exercise oversight in this domain, unlike in other areas where the Council's assent was necessary.

The Court of Justice enforced adherence to European Coal and Steel Community law through the interpretation of the Treaty. The appointment of judges was determined through a collective agreement among the national governments, with a term of six years.

The European Coal and Steel Community had quite little influence over the coal and steel as the initial influence was exercised by the global trends. The treaty did not achieve several fundamental goals in particular, it did not define the common energy policy. The representation at international organisations was not foreseen in the European Coal and Steel Community mainly due to the fact that the resources were located inside the community and the matter was related only to the founding states. The European Coal and Steel Community Treaty expired in 2002 and all the activities were taken by the European Community. After six years from the Treaty of Paris the Treaties of Rome were signed by the European Coal and Steel

[8] https://www.consilium.europa.eu/media/30558/qc3112311en.pdf.

Community members thus creating the European Economic Community and the European Atomic Energy Community and these treaties were adopted for the indefinite time unlike the ECSC.

Due to the fact that global trends primarily shaped the European Coal and Steel Community's initial influence, it has little influence over the coal and steel industries. The treaty failed to accomplish several fundamental objectives, notably the absence of a clear definition of a shared energy policy. The inclusion of representation at international organisations was not anticipated in the European Coal and Steel Community, primarily because the resources were confined within the community and the issue pertained solely to the founding states. The European Coal and Steel Community reached the end of its term in 2002, leading to the transfer of all its functions and responsibilities to the European Community. The Treaties of Rome were signed by the members of the European Coal and Steel Community six years after the Treaty of Paris. This event marked the establishment of the European Economic Community and the European Atomic Energy Community. Unlike the European Coal and Steel Community Treaty, which had a limited duration, these treaties were adopted with no specified end date.

2.3 Treaty Establishing the European Atomic Energy Community (Euratom Treaty)

The Euratom Treaty,[9] formally referred to as the Treaty establishing the European Atomic Energy Community, is an international agreement that was ratified on March 25, 1957, in Rome, concurrently with the Treaty of Rome. The latter treaty established the European Economic Community and laid the groundwork for the present-day European Union. The Euratom Treaty was implemented on January 1, 1958. The Euratom Treaty possesses distinct objectives and institutions that are independent of the EEC, which have since been integrated into the Treaty on the European Union and the Treaty on the Functioning of the European Union.

The central objective of the Euratom Treaty is to advance the utilisation of nuclear energy for peaceful and non-military applications.[10] This encompasses the provision of research support, guaranteeing the consistent availability of nuclear materials, and promoting the advancement of nuclear energy across the European Union member nations. The primary objective of the treaty is to establish a cohesive market for nuclear materials and technologies within the European Union, encompassing all member states. The objective is accomplished by implementing standardised protocols and guidelines governing the transportation and commercial transactions

[9]Treaty on the European Atomic Energy Community, of 25 March 1957—consolidated version (OJ C 203, 7.6.2016, pp. 1–112).

[10]Consolidated version of the Treaty establishing the European Atomic Energy Community. OJ C 203, 7.6.2016, pp. 1–112.

involving nuclear substances within the European Union. The Euratom treaty encompassed the advancement of research, the establishment of standardised technical norms with the aim of safeguarding the general public, the facilitation of research activities, and ensuring the non-utilisation of civil nuclear materials for military purposes.

The Euratom Treaty has undergone only a limited number of amendments, primarily as a result of the delicate nature of nuclear power utilisation and its impact on public sentiment. A number of minor modifications have been enacted as a result of the institutional alterations within the European Union. There is an ongoing argument suggesting that the Euratom Treaty has become outdated as a result of the absence of amendments. One of the primary objectives was to foster the advancement of nuclear industries and establish a unified nuclear market. The unrestricted transportation of nuclear fuels and materials, nuclear reactors, and associated equipment, as well as materials related to radiation protection, is guaranteed.

The Euratom Treaty establishes the fundamental principles pertaining to the unrestricted mobility of capital, services, goods, and individuals. The Treaty, despite its technical complexity, facilitates industrial collaboration by implementing measures such as the prohibition of exclusive access to nuclear products and the establishment of a Supply Agency with the authority to procure materials and negotiate supply contracts. The Agency is responsible for meeting the demand for the products as expressed by the customers. Further chapters will provide a detailed analysis of certain aspects pertaining to the application of competition law, with specific attention given to the role played by the Euratom Supply Agency.

The fundamental aim of the Euratom Treaty is to maintain high standards of nuclear safety and radiation protection across the European Union.[11] The provision of a legal framework facilitates the establishment of shared safety standards and coordinates efforts to effectively address potential nuclear emergencies. The treaty facilitates and encourages collaborative efforts in the field of nuclear research and development among member states of the European Union. The treaty facilitates collaboration in the domain of nuclear research and development among member states of the European Union. The objective of the treaty includes the creation of a unified marketplace for nuclear materials and technologies within the member states of the European Union. The primary objective of this initiative is to guarantee a consistent and fair distribution of nuclear materials, including fissile materials, in order to sustain the operational requirements of nuclear power plants and other related facilities. The European Atomic Energy Community's Joint Research Centre

[11] Consolidated version of the Treaty establishing the European Atomic Energy Community. OJ C 203, 7.6.2016, pp. 1–112. See Article 2.

was established with the purpose of conducting scientific and technical research to provide support for the European Union's nuclear energy objectives. The Euratom Treaty established a number of institutions with the purpose of fulfilling its objectives.

The European Commission functions as the executive body of the Euratom Treaty. It in question assumes the responsibility of formulating legislative proposals, executing policies, and overseeing the European Union's nuclear research initiatives. The Euratom Council, which operates as the Council of the European Atomic Energy Community within the framework of the European Union, serves as a representative body for the governments of member states. It assumes a significant role in the decision-making processes pertaining to nuclear energy affairs. The Euratom General Secretariat provides support to the European Commission in carrying out its responsibilities pertaining to the Euratom Treaty. The jurisdiction over disputes and legal matters arising from the application of the Euratom Treaty lies with the Court of Justice of the European Union. The Euratom Treaty continues to be an essential component of the legal framework of the European Union, in conjunction with the Treaties on the European Union and the Functioning of the European Union. It is important to acknowledge that the Euratom Treaty possesses distinct provisions and areas of competence that are separate from those found in other treaties of the European Union.

The treaty places significant emphasis on the principles of nuclear non-proliferation and the effective implementation of safeguards in order to deter the unauthorised diversion of nuclear materials for military objectives. The organisation engages in close collaboration with international entities such as the International Atomic Energy Agency in order to advance endeavours aimed at preventing the spread of nuclear weapons. The legal framework in question is characterised by its unique and separate nature. The Euratom Treaty, although linked to the European Union and possessing certain shared institutions, possesses distinct provisions and areas of competence that establish it as a separate legal framework governing nuclear energy cooperation among member states of the European Union. The fundamental objective of the Euratom Treaty is to promote the development of nuclear energy for non-military purposes, with a particular emphasis on ensuring the safe and secure use of nuclear materials. Additionally, the treaty aims to foster cooperation and facilitate research in the realm of nuclear science and technology among member states within the European Atomic Energy Community.

2.4 Treaty Establishing the European Economic Community (The Treaty of Rome)

The Treaty Establishing the European Community represents an important turning point in the progression of European integration.[12] The topic of the European Union is a subject of continuous scholarly inquiry, owing to its dynamic development, profound influence, and enduring importance in creating the European landscape. We shall provide a thorough examination of the Treaty, including its historical background, significant clauses, and significant impact on the European project, additionally, shall examine the impact of the Treaty's core concepts, namely economic cooperation, the establishment of the Common Market, and the creation of the European Atomic Energy Community, on the promotion of economic growth, political unity, and legal progress inside the European Union. Furthermore, we shall critically analyse the contemporary significance of the Treaty in the context of European governance, emphasising its influence on the institutional structure and policy goals of the European Union.

The Treaty of Rome, formally referred to as the Treaty Establishing the European Community, represents a significant milestone in the pursuit of European integration following the conclusion of World War II. The treaty, which was signed on March 25, 1957, by the six original member nations (Belgium, France, Italy, Luxembourg, the Netherlands, and West Germany), established the fundamental framework for the European Economic Community and Euratom. The subject under consideration holds significant importance for scholarly investigation due to its enduring impact on the development of the European Union.

A comprehensive grasp of the historical context of the treaty is essential in order to fully comprehend its significance. The profound impact of World War II and the ensuing urgent need for peace and economic revival served as catalysts for initiatives aimed at promoting collaboration among European nations. The Treaty of Rome represented the apex of these endeavours, placing significant emphasis on economic integration as a strategy to avert future conflicts and foster economic well-being.

This chapter examines the impact of the treaty on the development of the European Union's institutional structure. The text delineates the formation of pivotal organisations such as the European Commission, the Council of the European Union, and the European Parliament, which persistently influence the structure of European government in contemporary times. Furthermore, this analysis delves into the manner in which the aims of the Treaty, which first focused on economic cooperation, have evolved to cover a wider range of policy domains, including but not limited to environmental preservation, safeguarding consumer rights, and fostering social cohesion.

[12] Treaty establishing the European Community (Consolidated version 2002) OJ C 325, 24.12.2002, pp. 33–184.

The establishment of several fundamental pillars played a crucial role in influencing the process of European integration.[13] The aforementioned pillars encapsulated the fundamental goals and concepts of the treaty. The development of a unified market was a fundamental element of the Treaty of Rome. This entailed the elimination of trade impediments and the facilitation of unrestricted mobility of commodities, services, finances, and the workforce within the states comprising the membership. The primary objective of the common market was to provide a cohesive economic environment that would facilitate the development of competition and support economic growth.

A treaty established the Customs Union with the intention of establishing a unified customs zone among the member governments. This resulted in the establishment of shared external tariffs and the removal of internal customs levies by the group. The primary objective of the customs union was to enhance trade by establishing a harmonised external trade policy and enabling the unrestricted movement of products within the European Economic Community.

The Treaty of Rome established several significant institutions (Articles 137–188).[14]

- The Commission of the European Communities, commonly referred to as the European Commission, serves as the executive arm of the European Union. The entity in question was established under the Treaty of Rome and is tasked with the formulation of legislative proposals, the execution of European Union policies, and the enforcement of EU legal provisions. The composition of the Commission consists of Commissioners, with representation from each member state, who are selected by their respective governments. The nomination of the President of the Commission is a process wherein member states propose candidates who are afterwards subject to approval by the European Parliament. The role of the Commission has significant importance in the formulation and administration of the European Union's economic and regulatory framework.
- The Council of Ministers, commonly known as "the Council" holds significant importance as a pivotal decision-making entity within the European Union. The entity in question embodies the governing bodies of the member states and assumes the duty of enacting legislation, harmonising policies, and rendering significant determinations. The Council's composition and voting procedures have undergone changes over its history, resulting in the use of qualified majority voting for certain decisions. This approach fosters collaboration and consensus-building among member nations.
- The establishment of the European Parliamentary Assembly can be attributed to the Treaty of Rome, a pivotal agreement that subsequently underwent transformations leading to the formation of the European Parliament. At its inception,

---

[13]Treaty establishing European Economic Community (EEC Treaty) 1957. Three pillars cover: the European Communities including economic, social and environmental policies, the Common Foreign and Security Policy, Police and Judicial Cooperation in Security Matters.

[14]Treaty establishing European Economic Community (EEC Treaty) 1957.

the European Parliamentary Assembly possessed restricted authority and functioned primarily as an advisory entity. Nevertheless, as time elapsed, the power and authority of the subject in question experienced a substantial expansion. Presently, the European Parliament is democratically elected by the citizens of the European Union and assumes a pivotal function in the legislative proceedings, encompassing collaborative law making with the Council.
- The Court of Justice of the European Communities is an institution within the European Union that plays a crucial role in interpreting and applying EU law. The Court of Justice serves as the judicial arm of the European Union. The entity in question undertakes the task of interpreting European Union legislation, ensuring its consistent implementation, and resolving conflicts that may arise between member states and EU institutions. The Court is comprised of judges hailing from every member state and bears the responsibility of safeguarding the supremacy of the law throughout the European Union.

Over the course of time, successive treaties and agreements, including the Treaty of Lisbon, have implemented modifications and reforms to the institutional framework of the European Union, resulting in the evolution of the contemporary European Union, characterised by its broadened responsibilities, functions, and decision-making processes. Nevertheless, the establishments instituted by the Treaty of Rome have provided the fundamental foundation for the governance of the European Union and persistently fulfil crucial functions in shaping the process of European integration and policy formulation in the present era.

The development of a common market was a fundamental aspect of the Treaty of Rome. This entailed the elimination of trade obstacles and the facilitation of the unrestricted movement of commodities, services, capital, and labour within member states. The primary objective of the common market was to provide a cohesive economic environment that would facilitate the development of competition and support economic growth.

The Customs Union Agreement was enacted to form a customs union among the governments that are part of it. This resulted in the establishment of shared external tariffs and the removal of internal customs levies by the group. The primary objective of the customs union was to enhance trade by establishing a harmonised external trade policy and enabling the unrestricted movement of products within the European Economic Community.

The Treaty of Rome implemented competition regulations aimed at promoting equitable competition within the common market. The objective of these regulations was to mitigate anti-competitive behaviours, such as the formation of cartels and monopolistic practices, while simultaneously fostering economic efficiency. The pact established the foundation for the advancement of EU competition law, which continues to serve as a fundamental aspect of EU economic policy.

The treaty acknowledged the significance of agriculture, despite its primary emphasis on economic affairs.[15] The aforementioned initiative facilitated the establishment of the Common Agricultural Policy, which sought to guarantee consistent food provisions, equitable remuneration for agricultural producers, and affordable costs for consumers.

The aforementioned principles outlined in the Treaty of Rome played a crucial role in facilitating economic collaboration, expansion, and amalgamation among the states that were parties to the treaty. Over the course of time, these principles underwent a process of evolution and expansion, leading to their incorporation into a wider range of policy domains. The Treaty of Rome includes certain articles pertaining to energy, albeit with a rather restricted scope. As an illustration, Article 3 of the treaty stipulated the progressive formation of a unified market and the eradication of impediments to commerce. Although there were indirect implications for energy commerce, the document did not present any explicit energy-related aims or policies.

The primary aim of the Treaty of Rome was to establish a unified market and remove impediments to the unrestricted flow of commodities, services, capital, and labour within the member states. The establishment of this economic integration framework facilitated the organic development of energy commerce and cooperation.

The Treaty of Rome did not explicitly prioritise the energy sector; rather, it laid the foundation for European economic union and cooperation. This framework subsequently facilitated the inclusion of energy policy and regulation in future treaties and agreements. With the progression of European integration, the European Union's involvement in the energy sector has broadened, ultimately resulting in the establishment of a cohesive energy policy and a consolidated internal energy market. The central focus of the treaty was placed on the establishment of a unified market and the promotion of economic integration among the states comprising its membership. The Treaty of Rome, in its inception, laid the groundwork for a more extensive process of European integration and collaboration. This process was subsequently extended to include the energy sector through the following treaties and advancements.

2.5 The Single European Act

The Single European Act, which was signed in 1986 and came into effect in 1987, represented a significant milestone in the process of European integration. The Single European Act had a significant influence on the energy industry in the European Union, despite its primary focus on establishing the single European market. This chapter examines the influence of the Single European Act on the

[15]Treaty establishing European Economic Community (EEC Treaty) 1957.

development of energy policy and regulation within the European Union, with a particular focus on its contribution to the establishment of a more cohesive and competitive energy market. The Single European Act played a significant role in shaping the contemporary energy landscape of the European Union, encompassing various aspects like competitiveness, state aid, and environmental considerations.

The Single European Act[16] was a pivotal pact in the ongoing process of European integration. The main purpose of the initiative was to achieve the creation of a unified European market by the end of 1992. However, the provisions and objectives of this initiative had significant and wide-ranging ramifications for several policy domains, including the energy sector. This article aims to analyse the influence of the Single European Act on the energy policy of the European Union, with a particular focus on its contribution to the promotion of competition, the mitigation of environmental issues, and the enhancement of energy security.

The fostering of competition inside the European Union was a fundamental principle of the Single European Act. The concept of "qualified majority voting" was adopted, facilitating expedited and resolute decision-making in matters pertaining to the internal market. In the realm of the energy industry, this entailed the resolution of monopolistic practices and the rectification of market distortions.[17] The Single European Act played a pivotal role in establishing the initial framework for subsequent endeavours aimed at liberalising energy markets. This significant milestone ultimately led to the establishment of the domestic energy market.

The Single European Act region also acknowledged the issue of state aid, acknowledging that the provision of subsidies and preferential treatment had the potential to create distortions in competition.[18] The aforementioned development had notable ramifications within the energy sector, specifically pertaining to the allocation of financial resources and the provision of assistance for energy infrastructure. The pact facilitated the establishment of fair competition among enterprises and established the fundamental principles for regulating state assistance in the energy industry.

The significance of environmental issues increased during the deliberations of the Single European Act. The acknowledgment that the preservation of the environment should not be compromised in the pursuit of economic progress has had a significant impact on energy policy. Consequently, there was an increased prioritisation of sustainable energy sources, energy efficiency, and environmental impact assessments, establishing a foundation for forthcoming energy and environmental legislation within the European Union.

The significance of energy security was emphasised by the Single European Act through its recognition of the potential influence of external energy sources on the European Union's autonomy. This particular viewpoint exerted a significant influence on the energy strategy of the European Union, resulting in efforts to increase the

[16] Single European Act (OJ L 169, 29.6.1987, pp. 1–28).

[17] Single European Act (OJ L 169, 29.6.1987, pp. 1–28).

[18] Single European Act (OJ L 169, 29.6.1987, pp. 1–28).

variety of energy sources and suppliers as well as strengthen collaboration in the realm of international energy relations.[19]

The influence of the Single European Act on the energy industry inside the European Union is of significant importance and should not be underestimated. The inclusion of laws pertaining to competition, state aid, environmental considerations, and energy security establishes a framework conducive to the advancement of an energy market that is more integrated, competitive, and sustainable. Subsequent treaties and directives that built on the Single European Act initial framework for the European Union's energy policy have shaped the organisation today. These developments have not only influenced the current state of the EU energy landscape but also represent the changing priorities of European energy policy. Gaining a comprehensive understanding of the significance of the Single European Act in energy policy yields significant insights into the overarching trajectory of European integration and cooperation.

The concepts and clauses of the Single European Act laid the foundation for following treaties and agreements, such as the Treaty on the European Union (Maastricht Treaty). This treaty broadened the scope of European integration to encompass political, foreign policy, and security matters. The Single European Act was a pact of significant consequence that expedited the course of European integration. The fundamental objective of this initiative was to establish a cohesive domestic market, but it had significant ramifications for other policy domains, such as competition, state aid, the environment, and indirectly, energy. The influence of the Single European Act on energy policy and the wider European project highlights its significance in shaping the contemporary European Union and its policies.

2.6 The Maastricht Treaty

The Maastricht Treaty, also referred to as the Treaty on European Union, was ratified in 1992 and implemented in 1993, signifying a significant turning point in the progression of European integration.[20] The treaty's main emphasis on political and economic integration had noteworthy significance for the energy industry inside the European Union. This chapter analyses the fundamental principles and potential consequences of the Maastricht Treaty in relation to the energy policy of the European Union. The treaty had a diverse influence on the contemporary energy landscape of the European Union, ranging from its impact on the Common Energy Policy to the concepts of subsidiarity and shared competences.

The Maastricht Treaty was a significant agreement that furthered the process of European integration. It introduced the notion of European citizenship, established a unified foreign and security policy, and facilitated improved cooperation across

[19] Single European Act (OJ L 169, 29.6.1987, pp. 1–28).

[20] Treaty on European Union (OJ C 191, 29.7.1992, pp. 1–112).

multiple policy domains. Although the primary goals of the pact were centred around political and economic integration, it is important to acknowledge the substantial implications it had on the energy sector of the European Union.

The Maastricht Treaty introduced the concept of a common energy policy as a significant element. Although it may not possess the same level of comprehensiveness as other widely implemented programmes like the Common Agricultural Policy, this policy has established a fundamental basis for fostering collaboration and synchronisation within the energy sector. The treaty acknowledged energy as a mutually shared responsibility between the European Union and its member states, signifying a transition towards greater integration of energy policies.

The Maastricht Treaty implemented the principles of subsidiarity and proportionality (Article 5 and the application principles are laid down in the protocol No 2), which subsequently emerged as essential factors in the decision-making processes of the European Union. The principle of subsidiarity asserts that decisions need to be taken at the level of governance that is most suitable, whether it be at the European Union or national level. Within the framework of energy policy, this idea facilitated the member states in maintaining authority over certain areas of their energy sector while simultaneously collaborating on matters that have transnational ramifications.

The Maastricht Treaty delineated the domains in which the European Union and its constituent member states possess joint authorities. Within the energy sector, it can be observed that member states have maintained jurisdiction over their own national energy policies, while the European Union has assumed a role in facilitating the coordination and standardisation of energy-related issues, particularly those that possess a transnational nature. This approach established the foundation for following energy directives and legislation.

The document acknowledged the significance of energy security and the management of external relations.[21] The significance of fostering collaboration with energy-producing and transit nations was underscored, thereby establishing the foundation for the European Union's external energy strategy. The emphasis on energy security gained significance in subsequent years as the European Union endeavoured to enhance the variety of energy sources and transportation pathways.

The Maastricht Treaty holds significant importance as a pivotal instrument that not only propelled the process of European political and economic union but also laid the foundation for enhanced collaboration and harmonisation within the energy sector.[22] The trajectory of EU energy policy was significantly influenced by the adoption of a common energy policy, the incorporation of concepts such as subsidiarity and proportionality, the allocation of shared competences, and a strong emphasis on energy security. The concepts outlined in previous treaties and directives have served as a foundation for subsequent agreements, exerting a significant influence on the current energy landscape of the European Union. These efforts aim

[21] Treaty on European Union (OJ C 191, 29.7.1992, pp. 1–112). See Article 3, Article 8A, Article 130A-130E, 129B.

[22] Treaty on European Union (OJ C 191, 29.7.1992, pp. 1–112).

to foster a more cohesive, reliable, and environmentally friendly energy future. Gaining a comprehensive understanding of the Maastricht Treaty's significance in the realm of energy policy yields significant insights into the wider dynamics of European integration and cooperation.

2.7 The Amsterdam and Nice Treaties

The Amsterdam Treaty[23] of 1997 and the Nice Treaty[24] of 2001 represented significant milestones in the developmental course of the European Union. The treaties in question primarily revolved around institutional reforms and the necessary preparations for the enlargement of the European Union. However, it is important to note that these treaties also had significant implications for energy policy and its role in the process of European integration. This chapter examines the significance of energy considerations in the Amsterdam and Nice Treaties, highlighting their role in fostering the establishment of a cohesive and environmentally friendly energy framework within the European Union. The implementation of expanded cooperation mechanisms and the promotion of renewable energy sources have significantly invigorated the European Union's approach to energy-related issues.

The Amsterdam and Nice Treaties, subsequent to the Maastricht Treaty, played a crucial role in facilitating the necessary adjustments within the European Union to effectively incorporate its expanding membership and enhance the efficiency of its decision-making mechanisms. Nevertheless, they also implemented significant energy-related rules and concepts that propelled the European Union's energy policy agenda forward.

The Amsterdam Treaty, specifically, created the notion of enhanced cooperation, which permits a subset of member states to further integrate in particular domains, like energy, even in cases where unanimity among all member states is unattainable.[25] The utilisation of this mechanism played a crucial role in facilitating a more profound integration of energy systems since it enabled coalitions of member states to actively pursue ambitious energy policy goals, including the advancement of renewable energy sources.

Both accords placed significant emphasis on environmental problems, highlighting the imperative of incorporating environmental protection across multiple policy

[23]Treaty of Amsterdam amending the Treaty on European Union, the Treaties establishing the European Communities and certain related acts OJ C 340, 10.11.1997, pp. 1–144.

[24]Treaty of Nice amending the Treaty on European Union, the Treaties establishing the European Communities and certain related acts (OJ C 80, 10.3.2001, pp. 1–87).

[25]Treaty of Amsterdam amending the Treaty on European Union, the Treaties establishing the European Communities and certain related acts OJ C 340, 10.11.1997, pp. 1–144. See Article 46, Article 47.

domains.[26] Within the realm of energy, there has been an increasing emphasis on sustainability and the mitigation of greenhouse gas emissions. The Nice Treaty consolidated these obligations, facilitating the development of energy policies that placed a high emphasis on environmental accountability.

The Amsterdam and Nice Treaties played a crucial role in influencing the evolution of the internal energy market within the European Union. The authors emphasised the significance of competition within energy markets and facilitated the progression towards the liberalisation of the energy industry. The aforementioned development had substantial ramifications within the energy sector, as it fostered the facilitation of transnational commerce, the promotion of infrastructure investment, and the creation of a more linked energy grid across Europe.

The treaties additionally established the groundwork for the advancement and support of renewable energy sources.[27] The need for diversifying energy supplies and decreasing reliance on fossil fuels was acknowledged by the individuals. These principles had a significant impact on later energy directives and programmes that were designed to increase the proportion of renewable energy sources in the European Union's energy portfolio.

The Amsterdam and Nice Treaties, with their primary emphasis on institutional reforms and EU enlargement, exerted a significant influence on the formulation of the European Union's energy strategy. The authors implemented mechanisms to facilitate a more profound level of integration, strengthened their focus on environmental considerations, facilitated the growth of the internal energy market, and advocated for the use of renewable energy sources. The inclusion of energy-related provisions in the treaties has invigorated the European Union's dedication to fostering a more sustainable, competitive, and interconnected energy environment, thereby aligning with the changing focal points of European energy policy. Gaining an understanding of the significance of these treaties in terms of energy sheds light on the wider dynamics of European integration and cooperation.

The Amsterdam Treaty,[28] ratified in 1997, is a significant international agreement that holds great importance in the realm of European Union governance. The concept of improved collaboration was introduced in the European Union through the Amsterdam Treaty. Although the original purpose of this mechanism was directed towards different policy domains, it exerted a substantial influence on the realm of energy policy. Multiple groups of member states used enhanced collaboration to advance energy initiatives, including the promotion of renewable energy sources and the creation of cross-border electrical interconnections. This facilitated a

[26]Treaty of Amsterdam amending the Treaty on European Union, the Treaties establishing the European Communities and certain related acts OJ C 340, 10.11.1997, pp. 1–144. See Article 11, Article 6, 130R.

[27]Treaty of Amsterdam amending the Treaty on European Union, the Treaties establishing the European Communities and certain related acts OJ C 340, 10.11.1997, pp. 1–144. See Article 1, Article 2, Article 8, Article 9.

[28]Treaty of Amsterdam amending the Treaty on European Union, the Treaties establishing the European Communities and certain related acts OJ C 340, 10.11.1997, pp. 1–144.

greater degree of adaptability and customization in the formulation of energy policies among the European Union member states.

The Amsterdam Treaty[29] underlined the importance of incorporating environmental factors into European Union policies, particularly those pertaining to energy. This action established the foundation for the European Union's dedication to the advancement of sustainable energy development. This development started a transition towards cleaner and more ecologically sustainable energy sources, thereby linking energy policy with the overarching environmental objectives of the European Union.

The treaty recognises the significance of a fully operational internal energy market in ensuring the energy security and competitiveness of the European Union. The aforementioned statement serves to strengthen the dedication to the process of liberalising energy markets, fostering competition, and eliminating obstacles to the trade of energy products and services. The 1996 directive on electricity and gas liberalisation served as a forerunner to the subsequent establishment of the internal energy market.

The Nice Treaty was adopted in 2001 with the primary objective of addressing the institutional reforms required to facilitate the enlargement of the European Union while also considering the crucial aspect of energy security.[30] The issue of energy security gained prominence with the expansion of the European Union to encompass a greater number of member nations. The treaty acknowledges the necessity of guaranteeing a dependable and varied energy supply to every member state, especially those that rely significantly on a solitary energy source or supplier.

The Nice Treaty reaffirmed the European Union's dedication to the principles of environmental sustainability, particularly in the context of renewable energy.[31] The aforementioned dedication encompassed energy policy, hence bolstering the transition towards renewable energy sources. The framework made it easier for member states to work together to reach shared goals in the area of renewable energy. This laid the groundwork for later directives that set mandatory targets for the amount of renewable energy in the energy mix of the European Union.

The objective of the Nice Treaty was to enhance the efficiency of decision-making procedures within the European Union in anticipation of its enlargement. Although not directly pertaining to energy, these reforms have indirectly contributed to the enhancement of energy policy by establishing a more streamlined and proficient decision-making framework. The attainment of efficiency played a pivotal role in the resolution of intricate energy-related matters that necessitated the establishment of agreement among the governments comprising the membership.

---

[29] Treaty of Amsterdam amending the Treaty on European Union, the Treaties establishing the European Communities and certain related acts OJ C 340, 10.11.1997, pp. 1–144. See Article 2.

[30] Treaty of Nice amending the Treaty on European Union, the Treaties establishing the European Communities and certain related acts (OJ C 80, 10.3.2001, pp. 1–87).

[31] Treaty of Nice amending the Treaty on European Union, the Treaties establishing the European Communities and certain related acts (OJ C 80, 10.3.2001, pp. 1–87).

To summarise, the Amsterdam and Nice Treaties exerted a long-lasting influence on the energy policy of the European Union. The implemented structures to facilitate enhanced collaboration, strengthened the emphasis on environmental factors, encouraged the growth of the domestic energy market, and made progress towards achieving renewable energy targets. The aforementioned treaties demonstrate the European Union's dedication to aligning its energy framework with its overarching goals of sustainability, competitiveness, and security.

2.8 The Treaty on the Functioning of the European Union (The Treaty of Lisbon)

The Treaty of Lisbon, which served to modify and unify the pre-existing EU treaties, notably the Treaty establishing the European Community, carries noteworthy ramifications for the energy industry within the European Union.[32] The Treaty of Lisbon has exerted a significant influence on the European Union's energy policy, governance, and objectives through the implementation of various amendments. Several important factors contribute to the significance of the energy sector, including: the concept of energy as a shared competence: The Treaty of Lisbon established that energy policy is a shared competence between the European Union and its member states. This implies that although member states maintain their sovereignty over national energy policy, the European Union plays a role in coordinating and executing specific elements of energy policy to attain shared goals.

Article 194 of the TFEU, which became part of the Treaty of Lisbon, establishes the legal framework for the European Union's energy policy. The European Union's energy policy outlines its goals, which encompass the maintenance of a well-functioning energy market, the advancement of energy efficiency, and the promotion of the utilisation of renewable energy sources. The Treaty of Lisbon has strengthened the European Union's dedication to advancing renewable energy and energy efficiency through the incorporation of explicit provisions within Article 194 TFEU. Consequently, the Member States of the European Union have embraced ambitious objectives pertaining to renewable energy and energy efficiency. The Treaty of Lisbon enhanced the effectiveness of the European Union's external energy policy by establishing a stronger legal framework.[33] This development enabled the EU to present a more cohesive and coordinated stance on global energy issues. The measure bolstered the European Union's ability to engage in energy negotiations with non-member nations and effectively tackle issues related to energy security.[34]

---

[32] Treaty of Lisbon amending the Treaty on European Union and the Treaty establishing the European Community OJ C 306, 17/12/2007, pp. 1–271.

[33] Treaty of Lisbon amending the Treaty on European Union and the Treaty establishing the European Community OJ C 306, 17/12/2007, pp. 1–271.

[34] Huhta (2021).

The Treaty of Lisbon played a pivotal role in enabling the amalgamation of climate and energy policies within the European Union's overarching policy framework. The alignment of energy policy goals with the European Union's climate objectives, including the reduction of greenhouse gas emissions and the mitigation of climate change, proved to be beneficial. The Treaty of Lisbon served as the catalyst for the creation of the European External Action Service, which is a crucial organisation in charge of representing the interests of the European Union in the area of external energy relations. The European External Action Service assumes the responsibility of coordinating the European Union's diplomatic endeavours pertaining to energy-related affairs in collaboration with third countries and international organisations.

The Treaty of Lisbon placed significant emphasis on the significance of public access to information and public participation in energy-related affairs.[35] The legislation enhanced the entitlements of European Union citizens to receive information and participate in the formulation of energy policies, thereby promoting increased levels of transparency and accountability.[36] The Treaty of Lisbon implemented modifications to the decision-making mechanisms within the European Union, resulting in streamlined processes for the adoption of energy-related legislation and policies.[37] The implementation of qualified majority voting in certain domains of energy policy has facilitated expedited and resolute decision-making processes. In general, the amendments made to the Treaty of Lisbon have resulted in a more cohesive, coordinated, and ambitious framework for energy policy within the European Union. The Treaty of Lisbon has significantly influenced the energy sector of the European Union and its approach to energy challenges and opportunities. It has achieved this by establishing a well-defined legal foundation and outlining specific objectives for energy policy. Additionally, the treaty has facilitated the promotion of renewable energy sources and energy efficiency measures. Furthermore, it has strengthened the EU's external energy relations.[38] Overall, the Treaty of Lisbon has played a pivotal role in shaping the EU's energy sector and its response to various energy-related matters.

The Lisbon Treaty, formally referred to as the Treaty of Lisbon, is an extensive treaty of reform that was ratified on December 13, 2007, in Lisbon, Portugal.[39] The primary objective of this initiative was to optimise and improve the operational efficiency of the European Union and its mechanisms for making decisions. The treaty was ratified by all 27 member states of the European Union and subsequently

---

[35] Treaty of Lisbon amending the Treaty on European Union and the Treaty establishing the European Community OJ C 306, 17/12/2007, pp. 1–271.

[36] Pielow and Lewendel (2011).

[37] Treaty of Lisbon amending the Treaty on European Union and the Treaty establishing the European Community OJ C 306, 17/12/2007, pp. 1–271. See Article 2 C, Article 176 A.

[38] Sydow (2011).

[39] Treaty of Lisbon amending the Treaty on European Union and the Treaty establishing the European Community OJ C 306, 17/12/2007, pp. 1–271.

entered into force on December 1, 2009.[40] The Lisbon Treaty represents a noteworthy landmark in the progression of the European Union's institutional structure and policies. The treaty incorporates several significant elements and modifications, which are as follows. The Lisbon Treaty granted the European Union legal personality, enabling it to participate in international agreements and treaties on behalf of its constituent member states. This alteration has resulted in an enhanced level of prominence and impact for the European Union in matters pertaining to the international arena. The establishment of the position of President of the European Council is outlined in the treaty. This position is filled through the election process, wherein the members of the European Council select an individual to serve as President. The term of this position is renewable and spans a duration of two and a half years. The President assumes the responsibility of representing the European Union externally and presides over the meetings of the European Council. The Lisbon Treaty established the European Citizens' Initiative, which enables citizens of the European Union to directly propose legislation to the European Commission after reaching a predetermined signature threshold from numerous member states.

The treaty expanded the authority of the European Parliament by broadening its legislative function and granting it enhanced co-decision-making powers across multiple policy domains.[41] Additionally, it implemented a system wherein the President of the European Commission is elected based on the results of the European Parliament elections. The Lisbon Treaty introduced a more streamlined and inclusive framework for enhanced cooperation, enabling subsets of European Union member states to pursue specific policies even in the absence of unanimous agreement among all member states.[42] The treaty effectively integrated the Charter of Fundamental Rights of the European Union into the legal framework of the European Union. The charter serves to consolidate the fundamental rights and freedoms that are guaranteed to both citizens and residents of the European Union.

The Lisbon Treaty resulted in the elimination of the previous three-pillar structure of the European Union, which encompassed the European Community, Common Foreign and Security Policy, and Justice and Home Affairs. Instead, these pillars were consolidated into a unified legal framework. The establishment of the High Representative of the Union for Foreign Affairs and Security Policy has resulted in the appointment of an individual who assumes the role of the European Union's principal figure in matters pertaining to foreign policy and security. This individual also serves as the vice president of the European Commission. The Lisbon Treaty had a significant impact on the implementation of the double majority voting system within the Council of the European Union. This alteration aimed to enhance the

[40]Treaty of Lisbon amending the Treaty on European Union and the Treaty establishing the European Community OJ C 306, 17/12/2007, pp. 1–271.

[41]Treaty of Lisbon amending the Treaty on European Union and the Treaty establishing the European Community OJ C 306, 17/12/2007, pp. 1–271. See Article 9 A.

[42]Treaty of Lisbon amending the Treaty on European Union and the Treaty establishing the European Community OJ C 306, 17/12/2007, pp. 1–271.

efficiency of decision-making processes. In the context of decision-making processes within the European Union, it is stipulated that a qualified majority is achieved when a minimum of 55% of member states, representing no less than 65% of the total population of the European Union, support a particular decision.[43]

The primary objective of the Lisbon Treaty was to enhance the democratic nature, operational efficiency, and overall preparedness of the European Union in order to effectively tackle the various challenges arising in the twenty-first century. It perpetuates the impact on the operations of the European Union and exerts its sway over its policies and endeavours across diverse domains, encompassing foreign affairs, climate change, migration, and economic governance.

Following the ratification of the Lisbon Treaty, the energy sector was finally given a position in core European Union legislation. Despite this, a number of challenges relating to the past implementation of other articles acting as a legal framework nonetheless remain problematic. The energy sector was included in the primary law of the European Union, which specified the shared competence between the European Union and its member states in Article 4 TFEU.

The principle of shared competence between the European Union and its Member States is applicable in several key areas. These areas include the internal market, social policy (specifically as defined in the Treaty), economic, social, and territorial cohesion, agriculture and fisheries (excluding the conservation of marine biological resources), environment, consumer protection, transport, trans-European networks, energy, the area of freedom, security, and justice, as well as common safety concerns in public health matters (specifically as defined in the Treaty).

The energy article of the Treaty on the Functioning of the European Union, holds a crucial position within the Lisbon Treaty's framework for energy policy.[44] The European Union is granted the authority to adopt a unified energy policy with the objective of ensuring the effective operation of the energy market, advancing energy efficiency, and facilitating the growth of renewable energy sources. This article presents an analysis of the legal foundations underpinning significant energy directives and regulations, encompassing aspects such as the internal energy market, targets for renewable energy, and measures aimed at enhancing energy efficiency.

The Lisbon Treaty served to strengthen the ideas of subsidiarity and solidarity. The principle of subsidiarity asserts that decisions need to be taken at the level of governance that is most suitable, enabling member states to maintain authority over specific parts of their energy policies.[45] The aforementioned principle has played a crucial role in influencing the European Union's strategy towards regulating the

---

[43] Treaty of Lisbon amending the Treaty on European Union and the Treaty establishing the European Community OJ C 306, 17/12/2007, pp. 1–271.

[44] Treaty of Lisbon amending the Treaty on European Union and the Treaty establishing the European Community OJ C 306, 17/12/2007, pp. 1–271. See Article 176 A.

[45] Treaty of Lisbon amending the Treaty on European Union and the Treaty establishing the European Community OJ C 306, 17/12/2007, pp. 1–271.

energy market. It acknowledges and upholds the significance of accommodating the various national energy compositions and preferences within the member states.

In contrast, solidarity places emphasis on fostering collaboration and reciprocal assistance among member nations, particularly during instances of energy crises or disruptions in supply. The notion of solidarity has become increasingly significant within the realm of energy security as member nations engage in collaborative efforts to strengthen the resilience of their energy systems and infrastructure.[46] The Lisbon Treaty provided a clearer delineation of the distribution of powers and responsibilities pertaining to energy policy between the European Union and its member states. While individual member states retain jurisdiction over their own national energy decisions, the European Union has assumed a more expansive role in facilitating coordination and standardisation of energy-related matters, particularly those that have transnational ramifications. The allocation of competences has played a pivotal role in fostering the evolution of a more cohesive energy market within Europe.[47]

The accord effectively enhanced the European Union's ability to participate in external energy ties. This provision enables the European Union to engage in negotiations with third nations about energy accords, acting on behalf of its member states. Consequently, this provision strengthens the EU's overall negotiating capacity in the pursuit of diversified and dependable energy sources.

The Lisbon Treaty has invigorated the European Union's energy policy agenda by means of its fundamental articles. Article 194 of the TFEU has established the necessary legal framework for the advancement of a unified energy strategy. This provision has been vital in promoting the values of subsidiarity and solidarity, which have played a crucial role in fostering adaptability and collaboration within the European Union.[48] The aforementioned rules have played a significant role in fostering the development of a European energy market that is characterised by enhanced competitiveness, sustainability, and security. Consequently, the European Union has successfully aligned itself with its energy objectives for the twenty-first century. Gaining a comprehensive understanding of the significance of these fundamental articles is vital in order to fully comprehend the intricacies of European energy policy in the wider framework of European Union integration. The current form of Articles 114 and 192 of the TFEU was not in existence prior to the implementation of the Lisbon Treaty. The Lisbon Treaty, which was implemented in 2009, undertook the task of restructuring and renumbering certain articles within the EU Treaties.

Article 95 of the European Community Treaty, which has since been incorporated into the Treaty on the Functioning of the European Union as Article 114, primarily aimed to establish a legal framework for harmonising laws, regulations, and

---

[46] Delvaux (2011).

[47] Treaty of Lisbon amending the Treaty on European Union and the Treaty establishing the European Community OJ C 306, 17/12/2007, pp. 1–271.

[48] Johnston and Marel (2013).

administrative provisions among member states of the European Union. This harmonisation was intended to facilitate the smooth operation of the internal market. This article facilitated the European Union in achieving the harmonisation of regulations and the elimination of barriers that impede the unrestricted flow of goods, services, individuals, and capital within the internal market.

Article 174 of the EC Treaty, which has been subsequently included into the TFEU as Article 192, pertains to the domain of environmental policy. The document acknowledged the importance of environmental protection as a core purpose of the European Union and emphasised the need to incorporate environmental issues into the formulation and execution of various EU policies.

The Lisbon Treaty brought about significant alterations, which encompassed the renumbering of provisions and several adjustments to their substance.

Article 114 of the TFEU maintains the overarching objective that was previously established in Article 95 of the Treaty establishing the European Community (EC). The legal foundation is established to support the implementation of measures that promote harmonisation, with the goal of ensuring the development and operation of the internal market. Nevertheless, the Lisbon Treaty broadened the jurisdiction of Article 114 to encompass not only the unrestricted movement of products but also services and intellectual property.

Article 192 of the TFEU maintains the focus on environmental protection as a fundamental goal of the European Union, similar to its predecessor, Article 174 of the Treaty establishing the European Community (EC). Nevertheless, the Lisbon Treaty enhanced the significance of this particular article by explicitly stating that environmental policy should actively contribute to the promotion of sustainable development. Additionally, it emphasised the necessity of adhering to the precautionary principle and the principles of preventive action. Moreover, the treaty emphasised the importance of rectifying pollution at its source and ensuring that the party responsible for the environmental damage bears the cost of its restoration.

To summarise, prior to the implementation of the Lisbon Treaty, the European Union Treaties included corresponding provisions (Article 95 EC and Article 174 EC) that dealt with the harmonisation of the internal market and environmental policy, respectively. The renumbering of these articles as Article 114 TFEU and Article 192 TFEU was carried out by the Lisbon Treaty with the aim of preserving their fundamental aims and incorporating additional measures to enhance their significance within the framework of European Union law.

The commencement of legal actions by Poland with the aim of annulling Decision (EU) 2015/1814 holds considerable importance within the framework of European Union legislation and energy policy.[49] The subject matter of Decision (EU) 2015/1814 pertains to the regulations governing the provision of access to the OPAL natural gas pipeline. This pipeline serves as a conduit for the transportation of natural gas from the Nord Stream pipeline, facilitating the delivery of Russian-sourced natural gas to European destinations.

[49] Case C-5/16 *Poland v Parliament and Council*, EU:C:2018:483 para 13.

The OPAL pipeline holds significant importance within the European gas infrastructure since it forms an integral component of the broader Nord Stream project.[50] This project aims to facilitate the transportation of Russian natural gas to Europe by circumventing conventional transit routes.[51] In 2009, the European Commission issued an exemption to Germany, thereby permitting Gazprom, the state-owned Russian energy company, to utilise over 50% of the capacity of the OPAL pipeline.

In the year 2016, the European Commission made the decision to approve Decision (EU) 2016/1053, thereby granting Gazprom an expanded utilisation of the OPAL pipeline's capacity. This development consequently facilitated an enhanced level of Gazprom's market penetration within Europe.[52] The implementation of this decision encountered opposition from other European Union member states, including Poland and Ukraine, who contended that it would result in an excessive consolidation of authority over gas provisions under the control of Gazprom.

In November 2015, the Republic of Poland commenced legal actions with the aim of annulling Decision (EU) 2015/1814 before the General Court of the European Union. Poland's main argument focused on the claim that the European Commission had exceeded its authority by enforcing the decision without consulting Poland or other member states that it would affect. Poland argued that the aforementioned decision had a negative impact on energy security in Central and Eastern Europe, as it would heighten reliance on Russian gas and potentially result in interruptions of gas supplies in the region.[53]

Due to its potential to spark inquiries into the European Union's energy security strategy, competitive dynamics, and the delicate balance between the interests of individual member states and the interests of the EU as a whole, Poland's legal challenge is of great significance. The case also brought attention to the wider geopolitical ramifications of energy infrastructure choices, namely with respect to the European Union, Russia, and Ukraine.

In September 2019, the General Court issued a partial ruling in favour of Poland. The decision rendered some elements of Decision (EU) 2015/1814 null and void, as it determined that the European Commission had failed to perform a thorough evaluation of the potential consequences of granting Gazprom greater access to the OPAL pipeline on the availability of gas supplies to Central and Eastern Europe.[54]

---

[50] Yafimova (2017).

[51] Buschle and Talus (2019).

[52] Talus (2021).

[53] Action for annulment—Decision (EU) 2015/1814—Determination of legal basis—No taking into account of the effects of a measure—Article 192(1) TFEU—Article 192(2)(c) TFEU—Measures significantly affecting a Member State's choice between different energy sources and the general structure of its energy supply—Principle of sincere cooperation—Article 15 TEU—Powers of the European Council—Principles of legal certainty and protection of legitimate expectations—Principle of proportionality—Impact assessment.

[54] T-883/16 - Poland v Commission.

The court's decision served as an example of the significance of conducting in-depth studies and consultations when making decisions about energy infrastructure with the intention of preserving energy security and enhancing competitiveness within the European Union.

In brief, the act undertaken by Poland to initiate procedures aimed at annulling Decision (EU) 2015/1814 constituted a significant legal endeavour within the energy policy framework of the European Union. The statement emphasised the significance of maintaining an equilibrium between the interests of European Union member states and the broader concerns of energy security and competition, especially in relation to energy infrastructure projects that have geopolitical repercussions. The ensuing judicial decision underscored the necessity of thorough evaluations and consultations in similar circumstances.

2.9 The Fundamental Principles Guiding European Union Primary Law

The European Union's energy law encompasses a complex framework of regulations, directives, and decisions, which collectively determine its reach. These legal instruments depend mainly on the primary legislation of the European Union, which includes the European Union Treaties and fundamental principles that govern energy policy and regulation. The aim of this chapter is to comprehensively analyse the core principles inherent in the basic laws of the European Union, which form the basis for the development of energy law and policy within the European Union. These principles not only exert an impact on the legal framework but also serve as a manifestation of the European Union's commitment towards achieving a sustainable, secure, and competitive energy future.

The Treaty on the European Union and the Treaty on the Functioning of the European Union are two prominent legal agreements that provide the framework for governance inside the European Union. The aforementioned documents function as the foundational agreements that constitute the legal framework of the European Union. These treaties exhibit several important ideas related to energy law.

The notion of the internal market is outlined in Article 4 of the Treaty on the Functioning of the European Union. The fundamental premise underlying the internal market is the creation of a cohesive energy market within Europe. This statement underscores the imperative of removing barriers that impede the unimpeded movement of energy-related goods and services, thereby fostering equitable competition and affording consumers a broader array of choices. The fundamental tenet of energy legislation is to facilitate the advancement of a comprehensively interconnected and deregulated domestic energy market.

The notion of environmental sustainability is codified within Article 11 of the Treaty on the European Union and Article 191 of the Treaty on the Functioning of the European Union. The concept of environmental sustainability is a fundamental principle enshrined in the Treaties of the European Union. The fundamental emphasis resides in the integration of environmental objectives within the energy plan.[55] The main aim of the energy law is to promote the efficient use of resources, reduce emissions, and encourage the use of renewable energy sources in line with the environmental goals established by the European Union.

The notion of the "Four Freedoms of the Internal Market" pertains to the fundamental principles that serve as the foundation for the economic integration of the European Union. The freedoms in question pertain to the unrestricted mobility of goods, services, capital, and individuals among the member states of the European Union. The Four Freedoms, which encompass the unimpeded flow of goods, services, capital, and individuals, bear considerable significance in the domain of energy law.

The subject matter being deliberated pertains to the unrestricted transportation of commodities, as delineated in Articles 34–36 of the Treaty on the Functioning of the European Union. The idea of unfettered mobility governs energy commodities such as gas and electricity. The necessity of energy legislation stems from its ability to ensure the elimination of discriminatory practices in the trade of energy goods between member states. The subject matter under consideration pertains to the unrestricted provision of services, as delineated in Article 56 of the Treaty on the Functioning of the European Union. The concept of unrestricted mobility of services encompasses energy services, encompassing both the distribution and supply aspects. The discipline of energy law plays a crucial role in enabling the growth of international service provisions and fostering a robust environment of competition.

The subject matter under consideration pertains to the unrestricted transfer of financial resources, as delineated in Articles 63–66 of the Treaty on the Functioning of the European Union. The concept of unrestricted capital mobility governs the regulation and facilitation of energy projects and financial transactions. The primary objective of the energy law is to encourage the influx of financial resources to support the advancement of energy-related infrastructure.

The subject currently being examined pertains to the unrestricted mobility of individuals, as delineated in Articles 45–48 of the Treaty on the Functioning of the European Union. The notion of free mobility for humans embraces both energy professionals and labourers. The enactment of energy legislation promotes the enhancement of labour mobility within the energy industry.

The notion of non-discrimination and equitable treatment is a crucial tenet in promoting equity and justice within a given society. The concept of equality posits that every person should get equitable treatment, consideration, and entitlements, irrespective of their racial background, gender, age, or religious affiliation.[56] The restrictions on energy legislation are imposed by the principles of non-discrimination

---

[55] Affolter (2021).

[56] Consolidated Version of the Treaty on European Union arts. 3(3), 4(2), Oct. 26, 2012, 2012 O.J. (C 326) 01, Consolidated Version of the Treaty on the Functioning of the European Union art. 8, Oct. 26, 2012, 2012 OJ.

and equitable treatment, as articulated in Article 18 of the Treaty on the European Union. The implementation of measures to prevent discrimination on the basis of country of origin guarantees the provision of fair treatment to all participants within the energy market, thereby fostering principles of equity and equal access to opportunities.

Subsidiarity and proportionality are fundamental notions that hold significant importance within the realm of intellectual discourse. The concept of subsidiarity pertains to the notion that decision-making should be conducted at the most proximate or decentralised level feasible. The principles of subsidiarity and proportionality, as delineated in Article 5 of the Treaty on the European Union, have a significant impact on the development of energy legislation by determining the appropriate level of governance in decision-making processes related to energy policy. Decisions are made at the European Union level as judged necessary while also respecting the authority of member states.

The notion of solidarity is encompassed within Article 3 of the Treaty on the European Union and Article 122 of the Treaty on the Functioning of the European Union. The notion of solidarity holds great significance within the realm of energy law, notably among member nations.[57] The aforementioned idea holds significant importance in ensuring the security of the energy supply and enabling synchronised reactions to crises.[58] The basic legislation of the European Union serves as a robust foundation for the advancement of energy law and policy.

The aforementioned core principles demonstrate the European Union's commitment to promoting an integrated, environmentally sustainable, and economically viable energy framework. The discipline of energy law functions within the existing legal framework to promote a sustainable, efficient, and environmentally sensitive energy future for the entire population and economic entities of the European Union.

2.10 Conclusion

The European Coal and Steel Community played a crucial role in the establishment of the European Union and laid the groundwork for further economic and political cooperation among European nations. The primary aim of the community was to promote the harmonisation and consolidation of the coal and steel industries among its member states, aiming to promote economic recovery and stability in the post-war period. The European Coal and Steel Community foresaw four institutions: the High Authority, a Common Assembly, a Special Council, and the Court of Justice. The High Authority oversees the integration process and manages the common market, while the Common Assembly serves as the predecessor of the European Parliament. The Special Council of Ministers aims to harmonise the activities of the High

[57] Boute (2020).

[58] Bjornebye (2010).

Authority and national governments, while the Court of Justice enforces adherence to European Coal and Steel Community law through the interpretation of the Treaty. The Treaty of Rome expired in 2002, leading to the creation of the European Economic Community and the European Atomic Energy Community (Euratom). The Treaties of Rome were signed six years after the Treaty of Paris, marking the establishment of the European Economic Community and the European Atomic Energy Community.

The Euratom Treaty is an international agreement aimed at advancing nuclear energy use for peaceful and non-military purposes. It focuses on providing research support, ensuring consistent availability of materials, and promoting nuclear energy advancement across the European Union. The treaty establishes a cohesive market for nuclear materials and technologies, ensuring the unrestricted transportation of nuclear fuels, materials, and radiation protection. The treaty also promotes industrial collaboration by establishing a supply agency and a joint research centre. The European Commission and Euratom Council are responsible for formulating legislative proposals, executing policies, and overseeing nuclear research initiatives. The Euratom Treaty is an essential component of the legal framework of the European Union, with distinct provisions and areas of competence. The treaty emphasises nuclear non-proliferation and safeguards to deter the unauthorised diversion of materials for military purposes.

The Treaty Establishing the European Community (Treaty of Rome) established the foundation for the European Economic Community and Euratom. The Treaty's core concepts, such as economic cooperation, the establishment of the Common Market, and the creation of the European Atomic Energy Community, aimed to promote economic growth, political unity, and legal progress within the EU. The Treaty also influenced the development of the European Union's institutional structure, with key organisations such as the European Commission, the Council of the European Union, and the European Parliament influencing the structure of European government.

The Treaty of Rome established the European Parliamentary Assembly, which has since evolved into the European Parliament. The Court of Justice of the European Communities is responsible for interpreting and applying EU law, ensuring consistent implementation, and resolving conflicts between member states and EU institutions. The Treaty of Rome also facilitated the development of a common market, a customs union, competition regulations, and the Common Agricultural Policy. The treaty also laid the foundation for European economic union and cooperation, promoting economic integration among member states. The Treaty of Rome laid the groundwork for a more extensive process of European integration and collaboration, which has been extended to include the energy sector through subsequent treaties and advancements.

The Single European Act was a pivotal pact in the European integration process, aiming to create a unified European market by the end of 1992. The Act played a significant role in shaping the contemporary energy landscape, encompassing competitiveness, state aid, and environmental considerations. It facilitated the establishment of the domestic energy market and established the initial framework for liberalising energy markets.

The Single European Act also acknowledged the issue of state aid, facilitating fair competition among enterprises and establishing fundamental principles for regulating state assistance in the energy industry. The Act also highlighted the importance of environmental issues, prioritising sustainable energy sources, energy efficiency, and environmental impact assessments. The Single European Act also highlighted the potential influence of external energy sources on the European Union's autonomy, resulting in increased energy sources and suppliers and strengthened collaboration in international energy relations.

The Single European Act's influence on the energy industry is significant, as it laid the foundation for subsequent treaties and directives that have shaped the organisation today. These developments have influenced the current state of the EU energy landscape and represent the changing priorities of European energy policy. Gaining a comprehensive understanding of the Single European Act's significance in energy policy yields insights into the overarching trajectory of European integration and cooperation.

The Maastricht Treaty marked a significant turning point in European integration. It introduced the concept of European citizenship, unified foreign and security policies, and improved cooperation across multiple policy domains. The treaty introduced the concept of a common energy policy, which facilitated collaboration and synchronisation within the energy sector. The principles of subsidiarity and proportionality were implemented, enabling member states to maintain authority over certain areas of their energy sectors while collaborating on matters with transnational ramifications.

The treaty also delineated the domains in which the European Union and its constituent member states possess joint authorities, facilitating the coordination and standardisation of energy-related issues. The treaty acknowledged the importance of energy security and the management of external relations, establishing the foundation for the European Union's external energy strategy. The Maastricht Treaty's significance in energy policy has influenced the current energy landscape of the European Union, aiming to foster a more cohesive, reliable, and environmentally friendly energy future.

The Amsterdam and Nice Treaties were significant milestones in the development of the European Union, primarily focusing on institutional reforms and the preparations for enlargement. These treaties also had significant implications for energy policy and its role in European integration. The Amsterdam Treaty introduced the concept of enhanced cooperation, allowing member states to integrate in specific domains like energy even when unanimity among all states is unattainable. This mechanism played a crucial role in facilitating a more profound integration of energy systems, enabling coalitions of member states to pursue ambitious energy policy goals, including the advancement of renewable energy sources.

The Amsterdam Treaty underlined the importance of incorporating environmental factors into European Union policies, particularly those pertaining to energy, which established the foundation for the European Union's dedication to sustainable energy development. The treaty recognised the significance of a fully operational internal energy market in ensuring energy security and competitiveness.

The Nice Treaty aimed to enhance the efficiency of decision-making procedures within the European Union in anticipation of its enlargement. The attainment of efficiency played a pivotal role in the resolution of intricate energy-related matters that necessitated the establishment of agreement among the governments comprising the membership. Overall, the Amsterdam and Nice Treaties demonstrated the European Union's dedication to aligning its energy framework with its overarching goals of sustainability, competitiveness, and security.

The Treaty of Lisbon significantly impacted the European Union's energy sector by establishing a shared competence between the EU and its member states. The Treaty established Article 194 of the Treaty on the Functioning of the European Union as the legal framework for the EU's energy policy, focusing on maintaining a well-functioning energy market, advancing energy efficiency, and promoting renewable energy sources. The Treaty strengthened the EU's commitment to renewable energy and energy efficiency, enabling member states to pursue ambitious objectives.

The Treaty of Lisbon has significantly impacted the EU's energy sector and its response to various energy-related matters by establishing a well-defined legal foundation, outlining specific objectives for energy policy, and facilitating the promotion of renewable energy sources and energy efficiency measures. The energy sector was finally given a position in core European Union legislation, with the "energy article" of the Treaty on the Functioning of the European Union holding a crucial position within the framework for energy policy. The treaty strengthened the ideas of subsidiarity and solidarity, enabling member states to maintain authority over specific parts of their energy policies. The treaty provided a clearer delineation of powers and responsibilities pertaining to energy policy between the European Union and its member states, facilitating coordination and standardisation of energy-related matters.

The Lisbon Treaty aimed to renumber certain articles within the European Union Treaties, including Article 95 of the European Community Treaty and Article 174 of the EC Treaty. Article 114 of the TFEU aimed to establish a legal framework for harmonising laws, regulations, and administrative provisions among member states of the European Union, facilitating the smooth operation of the internal market. Article 192 of the TFEU focused on environmental policy, emphasising the importance of environmental protection and incorporating environmental issues into EU policies.

The Lisbon Treaty renumbered these articles as Article 114 TFEU and Article 192 TFEU to preserve their fundamental aims and incorporate additional measures to enhance their significance within the framework of European Union law. Poland initiated legal actions to annul Decision (EU) 2015/1814, which pertains to the regulations governing access to the OPAL natural gas pipeline. The decision, approved in 2016, granted Gazprom expanded use of the pipeline's capacity, facilitating Gazprom's market penetration within Europe. However, opposition from other EU member states, including Poland and Ukraine, argued that the decision would result in excessive consolidation of authority over gas provisions under Gazprom's control.

Poland's legal challenge is significant due to its potential to spark inquiries into the European Union's energy security strategy, competitive dynamics, and the delicate balance between individual member states' interests and the EU's interests. In September 2019, the General Court issued a partial ruling in favour of Poland, rendering some elements of Decision (EU) 2015/1814 null and void and highlighting the importance of thorough evaluations and consultations when making decisions about energy infrastructure to preserve energy security and enhance competitiveness.

The European Union's energy law is a complex framework of regulations, directives, and decisions that determine its reach. These legal instruments are based on the primary legislation of the European Union, including the Treaty on the European Union, and fundamental principles that govern energy policy and regulation. The core principles of energy law include the internal market, environmental sustainability, the four freedoms of the internal market, unrestricted mobility of goods, services, capital, and individuals, unrestricted transportation of commodities, provision of services, transfer of financial resources, and free mobility of individuals.

The concepts of non-discrimination and equitable treatment are crucial to promoting equity and justice within society. The principles of non-discrimination and equitable treatment ensure fair treatment for all participants in the energy market, fostering equity and equal access to opportunities. Subsidiarity and proportionality are fundamental notions that impact the development of energy legislation by determining the appropriate level of governance in decision-making processes related to energy policy.

Solidarity and proportionality are fundamental notions that hold significant importance within the realm of energy law, ensuring the security of the energy supply and enabling synchronised reactions to crises. The basic legislation of the European Union serves as a robust foundation for the advancement of energy law and policy. The European Union's commitment to a sustainable, secure, and competitive energy future is demonstrated through its core principles.

References

Affolter S (2021) The subsidiarity principle in EU environmental law. E-International Relations in Walzenbach G, Alleweldt R (eds) Varieties of European subsidiarity. A multidisciplinary approach. E-International Relations Publishing

Bjornebye H (2010) Investing in EU energy security: exploring the regulatory approach to tomorrow's electricity production. Kluwer Law International

Boute A (2020) The principle of solidarity and the geopolitics of energy: Poland v Commission (OPAL pipeline). Common Mark Law Rev 57:889–914

Buschle D, Talus K (2019) One for all and all for one? The General Court Ruling in the OPAL Case. OGEL 2019/5

Delvaux B (2011) EU law and the developments of sustainable, competitive and secure energy policy – opportunities and shortcomings. Intersentia

Huhta K (2021) The scope of State sovereignty under Article 194(2) TFEU and evolution of competences in the energy sector. Cambridge University Press

Johnston A, Marel E (2013) Ad Lucem? Interpreting the new EU energy provision, and in particular the meaning of Article 194(2) TFEU. EEELR 22(5)

Pielow JC, Lewendel J (2011) Beyond Lisbon: EU competences in the field of energy policy. In: Delvaux B, Hunt M, Talus K (eds) EU energy law and policy issues. Intersentia

Sydow H (2011) The dancing procession of Lisbon: legal bases for European energy policy. Eur Energy J 1(1)

Szabo V (2016) The EU Member States right to energy mix. Masaryk Univ J Law Technol 10:1

Talus K (2021) The interpretation of the principle of energy solidarity - a critical comment on the Opinion of the Advocate General on OPAL. The Oxford Institute for Energy Studies

Yafimova K (2017) The OPAL Exemption Decision: past, present, and future. Oxford Institute for Energy Studies. 2017/117

Chapter 3
Energy Sector Specific Regulation

Abstract The energy markets in the European Union have experienced substantial changes as a result of the liberalisation process brought about by the implementation of the first and second energy packages. The initial package sought to create a cohesive domestic energy market, promoting competition, energy stability, and consumer choices. The primary objective of the second package was to streamline cross-border energy trading and foster cooperation among member states. The Second Energy Package's primary goal was to facilitate the deregulation and harmonization of energy markets throughout the European Union. The purpose of the package was to tackle persistent monopolistic behaviours in the energy sector and foster a more competitive environment. The goal was to eliminate obstacles that hinder the entry of new competitors into the market and enhance the flow of energy across international borders. The Third Energy Package's primary goal was to facilitate energy industry deregulation and harmonization. The primary goal was to ensure regulatory autonomy, promote consumer empowerment, and foster a secure investment climate. The package's objective was to simplify the integration of renewable energy sources into power grid infrastructure and encourage investments in environmentally sustainable energy technologies.

3.1 Introduction

The European Union is at the forefront of worldwide endeavours to tackle the diverse issues presented by the energy industry in the twenty-first century. Energy is a crucial component of modern societies, playing a significant role in supporting economic growth, promoting societal welfare, and enhancing industrial efficiency. The regulation of energy within the European Union framework holds great importance due to its intersection with sustainable energy security, environmental conservation, and economic competitiveness. The purpose of this initial chapter is to provide a fundamental examination of energy regulation within the European Union, offering a clear understanding of the primary factors, goals, and intricacies that form the basis of this crucial domain.

L. Rimšaitė, *The Crossroads of Competition Law and Energy Regulation*,
https://doi.org/10.1007/978-3-031-73238-6_3

The undeniable importance of energy in driving economic development and improving societal well-being is widely recognised. Energy sources play a crucial role in driving various sectors, facilitating efficient transportation networks, and maintaining favourable living conditions inside the European Union. Consequently, the availability and utilisation of energy resources significantly contribute to the overall well-being and economic success of European Union residents. The topic of discussion is the global energy transition. The current energy environment is marked by a significant and transformative shift towards sustainability and the reduction of carbon emissions. The imperative to address climate change, optimise energy efficiency, and diversify energy sources together motivates this dramatic energy transition.

The European Union developed the European Energy Policy Framework as a comprehensive and strategic approach to address the opportunities and challenges in the energy sector. This framework aims to ensure a sustainable, secure, and competitive energy system for the Member States. The energy regulatory paradigm of the European Union is characterised by a strong emphasis on integration and interconnection. This commitment extends beyond national borders and aims to establish a cohesive European energy market.

The foundation of European Union energy policy is rooted in three fundamental principles: energy efficiency, renewable energy, and the establishment of a competitive internal energy market. The aforementioned pillars jointly function as crucial means for achieving the overarching goals of energy security, sustainability, and affordability within the European Union.

The European Union enforces energy rules through a collection of directives and regulations that establish legally binding standards for member states. Prominent directives encompass the Renewable Energy Directive,[1] Energy Efficiency Directive,[2] and Gas Directive,[3] among other notable ones. The indispensable nature of the joint endeavours between the Agency for the Cooperation of Energy Regulators and the European Network of Transmission System Operators lies in their ability to facilitate cooperation among national energy regulatory agencies and guarantee the smooth functioning of electricity grids.

The internal energy market of the European Union is strategically designed to promote competition, encourage investments, and offer consumers the freedom to choose in both wholesale and retail markets. The wholesale and retail markets provide the platform for energy producers, suppliers, and consumers to participate in transparent and fair transactions. The harmonisation of grid codes and the

[1]Directive (EU) 2023/2413 of the European Parliament and of the Council of 18 October 2023 amending Directive (EU) 2018/2001, Regulation (EU) 2018/1999 and Directive 98/70/EC as regards the promotion of energy from renewable sources, and repealing Council Directive (EU) 2015/652.

[2]Directive (EU) 2023/1791 of the European Parliament and of the Council of 13 September 2023 on energy efficiency and amending Regulation (EU) 2023/955 (recast).

[3]Directive 2009/73/EC of the European Parliament and of the Council of 13 July 2009 concerning common rules for the internal market in natural gas and repealing Directive 2003/55/EC.

expansion of cross-border electricity and gas infrastructure play a crucial role in achieving the goal of establishing a fully linked European energy market.

Energy security is a fundamental aspect of the European Union's energy policy, as it encompasses the maintenance of a reliable and varied energy supply.[4] The strategic diversification of energy sources and supply routes is a fundamental aspect of this endeavour. The ambitious climate goals of the European Union necessitate a quick shift towards energy sources that are both low in carbon emissions and renewable in nature, making decarbonization a crucial undertaking. The urgency resides in the need to achieve a balance between decarbonization, energy affordability, and reliability.

Innovation and digitization are driving a significant transition in the energy environment as a result of notable technological developments. This shift holds potential for the implementation of intelligent electricity distribution networks, the use of demand-side management strategies, and the promotion of enhanced energy efficiency. The energy regulatory system inside the European Union serves as a strong demonstration of the EU's unwavering dedication to promoting sustainability, competitiveness, and energy security.[5] In the forthcoming chapters, a comprehensive analysis will be undertaken to examine various aspects of energy regulation within the European Union. This examination will encompass the policies, challenges, and advancements that shape the current energy framework in Europe. The pursuit of energising Europe extends beyond a mere vision, including a collaborative effort and serving as an unwavering witness to the European Union's determined guidance in the worldwide shift towards sustainable energy.

The inadequate state of energy security can be attributed to the reliance on external energy suppliers. However, this highlights the imperative for Member States to pursue the diversification of energy resources to ensure a continuous supply in the event of unforeseen disruptions. The secondary legislation has been enacted to facilitate the implementation of a unified energy market and to establish regulations for market participants, with the aim of promoting market liberalisation.

[4] Regulation (EU) 2019/941 of the European Parliament and of the Council of 5 June 2019 on risk-preparedness in the electricity sector and repealing Directive 2005/89/EC. Regulation (EU) 2017/1938 of the European Parliament and of the Council of 25 October 2017 concerning measures to safeguard the security of gas supply and repealing Regulation (EU) No 994/2010. Directive (EU) 2018/2001 of the European Parliament and of the Council of 11 December 2018 on the promotion of the use of energy from renewable sources. Regulation (EU) 2018/1999 of the European Parliament and of the Council of 11 December 2018 on the Governance of the Energy Union and Climate Action.

[5] Regulation (EU) 2019/941 of the European Parliament and of the Council of 5 June 2019 on risk-preparedness in the electricity sector and repealing Directive 2005/89/EC. Regulation (EU) 2017/1938 of the European Parliament and of the Council of 25 October 2017 concerning measures to safeguard the security of gas supply and repealing Regulation (EU) No 994/2010. Directive (EU) 2018/2001 of the European Parliament and of the Council of 11 December 2018 on the promotion of the use of energy from renewable sources. Regulation (EU) 2018/1999 of the European Parliament and of the Council of 11 December 2018 on the Governance of the Energy Union and Climate Action.

3.2 EU Energy Market Liberalisation and the Adoption of the First Energy Package

The European energy landscape has undergone significant transformation as a result of the liberalisation of energy markets facilitated by the implementation of the first and second energy packages. This transformation has led to the emergence of a more competitive, networked, and consumer-centric environment. This chapter aims to analyse the multifaceted nature of regulatory actions, examining the accomplishments and obstacles that have shaped the European Union's progression towards establishing a comprehensive, sustainable internal energy market. In this chapter, we explore the intricacies of a profound expedition that has influenced the prospective energy landscape of the European Union.

The impetus behind the development of the first energy package in the European Union stemmed from various pivotal elements and aims, with the primary purpose of effecting reform and fostering liberalisation within the energy sector throughout the Member States. Monopolistic energy markets were prevalent in several Member States prior to the implementation of the First Energy Package.[6] This resulted in a scenario where a singular or limited number of influential energy corporations held authority over the production, conveyance, and dispersal of electricity and gas. The presence of monopolies frequently led to a decrease in competition, an increase in pricing, and a restriction in consumer options.

During the late 1990s and early 2000s, the European Union underwent a process of expansion when it sought to incorporate multiple new member states originating from Eastern and Central Europe. The energy market liberalisation and regulatory frameworks in these newly admitted member states exhibited a range of degrees of variation. The European Union aimed to establish a cohesive and standardised energy market encompassing all members.

The fundamental purpose of the European Union was to establish a unified internal market for energy, mirroring the existing single market for goods and services. The primary objective of this internal energy market was to foster competition, enhance energy security, and offer consumers a wider range of options and competitive pricing.[7] The European Union has acknowledged the imperative of incorporating renewable energy sources into the energy portfolio and mitigating the release of greenhouse gas emissions.[8] The establishment of a competitive energy market was perceived as a means to stimulate investments in renewable energy sources and enhance energy efficiency.

The facilitation of cross-border energy trading was a primary objective. The European Union sought to facilitate the unrestricted movement of electricity and gas across national boundaries, fostering energy security and affording member

---

[6]Cameron (2005).

[7]Jones (2019).

[8]Directive (EU) 2018/2001 of the European Parliament and of the Council of 11 December 2018 on the promotion of the use of energy from renewable sources. OJ L 328, 21.12.2018, pp. 82–209.

states the opportunity to tap into a wide range of energy resources.[9] The Treaty on the Functioning of the European Union (TFEU) established the necessary legislative framework for the formulation and implementation of energy policy within the European Union. The utilisation of Articles 101 and 102 of the Treaty on the Functioning of the European Union, which specifically pertain to competition law, was employed as a means to tackle anti-competitive practices within the energy sector.

The European Union has acknowledged the necessity of establishing a unified regulatory framework to effectively supervise and govern energy markets. This encompassed the establishment of autonomous regulatory bodies at the domestic level and the promotion of collaboration among these entities. The introduction of the First Energy Package was motivated by various circumstances and aims, aiming to commence the process of liberalisation and harmonisation in the energy market.[10] The aforementioned package encompassed a set of laws and rules that established the fundamental framework for fostering enhanced competition and integration within the energy markets of the European Union. Subsequent energy packages have further developed and expanded upon these initial changes.

Limited market competition results in consumers not having the freedom to choose their energy supplier, leading to increased energy prices.[11] Following this background, and with a view to creating a competitive market that provides sustainable, secure energy supplies to consumers and businesses, special energy legislation was adopted.[12] Consumers are subjected to higher energy prices as a result of limited competition in the market, which restricts their ability to select alternative energy suppliers. In light of the aforementioned context and with the objective of establishing a market that fosters competition and ensures the provision of sustainable and reliable energy resources to both consumers and businesses, specific legislation pertaining to the energy sector was enacted.

The First Energy Package within the European Union encompassed a series of legislative measures designed to promote the liberalisation and integration of the energy markets across the EU. The adoption of this policy occurred in 1996 and

---

[9] Communication from the Commission to the European Parliament, the Council, the European Economic and Social Committee and the Committee of the Regions. Progress towards completing the Internal Energy Market. COM (2014) 634 final.

[10] Directive 96/92/EC of the European Parliament and of the Council of 19 December 1996 concerning common rules for the internal market in electricity. OJ L 027, 30.1.1997, pp. 20–29. Directive 98/30/EC of the European Parliament and of the Council of 22 June 1998 concerning common rules for the internal market in natural gas. OJ L 204, 21.7.1998, pp. 1–12.

[11] Green Paper. Towards a European strategy for the security of energy supply. COM (2000) 769 final.

[12] Communication from the Commission to the Council and the European Parliament. Completing the internal energy market. Proposal for a Directive of the European Parliament and of the Council amending Directives 96/92/EC and 98/30/EC concerning common rules for the internal market in electricity and natural gas. Proposal for a Regulation of the European Parliament and of the Council on conditions for access to the network for cross-border exchanges in electricity. COM (2001) 125 final.

marked a notable milestone in the progression towards the establishment of a unified energy market within Europe. The First Energy Package marked a substantial transition from monopolistic and controlled energy markets to enhanced competition and openness in the European Union.[13] The primary objective of this initiative was to foster the emergence of new participants in the market, enhance the range of options available to consumers, and ultimately result in heightened competition within the energy sector, thereby potentially driving down prices.

It is noteworthy to acknowledge that the first energy package established the groundwork for succeeding energy packages and directives, which subsequently propelled the European Union's endeavours towards liberalising its energy market. This progress was further augmented by the implementation of the Second and Third Energy Packages. The successive packages implemented various initiatives, including the development of regulatory authorities, the promotion of renewable energy, and enhanced cross-border collaboration within the energy industry.

The First Energy Package contained two Directives. The Electricity Directive (96/92/EC)[14] is a legislative measure that pertains to the regulation of electricity within the European Union. The objective of this directive was to establish a competitive electricity market within the European Union by facilitating the introduction of competition in the generation and supply of electricity. The legislation implemented regulations pertaining to the issuance of authorizations for electricity generators, mandated the separation of transmission and distribution activities from production and supply, and promoted the formation of autonomous regulatory bodies. The Gas Directive (98/30/EC)[15] shares similarities with the Electricity Directive in its objective of establishing a competitive market for natural gas within the European Union. The policy implemented principles pertaining to third-party access to gas transmission networks, regulated the criteria for authorising gas undertakings, and promoted the establishment of autonomous gas regulatory bodies.

3.3 Energy Trade Across Borders: The Priority of the Second Energy Package

A variety of fundamental goals and concerns relating to the energy industry drove the implementation of the Second Energy Package within the European Union.[16] The adoption of the second energy package in 2003 was driven by the objective of

---

[13] Dorigoni and Pontoni (2008).

[14] Directive 96/92/EC of the European Parliament and of the Council of 19 December 1996 concerning common rules for the internal market in electricity. OJ L 27, 30.1.1997, pp. 20–29.

[15] Directive 98/30/EC of the European Parliament and of the Council of 22 June 1998 concerning common rules for the internal market in natural gas. OJ L 204, 21.7.1998, pp. 1–12.

[16] Directive 2003/54/EC of the European Parliament and of the Council of 26 June 2003 concerning common rules for the internal market in electricity and repealing Directive 96/92/EC. OJ L

advancing the liberalisation and harmonisation of the energy markets inside the European Union. In spite of the regulatory measures implemented under the First Energy Package, certain member states continued to exhibit the presence of dominating energy firms that had substantial control over the market. The primary objective of the Second Energy Package was to effectively tackle the persistent monopolistic practices within the energy sector and foster a more competitive environment.

The European Union has demonstrated its dedication to fostering competition in energy markets, with the aim of offering customers an expanded range of energy suppliers and competitive pricing options. The primary objective of the Second Energy Package was to eliminate any remaining obstacles that hindered the ability of new market participants to enter the market. The European Union has acknowledged the significance of cross-border competition and trade within the energy sector. The primary objective of the Second Energy Package was to enhance the facilitation of cross-border energy flows and remove barriers that impeded the unrestricted transmission of electricity and gas among member states.

The equitable and non-discriminatory provision of network access to energy infrastructure, including transmission and distribution networks, was a primary focal point. The primary objective of the Second Energy Package was to establish a set of transparent regulations pertaining to network access and prices, with the intention of preventing any form of discriminatory practice.[17] The package emphasised the importance of establishing autonomous national regulatory authorities (NRAs) that are entrusted with the task of supervising the energy sector in member states. The text underscored the significance of regulatory autonomy in guaranteeing equitable competition and effective market supervision.

The European Union has established environmental targets aimed at mitigating greenhouse gas emissions and enhancing the proportion of renewable energy sources within the energy portfolio.[18] The Second Package facilitated the advancement of cleaner and more sustainable energy technology through the promotion of investments. The prioritisation of ensuring the security of the electricity supply was of utmost importance. The primary objective of the package was to bolster the resilience of energy systems through the promotion of investments in infrastructure and the diversity of energy sources.

The Second Energy Package demonstrated adherence to the provisions outlined in the European Union (EU) Treaty, specifically those pertaining to competition

---

176, 15.7.2003, pp. 37–55. Directive 2003/55/EC of the European Parliament and of the Council of 26 June 2003 concerning common rules for the internal market in natural gas and repealing Directive 98/30/EC. OJ L 176, 15.7.2003, pp. 57–78. Regulation (EC) No 1228/2003 of the European Parliament and of the Council of 26 June 2003 on conditions for access to the network for cross-border exchanges in electricity. OJ L 176, 15.7.2003, pp. 1–10.

[17] Article 20 of the Electricity Directive 2003/54/EC and Article 18 of the Gas Directive 2003/55/EC.

[18] Regulation (EU) 2018/1999 of the European Parliament and of the Council of 11 December 2018 on the Governance of the Energy Union and Climate Action. OJ L 328, 21.12.2018, pp. 1–77.

(Articles 101 and 102 of the TFEU) and the establishment of a unified internal energy market (Article 194 TFEU). In a broader context, the second energy package was implemented as a component of a comprehensive initiative aimed at establishing a more competitive, interconnected, and sustainable energy market inside the European Union. The aforementioned development expanded upon the principles set forth in the First Energy Package and formed the necessary framework for succeeding energy packages and directives, which further advanced the objectives of energy market liberalisation and regulatory harmonisation.

The Second Energy Package within the European Union pertains to a collection of legislative measures that were enacted in 2003 with the aim of advancing the liberalisation and integration of the energy markets across the European Union. The Second Energy Package encompassed several fundamental components, which can be identified as the key elements.

The Electricity Directive (2003/54/EC)[19] is a legislative measure that pertains to the regulation of electricity within the European Union. This directive facilitated increased competition within the electricity market of the European Union. The aforementioned policy initiative expanded upon the principles of granting third-party access to both transmission and distribution networks. It also established regulations to ensure transparent and non-discriminatory access to these networks. The Gas Directive (2003/55/EC)[20] shares similarities with the Electricity Directive as it seeks to enhance competition within the gas market of the European Union. The aforementioned measures expanded the scope of third-party utilisation of gas transmission and storage facilities, bolstered the authority of regulatory bodies, and implemented regulations pertaining to the accreditation of transmission system operators.

The Regulation on Cross-Border Exchanges in Electricity (1228/2003/EC)[21] seeks to enhance the efficiency of cross-border electricity exchanges and promote collaboration among transmission system operators. It is an extension of the earlier iteration of the regulation, which was part of the initial energy package. The Regulation on Cross-Border Exchanges in Gas (1775/2005/EC)[22] shares similarities with the regulation pertaining to electricity exchanges. Its primary objective is to

[19] Directive 2003/54/EC of the European Parliament and of the Council of 26 June 2003 concerning common rules for the internal market in electricity and repealing Directive 96/92/EC - Statements made with regard to decommissioning and waste management activities. OJ L 176, 15.7.2003, pp. 37–56.

[20] Directive 2003/55/EC of the European Parliament and of the Council of 26 June 2003 concerning common rules for the internal market in natural gas and repealing Directive 98/30/EC. OJ L 176, 15.7.2003, pp. 57–78.

[21] Regulation (EC) No 1228/2003 of the European Parliament and of the Council of 26 June 2003 on conditions for access to the network for cross-border exchanges in electricity (Text with EEA relevance). OJ L 176, 15.7.2003, pp. 1–10.

[22] Regulation (EC) No 1775/2005 of the European Parliament and of the Council of 28 September 2005 on conditions for access to the natural gas transmission networks (Text with EEA relevance) OJ L 289, 03/11/2005, pp. 1–13.

enhance the efficiency of cross-border gas exchanges and foster collaboration among gas transmission system operators.

The Second Energy Package played a pivotal role in the advancement of the European Union's internal energy market and the facilitation of competition within the electricity and gas sectors.[23] The package aimed to augment the regulatory framework and promote transparency in market operations with the objective of expanding consumer choice, mitigating energy costs, and enhancing supply security.[24] These measures were implemented as part of a larger endeavour to establish a functional and interconnected energy market in Europe, which ultimately resulted in the formulation and implementation of the Third and Fourth Energy Packages in subsequent years.

This legislation package introduced regulated third-party access requirements and obliged the transmission system operators to publish network access tariffs and other conditions on a non-discriminatory basis, which had to be approved by the national regulatory authorities. In the absence of a clear ownership unbundling, there was a real opportunity for companies to take advantage of their position by refusing to grant access and implying other hardcore restrictions such as cross-subsidization.[25] Under the Second Energy Package, vertically integrated companies had to be separated at least by functional, legal or accounting separation, but this model of market liberalization did not produce the desired results.[26] The separation of vertically integrated companies through legal, functional or accounting separation has failed to liberalize the market.[27] This problem persisted because the companies retained previous contacts and access to relevant information.[28] Therefore, functional, legal and accounting unbundling has created the prerequisites for purely formal partitioning without achieving the desired results of market liberalization. By the deadline for implementing the directives, the problem of market liberalization had still not been resolved,[29] and further steps had to be taken to improve the situation in market.

---

[23] Directive 2003/54/EC of the European Parliament and of the Council of 26 June 2003 concerning common rules for the internal market in electricity and repealing Directive 96/92/EC. OJ L 176, 15.7.2003, pp. 37–56. See Article 1. Directive 2003/55/EC of the European Parliament and of the Council of 26 June 2003 concerning common rules for the internal market in natural gas and repealing Directive 98/30/EC. OJ L 176, 15.7.2003, pp. 57–78. See Article 1.

[24] Directive 2003/54/EC of the European Parliament and of the Council of 26 June 2003 concerning common rules for the internal market in electricity and repealing Directive 96/92/EC. OJ L 176, 15.7.2003, pp. 37–56. See Article 1. Directive 2003/55/EC of the European Parliament and of the Council of 26 June 2003 concerning common rules for the internal market in natural gas and repealing Directive 98/30/EC. OJ L 176, 15.7.2003, pp. 57–78. See Article 1.

[25] Dralle (2018).

[26] Cameron (2005).

[27] Jones (2019).

[28] Davies and Price (2007).

[29] Communication from the Commission. Delivering the internal electricity market and making the most of public intervention. SWD (2013) 438 final, SWD (2013) 439 final, SWD (2013) 440 final, SWD (2013) 441 final, SWD (2013) 442 final. C (2013) 7243 final.

Following the provisions of the Second Energy Package, it was mandated that vertically integrated companies undergo separation through functional, legal, or accounting means.[30] However, it is worth noting that this particular approach to market liberalisation did not yield the intended outcomes. The attempt to liberalise the market through the separation of vertically integrated companies, whether through legal, functional, or accounting means, has proven to be ineffective. The persistence of this problem can be attributed to the companies' retention of previous contacts and continued access to pertinent information. Hence, the implementation of functional, legal, and accounting unbundling has established the necessary conditions for a purely formal separation, yet it has failed to accomplish the intended outcomes of market liberalisation. Despite the approaching deadline for the implementation of the directives, the issue of market liberalisation remained unresolved, necessitating additional measures to enhance the market situation.

3.4 Advancing Integration of Energy Markets: The Third Energy Package

The implementation of the Third Energy Package within the European Union was prompted by various significant rationales and goals, with the intention of advancing the liberalisation and standardisation of the European Union's energy markets. The adoption of the Third Energy Package, comprising a collection of directives and regulations, was undertaken to effectively tackle a range of difficulties and concerns within the energy industry. The European Union tried to enhance the integration of its energy markets and establish an authentic internal energy market. The objective of the Third Energy Package was to further advance the achievements of the First and Second Energy Packages, with the primary goal of facilitating unobstructed cross-border energy transmission.

The promotion of competition has consistently been a key goal within the energy sector. The objective of the package was to enhance competition by eliminating obstacles that hindered the entry of new players into the market.[31] This would subsequently result in a wider range of options for consumers and more competitive pricing. The issue of preventing market abuse was addressed by addressing concerns regarding potential instances of market abuse, including anti-competitive practices. The package encompasses rules aimed at mitigating market manipulation, enhancing market transparency, and fortifying the regulatory system.

The Third Energy Package has further strengthened the process of unbundling energy activities, specifically by enhancing the segregation of energy generation, transmission, and distribution operations. The primary objective was to mitigate any conflicts of interest and enhance the autonomy of transmission system operators

[30] Article 10 of the Electricity Directive 2003/54/EC and Article 9 of the Gas Directive 2003/55/EC.

[31] Cameron (2007).

(TSOs) and distribution system operators (DSOs). The prioritisation of regulatory independence has been underscored as a means to guarantee the efficient supervision of the energy industry through national regulatory bodies. The National Regulatory Authorities (NRAs) were bestowed with enhanced jurisdiction to oversee and implement regulations pertaining to market norms. The primary objective of the package was to enhance the empowerment of energy customers through the provision of improved information, simplified provider switching processes, and increased autonomy in managing their energy consumption. It advocated for initiatives aimed at enhancing consumer consciousness and safeguarding.

The intention was to encourage investment by focusing on creating a secure investment climate in the energy sector. One of the goals of the package was to establish a set of regulations that would promote trust and stability, therefore encouraging investments in infrastructure, renewable energy, and energy efficiency. The European Union has established ambitious targets to increase the number of renewable energy sources in its energy portfolio. The main goal of the third energy package was to promote the smooth integration of renewable energy sources into the current power grid infrastructure while also encouraging investments in ecologically sustainable energy technologies.

The maintenance of energy supply security continued to be a significant concern. The package encompassed provisions aimed at bolstering supply security through the enhancement of infrastructure, the promotion of energy source diversification, and the implementation of emergency response measures.[32] The Third Energy Package demonstrated alignment with pertinent articles of the Treaty on the Functioning of the European Union, namely those pertaining to competition (Articles 101 and 102 TFEU) and the internal energy market (Article 194 TFEU). In its entirety, the third energy package constituted a notable advancement in the European Union's endeavours to establish a more competitive, interconnected, and sustainable energy market. The primary objective of this initiative was to effectively tackle the dynamic difficulties and potential advantages within the energy industry, all the while guaranteeing adherence to the legal frameworks and treaty requirements established by the European Union.

The Third Energy Package consists of these Directives and Regulations:

- Directive 2009/72/EC of the European Parliament and of the Council of 13 July 2009 concerning common rules for the internal market in electricity and repealing Directive 2003/54/EC.
- Directive 2009/73/EC of the European Parliament and of the Council of 13 July 2009 concerning common rules for the internal market in natural gas and repealing Directive 2003/55/EC
- Regulation (EC) No 714/2009 of the European Parliament and of the Council of 13 July 2009 on conditions for access to the network for cross-border exchanges in electricity and repealing Regulation (EC) No 1228/2003.

[32] Bjornebye (2010).

- Regulation (EC) No 715/2009 of the European Parliament and of the Council of 13 July 2009 on conditions for access to the natural gas transmission networks and repealing Regulation (EC) No 1775/2005.
- Regulation (EC) No 713/2009 of the European Parliament and of the Council of 13 July 2009 establishing an Agency for the Cooperation of Energy Regulators.

The European Union's Third Energy Package refers to a collection of legislative measures that were enacted in 2009 with the aim of promoting the continued liberalisation and integration of the energy markets within the EU.[33] The objective of the package was to promote competition, strengthen consumer rights and protection, and enhance the efficiency of the internal energy market. The documents aimed to tackle significant concerns within the electricity and gas industries, with the objective of establishing a European energy market that is characterised by enhanced transparency, efficiency, and interconnectivity. The primary constituents of the third energy package encompass the following legislation that is elaborated bellow.

The Electricity Directive (2009/72/EC) is a legislative measure that pertains to the regulation of electricity within the European Union. The revised Electricity Directive was designed with the objective of enhancing competition within the electricity market of the European Union. The reinforcement of the unbundling of generation, transmission, and distribution activities serves the purpose of preventing conflicts of interest, increasing the independence of system operators, and fostering equitable market conditions.

The Gas Directive (2009/73/EC) shares similarities with the Electricity Directive in its objective to enhance competition within the European Union gas market. The legislation implemented measures to reinforce the unbundling obligations imposed on gas transmission system operators, with the objective of improving the transparency and oversight of gas infrastructure.

The Regulation on Cross-Border Electricity Exchanges (714/2009/EC) was implemented with the objective of bolstering cross-border electricity exchanges and fostering collaboration among transmission system operators.[34] The implementation of standardised regulations for the allocation of capacity and management of congestion was undertaken with the aim of enhancing market efficiency.

The Regulation on Conditions for Access to Gas Transmission Networks (715/2009/EC) shares similarities with the regulation governing electricity exchanges. Its primary objective is to enhance cross-border gas exchanges and foster collaboration among gas transmission system operators. The implementation of standard regulations for capacity allocation and tariff regulation was initiated.

Regulation (713/2009/EC) mandated the creation of the Agency for the Cooperation of Energy Regulators (ACER) as an independent regulatory body at the European Union (EU) level. The primary objective of ACER is to facilitate and enhance regulatory cooperation, monitor market dynamics, and effectively tackle

[33] Article 1 of both the Electricity Regulation (EC) No 713/2009 and the Gas Regulation (EC) No 714/2009.

[34] Article 1 of the Gas Regulation (EC) No 714/2009.

cross-border challenges within the energy sector.[35] The Directive on Energy End-Use Efficiency and Energy Services (2006/32/EC) underwent amendments as a component of the third energy package, with the aim of enhancing energy efficiency initiatives and establishing a fresh indicative objective for energy conservation by the year 2020.[36]

The Electricity and Gas Directives (2009/72/EC and 2009/73/EC) was implemented with the objective of bolstering consumer rights and safeguarding the energy market. Its primary goals included facilitating consumer access to transparent information, ensuring ease of supplier switching, and establishing safeguards against unfair practises. The Electricity and Gas Directives play a pivotal role in the European Union's comprehensive initiative to promote liberalisation and harmonisation within its energy markets. These regulations were implemented as a component of the wider EU energy market liberalisation initiatives with the objective of establishing an internal energy market for electricity and gas that is competitive, focused on consumers, and sustainable.

The adoption of the Third Energy Package represented notable progress in the European Union's efforts to develop a complete and competitive internal energy market. The main aim of this project was to address the ongoing challenges in the electricity and gas sectors, with the ultimate purpose of allowing customers to benefit from a more efficient and competitive energy market. The implementation of the package was crucial in promoting the European Union's energy policy objectives, which included promoting renewable energy, improving energy efficiency, and strengthening energy security.

The primary distinction lies in the implementation of more stringent regulations compared to the previous iterations. This legislation implemented more stringent measures, including the complete separation of transmission networks from production or supply, as well as the creation of a mechanism for collaboration between independent energy regulators and European transmission system operators. It also emphasised the importance of transparency and cooperation to guarantee the security of the energy supply. The government has granted enhanced authority and autonomy to energy regulators. These initiatives failed to establish a highly effective domestic market. The process of market liberalisation has followed a continuous pattern, with the gradual integration of national markets starting at the regional level and progressing towards the establishment of the EU single market. The process of liberalising the electricity sector in the Scandinavian countries commenced in 1990 and has since evolved into a successful power trading exchange known as Nord Pool Spot. Although in the early Commission decisions on concentrations, the Scandinavian electricity market was considered to be national in scope, the parties

[35] Article 1 of the Regulation (EC) No 713/2009.

[36] Directive 2012/27/EU of the European Parliament and of the Council of 25 October 2012 on energy efficiency, amending Directives 2009/125/EC and 2010/30/EU, and repealing Directives 2004/8/EC and 2006/32/EC. J L 315, 14.11.2012, pp. 1–56. Directive 2006/32/EC of the European Parliament and of the Council of 5 April 2006 on energy end-use efficiency and energy services and repealing Council Directive 93/76/EEC. OJ L 114, 27.4.2006, pp. 64–85. See Article 1, Article 3.

also traded electricity across borders, allowing consumers to choose the foreign electricity undertaking.[37]

The Third Energy Package seeks for the general objective to create internal energy market and include the respective provisions for the achievement of this target:

- The unbundling of the vertically integrated utilities.
- Strengthened the independence of regulators.
- Established Agency for the Cooperation of Energy Regulators (ACER).
- Enhanced the cross-border cooperation between transmission system operators, ENTSOE, ENTSOG to create the network codes, monitor the security of supply.
- Third party access to the essential facilities.
- The capacity allocation determined in a proper way.
- Enhanced consumer protection.

In the following section we provide the overview of each pillar.

3.4.1 The Unbundling Models

Unbundling pertains to the detachment of distinct components of the energy supply chain with the aim of mitigating conflicts of interest, fostering competition, and cultivating equitable market conditions within the energy sector of Europe.[38] The European Union has implemented various unbundling models with the aim of promoting fair competition and fostering a balanced market environment within the electricity and gas sectors.[39] The primary models of unbundling within the energy sector of the European Union are elaborated below.

Vertical unbundling, or ownership unbundling, is a paradigm that requires energy businesses with vertical integration to separate their ownership and operational management of transmission and distribution networks. The goal is to separate the generation and supply activities from the ownership and operation of transmission and distribution infrastructure. This method ensures the independence of network operators, promotes fair network access, and minimises any kind of bias against other participants in the market. The ISO model involves the establishment of an independent system operator where vertically integrated energy companies maintain

[37] Case IV/M.931 *Neste/Ivo*, Case IV/M.1231 *Ivo/Stockholm Energi*, Case COMP/M.3268 *Sydkraft/Graninge*.

[38] Directive 2009/72/EC of the European Parliament and of the Council of 13 July 2009 concerning common rules for the internal market in electricity and repealing Directive 2003/54/EC. OJ L 211, 14.8.2009, pp. 55–93. See Article 9. Directive 2009/73/EC of the European Parliament and of the Council of 13 July 2009 concerning common rules for the internal market in natural gas and repealing Directive 2003/55/EC. OJ L 211, 14.8.2009, pp. 94–136. See Article 10.

[39] Berge et al. (2012).

ownership of their transmission and distribution networks.[40] The responsibility for the operation and management of the transmission network lies with the independent system operator. The primary objective of this arrangement is to uphold the autonomy and impartiality of the system operator, thereby facilitating effective grid management and equitable access to the network.

The ITO concept, commonly referred to as Independent Transmission Operator unbundling, exhibits resemblances to the ISO paradigm.[41] However, it entails the creation of an independent transmission operator to supervise and manage the transmission network. In this situation, the independent operator can appear as either a separate legal organization or a functionally separate department within the vertically integrated energy company.

The legal unbundling model, also known as functional unbundling, involves vertically integrated energy companies retaining ownership of transmission and distribution networks while functionally separating these activities from their generation and supply businesses. The primary objective is to prevent any form of discriminatory behaviour or preferential treatment in terms of network access.

According to the Ownership Control Unbundling (OCU) model, energy corporations must retain ownership of the transmission network while delegating operational control to an independent body.[42] Even if the vertically integrated firm still owns the transmission system, this model ensures autonomous control. European Union member states adopt varying unbundling approaches due to their autonomy in selecting how to enforce unbundling obligations, which are contingent upon their unique energy market structure and regulatory environment. The main goal of these unbundling models is to promote competition, improve transparency, and stimulate investment in the energy sector of the European Union while giving priority to safeguarding consumer interests and guaranteeing a reliable and secure energy supply.

Unbundling refers to the process of separating energy supply and generation activities from the transmission networks. The Electricity Directive offered three unbundling models. The decision on the model preference was delegated to the Member States. Vertically integrated firms, operating at all levels, implement unbundling. Control over the entire energy chain diminishes market competition and creates artificial obstacles to prevent entry into the market. The transportation of

---

[40] Balmert and Brunerkreeft (2010).

[41] Directive 2009/72/EC of the European Parliament and of the Council of 13 July 2009 concerning common rules for the internal market in electricity and repealing Directive 2003/54/EC. OJ L 211, 14.8.2009, pp. 55–93. See Article 13. Directive 2009/73/EC of the European Parliament and of the Council of 13 July 2009 concerning common rules for the internal market in natural gas and repealing Directive 2003/55/EC. J L 211, 14.8.2009, pp. 94–136. See Article 15.

[42] Directive 2009/72/EC of the European Parliament and of the Council of 13 July 2009 concerning common rules for the internal market in electricity and repealing Directive 2003/54/EC. OJ L 211, 14.8.2009, pp. 55–93. See Article 13. Directive 2009/73/EC of the European Parliament and of the Council of 13 July 2009 concerning common rules for the internal market in natural gas and repealing Directive 2003/55/EC. J L 211, 14.8.2009, pp. 94–136. See Article 15.

energy to consumers necessitates essential components: generation, transmission, distribution, and supply. Power plants generate electricity and then transmit it to transmission lines. Transmission networks transport energy over great distances using high voltages. Transmission system operators typically provide balancing services to ensure that the supply of electricity aligns with the demand. The distribution system operates at lower voltages, transferring electricity from the high-voltage transmission system to consumers and houses. The gas sector employs similar techniques. Energy supply is a separate process that involves exchanging electricity in wholesale marketplaces before selling it to customers.

The concept of unbundling refers to the process of separating energy supply and generation activities from the transmission networks. The Electricity Directive introduced three distinct models of unbundling.[43] The decision regarding model preference was delegated to the Member States. The process of unbundling is commonly implemented in vertically integrated firms that engage in operations across multiple levels. The exertion of such control over the entirety of the energy chain consequently diminishes competition within the market and establishes artificial barriers to market entry.

The delivery of energy to consumers requires multiple crucial elements, including the generation, transmission, distribution, and supply processes. Power plants produce electricity, which is then sent over transmission lines. Transmission networks transport energy over vast distances, typically at elevated voltages. Transmission system operators are normally responsible for maintaining a balanced electrical supply that is in line with demand.[44] The distribution system functions at lower voltages and enables the transmission of energy from the high-voltage transmission system to end-users, such as consumers and houses. The gas industry employs similar techniques.

3.4.1.1 The Full Ownership Unbundling

The implementation of full ownership unbundling in the energy sector of the European Union serves as a crucial regulatory strategy aimed at fostering competition, ensuring equitable market conditions, and facilitating efficient grid management. The European Union's dedication to establishing a unified energy market across Europe resulted in the implementation of the third energy package in 2009.[45]

---

[43] Directive 2009/72/EC of the European Parliament and of the Council of 13 July 2009 concerning common rules for the internal market in electricity and repealing Directive 2003/54/EC. OJ L 211, 14.8.2009, pp. 55–93. See Article 9.

[44] Directive 2009/72/EC of the European Parliament and of the Council of 13 July 2009 concerning common rules for the internal market in electricity and repealing Directive 2003/54/EC. OJ L 211, 14.8.2009, pp. 55–93. See Article 12.

[45] Regulation (EC) No 713/2009 of the European Parliament and of the Council of 13 July 2009 establishing an Agency for the Cooperation of Energy Regulators. OJ L 211, 14.8.2009, pp. 1–14. See Article 1. Regulation (EC) No 714/2009 of the European Parliament and of the Council of

This package encompasses measures for complete ownership unbundling. The present chapter delves into the notion of full ownership unbundling, elucidating its aims, principal characteristics, benefits, and obstacles within the framework of the European Union's endeavours to establish a proficient and unified energy market.

Full ownership unbundling refers to the comprehensive separation of energy generation and supply operations from the ownership and operational control of transmission and distribution networks.[46] According to this framework, energy companies that possess vertical integration must divest their ownership stakes in the network infrastructure and establish distinct legal entities to oversee transmission and distribution operations.[47] By establishing independent transmission and distribution network operators, full ownership unbundling achieves the promotion of competition. This measure effectively eliminates the possibility of engaging in anti-competitive conduct, discriminatory practises, or providing preferential treatment to the vertically integrated company's own generation assets.

To ensure network neutrality, it is imperative to separate the ownership and operation of the network from energy generation and supply businesses. This separation guarantees a neutral and non-discriminatory management of the grid. The network ensures equitable and unbiased access for all market participants, including both new entrants and existing competitors. The promotion of competition and establishment of equitable conditions through full ownership unbundling serve to stimulate investment in energy infrastructure and foster innovation within the energy sector. Independent network operators have the capacity to prioritise the enhancement of grid reliability, efficiency, and integration with renewable energy sources.

The implementation of full ownership unbundling necessitates vertically integrated energy companies establishing distinct legal entities for their transmission and distribution operations in order to achieve separation of activities.[48] It is imperative that the ownership of these entities remain separate from any ownership interests in energy generation and supply activities. The independence of system operators is a

---

13 July 2009 on conditions for access to the network for cross-border exchanges in electricity and repealing Regulation (EC) No 1228/2003. OJ L 211, 14.8.2009, pp. 15–35. See Article 1. Directive 2009/72/EC of the European Parliament and of the Council of 13 July 2009 concerning common rules for the internal market in electricity and repealing Directive 2003/54/EC. OJ L 211, 14.8.2009, pp. 55–93. See Article 1. Directive 2009/73/EC of the European Parliament and of the Council of 13 July 2009 concerning common rules for the internal market in natural gas and repealing Directive 2003/55/EC. OJ L 211, 14.8.2009, pp. 94–136. See Article 1.

[46] Directive 2009/72/EC of the European Parliament and of the Council of 13 July 2009 concerning common rules for the internal market in electricity and repealing Directive 2003/54/EC. OJ L 211, 14.8.2009, pp. 55–93. See Article 9. Directive 2009/73/EC of the European Parliament and of the Council of 13 July 2009 concerning common rules for the internal market in natural gas and repealing Directive 2003/55/EC. OJ L 211, 14.8.2009, pp. 94–136. See Article 10.

[47] Davies and Price (2007).

[48] Commission staff working paper. Interpretative note on Directive 2009/72/EC concerning common rules for the internal market in electricity and Directive 2009/73/EC concerning common rules for the internal market in natural gas. The unbundling regime. 22. January 2010.

crucial aspect of ensuring the fair and unbiased operation of transmission and distribution networks. These operators are required to conduct their activities in a transparent and non-discriminatory manner, thereby upholding the principles of impartiality. The individuals in question bear the responsibility of overseeing grid management, maintenance, and expansion. Regulatory oversight is a crucial aspect of ensuring compliance with unbundling requirements and market regulations by network operators. Regulatory authorities, which may include national energy regulators and the ACER at the European Union level, are in charge of carrying out this duty.[49] These authorities are responsible for monitoring and enforcing compliance in the energy sector.

One of the benefits of full ownership unbundling is the promotion of competition in the energy market. This policy allows for the participation of new entrants and smaller players, enabling them to compete on an equal basis with established energy companies. Enhanced grid efficiency is achieved when independent network operators prioritise the effective management and enhancement of transmission and distribution infrastructure, resulting in a more dependable and robust energy grid. The process of unbundling encourages the development of energy infrastructure, such as smart grid technologies and the integration of renewable energy, which in turn facilitates investment and innovation. This is achieved through the establishment of a market environment that is both transparent and competitive. Transition costs are a significant consideration when implementing full ownership unbundling in vertically integrated companies. This process necessitates restructuring operations and establishing new legal entities, which can be both challenging and expensive. Regulators are tasked with the responsibility of ensuring rigorous adherence to unbundling requirements in order to prevent any attempts to bypass or violate the essence of the regulation.

Market fragmentation may occur as a result of full ownership unbundling, leading to the presence of multiple independent network operators that lack coordination.[50] This lack of coordination has the potential to impact the flow of electricity and gas across borders. In conclusion, the implementation of full ownership unbundling has had a substantial impact on the European energy sector, as it has effectively stimulated competition, improved grid efficiency, and fostered investments in sustainable energy infrastructure. The European Union is currently progressing towards the establishment of a unified energy market within its member states. In order to

[49] Regulation (EC) No 713/2009 of the European Parliament and of the Council of 13 July 2009 establishing an Agency for the Cooperation of Energy Regulators. OJ L 211, 14.8.2009, pp. 1–14. See Article 1. Directive 2009/72/EC of the European Parliament and of the Council of 13 July 2009 concerning common rules for the internal market in electricity and repealing Directive 2003/54/EC. OJ L 211, 14.8.2009, pp. 55–93. See Article 35. Directive 2009/73/EC of the European Parliament and of the Council of 13 July 2009 concerning common rules for the internal market in natural gas and repealing Directive 2003/55/EC. OJ L 211, 14.8.2009, pp. 94–136. See Article 39.

[50] Commission staff working document. Ownership unbundling. The Commission's practice in assessing the presence of a conflict of interest including in case of financial investors. SWD (2013) 177 final.

attain energy security, sustainability, and consumer welfare, the adoption of complete ownership unbundling is regarded as a crucial policy measure.[51]

The third energy package sets out the criteria for full ownership unbundling of the vertically integrated companies. A vertically integrated undertaking within the meaning of the gas directive is a natural gas undertaking or group of natural gas undertakings in which the same person or persons have the power, directly or indirectly, to exercise control and perform at least one of the functions of production or supply of natural gas. Under the Electricity Directive, a vertically integrated undertaking is defined in a similar way, except that the specificity of the sector excludes direct or indirect control of the transmission or distribution and production and supply activities. Article 9 of the Electricity and Gas Directives provides that the same person or persons are not entitled to exercise control or any right over the transmission system operator or over the transmission system operator in relation to any of the functions of production or supply. Article 2 (34) of the electricity Directive and the gas directive clarifies the concept of control, which means that rights, contracts or any other means give the enterprise decisive influence over: the ownership or the right to use all or part of the assets of an undertaking and the rights or contracts which company bodies, voting or decision making. In other words, a company active in the supply or production business may not hold any shares in the transmission company, nor may it appoint any members of the board of directors or voting rights. Supply and production companies have the right to choose who to sell their shares to. Such requirements ensure the implementation of a model of full ownership unbundling from production or supply functions.[52]

According to Article 9 (1)(a) of the electricity and gas directives, it is stipulated that any entity that possesses a transmission system is required to function as a transmission system operator. As stipulated in Article 9 (1)(c), individuals or entities are prohibited from appointing or exercising authority over the entity responsible for carrying out generation or supply functions, either directly or indirectly. This prohibition extends to the appointment of members to the transmission system operator, the supervisory body, the administrative or management body of the transmission system, or any claims against said company. According to Article 9 (1)(d), it is stipulated that an individual should not be qualified to serve as a member of any entity engaged in the activities of production or supply, nor should they hold a position on the supervisory board, management board, or legal bodies of a transmission system operator or a transmission system. The entitlements outlined in Article 9 (1)(b)(c) encompass the authority to exercise voting privileges and the authority to designate individuals to hold positions on the supervisory board, administrative board, or other bodies that represent the enterprise or the controlling

[51] Directive 2009/72/EC of the European Parliament and of the Council of 13 July 2009 concerning common rules for the internal market in electricity and repealing Directive 2003/54/EC. OJ L 211, 14.8.2009, pp. 55–93. See Article 9. Directive 2009/73/EC of the European Parliament and of the Council of 13 July 2009 concerning common rules for the internal market in natural gas and repealing Directive 2003/55/EC. OJ L 211, 14.8.2009, pp. 94–136. See Article 10.

[52] Dorigoni and Pontoni (2008).

stake. The implementation of the complete ownership unbundling concept is expected to guarantee equitable and unbiased access to energy networks.

This paradigm facilitates enhanced market competition by establishing distinct entities involved in transmission, production, or distribution activities. As an integrated corporation working across several business areas, it is worth noting that while transmission maintains a monopoly, production is a competitive aspect. This particular market structure poses challenges for new entrants, as the company in question has a vested interest in providing for its own generation. Full ownership unbundling refers to the concept of dividing the roles of management and ownership. The transmission system operator assumes the roles of both system owner and system administrator, functioning as an independent operator separate from the business interests of other activities. In the context of ownership unbundling, the vertically integrated enterprise is required to transfer ownership to an independent investor or to a separate organisation that is not associated with the vertically integrated corporation.[53] The aforementioned endeavour should refrain from exerting any form of substantial control over the investor, whether through direct or indirect means. This includes, but is not limited to, exercising veto power, appointing individuals to the board or supervisory board of the company, or possessing sole shareholder rights.

The assurance of independence for the members of the supervisory and management bodies of the transmission system operator from the interests of the vertically integrated company shall be achieved via the implementation of the following measures. The vertically integrated enterprise is not eligible to designate individuals to serve on the supervisory board, management body, or any other governing body of the transmission system operator. Members of the transmission system operator's bodies who are already in office are prohibited from simultaneously holding positions as members of the body of the vertically integrated undertaking or any of its divisions. The decision-making authority for the operation of the transmission system operator is with the management bodies, which are responsible for making direct decisions within their designated scope of authority. It is important to ensure that the vertically integrated undertaking does not exceed the rights of minority shareholders in terms of its impact.

According to Council Regulation (EC) No. 139/2004,[54] which pertains to the regulation of concentrations between undertakings, the term control is defined as the capacity to exert a significant influence over an undertaking by means of ownership, the entitlement to utilise an asset, or the authority to exert a decisive impact on the organisational structure of said undertaking. Ownership unbundling is further

[53] Directive 2009/72/EC of the European Parliament and of the Council of 13 July 2009 concerning common rules for the internal market in electricity and repealing Directive 2003/54/EC. OJ L 211, 14.8.2009, pp. 55–93. See Article 9. Directive 2009/73/EC of the European Parliament and of the Council of 13 July 2009 concerning common rules for the internal market in natural gas and repealing Directive 2003/55/EC. OJ L 211, 14.8.2009, pp. 94–136. See Article 10.

[54] Council Regulation (EC) No 139/2004 of 20 January 2004 on the control of concentrations between undertakings (the EC Merger Regulation) OJ L 24, 29.1.2004, pp. 1–22.

underscored by its significance as a crucial component. Control refers to the legal or transactional entitlements possessed by an individual that, either independently or collectively, grant them the authority to significantly influence the functioning of an organisation. These rights encompass a range of entitlements, such as the ownership of either the entirety or a portion of the assets belonging to the entity or the privilege to utilise all or a portion of said assets. Additionally, these rights may also confer upon the individual a significant influence over the composition of the company's management bodies, the decisions made by said bodies, or the manner in which the company is operated.

Various methods, such as acquiring firm shares and entering into long-term contracts with management implications, are deemed permissible for achieving control. Competition law posits that the acquisition of 50% of shares, votes, or assets implies the acquisition of control; however, this presumption can be challenged based on the specific circumstances.[55] Control can manifest in various ways, including direct control, control through intermediaries, individual control, joint control, proactive control where decision-making authority lies with an individual, passive control where an individual has the power to veto decisions, unilateral control where control is held by a single person, and joint control where control is shared among multiple individuals, such as in the case of a shareholders' agreement.

The Commission's paper on ownership unbundling provides a comprehensive analysis of the requirements pertaining to the absence of other rights.[56] The aforementioned rights encompass voting rights, the authority to designate individuals to the management body, possessing a controlling interest, and the entitlement of passive shareholders to dividends, without the inclusion of voting rights. The rigidity of this approach becomes apparent when confronted with the challenge of separating state-owned energy companies, specifically in relation to the stringent enforcement of control separation requirements. It is worth noting that achieving a complete separation of ownership, encompassing both management and control, may not always be feasible.

The paradigm of total ownership unbundling has established the necessary prerequisites for fostering a competitive energy market through the segregation of vertically integrated operations, thereby enabling consumers to exercise their freedom of choice in selecting an energy provider. Nevertheless, it is important to consider that while the fragmentation of enterprises may contribute to the advancement of the internal market to some extent, it is imperative to uphold an integrated approach towards diversifying energy sources, ensuring security of supply, and fostering the creation of new generation capacity. Furthermore, over an extended period, this could potentially lead to a rise in prices.

---

[55] Council Regulation (EC) No 139/2004 of 20 January 2004 on the control of concentrations between undertakings (EC Merger Regulation). OJ L 24, 29.1.2004, pp. 1–22. See Article 3 (1) (b).

[56] Commission staff working paper. Interpretative note on Directive 2009/72/EC concerning common rules for the internal market in electricity and Directive 2009/73/EC concerning common rules for the internal market in natural gas. The unbundling regime. 22. January 2010.

3.4.1.2 The Independent System Operator (ISO)

The Independent System Operator (ISO) plays a crucial role in contemporary energy markets by ensuring the effective and trustworthy functioning of electricity transmission systems. ISOs, as a crucial component of the European Union's endeavours to establish a unified energy market, assume a pivotal function in upholding grid stability, fostering competition, and integrating renewable energy sources.[57] This chapter delves into the concept of the ISO, examining its functions, benefits, challenges, and significance within the framework of the European Union's energy policy objectives. An ISO is an entity that assumes the responsibility of ensuring the secure, non-discriminatory, and efficient operation of the electricity transmission network in an impartial manner. The entity functions as the central coordinator of the energy grid, responsible for maintaining a real-time equilibrium between the supply and demand of electricity.

Grid management involves the ongoing monitoring of the electricity grid by the ISO, with the objective of maintaining a state of equilibrium between supply and demand. The system is responsible for the management of power flows, the resolution of congestion, and the implementation of corrective measures in order to ensure the stability of the grid.[58] Market facilitation is one of the key functions performed by the ISO, which involves the supervision of electricity market operations. This includes activities such as the scheduling and dispatch of power generation. The system enables the smooth execution of market transactions and guarantees equitable grid access for all participants. Grid planning is a significant responsibility undertaken by an ISO, as it involves evaluating the necessity for expanding infrastructure and incorporating emerging renewable energy sources into the grid.

Grid stability and reliability are crucial aspects of the ISO's operations. Through real-time grid management, the ISO effectively balances the electricity supply with the demand, thereby mitigating the potential occurrence of blackouts and ensuring a consistent and dependable energy supply. Efficient resource allocation is achieved through the market facilitation provided by the ISO, which optimises the dispatch of power generation. This approach encourages the utilisation of generation sources that are both cost-effective and environmentally friendly. The integration of renewable energy sources is facilitated by an ISO, which effectively manages their intermittent characteristics and maximises their utilisation within the power grid.

ISOs are entities responsible for the operation, control, and coordination of the transmission system in a given region. They play a crucial role in ensuring reliable and efficient The European Network of Transmission System Operators for Electricity (ENTSOE) serves as the overarching entity responsible for coordinating the

[57] Regulation (EC) No 714/2009 of the European Parliament and of the Council of 13 July 2009 on conditions for access to the network for cross-border exchanges in electricity and repealing Regulation (EC) No 1228/2003. OJ L 211, 14.8.2009, pp. 15–35. See Article 13.

[58] Regulation (EC) No 714/2009 of the European Parliament and of the Council of 13 July 2009 on conditions for access to the network for cross-border exchanges in electricity and repealing Regulation (EC) No 1228/2003. OJ L 211, 14.8.2009, pp. 15–35. See Article 13.

operations of individual ISOs and transmission system operators (TSOs) throughout Europe.[59] ENTSOE plays a crucial role in promoting collaboration and harmonisation among ISOs in order to establish a well-integrated and interconnected electricity grid across Europe. Regional Coordination Centres play a crucial role within the ENTSOE by promoting effective cross-border coordination and enhancing the efficiency of electricity transmission between adjacent countries.[60] The Agency for the Cooperation of Energy Regulators (ACER) plays a significant role in monitoring the operations of ISOs and TSOs to ensure adherence to European Union regulations and facilitate the effective functioning of energy markets.[61]

The integration of renewable energy sources into the grid presents significant challenges for ISOs, as they must effectively manage this integration while maintaining grid stability in the face of the inherent variability of these sources. Grid modernization is a crucial investment for ISOs in order to adapt to the rapid advancements in technology. This is necessary to effectively integrate emerging technologies like energy storage and demand response.

In order to accomplish the objective of establishing a comprehensive and unified energy market in Europe, it is imperative for ISOs to strengthen cross-border coordination and facilitate smooth electricity exchanges among Member States. ISOs are a vital component of the European Union's energy market design, as they are responsible for ensuring the reliability, competitiveness, and sustainability of the energy system. ISOs play a crucial role in the attainment of the European Union's energy policy goals, namely energy security, decarbonization, and consumer welfare, through their efficient management of the electricity grid, facilitation of market transactions, and integration of renewable energy sources.[62] The role of ISOs in fostering a resilient and interconnected European energy market will become increasingly vital as the energy landscape continues to evolve.

The choice of an independent system operator represents an additional approach that can be employed as a potential solution for the execution of the energy market liberalisation outlined in the third energy package. The aforementioned model is comparatively more permissive, as it allows the corporation to exercise control over

---

[59] Commission staff working document. Enforcement of the Third Energy Market Package. Accompanying the document Communication from the Commission to the European Parliament, the Council, the European Economic and Social Committee and the Committee of the Regions. Progress towards completing the Internal Energy Market. COM (2014) 634 final. SWD (2014) 310 final, SWD (2014) 311 final, SWD (2014) 312 final, SWD (2014) 313 final, SWD (2014) 314 final. SWD (2014) 315 final.

[60] Regulation (EC) No 714/2009 of the European Parliament and of the Council of 13 July 2009 on conditions for access to the network for cross-border exchanges in electricity and repealing Regulation (EC) No 1228/2003. OJ L 211, 14.8.2009, pp. 15–35. See Article 8.

[61] Regulation (EU) No 1227/2011 of the European Parliament and of the Council of 25 October 2011 on wholesale energy market integrity and transparency Text with EEA relevance. OJ L 326, 8.12.2011, pp. 1–16.

[62] Regulation (EC) No 714/2009 of the European Parliament and of the Council of 13 July 2009 on conditions for access to the network for cross-border exchanges in electricity and repealing Regulation (EC) No 1228/2003. OJ L 211, 14.8.2009, pp. 15–35. See Article 13.

the transmission networks through ownership. However, the company is required to outsource the tasks of operation, maintenance, and investment pertaining to these networks.

There are two well-defined models of independent system operators, known as "deep ISO" and "shallow ISO".[63] This chapter will provide a thorough analysis of both models. It is crucial to acknowledge that the profound ISO model delegated all functions to a third party. The corporation owns all of the shares, but ISO is responsible for carrying out the network operator's tasks, making investment decisions, and maintaining direct communication with customers. However, according to the ISO model, the transmission company is responsible for all additional system operator requirements. Under the current model, the system operator is solely responsible for the gearbox function. Therefore, the ISO model can be considered a type of partial separation that falls between complete ownership unbundling and legal separation. An important advantage of using this technique is that it allows corporations to avoid the need to sell their shares, thereby allowing them to maintain ownership of the networks. The shallow ISO model may not effectively support market liberalisation due to its narrow focus, where the gearbox firm retains all rights and the ISO only performs a single function. As a result, market liberalization integration would not be viable within the confines of this specific paradigm.

The Commission endorses the concept of complete ownership unbundling as the optimal approach to guaranteeing market competitiveness in the energy sector, specifically in relation to the separation of generation and transmission activities.[64] Furthermore, it serves to guarantee the security of the energy supply and promote the diversification of energy sources. Excessive market concentration engenders concerns that impede market participants from effectively reducing prices. Based on the ISO model, the vertically integrated enterprise retains ownership of the networks despite transferring ownership to a third party with a legally separate structure from that of the network owner. The academic literature distinguishes between various geographical components of the ISO. There is a requirement for a single ISO for each transmission system operator. National ISOs are responsible for overseeing all

[63] ENTSOE Ten-Year Network Development Plan (TYNDP). Annual Report on the Results of Monitoring the Internal Electricity and Natural Gas Markets in 2022. Guidelines on the application of Regulation (EC) No 714/2009 on conditions for access to the network for cross-border exchanges in electricity SWD (2011) 211 final. EER Status Review of the Internal Electricity and Gas Markets 2020. Regulation (EC) No 714/2009 of the European Parliament and of the Council of 13 July 2009 on conditions for access to the network for cross-border exchanges in electricity and repealing Regulation (EC) No 1228/2003. OJ L 211, 14.8.2009, pp. 15–35. See Article 13. Directive 2009/72/EC of the European Parliament and of the Council of 13 July 2009 concerning common rules for the internal market in electricity and repealing Directive 2003/54/EC. OJ L 211, 14.8.2009, pp. 55–93. See Article 9.

[64] Directive 2009/72/EC of the European Parliament and the Council of 13 July 2009 concerning common rules for the internal market in electricity and repealing Directive 2003/54/EC (OJ L 211, 14.8.2009, p. 55). Directive 2009/73/EC of the European Parliament and the Council of 13 July 2009 concerning common rules for the internal market in natural gas and repealing Directive 2003/55/EC (OJ L 211, 14.8.2009, p. 94).

networks within a specific country, regardless of their ownership structure. Regional ISOs involve a supranational system operator that coordinates multiple national networks.

It is imperative to emphasise that the use of the ISO model aims to mitigate the prevalence of discrimination within the financial transactions of vertically integrated enterprises. The establishment of an internal market and its subsequent liberalisation are facilitated by the adoption of a regional ISO model. The implementation of the ISO model gives rise to several complexities. Firstly, it is important to acknowledge the presence of a conflict of interest between the corporate entity that possesses ownership of the organisation and the ISO regarding the allocation and dissemination of the organisation's competencies.[65] The decision regarding the ISO may ultimately rest with the ISO itself; however, it is possible that the financial burden of the investment may be imposed upon the owner of the gearbox system. This situation has the potential to generate conflict in a specific context.

The allocation of responsibilities, financial accountability, and establishment of a profit-sharing mechanism in situations involving disputes regarding network growth and management lack clarity. This presents another issue of concern. Who bears the financial responsibility in the event that the actions undertaken by the ISO fail to achieve their intended outcomes? The aforementioned query is the subject of contemplation. The issue of liability arises due to a lack of clarity regarding which companies would bear responsibility in the event of an incident and determining whose culpability can be attributed to inadequate investment. This situation presents a challenge in ascertaining the party accountable for the financial restitution.

The term "deep ISO" refers to a situation where the owner of a network loses control over investment planning and is no longer responsible for providing access to a third party. In this context, deep ISO can be considered equivalent to de facto expropriation. ISO assumes responsibility for the implementation of all of these functions. There exists a scenario wherein an ISO may formulate an investment plan, yet the network owner may express disagreement with the proposed plan. Despite the network owner's original intent, investment planning is conducted by the ISO, as it assumes responsibility for this function, while the owner is solely accountable for executing projects that have been successfully finalised. Despite the prevalence of the deep ISO model in the United States, a comparable model with similar characteristics can be found in the United Kingdom. In the context of the electrical industry in Scotland, it is worth noting that National Grid, an operator based in England and Wales, assumes the role of an ISO for the Scottish transmission networks. These networks, on the other hand, are under the control of a vertically integrated firm located in Scotland. This serves as a singular illustration of the potential operational dynamics of vertical integration. The shallow ISO model is implemented in practise,

[65] Commission Staff Working Paper. Interpretative Note on Directive 2009/72/EC Concerning Common Rules for the Internal Market in Electricity and Directive 2009/73/EC Concerning Common Rules for the Internal Market in Natural Gas. The Unbundling Regime. 2010.

as the responsibility for managing network investments is delegated to the owner of the network rather than being held by National Grid.[66]

The ISO concept has emerged as a crucial component in the dynamic energy sector.[67] The significance of its function in maintaining equilibrium among the objectives of efficiency, competition, and reliability cannot be overstated. Despite the existence of ongoing problems, ISOs remain integral to influencing the trajectory of energy markets, thereby guaranteeing a sustainable and resilient energy landscape for the future.

3.4.1.3 The Independent Transmission Operator (ITO)

The emergence and evolution of independent transmission operators throughout history provide compelling evidence of the ongoing and dynamic transition taking place within the energy industry. A comprehensive understanding of the historical context is necessary to fully comprehend the function and significance of independent transmission operators within modern energy networks. The concept of centralised grid management may be traced back to the early phases of electrification, when local utilities were tasked with the operation of their respective generation, transmission, and distribution networks. The utilities, often identified by their vertical integration, were assigned the duty of supplying electricity to their respective geographic regions.

Technology advancements and growing power demand made it clear that the grid needed expansion. Utilities began the process of constructing interconnections between their systems in order to improve resource sharing and increase dependability. The introduction of this interconnection laid the groundwork for both regional and national grid growth. The increasing intricacy and need for expert grid management have propelled the rise of grid operators. The operators primarily concentrated on managing high-voltage transmission networks, ensuring a steady and stable electricity flow, and effectively handling congestion-related difficulties. Many countries introduced regulatory reforms in the late twentieth century to promote competition in the energy sector. As a result, the vertically integrated

---

[66] UK Department for Business, Energy & Industrial Strategy (BEIS). Electricity Market Reform: Policy Overview. UK Government. Available at: https://www.gov.uk/government/publications/electricity-market-reform-policy-overview. Ofgem. National Grid's Role as System Operator. Ofgem Publications. Available at: https://www.ofgem.gov.uk/publications/national-grid-role-system-operator. UK Government. Energy White Paper: Powering our Net Zero Future. December 2020. Available at: https://www.gov.uk/government/publications/energy-white-paper-powering-our-net-zero-future.

[67] Directive 2009/72/EC of the European Parliament and of the Council of 13 July 2009 concerning common rules for the internal market in electricity and repealing Directive 2003/54/EC. OJ L 211, 14.8.2009, pp. 55–93. See Article 13. Regulation (EC) No 714/2009 of the European Parliament and of the Council of 13 July 2009 on conditions for access to the network for cross-border exchanges in electricity and repealing Regulation (EC) No 1228/2003. OJ L 211, 14.8.2009, pp. 15–35. See Article 12.

utilities broke apart, leading to the separation of generating, transmission, and distribution activities. Furthermore, it necessitated the creation of independent entities responsible for grid management.[68] The emergence of autonomous transmission operators as separate entities responsible for the functioning, optimization, and maintenance of transmission networks was a significant advancement in the late twentieth and early twenty-first centuries. The aim of this modification was to enhance the impartiality, equity, and effectiveness of the grid.

Regional independent system operators assumed the role of overseeing transmission activities across larger geographical regions, facilitating the exchange of energy between different countries, and ensuring the stability of the power system. The use of various grid management technologies, including real-time monitoring, control systems, and grid analytics, has provided independent transmission operators with the ability to enhance the efficiency of grid operations, facilitate the integration of renewable energy sources, and effectively address fluctuations in energy demand.

Independent Transmission Operators have encountered a range of obstacles, such as the need to guarantee the durability of power grids in the presence of severe weather occurrences, mitigating cybersecurity risks, and adapting to the incorporation of distributed energy resources.[69] The capacity to adapt and develop has played a crucial role in ensuring their sustained relevance. With the ongoing decarbonisation, decentralisation, and digitalization of the energy sector, there is an increasing recognition of the crucial role played by independent transmission operators in maintaining the dependability and sustainability of electricity networks. The historical development of independent transmission operators demonstrates the industry's dedication to improving the efficiency, dependability, and equity of the power grid while also adjusting to the changing energy environment. Furthermore, this highlights the continuous significance of ITOs in influencing the trajectory of energy systems in the future.

An independent transmission operator plays a crucial role in the energy industry by assuming responsibility for the independent operation and management of electricity transmission networks.[70] The emergence of independent transmission

[68] Commission Staff Working Paper. Interpretative Note on Directive 2009/72/EC Concerning Common Rules for the Internal Market in Electricity and Directive 2009/73/EC Concerning Common Rules for the Internal Market in Natural Gas. The Unbundling Regime. 2010.

[69] Directive 2009/72/EC of the European Parliament and of the Council of 13 July 2009 concerning common rules for the internal market in electricity and repealing Directive 2003/54/EC. OJ L 211, 14.8.2009, pp. 55–93. See Article 17. Regulation (EU) 2019/943 of the European Parliament and of the Council of 5 June 2019 on the internal market for electricity (recast). OJ L 158, 14.6.2019, pp. 54–124. See Article 40. Directive (EU) 2019/944 of the European Parliament and of the Council of 5 June 2019 on common rules for the internal market for electricity and amending Directive 2012/27/EU. OJ L 158, 14.6.2019, pp. 125–199. See Article 54.

[70] Commission staff working document. Report on the ITO Model Accompanying the document Communication from the Commission to the European Parliament, the Council, the European Economic and Social Committee and the Committee of the Regions. Progress towards completing the Internal Energy Market. COM (2014) 634 final. SWD (2014) 310 final, SWD (2014) 311 final, SWD (2014) 313 final, SWD (2014) 314 final, SWD (2014) 315 final. SWD (2014) 312 final.

operators has become a crucial element in energy market reforms. Their primary objectives include improving grid reliability, fostering competition, and facilitating the integration of renewable energy sources.[71] This chapter explores the concept of independent transmission operators, examining their roles, advantages, difficulties, and importance within the framework of the European Union's ambitious energy policy objectives. An independent transmission operator is a legally separate and self-governing company that assumes responsibility for the technical and operational administration of electricity transmission networks. The entity functions autonomously from energy generation and supply enterprises, thereby guaranteeing an impartial and open approach to the management of the grid.

The ITO is in charge of overseeing the transmission grid's operation, ensuring its reliability, efficiency, and safety. The primary objective is to optimise power flows and minimise congestion in order to uphold grid stability. Grid planning is a crucial aspect of the development and expansion of transmission infrastructure, wherein independent transmission operators assume a substantial role. Market facilitation refers to the role of independent transmission operator in promoting fair and equal access to the transmission network for all participants in the market. This ensures that market transactions are conducted without any form of discrimination. Electricity trading and dispatch are facilitated by these entities, which promote competition and optimise resource allocation for enhanced efficiency.

Grid reliability is ensured by the autonomy of an independent transmission operator from energy generation and supply enterprises. This autonomy allows the independent transmission operator to concentrate exclusively on the preservation of grid reliability and stability, thereby reducing the likelihood of blackouts and disturbances. The independent transmission operators facilitate market competition by ensuring that all participants in the electricity market have fair and unbiased access to the transmission grid.[72] This practise promotes equitable market conditions and incentivizes the entry of new participants into the market. Renewable energy integration is a pivotal aspect of grid management, and in this regard, ISOs and TSOs assume a critical role.[73] Their specialised knowledge enables the seamless integration of intermittent renewable energy generation, resulting in enhanced efficiency and effectiveness.

---

[71] Directive 2009/72/EC of the European Parliament and of the Council of 13 July 2009 concerning common rules for the internal market in electricity and repealing Directive 2003/54/EC. OJ L 211, 14.8.2009, pp. 55–93. See Article 13, Article 17. Regulation (EU) 2019/943 of the European Parliament and of the Council of 5 June 2019 on the internal market for electricity (recast). OJ L 158, 14.6.2019, pp. 54–124. See Article 40.

[72] Directive 2009/72/EC of the European Parliament and of the Council of 13 July 2009 concerning common rules for the internal market in electricity and repealing Directive 2003/54/EC. OJ L 211, 14.8.2009, pp. 55–93. See Article 13, Article 17.

[73] Commission Staff Working Paper. Interpretative Note on Directive 2009/72/EC Concerning Common Rules for the Internal Market in Electricity and Directive 2009/73/EC Concerning Common Rules for the Internal Market in Natural Gas. The Unbundling Regime. 2010.

European countries have used several approaches for independent transmission operators, such as creating separate legal organisations or establishing functionally independent divisions inside vertically integrated utilities. Regional collaboration is critical to the functioning of autonomous gearbox operators. These entities participate in cooperative endeavors through regional coordination centers, with the primary goal of maximizing power transmission across national boundaries. Moreover, these centers have a vital function in guaranteeing the security of the power grid and enabling efficient regional collaboration among autonomous transmission providers. The ENTSOE plays a crucial role in coordinating independent transmission operators and transmission system operators across Europe. Its main goal is to promote grid integration and facilitate cooperation.[74]

Grid modernization poses a significant challenge for independent transmission operator as they strive to upgrade the electricity grid to effectively integrate emerging technologies, including smart grids, energy storage, and demand response. It is imperative to sustain ongoing endeavours aimed at bolstering cross-border collaboration among independent transmission operator in order to fortify regional energy security and facilitate the advancement of electricity trading. In pursuit of its decarbonization objectives, the European Union must effectively oversee the incorporation of an increasing proportion of renewable energy sources within its energy infrastructure while simultaneously ensuring the stability of the grid.[75]

It can be observed that independent transmission operators have emerged as significant entities in influencing the trajectory of the European energy sector. The grid management system employed by the organisation is characterised by its autonomy and transparency, which effectively guarantee a dependable provision of electricity. Moreover, this system actively promotes market competition and facilitates the seamless integration of renewable energy sources. The European Union's ongoing pursuit of its ambitious energy policy objectives necessitates the crucial involvement of independent transmission operators in order to facilitate the development of a resilient, sustainable, and interconnected energy market within Europe.

The most liberal unbundling approach for a vertically integrated corporation entails the retention of transmission network exploitation and ownership by the company overseeing the network while delegating network management responsibilities to a subsidiary of the transmission company.[76] This particular organisation has the autonomy to independently make financial and technological decisions,

---

[74] Regulation (EC) No 714/2009 of the European Parliament and of the Council of 13 July 2009 on conditions for access to the network for cross-border exchanges in electricity and repealing Regulation (EC) No 1228/2003. OJ L 211, 14.8.2009, pp. 15–35. See Article 4.

[75] Directive (EU) 2018/2001 of the European Parliament and of the Council of 11 December 2018 on the promotion of the use of energy from renewable sources (recast). OJ L 328, 21.12.2018, pp. 82–209. See Article 3, Article 16, Article 18.

[76] Directive 2009/72/EC of the European Parliament and of the Council of 13 July 2009 concerning common rules for the internal market in electricity and repealing Directive 2003/54/EC. OJ L 211, 14.8.2009, pp. 55–93. See Article 9, Article 13.

separate from the influence or control of its parent corporation. The primary objective of the oversight function is to be executed by an autonomous regulatory body, with the aim of safeguarding against potentially detrimental outcomes for the parent firm resulting from decision-making processes. In this particular arrangement, the transmission system operator continues to be a component of the vertically integrated enterprise, while specific regulations pertaining to unbundling are outlined in Articles 17 to 23 of the electricity and gas directives. The vertically integrated enterprise will retain its position as the gearbox system operator, but it must implement robust measures to ensure that decision-making processes are not compromised. This approach necessitates the autonomy of the system operator, obviating the necessity of corporate division or delegation of pertinent functions to an external organisation.

The implementation of full ownership unbundling may potentially encounter conflicts with national constitutional rules and impede the free movement of capital. Additionally, the anticipated effects on prices remain uncertain, and there is a possibility that these reforms could negatively affect investment. The ITO model is recognised as a very successful and efficient system for unbundling, which surpasses the alternative of outsourcing network administration to an independent system operator in terms of achieving more efficiency. Additionally, it is worth mentioning that this measure will effectively promote equitable competition and encourage investment, facilitating the entry of new market players and fostering competition among established firms.[77]

Vertically integrated enterprises are characterised by the consolidation of generation, transmission, distribution, and supply activities under a single corporate entity. These corporations face criticism due to market foreclosure and competitive restrictions resulting from their management approach. These corporations exert dominance over transportation networks and wield influence in both the wholesale and retail sectors, posing significant barriers for emerging or smaller enterprises seeking to establish a foothold in the market.

The timely transposition of directives into national laws by the Member States was not actively pursued, leading the Commission to commence a series of infringement procedures. While the Third Energy Package has been implemented with the intention of promoting competition in the energy market, it is important to note that simply meeting legislative requirements does not guarantee the establishment of a truly competitive internal market. In order to effectively attain these objectives, it is imperative to strike a harmonious equilibrium between the provisions of competition law and energy law processes, thereby mitigating the issue of duplicative application. In the subsequent section, we will examine the determinants contributing to the bolstering of autonomy within national regulatory authorities as well as the efficacy of their activities in attaining objectives related to market liberalisation.

[77] Directive 2009/72/EC of the European Parliament and of the Council of 13 July 2009 concerning common rules for the internal market in electricity and repealing Directive 2003/54/EC. OJ L 211, 14.8.2009, pp. 55–93. See Article 13.

3.4.2 *Independency of National Energy Regulators*

The crucial function of national energy regulators in the European Union is to ensure the attainment of the objectives outlined in the third energy package. These regulators are responsible for promoting efficient and transparent operations within energy markets, with a primary focus on safeguarding the interests of consumers. The Third Energy Package outlines the primary functions and obligations of national energy regulators. The oversight and regulation of energy markets within individual nations is entrusted to national energy regulatory bodies. The researchers engage in the examination of market behaviour, the evaluation of competition levels, and the exploration of any instances of anti-competitive practices or market abuse. This encompasses the surveillance of electricity and gas wholesale and retail markets in order to promote equitable competition.

Tariff regulation refers to the governmental policies and measures implemented to control and manage the imposition of tariffs on imported goods. Regulatory bodies are responsible for the determination and authorization of network tariffs, which encompass the fees that network operators are permitted to levy upon market players for their utilisation of transmission and distribution infrastructure. It is imperative that the tariffs adhere to the principles of non-discrimination, cost-reflectiveness, and transparency.[78]

Regulatory bodies are responsible for enforcing the provision of third-party access to energy infrastructure by network operators in a manner that is fair and unbiased. The regulatory body is responsible for establishing and implementing regulations that control the accessibility of transmission and distribution networks. Their primary objective is to ensure equitable opportunities for all market participants, including new entrants, to utilise the infrastructure.[79] Regulatory bodies possess the jurisdiction to conduct investigations and enforce measures in response to instances of anti-competitive conduct, market manipulation, or infringements upon competition regulations. This encompasses the examination of matters pertaining to market dominance, collusion, and the exploitation of market power.

Consumer protection is a field of study that focuses on safeguarding the rights and interests of consumers in various economic transactions. Safeguarding the interests of consumers constitutes a fundamental duty of national regulatory bodies. Their primary objective is to guarantee that individuals have readily available and easily understandable information regarding energy costs, contractual agreements, and

[78] Directive 2009/72/EC of the European Parliament and of the Council of 13 July 2009 concerning common rules for the internal market in electricity and repealing Directive 2003/54/EC. OJ L 211, 14.8.2009, pp. 55–93. See Article 37.

[79] Directive 2009/72/EC of the European Parliament and of the Council of 13 July 2009 concerning common rules for the internal market in electricity and repealing Directive 2003/54/EC. OJ L 211, 14.8.2009, pp. 55–93. See Article 32, Article 37.

energy suppliers. Regulators also handle customer complaints and disputes, thereby ensuring equitable treatment.[80]

Regulatory bodies are responsible for the approval and supervision of investments in energy infrastructure, including interconnectors and smart grid initiatives. The authors evaluate the necessity of infrastructure development in order to improve market competition and ensure the security of supply. Regulators play a crucial role in enabling the seamless integration of renewable energy sources into the electrical system. The establishment of regulations and methods is undertaken to facilitate the integration of renewable energy generators into the existing network infrastructure while also ensuring equitable remuneration for their electricity generation.

The third energy package aims to foster regional and cross-border collaboration among national regulators in order to facilitate market integration and effectively tackle regional energy-related issues. This encompasses collaborative efforts in market coupling, capacity mechanisms, and regulatory harmonisation. The concept of "security of supply" refers to the assurance and reliability of the availability of essential resources or goods.[81] Regulatory bodies evaluate and mitigate any threats to the stability and reliability of energy provision. The individuals collaborate with network operators and market participants in order to formulate emergency plans and establish methods for effectively managing supply outages or emergencies. Regulatory independence refers to the ability of regulatory bodies to operate autonomously and free from external influence or interference.

In order to ensure impartial decision-making, it is imperative for regulators to uphold their independence from both political influence and business interests. The individuals in question bear responsibility towards their respective national governments while also being required to prioritise the welfare of the energy market and customers. It is imperative for national regulators to guarantee that their actions and decisions are in accordance with the norms and directives set forth by the European Union. The coordination of cross-border regulatory matters is facilitated through collaboration with the ACER[82] and the ENTSOE.

Regulatory bodies are obligated to provide frequent reports on their operational undertakings, market dynamics, and adherence to European Union regulatory frameworks. The establishment of transparency in decision-making processes is of utmost

---

[80] Directive 2009/72/EC of the European Parliament and of the Council of 13 July 2009 concerning common rules for the internal market in electricity and repealing Directive 2003/54/EC. OJ L 211, 14.8.2009, pp. 55–93. See Article 3, Article 37.

[81] Regulation (EC) No 713/2009 of the European Parliament and of the Council of 13 July 2009 establishing an Agency for the Cooperation of Energy Regulators (ACER). OJ L 211, 14.8.2009, pp. 1–14. See Article 1, Article 4. Regulation (EC) No 714/2009 of the European Parliament and of the Council of 13 July 2009 on conditions for access to the network for cross-border exchanges in electricity and repealing Regulation (EC) No 1228/2003. OJ L 211, 14.8.2009, pp. 15–35. See Article 6.

[82] Regulation (EU) 2019/942 of the European Parliament and of the Council of 5 June 2019 establishing a European Union Agency for the Cooperation of Energy Regulators. PE/83/2018/REV/1. OJ L 158, 14.6.2019, pp. 22–53.

importance in order to foster trust among market participants and the general public. The involvement of national energy regulators is crucial to the implementation and enforcement of the provisions outlined in the third energy package.[83] Regulatory bodies play a crucial role in upholding competition, safeguarding consumer interests, maintaining market transparency, and fostering efficient and sustainable operations within the energy markets of their various nations. The attainment of the package's aims, which involve the establishment of a proficient European energy market, heavily relies on the collaboration of regulators at both the regional and European Union levels.

The Third Energy Package introduced the increased independency of national energy regulators.[84] Although some provisions were introduced in the second electricity and gas directives, with the adoption of third package the functions were broadened.[85] The independency of national regulators was seen as important element to ensure proper functioning of the internal market. Therefore, the regulators needed to become independent bodies from the industries and governments. They own a legal entity, have the authority and budget. Governments were also obliging to supply the regulators with the sufficient resources to carry out the operations.

Regulators have the authority to issue legally binding decisions and impose fines on businesses that fail to comply with their legal duties. The authorities obligated market participants to provide precise data for market monitoring and surveillance. We also anticipated the cooperation of the regulators. Articles 39–44 and 35–37 of the Gas Directive established and protected the powers of the national regulatory authorities. The Gas Directive specifically assigned responsibilities to the regulatory authorities. The regulatory authority is responsible for establishing or endorsing transmission or distribution tariffs and procedures based on transparent criteria. The regulatory body ensures that transmission and distribution system operators, system owners, and natural gas undertakings comply with their obligations under this Directive and other relevant European Union legislation, particularly in cross-border matters. The reports must provide a detailed record of the actions taken and the results attained for each of the responsibilities specified in this article. It is crucial to ensure that there are no financial transactions between the transmission, distribution, storage, LNG, and supply operations. It is important to carefully observe transmission system operators' investment strategies. In its yearly report, the regulatory authority should look at these plans and see if they are in line with the community's

[83] Pielow and Lewendel (2011).

[84] Regulation (EC) No 713/2009 of the European Parliament and of the Council of 13 July 2009 establishing an Agency for the Cooperation of Energy Regulators (ACER). OJ L 211, 14.8.2009, pp. 1–14. See Article 1, Article 4. Directive 2009/72/EC of the European Parliament and of the Council of 13 July 2009 concerning common rules for the internal market in electricity and repealing Directive 2003/54/EC. OJ L 211, 14.8.2009, pp. 55–93. See Article 35.

[85] Delvaux et al. (2017).

overall network development plan, as stated in Article 8(3)(b) of Regulation (EC) No. 715/2009.[86]

The task involves overseeing adherence to and evaluating the historical effectiveness of regulations pertaining to network security and reliability. This includes establishing or endorsing benchmarks and criteria for service quality and provision, either independently or in collaboration with other competent entities. The monitoring of transparency levels, specifically regarding wholesale prices, and the enforcement of transparency obligations for natural gas companies.[87] The monitoring of market opening and competition levels, both at the wholesale and retail levels, includes activities on natural gas exchanges, pricing for household customers (including prepayment systems), rates of customer switching, disconnection rates, charges for maintenance services, and execution of maintenance services. The objective is to observe and track the prevalence of restrictive contractual practices, specifically exclusivity clauses that may hinder large non-household customers from engaging with multiple suppliers simultaneously or limit their options to do so. Additionally, if deemed necessary, relevant information regarding these practices will be communicated to the national competition authorities.

In order to uphold contractual autonomy, it is important to acknowledge the significance of both interruptible supply contracts and long-term contracts, as long as they align with community law and adhere to community policy. The act of monitoring and evaluating the conditions of access to storage and other ancillary services, as outlined in Article 33, is necessary. If the access regime to storage is determined in accordance with Article 33(3), the aforementioned work shall specifically exclude the examination of rates.

Assisting in the collaborative effort with other pertinent authorities to guarantee the effectiveness and enforcement of consumer protection measures Publishing suggestions, with a frequency of at least once a year, regarding the conformity of supply prices, and then presenting these recommendations to the relevant competition authorities, if deemed necessary. In order to guarantee access to consumer consumption data, it is necessary to provide an optional use of a standardised format that is clearly comprehensible at the national level.

The responsibilities include overseeing the enforcement of regulations pertaining to the duties and obligations of transmission system operators, distribution system operators, suppliers, customers, and other market participants as outlined in Regulation (EC) No 715/2009. Additionally, ensuring proper adherence to the criteria that determine whether a storage facility falls under Article 33(3) or (4) is monitored.

---

[86] Regulation (EC) No 715/2009 of the European Parliament and of the Council of 13 July 2009 on conditions for access to the natural gas transmission networks and repealing Regulation (EC) No 1775/2005. OJ L 211, 14.8.2009, pp. 36–54.

[87] Directive 2009/72/EC of the European Parliament and of the Council of 13 July 2009 concerning common rules for the internal market in electricity and repealing Directive 2003/54/EC. OJ L 211, 14.8.2009, pp. 55–93. See Article 37. Regulation (EC) No 713/2009 of the European Parliament and of the Council of 13 July 2009 establishing an Agency for the Cooperation of Energy Regulators (ACER). OJ L 211, 14.8.2009, pp. 1–14. See Article 4.

Lastly, the implementation of safeguard measures as mentioned in Article 46 is also mandatory. Contributing to the enhancement of data interchange processes to ensure compatibility for crucial market operations at the regional level.

The directives have expanded the range of functions assigned to national regulatory authorities. The interpretative note pertaining to the directives on gas and electricity provided clarification regarding the scope of the rights and obligations associated with these directives. Furthermore, in 2016, ACER implemented proposals aimed at enhancing the autonomy of national regulatory bodies. Specifically, it has been suggested that in order to clarify the description in legislation of the functions of Member States and regulatory authorities, accountability should be established towards national parliaments rather than governments. It is imperative to establish unambiguous and transparent guidelines for the appointment of board members or top-level executives. There is a need for enhancement in the realm of financial independence.

The introduction of the third energy package led to a notable enhancement in the level of autonomy for national energy regulators. The requirements related to the electricity and gas directives were strengthened with the approval of the third package, in addition to the specific regulations outlined in the second set of directives. The need to ensure the smooth operation of the internal market prompted the recognition of the necessity of independent national regulators. The determination was taken from the findings obtained from a study conducted. Consequently, regulatory bodies were pushed to undergo a transformation, adopting a structure that demonstrates autonomy from both governmental influence and the firms under their purview.[88] The individuals in question adopt the position of proprietors of a legally acknowledged entity, thereby obtaining both authoritative powers and a commensurate financial plan. Moreover, it was imperative for the governments to allocate the requisite resources to regulatory bodies in order to efficiently carry out their obligations.

Regulatory authorities are vested with the legal authority to issue legally binding decisions and impose financial penalties on enterprises that fail to comply with the prescribed legal requirements. The necessity of market participants providing precise data to regulators was considered crucial to enabling efficient market surveillance and oversight by the authorities. Moreover, the intention was for regulatory authorities to engage in a coordinated effort.

[88] Directive 2009/72/EC of the European Parliament and of the Council of 13 July 2009 concerning common rules for the internal market in electricity and repealing Directive 2003/54/EC. OJ L 211, 14.8.2009, pp. 55–93. See Article 35. Directive 2009/73/EC of the European Parliament and of the Council of 13 July 2009 concerning common rules for the internal market in natural gas and repealing Directive 2003/55/EC. OJ L 211, 14.8.2009, pp. 94–136. See Article 39. Regulation (EC) No 713/2009 of the European Parliament and of the Council of 13 July 2009 establishing an Agency for the Cooperation of Energy Regulators (ACER). OJ L 211, 14.8.2009, pp. 1–14. See Article 4.

3.4.3 *Agency for the Cooperation of Energy Regulators (ACER)*

The ACER holds a crucial role as an agency within the energy sector of the European Union.[89] The key goals of this initiative encompass the promotion of regulatory collaboration and the facilitation of efficient operations within energy markets. The facilitation of market integration, the encouragement of competition, and the defence of consumer interests served as the foundation for ACER's establishment. Nevertheless, ACER encounters numerous challenges in completing its mandated responsibilities.

This chapter aims to provide a critical evaluation of the issues encountered by ACER, encompassing the existence of divergent national interests and disparities in regulatory practices. Furthermore, the document explores the potential of the agency to promote the energy objectives of the European Union. It places particular focus on the agency's role in facilitating the transition towards sustainable energy sources and fostering collaboration among various countries. The objective of this study is to examine the impact of social media usage on individuals' mental well-being. The successful attainment of the European Union's ambitious energy policy goals, which include the creation of a consolidated internal energy market and the transition towards cleaner and more sustainable energy sources, relies on the effective enforcement of regulatory oversight and cooperation. The crucial role that ACER plays as the regulatory cornerstone is essential to the successful completion of these objectives. This chapter examines the challenges encountered by ACER, the European Agency for the Cooperation of Energy Regulators, in effectively carrying out its mandate. Additionally, it emphasises the unexplored possibilities of the agency in steering the European Union towards a more competitive, networked, and environmentally friendly energy industry.

The ACER, founded in 2010 in accordance with Regulation (EC) No 713/2009, has been entrusted with the task of promoting market integration, encouraging competition, and safeguarding consumer interests within the diverse energy markets of the European Union.[90] The founding of the agency was a noteworthy milestone in the European Union's pursuit of creating a unified and consumer-oriented energy market.

National regulatory authorities (NRAs) are government bodies that have the primary responsibility of supervising and enforcing regulations across different sectors within the authority of a nation. NRAs frequently function with unique national priorities, resulting in varying methodologies and policies in their

[89]Regulation (EU) 2019/942 of the European Parliament and of the Council of 5 June 2019 establishing a European Union Agency for the Cooperation of Energy Regulators. PE/83/2018/REV/1. OJ L 158, 14.6.2019, pp. 22–53.

[90]Regulation (EC) No 713/2009 of the European Parliament and of the Council of 13 July 2009 establishing an Agency for the Cooperation of Energy Regulators (ACER). OJ L 211, 14.8.2009, pp. 1–14. See Article 1, Article 4.

regulatory practices. The effectiveness of ACER relies on its cooperation with NRAs, which might be influenced by their respective national energy interests.[91] Conflicts of interest can potentially emerge when regulatory measures have consequences that transcend national boundaries. The endeavour to harmonise the interests of member state with the overarching goals of the European Union may be a complex and diverse issue.

The energy mix of member states within the European Union display a diverse spectrum, comprising varying quantities of fossil fuels, renewable sources, and nuclear energy. The presence of these discrepancies may potentially lead to disagreements over common energy policy objectives, such as the mitigation of carbon emissions and the achievement of renewable energy targets.

The concept of regulatory fragmentation refers to the presence of numerous and varied regulatory frameworks within a specific sector or market. Fragmentation can occur as a result of multiple factors, including disparities in national or regional rules as well as differences in norms and requirements. The existence of disparate market structures, such as capacity mechanisms and renewable energy support programmes, can hinder the formation of a cohesive internal energy market. ACER is confronted with the task of effectively correcting these disparities in a manner that adheres to the principles of equitable competition and sustains a just environment for all individuals involved.

The presence of regulatory discrepancies pertaining to grid planning, access, and tariffs has the potential to hinder the progress of cross-border electricity and gas infrastructure development. The incorporation of these practices is essential in order to attain seamless market harmonisation. The present discourse pertains to the subject matter of political sensitivities. The issue of energy supply security holds significant importance for many member states inside the European Union. Geopolitical factors, such as the imperative to enhance energy source diversity and the dependence on external providers, possess the capacity to impact regulatory decisions. ACER must adeptly harmonise these considerations with the objectives of market liberalisation and competitiveness. The effect of popular emotion and political circumstances frequently shapes energy policy, highlighting the major importance that popular opinion plays in this domain. Potential conflicts can emerge between national and European Union energy policies as a result of various circumstances, including the utilisation of nuclear energy, the exploitation of shale gas, and issues related to the environment.

The notion of capacity limits pertains to the inherent limitations or restrictions on the highest quantity of resources, commodities, or services that can be generated. ACER operates within the parameters of constrained resources, including both financial and personnel capabilities. The complex and evolving nature of the energy sector presents considerable obstacles to effectively fulfilling its regulatory responsibilities. The energy industry generates significant amounts of data related to market

[91] Commission evaluation of 22.1.2014 of the activities of the Agency for the Cooperation of Energy Regulations (ACER) under article 34 of Regulation (EC) 713/2009. C (2014) 242 final.

transactions, grid operations, and consumption patterns, hence requiring efficient solutions for data management.[92] The efficient management and analysis of this data to support regulatory decision-making may pose considerable obstacles. The subject of inquiry concerns the implementation and oversight strategies. The multidimensional undertaking of ensuring conformity of member states with energy legislation and regulations of the European Union falls under this duty. It is crucial that ACER demonstrate the capacity to effectively monitor, investigate, and implement these restrictions. The notion of a dynamic energy landscape pertains to the fluctuating states of potential energy that a system can inhabit, which are subject to the influence of both internal and external influences.[93]

Technological innovation encompasses the systematic progression and integration of novel or enhanced technology across various businesses and areas. The development and swift advancement of energy technologies, encompassing smart grids, energy storage, and decentralised generation, provide notable regulatory challenges. ACER should implement the requisite adaptations in light of these developments and ensure that regulations remain relevant and effective. The ongoing transition towards a future typified by the utilisation of low-carbon and renewable energy sources requires the deployment of regulatory measures that are flexible and may be adjusted as needed. The ongoing challenge is attaining a balanced state of harmony between the integration of intermittent renewable sources, guaranteeing energy security, and upholding market stability.

ACER operates amid a complex and dynamic energy landscape characterised by diverse national interests, regulatory disparities, political sensitivities, resource constraints, and evolving technical advancements.[94] Effectively tackling these challenges requires a meticulous balance between objectives that encompass the entirety of the European Union and considerations unique to each member state, as well as robust cooperation with national regulatory authorities.[95] The significance of ACER in the attainment of the European Union's energy market integration and sustainability goals is contingent upon its ability to effectively adapt, harmonise legislation, and enforce the energy policies of the EU.

ACER has the capability to facilitate the integration of renewable energy sources into the electricity grid by fostering cross-border cooperation in initiatives related to

[92] Regulation (EC) No 713/2009 of the European Parliament and of the Council of 13 July 2009 establishing an Agency for the Cooperation of Energy Regulators (ACER). OJ L 211, 14.8.2009, pp. 1–14. See Article 1, Article 5, Article 6.

[93] Regulation (EC) No 713/2009 of the European Parliament and of the Council of 13 July 2009 establishing an Agency for the Cooperation of Energy Regulators (ACER). OJ L 211, 14.8.2009, pp. 1–14. See Article 1, Article 3.

[94] Regulation (EC) No 713/2009 of the European Parliament and of the Council of 13 July 2009 establishing an Agency for the Cooperation of Energy Regulators (ACER). OJ L 211, 14.8.2009, pp. 1–14. See Article 1, Article 3, Article 4.

[95] Proposal for a Regulation of the European Parliament and of Council on energy market integrity and transparency. SEC (2010) 1510 final, SEC (2010) 1511 final. COM (2010) 726 final. 2010/0363 (COD) C7-0407/10.

renewable energy. The aforementioned methodology possesses the capacity to alleviate the fluctuation of intermittent renewable energy sources and enhance the reliability of the power system. The potential of the ACER to make substantial contributions towards the advancement and installation of smart grid technology is noteworthy. These technologies play a critical role in enabling the efficient distribution of energy, overseeing energy consumption patterns, and integrating decentralised energy sources. Academic scholars have dedicated their research efforts to investigating the phenomenon of market integration and analysing its effects on competitiveness.[96] The agency possesses the capacity to accelerate the progress of transnational infrastructure projects, including interconnectors and pipelines, thereby promoting market integration and the unimpeded flow of energy between member states. Price convergence is a prospective approach that ACER, the Agency for the Cooperation of Energy Regulators, can utilise in order to attain the harmonisation of electricity and gas prices across the European Union. The objective of this technique is to reduce price disparities and enhance consumer advantages in competitive energy markets. The process of market monitoring is of utmost importance as it serves to detect and rectify instances of market abuse, thereby ensuring the preservation of fair and transparent market competition. The monitoring actions conducted by ACER make a substantial contribution towards achieving this objective. The potential for increased accessibility to energy consumption data exists within the Agency for the Cooperation of Energy Regulators (ACER), which could facilitate informed decision-making by consumers regarding their energy usage and foster the adoption of energy-efficient practices.[97]

The organisation possesses the capability to commence educational activities with the objective of augmenting consumer comprehension pertaining to their rights and choices within the energy industry. The subject matter under consideration belongs to the domain of energy security and crisis management, with a specific emphasis on the involvement of the ACER in the coordination of measures aimed at addressing energy crises. The participation of ACER in this matter has the potential to increase energy security by fostering cross-border collaboration and facilitating the pooling of resources.[98] This holds special significance in circumstances characterised by supply outages or instances of extreme weather events. The agency possesses the capability to efficiently supervise and manage strategic reserves of energy resources, thereby ensuring their availability during unanticipated events.

Regulatory harmonisation pertains to the endeavour of attaining more uniformity in the regulatory practices of individual nations, with the objective of ensuring the consistent implementation of regulations established by the European Union and

---

[96] Hogan (2021), Newbery (2019), and Green (2021).

[97] Regulation (EC) No 713/2009 of the European Parliament and of the Council of 13 July 2009 establishing an Agency for the Cooperation of Energy Regulators (ACER). OJ L 211, 14.8.2009, pp. 1–14. See Article 1, Article 3, Article 6.

[98] Regulation (EC) No 713/2009 of the European Parliament and of the Council of 13 July 2009 establishing an Agency for the Cooperation of Energy Regulators (ACER). OJ L 211, 14.8.2009, pp. 1–14. See Article 1, Article 3, Article 6.

reducing discrepancies in regulatory frameworks. The promotion of convergence of practices can be facilitated via the ACER. The agency has the capacity to regularly synchronise market laws, therefore ensuring fair conditions for all participants in the market among member states. The ACER's alignment of regulatory practices with EU emissions reduction targets allows for the effective contribution of energy market operations towards broader sustainability objectives. Data-driven decision-making is a strategic methodology that depends on the systematic study and interpretation of data to inform and lead decision-making processes. The application of big data analytics by ACER holds the capacity to yield significant insights into market behaviour, support evidence-based decision-making, and expedite the detection of market irregularities.

ACER possesses the capability to foster innovation within the energy industry by offering support for research and development endeavours and actively advocating for the incorporation of emerging technology.[99] ACER possesses the capacity to enhance its worldwide impact by establishing partnerships with international energy regulatory bodies. This would facilitate the progression of global norms and promote the dissemination of European Union energy expertise on a global level. ACER exhibits substantial potential to exert influence on the energy landscape of the European Union through its endeavours to facilitate the transition towards sustainable energy sources, foster market integration and competition, empower consumers, enhance energy security, promote regulatory harmonisation, and contribute to environmental sustainability. The acknowledgement of this potential necessitates the implementation of a proactive approach, the allocation of adequate resources, and the formation of robust partnerships with national regulatory entities and other pertinent stakeholders. The efforts of ACER play a vital role in achieving the energy goals set by the European Union while also ensuring the resilience, sustainability, and competitiveness of the European energy industry in a dynamic global context.

In conclusion, it can be deduced that ACER, the entity entrusted with the task of coordinating energy regulation within the European Union, faces substantial challenges stemming from divergent national interests and regulatory methodologies. However, the considerable potential of this technology to make a significant contribution towards the attainment of the energy objectives set by the European Union is evident. The European Union's pursuit of a competitive, integrated, and sustainable energy framework can be significantly influenced by the activities of ACER. This influence stems from ACER's focus on regulatory harmonisation, crisis management, and consumer empowerment. The European Union is presently confronted with the complexities of a diverse energy transformation. The proper functioning of the ACER is of increasing importance in this particular environment, as it plays a critical role in achieving the energy objectives of the European Union.

---

[99] Regulation (EC) No 713/2009 of the European Parliament and of the Council of 13 July 2009 establishing an Agency for the Cooperation of Energy Regulators (ACER). OJ L 211, 14.8.2009, pp. 1–14. See Article 3, Article 5. Regulation (EU) 2019/942 of the European Parliament and of the Council of 5 June 2019 on the internal market for electricity. OJ L 158, 14.6.2019, pp. 1–40. See Article 58, Article 59.

The Council of European Energy Regulators (CEER) was created in 2000 with the primary aims of facilitating the exchange of knowledge and expertise among its members, promoting coordination of various initiatives, and undertaking additional responsibilities when required. The Commission has undertaken the organisation of the Florence and Madrid forums in order to establish a direct connection with national energy regulators.[100] The European Regulatory Group on Electricity and Gas (ERGEG) was established by the Commission in 2003. The establishment of the ACER in 2011 was a result of the implementation of the third energy package. ACER was created as an autonomous entity with the purpose of promoting the integration and harmonisation of energy markets. Furthermore, the Regulation on Energy Market Integrity and Transparency (REMIT) expanded the scope of ACER's responsibilities.

The establishment of this agency has resulted in the discontinuation of ERGEG, as its operations were deemed inadequate in achieving the objectives of the internal energy market. The functions of the ACER were officially established and outlined in Regulation 713/2009.[101] These functions encompassed several key areas, such as offering advice on the formulation of network codes, providing opinions on the creation of 10-year network development plans, conducting market monitoring activities, and issuing recommendations pertaining to cross-border networks.[102] ACER collaborates with national regulatory agencies to effectively execute its supervisory function within the internal market and diligently oversees instances of market abuse. It is important to acknowledge that ACER operates independently from both the Commission and the Member States.

ACER possesses the authority to render legally enforceable determinations. ACER has the authority to determine capacity allocation procedures and the distribution of profits generated from the sale of capacity and charges imposed on network users in cases where national regulators are unable to reach a consensus on the regulation of cross-border infrastructure. Additionally, ACER has the power to grant exemptions to newly established cross-border networks from internal market regulations. The standards established by the Australian Council for Educational Research (ACER) delineate the overarching concepts of the network codes. These

---

[100] Directive 2003/54/EC of the European Parliament and of the Council of 26 June 2003 concerning common rules for the internal market in electricity and repealing Directive 96/92/EC. OJ L 176, 15.7.2003, pp. 37–55. Directive 2003/55/EC of the European Parliament and of the Council of 26 June 2003 concerning common rules for the internal market in natural gas and repealing Directive 98/30/EC. OJ L 176, 15.7.2003, pp. 57–78. Regulation (EC) No 713/2009 of the European Parliament and of the Council of 13 July 2009 establishing an Agency for the Cooperation of Energy Regulators (ACER). OJ L 211, 14.8.2009, pp. 1–14. Regulation (EU) 2019/942 of the European Parliament and of the Council of 5 June 2019 on the internal market for electricity and amending Regulation (EC) No 713/2009, Regulation (EC) No 714/2009, and Regulation (EU) No 715/2009. OJ L 158, 14.6.2019, pp. 1–40.

[101] Regulation (EC) No 713/2009 of the European Parliament and of the Council of 13 July 2009 establishing an Agency for the Cooperation of Energy Regulators (ACER). OJ L 211, 14.8.2009, pp. 1–14. See Article 1.

[102] Schittekatte et al. (2020).

network codes, in turn, are formulated by the European Network of Transmission System Operators for Gas (ENTSOG)[103] for natural gas and the European Network of Transmission System Operators for Electricity (ENTSOE) for electricity. Network codes have the potential to acquire legal enforceability subsequent to a decision made by the Commission. When examining the functions of ACER, it is important to acknowledge that the inclusion of the Third Energy Package aimed to empower ACER not only to offer advisory opinions but also to grant it the ability to make legally binding determinations regarding tariffs and investment plans. However, ACER was ultimately denied this authority during the course of the discussions.

The ACER possesses the authority to make decisions that carry legal weight in situations where national regulatory agencies encounter difficulties in reaching a consensus about the regulation of cross-border infrastructure. Additionally, it could provide a provision for the exclusion of the application of internal market regulations in situations where the construction of new infrastructure is involved. The rationale for this clause is to ensure the effective implementation of additional investments. Nevertheless, the ultimate authorization must be granted by both the Commission and the respective national regulatory agencies.

The inquiry revolves around the potential effectiveness of market opening and liberalisation through the establishment of supranational regulators and the provision of specific coordination functions. The energy sector has a closed market structure wherein vertically integrated firms hold significant market power, hence exacerbating challenges for consumers in selecting their energy provider and impeding the entry of new firms into the market. The justification for regulating the energy sector in order to ensure a secure energy supply is frequently grounded in considerations of the public interest.[104] The creation of a paradoxical situation is subject to scrutiny, as the implementation of energy legislation may lead to heightened administrative burdens, thereby diminishing market competitiveness. The necessity of a regulatory body in the market is partially acknowledged based on the aforementioned rationale; yet the validity of such a requirement becomes debatable following the process of market liberalisation.

The independence of regulatory agencies, as outlined in the electricity and gas directives, is compromised due to their significant reliance on governments, limited autonomy, and constrained powers. The Commission emphasised the importance of legislative proposals that seek to achieve harmonisation of competences and enhance the autonomy of national regulatory institutions.[105] In order to effectively facilitate

---

[103] Regulation (EU) 2017/1938 of the European Parliament and of the Council of 25 October 2017 concerning measures to safeguard the security of gas supply and repealing Regulation (EU) No 994/2010. OJ L 280, 28.10.2017, pp. 1–56.

[104] Delvaux (2011).

[105] Directive 2009/72/EC of the European Parliament and of the Council of 13 July 2009 concerning common rules for the internal market in electricity and repealing Directive 2003/54/EC. OJ L 211, 14.8.2009, pp. 55–93 See Article 35. Directive 2009/73/EC of the European Parliament and of the Council of 13 July 2009 concerning common rules for the internal market in natural gas and

the development and operation of the internal market, it is imperative to enhance the authority of regulatory organisations in relation to strategic determinations. These bodies should possess independence from both public and private entities and be endowed with their own financial resources. Although national regulatory authorities possess the authority to establish tariffs that are fair and realistic in terms of costs, as well as techniques to facilitate the operation of the internal market, concerns persist over the true autonomy of these regulators and their capacity to make crucial strategic choices. There is also scepticism over the potential of enhanced regulatory independence to foster greater chances for a competitive internal market.

The Commission has recognised the necessity of market integration and has consequently implemented explicit regulations for market players in order to facilitate monitoring and reporting processes. The adoption of the regulation on wholesale energy market integrity and transparency (REMIT)[106] occurred on December 28, 2011. According to this legislation, it is incumbent upon market players to provide notification to both the Agency for the Cooperation of Energy Regulators (ACER) and the national regulatory bodies. Additionally, it implemented regulations against insider trading and market manipulation pertaining to wholesale products.

Market participants are required to disclose information pertaining to transactions made by electricity and natural gas producers, operators of natural gas storage facilities, or operators of LNG import facilities. These transactions are specifically aimed at mitigating immediate physical losses resulting from unforeseen disruptions. This regulation facilitates the early detection of potential market abuses, thereby prohibiting the manipulation of wholesale markets. It establishes regulations to prevent market abuse and imposes suitable restrictions on insider trading, which has frequently led to excessive costs for consumers in relation to their energy consumption. The objective of these trading regulations is to promote equitable energy pricing and enhance market trust through the implementation of measures that enhance market transparency. The regulation establishes sanctions for failure to comply. Energy traders have a legal obligation to submit reports of their transactions to the ACER.

ACER, in the event that primary data show probable market abuse, contacts the national regulatory authorities for an investigation after monitoring and analysing

repealing Directive 2003/55/EC. OJ L 211, 14.8.2009, pp. 94–136. See Article 39. Regulation (EC) No 713/2009 of the European Parliament and of the Council of 13 July 2009 establishing an Agency for the Cooperation of Energy Regulators (ACER). OJ L 211, 14.8.2009, pp. 1–14. See Article 1. Regulation (EC) No 714/2009 of the European Parliament and of the Council of 13 July 2009 on conditions for access to the network for cross-border exchanges in electricity and repealing Regulation (EC) No 1228/2003. OJ L 211, 14.8.2009, pp. 15–35. See Article 6. Regulation (EC) No 715/2009 of the European Parliament and of the Council of 13 July 2009 on conditions for access to the natural gas transmission networks and repealing Regulation (EC) No 1775/2005. OJ L 211, 14.8.2009, pp. 36–55. See Article 7.

[106] Regulation (EU) No 1227/2011 of the European Parliament and of the Council of 25 October 2011 on wholesale energy market integrity and transparency Text with EEA relevance. OJ L 326, 8.12.2011, pp. 1–16.

transactions, if deemed necessary.[107] In instances where infringements are identified, it is the responsibility of national regulatory agencies to levy fines that are commensurate with the extent of consumer losses incurred. From our perspective, this regulation introduces a level of uncertainty in its implementation. On the one hand, it aims to enhance market transparency by mandating the disclosure of specific information. However, it is important to consider the potential conflict between the requirements of competition law and REMIT, particularly regarding the sharing of information among competitors. Based on the recommendations provided by the Commission regarding the exchange of information, the presence of transparency in markets characterised by oligopoly may be perceived in a negative light due to the underlying assumption of coordination among the participants in the market. The concentration of energy markets necessitates a cautious approach.

The GDF/International Power[108] case serves as a pertinent example of the aforementioned scenario, wherein the Commission discerned potential risks to competition due to the dominant undertaking's potential access to confidential information pertaining to a rival entity. In accordance with the regulatory obligations outlined in the REMIT, it is expected that certain information obtained by GDF should have been disclosed to the public. From a regulatory perspective, the Commission aims to enhance transparency to address the current lack of information sharing among economic operators. By implementing REMIT, operators can establish measures to prevent abuse and collusion among competitors in concentrated markets.

The introduction of REMIT also raises questions about the allocation and distribution of powers between national regulators and competition authorities, leading to a certain level of ambiguity. In this particular scenario, there exists a circumstance where national regulatory bodies, in conjunction with competition authorities, undertake the responsibility of ensuring that market participants adhere to the regulations pertaining to competition.[109] In practical application, enterprises often encounter varying regulatory frameworks that necessitate compliance with energy sector regulations. However, concurrently, the Commission initiates investigations in accordance with competition legislation.

The issue of enforcing regulatory commitments and the interplay between competition law and the regulatory framework in the energy industry are brought to the forefront by the REMIT. The presence of more transparency within the market should be regarded in a favourable light, as it serves to prevent market manipulation

---

[107] Regulation (EC) No 713/2009 of the European Parliament and of the Council of 13 July 2009 establishing an Agency for the Cooperation of Energy Regulators (ACER). OJ L 211, 14.8.2009, pp. 1–14. See Article 7 (1).

[108] Case COMP/M.5978 – GDF Suez/ International Power.

[109] Regulation (EU) No 1227/2011 of the European Parliament and of the Council of 25 October 2011 on wholesale energy market integrity and transparency. OJ L 326, 8.12.2011, pp. 1–16. See Article 9 (3).

and facilitates the emergence of competitive dynamics.[110] However, it is imperative not to disregard the current legislative framework governing the sharing of information among market participants operating at the same level and who may be competitors, whether presently or potentially. From a competition law standpoint, the revelation and exchange of information in question could potentially be deemed to be in violation of competition law. Despite the stated objective of establishing a transparent and competitive internal market, the energy market continues to exhibit a significant level of concentration. Market participants, through the selective disclosure of information, create conditions that enable other participants to exploit this situation. Hence, it is advisable to take caution while managing the information needs of various entities, ensuring that the requirements do not harm the information provider or the customers due to the actions of other participants in the market. In the subsequent section, we shall undertake an analysis and evaluation of the implementation of third-party access rights and the associated challenges pertaining to market integration.

The Clean Energy Package introduced revisions pertaining to resource adequacy evaluations and risk preparedness.[111] The amendment to Regulation 713/2009 was carried out through the enactment of Regulation 2019/942.[112] It is imperative to conduct resource sufficiency assessments at the national, regional, and European levels. It is mandatory for Member States to conduct assessments prior to establishing capacity mechanisms. In this scenario, it is imperative for ACER to grant approval for the requisite procedures and specifications that are essential for facilitating cross-border involvement in capacity mechanisms.

The field of risk preparedness and crisis management has experienced certain modifications pertaining to the identification of crisis scenarios. In this regard, the ACER is authorised to endorse the methodologies devised by the ENTSOE for the purpose of identifying regional scenarios and conducting assessments of seasonal generation adequacy.[113] In addition, ACER will have the authority to grant approval for the techniques employed by ENTSOE in implementing the bidding zone in the event that the national regulatory agencies fail to reach a unanimous judgement within the specified timeframe.

---

[110] Regulation (EU) No 1227/2011 of the European Parliament and of the Council of 25 October 2011 on wholesale energy market integrity and transparency. OJ L 326, 8.12.2011, pp. 1–16. See Article 2, Article 3, Article 5.

[111] Nouicer and Meeus (2019).

[112] Regulation (EU) 2019/942 of the European Parliament and of the Council of 5 June 2019 establishing a European Union Agency for the Cooperation of Energy Regulators. PE/83/2018/REV/1. OJ L 158, 14.6.2019, pp. 22–53.

[113] Regulation (EC) No 714/2009 of the European Parliament and of the Council of 13 July 2009 on conditions for access to the network for cross-border exchanges in electricity. OJ L 211, 14.8.2009, pp. 15–35. See Article 8 (1). Regulation (EU) No 347/2013 of the European Parliament and of the Council of 17 April 2013 on guidelines for trans-European energy infrastructure. OJ L 115, 25.4.2013, pp. 39–75. See Article 10 (2). Regulation (EU) No 1227/2011 of the European Parliament and of the Council of 25 October 2011 on wholesale energy market integrity and transparency. OJ L 326, 8.12.2011, pp. 1–16. See Article 10 (3).

Additionally, ACER will have the authority to grant approval for the utilisation of congestion revenues. This approval will ensure that measures are in place to ensure the allocated capacity is actually available or to maintain cross-zone capacity by optimising the usage of existing interconnections through remedial actions. Furthermore, the costs associated with network investments aimed at reducing interconnector congestion can also be covered using these revenues.[114] The network code determination underwent adjustments, wherein ACER was previously permitted to express opinions on the network codes created by ENTSOE but was not authorised to make any modifications to the draft text. The aforementioned scenario resulted in delays, as ACER was required to reject the draft network codes or, in certain instances, submit the Commission with comprehensive requirements along with suggested revisions. The newly implemented regulation grants ACER the authority to make revisions to the draft network codes that are thereafter submitted directly to the Commission.

The responsibility for adopting the terms, conditions, and methodology lies directly with the board of regulators at ACER. The national regulatory bodies of Member States no longer attempt to reach unanimity; instead, they use a qualified majority voting system among their members to accomplish this. The adoption of regional terms, conditions, and methodologies by national regulatory authorities is necessary. In cases where unanimous consensus is not reached or if the decision has implications for the internal market or security of supply, ACER will be responsible for making the decision.

In the past, ACER possessed the authority to oversee the activities of ENTSOE but lacked the ability to make any substantive decisions. The scope of monitoring encompasses the Regional Coordination Centres, the Nominated Electricity Market Operators, and the European Organisation of Distribution System Operators.[115] In the event that ACER offers an opinion indicating a probable infringement, it becomes the responsibility of the national regulatory authorities to make a judgement about the breach and implement appropriate measures. If the decision is not adopted by regional authorities, it is assumed by ACER. The newly implemented regulation enhances the decision-making authority of the ACER, particularly in matters pertaining to cross-border concerns.

---

[114] Rumpf and Hancher (2020).

[115] Regulation (EC) No 713/2009 of the European Parliament and of the Council of 13 July 2009 establishing an Agency for the Cooperation of Energy Regulators. OJ L 211, 14.8.2009, pp. 1–14. See Article 3 (1), Article 6. Regulation (EU) No 1227/2011 of the European Parliament and of the Council of 25 October 2011 on wholesale energy market integrity and transparency. OJ L 326, 8.12.2011, pp. 1–16. See Article 8 (1). Regulation (EU) No 347/2013 of the European Parliament and of the Council of 17 April 2013 on guidelines for trans-European energy infrastructure. OJ L 115, 25.4.2013, pp. 39–75. See Article 5 (4).

3.4.4 Cross-Border Cooperation, ENTSOE, ENTSOG and Network Codes

The European Union has embarked on a significant initiative to create a unified and coordinated energy market with the goal of ensuring a dependable, eco-friendly, and economically efficient energy supply for its member states. Collaboration across international boundaries is a pivotal element in this endeavour, facilitated by esteemed associations such as the European Network of Transmission System Operators for Electricity (ENTSOE) and Gas (ENTSOG), in conjunction with the design and implementation of network codes. This study thoroughly examines the intricacies and significance of these elements within the broader context of European energy policy.

The ENTSOE is comprised of national transmission system operators (TSO) and operates as an association. The primary objectives of the key functions are to guarantee the effective coordination of the functioning of the European power system inside the linked grid. One of the primary responsibilities includes the maintenance of power system security and the effective operation of interconnected markets. ENTSOE is entrusted with the responsibility of developing and implementing standards, network codes, and platforms to ensure the secure functioning of the system. Additionally, it is important to evaluate the sufficiency of the system across different temporal intervals and effectively coordinate the strategic planning for the advancement of the European infrastructure, specifically focusing on the formulation of ten-year network development plans. The provision of tools that facilitate the transparent sharing of data among market participants is also anticipated. The responsibilities outlined in Regulation 714/2009 were anticipated, but they were subsequently modified with the implementation of the Clean Energy Package, specifically through the amendment introduced by Regulation (EU) 2019/943,[116] which became effective in 2020.

The European Network of Transmission System Operators for Gas (ENTSOG) shares a common objective of fostering collaboration among national operators in Europe, advancing the development of the internal market, and bolstering cross-border trade.[117] Regulation 715/2009 delineated the fundamental duties. The advancement of network codes encompasses the establishment of regulations governing the integration of markets, the operation of systems, the allocation of capacity, the interconnection of networks, and the security of the overall system.

[116] Regulation (EU) 2019/943 of the European Parliament and of the Council of 5 June 2019 on the internal market for electricity. PE/9/2019/REV/1. OJ L 158, 14.6.2019, pp. 54–124.

[117] Regulation (EC) No 715/2009 of the European Parliament and of the Council of 13 July 2009 on conditions for access to the natural gas transmission networks and repealing Regulation (EC) No 1775/2005. OJ L 211, 14.8.2009, pp. 1–30. See Article 4 (1). Regulation (EU) No 347/2013 of the European Parliament and of the Council of 17 April 2013 on guidelines for trans-European energy infrastructure. OJ L 115, 25.4.2013, pp. 39–75. See Article 4 (1). Regulation (EU) No 1227/2011 of the European Parliament and of the Council of 25 October 2011 on wholesale energy market integrity and transparency. OJ L 326, 8.12.2011, pp. 1–16. See Article 8 (1).

Network codes play a crucial role in the establishment of a competitive energy market. The elaboration of these concepts was undertaken within the framework of the third energy package. Network codes are a set of technological regulations that facilitate market competitiveness.[118] The authors discuss the grid connection criteria and standards, as well as the implications for cross-border infrastructure investments. The network codes were developed through collaboration among key entities, including the ENTSOE, ENTSOG, the ACER, the European Commission, and other relevant stakeholders.

In Electricity there are eight adopted network codes which can be divided in three major groups:

- The Market codes:[119]
  - Forward Capacity Allocation guidelines (FCA GL) EU Regulation 2016/1719—includes the requirements for long- term transmission rights.
  - Capacity Allocation and Congestion Management guidelines (CACM GL) EU Regulation 1222/2015—includes the management of power exchanges, allocation of transmission capacity.
  - Electricity Balancing guidelines (EB GL) EU Regulation 2017/2195—harmonises and balances the energy market includes the imbalance settlements and capacity for the balancing timeframe.
- The System operation codes:[120]
  - The electricity transmission system operation guidelines (SO GL) EU Regulation 2017/1485—implies the system security and operational requirements, frequency management.
  - Emergency and Restoration (ER NC) EU Regulation 2017/2196—sets out the process to be followed when operator is facing the system incident on the grid.
- The Grid connection codes:[121]

---

[118] Regulation (EC) No 714/2009 of the European Parliament and of the Council of 13 July 2009 on conditions for access to the network for cross-border exchanges in electricity and repealing Regulation (EC) No 1228/2003. OJ L 211, 14.8.2009, pp. 15–35. See Article 6 (1). Regulation (EC) No 715/2009 of the European Parliament and of the Council of 13 July 2009 on conditions for access to the natural gas transmission networks and repealing Regulation (EC) No 1775/2005. OJ L 211, 14.8.2009, pp. 36–54. See Article 8 (2).

[119] Commission Regulation (EU) 2016/1719 of 26 September 2016 establishing a guideline on forward capacity allocation. OJ L 259, 27.9.2016, pp. 42–68. Commission Regulation (EU) 2015/1222 of 24 July 2015 establishing a guideline on capacity allocation and congestion management. OJ L 197, 25.7.2015, pp. 24–72. Commission Regulation (EU) 2017/2195 of 23 November 2017 establishing a guideline on electricity balancing. OJ L 312, 28.11.2017, pp. 6–53.

[120] Commission Regulation (EU) 2017/1485 of 2 August 2017 establishing a guideline on electricity transmission system operation. OJ L 220, 25.8.2017, pp. 1–120. Commission Regulation (EU) 2017/2196 of 24 November 2017 establishing a network code on electricity emergency and restoration. OJ L 312, 28.11.2017, pp. 54–98.

[121] Commission Regulation (EU) 2016/1388 of 17 August 2016 establishing a network code on demand connection. OJ L 223, 18.8.2016, pp. 10–54. Commission Regulation (EU) 2016/1447 of

- The demand connection network code (DCC NC) EU Regulation 2016/1388—targeted to ensure the connectivity, avoid voltage limitations.
- The requirements for grid connection of high voltage direct current systems and direct current—connected power park modules network code (HVDC NC) EU Regulation 2016/1447—sets the requirements for long distance connections and tackles to the level playing field in the interconnections.
- The network code on requirements for grid connection of generators (RfG NC) EU Regulation 2016/631—provides the connection requirements for producers.

Regulation (EC) 715/2009 includes network codes that have been implemented in the natural gas sector. Specifically, in accordance with the yearly prioritised areas and considering the feedback from ACER and the ENTSOG, the Commission approves the network code proposals aimed at establishing a fully operational energy market and ensuring affordable energy for customers. ENTSOG adopts network codes and thereafter monitors, assesses, and studies their application and impact on market integration and liberalisation.

Currently there are adopted network codes in natural gas sector:[122]

- The network code on interoperability—sets harmonised rules for the operation of gas transmission system, data exchange.
- The capacity allocation mechanism network code (CAM NC) EU Regulation 459/2017—is applicable to the interconnections, the entry and exit points from the third countries, the rules providing the interruptible capacity the auction dates are included.
- Balancing network code (BAL NC) EU Regulation 312/2014—provides balancing rules, requirements for the imbalance charges, operational balancing.
- Tariff network code (TAR NC) EU Regulation 460/2017—introduces the transmission tariff structure, methodologies allowing to ensure the transparency and non – discrimination in the market.

26 August 2016 establishing a network code on requirements for grid connection of high voltage direct current systems and direct current-connected power park modules. OJ L 241, 8.9.2016, pp. 1–65. Commission Regulation (EU) 2016/631 of 14 April 2016 establishing a network code on requirements for grid connection of generators. OJ L 112, 27.4.2016, pp. 1–68.

[122]Commission Regulation (EU) 2017/459 of 16 March 2017 establishing a network code on capacity allocation mechanisms in gas transmission systems. OJ L 72, 17.3.2017, pp. 1–28. Commission Regulation (EU) No 312/2014 of 26 March 2014 establishing a Network Code on Gas Balancing of Transmission Networks. OJ L 91, 27.3.2014, pp. 15–35. Commission Regulation (EU) 2017/460 of 16 March 2017 establishing a network code on harmonised transmission tariff structures for gas. OJ L 72, 17.3.2017, pp. 29–56. Commission Regulation (EU) 2015/703 of 30 April 2015 establishing a network code on interoperability and data exchange rules. OJ L 113, 1.5.2015, pp. 13–26. European Commission Decision of 2012 amending the Annex I to Regulation (EC) No 715/2009 on conditions for access to the natural gas transmission networks. OJ L 211, 14.8.2009, pp. 36–54.

- Interoperability and Data Exchange network code (INT NC) EU Regulation 703/2015—provides the degree of technical harmonisation of the interconnection agreements, gas quality management, data exchange particularities.
- Congestion management procedure guidelines (CMP Guidelines) EC Decision of 2012 amending the Annex I to EC Regulation 715/2009—targeted at contractual congestions and setting back the unused capacity to market.

The Clean Energy Package, specifically EU Regulation 2019/943, made amendments to the previous Regulation 714/2009 pertaining to electricity as well as EU Regulation 2019/941 on risk preparedness. Additionally, EU Regulation 2019/942, which established a European Union Agency for the Cooperation of Energy Regulators, introduced notable enhancements to the implementation of the competitive energy market. These improvements aim to enhance transparency, accessibility, and energy efficiency.

3.4.5 Third Party Access to the Infrastructure Facilities

The primary emphasis of the international energy transition has been on the liberalisation and deregulation of energy markets, aiming to improve efficiency, reduce costs, and increase the use of renewable energy sources. A fundamental component of this transformation encompasses the notion of third-party entry into energy infrastructure, enabling the involvement of diverse market participants in gaining access to essential energy assets such as pipelines, grids, and storage facilities.

The inclusion of third-party entities in infrastructure access is a fundamental component of guaranteeing the effective functioning of the market. The provision of this criterion was anticipated in the initial gas and electricity directives, granting Member States the option to implement either a regulated or negotiated access regime.[123] In accordance with the negotiated access model, infrastructure companies are required to engage in negotiations with eligible customers to establish the terms and circumstances of access. Additionally, they are obligated to publicly disclose the primary conditions governing access.

The facilitation of market infrastructure access for third parties is a crucial component in ensuring the efficient operation of the market. The first gas and electricity directives contained provisions for this specific criterion, allowing Member States the option to adopt either a regulated or negotiated access system. As per the negotiated access model, infrastructure companies have a responsibility to initiate agreements with qualifying customers concerning the conditions of

[123] Directive 96/92/EC of the European Parliament and of the Council of 19 December 1996 concerning common rules for the internal market in electricity. OJ L 27, 30.1.1997, pp. 20–29. Directive 98/30/EC of the European Parliament and of the Council of 22 June 1998 concerning common rules for the internal market in natural gas. OJ L 204, 21.7.1998, pp. 1–12.

infrastructure access.[124] Furthermore, it is necessary for them to publish the fundamental terms and conditions pertaining to the accessibility of the infrastructure.

As per the provisions outlined in Article 32 (1) of the Electricity Directive, it is mandatory for Member States to establish a framework facilitating third-party access to transmission and distribution systems. The proposed system ought to be founded on openly accessible tariffs that are applicable to all qualified customers. It should be executed in an impartial and non-discriminatory way, ensuring equal treatment for all users of the system.[125] Member States must ensure that tariffs, as well as the methodology employed to ascertain them, are permitted prior to their implementation in accordance with the provisions set forth in Article 37. In addition, it is imperative for Member States to guarantee the public availability of both the authorised tariffs and methodologies (if only methodologies are approved) before their implementation.

The identical clause is incorporated in Article 32 (1) of the Gas Directive. It is crucial for Member States to ensure the regulatory framework that facilitates third-party access to both the transmission and distribution systems, as well as liquefied natural gas (LNG) facilities.[126] Access to this service should be facilitated by implementing publicly stated tariffs that are accessible to all qualifying consumers, including supply undertakings. Furthermore, it is critical that these tariffs be applied in a fair and objective manner, without prejudice or distinction between them. It is critical for Member States to guarantee that tariffs, including the methods used to determine them, are sanctioned by a regulatory body, as required by Article 39(1), and that they are made publicly available prior to implementation, as required by Article 41.[127]

The aforementioned rules establish the key conditions for stated rates in order to potentially prohibit discriminatory practices in which infrastructure usage prices are disproportionately biased towards certain activities, either excessively expensive or low. The major goal of regulated tariffs is to prevent unreasonable pricing and network exploitation while simultaneously encouraging new infrastructure

---

[124] Directive 96/92/EC of the European Parliament and of the Council of 19 December 1996 concerning common rules for the internal market in electricity. OJ L 27, 30.1.1997, pp. 20–29. See Article 17. Directive 98/30/EC of the European Parliament and of the Council of 22 June 1998 concerning common rules for the internal market in natural gas. OJ L 204, 21.7.1998, pp. 1–12. See Article 16.

[125] Directive 2009/72/EC of the European Parliament and of the Council of 13 July 2009 concerning common rules for the internal market in electricity. OJ L 211, 14.8.2009, pp. 55–93. See Article 32 (1).

[126] Directive 2009/73/EC of the European Parliament and of the Council of 13 July 2009 concerning common rules for the internal market in natural gas. OJ L 211, 14.8.2009, pp. 94–136. See Article 32 (1).

[127] Directive 2009/72/EC of the European Parliament and of the Council of 13 July 2009 concerning common rules for the internal market in electricity. OJ L 211, 14.8.2009, pp. 55–93. See Article 39 (1), Article 41. Directive 2009/73/EC of the European Parliament and of the Council of 13 July 2009 concerning common rules for the internal market in natural gas. OJ L 211, 14.8.2009, pp. 94–136. See Article 39 (1), Article 41.

investments. The employment of tariff-calculating methodology promotes commerce and competition while preventing cross-subsidisation among users. Regulation (EC) 715/2009[128] was adopted to establish the entry-exit model for tariff determination, with the goal of allowing network users to reserve network capacity autonomously. Access to information and physical access to systems are important factors in determining demand and supply.

In accordance with Article 1 of Regulation (EC) 715/2009, the primary goal is to adopt laws that are just and impartial in order to facilitate access to natural gas transmission lines, taking into account the distinct characteristics of both national and regional markets. The primary objective of this endeavour is to guarantee the efficient functioning of the domestic gas market. Furthermore, the objective is to design regulations that are just and impartial in order to facilitate access to LNG and storage facilities while also considering the unique attributes of both national and regional markets. Ultimately, the objective is to facilitate the establishment of a proficient and accountable wholesale gas market while simultaneously guaranteeing a dependable gas supply. The objective is to attain this goal through the implementation of protocols that standardise the regulations governing network access for transnational gas transactions.

Ensuring equitable access to infrastructure is of utmost importance, as it entails providing equal services to all users of the system. The significance of these criteria arises from the distinct attributes of the transmission network or LNG facilities, which often play a vital role in the provision of services to clients. In the event that the network operator does not ensure equitable and unbiased circumstances, the market may either remain unavailable or solely serve particular entities, thereby impeding end consumers' ability to choose their energy provider.

According to Article 13 (1) of Regulation (EC) 715/2009, the methods used by transmission system operators to set tariffs, which are then approved by regulatory authorities according to Article 41(6) of Directive 2009/73/EC,[129] and which are published according to Article 32(1) of the same Directive, must follow certain rules. The implementation of these principles, such as transparency, consideration of system integrity and improvement, and reflection of tariffs or their determination methods, should be carried out in a manner that prevents any kind of discrimination.

In the event that the regulatory authority grants approval for these agreements and the subsequent income, Member States possess the jurisdiction to establish tariffs through market-driven processes, such as auctions. Tariffs, or the processes utilised for their determination, are designed to facilitate efficient gas trade and encourage

---

[128] Regulation (EC) No 715/2009 of the European Parliament and of the Council of 13 July 2009 on conditions for access to the natural gas transmission networks and repealing Regulation (EC) No 1775/2005. OJ L 211, 14.8.2009, pp. 36–54.

[129] Directive 2009/73/EC of the European Parliament and of the Council of 13 July 2009 concerning common rules for the internal market in natural gas and repealing Directive 2003/55/EC. OJ L 211, 14.8.2009, pp. 94–136.

competition while also limiting cross-subsidisation among network users.[130] Furthermore, tariffs are implemented with the objective of stimulating investment and guaranteeing the preservation or establishment of interoperability for transmission networks.

The tariffs levied on network users should conform to the principle of non-discrimination and ought to be determined on a case-by-case basis for each ingress or egress point of the transmission system. The endorsement of national regulatory bodies is necessary for the implementation of cost-allocation systems and rate-setting strategies related to entry points and exit points. There exist many factors that necessitate careful examination when endeavouring to enhance competitiveness in energy marketplaces.[131] The major responsibility rests with the national regulatory bodies, which are entrusted with the task of formulating the parameters and techniques for tariff computations.

3.4.5.1 Exemptions and Derogations

The Electricity and Gas Directives[132] stipulates provisions on exemptions from the requirement to provide access to third parties. The specifications are outlined in Article 32(2). If the system lacks the necessary capacity, the system operator may deny access to the transmission or distribution system. Acts of refusal must be backed up with good reasons, especially in light of the rules in Article 3. They must also be based on objective, well-supported criteria that have to do with technical and economic aspects.

The regulatory authorities, as mandated by Member States, bear the responsibility of ensuring the uniform implementation of the criteria and establishing a mechanism for resolving disputes for system users who have been denied access. The regulatory authorities have the responsibility of ensuring that, in situations where access is prohibited, the transmission or distribution system operator furnishes relevant information pertaining to the necessary measures for enhancing the network. The individual making the request may be subject to a reasonable fee, which corresponds to the costs associated with providing the requested information.

---

[130] Directive 2009/73/EC of the European Parliament and of the Council of 13 July 2009 concerning common rules for the internal market in natural gas and repealing Directive 2003/55/EC. OJ L 211, 14.8.2009, pp. 94–136. See Article 41.

[131] Directive 2009/73/EC of the European Parliament and of the Council of 13 July 2009 concerning common rules for the internal market in natural gas and repealing Directive 2003/55/EC. OJ L 211, 14.8.2009, pp. 94–136. See Article 41 (2).

[132] Directive 2009/72/EC of the European Parliament and the Council of 13 July 2009 concerning common rules for the internal market in electricity and repealing Directive 2003/54/EC (OJ L 211, 14.8.2009, p. 55). Directive 2009/73/EC of the European Parliament and the Council of 13 July 2009 concerning common rules for the internal market in natural gas and repealing Directive 2003/55/EC (OJ L 211, 14.8.2009, p. 94).

In specific instances, such as the establishment of cross-border pipelines or LNG terminals, as well as electrical interconnections, there may be exemptions to the necessity of granting access rights. In order to facilitate the completion of significant infrastructure projects, utility companies are required to make substantial investments. Consequently, the conventional regulations governing market operations may not be fully relevant in these cases.

There is a requirement for enhancing the security of supply through investment. The infrastructure owner must adhere to the unbundling rules. The implementation of the investment is contingent upon the application of an exemption, as the project carries significant risks. The users of the infrastructure are responsible for covering the costs of access. It is asserted that such an exemption would not adversely impact the functioning of the market. It is not feasible to finance the investment solely. The aforementioned provisions are encompassed within Article 63(1) of Regulation 2019/943,[133] which can be summarised as follows: Under some conditions, such as the introduction of a novel investment for the creation of cross-border pipelines, LNG terminals, or electrical interconnections, there is a possibility of entirely waiving the obligation to provide access rights. In light of the need for utilities to make major investments by building significant new infrastructure, the traditional market rules that typically regulate their operations may not be appropriate in this specific context.

The improvement of the security of supply requires financial investment, while the implementation of unbundling legislation is crucial for the entity responsible for the infrastructure.[134] The successful implementation of the investment is dependent on the utilisation of an exemption, as the project involves significant levels of risk. The imposition of user fees should be considered a prerequisite for accessing infrastructure. The introduction of such an exception would not have a negative impact on market operations. Furthermore, it is crucial to note that the investment's funding cannot come from the revenue the transmission system generates.

The provisions delineated in Article 63(1) of Regulation 2019/943 are given in the following manner: under certain conditions, it is feasible for recently created direct current interconnectors to receive an exemption from particular provisions delineated in Articles 19(2) and (3) of this Regulation, along with Articles 6 and 43, Article 59(7), and Article 60(1) of Directive (EU) 2019/944.[135] Nevertheless, this exemption is contingent upon the satisfaction of specific conditions. The investment is intended to foster competition within the electricity supply industry. The investment entails a substantial degree of risk, hence requiring an exemption in order to proceed. The proprietor of the interconnector, regardless of whether they are an individual or a legal entity, is distinct from the system operators responsible for

[133] Regulation (EU) 2019/943 of the European Parliament and of the Council of 5 June 2019 on the internal market for electricity. OJ L 158, 14.6.2019, pp. 54–124.

[134] Nardi (2010).

[135] Regulation (EU) 2019/943 of the European Parliament and of the Council of 5 June 2019 on the internal market for electricity. OJ L 158, 14.6.2019, pp. 54–124. See Article 63 (1).

constructing the interconnector within their separate systems, particularly in relation to their legal frameworks. Fees are levied on individuals who use the interconnector. According to Article 19 of Directive 96/92/EC of the European Parliament and the Council,[136] after the partial market opening, none of the costs related to the capital or operation of the interconnector have been recovered from the fees collected for using the transmission or distribution systems that are linked by the interconnector. Granting an exception would not result in any adverse effects on competition or the effective functioning of the internal market for electricity. Additionally, it would not impede the efficient operation of the regulated system linked to the interconnector.

The decisions regarding exemptions for the new electricity infrastructure were made in support of several projects, namely EstLink, BritNED, East-West Cable, Arnoldstein/Tarvisio, ElecLink, SI-IT Interconnectors, ElecLink (Decisions of 2014, 2020, and 2021), Piemonte Svoia Interconnector (Decisions of 2016 and 2020), SI-IT Interconnectors (Decisions of 2017, 2019, and 2021), and Resia Interconnector.[137]

The decisions regarding exemptions for new gas infrastructure projects were made in support of the following initiatives: BBL, Poseidon, Nabucco AT-CAB, AT-C (Decisions made in 2008 and 2013), RO-C, BG-C, HU-C, OPAL (Decisions made in 2009 and 2016), Gazelle, Gazelle II, Trans Adriatic Pipeline, and Interconnector Greece-Bulgaria IGB.[138]

[136] Directive 96/92/EC of the European Parliament and of the Council of 19 December 1996 concerning common rules for the internal market in electricity. OJ L 27, 30.1.1997, pp. 20–29.

[137] Decision 2012/263/EU: Commission Decision of 20 December 2011 on the exemption of the EstLink 2 electricity interconnection between Estonia and Finland from the regulatory framework for cross-border electricity exchanges. Decision 2011/640/EU: Commission Decision of 12 September 2011 on the exemption of the BritNED interconnector between the Netherlands and the United Kingdom. Decision 2011/274/EU: Commission Decision of 22 April 2011 on the exemption of the East-West Interconnector between Ireland and Wales. Decision 2014/736/EU: Commission Decision of 27 November 2014 on the exemption of the Arnoldstein/Tarvisio interconnector. Decision 2014/709/EU: Commission Decision of 30 September 2014 on the exemption of the ElecLink interconnector between the United Kingdom and France. Decision 2020/418/EU: Commission Decision of 11 March 2020 on the modification of the exemption granted to the ElecLink interconnector. Decision 2021/647/EU: Commission Decision of 19 April 2021 on further modifications to the exemption of the ElecLink interconnector. Decision 2017/1401/EU: Commission Decision of 26 July 2017 on the exemption of the Slovenia-Italy interconnectors. Decision 2019/322/EU: Commission Decision of 12 February 2019 on the modification of the exemption granted to the SI-IT Interconnectors. Decision 2021/2263/EU: Commission Decision of 9 December 2021 on further amendments to the exemptions of the SI-IT Interconnectors. Decision 2016/743/EU: Commission Decision of 25 May 2016 on the exemption of the Piemonte Svoia interconnector. Decision 2020/568/EU: Commission Decision of 21 April 2020 on the modification of the exemption granted to the Piemonte Svoia Interconnector. Decision 2016/159/EU: Commission Decision of 12 February 2016 on the exemption of the Resia interconnector.

[138] Decision 2008/792/EC: Commission Decision of 29 September 2008 on the exemption of the BBL gas interconnector from the regulatory framework. Decision 2008/138/EC: Commission Decision of 18 January 2008 on the exemption of the Poseidon gas pipeline. Decision 2008/831/

The exemption decision has been granted for a number of LNG Terminals, including LNG Grain (UK), South Hook (UK), Rovigo (IT), Dragon (UK), LNG Brindisi (IT), Gate Terminal (NL), LionGas (NL), LNG Eemshaven (NL), LNG Livorno (IT), LNG Shannon (IE), LNG Dunkerque (FR), LNG Porto Empedocle (IT), National Grid Grain LNG (UK), LNG Toscana (Livorno) (IT), LNG Alexandroupolis (GR), LNG South Hook (UK), and German LNG Terminal (DE). The exemption was also granted to a gas storage facility located in Damborice, Czech Republic. The derogation decisions pertaining to small electricity systems, as outlined in Article 64 of Regulation 2019/943 and Article 66 of Directive (EU) 2019/944, were granted in support of various regions, namely the Azores, Madeira, Cyprus, Malta, the Greek Islands, and Kriegs Flak.[139]

EC: Commission Decision of 14 October 2008 on the exemption of the Nabucco gas pipeline from the regulatory framework. Decision 2008/232/EC: Commission Decision of 16 December 2008 on the exemption of the AT-C gas interconnector. Decision 2013/392/EU: Commission Decision of 27 June 2013 on the modification of the exemption granted to the AT-C gas interconnector. Decision 2009/708/EC: Commission Decision of 28 July 2009 on the exemption of the RO-C gas interconnector. Decision 2009/709/EC: Commission Decision of 28 July 2009 on the exemption of the BG-C gas interconnector. Decision 2009/710/EC: Commission Decision of 28 July 2009 on the exemption of the HU-C gas interconnector. Decision 2009/548/EC: Commission Decision of 16 July 2009 on the exemption of the OPAL gas pipeline. Decision 2016/1672/EU: Commission Decision of 28 September 2016 on the modification of the exemption granted to the OPAL gas pipeline. Decision 2008/759/EC: Commission Decision of 17 September 2008 on the exemption of the Gazelle gas pipeline. Decision 2009/165/EC: Commission Decision of 27 January 2009 on the exemption of the Gazelle II gas pipeline. Decision 2013/404/EU: Commission Decision of 29 July 2013 on the exemption of the Trans Adriatic Pipeline (TAP). Decision 2015/2053/EU: Commission Decision of 28 October 2015 on the exemption of the Interconnector Greece-Bulgaria (IGB).

[139]Decision 2005/750/EC: Commission Decision of 18 October 2005 on the exemption of the Grain LNG terminal in the UK. Decision 2006/180/EC: Commission Decision of 15 February 2006 on the exemption of the South Hook LNG terminal in the UK. Decision 2007/296/EC: Commission Decision of 12 March 2007 on the exemption of the Rovigo LNG terminal in Italy. Decision 2007/727/EC: Commission Decision of 21 November 2007 on the exemption of the Dragon LNG terminal in the UK. Decision 2009/19/EC: Commission Decision of 8 January 2009 on the exemption of the Brindisi LNG terminal in Italy. Decision 2009/573/EC: Commission Decision of 25 June 2009 on the exemption of the Gate LNG terminal in the Netherlands. Decision 2009/759/EC: Commission Decision of 24 September 2009 on the exemption of the LionGas LNG terminal in the Netherlands. Decision 2011/902/EU: Commission Decision of 20 December 2011 on the exemption of the LNG Eemshaven terminal in the Netherlands. Decision 2012/435/EU: Commission Decision of 26 June 2012 on the exemption of the LNG Livorno terminal in Italy. Decision 2012/685/EU: Commission Decision of 25 October 2012 on the exemption of the LNG Shannon terminal in Ireland. Decision 2013/433/EU: Commission Decision of 10 July 2013 on the exemption of the LNG Dunkerque terminal in France. Decision 2013/791/EU: Commission Decision of 17 December 2013 on the exemption of the LNG Porto Empedocle terminal in Italy. Decision 2014/416/EU: Commission Decision of 27 June 2014 on the exemption of the National Grid Grain LNG terminal in the UK. Decision 2014/710/EU: Commission Decision of 16 October 2014 on the exemption of the LNG Toscana (Livorno) terminal in Italy. Decision 2017/1316/EU: Commission Decision of 27 July 2017 on the exemption of the LNG Alexandroupolis terminal in Greece. Decision 2019/567/EU: Commission Decision of 26 March 2019 on the exemption of the German LNG terminal. Decision 2014/939/EU: Commission Decision of 15 December 2014 on the exemption of the Damborice gas storage facility in the Czech Republic. Decision 2013/228/EU:

It is imperative to conduct a more comprehensive examination of the Nord Stream 2 project and its compliance with the provisions outlined in the third energy package pertaining to third-party access and unbundling.[140] The Nord Stream comprises a system of offshore natural gas pipelines that were strategically developed to build a direct linkage between the nations of Russia and Germany beneath the Baltic Sea. The Nord Stream infrastructure is comprised of a pair of pipelines that establish a connection between the locations of Vyborg and Lubmin. In contrast, the Nord Stream 2 project encompasses two pipelines that establish a linkage between Ust-Luga and Lubmin. The first established target date for the conclusion of the second pipeline was the end of 2019. Nevertheless, the project faced substantial criticism and incurred delays.[141] The adherence of the Nord Stream 2 project to the regulations stipulated in the Third Energy Package is crucial, particularly with respect to the principles of unbundling, third-party access rights, and non-discriminatory rate fixing. This necessitates the responsibility to provide tariffs that are uniformly applied to all consumers, devoid of any discriminatory practices. In compliance with the gas directive, a provision is in place that provides derogations, enabling the temporary use of exemptions to safeguard the security of supply for recently constructed pipelines that facilitate the transportation of natural gas from third country. The Nord Stream pipeline is connected to the southern pipeline OPAL, which spans from Greifswald to Olbernhau in Germany and is situated in close proximity to the Czech border. The pipeline listed above functions as a link connecting the Nord Stream pipeline with the JAGAL and STEGAL transmission pipelines. The NEL pipeline, located in the western region, functions as a connection between the cities of Greifswald and Achim. Moreover, it establishes a linkage with the MIDAL pipeline, leading to the creation of the Greifswald-Bunde connection. The Nord Stream 2 route covers a distance of 1200 km, with an anticipated total capacity of around 55 billion cubic metres. In the year 2012, the examination of the findings from the feasibility study was carried out by the shareholders of Nord Stream, leading to the final determination of the project's economic and technical feasibility. In the year 2017, Nord Stream 2 AG established a financial agreement with ENGIE, OMV, Royal Dutch Shell, Uniper, and Withershell, jointly providing 50 percent of the total project expenses. The building project began in the year 2018 and successfully attained its completion in the month of September in the year

Commission Decision of 25 April 2013 on derogation for the electricity system in the Azores. Decision 2014/710/EU: Commission Decision of 16 October 2014 on derogation for the electricity system in Madeira. Decision 2014/643/EU: Commission Decision of 11 September 2014 on derogation for the electricity system in Cyprus. Decision 2013/709/EU: Commission Decision of 14 November 2013 on derogation for the electricity system in Malta. Decision 2013/731/EU: Commission Decision of 20 November 2013 on derogation for the electricity systems in Greek Islands. Decision 2013/745/EU: Commission Decision of 20 November 2013 on derogation for the electricity system in Kriegs Flak.

[140] Dudek and Piebalgs (2017).

[141] Kotek et al. (2017).

2021.[142] Nord Stream 2 exhibits similarities to its antecedent, the pre-existing initial pipeline. The project has faced preliminary political and legal obstacles in recent times. The project's lack of adherence to German legal requirements has resulted in the regulatory authority in Germany suspending the certification procedure.[143] Currently, Nord Stream AG, a Switzerland-based firm, has the intention to establish a subsidiary in compliance with the legal framework of Germany. The aim is to effectively allocate both tangible and intangible resources, including assets and human capital, to the recently established subsidiary. The certification process was temporarily suspended by the German regulatory authorities before reaching its conclusion.

The owner of the Nord Stream pipeline is required to comply with unbundling restrictions as stipulated by the gas directive and its subsequent revision in 2019.[144] This necessitates the obligation to divest the pipeline to an external entity while also guaranteeing the provision of access to competitors such as Novatek and Rosneft. Furthermore, it is imperative to establish a system that guarantees openness in tariff structures, allowing customers to easily access published tariffs and request price evaluations for their contractual agreements. The relevance of Article 11 of the Gas Directive stems from its classification as a third-country enterprise. In the present scenario, it is imperative for the German regulatory body to perform a comprehensive evaluation of supply security risks prior to granting certification. Given the current understanding of the solidarity principle as emphasised in Article 194(1) of the TFEU, it is imperative to duly acknowledge the interests of Member States. The principle established in the case C-848/19P, *Germany v. Poland*, has been upheld by the Court of Justice of the European Union (CJEU).[145]

The TFEU and secondary laws lay considerable emphasis on ensuring the security of supply, rendering it an essential feature that the project must adhere to

[142] Nord Stream AG. (2012). Feasibility Study and Project Evaluation. Retrieved from Nord Stream Project History. Nord Stream 2 AG. (2017). Financial Agreement and Project Funding. Retrieved from Nord Stream 2 Financing. Nord Stream 2 AG. (2021). Completion of Nord Stream 2 Pipeline. Retrieved from Nord Stream 2 Project Milestones.

[143] EurActiv. (2021). "Nord Stream 2 faces regulatory hurdles and political backlash." Retrieved from EurActiv Nord Stream 2. Reuters. (2021). "Germany suspends Nord Stream 2 pipeline certification." Retrieved from Reuters Nord Stream 2 Certification.

[144] Directive 2009/73/EC of the European Parliament and of the Council of 13 July 2009 concerning common rules for the internal market in natural gas. OJ L 211, 14.8.2009, pp. 94–136. See Article 9 (1), Article 9 (2). Directive (EU) 2019/944 of the European Parliament and of the Council of 5 June 2019 on common rules for the internal market for electricity. OJ L 158, 14.6.2019, pp. 125–199. See Article 54. Directive 2009/73/EC of the European Parliament and of the Council of 13 July 2009. OJ L 211, 14.8.2009, pp. 94–136. See Article 32. Directive (EU) 2019/944 of the European Parliament and of the Council of 5 June 2019 on common rules for the internal market for electricity. OJ L 158, 14.6.2019, pp. 125–199. See Article 31. Regulation (EU) 2019/943 of the European Parliament and of the Council of 5 June 2019 on the internal market for electricity. OJ L 158, 14.6.2019, pp. 54–124. See Article 63. Commission Decision (EU) 2018/2072 of 27 November 2018 on the exemption of the Nord Stream 2 gas pipeline project. OJ L 322, 29.11.2018, pp. 32–54.

[145] Judgment of the Court of Justice of the European Union (Grand Chamber) of 6 October 2021 in Case C-848/19P, Germany v. Poland. Official Journal C 462, 30.11.2021, p. 5–5.

and conform to. The assurance of supply security cannot be guaranteed by the implementation of Nord Stream 2, as the existing demand is currently fulfilled by pipelines that pass-through Belarus, Poland (particularly the Yamal pipeline), and Ukraine. In light of the present circumstances pertaining to capacity allocation in Opal, Eugal, and the development of Turkish Stream, there exists a potential scenario wherein the transit pipes may be rendered inactive, hence leading to Ukraine's deprivation of its natural gas provision. When evaluating the Nord Stream 2 route, it is probable that the central and eastern European countries will cease to function as the principal links to the western European markets, which might potentially lead to a deprivation of access to virtual reverse flows.[146]

The primary objective of the Nord Stream 2 project is to counterbalance the increasing influence of Gazprom by alleviating the potential consequences of diminishing natural gas reserves in the United Kingdom and the Netherlands on the European Union's capacity for natural gas extraction. Furthermore, there is a possibility that it may diminish the incentive to undertake the essential financial commitments required to entice more providers of liquefied natural gas (LNG). Moreover, the conveyance of natural gas via a direct pipeline to Germany is anticipated to lead to an increase in natural gas prices across Western, Central, and Southern Europe.

In July 2021, a joint statement was released by the United States and Germany, emphasising the importance of energy security and the pursuit of climate objectives.[147] It is contended that economic sanctions may potentially be employed if Russia were to utilise energy projects as a mechanism of aggressive coercion towards Ukraine. There is a possibility of implementing restrictions on the exportation of natural gas. The statement acknowledges the importance of energy security and the promotion of a diverse range of energy sources, as highlighted in the third energy package. Moreover, a proactive measure was implemented to augment the determination and commitment to addressing the issue of climate change, with a particular emphasis on accelerating the global transition towards sustainable methodologies and reducing greenhouse gas emissions. Efforts to address climate change involve implementing strategies to enhance energy security in Europe, thereby reducing dependence on Russian natural gas. Germany has undertaken a commitment to establish a green fund with the objective of offering assistance to Ukraine in its endeavours to shift towards renewable energy sources. The establishment of this fund will additionally support the advancement of hydrogen technology, bolster energy efficiency, accelerate the transition away from coal, and contribute to the objective of attaining carbon neutrality.

The inclusion of the gas directive was a crucial aspect of the third energy package, which was implemented prior to the introduction of the new energy chapter in the TFEU. The fundamental elements comprise the unbundling of ownership, the

[146] Chyong (2017).

[147] https://www.state.gov/joint-statement-of-the-united-states-and-germany-on-support-for-ukraine-european-energy-security-and-our-climate-goals/.

imposition of third-party access restrictions, and the implementation of laws for the certification of gearbox system operators, among other factors. The procedural requirements for certifying transmission system operators from non-EU countries are delineated in Article 11 of the Directive. The provision regarding an exemption clause is encompassed under Article 36 of the Gas Directive.[148]

The primary issue raised in relation to the Nord Stream 2 project was its adherence to the Gas Directive. This problem arises from the ambiguity surrounding the degree to which the project must comply with legal laws. The presence of uncertainty stems from the project's physical location beyond the boundaries of the European Union, despite its connecting points and claimed purpose of supplying natural gas to Europe. In 2017, the legal services of both the Commission and the Council found that the project's adherence to EU law fell outside the established boundaries. Applying the Gas directive to the Exclusive Economic Zone would deviate from the stipulations delineated in Articles 56 and 58 of the United Nations Convention on the Law of the Sea. The argument has been presented by the Commission that the enforcement of EU legal requirements within the Exclusive Economic Zone is permissible under Article 79(4) of the United Nations Convention on the Law of the Sea.[149] According to the statement provided by the Council, the specified article confers upon the coastal state the power to specify requirements for pipelines that pass through its territory or territorial sea. A recommendation was made to engage in international negotiations with Russia as a means to overcome the prevailing uncertainties and legal deficiencies. However, the mandate for these negotiations necessitated a unanimous vote from the Member States, given the contentious nature of the project, with some countries expressing support while others strongly opposed it.

In 2017, the Commission initiated the proposal for a Directive of the European Parliament and the Council with the objective of modifying the existing Gas directive 2009/73, which pertains to the creation of uniform regulations for the internal gas market.[150] The main aim of this plan was to expand the legislative framework to include other countries, particularly pipelines that enter the European Union. Furthermore, a provision was established to grant an exception for pre-existing initiatives such as Nord Stream 1. As per the amendment, it is incumbent upon the German authorities to guarantee that the project adheres to the regulations stipulated by the European Union. The amendment outlines the specific

---

[148] Directive 2009/73/EC of the European Parliament and of the Council of 13 July 2009 concerning common rules for the internal market in natural gas and repealing Directive 2003/55/EC OJ L 211, 14.8.2009, pp. 94–136. See Article 11, Article 36.

[149] United Nations Convention on the Law of the Sea (UNCLOS). See Article 56, Article 58, Article 79 (4).

[150] Commission staff working document. Assessing the amendments to Directive 2009/73/EC setting out rules for gas pipelines connecting the European Union with third countries accompanying the document "Proposal for a Directive of the European Parliament and of the Council amending Directive 2009/73/EC concerning common rules for the internal market in natural gas. COM (2017) 660 final.

requirements on unbundling, third-party access, and transparency that third countries operating pipelines within the European Union must comply with, regardless of whether the pipelines are now in operation or are planned for the future. As per the specifications delineated in paragraph 9 of the amendment containing Article 49a, the inclusion of the derogation provision was implicitly acknowledged, so permitting its prospective bestowal by the Member State in which the original interconnection point is located.

The following part elaborates on derogations pertaining to the establishment and operation of transmission lines connecting to and from countries outside of the primary jurisdiction. Regarding gas transmission lines between a Member State and a third country that were completed prior to May 23, 2019, the Member State where the initial connection point of such a transmission line with a Member State's network is situated has the option to deviate from certain articles, namely Articles 9, 10, 11, 32, and Articles 41(6), (8), and (10), for the sections of the gas transmission line located within its territory and territorial sea. This deviation can be justified by objective reasons.[151]

The duration of the derogation shall be restricted to a maximum of 20 years, contingent upon the presence of a valid and substantiated rationale. It may be extended if deemed necessary and must adhere to any stipulations that aid in the fulfilment of the aforementioned conditions. The aforementioned derogations shall not be applicable to the transmission lines connecting a Member State with a third country that is obligated to incorporate this Directive and has successfully implemented it within its legal framework through an agreement reached with the European Union. In cases where a transmission line is situated within the territories of multiple Member States, the Member State in which the initial connection point with the network of Member States is located holds the authority to determine whether to provide an exemption for said transmission line. Prior to making this decision, the member state must engage in consultations with all relevant member states.

At the behest of the relevant Member States, the Commission has the authority to assume the role of an observer in the consultation process between the Member State hosting the initial connection point and a third country. The purpose of this consultation is to ensure the uniform implementation of this directive within the territory and territorial sea of the Member State where the initial interconnection point is situated. This includes the possibility of granting exceptions for transmission limitations.

The application for exemption for the Nord Stream 2 project was denied by the German authorities in 2020. Subsequently, a number of grievances were filed in the German judicial system pertaining to the regulatory authority's determination to

[151] Regulation (EU) 2019/943 of the European Parliament and of the Council of 5 June 2019 on the internal market for electricity. OJ L 158, 14.6.2019, pp. 54–124. See Article 49.

deny the petition for an exemption.[152] Furthermore, the complainant initiated legal proceedings before the General Court, which ultimately deemed the complaint inadmissible based on procedural reasons rather than its substance. In addition, an appeal was made to the CJEU. Furthermore, the initiation of the proceedings in the arbitration was carried out in accordance with the provisions of the Energy Charter Treaty.

Nord Stream 2 AG, a subsidiary of the Russian state-owned business Gazprom, initiated the legal proceedings. The entity in question exercises authority over a natural gas conduit that spans from Russia to Germany. This conduit receives financial support from energy corporations within the European Union. The context of this case holds immense political significance for the EU and Europe as a whole, according to the applicant. Indeed, the applicant went bankrupt earlier this year, in close proximity to Russia's invasion of Ukraine. The matter currently under consideration by the Court of Justice is admissibility. In simpler terms, the question is whether Nord Stream 2 AG, a private entity, has the legal right to challenge an EU directive before the CJEU. In essence, the case remains unresolved. This post solely discusses the constitutional significance of the Court's decision on the eligibility requirements outlined in Article 263(4) TFEU.[153]

In 2019, Nord Stream 2 AG contested the legality of Directive 2019/692[154] ("2019 Directive") in front of the General Court. The 2019 Directive expands the regulations outlined in Directive 2009/73 to include gas pipelines that connect a Member State with a third nation. On May 23, 2019, the disputed directive came into effect, applying to all pipelines completed after that date (Article 49a). According to the company's statement, the Gas Directive's regulations now bind the nearly completed Nord Stream 2 pipeline.

The General Court deemed the applicant's challenge inadmissible and thus dismissed it. The argument states that directives have no direct impact on a private petitioner's legal circumstances before their transposition deadline. Directives can only impose legal obligations on a private party through national transposition measures. In relation to this particular issue, the General Court emphasised that the Member States have a significant amount of freedom in implementing specific aspects of the Directive in question.[155] Germany, the involved Member State in this situation, had not implemented the Directive at the time of initiating the annulment action, according to the analysis. As a result, the applicant did not possess

[152] Case Bundesnetzagentur's decision on Nord Stream 2. The decision was made by the Bundesnetzagentur on January 15, 2020. Available https://www.bundesnetzagentur.de/EN/Areas/Energy/Companies/Certification/Procedures/NordStream2/NordStream2_node.html.

[153] Court of Justice of the European Union, Nord Stream 2 AG v. European Commission, Case C-848/19 P, [2021] ECLI:EU:C:2021:740.

[154] Directive (EU) 2019/692 of the European Parliament and of the Council of 17 April 2019 amending Directive 2009/73/EC concerning common rules for the internal market in natural gas. OJ L 117, 3.5.2019, pp. 1–7.

[155] General Court of the European Union, Nord Stream 2 AG v. European Commission, Case T-526/14, [2019] ECLI:EU:T:2019:846.

the legal right to bring the case under Article 263(4) TFEU. The Court of Justice received an appeal from Nord Stream 2 AG challenging the General Court's order.

The Grand Chamber favored the appellant, overturning the order. The court determined that the appellant satisfied both the requirements of direct and individual concern and, therefore, referred the case back to the General Court to make a decision based on its substance. The Court of Justice interprets the General Court's order as explicitly removing directives from the scope of actions under Article 263(4) TFEU.[156] The order implies that directives cannot directly influence an individual's legal status without transforming into national legislation. In this case, the Court of Justice aimed to clarify that directives can directly affect individuals. Directives have a direct impact on an individual's legal position, rather than just an indirect impact through the implementation steps taken by their country. The Court emphasised the importance of assessing an individual's direct involvement by taking into account the act's actual impact and consequences, the circumstances surrounding its enactment, and the authority of the institutions responsible for its adoption.[157] It is not permissible to deny an individual standing solely because the challenged conduct takes the form of a direction. Only when the directive grants Member States some flexibility in determining the immediate legal consequences for individuals can we question the direct correlation between the directive and its legal implications.

The Grand Chamber also confirmed that the General Court erred in its assessment that the 2019 Directive provides Member States with some discretion in making decisions.[158] It reiterates that the requirement to transpose a directive does not necessarily imply that it allows any room for interpretation by those who receive it. It is critical to assess whether the Member States have flexibility in implementing the specified regulations and whether it genuinely impacts the applicant's legal status. According to the revised Gas Directive, Member States have the ability to give exclusions and derogations to pipelines that meet specific requirements. The Directive provides comprehensive regulations for these standards, leaving no room for member states to use discretion when applying exclusions and derogations to the Nord Stream 2 project. This is because the corporation did not meet the specified conditions. The national authorities lack genuine discretion, as stated in Advocate General Bobek's Opinion. The Member States' actions will unavoidably alter the appellant's legal status.

The Court of Justice further established the appellant's individual impact. The Court used the Plaumann test to determine that the appellant was clearly identifiable at the time the 2019 Directive was implemented. The Court is referring to the exceptions and exclusions provided by the revised Gas Directive. Article 49a grants a derogation to pipelines completed before May 23, 2019, the date the 2019 Directive became effective. Article 36 grants an exemption to new gas infrastructure projects that have not yet made a final investment decision. Upon implementation of

---

[156] Case C-348/20 P Nord Stream 2 v Parliament and Council.

[157] Case C-348/20 P Nord Stream 2 v Parliament and Council. Paras 82, 90–95.

[158] Case C-348/20 P Nord Stream 2 v Parliament and Council. Para 87.

the 2019 Directive, Nord Stream 2 stood out as the only pipeline that had advanced significantly beyond the initial investment phase, despite its incomplete construction. Therefore, neither the derogation nor the exemption included this particular pipeline.[159] The information provided was adequate to differentiate the appellant, and the Court of Justice concluded that Articles 36 and 49a specifically pertain to them. The Court has affirmed the acceptability of the appellant's objection to the two regulations and has sent the case back to the General Court to make a decision based on its substance.

Despite the stated objective of achieving decarbonisation in Europe by the year 2050, it is evident that natural gas continues to occupy a significant position in the ongoing decarbonisation efforts. The rationale behind this phenomenon can be attributed to the progressive phasing out of coal as a primary energy source, coupled with the limited readiness of renewable energy sources to acquire a predominant position in the energy mix, mostly due to inadequate installed capacities. Given the current situation, it is worth noting that Europe is heavily dependent on the importation of natural gas. It is crucial for Europe to undertake an examination of alternative strategies aimed at diversifying its natural gas sources in order to adequately address the escalating demand.[160] The European Union has implemented measures aimed at augmenting the diversification of its energy sources and investigating alternative import prospects. In light of the European Union's goal to actively reduce the utilisation of natural gas, efforts are being made to undertake investments. Natural gas and methane are commonly considered to be the preferred fuel choices for enabling the transition towards renewable energy sources. Nevertheless, it is crucial to acknowledge that these fuel sources continue to produce emissions, contributing to the release of carbon dioxide into the Earth's atmosphere. Hydrogen is commonly acknowledged as a transitional fuel in the context of decarbonisation, particularly in regions where the adoption of electricity presents obstacles. Both hydrogen as an energy carrier and green hydrogen are widely regarded as potential solutions to address this problem.

3.4.6 Capacity Allocations and Congestion Management

Capacity allocation and congestion management play a crucial role in facilitating the efficient operation of the internal energy market. Consequently, the recommendations pertaining to capacity allocation and congestion management for both electricity and natural gas were officially adopted by the Framework.[161] The

[159] General Court of the European Union, Nord Stream 2 AG v. European Commission, Case T-526/14, [2019] ECLI:EU:T:2019:846, paras 79–82.

[160] Hancher and Marhold (2019).

[161] Regulation (EU) 1222/2015 of the European Parliament and of the Council of 25 November 2015 on Capacity Allocation and Congestion Management. OJ L 330, 16.12.2015, pp. 24–50.

implementation of flow-based market coupling has established the necessary circumstances for enhancing price convergence among different regions and improving congestion management.

The capacity allocation mechanism refers to the procedure by which requests for network capacity from users are handled. There exist various sorts of allocation mechanisms, like first-come, first-served, pro rata, auctions, and open seasons.[162] The first-come, first-served approach is representative of a scenario where capacity is allocated based on the order in which market participants make their demands. The programme is characterised by its simplicity, allowing users to quickly and easily utilise its full capability upon payment of the appropriate regulated price. Nevertheless, this particular model lacks a market-based approach that would effectively integrate the capacity requirements of the market. Potential prejudice may arise due to the lack of awareness among certain market participants of the requisite information needed to request capacity.

The pro-rata capacity allocation model incorporates several characteristics of the previously mentioned model. However, in this model, all requests are executed simultaneously. If the demand exceeds the available capacity, the requests are proportionally reduced based on the pro rata principle in order to fulfil the present demand.[163] The current paradigm has the potential to create a bias against smaller market participants and provide preferential treatment to larger ones as a result of the required financial assurances for capacity. Risk mitigation often involves the implementation of supplementary measures, such as the imposition of constraints on the maximum allocated capacity within the market.

Auctions are conducted wherein market participants submit requests specifying the desired amount of capacity and the maximum price they are willing to pay for this capacity. In the event that the aggregate requested capacity of all tender participants falls below the total available capacity, the requests are deemed fulfilled. Conversely, if the requested capacity exceeds the whole available capacity, the winners are chosen based on the descending order of the highest offered bid. Auctions are typically characterised by transparency and non-discrimination, as

---

Regulation (EU) 2019/943 of the European Parliament and of the Council of 5 June 2019 on the internal market for electricity. OJ L 158, 14.6.2019, pp. 54–124. Regulation (EU) No 984/2013 of the European Parliament and of the Council of 14 October 2013 on the internal gas market. OJ L 273, 15.10.2013, pp. 32–62. Regulation (EU) 2017/1938 of the European Parliament and of the Council of 25 October 2017 concerning measures to safeguard the security of gas supply. OJ L 280, 28.10.2017, pp. 1–46.

[162] Regulation (EU) 1222/2015 of the European Parliament and of the Council of 25 November 2015 on Capacity Allocation and Congestion Management. OJ L 330, 16.12.2015, pp. 24–50. Regulation (EU) No 984/2013 of the European Parliament and of the Council of 14 October 2013 on the internal gas market. OJ L 273, 15.10.2013, pp. 32–62.

[163] Regulation (EU) 1222/2015 of the European Parliament and of the Council of 25 November 2015 on Capacity Allocation and Congestion Management, OJ L 330, 16.12.2015, pp. 24–50. See Article 19. Regulation (EU) No 984/2013 of the European Parliament and of the Council of 14 October 2013 on the internal gas market, OJ L 273, 15.10.2013, pp. 32–62. See Article 8.

they operate on the basis of an individual's ability to financially support a specific capability.

The concept of "open season" refers to a specific timeframe in which market participants can make requests for capacity without the requirement of including a bid price. The determination of the latter is contingent upon the actions and decisions made by the market regulator. This particular process consists of multiple stages. During the non-binding phase, market participants engage in the submission of non-binding requests. Following this stage, the operator possesses the ability to ascertain future market demand. During the subsequent stage, market participants who had previously submitted non-binding offers are requested to present binding bids for the newly available capacity, taking into account the outcomes of the initial phase. The participants establish contractual agreements with the network operator, and it is the network operator who determines the extent of the investment based on these agreements. In the event that capacity is established, the allocation of capacity becomes obligatory. If a market player fails to execute any investment, the network operator retains the authority to revoke the allocation.

The auctions under consideration involve participants submitting requests that include both the desired capacity amount and the maximum price they are willing to pay for said capacity. If all tender participants have submitted requests for a capacity that is less than the total available capacity, then the requests will be fulfilled. If the desired capacity exceeds the overall available capacity, the selection of winners will be determined by the highest bid made. Auctions typically adhere to the ideals of transparency and non-discrimination as they rely on the capacity to pay for a specific item or service.

To optimise the operational efficiency of the internal energy market, it is crucial to employ procedures such as capacity allocation and congestion management. The aforementioned consequence arose as a result of the approval granted for the implementation of the Framework Rules on Capacity Allocation and Congestion Management for Natural Gas and Electricity.[164] The introduction of flow-based market coupling has created the requisite circumstances for attaining heightened price convergence among diverse regions and increased congestion management. This phenomenon can be attributed to the improvement of congestion management.

Mitigating congestion is a crucial approach that can be employed to decrease the level of physical congestion within infrastructure. When there is a discrepancy between the actual demand and the potential capacity of market participants, optimisation tools are employed to implement specific procedures aimed at mitigating contractual congestion.

[164] Commission Regulation (EU) 2015/1222 of 24 July 2015 establishing a guideline on capacity allocation and congestion management.

3.4.7 Enhanced Consumer Protection

The significance of safeguarding consumer interests within the energy sector has witnessed a notable rise due to the continual transformations occurring in energy markets. In a time of abundant renewable energy, cutting-edge technologies, and shifting customer expectations, the goals of ensuring fair pricing, accessible information, and conflict resolution have grown more complex. This chapter presents a comprehensive review of the historical development of consumer protection in the energy sector, evaluating both its accomplishments and inherent limitations. The third energy package has also garnered attention for customer rights and their protection.

The consumer rights are also deprived in:

- Directive 2012/27/EU of the European Parliament and of the Council of 25 October 2012 on energy efficiency, amending Directives 2009/125/EC and 2010/30/EU and repealing Directives 2004/8/EC and 2006/32/EC. (Energy Efficiency Directive).
- Directive 2011/83/EU of the European Parliament and of the Council of 25 October 2011 on consumer rights, amending Council Directive 93/13/EEC and Directive 1999/44/EC of the European Parliament and of the Council and repealing Council Directive 85/577/EEC and Directive 97/7/EC of the European Parliament and of the Council. (Consumer Rights Directive).
- Council Directive 93/13/EEC of 5 April 1993 on unfair terms in consumer contracts. (Unfair Contract Terms Directive).
- Directive 2005/29/EC of the European Parliament and of the Council of 11 May 2005 concerning unfair business-to-consumer commercial practices in the internal market and amending Council Directive 84/450/EEC, Directives 97/7/EC, 98/27/EC and 2002/65/EC of the European Parliament and of the Council and Regulation (EC) No 2006/2004 of the European Parliament and of the Council. (Unfair Commercial Practices Directive).[165]

The implementation of horizontal laws aimed at consumer protection in the electricity and gas sectors did not provide the anticipated outcomes in terms of enhancing

---

[165] Directive 2012/27/EU of the European Parliament and of the Council of 25 October 2012 on energy efficiency, amending Directives 2009/125/EC and 2010/30/EU and repealing Directives 2004/8/EC and 2006/32/EC, OJ L 315, 14.11.2012, pp. 1–56. Directive 2011/83/EU of the European Parliament and of the Council of 25 October 2011 on consumer rights, amending Council Directive 93/13/EEC and Directive 1999/44/EC of the European Parliament and of the Council and repealing Council Directive 85/577/EEC and Directive 97/7/EC of the European Parliament and of the Council, OJ L 304, 22.11.2011, pp. 64–88. Council Directive 93/13/EEC of 5 April 1993 on unfair terms in consumer contracts, OJ L 95, 21.04.1993, pp. 29–34. Directive 2005/29/EC of the European Parliament and of the Council of 11 May 2005 concerning unfair business-to-consumer commercial practices in the internal market and amending Council Directive 84/450/EEC, Directives 97/7/EC, 98/27/EC and 2002/65/EC of the European Parliament and of the Council and Regulation (EC) No 2006/2004 of the European Parliament and of the Council, OJ L 149, 11.06.2005, pp. 22–39.

consumer empowerment. Provisions were implemented to enable clients to change their supplier within a three-week timeframe. The suppliers were required to furnish information to consumers in addition to establishing an effective mechanism for addressing complaints. The package incorporated explicit provisions pertaining to vulnerable clients and the accessibility of energy supplies.

Prior to the implementation of the third package, the provision of electricity to all users was not guaranteed, resulting in customers frequently encountering challenges while attempting to exercise their entitlements. In accordance with the stipulations, there exists a responsibility to furnish impartial and dependable information regarding the range of offerings present in the market, thereby facilitating the comparison of diverse alternatives. The contractual provisions needed to exhibit transparency and fairness. The incorporation of the capacity to access and modify consumption patterns was implemented with the aim of enhancing energy efficiency and minimising expenses.

It is critical to provide clients with a full breakdown of services related to the various offers so that they may examine the necessary information and make an informed decision. It is critical that the contract's terms and conditions are given clearly and without any false aspects. Customers should not be limited to a single vendor. The development of the energy consumer checklist was a crucial element in the third energy package, with the goal of providing consumers with accurate and reliable information about their rights in the energy industry. The rights and obligations pertaining to these specific matters were evident in the recast electricity directive of the Clean Energy package, as well as in the newly introduced gas directive, which accompanied the legislation of the hydrogen package.[166]

The present condition of consumer protection in the energy sector is currently at a pivotal point. Despite significant progress in enhancing consumer empowerment and advancing their rights, there are still enduring challenges that need to be addressed. The present imperative to shift towards cleaner and more sustainable energy sources, coupled with technological improvements and shifts in market dynamics, calls for a re-evaluation of existing policies and the development of innovative initiatives. These policies and tactics should not only serve to protect customers but also actively engage them in the process of transitioning.

[166]Directive (EU) 2019/944 of the European Parliament and of the Council of 5 June 2019 on common rules for the internal market for electricity and amending Directive 2012/27/EU. OJ L 158, 14.6.2019, pp. 125–199. Directive (EU) 2023/451 of the European Parliament and of the Council of 14 March 2023 on common rules for the internal markets in renewable and natural gases and in hydrogen, amending Directive 2009/73/EC and repealing Directive 2009/73/EC. OJ L 79, 21.3.2023, pp. 1–119.

3.5 Competition Law Role in Energy Sector

The enhancement of *ex-ante* controls is being implemented to bolster the establishment of the internal energy market. The Commission's investigation into the energy sector has revealed that the market continues to exhibit a lack of competition, leading to a situation where consumers are unable to access competitive pricing options. Vertical integration enables established organisations to create barriers to entry, thus impeding the entry of new competitors and safeguarding their market position. The initial energy package laid the groundwork for the establishment of competition legislation within the energy industry. However, it became apparent that the existing regulatory measures and market liberalisation tools were inadequate to fully achieve the objectives of the internal market. Ten years later, the Member States have reached a consensus to progressively liberalise electricity markets, employing not just energy regulatory measures but also competition law instruments. The jurisdiction to evaluate the level of commercial discretion pertaining to sector-specific regulations is retained by both national competition authorities and the Commission. The energy sector is subject to oversight by national regulatory authorities, while compliance with competition law requirements under the TFEU is supervised by national competition authorities in conjunction with the Commission. However, it is important to note that these institutions do not possess the jurisdiction to enforce sector-specific oversight. A potential conflict may arise between competition law regulation and sector-specific regulation. These conflicts can be categorised as either vertical or horizontal in character. Vertical conflicts involve the sharing of jurisdiction between the European Union and the national level. In instances of a horizontal dispute, there may arise a scenario wherein the delineation between competition law and energy law becomes ambiguous. According to several scholars, the implementation of *ex ante* regulation within the energy sector is seen as necessary to effectively realise a liberalised internal market. Several other scholars perceive the role of competition law in the regulation of the energy sector as supplementary.[167] This stance is justifiable, as regulatory measures within the realm of energy law are crucial elements that necessitate diligent monitoring and enforcement.

Several scholars contend that regulatory frameworks are formulated with consideration for competition law and that these two legal branches function cohesively to govern these features in an interconnected manner.[168] Competition law is delineated within the fundamental legislation of the European Union, whereas the regulation of the energy sector is established through secondary legislation, specifically directives and regulations. From a hierarchical perspective, the problem is readily comprehensible; however, the level of practical implementation gives rise to doubts. Competition law serves the objective of governing the interactions that arise among economic organisations as they engage in competitive activities. One of the primary objectives of competition law is to govern the interactions between participants in

[167] Growitsch and Stronzik (2011).

[168] Berge et al. (2012).

equitable relationships through the use of regulatory measures. This serves to safeguard the interests of consumers and competitors while also facilitating the integration of national markets within the framework of establishing an internal market.

Within the realm of economics, competition is commonly conceptualised as a competitive event wherein both natural and legal entities engaged in commercial activities limit their capacity to exert dominance over the market. This competition is designed to yield economic advantages that are not invariably linked to increased profitability. Competition law includes provisions that aim to prevent the abuse of market dominance, particularly in cases where a firm holds a significant share of the market.[169] Additionally, it forbids the formation of agreements that are seen to be anti-competitive in nature. Incompatibilities with the internal market can arise due to constraints associated with state aid. The authority responsible for overseeing competition has the jurisdiction to intervene in mergers and acquisitions that have the potential to impact competition. This intervention is warranted when such transactions have the potential to enhance or establish a dominant market position or when they severely impede competition in the relevant market. The use of competition regulations prompts an inquiry into whether the company possesses market power capable of exerting an effect on competition.

Despite the existence of special regulations within the energy sector, the Commission retains the authority to intervene in disputes based on violations of competition rules outlined in the TFEU. The exercise of these rights gives rise to a dual regulatory framework. The obligation for Deutsche Telekom to offer network access rights to its competitors was already established in the case law of the CJEU, namely in the case of *Deutsche Telekom*.[170] Consequently, the company refrained from establishing its own pricing structure, as the wholesale rates were determined by the regulatory authority. The company, however, had the discretion to impose a retail tariff within the confines of the predetermined price range. Deutsche Telekom has faced allegations of engaging in anti-competitive practices through the exploitation of its strong market position, namely by maintaining an insufficient buffer between wholesale and retail prices. In this particular instance, the CJEU determined that while the regulator established the prices, the corporation possessed the authority to exercise discretion in setting rates for end users, even though the wholesale price was subject to regulation.[171] Prior to the completion of an inquiry conducted by the

---

[169] Treaty on the Functioning of the European Union (TFEU), Article 102, OJ C 326, 26.10.2012, pp. 47–390. Council Regulation (EC) No 1/2003 of 16 December 2002 on the implementation of the rules on competition laid down in Articles 81 and 82 of the Treaty, OJ L 1, 4.1.2003, pp. 1–25. Directive (EU) 2019/1 of the European Parliament and of the Council of 11 December 2018 to empower the competition authorities of the Member States to be more effective enforcers and to ensure the proper functioning of the internal market, OJ L 11, 14.1.2019, pp. 3–33.

[170] Case COMP/C-1/37.451, 37.578, 37.579, *Deutsche Telekom AG*.

[171] Joined cases 209/78, 215/78, 218.78, *Van Landewyck and Others v Commission*; Joined Cases 240/82, 261/82, 269/82, *Stichting Sigarettenindustrie and Others v Commission*; Case C-219/95 *P Ferriere Nord v Commission*; Joined cases C-359/95 and C-379/95 *P, Commission and French*

Commission on the energy sector, it had been able to operate without any obstacles, despite the prior intervention of competition authorities in addressing the dispute.

A comparable scenario arose in the *HFC Bank plc/British Gas Trading Ltd* case when the UK energy regulator addressed the dispute.[172] However, the Commission noted a potential concern related to tying in the same case within the context of competition law. In this instance, the Commission was anticipating the ultimate determination from the regulator, who additionally affirmed the absence of any potential for tying. Consequently, the Commission proceeded to conclude the case.

National energy regulators possess the authority to enforce precise regulations and have jurisdiction to impose punishment upon the identification of infractions. Nevertheless, a thorough examination of the provisions within the second energy package pertaining to the authorities' jurisdiction reveals their role in upholding competition law, as stipulated in Article 102 of the TFEU.[173] The pursuit of energy market liberalisation through a blend of regulatory measures can occasionally yield unintended consequences. These requirements suggest a more stringent approach to regulation and control rather than granting enterprises the autonomy to function within the market. The prevalent argument regarding market over-concentration and the subsequent imperative for sectoral reform give rise to a situation where double standards are observed, leading operators to prioritise adherence to certain regulatory standards rather than engaging in competitive practices. Otherwise, individuals will face penalties for their failure to uphold regulatory standards. The issue becomes more pronounced when there is a clash between the specific regulations of energy law and competition law regulations, placing the business in a state of uncertainty as it attempts to execute these rules.

The primary objective of the energy law is to foster competitive market conditions by establishing a regulatory framework that includes ex ante requirements and a supervisory mechanism. The Commission assumes a significant responsibility for overseeing the application of European Union law within the national legal systems of its member states, as stipulated by the Treaty on the Functioning of the European Union.[174] Upon deeper examination of the Commission's position, specifically

---

Republic v Ladbroke Racing; Case T-228/97 *Irish Sugar v Commission*; Case T-513/93 *Consiglio Naxionale Degli Spedizionieri Doganali.*

[172] European Commission, XXVIIth Report on Application of Competition Rules in the European Union, 1997.

[173] Treaty on the Functioning of the European Union (TFEU), Article 102, OJ C 326, 26.10.2012, pp. 47–390.

[174] Treaty on the Functioning of the European Union (TFEU) OJ C 326, 26.10.2012, pp. 47–390. Directive 2012/27/EU of the European Parliament and of the Council of 25 October 2012 on energy efficiency, amending Directives 2009/125/EC and 2010/30/EU and repealing Directives 2004/8/EC and 2006/32/EC (Energy Efficiency Directive). OJ L 315, 14.11.2012, pp. 1–56. Directive 2011/83/EU of the European Parliament and of the Council of 25 October 2011 on consumer rights, amending Council Directive 93/13/EEC and Directive 1999/44/EC of the European Parliament and of the Council and repealing Council Directive 85/577/EEC and Directive 97/7/EC of the European Parliament and of the Council (Consumer Rights Directive). OJ L 304, 22.11.2011, pp. 64–88. Council Directive 93/13/EEC of 5 April 1993 on unfair terms in consumer contracts

focusing on the powers vested in the Directorate - General for Competition, it becomes evident that the latter possesses comprehensive authority to take action against corporations that fail to adhere to competition law. The Commission has the exclusive authority to enforce Article 101 TFEU and is vested with the discretionary power to bestow exemptions. The implementation of this system aims to establish a standardised process for the approval of exemptions. The Commission held the viewpoint that it possessed the capability to evaluate the economic inconsistencies that arise and harmonise the many objectives outlined in the TFEU.

Efforts have been undertaken to streamline the current system with the aim of enhancing its modernity. These adjustments seek to alleviate the administrative workload and simultaneously offer businesses a higher degree of legal assurance.[175] The aforementioned modifications have been enacted with the purpose of conferring enforcement responsibilities upon national competition authorities and courts. In the *Synergen* case,[176] the Commission exercised its conferred powers to direct the Irish regulatory body to resolve the issue in alignment with Regulation No. 1/2003 and guarantee adherence to the associated responsibilities. The justification for employing *lex specialis* in the energy sector in this particular instance stems from the specialised authority's jurisdiction over regulations specific to the energy industry, encompassing technical matters, pricing, and access concerns that fall outside the purview of competition authorities.

The Commission has highlighted the primary barriers pertaining to the advancement of the internal market within the energy sector inquiry. Companies that were vertically integrated, meaning they had control over all aspects of natural gas production, electricity generation, transmission, distribution networks, and supply activities, exposed several problems. The efficient structuring of a corporation facilitates cost optimisation while concurrently establishing market dominance. However, such companies may impede market entry for potential new competitors. Through this approach, big corporations uphold their market dominance and independently establish their energy pricing. Consequently, the Commission has implemented measures to alleviate the adverse consequences. The third energy package offers different measures to address the issue of ownership unbundling inside vertically integrated firms.[177] One of the most contentious issues pertains to the implementation of the entire ownership unbundling model inside vertically

(Unfair Contract Terms Directive). OJ L 95, 21.4.1993, pp. 29–34. Directive 2005/29/EC of the European Parliament and of the Council of 11 May 2005 concerning unfair business-to-consumer commercial practices in the internal market and amending Council Directive 84/450/EEC, Directives 97/7/EC, 98/27/EC, and 2002/65/EC of the European Parliament and of the Council and Regulation (EC) No 2006/2004 of the European Parliament and of the Council (Unfair Commercial Practices Directive). OJ L 149, 11.6.2005, pp. 22–39.

[175] Berge et al. (2012).

[176] IP/02/792 of May 2002, Commission clears Synergen Venture between ESB and Statoil following strict commitments.

[177] Growitsch and Stronzik (2011).

integrated companies, which prohibits the consolidation of control over transmission and/or distribution operations with supply and production.

According to the Commission's assertion, adopting this approach is the most efficient means to facilitate the establishment of the internal energy market and to eradicate monopolistic practices that primarily disadvantage consumers. There exists a significant discourse surrounding the efficacy of this paradigm in establishing both theoretical and practical conditions necessary for the operation of the internal market. The tight regulations pose several challenges in cases where enterprises with vertical integration are under state ownership. In this scenario, the fulfilment of unbundling standards is necessary to assure the absence of control across organisations. The implementation of such a mandate raises concerns due to institutional subordination and the principles of separation of powers and accountability.[178] The concept of absence of control encompasses various aspects, such as the rights associated with shareholding, including the ability to appoint board or supervisory board members. Additionally, it could potentially encompass the passive shareholder's entitlement to receive dividends, although this interpretation may vary. This viewpoint is justifiable due to the fact that, even with a minimal ownership stake in the company, the lack of a shareholder in the decision-making process allows for comprehensive access to information regarding decisions made by the management bodies. When examining the scenario in which energy corporations are overseen by the state through relevant regulatory bodies, one may raise concerns regarding the extent of control and the degree of separation observed when governmental decisions are taken, particularly considering the hierarchical relationship between the two entities.

Another scenario occurs when privately owned enterprises are obligated to adhere to ownership unbundling regulations. In this particular scenario, it is necessary to assess the stipulations outlined in bilateral foreign investment protection treaties as well as the obligations pertaining to foreign investor protection as mandated by the Energy Charter Treaty.[179] The equitable involvement of the state should be ensured in relation to the company's shares while safeguarding the legal interests of investors. The inclusion of unbundling requirements in energy legislation for vertically integrated enterprises establishes the necessary conditions for the emergence of a

[178] Directive 2009/72/EC of the European Parliament and of the Council of 13 July 2009 concerning common rules for the internal market in electricity and repealing Directive 2003/54/EC. OJ L 211, 14.8.2009, pp. 55–93. Directive 2009/73/EC of the European Parliament and of the Council of 13 July 2009 concerning common rules for the internal market in natural gas and repealing Directive 2003/55/EC. OJ L 211, 14.8.2009, pp. 94–136. Regulation (EC) No 714/2009 of the European Parliament and of the Council of 13 July 2009 on conditions for access to the network for cross-border exchanges in electricity and repealing Regulation (EC) No 1228/2003. OJ L 211, 14.8.2009, pp. 15–35. Regulation (EC) No 715/2009 of the European Parliament and of the Council of 13 July 2009 on conditions for access to the natural gas transmission networks and repealing Regulation (EC) No 1775/2005. OJ L 211, 14.8.2009, pp. 36–54. Treaty on the Functioning of the European Union (TFEU), particularly Article 102, addressing the abuse of a dominant position. Consolidated version: OJ C 326, 26.10.2012, pp. 47–390.

[179] Energy Charter Treaty, signed on 17 December 1994. OJ L 69, 9.3.1998, pp. 3–60.

liberalised and competitive internal market. However, it is important to note that the mere presence of these requirements does not automatically ensure the successful establishment of a well-functioning market. The necessity lies not only in eliminating horizontal and vertical connections between enterprises but also in making efforts to diversify energy sources in order to develop a competitive internal market.

3.5.1 Conclusions

The European Union's energy landscape has undergone significant transformation due to the liberalisation of energy markets through the implementation of the first and second energy packages. The first package aimed to establish a unified internal energy market, fostering competition, energy security, and consumer options. The second package aimed to facilitate cross-border energy trading and promote collaboration among member states. The first energy package established the groundwork for subsequent packages, which aimed to promote renewable energy, cross-border collaboration, and the development of regulatory authorities. The first energy package contained two directives that aimed to establish a competitive electricity market and promote renewable energy, ultimately driving down prices.

The primary objective of the Second Energy Package was to promote the liberalisation and standardisation of energy markets across the European Union. The objective of the package was to address enduring monopolistic practices in the energy sector and promote a more competitive atmosphere. The objective was to remove barriers that impede the entry of new competitors into the market and improve the movement of energy across national borders. The package underscored the significance of independent national regulatory bodies and the creation of a cohesive domestic energy market. The primary objective of the package was to facilitate the advancement of cleaner and more sustainable energy technology through investments in infrastructure and energy sources. The second energy package was essential in promoting the development of the internal energy market of the European Union and fostering competition in the electricity and gas industries. Nevertheless, the execution of functional, legal, and accounting unbundling proved ineffective in attaining the intended results of market liberalisation, necessitating additional measures to enhance market conditions.

The Third Energy Package's main goal was to promote the liberalization and standardization of the energy market. This would facilitate the transmission of energy across national borders, mitigate obstacles, prevent market manipulation, and enhance the efficiency of separating energy operations. The main objective was to guarantee regulatory independence, encourage consumer empowerment, and cultivate a stable investment environment. The package sought to streamline the incorporation of renewable energy sources into power grid infrastructure and promote investments in environmentally sustainable energy technologies. Furthermore, it addressed the problem of ensuring energy supply security by improving infrastructure, expanding the range of energy sources, and establishing mechanisms for emergency response.

The unbundling models aim to foster competition, enhance transparency, and encourage investment while prioritising consumer interests and ensuring a reliable and secure energy supply. Unbundling refers to the procedure of separating discrete elements within the energy supply chain with the aim of fostering equitable competition and establishing a harmonised market framework within the domains of electricity and gas. This practice aims to diminish competitive forces and establish contrived obstacles for potential market entrants. The delivery of energy to final consumers necessitates a series of interconnected activities, including generation, transmission, distribution, and supply. The authority to choose a model preference is assigned to each Member State.

The objective of the Third Energy Package in the European Union is to create a highly effective energy market in Europe by encouraging the use of efficient and transparent practices within energy markets. National energy regulators have the authority to supervise energy markets, set rates, ensure that third parties have access to energy infrastructure, and protect consumer rights. In addition, they supervise investments in energy infrastructure, guaranteeing fair access to renewable energy sources and compensation. The package aims to promote cooperation among regulators in different regions and across borders, facilitate market integration, and tackle energy-related challenges specific to each region. Regulatory autonomy is of utmost importance, and it is imperative for national regulators to uphold their independence from political interference and commercial interests. The package additionally grants national energy regulators enhanced autonomy, enabling them to issue legally binding decisions and enforce penalties in cases of non-compliance with legal responsibilities. Furthermore, it addressed the problem of ensuring energy supply security by improving infrastructure, expanding the range of energy sources, and establishing mechanisms for emergency response.

National regulatory authorities are responsible for establishing or approving transmission or distribution tariffs and methodologies, following transparent criteria. They ensure compliance with obligations under the Gas Directive and other European Union legislation, particularly on cross-border issues. The regulatory body monitors the investment plans of transmission system operators, ensures adherence to network security and reliability regulations, and monitors market opening and competition levels. They also monitor consumer protection measures, consumer access to storage, and consumer consumption data. The Third Energy Package strengthened the autonomy of national energy regulators, requiring them to adopt a structure that demonstrates autonomy from both governmental influence and firms. Regulatory authorities are vested with the legal authority to issue legally binding decisions and impose financial penalties on enterprises that fail to comply with legal requirements. Market participants provide precise data to regulators, enabling efficient market surveillance and oversight.

The Agency for the Cooperation of Energy Regulators (ACER) plays an important role within the energy sector of the European Union by actively fostering market integration and competition and safeguarding consumer interests. The organisation encounters several obstacles in fulfilling its prescribed obligations, such as conflicting national interests and discrepancies in regulatory methodologies. The fundamental significance of the agency lies in its facilitation of the transition towards sustainable energy sources and promotion of collaborative efforts across nations, hence playing a vital role in the achievement of the European Union's energy policy objectives. In order to promote fair competition and establish a competitive environment, it is imperative for the agency to tackle issues such as regulatory fragmentation, grid planning, access, and rates. In order to ensure efficient monitoring, investigation, and implementation of rules, the agency must also take into consideration political sensitivities, capacity limitations, and the ever-changing energy landscape. For the energy policy objectives, the agency's involvement in promoting a unified and consumer-oriented energy market is vital.

The independence of regulatory agencies is compromised due to their reliance on governments and limited autonomy. The Commission emphasises the need for legislative proposals to harmonise competencies and enhance the autonomy of national regulatory institutions. The European Union is working to create a unified and coordinated energy market to ensure a reliable, eco-friendly, and economically efficient energy supply for its member states. Collaboration across international boundaries is crucial, with entities like ENTSOE and ENTSOG facilitating this effort by focusing on maintaining power system security and operating interconnected markets and aiming to foster collaboration among national operators in Europe, advance the internal market, and strengthen cross-border trade.

The international energy transition focuses on liberalising and deregulating energy markets to improve efficiency, reduce costs, and increase renewable energy use. Third-party entry into energy infrastructure is essential for effective market functioning. The initial gas and electricity directives provided Member States with the option to implement either a regulated or negotiated access regime. Infrastructure companies must engage in negotiations with eligible customers and publicly disclose access conditions. The Electricity Directive mandates Member States to establish a framework for third-party access to transmission and distribution systems based on openly accessible tariffs applicable to all qualified customers. This should be impartial and non-discriminatory, ensuring equal treatment for all users. Member States must ensure the public availability of authorised tariffs and methodologies before implementation.

The Gas Directive requires Member States to construct a regulatory framework that facilitates third-party access to transmission and distribution systems as well as liquefied natural gas (LNG) facilities. These systems should be publicly stated and objective, without prejudice or differentiation. Regulations aim to prevent discriminatory practices, promote trade and competition, and prevent cross-subsidisation among users. Access to information and physical access to systems are crucial for evaluating demand and supply. Regulations aim to prevent discriminatory practices in infrastructure utilisation by promoting competition and reducing cross-subsidisation among different user groups. These regulations use the entry-exit model for price determination, ensuring network users have the ability to allocate network capacity. Infrastructure companies must openly disclose the terms and conditions of infrastructure access and make the necessary requirements accessible to the public.

Regulation 715/2009 aims to adopt just and impartial laws to facilitate access to natural gas transmission lines, considering the unique characteristics of national and regional markets. This aims to ensure the efficient functioning of the domestic gas market and establish a competent and accountable wholesale gas market while ensuring a reliable gas supply. Equitable access to infrastructure is crucial, as it ensures all users receive the same level of service without discrimination. Network operators must ensure equitable and unbiased conditions, as the market may remain inaccessible or cater exclusively to specific entities, restricting end consumers' ability to choose their energy provider. Tariffs are established through market-driven processes, such as auctions, to facilitate efficient gas trade, encourage competition, and limit cross-subsidisation among network users. They are implemented to foster investment and ensure interoperability for transmission networks. Tariffs must conform to the principle of non-discrimination and be determined on a case-by-case basis for each ingress or egress point of the transmission system. National regulatory bodies must endorse cost-allocation systems and rate-setting strategies related to entry and exit points.

Recent years have witnessed substantial transformations in the energy sector, resulting in an increasing demand for safeguarding the interests of consumers. The Third Energy Package has prioritised customer rights and protection, but it has encountered difficulties in strengthening consumer empowerment. The package encompasses procedures for supplier substitution within a three-week period, dissemination of information to consumers, and resolution of grievances. However, the failure to ensure the provision of energy to all consumers resulted in customers facing challenges in exercising their entitlements. The primary objective of the third package is to deliver unbiased and reliable information regarding the products available on the market, enable easy comparisons, and improve energy efficiency. The energy consumer checklist is a crucial component of the package, guaranteeing precise and dependable information regarding customers' entitlements in the energy industry. The current status of consumer protection in the energy sector is at a critical juncture, with notable advancements in bolstering consumer empowerment and promoting their entitlements. The transition towards more environmentally friendly and enduring energy sources, advancements in technology, and changes in market conditions necessitate a reassessment of current regulations and the creation of inventive initiatives. These regulations should not only ensure clients' safety and well-being, but also actively involve them in the transition process.

The Commission's investigation into the energy sector has revealed a lack of competition, causing consumers to be unable to access competitive pricing options. Vertical integration enables established organisations to create barriers to entry, impeding new competitors and safeguarding their market position. The initial energy package laid the groundwork for competition legislation within the energy industry, but the existing regulatory measures and market liberalisation tools were inadequate to fully achieve the objectives of the internal market. Ten years later, the Member States have reached a consensus to progressively liberalise electricity markets, employing not just energy regulatory measures but also competition law instruments. National competition authorities and the Commission both retain the authority to judge the degree of commercial discretion pertaining to sector-specific regulations.

The energy sector is subject to oversight by national regulatory authorities, while compliance with competition law requirements under the Treaty on the Functioning of the European Union (TFEU) is supervised by national competition authorities in conjunction with the Commission. However, these entities do not possess the jurisdiction to enforce sector-specific oversight. A potential conflict may arise between competition law regulation and sector-specific regulation, which can be vertical or horizontal in character. Regulatory frameworks are formulated with consideration for competition law, with competition law delineated within the fundamental legislation of the European Union and energy sector regulation through secondary legislation, specifically directives and regulations. The Commission retains the authority to intervene in disputes based on violations of competition rules outlined in the TFEU, giving rise to a dual regulatory framework.

National energy regulators have the authority to enforce precise regulations and impose sanctions for infractions. However, their role in upholding competition law, as stipulated in Article 102 of the TFEU, is emphasised in the second energy package. The primary objective of the energy law is to foster competitive market conditions by establishing a regulatory framework with *ex ante* requirements and a supervisory mechanism. The Commission assumes significant responsibility for overseeing the application of European Union law within the national legal systems of its member states.

Efforts have been undertaken to streamline the current system, alleviating administrative workload and offering businesses a higher degree of legal assurance. The Commission has highlighted the primary barriers pertaining to the advancement of the internal market within the energy sector inquiry. Companies that were vertically integrated, meaning they had control over all aspects of natural gas production, electricity generation, transmission, distribution networks, and supply activities, exposed several problems. The Commission has implemented measures to alleviate the adverse consequences. The third energy package offers different measures to address the issue of ownership unbundling inside vertically integrated firms. The Commission asserts that adopting this approach is the most efficient means to facilitate the establishment of the internal energy market and eradicate monopolistic practices that primarily disadvantage consumers. However, tight regulations pose challenges in cases where enterprises with vertical integration are under state ownership. The implementation of unbundling standards is necessary to assure the absence of control across organisations, but concerns arise due to institutional subordination and the principles of separation of powers and accountability. In addition to unbundling requirements in energy legislation for vertically integrated enterprises, it is necessary to eliminate horizontal and vertical connections between enterprises and diversify energy sources to develop a competitive internal market.

References

Balmert D, Brunerkreeft G (2010) Deep - ISOs and network investment. Compet Regul Netw Ind, Intersentia 11(1):27–50

Berge H, Bernaerts I et al (2012) EU energy law and policy yearbook. Claeys and Casteels

Bjornebye H (2010) Investing in EU energy security: exploring the regulatory approach to tomorrow's electricity production. Kluwer Law International

Cameron P (2005) The legal aspects of EU energy regulation. Implementing the new Directives on Electricity and Gas across Europe. Oxford University Press, New York

Cameron P (2007) Competition in energy markets: law and regulation in the European Union. Oxford University Press

Chyong CK (2017) An assessment of Gazprom's proposed commitments concerning Central and Eastern European gas markets using a global gas market simulation model. Energy Policy Research Group, Cambridge

Davies SW, Price C (2007) Does ownership unbundling matter? Evidence from UK energy markets. Inter - economics 42(6):297–301

Delvaux B (2011) EU law and the developments of sustainable, competitive and secure energy policy – opportunities and shortcomings. Intersentia

Delvaux B, Hunt M, Talus K (eds) (2017) EU energy law and policy issues. Intersentia

Dorigoni S, Pontoni F (2008) Ownership separation of the gas transportation network: theory and practice. Working paper series. 9

Dralle MT (2018) Ownership unbundling and related measures in the EU energy sector: foundations, the impact of WTO law and investment protection. Springer

Dudek J, Piebalgs A (2017) Nord Stream 2 and the EU regulatory framework: challenges ahead. Policy Brief. RSCAS. 26

Green R (2021) Competitive effects of market integration in European electricity markets. Energy Econ 95:105070

Growitsch C, Stronzik M (2011) Ownership unbundling of gas transmission networks – empirical evidence. J Regul Econ 46(2)

Hancher L, Marhold A (2019) A common EU framework regulating import pipelines for gas? Exploring the Commission's proposal to amend the 2009 Gas Directive. J Energy Nat Resour Law. Taylor and Francis Online 37(3)

Hogan WW (2021) Market design for decarbonization: integrating renewables and managing grid stability. Harvard Kennedy School

Jones C (ed) (2019) EU energy law vol. II EU competition law and energy markets, 5th edn. Claeys and Casteels

Kotek P, Selei A, Takacsne TB (2017) The impact of construction of the Nord Stream 2 gas pipeline on gas prices and competition. Regional Centre for Energy Policy Research

Nardi P (2010) The interplay between the European Commission, Member States and utilities in the debate on transmission network unbundling. Working paper series

Newbery D (2019) The role of market integration in the European Union's energy transition. Oxford Rev Econ Policy 35(2):229–246

Nouicer A, Meeus L (2019) The EU Clean Energy Package. RSCAS. Technical Report

Pielow JC, Lewendel J (2011) The EU energy policy after the Lisbon Treaty. In: Dorsman A, Westerman W, Baha Karan M, Arslan-Ayaydin O (eds) Financial aspects in energy: a European perspective. Springer, Heidelberg, pp 147–165

Rumpf J, Hancher L (2020) Single interconnectors and congestion management challenges – the legal framework? RSCAS 2020/73

Schittekatte T, Reif V, Meeus L (2020) The EU Electricity Network Codes. RSCAS. Technical Report

Chapter 4
Europe's Journey to Carbon Neutrality: Pioneering a Continent Without Emissions

Abstract The Paris Agreement is a significant international agreement aimed at limiting the rise in global temperatures to less than 2 °C and achieving carbon neutrality by 2050. The global effort to address climate change and establish a framework for collaborative initiatives across nations is a universal activity. The agreement prioritises the importance of adaptive capacity, resilience, and vulnerability mitigation in relation to the effects of climate change, especially for nations that are weak and undergoing development. The Paris Agreement is highly significant in the areas of international law and climate policy, highlighting the effectiveness of multilateral approaches in tackling complex global concerns. The effectiveness of the effort depends on strong enforcement mechanisms and the steadfast dedication of states, civil society, and the corporate sector to execute their obligations and facilitate significant changes in the pursuit of a sustainable, low-carbon global environment. In 2019, the European Union conducted a comprehensive evaluation of its energy policy framework with the aim of shifting away from fossil fuels and towards more environmentally friendly and sustainable energy sources.

4.1 Introduction

Europe finds itself at a critical juncture in light of the increasingly pressing global issues presented by climate change and environmental deterioration. The pressing necessity to confront the climate catastrophe has spurred a profound process, envisioning a future in which a continent that was formerly dependent on fossil fuels emerges as a model of sustainability. This endeavour, also known as the "pursuit of carbon neutrality", represents an unparalleled dedication to significantly diminish the release of greenhouse gases, ultimately attaining a condition of equilibrium between emissions generated and sequestered from the environment. In this initial chapter, we commence an examination of Europe's ambitious endeavour to

L. Rimšaitė, *The Crossroads of Competition Law and Energy Regulation*,
https://doi.org/10.1007/978-3-031-73238-6_4

lead the way in establishing a continent with zero emissions.[1] This formidable undertaking covers various aspects, including technological advancements, legislative restructuring, public involvement, and international collaboration.

The pursuit of carbon neutrality in Europe is based on the acknowledgement that climate change presents a significant peril to the ecosystems, economies, and communities of our planet. The escalation of global temperatures, alterations in weather patterns, and increased frequency and intensity of catastrophic events serve as evident signs of the current situation. In order to prevent severe repercussions, the worldwide community, including the European Union, has made a commitment to the objective of the Paris Agreement, which is to restrict the increase in global temperatures to a level much below 2 °C compared to pre-industrial times. The attainment of this objective requires a comprehensive overhaul of energy systems, transportation infrastructure, industrial practices, agricultural methods, and land use.[2]

Central to Europe's pursuit of carbon neutrality is a forward-thinking dedication to restructuring its energy infrastructure, reducing carbon emissions in its economies, and promoting sustainable lifestyles among its populace. The attainment of carbon neutrality in Europe is predicated on a number of fundamental pillars. The process of achieving carbon neutrality entails a crucial element known as decarbonising the energy mix. This involves shifting away from the use of fossil fuels and concurrently expanding the deployment of renewable energy sources, including wind, solar, and hydropower. The transition towards an environmentally friendly and sustainable energy combination plays a pivotal role in mitigating carbon emissions originating from power production and other sectors that consume significant amounts of energy.[3] Europe is dedicated to transforming its transport industry through the promotion of electric mobility, the expansion of public transport networks, and investments in sustainable urban design. The objective of this initiative is to significantly mitigate emissions stemming from transportation via road, air, and sea channels. The adoption of cleaner production techniques and technology poses a problem for heavy industrial sectors, including manufacturing and heavy-duty transportation. Europe is actively promoting innovation and sustainability in these areas in order to connect them with the objective of achieving carbon neutrality.

[1]Communication from the Commission to the European Parliament, the European Council, the Council, the European Economic and Social Committee and the Committee of the Regions. State of Energy Union 2015. SWD (2015) 208, SWD (2015) 209, SWD (2015) 217 a 243. COM (2015) 572 final.

[2]Paris Agreement. Adopted on 12 December 2015. Full text available in the Official Journal of the European Union: OJ L 282, 19.10.2016, pp. 4–16. Regulation (EU) 2021/1119 of the European Parliament and of the Council of 30 June 2021 on the European climate law. Establishes the framework for achieving climate neutrality. OJ L 243, 9.7.2021, pp. 1–17.

[3]Communication from the Commission to the European Parliament, the European Council, the Council, the European Economic and Social Committee and the Committee of the Regions. Delivering the internal electricity market and making the most of public intervention. SWD (2013) 438 final, SWD (2013) 439 final, SWD (2013) 440 final, SWD (2013) 441 final, SWD (2013) 442 final. C (2013) 7243 final.

The notion of a circular economy is a pivotal element in achieving carbon neutrality since it serves to minimise waste and optimise the utilisation of resources, thereby enhancing efficiency.[4] The European region is actively pursuing the concept of circularity in various aspects of its operations, including product design, manufacturing processes, and waste management. The importance of sustainable agriculture, forestry, and land use in relation to carbon sequestration and conservation cannot be overstated. The European continent is currently engaged in the exploration of regenerative agricultural practices and afforestation as means to attain carbon neutrality, all the while ensuring the preservation of food security. The attainment of carbon neutrality necessitates the active participation of diverse societal entities, encompassing enterprises, local governments, and individuals. The inclusion of public awareness, education, and engagement is vital to the progression of this endeavour. Europe aims to set a precedent and foster global collaboration in addressing climate change. Europe is actively promoting the worldwide shift towards a sustainable and carbon-neutral future by employing diplomatic efforts, establishing trade agreements, and providing development aid.

Although the European Union's aspiration to achieve carbon neutrality is commendable, it is not devoid of inherent obstacles and complexities. The successful implementation of the transition necessitates substantial financial investments, advancements in technology, and comprehensive systemic transformations.[5] Achieving a harmonious equilibrium between economic growth, social fairness, and environmental sustainability poses a multifaceted challenge. The European continent's commitment to achieving carbon neutrality is fostering innovation, generating employment opportunities, ameliorating air quality, and bolstering its capacity to withstand forthcoming adversities.

The European Union's aspiration to achieve carbon neutrality by 2050 represents a significant and ambitious undertaking. This statement denotes a significant change in the way societies see and address the generation, utilisation, and preservation of energy resources, as well as their impact on the environment.[6] This chapter aims to examine Europe's endeavour towards achieving carbon neutrality, encompassing an analysis of the underlying motivations, methods, problems, and worldwide ramifications associated with this pioneering initiative.

---

[4]Communication from the Commission to the European Parliament, the European Council, the Council, the European Economic and Social Committee and the Committee of the Regions. Circular Economy Action Plan: For a cleaner and more competitive Europe. COM (2020) 98 final. European Commission. The European Green Deal. COM (2019) 640 final. Directive (EU) 2018/851 of the European Parliament and of the Council of 30 May 2018 amending Directive 2008/98/EC on waste. OJ L 150, 14.6.2018, pp. 109–140.

[5]Communication from the Commission to the European Parliament, the European Council, the Council, the European Economic and Social Committee and the Committee of the Regions. Clean Planet for All: A European strategic long-term vision for a prosperous, modern, competitive and climate neutral economy. COM (2018) 773 final.

[6]Communication from the Commission to the European Parliament, the European Council, the Council, the European Economic and Social Committee and the Committee of the Regions. The European Green Deal. COM (2019) 640 final.

One could argue that Europe's commitment to carbon neutrality is a calculated response to the existential threat that climate change presents. The increasing frequency and intensity of climate-related disasters have underscored the imperative to mitigate greenhouse gas emissions. The European Union, being a prominent actor in the global economic and political arena, endeavours to impose its influence through the establishment of favourable precedents. The European Union's dedication to attaining carbon neutrality serves as a noteworthy example for other entities to follow, strengthening the European Union's standing as a prominent leader in tackling the issue of climate change. Europe is presently experiencing a notable surge in the implementation of renewable energy sources, such as wind, solar, and hydropower, in an effort to replace traditional energy sources reliant on fossil fuels. Investments in research and development have a crucial role in facilitating technological innovation within these domains.

Improving energy efficiency in several sectors, such as industry, transportation, and buildings, plays a crucial role in mitigating emissions. The European Union has established high objectives with regards to the reduction of energy usage. Two important mechanisms, namely the Carbon Border Adjustment Mechanism (CBAM) and the EU Emissions Trading System (EU ETS), effectively facilitate the price of carbon emissions.[7] These mechanisms are crucial in establishing appropriate carbon pricing and creating incentives for the reduction of emissions. The adoption of a circular economy model facilitates the optimisation of resource utilisation, the mitigation of waste generation, and the reduction of emissions resulting from both production and consumption activities. Transition costs refer to the significant financial commitments necessary for the achievement of carbon neutrality, which entail expenditures on environmentally friendly technologies and the development of sustainable infrastructure. The task of guaranteeing the economic viability and social equity of these investments presents a significant challenge.

The growing dependence on intermittent renewable sources gives rise to apprehensions over energy security in times of diminished renewable supply. The importance of storage and grid flexibility cannot be overstated. Certain industries, particularly those that heavily depend on fossil fuels, are confronted with economic upheaval. The implementation of just transition policies aimed at providing support to communities and employees affected by various socio-economic changes is of utmost importance. The global implications of a given phenomenon refer to the wide-ranging consequences and effects that it has on a global scale.

[7]Communication from the Commission to the European Parliament, the European Council, the Council, the European Economic and Social Committee and the Committee of the Regions. Proposal for a Regulation of the European Parliament and of the Council establishing a Carbon Border Adjustment Mechanism. COM (2021) 564 final. Directive 2003/87/EC of the European Parliament and of the Council of 13 October 2003 establishing a scheme for greenhouse gas emission allowance trading within the Community and amending Council Directive 96/61/EC. OJ L 275, pp. 32–46.

The pursuit of carbon neutrality in Europe signifies a momentous and bold dedication to tackle the pressing issue of climate change. Although there are numerous obstacles on the path ahead, the European Union's unwavering commitment to achieving a sustainable and carbon-neutral future possesses the capacity to fundamentally transform worldwide energy systems, stimulate ground-breaking advancements, and cultivate international cooperation. As Europe takes the lead in establishing a continent with zero emissions, the knowledge gained, and accomplishments attained will have a profound impact extending beyond its geographical boundaries. These experiences will leave a lasting impression on the trajectory towards a sustainable and resilient future for global society.

In an epoch characterised by unparalleled ecological predicaments, the European Union has undertaken a forward-thinking endeavour aimed at achieving a formidable objective: to establish itself as the foremost region in attaining a state of equilibrium between greenhouse gas emissions produced and those removed from the atmosphere.[8] The daring promise mentioned, which is included in the European Green Deal and supported by all 27 Member States, represents an exceptional advancement towards achieving sustainability, climate resilience, and assuming a worldwide leadership role in addressing climate change. The endeavour to achieve carbon neutrality in Europe extends beyond physical borders and represents a hopeful emblem for a worldwide society grappling with the urgent issue of climate change. The European Union is presently engaged in substantial efforts to reinvent its energy infrastructure, mitigate carbon emissions within its industries, and transition towards a circular and sustainable economic paradigm. This significant juncture in history affords the European Union the chance to make determinations that will have profound implications for the global environment.

The European Green Deal, a comprehensive and innovative policy framework, is crucial in Europe's pursuit of achieving carbon neutrality. This endeavour not only places climate action as a top priority but also encompasses a wide range of sustainability-related topics, including the preservation of biodiversity and the incorporation of circular economy ideas. The aforementioned transformative agreement acts as a strategic framework for the European continent's shift towards sustainability, with the goal of attaining carbon neutrality within the European Union by 2050.[9] The goal of carbon neutrality is a complex and intricate effort involving a wide range of policies that have significant effects on many aspects of society and the economy. The term pertains to a substantial shift in energy generation, wherein renewable sources supplant fossil fuels and the emphasis on energy efficiency becomes paramount. This necessitates a reassessment of transport, with a focus on electric mobility and the implementation of sustainable urban design

[8]International Energy Agency. Net Zero by 2050. A roadmap for the Global Energy Sector. Revised version October 2021.

[9]Communication from the Commission to the European Parliament, the European Council, the Council, the European Economic and Social Committee and the Committee of the Regions: The European Green Deal. COM (2019) 640 final.

principles. Implementing circular economic models is critical because they effectively minimize waste and optimize resource use. Furthermore, it emphasises the need for a fair and unbiased transition, guaranteeing the involvement of all individuals in the effort to move towards a more environmentally sustainable economy. Currently, the European Union is actively working to modernise its energy framework, reduce carbon emissions in its industries, and shift towards a circular and sustainable economy. The present moment in history presents a crucial chance to choose a path that has far-reaching consequences for the overall well-being of our planet.

The Framework Strategy for a Resilient Energy Union is a significant document within the European Union's efforts to achieve a sustainable, secure, and interconnected energy future.[10] This framework was implemented as a component of the Energy Union effort, and it outlines a comprehensive approach designed to improve energy resilience, strengthen security of supply, and promote the climate objectives of the European Union. The Energy Union plan, which was introduced in 2015, aims to ensure the provision of secure, sustainable, competitive, and affordable energy to both European citizens and enterprises. The primary objective of the Framework Strategy for a Resilient Energy Union is to attain five interconnected dimensions that work together to support its goals. The concept of energy security encompasses the objectives of maintaining a consistent and dependable energy supply, diminishing reliance on foreign sources, and improving methods for responding to energy-related crises. The completion of the internal energy market aims to enhance competition, foster innovation, and enhance consumer choice. The prioritisation of energy efficiency solutions is crucial in order to effectively cut energy usage, minimise costs, and mitigate greenhouse gas emissions.

Decarbonisation refers to the process of facilitating the shift towards a low-carbon energy system by means of augmenting the utilisation of renewable energy sources, enhancing energy efficiency, and establishing a more adaptable energy framework.[11] The promotion of innovation and investments in research and development is crucial for driving technical developments and enhancing energy technologies. The plan places emphasis on the cooperation of Member States in order to facilitate the development of integrated national energy and climate plans. This initiative establishes a foundation for a more integrated strategy towards energy and climate policies, promoting the principles of openness and responsibility. The energy security plan emphasises the importance of diversifying energy sources, channels, and suppliers. The document also presents strategies for bolstering crisis response

---

[10]The Communication from the Commission to the European Parliament, the Council, the European Economic and Social Committee, the Committee of the Regions and the European Investment Bank "A Framework Strategy for a Resilient Energy Union with a Forward – Looking Climate Change Policy" COM/2015/080 final.

[11]The Communication from the Commission to the European Parliament, the Council, the European Economic and Social Committee, the Committee of the Regions and the European Investment Bank "A Framework Strategy for a Resilient Energy Union with a Forward – Looking Climate Change Policy" COM/2015/080 final.

mechanisms, enhancing infrastructure, and fortifying energy diplomacy. The completion of the internal energy market continues to be a primary focus. The strategy places significant emphasis on the development of cross-border infrastructure projects, the establishment of harmonised market rules, and the elimination of regulatory barriers in order to facilitate the creation of an integrated and efficient energy market.[12]

Ambitious targets are established to improve energy efficiency across multiple sectors, including buildings, industry, and transportation. The emphasis is placed on initiatives aimed at refurbishing current structures, implementing energy-efficient technologies, and advocating for sustainable modes of transportation. The concept of decarbonisation emphasises the significance of shifting towards an energy mix that has reduced carbon emissions.[13] The plan encompasses ambitious objectives for the implementation of renewable energy, advancements in energy storage technologies, and efforts to reduce carbon emissions in the transportation industry. The implications and challenges associated with the topic at hand are of significant importance and warrant careful consideration. The strategy's primary objective of diminishing reliance on external suppliers and augmenting energy security carries significant ramifications for the European Union's diplomatic relations and trade policy. To effectively accomplish the objectives of the strategy, significant financial resources must be allocated towards energy infrastructure improvements, thereby prompting inquiries regarding the means of finance and the equitable distribution of costs. The successful transition to a low-carbon energy system while ensuring energy security necessitates the adept handling of intermittent renewable energy sources and the implementation of a resilient grid infrastructure. The diversification of energy sources has the potential to generate geopolitical consequences, which might influence the dynamics of relationships with energy suppliers and transit countries.

The Framework Strategy for a Resilient Energy Union signifies the European Union's dedication to achieving a sustainable, secure, and interconnected energy future.[14] Although the strategy sets forth high objectives, it duly recognises the intricate issues that confront the energy sector. The achievement of successful implementation is contingent upon the establishment of strong governance structures, the fostering of effective cooperation among stakeholders, the allocation of significant financial resources, and a steadfast dedication to fostering innovation.

[12]The Communication from the Commission to the European Parliament, the Council, the European Economic and Social Committee, the Committee of the Regions and the European Investment Bank "A Framework Strategy for a Resilient Energy Union with a Forward – Looking Climate Change Policy" COM/2015/080 final.

[13]The Communication from the Commission to the European Parliament, the Council, the European Economic and Social Committee, the Committee of the Regions. The European Green Deal. COM (2019) 640 final.

[14]The Communication from the Commission to the European Parliament, the Council, the European Economic and Social Committee, the Committee of the Regions and the European Investment Bank "A Framework Strategy for a Resilient Energy Union with a Forward – Looking Climate Change Policy" COM/2015/080 final.

The European Union endeavours to set a precedent in the worldwide energy transition with the objective of fostering a more durable and environmentally friendly energy framework for forthcoming cohorts.

4.2 The Paris Agreement

The Paris Agreement is a significant international pact that encompasses the legal, technological, and intellectual dimensions of worldwide climate action.[15] In this analysis, we explore the primary legal facets of the subject and provide scholarly perspectives on its importance.

The European Union's objective to position itself as the foremost region worldwide in attaining full elimination of emissions is closely interconnected with the commitments it has delineated in the Paris Agreement. The Paris Agreement, an international convention adopted within the framework of the United Nations Framework Convention on Climate Change in 2015, is a notable endeavour on a worldwide scale to tackle the issue of climate change. The major aim of this initiative is to effectively limit the rise in global temperatures to a magnitude that is notably lower than 2 °C over the levels observed during the pre-industrial period. Furthermore, it establishes the lofty objective of constraining the increase in temperature to 1.5 °C. This aspiration demonstrates a high level of ambition. To achieve this goal, countries, including those inside the European Union, put forth their emissions reduction targets and strategies, commonly known as nationally determined contributions.[16] The European Union's commitment to achieving carbon neutrality by 2050 aligns with the long-term temperature goal outlined in the Paris Agreement. The European Union's dedication to addressing climate change is apparent through its endeavours to exceed the established baseline goals, demonstrating its ambition to take on a prominent position in this field. The origins of the Paris Agreement can be attributed to a series of international negotiations spanning several decades, with the primary objective of tackling the escalating challenge posed by climate change.[17] This agreement builds upon previous climate agreements, including the Kyoto Protocol. The acknowledgment of the pressing necessity to enhance the worldwide reaction to climate change acted as a stimulus for its implementation.

The agreement sets a comprehensive structure that prioritises transparency and accountability. It mandates countries to consistently provide reports on their emissions and the extent to which they are meeting their Nationally Determined Contributions. The global stocktake procedure is undertaken on a quinquennial basis in

[15] Paris Agreement (2015) – United Nations Framework Convention on Climate Change, Paris, France, Dec. 12, 2015.

[16] Hoffmann (2011).

[17] Paris Agreement (2015) – United Nations Framework Convention on Climate Change, Paris, France, Dec. 12, 2015.

order to evaluate the overall advancement made collectively. Developed nations have made a commitment to mobilise financial resources in order to provide support for climate mitigation and adaptation endeavours in developing nations. The Paris Agreement places significant importance on the enhancement of adaptive capacity, the reinforcement of resilience, and the reduction of susceptibility to the effects of climate change, with a special focus on nations that are fragile and in the process of development. The agreement recognises the notion of loss and damage pertaining to the adverse effects of climate change that go beyond the capacity for adaptation. The system is established to effectively mitigate and manage the negative impacts and consequences resulting from climate change.

The Paris Agreement holds considerable significance due to multiple factors. The statement signifies widespread agreement at the global level regarding the imperative nature of addressing climate change promptly as well as establishing a structure for collaborative efforts among nations. The remarkable level of dedication displayed by its near-universal acceptance highlights the inclusivity of this phenomenon. Nevertheless, the subject at hand encounters various obstacles, such as the imperative for heightened ambition in Nationally Determined Contributions, the necessity to reconcile disparities between pledged commitments and actual implementation, and the task of tackling financial and equality concerns.

The Paris Agreement carries significant implications for the realm of international law and the governance of climate-related matters.[18] This statement highlights the efficacy of multilateralism in tackling intricate global issues. Furthermore, this action establishes a precedent for the use of voluntary, nationally determined obligations within the context of international accords. The success of the initiative is contingent upon the implementation of strong enforcement mechanisms, and its influence on shaping the international climate agenda is expected to have an impact on forthcoming climate negotiations. The Paris Agreement serves as a tribute to the shared dedication of humanity to facing the profound challenge posed by climate change. As nations strive to execute their Nationally Determined Contributions and enhance their climate ambition, the accord continues to serve as a source of optimism and a vital mechanism for protecting the planet's long-term well-being. The sustained progression and achievement of this endeavour will rely on the determination of states, civic society, and the corporate sector to uphold their obligations and facilitate profound alterations in the quest for a sustainable, low-carbon global environment.

The Paris Agreement has legal force and is an international treaty pursuant to the Vienna Convention on the Law of Treaties. This form is of the essential importance to ensure the binding obligations to the contracting parties.[19] The long-term goals and the reporting provisions are legally binding however, targets itself are not of the binding nature, rather of the nature of strong commitment. The higher values and goals were beyond as the strict wording of this agreement would have led that it

[18] Paris Agreement (2015) – United Nations Framework Convention on Climate Change, Paris, France, Dec. 12, 2015.

[19] Andresen (2015).

would not have come in force due to the lack of ratifying countries.[20] This document creates obligations but does not explicitly set the implementing measure. The contracting parties have to submit their nationally determined contributions with exact measure for the five-year cycle. This document reflects global understanding of the changing climate and the measures taken by every country.

To meet the set put climate goals the coal phase-out is at the utmost important. This fuel is the most carbon intensive fuel which is widely used in the generation of electricity. The burning of coal is a source of nitrogen oxides, sulphur dioxide and heavy metals in the air. To achieve the target the option is to limit the new constructions of the coal-fired plants and mitigating the decrease of the emissions in existing power plants.

The primary means by which the level of ambition in the climate regime can be heightened is through the implementation of periodic evaluations to assess the advancements made in relation to the agreement's temperature objective. In 2018, a preliminary evaluation, commonly referred to as the "facilitative discussion", is scheduled to occur before the anticipated implementation of the agreement. The initial official evaluation, known as the "global stocktake" (Article 14(1)), as stated in the agreement, was planned to take place in 2023, followed by subsequent assessments every five years. The purpose of these evaluations is to provide information to stakeholders as they develop future nationally determined contributions, with the intention of revising and improving their commitments (as stated in Article 14(3)).

The Paris Agreement incorporates a mandatory framework for national reporting, encompassing data on emissions from various sources and the removal of greenhouse gases through carbon sinks. This emphasis on transparency serves as a crucial regulatory mechanism, fostering trust among participating nations and facilitating the evaluation of individual commitments (as outlined in Article 13). The Paris Agreement diverges from the regulatory strategy of the Kyoto Protocol by encompassing all nations in its mitigation endeavour. While the Kyoto deal exclusively imposed emission reduction responsibilities on Annex I countries, the new accord mandates all emitters to undertake nationally determined measures in order to mitigate global warming. The concept of inclusiveness signifies a major progression in the realm of international climate negotiations. These negotiations have historically been marked by a substantial division between the northern and southern hemispheres regarding the interpretation of the principle of common but differentiated responsibilities and respective capabilities outlined in the UNFCCC.[21] Europe's dedication to achieving carbon neutrality can be construed as a strategic reaction to the profound existential peril presented by climate change.

[20] Hoffmann (2011).

[21] United Nations Framework Convention on Climate Change (UNFCCC). The United Nations Framework Convention on Climate Change. United Nations, 1992. Paris Agreement (2015) – United Nations Framework Convention on Climate Change, Paris, France, Dec. 12, 2015.

The establishment of widespread endorsement for the Paris agreement can be attributed, in part, to the meticulous design of its legal framework. This framework strategically incorporates elements that are either vaguely defined, unenforceable, or beyond the jurisdiction of domestic courts. It became evident throughout the preliminary discussions leading up to the Paris summit that the Paris Agreement would be classified as an international treaty in accordance with the provisions outlined in the Vienna Convention on the Law of Treaties. Nevertheless, one important aspect of the Paris Agreement is its flexibility in allowing individual nations to determine the necessary process for ratification, whether it be by parliamentary approval or presidential decision, thus addressing longstanding requests from the United States (as stated in Article 20). However, it is important to note that non-compliance with their own national climate plans will not be considered a violation of international law. The compliance process of the agreement is clearly intended to be expert-based and facilitative, operating in a transparent, non-adversarial, and non-punitive way (Article 15(2)). Even in cases where parties violate treaty provisions, they will not be subject to harsh measures as they would be in other international agreements, such as those established by the World Trade Organisation. As a result, several analysts have disputed the Paris Agreement's legal bindingness, which is the subject of the inquiry. The central concern revolves around the potential impact of its unique legal framework, which primarily focuses on procedural matters and grants countries autonomy in determining their contributions to global climate mitigation. The question at hand is whether this approach can effectively contribute to global efforts aimed at preventing hazardous climate change.

4.3 The Clean Energy Package

In the year 2019, the European Union (EU) undertook a complete review of its energy policy framework in order to facilitate a shift from fossil fuels to more ecologically sustainable energy sources. The reform of the policy was primarily motivated by the European Union's dedication to the Paris Agreement, which advocates for substantial reductions in greenhouse gas emissions.[22] The agreement obtained on the Clean Energy for All Europeans package notes a significant progression in the implementation of the energy union initiative, which was introduced

[22] Regulation (EU) 2018/1999 of the European Parliament and of the Council of 11 December 2018 on the Governance of the Energy Union and Climate Action. OJ L 328, pp. 1–77. Directive (EU) 2018/2001 of the European Parliament and of the Council of 11 December 2018 on the promotion of the use of energy from renewable sources (recast). OJ L 328, pp. 82–209. Directive (EU) 2018/844 of the European Parliament and of the Council of 30 May 2018 amending Directive 2010/31/EU on the energy performance of buildings and Directive 2012/27/EU on energy efficiency. OJ L 156, pp. 75–91.

in 2015.[23] Based on the proposals made by the Commission in 2016, the package comprises a comprehensive set of eight proposed laws.[24] It is anticipated that the adoption of the new regulations will result in substantial benefits for consumers, the environment, and the economy. By implementing these modifications at the European Union level, the legislation not only highlights the EU's leadership in tackling the problem of global warming but also significantly contributes to the EU's overarching goal of achieving carbon neutrality (reaching net-zero emissions) by 2050.

The European Union's Clean Energy Package is a significant legal framework that aims to hasten the transition to a carbon-emissions-reduced, environmentally sustainable energy system. With a comprehensive range of regulations and directives, the objective is to fundamentally transform the energy sector, facilitate the use of renewable energy sources, optimise energy efficiency, and strengthen energy markets. Nevertheless, like every ambitious policy endeavour, the Clean Energy Package is not devoid of its inherent limitations and obstacles. This chapter examines the various aspects of the legislative process, including its goals, achievements, and challenges that affect its execution.

The Clean Energy Package serves as a pivotal framework in the realm of sustainable energy. It establishes a comprehensive set of policies and regulations aimed at promoting the adoption and utilisation of clean energy sources. The Clean Energy Package encompasses a range of policy objectives, including the promotion of renewable energy integration, enhancement of energy efficiency, and establishment of a more competitive energy market. These objectives are in accordance with the overarching objectives of the European Green Deal and the endeavour to achieve a carbon-neutral continent by the year 2050.[25] The package encompasses a variety of directives and laws that specifically address various facets of the energy industry, spanning from energy efficiency and renewable energy to market design and governance. The comprehensiveness of the subject matter is indicative of the intricate nature of the energy transition. The package introduces aggressive targets and initiatives for energy efficiency, with the aim of promoting energy savings across diverse industries. The recognition of the pivotal role of energy efficiency in attaining climate objectives and mitigating energy expenses is acknowledged.

The promotion of renewable energy sources is a key component of the package, which includes enforceable targets and methods to enable their integration into the overall energy portfolio. The primary goal is to mitigate reliance on fossil fuels and advance the development of a more sustainable energy landscape.[26] The successful

[23]The Communication from the Commission to the European Parliament, the Council, the European Economic and Social Committee, The Committee of the Regions and the European Investment Bank "Clean Energy for All Europeans". COM (2016) 860 final. 30.11.2016.

[24]Nouicer et al. (2020).

[25]Fetting (2020).

[26]Directive (EU) 2018/2001 of the European Parliament and of the Council of 11 December 2018 on the promotion of the use of energy from renewable sources (recast). OJ L 328, 21 December 2018, pp. 82–209. See Article 3, Article 7, Article 8.

implementation of the Clean Energy Package is accompanied by a multitude of hurdles. It is imperative for Member States to ensure the harmonisation of their domestic policies with the directives established by the European Union, a task that often entails intricate and protracted procedures. The financing of the transition to a clean energy system necessitates significant allocations of funds towards the development of infrastructure, technology, and research. The task of identifying sufficient funding sources and mechanisms continues to pose a significant obstacle. The integration of intermittent renewable sources into the electricity grid requires substantial enhancements in grid infrastructure and energy storage systems. The significance of these expenditures lies in their crucial role in maintaining grid stability.

Social equity is a significant concern in the context of the energy transition since it has the potential to disproportionately impact underprivileged communities and workers within industries that are experiencing transformation. The urgent matter at hand is the resolution of social and economic disparities that have emerged as a result of the transition. The interplay between market dynamics and the need for climate action and energy security presents a multifaceted policy challenge. The Clean Energy Package represents a crucial legal framework that embodies the European Union's dedication to tackling climate change and attaining a sustainable energy future. The praiseworthy nature of its objectives is contingent upon its ability to navigate the inherent complications and risks associated with a significant energy transition. As we go to examine the subsequent chapters, we will undertake a more comprehensive exploration of these dimensions, therefore illuminating the transformative trajectory that the European Union has undertaken and the resilience necessary to surmount its inherent vulnerabilities.

The importance of energy performance in buildings is widely acknowledged within this framework. The directive revises and modifies certain provisions that were previously in effect. The proposed modifications encompass additional obligations pertaining to the modernization of antiquated structures that consume a substantial share of energy. The recent advancements are intricately linked to the refurbishment, hence augmenting the potential for energy conservation. The refurbishment strategies establish overarching objectives that are to be achieved over an extended period of time while also delineating specific intermediate targets to be reached along the way. Member States are also obligated to implement the most efficient energy performance requirements. Starting December 31, 2020, it was mandatory for all buildings to adhere to the "nearly zero-energy" standard. Additionally, it is required that an energy performance certificate be issued throughout the transfer process. The documents were updated to incorporate provisions for air quality, ventilation, and temperature regulation systems.

Renewable energy enhancements constitute an additional objective in the Clean Energy Package. Given that the energy industry is accountable for greenhouse gas emissions, the adoption of renewable energy sources effectively addresses this concern from the outset. The updated regulation establishes lofty objectives, including a minimum requirement of 32% renewable energy integration into the energy mix by the year 2030.[27] This provision is subject to change by the year 2023 and exhibits variation among certain sectors. The use of renewable fuels in the transportation sector has been augmented to reach a proportion of 14%, enhancing the overall sustainability of bioenergy.

The Clean Energy Package also aimed to address energy efficiency. The revised regulation has implemented a target for energy efficiency to be attained by 2030, which is set at a minimum of 32.5%. All of the European Union's member states are working together to achieve this goal. This entails a reduction in basic energy use as well. In order to meet the objectives, set forth, it is imperative for Member States to attain an annual energy savings rate of 0.8% over the designated timeframe. In accordance with the established objectives, Member States are required to develop decennial national energy and climate plans that include specific policies aimed at attaining the aforementioned targets.[28] The increased knowledge among consumers is also positively received, as the directive mandates the provision of information to consumers regarding their energy consumption in order to enhance their understanding of energy conservation. The provisions also encompassed a detailed review of the enhanced efficiency of heating and cooling systems. The modification of this directive is anticipated to take place in 2024, with the purpose of evaluating the progress made towards the established targets and determining the necessary actions to be implemented in order to fulfil the overarching objectives of energy conservation. In order to ensure the effective implementation of the anticipated requirements, the Commission has also released a number of instructional materials.

The Clean Energy Package encompassed the introduction of both directives and regulations. The adoption of the regulation pertaining to the governance of the Energy Union and the attainment of climate objectives has taken place. This document explains the procedures and measures employed to evaluate the achieved targets. Furthermore, it fosters collaboration among Member States in order to effectively attain the climate objectives and meet the targets set by the Energy Union. Furthermore, this topic is strongly interconnected with the objectives outlined in the Paris Agreement, encompassing the strategies employed to attain these goals as well as the processes involved in monitoring and assessing the effectiveness of the implemented measures. The administrative load is mitigated by the process of streamlining the action plans and assigning the responsibility of monitoring their implementation to the Commission. An essential aspect pertains to transparency, which is guaranteed through the beginning of public consultations concerning the national energy and climate strategies.[29]

[27] Directive (EU) 2018/2001 of the European Parliament and of the Council of 11 December 2018 on the promotion of the use of energy from renewable sources (recast). Official Journal of the European Union, L 328, pp. 82–209. See Article 3 (1), Article 7.

[28] Directive (EU) 2018/2001 of the European Parliament and of the Council of 11 December 2018 on the promotion of the use of energy from renewable sources (recast). Official Journal of the European Union, L 328, pp. 82–209. See Article 1 (1), Article 3, Article 7.

[29] Cameron and Heffron (2016).

The final component is commonly referred to as the electricity market design, encompassing the regulation of electricity, the amendment of the electricity directive, the regulation of risk preparedness, and the Agency for the Cooperation of Energy Regulators (ACER) regulation.[30] The revised directives were intended to bring about the completion of the internal market liberalisation process, promote competition in the energy market, offer consumers affordable energy options, raise consumer awareness regarding electricity consumption, and improve overall energy savings. Regarding the escalating proportions of renewable energy, it is imperative to also address the issue of balancing, as stipulated by the regulations.

Additional regulations were implemented concerning the emissions of power plants and the provision of subsidies as capacity measures, ensuring compliance with climate objectives. The agenda also included the implementation of an action plan to address future electrical problems and shortages.[31] The significance of this aspect lies in the assurance of adequate energy supply to consumers while minimising any negative effects on the energy market. Consequently, it is imperative for Member States to assess and establish adequate energy reserves and crisis management mechanisms. It is imperative to implement risk preparedness plans, and it is essential for Member States to engage in coordination and cooperation during times of crisis.

The establishment of the Electricity Coordination Group involved the inclusion of officials from national government bodies, the ACER, and the European Network of Transmission System Operators for Electricity (ENTSOE). The primary objective of the group is to facilitate the effective coordination and exchange of information pertaining to actions that have a significant impact on the member states. Despite

---

[30] Regulation (EU) 2019/943 of the European Parliament and of the Council of 5 June 2019 on the internal market for electricity. OJ L 158, pp. 54–124. See Article 1. Directive (EU) 2019/944 of the European Parliament and of the Council of 5 June 2019 on common rules for the internal market for electricity. OJ L 158, 14 June 2019, pp. 125–199. See Article 1. Regulation (EC) No 713/2009 of the European Parliament and of the Council of 13 July 2009 establishing an Agency for the Cooperation of Energy Regulators (ACER). OJ L 211, 14 August 2009, pp. 1–14. See Article 1. Regulation (EU) 2017/2196 of the European Parliament and of the Council of 30 November 2017 establishing a network code on emergency and restoration. OJ L 334, 14 December 2017, pp. 1–24. See Article 1.

[31] Regulation (EU) 2018/1999 of the European Parliament and of the Council of 11 December 2018 on the Governance of the Energy Union and Climate Action. OJ L 328, pp. 1–77. See Article 1. Directive (EU) 2018/2001 of the European Parliament and of the Council of 11 December 2018 on the promotion of the use of energy from renewable sources (recast). OJ L 328, pp. 82–209. See Article 1. Directive (EU) 2019/944 of the European Parliament and of the Council of 5 June 2019 on common rules for the internal market for electricity. OJ L 158, pp. 125–199. See Article 1. Regulation (EU) 2019/943 of the European Parliament and of the Council of 5 June 2019 on the internal market for electricity. OJ L 158, pp. 54–124. See Article 1. Regulation (EU) 2018/410 of the European Parliament and of the Council of 14 March 2018 amending Directive 2003/87/EC to enhance cost-effective emission reductions and low-carbon investments. OJ L 76, pp. 3–27. See Article 1. Regulation (EU) 2020/852 of the European Parliament and of the Council of 18 June 2020 on the establishment of a framework to facilitate sustainable investment. OJ L 198, 22 June 2020, pp. 13–43. See Article 1.

being founded under the Third Energy Package, ACER's functions and powers required revision. Under the newly implemented regulation, ACER will be granted more responsibilities and authority. In addition to its existing advisory and monitoring activities, ACER's powers will be expanded to address the issue of market fragmentation and promote its reduction and exercises the authority to engage in regulatory proceedings.

The Clean Energy Package comprises a series of legislation and directives aimed at attaining climate objectives, enhancing coordination and collaboration among Member States, and transitioning from fossil fuels to renewable energy objectives. The aforementioned bundle serves as a precursor to the forthcoming Commission Green Deal, which will be further discussed in subsequent sections.

4.4 The Green Deal

The European Green Deal, which the European Commission unveiled in late 2019, marks a significant turning point in the European Union's commitment to combating climate change and promoting sustainable development.[32] The Green Deal aims to achieve a climate-neutral, resource-efficient, and socially inclusive economy in the European Union by 2050, building upon a robust legislative framework. This chapter delves into the legal foundations of the Green Deal, analyses its fundamental results, and provides a critical evaluation of significant criticisms and issues related to its execution. This chapter offers a comprehensive analysis of the European Green Deal, focusing on its legal dimensions, the challenges associated with its implementation, and its potential for transformative change.

The European Green Deal finds its foundation in the Treaty on the European Union and the Treaty on the Functioning of the European Union. The commitment to seek sustainable development is enshrined in Article 3 of the Treaty on the European Union, while Article 191 of the Treaty on the Functioning of the European Union sets the objectives of the EU's environmental policy. Furthermore, Article 194 of the Treaty on the Functioning of the European Union pertains to the regulation of energy policy, a domain that is intricately linked with the achievement of climate objectives.

The achievement of the Green Deal's objectives is being facilitated through the introduction or modification of a range of legislative measures.[33] The aforementioned initiatives encompass the European Climate Law, the European Green Deal Investment Plan, the Farm to Fork Strategy, and the Biodiversity Strategy, as well as a range of directives and regulations pertaining to energy, transport, and the circular

[32] The Communication from the Commission to the European Parliament, the Council, the European Economic and Social Committee, the Committee of the Regions. The European Green Deal. COM (2019) 640 final.

[33] Fetting (2020).

economy. The Green Deal encompasses a set of crucial objectives that are deemed essential for its successful implementation.

The major objective of the Green Deal is the attainment of climate neutrality by the year 2050. This entails the delicate equilibrium between greenhouse gas emissions and removals, thereby making a significant contribution to the international endeavours aimed at constraining global warming to a level significantly below 2 °C. The Green Deal prioritises the augmentation of renewable energy sources and enhancements in energy efficiency. The policy establishes mandatory objectives for the proportion of renewable energy sources and energy conservation measures.

In order to acknowledge and address the social and economic effects of the transition, the Green Deal includes a Just Transition Fund that offers support to regions and industries that are most negatively affected by these changes. The Green Deal places considerable emphasis on the preservation and restoration of biodiversity, as well as the promotion of circular economy practices aimed at mitigating waste generation and resource consumption. Critics contend that the allocated funds for the Green Deal may be inadequate in realising its lofty objectives, necessitating the provision of more considerable financial resources. The achievement of social equity poses a persistent challenge, as it necessitates an equitable and fair transition for all individuals and geographical areas. This challenge is compounded by apprehensions regarding the potential ramifications of job displacement and economic inequalities. The legislative structure of the Green Deal exhibits a high degree of complexity, which gives rise to many obstacles in its execution. These challenges mostly stem from the possible conflicts that may arise between different policy objectives. The attainment of climate neutrality necessitates the establishment of global cooperation.

The European Green Deal signifies a crucial juncture in international efforts to address climate change. The statement reflects the European Union's dedication to harmonising its economic and environmental objectives, acknowledging that sustainability is a fundamental aspect of a thriving future. The Paris Agreement and international commitments refer to global efforts and agreements made by countries to address climate change and reduce greenhouse gas emissions. These agreements aim to mitigate the impacts of climate change and promote sustainable development on a global scale. The European Green Deal is in accordance with the objectives and principles of the Paris Agreement, thereby strengthening the European Union's dedication to international efforts in addressing climate change. This section examines the manner in which the agreement enhances the European Union's position within the realm of global climate governance. The topic of discussion pertains to the legislative and regulatory framework of the European Union. An in-depth look at the existing laws of the European Union, such as the 2030 Climate and Energy Framework,[34] the Emissions Trading System (ETS), and the Renewable Energy Directive,

[34]Communication from the Commission to the European Parliament, the Council, the European Economic and Social Committee and the Committee of the Regions. A policy framework for climate and energy in the period from 2020 to 2030. COM/2014/015 final.

shows how the European Green Deal not only builds on but also strengthens existing laws. A comprehensive analysis of the Just Transition Fund and the Just Transition Mechanism Regulation highlights the European Union's commitment to facilitating an equitable and all-encompassing shift towards a sustainable economy while effectively tackling social and economic inequalities across member states.[35] One of the key challenges in implementing the European Green Deal is the mobilisation of financial resources. A comprehensive analysis of the financial aspects of the deal, such as the allocation of funds, the Multiannual Financial Framework, and the utilisation of innovative financial instruments, sheds light on the difficulties faced in securing the required investments for this ambitious agenda. The process of sectoral transformation involves a comprehensive examination of the unique issues faced by different sectors. This includes the decarbonisation of the energy sector and the rehabilitation of rural communities through sustainable agriculture. These examples highlight the complex nature of altering entire industries.

The convergence of innovation and green technology has emerged as an important field of study and research. An overview highlights the potential of the European Green Deal's focus on research, innovation, and the development of green technologies to stimulate economic growth and improve competitiveness. The analysis of possible social and environmental benefits, such as the improvement of air and water quality, conservation of biodiversity, and enhancement of quality of life, highlights the all-encompassing nature of the agreement. The European Green Deal is a significant shift in policy and strategy for the European Union, with far-reaching implications for global endeavours to address climate change. However, the execution of this project poses numerous challenges, including securing sufficient funding and successfully adapting to industry changes. This book examines the legal basis of the European Green Deal and provides an analytical perspective on its potential to transform the economic, social, and environmental landscape of the European Union. Participating in this process offers unique insights into the profound influence of climate policy and the imperative of aligning sustainability, economic growth, and social equity in the present period.

[35] Directive 2009/72/EC of the European Parliament and of the Council of 13 July 2009 concerning common rules for the internal market in electricity and repealing Directive 2003/54/EC. OJ L 211, 14.8.2009, pp. 55–93. Directive 2009/73/EC of the European Parliament and of the Council of 13 July 2009 concerning common rules for the internal market in natural gas and repealing Directive 2003/55/EC. OJ L 211, 14.8.2009, pp. 94–136. Regulation (EC) No 714/2009 of the European Parliament and of the Council of 13 July 2009 on conditions for access to the network for cross-border exchanges in electricity and repealing Regulation (EC) No 1228/2003. OJ L 211, 14.8.2009, pp. 15–35. Regulation (EC) No 715/2009 of the European Parliament and of the Council of 13 July 2009 on conditions for access to the natural gas transmission networks and repealing Regulation (EC) No 1775/2005. OJ L 211, 14.8.2009, pp. 36–54. Treaty on the Functioning of the European Union (TFEU), particularly Article 102, addressing the abuse of a dominant position. Consolidated version: OJ C 326, 26.10.2012, pp. 47–390.

The Green Deal[36] is the ambitious roadmap towards sustainable zero carbon community by 2050. The Commission has previously identified the roadmap targets whereas the decarbonisation, resource efficiency was introduced.[37] This roadmap provides actions need to be taken as well as necessary investments for proper implementation. This document covers all economic sectors, in particular, energy, transport, buildings, industries etc. For the further implementation of the targeted goals the Commission has introduced the first European Climate Law proposal,[38] the Industrial Strategy for 2030, the Industrial Strategy and Circular Economy Action Plan and the Strategy from Farm to Fork,[39] the Strategy for Energy System Integration, Offshore renewable strategy,[40] Methane strategy,[41] Chemicals strategy for

[36]The Communication from the Commission to the European Parliament, The European Council, The Council, The European Economic and Social Committee and the Committee of the Regions. The European Green Deal COM/2019/640 final.

[37]Communication from the Commission to the European Parliament, the Council, The European Economic and Social Committee and the Committee of the Regions. Energy Roadmap 2050. SEC (2011) 1565 final, SEC (2011) 1566 final, (2011) 1569 final. COM (2011) 885 final. Communication from the Commission to the European Parliament, the Council, the European Economic and Social Committee and the Committee of the Regions. A Roadmap for moving to a competitive low carbon economy in 2050. SEC (2011) 287 final, SEC (2011) 288 final, SEC (2011) 289 final. COM (2011) 112 final. Communication from the Commission to the European Parliament, the Council, the European Economic and Social Committee and the Committee of the Regions. A resource – efficient Europe – Flagship initiative under the Europe 2020 Strategy. COM (2011) 21 final. Communication from the Commission. Europe 2020. A strategy for smart, sustainable and inclusive growth. COM (2010) 2020 final.

[38]The Proposal for a Regulation of the European Parliament and of the Council establishing the framework for achieving climate neutrality and amending Regulation (EU) 2018/1999 (European Climate Law) COM/2020/80 final.

[39]The Communication from the Commission to the European Parliament, The European Council, The Council, The European Economic and Social Committee and the Committee of the Regions. A Farm to Fork Strategy for a fair, healthy and environmentally friendly food system. COM/2020/381 final.

[40]The Communication from the Commission to the European Parliament, The European Council, The Council, The European Economic and Social Committee and the Committee of the Regions. An EU Strategy to harness the potential of offshore renewable energy for a climate neutral future. COM/2020/741 final.

[41]The Communication from the Commission to the European Parliament, The European Council, The Council, The European Economic and Social Committee and the Committee of the Regions. On an EU strategy to reduce methane emissions. COM/2020/663 final.

sustainability,[42] 2030 Climate Target Plan,[43] the European Battery Alliance,[44] the Renovation Wave.[45]

The Industrial Strategy[46] introduced several initial targets, in particular, it tackles the review of the competition rules with the current merger control and revision of State aid guidelines ensuring that these rules reflect the fast-changing needs of market. Moreover, it introduces the measures for modernisation and decarbonisation of energy industries, the promotion of low-carbon energy at affordable prices, the legislation on green public procurement rules, the innovation and investment.

The EU Strategy for Energy System Integration[47] draws attention to the enhancement of the circular economy including the energy efficiency, the direct electrification thus to use as much as possible the electricity instead of other sources, in particular the enhancement of electric vehicles usage, increase the installation of the charging points for the transport, continue the expansion of the wind and solar electric producing installations. Additionally, the promotion of the usage of renewable and low-carbon fuels was elaborated.

The European Green Deal represents a robust and all-encompassing policy framework that has positioned the European Union on a path towards a sustainable and climate-neutral future. In conclusion, our analysis of the legal underpinnings, key achievements, complaints, and obstacles surrounding the Green Deal demonstrates the profound impact of this programme on the European Union's environmental and climatic agenda. In the final part of this study, we engage in a retrospective analysis of the accomplishments, ramifications, and potential trajectories of the European Green Deal.

[42]The Communication from the Commission to the European Parliament, The European Council, The Council, The European Economic and Social Committee and the Committee of the Regions. Chemicals Strategy for Sustainability Towards a Toxic-Free Environment. COM/2020/667 final.

[43]The Communication from the Commission to the European Parliament, The European Council, The Council, The European Economic and Social Committee and the Committee of the Regions. Stepping up Europe's 2030 climate ambition. Investing in a climate-neutral future for the benefit of our people. COM/2020/562 final.

[44]The Commission proposal for a Regulation of the European Parliament and of the Council concerning batteries and waste batteries, repealing Directive 2006/66/EC and amending Regulation (EU) No 2019/1020/ COD/2020/353, COM/2020/798/3.

[45]The Communication from the Commission to the European Parliament, The European Council, The Council, The European Economic and Social Committee and the Committee of the Regions. A Renovation Wave for Europe - greening our buildings, creating jobs, improving lives. COM/2020/662 final.

[46]The Communication from the Commission to the European Parliament, The European Council, The Council, The European Economic and Social Committee and the Committee of the Regions. A New Industrial Strategy for Europe. COM/2020/102 final.

[47]The Communication from the Commission to the European Parliament, The European Council, The Council, The European Economic and Social Committee and the Committee of the Regions. Powering a climate-neutral economy: An EU Strategy for Energy System Integration. COM/2020/299 final.

The commitment to achieving climate neutrality by 2050 demonstrates a firm and unwavering determination to face the serious and immediate challenge that climate change poses. This measure establishes a precedent for international efforts to address climate change and reinforces the European Union's position as a prominent advocate for climate-related initiatives. The Green Deal's comprehensive approach has facilitated the integration of several policy domains, acknowledging the inherent interconnectedness between environmental sustainability, economic prosperity, and social welfare.

The Green Deal has initiated a paradigm shift in environmental legislation within the European Union, encompassing a range of directives and regulations aimed at facilitating the transition towards a sustainable and environmentally friendly economy. The European Union's dedication to the Green Deal has exerted a significant impact on international climate deliberations, thereby fostering the inclination of other states to enhance their climate aspirations. The implications and challenges associated with the subject matter are of significant importance and warrant careful consideration.[48] The execution of the Green Deal is characterised by its intricate nature, which gives rise to several problems, such as the need to effectively coordinate policy objectives and ensure a uniform and steady advancement of the initiative throughout member states.

The prioritisation of social equity is of utmost importance, as it pertains to guaranteeing a fair and equitable transition for all individuals and areas. The intricate challenge is effectively addressing the social and economic inequalities that arise as a consequence of this shift. The attainment of climate neutrality necessitates the establishment of global collaboration, hence necessitating the European Union's ongoing commitment to engaging with international counterparts in order to facilitate a synchronised global approach to addressing climate change.

The pursuit of sustainability transition, as outlined in the Green Deal, encompasses a vision for a sustainable future that necessitates a commitment to long-term efforts. During the process of transition, it is imperative for the European Union to maintain a high level of adaptability, responsiveness, and commitment towards its climate objectives. The imperative for technological innovation lies in the ongoing commitment to invest in research and development, since it is crucial for the advancement and implementation of the necessary technologies to attain climate neutrality.

The role of the European Union as a global climate leader necessitates the continuous exertion of pressure on other states to enhance their climate ambitions and engage in collaborative efforts towards achieving global climate objectives. The task of policy integration, which entails ensuring the cohesive functioning of the diverse policy domains contained in the Green Deal, will persistently present a challenge that necessitates constant monitoring and adjustment.

---

[48] The Communication from the Commission to the European Parliament, The European Council, The Council, The European Economic and Social Committee and the Committee of the Regions. The European Green Deal COM/2019/640 final.

The European Green Deal signifies a fundamental transformation in the European Union's strategy towards environmental and climate policies.[49] The aforementioned statement reflects a dedication to confronting the issue of climate change, safeguarding the natural environment, and promoting sustainable development within a comprehensive legislative structure. In the culmination of our examination of this paradigm-shifting endeavour, we duly recognise the accomplishments of the Green Deal while also recognising the obstacles it has encountered. Moving forward, we approach the future with a sense of hopefulness and resolute resolve. The pursuit of a sustainable and climate-neutral Europe remains a continuing endeavour, with the European Green Deal serving as a definitive and determined roadmap towards achieving this objective. The document functions as a strategic plan for the European Union and acts as a source of motivation for the global community as we collaboratively endeavour to protect our planet for the well-being of future generations.

4.5 Legally Binding Provisions Delivering the Green Deal Policy Objectives

In order to effectively achieve the policy objectives outlined in the European Green Deal, it is crucial to include legally binding components. These regulations build the necessary legal framework to ensure the successful execution of the lofty goals stated in the Green Deal, ensuring that member states and stakeholders are accountable for meeting their obligations. The following are many legally binding provisions that are essential elements in the execution of the Green Deal policy objectives.

The European Climate Law,[50] which was ratified in June 2021, serves as a fundamental legal mechanism that codifies the European Union's dedication to achieving climate neutrality by the year 2050. The European Union is legally obligated to pursue the goal of attaining net-zero greenhouse gas emissions by the year 2050. Additionally, it sets forth a provisional objective of achieving a 55% decrease in emissions by the year 2030 in relation to the levels observed in 1990. This target holds significant importance in the pursuit of the climate objectives outlined in the Green Deal. This objective establishes a distinct path for reducing emissions and guarantees that member nations undertake substantial measures to address climate change.

[49] The Communication from the Commission to the European Parliament, The European Council, The Council, The European Economic and Social Committee and the Committee of the Regions. The European Green Deal COM/2019/640 final.

[50] Regulation (EU) 2021/1119 of the European Parliament and of the Council of 30 June 2021 establishing the framework for achieving climate neutrality and amending Regulations (EC) No 401/2009 and (EU) 2018/1999 ('European Climate Law'). PE/27/2021/REV/1. OJ L 243, 9.7.2021, pp. 1–17.

The amended Renewable Energy Directive,[51] which was incorporated as a component of the Green Deal, encompasses legally enforceable objectives pertaining to the capacity of renewable energy inside the European Union. The European Union is obligated to attain a 32% proportion of renewable energy in its overall energy consumption by the year 2030. The Energy Efficiency Directive[52] establishes obligatory objectives for enhancing energy efficiency within the European Union.

Circular economy legislation is being implemented through a range of legislative initiatives as part of the Green Deal initiative. The aforementioned measures encompass regulations pertaining to waste management, the reduction of single-use plastics, and the establishment of eco-design criteria. The aforementioned legally enforceable measures set regulations pertaining to product design, recycling practises, and waste management, promoting a more sustainable approach to the utilisation of resources.

The ETS is an established and legally enforceable mechanism within the European Union aimed at mitigating greenhouse gas emissions in sectors like industry and aviation. The primary objective of the Green Deal is to enhance the effectiveness of the ETS through the enhancement of its ambition and the extension of its scope to encompass supplementary industries.[53]

The Just Transition Fund Regulation has been established with the aim of facilitating an equitable and all-encompassing shift towards a sustainable economy. This regulation outlines a set of legally enforceable criteria and processes that govern the allocation of funding to regions that are most significantly impacted by this transition. This provision is designed to ensure that the objectives of the Green Deal are achieved in a way that is socially equitable. The EU Biodiversity Strategy for 2030[54] encompasses legally obligatory elements aimed at ceasing and reversing the decline in biodiversity. The aforementioned requirements encompass the creation of legally safeguarded regions, objectives for restoration, and strategies to mitigate the factors contributing to the reduction of biodiversity.

The Farm to Fork Strategy endeavours to enhance the sustainability of food systems and imposes legally binding obligations on the European Union (EU) to

---

[51] Directive (EU) 2023/2413 of the European Parliament and of the Council of 18 October 2023 amending Directive (EU) 2018/2001, Regulation (EU) 2018/1999 and Directive 98/70/EC as regards the promotion of energy from renewable sources, and repealing Council Directive (EU) 2015/652 PE/36/2023/REV/2. OJ L, 2023/2413, 31.10.2023.

[52] Directive (EU) 2023/1791 of the European Parliament and of the Council of 13 September 2023 on energy efficiency and amending Regulation (EU) 2023/955 (recast) (Text with EEA relevance). PE/15/2023/INIT. OJ L 231, 20.9.2023, pp. 1–111.

[53] Regulation (EU) 2021/1119 of the European Parliament and of the Council of 30 June 2021 establishing the European Climate Law and amending Regulation (EU) 2018/1999. OJ L 243, 9.7.2021, pp. 1–17.

[54] Communication from the Commission to the European Parliament, the Council, the European Economic and Social Committee and the Committee of the Regions EU. Biodiversity Strategy for 2030 Bringing nature back into our lives. COM/2020/380 final.

achieve certain objectives. These objectives encompass a decrease in the use of chemical pesticides and fertilisers as well as an augmentation in the practise of organic farming. The aforementioned legally enforceable measures serve as the fundamental framework of the European Green Deal, guaranteeing that the objectives of the policy are not solely aspirational but are firmly established in legislation. The framework established facilitates the implementation of actions, establishes precise objectives, and establishes systems to track advancements and ensure adherence, thereby propelling the European Union towards a future characterised by sustainability, resilience, and carbon neutrality.

The European Union vision of becoming climate-neutral energy system using renewables including hydrogen as well as having improved energy efficiency, was outlined in the Green Deal and particular revision of existing legislation was foreseen in the Commission work programme.[55] The amendments cover systemic changes towards green transition, puts forward the measures for the smart and sustainable transport, the circular economy action plan, eco-design, sustainable products, circular electronics, improving reuse of the mobiles and other devices. The Green Deal goes beyond the emission cut, it thus follows the biodiversity strategy for 2030, reducing environmental impact of the livestock farming.

4.5.1 The Climate Law

The European Climate Law, which is a fundamental element of the European Green Deal, reflects the resolute dedication of the European Union to tackling the pressing issue of climate change.[56] The legislation, which was implemented in July 2021, sets up a comprehensive and enforceable system aimed at attaining carbon neutrality by the year 2050. This chapter explores the implications and relevance of the European Climate Law. It thoroughly examines the essential provisions of the law, analyses its legal and policy consequences, and assesses its broader impact on global climate action.

The European Climate Law, officially known as Regulation (EU) 2021/1119, integrates the objectives outlined in the European Green Deal into a legally enforceable document. One of the key objectives established by this law is the commitment to achieve carbon neutrality by the year 2050. The legislation additionally established a mandatory objective for the European Union to achieve a 55% reduction in greenhouse gas emissions by 2030, relative to the levels observed in 1990.

---

[55] Piebalgs et al. (2021).

[56] Regulation (EU) 2021/1119 of the European Parliament and of the Council of 30 June 2021 establishing the framework for achieving climate neutrality and amending Regulations (EC) No 401/2009 and (EU) 2018/1999 ('European Climate Law'). PE/27/2021/REV/1. OJ L 243, 9.7.2021, pp. 1–17.

This target supersedes the prior goal of a 40% reduction.[57] The European Climate Law is a fundamental component of the European Green Deal, serving as a foundation for the implementation of green regulatory measures aimed at attaining the climate objectives of the European Union. While the Climate Law does not prescribe specific actions for the European Union and Member States to adopt in order to achieve zero emissions, it does provide a guiding framework towards attaining these objectives.

These aims establish a distinct path towards achieving climate neutrality. It also establishes a legally enforceable obligation to achieve climate neutrality, strengthening responsibility and guaranteeing that climate objectives are of utmost importance in the formulation of European Union policy choices. The legal framework mandates the incorporation of climate-related factors into several policy domains, encompassing energy, transportation, agriculture, and industry. The integration of several components facilitates a more cohesive and inclusive strategy for addressing climate change. Member States are obligated to formulate and execute National Energy and Climate Plans that delineate their intended contributions towards the climate targets of the European Union. This promotes collaborative endeavours and shared responsibility. The concept of a just transition is emphasised in legislation, which recognises the imperative for climate measures to incorporate principles of socioeconomic equity. The policy requires providing assistance to regions and industries that are disproportionately impacted by the transformation. The European Climate Law establishes the European Union as a prominent global leader in the realm of climate action. The establishment of enforceable commitments and the adoption of ambitious targets by a nation serve as a standard for other countries, fostering increased global efforts towards more significant climate ambitions.

International diplomacy is inevitable in enhancing the European Union's standing in global climate discussions, including those conducted under the United Nations Framework Convention on Climate Change and the Paris Agreement.[58] Private sector engagement is facilitated by a robust legal framework and well-defined objectives, which create a stable atmosphere conducive to attracting private sector investments in environmentally friendly technologies and sustainable practices. The legislation highlights the European Union's dedication to enhancing climate resilience by mitigating the effects of climate change and protecting communities, ecosystems, and the economy.

The European Climate Law holds a pivotal position within the climate policy framework of the European Union, as it establishes ambitious objectives and imposes legally binding obligations to address the challenges posed by climate

---

[57] Regulation (EU) 2021/1119 of the European Parliament and of the Council of 30 June 2021 establishing the framework for achieving climate neutrality and amending Regulations (EC) No 401/2009 and (EU) 2018/1999 ('European Climate Law'). PE/27/2021/REV/1. OJ L 243, 9.7.2021, pp. 1–17. See Article 1, Article 2, Article 4, Article 5.

[58] Andresen (2015).

change.[59] The relevance of this extends beyond the geographical boundaries of Europe, as it establishes the European Union as a prominent figure in global climate leadership and fosters international collaboration. Upon careful examination of the ramifications and importance of this legislation, it becomes apparent that it not only moulds the European Union's path towards addressing climate issues but also exerts an impact on the wider international reaction to the prevailing and critical issue of climate change.

The legal framework establishes a comprehensive governance structure to ensure that the European Union and its Member States effectively adhere to their climate objectives. The framework encompasses the systematic practise of regular reporting, monitoring, and evaluation to assess the progress made in achieving climate targets. Member states are obligated to formulate and present National Energy and Climate Plans (NECPs), which delineate their respective contributions towards achieving the European Union's collective climate objectives. The plans should encompass comprehensive strategies outlining the specific measures that each member state will undertake to effectively attain carbon reductions, foster the adoption of renewable energy sources, and bolster energy efficiency.

The establishment of a target for the year 2040 has not yet been determined. However, in accordance with Article 4 of the European Climate Law, the formulation of this target should consider various factors, such as the utilisation of relevant data, including the most up-to-date and reliable scientific evidence, as well as the assessment of social, economic, and environmental consequences. Additionally, the principles of cost-effectiveness, economic efficiency, and competitiveness should be taken into account during the target-setting process.[60] The Commission is required to release a greenhouse gas emissions budget that maximises the allowable amount of greenhouse gases for the period of 2030–2050 while ensuring that the European Union's commitment to the Paris Agreement is not compromised and the objectives for the year 2040 are established.

The Commission enacted a set of legislative measures called EU fit for 55 on July 14, 2021, as part of the European Green Deal. This effort aims to strengthen the European Union's position as a significant actor in global climate governance. The package's main goal is to update current legislation to comply with the climate target that the European Union has set for the year 2030. Additionally, it seeks to include policy measures that would enable the required modifications in the economy, society, and industry. Furthermore, the proposed package endeavours to achieve a reduction in net emissions of at least 55% (relative to 1990 levels) by the year 2030, thereby offering assistance in attaining climate neutrality. EU fit for 55 was designed

[59]Regulation (EU) 2021/1119 of the European Parliament and of the Council of 30 June 2021 establishing the framework for achieving climate neutrality and amending Regulations (EC) No 401/2009 and (EU) 2018/1999 ('European Climate Law'). PE/27/2021/REV/1. OJ L 243, 9.7.2021, pp. 1–17.

[60]Cameron (2007).

to implement the ambitious targets set out in the Climate Law which shall be elaborated in the following chapter.

4.5.2 *The EU Fit for 55*

The EU Fit for 55 package encompasses a comprehensive legislative proposal aimed at attaining climate and energy objectives. In accordance with the Paris Agreement, the established objective is to reduce emissions by 40% relative to the levels observed in 1990, with a further target of achieving an 80% reduction by the year 2050.[61] In December 2020, an agreement was reached to achieve a reduction of at least 55% in greenhouse gas emissions by 2030, relative to the levels seen in 1990. Furthermore, the accord aims to transform the continent into a zero-emission entity by the year 2050. The targets mentioned were given legal force with the adoption of the European Climate Law. Additionally, the nationally decided contribution to the Paris Agreement was amended in light of these new obligations.

The European Union Emissions Trading System (EU ETS)[62] has been revised to impose tighter regulations on the aviation sector, including the elimination of free allowances.[63] Additionally, the scope of the EU ETS has been expanded to include the maritime, road, and transport sectors. The ETS system operates on the idea of cap and trade, wherein it establishes a limit on the annual emissions of greenhouse gases. The permissible emission levels have been reduced, resulting in significant emission reductions within the power industry prior to the implementation of the new laws. In accordance with the European Trading Scheme (ETS), regulated entities are obligated to purchase emissions permits, which can also be traded with other market players if necessary. The newly presented plans aim to expand coverage to more sectors by implementing a new mechanism. In the initial year, the fuel suppliers will possess the right to get the emission permits and fulfil the obligation of reporting the emissions for the years 2024 and 2025. The responsibility of regulating fuel suppliers, with the exception of homes and car owners, lies with the upstream system. The suppliers are required to monitor and report the quantities of fuel they supply to

[61] Regulation (EU) 2021/1119 of the European Parliament and of the Council of 30 June 2021 on the European Climate Law, OJ L 243, pp. 1–17. Directive (EU) 2018/2001 of the European Parliament and of the Council of 11 December 2018 on the promotion of the use of energy from renewable sources, OJ L 328, pp. 82–209. Regulation (EU) 2018/842 of the European Parliament and of the Council of 30 May 2018 on the effort of Member States to reduce their greenhouse gas emissions, OJ L 156, pp. 26–42. Regulation (EU) 2019/943 of the European Parliament and of the Council of 5 June 2019 on the internal market for electricity, OJ L 158, 14.6.2019, pp. 54–124.

[62] Directive (EU) 2023/959 of the European Parliament and of the Council of 10 May 2023 amending Directive 2003/87/EC establishing a system for greenhouse gas emission allowance trading within the Union and Decision (EU) 2015/1814 concerning the establishment and operation of a market stability reserve for the Union greenhouse gas emission trading system (Text with EEA relevance). PE/9/2023/REV/1. OJ L 130, 16.5.2023, pp. 134–202.

[63] Schittekatte et al. (2021).

the market, as well as possess emission allowances corresponding to the carbon intensity of the fuels. The suppliers should be improved in order to reduce carbon emissions from fuel, resulting in cost reductions for emission trading.

It is imperative to reduce emissions by 61% by the year 2030, in comparison to the emissions levels seen in 2005. The Commission has put forth a proposal to increase the annual emission reduction to 4.2% within the current framework along with a single reduction of the overall emissions cap by 117 million permits in order to achieve the desired objective. The move toward complete auctioning by the year 2027 coincided with the launch of the initiative to gradually end the provision of complimentary allowances for the aviation industry. The revision of the market stability reserve has enabled it to promptly withdraw the historical surplus allowances. Once the implementation of carbon pricing measures in the building and road transport sectors is initiated, the Social Climate Fund will commence its operations with the aim of addressing the social issues faced by vulnerable populations. The Effort Sharing Regulation remains in effect, with national policies determining the contributions towards carbon reduction.

The following proposals were introduced regarding the amendments to the EU ETS, energy taxation, energy efficiency, renewable energy, carbon border adjustment mechanisms, effort sharing, land use, forestry, agriculture, transport, social climate fund, in particular:[64]

[64] Proposal for a Directive of the European Parliament and of the Council amending Directive 2003/87/EC establishing a system for greenhouse gas emission allowance trading within the Union, Decision (EU) 2015/1814 concerning the establishment and operation of a market stability reserve for the Union greenhouse gas emission trading scheme and Regulation (EU) 2015/757. COM (2021) 551 final. Proposal for a Directive of the European Parliament and of the Council amending Directive 2003/87/EC as regards aviation's contribution to the Union's economy-wide emission reduction target and appropriately implementing a global market-based measure. COM (2021) 551 final. Proposal for a Decision of the European Parliament and of the Council amending Directive 2003/87/EC as regards the notification of offsetting in the respect of a global market-based measure for aircraft operators based in the Union COM (2021) 551 final. Proposal for a Decision of the European Parliament and of the Council amending Decision (EU) 2015/1814 as regards the amount of allowances to be placed in the market stability reserve for the Union greenhouse gas emission trading scheme until 2030. COM (2021) 551 final. Proposal for a Council Directive restructuring the Union framework for the taxation of energy products and electricity. COM (2021) 563 final. Proposal for a Directive of the European Parliament and of the Council on energy efficiency. COM (2021) 558 final. Proposal for a Directive of the European Parliament and of the Council amending Directive (EU) 2018/2001 of the European Parliament and of the Council, Regulation (EU) 2018/1999 of the European Parliament and of the Council and Directive 98/70/EC of the European Parliament and of the Council as regards the promotion of energy from renewable sources and repealing Council Directive (EU) 2015/652. COM (2021) 557 final. Proposal for a Regulation of the European Parliament and of the Council establishing a carbon border adjustment mechanism. COM (2021) 564 final. Proposal for a Regulation of the European Parliament and of the Council amending Regulation (EU) 2018/842 on binding annual greenhouse gas emission reductions by Member States from 2021 to 2030 contributing to climate action to meet commitments under the Paris Agreement. COM (2021) 556 final. Proposal for a Regulation of the European Parliament and of the Council amending Regulations (EU) 2018/841 as regards the scope, simplifying the compliance rules, setting out the targets of the Member States for 2030 and committing to

- The Proposal for a Directive of the European Parliament and of the Council amending Directive 2003/87/EC establishing a system for greenhouse gas emission allowance trading within the Union, Decision (EU) 2015/1814 concerning the establishment and operation of a market stability reserve for the Union greenhouse gas emission trading scheme and Regulation (EU) 2015/757.
- The Proposal for a Directive of the European Parliament and of the Council amending Directive 2003/87 as regards aviation's contribution to the Union's economy-wide emission reduction target and appropriately implementing a global market-based measure.
- The Proposal for a Decision of the European Parliament and of the Council amending Directive 2003/87/EC as regards the notification of offsetting in the respect of a global market-based measure for aircraft operators based in the Union.
- The Proposal for a Decision of the European Parliament and of the Council amending Decision (EU) 2015/1814 as regards the amount of allowances to be placed in the market stability reserve for the Union greenhouse gas emission trading scheme until 2030.
- The Proposal for a Council Directive restructuring the Union framework for the taxation of energy products and electricity.
- The Proposal for a Directive of the European Parliament and of the Council on energy efficiency.
- The Proposal for a Directive of the European Parliament and of the Council amending Directive (EU) 2018/2001 of the European Parliament and of the Council, Regulation (EU) 2018/1999 of the European Parliament and of the Council and Directive 98/70/EC of the European Parliament and of the Council as regards the promotion of energy from renewable sources and repealing Council Directive (EU) 2015/652.
- The Proposal for a Regulation of the European Parliament and of the Council establishing a carbon border adjustment mechanism.

---

the collective achievement of climate neutrality by 2035 in the land use, forestry and agriculture sector, and (EU) 2018/1999 as regards improvement in monitoring, reporting, tracking of progress and review. COM (2021) 555 final. Communication from the Commission to the European Parliament, the Council, the European Economic and Social Committee and the Committee of the Regions "A strategic rollout plan to outline a set of supplementary actions to support the rapid deployment of alternative fuels infrastructure". COM (2021) 556 final. Proposal for a Regulation of the European Parliament and of the Council on the deployment of the alternative fuels infrastructure and repealing Directive 2014/94/EU of the European Parliament and of the Council. COM (2021) 557 final. Proposal for a Regulation of the European Parliament and of the Council amending Regulation (EU) 2019/631 as regards strengthening the CO2 emission performance standards for new passenger cars and new light commercial vehicles in line with the Union's increased climate actions. COM (2021) 554 final. Proposal for a Regulation of the European Parliament and of the Council on ensuring a level playing field for sustainable air transport. COM (2021) 556 final. Proposal for a Regulation of the European Parliament and of the Council on the use of renewable and low-carbon fuels in maritime transport and amending Directive 2009/16/EC. COM (2021) 556 final. Proposal for a Regulation of the European Parliament and of the Council establishing a Social Climate Fund. COM (2021) 557 final.

- The Proposal for a Regulation of the European Parliament and of the Council amending Regulation (EU) 2018/842 on binding annual greenhouse gas emission reductions by Member States from 2021 to 2030 contributing to climate action to meet commitments under the Paris Agreement.
- The Proposal for a Regulation of the European Parliament and of the Council amending Regulations (EU) 2018/841 as regards the scope, simplifying the compliance rules, setting out the targets of the Member States for 2030 and committing to the collective achievement of climate neutrality by 2035 in the land use, forestry and agriculture sector, and (EU) 2018/1999 as regards improvement in monitoring, reporting, tracking of progress and review.
- Communication from the Commission to the European Parliament, the Council, the European Economic and Social Committee and the Committee of the Regions "A strategic rollout plan to outline a set of supplementary actions to support the rapid deployment of alternative fuels infrastructure".
- The Proposal for a Regulation of the European Parliament and of the Council on the deployment of the alternative fuels infrastructure and repealing Directive 2014/94/EU of the European Parliament and of the Council.
- The Proposal for a Regulation of the European Parliament and of the Council amending Regulation (EU) 2019/631 as regards strengthening the CO2 emission performance standards for new passenger cars and new light commercial vehicles in line with the Union's increased climate actions.
- The Proposal for a Regulation of the European Parliament and of the Council on ensuring a level playing field for sustainable air transport.
- The Proposal for a Regulation of the European Parliament and of the Council on the use of renewable and low-carbon fuels in maritime transport and amending Directive 2009/16/EC.
- The Proposal for a Regulation of the European Parliament and of the Council establishing a Social Climate Fund.

Alongside the changes made to the EU ETS, the Commission has suggested a distinct emissions trading system called ETS2. This system will address emissions from activities that are not currently included in the EU ETS, such as emissions from commercial and residential buildings (including those supplied by district heat networks), road transport, and specific sectors like fuel combustion in energy industries, manufacturing, and construction. Starting in 2025, ETS2's structure and compliance criteria will include the establishment of a distinct and independent system. The new system will mostly adhere to the same cap-and-trade structure as the current EU ETS, which includes a compliance period that spans the duration of a calendar year. Organisations that are part of ETS2 must fulfil the following obligations: Acquire a GHG emissions permit by January 1, 2025. Report emissions starting on January 1, 2025, covering the calendar years 2024 and 2025. Participate in auctions to purchase allowances for the first time in 2027 and submit them by May 31 each year, starting in 2028. However, we may extend these deadlines by one year if energy prices are exceptionally high.[65] Importantly, the Emissions Trading Scheme 2 (ETS2) will not allow for the free distribution of credits; instead, it will sell all allowances through auctions. ETS2 implements a yearly linear reduction trajectory to achieve the 2030 reduction targets of a 42% decrease in emissions compared to the levels recorded in 2005. Member States have the option to grant a temporary exemption to a regulated entity from surrendering allowances under ETS2 until December 31, 2030, as long as the company pays a national carbon price for its emissions that is higher than its ETS2 responsibility. Regulated entities must comply with obligations for their emissions, and they will establish a unique market stability reserve.

The EU ETS I now includes maritime transport, marking a significant achievement. The system will incorporate maritime transport emissions for the first time. Shipping businesses will be required to progressively relinquish emission allowances, starting with 40% of confirmed emissions in 2024, followed by 70% in 2025, and ultimately reaching 100% in 2026. This action intends to hold the EU accountable for reducing emissions in maritime shipping. In the EU ETS, there is also the possibility of incorporating municipal waste incineration units, commonly known as waste incineration. The Commission will use reports on emissions from EU Member States starting in 2024 to assess their eligibility for EU ETS participation starting in 2028. 028. The Commission is also considering the possibility of including additional waste management activities under the EU ETS, specifically landfills, which are responsible for EU methane and nitrous oxide emissions.

The December package, also known as the "Hydrogen and Gas Package" of EU Fit for 55, covers the legislative and policy proposals related to gas and buildings enabling them to meet the new targets. The following proposals were included in the package:[66]

[65] Proposal for a Regulation of the European Parliament and of the Council amending Regulation (EU) 2018/842, COM (2021) 555 final, OJ C 265, 5.7.2021, pp. 1–12. See Article 1, Article 3. Proposal for a Regulation of the European Parliament and of the Council establishing a carbon border adjustment mechanism, COM (2021) 564 final, OJ C 265, 5.7.2021, pp. 13–29. See Article 6, Article 9. Regulation (EU) 2021/1119 of the European Parliament and of the Council of 30 June 2021 on the European Climate Law, OJ L 243, 9.7.2021, pp. 1–17. See Article 4, Article 6.

[66] Proposal for a Directive of the European Parliament and of the Council on common rules for the internal markets in renewable and natural gases and in hydrogen, COM (2021) 803 final, OJ C 348, 19.10.2022, pp. 1–43. Annexes to the Proposal for a Directive of the European Parliament and of the Council on common rules for the internal markets in renewable and natural gases and in hydrogen, COM (2021) 803 final, OJ C 348, 19.10.2022, pp. 44–99. Proposal for a Regulation of the European Parliament and of the Council on internal markets for renewable and natural gases and for hydrogen (recast), COM (2021) 804 final, OJ C 348, 19.10.2022, pp. 100–125. Annexes to the Proposal for a Regulation of the European Parliament and of the Council on internal markets for renewable and natural gases and for hydrogen, COM (2021) 804 final, OJ C 348, 19.10.2022, pp. 126–145. Proposal for a Regulation of the European Parliament and of the Council on methane emissions reduction in the energy sector and amending Regulation (EU) 2019/942, COM (2021) 805 final, OJ C 348, 19.10.2022, pp. 146–174. Proposal for a Directive of the European Parliament and of the Council on the energy performance of buildings (recast), COM (2021) 802 final, OJ C 348, 19.10.2022, pp. 175–205. Annexes to the Proposal for a Directive of the European Parliament

- The Proposal for a Directive of the European Parliament and of the Council on common rules for the internal markets in renewable and natural gases and in hydrogen.
- Annexes to the Proposal for a Directive of the European Parliament and of the Council on common rules for the internal markets in renewable and natural gases and in hydrogen.
- The Proposal for a Regulation of the European Parliament and of the Council on internal markets for renewable and natural gases and for hydrogen (recast).
- Annexes to the Proposal for a Regulation of the European Parliament and of the Council on the internal markets for renewable and natural gases and for hydrogen.
- The Proposal for a Regulation of the European Parliament and of the Council on methane emissions reduction in the energy sector and amending Regulation (EU) 2019/942.
- The Proposal for a Directive of the European Parliament and of the Council on the energy performance of buildings (recast).
- Annexes to the Proposal for a Directive of the European Parliament and of the Council on the energy performance of buildings (recast).

Other proposals:

- The Communication from the Commission to the European Parliament and the Council "Sustainable Carbon Cycles".
- The Proposal for a Regulation of the European Parliament and of the Council on Union guidelines for the development of the trans-European transport network, amending Regulation (EU) 2021/1153 and Regulation (EU) No 913/2010 and repealing Regulation (EU) 1315/2013.
- The Communication from the Commission to the European Parliament and the Council on the extension of the trans-European transport network (TEN-T) to neighbouring third countries.

---

and of the Council on the energy performance of buildings (recast), COM (2021) 802 final, OJ C 348, 19.10.2022, pp. 206–225. Communication from the Commission to the European Parliament and the Council "Sustainable Carbon Cycles", COM (2021) 800 final, OJ C 348, 19.10.2022, pp. 226–240. Proposal for a Regulation of the European Parliament and of the Council on Union guidelines for the development of the trans-European transport network, COM (2021) 799 final, OJ C 348, 19.10.2022, pp. 241–265. Communication from the Commission to the European Parliament and the Council on the extension of the trans-European transport network (TEN-T) to neighbouring third countries, COM (2021) 798 final, OJ C 348, 19.10.2022, pp. 266–280. Proposal for a Directive of the European Parliament and of the Council amending Directive 2010/40/EU, COM (2021) 797 final, OJ C 348, 19.10.2022, pp. 281–300. Communication from the Commission to the European Parliament and the Council "Action plan to boost long distance and cross-border passenger rail", COM (2021) 796 final, OJ C 348, 19.10.2022, pp. 301–320. Communication from the Commission to the European Parliament, the Council, the European Economic and Social Committee and the Committee of the Regions "The New EU Urban Mobility Framework", COM (2021) 795 final, OJ C 348, 19.10.2022, pp. 321–340. Proposal for a Directive of the European Parliament and of the Council on the Protection of the environment through criminal law, COM (2021) 794 final, OJ C 348, 19.10.2022, pp. 341–360. Communication from the Commission to the European Parliament and the Council "Sustainable Carbon Cycles", COM (2021) 800 final, OJ C 348, 19.10.2022, pp. 361–380.

- The Proposal for a Directive of the European Parliament and of the Council amending Directive 2010/40/EU on the framework for the deployment of Intelligent Transport Systems in the field of road transport and for interfaces with other modes of transport.
- The Communication from the Commission to the European Parliament and the Council "Action plan to boost long distance and cross-border passenger rail".
- The Communication from the Commission to the European Parliament, the Council, the European Economic and Social Committee and the Committee of the Regions "The New EU Urban Mobility Framework".
- The Proposal for a Directive of the European Parliament and of the Council on the Protection of the environment through criminal law and replacing Directive 2008/99/EC.
- The Communication from the Commission to the European Parliament and the Council "Sustainable Carbon Cycles".

The legislative measures implemented in July encompass a focused initiative aimed at mitigating methane emissions within the energy industry. The countries have made a commitment, through the EU Methane Strategy and a global initiative, to decrease methane emissions by 30% by the year 2030 in comparison to the levels observed in 2020. Hence, the legislative measures establish a novel framework for the quantification, disclosure, and validation of methane emissions. Furthermore, it is mandatory for Member States to develop national strategies aimed at mitigating methane emissions originating from coal mines, fossil gas, and inactive oil sources. It is imperative that corporations be mandated to assess and quantify the levels of methane emissions they produce. Additionally, they should be obligated to identify and rectify any instances of methane leakage within their operational processes. This necessitates a transition from approximations to precise measurements, which should be verified by impartial third-party entities. The newly enacted regulation additionally incorporates the provision for anyone to lodge complaints with national authorities in cases where there are suspicions of methane leakage.

The plan aims to address the issue of methane emissions from imports by mandating that importers of fossil fuels provide information regarding the measurement performance, reporting, verification, and mitigation of these emissions. The establishment of the transparency database is anticipated to be undertaken by the Commission, with the objective of publicly disclosing the data submitted by importers. This initiative aims to enhance transparency and promote greater public awareness. The Commission is expected to commence the process of evaluating the methane rule by 2025, hence proposing more stringent regulations pertaining to the importation of fossil fuels. Given that the European Union only accounts for a small portion of global methane emissions, the implementation of the global methane pledge is anticipated to provide significant outcomes in terms of evaluating worldwide emissions.

The change to the recently implemented renewable energy directive was introduced as a component of the legislative package in July. The aforementioned regulation was implemented as part of the Clean Energy Package in 2019, and the deadline for its transposition had recently lapsed just before the release of the July package. The revised targets have been elevated both in terms of overall objectives and sub-objectives, specifically in relation to the trajectory leading to climate neutrality.

The proposed sub-targets encompass a recommendation to the industrial sector to progressively augment the proportion of renewable energy utilised on a yearly basis, as well as a stipulation that at least 50% of hydrogen consumption should originate from renewable sources by the year 2030. The objective was also established for the heating and cooling industry with the aim of enhancing the proportion of renewable sources in district heating and cooling systems. Renewable energy sources account for approximately 49% of the final energy consumption in the building industry across Member States. The objectives of the transport sector were revised to prioritise a reduction in greenhouse gas emissions by at least 13% compared to diesel and petrol by the year 2030 rather than aiming for a 14% share of final energy consumption in the motor vehicle segment.[67]

The Commission has extended the use of energy derived from non-biological renewable sources, such as green hydrogen, to be accounted for within the sector where it is consumed. Additionally, this expansion encompasses sectors beyond transportation, specifically targeting the industrial sector. The present total rated thermal input for producers of electricity, heating, and cooling from biomass is 20 MW. However, it is necessary for these producers to align their requirements with the specific sustainability standards, which should be consistent with a total rated thermal input of 5 MW. The utilisation of forest biomass as a resource for energy generation is anticipated to encounter significant limitations beyond the year 2026.[68]

The transparency criteria were further extended with the aim of furnishing clients with essential information pertaining to their energy selection. Furthermore, it is imperative that electrical grid operators are mandated to furnish customers with up-to-date information and future projections regarding the proportion of renewable electricity and the associated greenhouse gas emissions of the energy being supplied. Electric car manufacturers are required to offer real-time information on the installed batteries, the location of the vehicles, and essential details regarding energy consumption and management. The provision of information regarding the proportion of renewable sources in district heating and cooling systems was also introduced to customers.

There is a need to enhance the effectiveness of renewable power purchase agreements in light of the anticipated removal of regulatory restrictions. The issuance of guarantees of origin is anticipated to be carried out by certain Member States. Additionally, a stipulation was implemented that prohibits the instant revocation of

[67] Directive (EU) 2018/2001 of the European Parliament and of the Council of 11 December 2018 on the promotion of the use of energy from renewable sources, amending Directive 2012/27/EU, and repealing Directive 2009/28/EC. See Article 3 (1), Annex VII.

[68] Proposal for a Directive of the European Parliament and of the Council on the promotion of the use of energy from renewable sources (recast), COM (2021) 805 final. OJ C 348, pp. 146–174.

the guarantee of origin once it has been provided. Furthermore, the guarantees of origin are anticipated to be transferable in accordance with the conditions outlined in the renewable power purchase agreements.

The amendments were implemented to regulate the suppliers of electricity from renewable sources for electric vehicle charging sites. The purpose of these credits was to enable fuel suppliers to fulfil their responsibility of including renewable energy sources into the energy mix by purchasing them. District heating systems with a capacity above 25 MW are required to comply with the efficiency standards outlined in the relevant energy efficiency directive. Failure to meet these requirements necessitates the implementation of mandatory obligations. It is incumbent upon Member States to establish the initial prerequisites for the utilisation of renewable energy sources in architectural structures. Member States should aim to participate in at least one cooperative energy project by the year 2026.

The inclusion of the carbon border adjustment mechanism proposed in the package aims to ensure that the European Union effectively achieves its greenhouse gas reduction commitments. The proposed mechanism is intended to be applied to the cost associated with carbon imports of various items, which would be computed based on the carbon emissions generated during the manufacturing process of specific products, including steel, iron, cement, fertilisers, aluminium, and power. The transition phase is implicitly understood to extend until 2026, during which only the act of reporting is required. Following the conclusion of the transition period, importers of the aforementioned products are required to obtain authorization from national authorities in order to procure certifications associated with the carbon border adjustment system. The determination of the certificate price shall be based on the weekly average auction price of the EU ETS allowances.[69]

It is imperative to disclose both the quantity of items and their corresponding total embedded emissions. Importers have the option to provide evidence of having paid the carbon price in third countries, enabling them to deduct the corresponding sum. China has expressed certain criticisms of the measure. Russia and Turkey have been accused of breaking the standards set forth by the World Trade Organisation (WTO) and engaging in discriminatory practices towards third-party nations. The European Union has the perspective that the measures adopted are equally applicable to both its member states and third countries. Furthermore, it is anticipated by the Commission that the implementation of EU policies will serve as a catalyst for third countries to enhance their carbon pricing standards.[70]

[69] Proposal for a Regulation of the European Parliament and of the Council on the Carbon Border Adjustment Mechanism (COM/2021/564 final). See Article 1, Article 4, Article 6, Article 10, Article 15.

[70] Proposal for a Regulation of the European Parliament and of the Council on the Carbon Border Adjustment Mechanism (COM/2021/564 final). See Article 1, Article 4, Article 6, Article 10, Article 15. General Agreement on Tariffs and Trade (GATT) 1994, particularly Article III (National Treatment on Internal Taxation and Regulation) and Article XI (General Elimination of Quantitative Restrictions). See Article III.

The proposed Energy Taxation Directive seeks to establish minimum tax rates for fuels and assess their implications for the energy environment. The tax rates have been restructured to categorise energy items and electricity based on their respective kinds. The highest tax rates are intended to be levied on products with the highest levels of pollution, specifically conventional fossil fuels and non-sustainable biofuels. Conversely, the lowest tax rate is applicable to electricity, advanced sustainable biofuels, biogas, and renewable fuels such as renewable hydrogen.[71] The tax reductions will be applicable to the sectors of renewable energy and agriculture. It is anticipated that the minimum rates within the aviation sector will experience a progressive increase over the transition period. In contrast, it is imperative that sustainable fuels be implemented with a zero-minimum rating during the transition period.

The EU fit for 55 package has also addressed the issue of energy efficiency. The modified suggestions for the new directive and the renewable directive were recently introduced. Energy efficiency has emerged as a primary objective across various industries, with a focus on reducing both primary and final energy consumption. This objective is pursued through the implementation of measures such as enhanced energy savings and building modifications. The refurbishment was motivated by the objective of renovating a minimum of 3% of the total ground area of public entities annually, with the aim of transforming them into zero-energy buildings. The energy performance contracts have been modified specifically for use in large non-residential buildings. Therefore, it is recommended that Member States establish a centralised entity to streamline processes and engage in partnerships with the private sector when developing specific projects that are eligible for funding. The proposal aims to address the needs of disadvantaged consumers by granting them specific minimum contractual rights related to heating and cooling services. Additionally, the proposal establishes an out-of-court method for resolving disputes. The notion of prioritising energy efficiency is deemed appropriate for implementation by both transmission and distribution system operators as well as national regulatory agencies.[72]

The regulatory framework governing the gas market encompasses provisions pertaining to natural gas, including renewable and low-carbon gases, as well as

[71] Proposal for a Directive of the European Parliament and of the Council restructuring the Union framework for the taxation of energy products and electricity, COM (2021) 563 final OJ C 328, 24.7.2023, pp. 42–65.

[72] Directive (EU) 2018/2001 on the Promotion of the Use of Energy from Renewable Sources (Renewable Energy Directive) OJ L 328, 21.12.2018, pp. 82–209. Directive (EU) 2012/27/EU of the European Parliament and of the Council of 25 October 2012 on energy efficiency, amending Directives 2009/125/EC and 2010/30/EU, and repealing Directives 2004/8/EC and 2006/32/EC. OJ L 315, 14.11.2012, pp. 1–56. Regulation (EU) 2021/1119 of the European Parliament and of the Council of 30 June 2021 on the European Climate Law and amending Regulation (EU) 2018/1999. OJ L 243, 9.7.2021, pp. 1–17. Proposal for a Directive of the European Parliament and of the Council on energy efficiency (recast) COM(2021) 558 final. Proposal for a Directive of the European Parliament and of the Council on the energy performance of buildings (recast) COM (2021) 802 final.

hydrogen. The recasts encompass the introduction of revised definitions for renewable and low-carbon gases, as well as the establishment of certification processes and standardised regulations for the integration of these low-carbon gases into existing gas infrastructure.[73] The newly proposed legislation seeks to enhance the rights of consumers by matching them with electricity customers and introducing active customers. Additionally, the legislation outlines the necessary billing criteria and the information that should be provided to gas customers. The hydrogens also witnessed the implementation of unbundling laws, third-party access, and tariff control. New regulatory measures have been implemented to ensure the security of gas supply, with a specific focus on the voluntary joint procurement plan for transmission system operators. The inclusion of the plan for building renovation in the winter package is intended to increase renovation rates and establish minimum energy performance criteria for buildings. It is mandatory for the Member States to furnish the national building renovation action plans. Furthermore, the proposed plan specifically addresses the development of electric car infrastructure, particularly focusing on the establishment of charging stations at construction sites.

The Winter Legislation of the EU Fit for 55 Package aims to promote the advancement of renewable and low-carbon gases within the energy composition.[74] Its objectives include ensuring supply security, addressing pricing concerns, implementing modifications to regulatory bodies, and conducting a comprehensive review of their roles and responsibilities.[75] The establishment of a hydrogen internal market represents a distinctive initiative that now lacks any comparable counterparts on a global scale. Additionally, the establishment of the European Network for Network Operators of Hydrogen will involve the assignment of specific responsibilities, including the preparation of network codes and non-binding ten-year network development plans for the hydrogen sector.[76] The responsibility for the development plans of the gas and hydrogen networks shall lie with the ENTSOG until the organisation is established. The hydrogen projects should be eligible for financing as interconnection projects within the framework of the ten-year network development plans. Despite the introduction of new legislation, the unbundling requirements and implications of third-party access remain relevant. However, the new legislation includes a provision for investment augmentation. Specifically, Member States have the option to deny third-party access to their hydrogen networks until the year 2031. The proposed policy lacks clarity in differentiating between low-carbon and renewable fuels or gases. In terms of supporting the growth of

[73] Proposal for a Directive of the European Parliament and of the Council on common rules for the internal markets in renewable and natural gases and in hydrogen (recast), COM (2021) 804 final OJ C 328, 24.7.2023, pp. 66–85.

[74] Hancher and Winters (2017).

[75] Proposal for a Regulation of the European Parliament and of the Council on internal markets for renewable and natural gases and for hydrogen (recast), COM (2021) 805 final. OJ C 328, 24.7.2023, pp. 86–106.

[76] Ali et al. (2021).

renewable energy sources, a 75% discount on entry or exit tariffs will be provided, and transmission charges will be waived until 2031.

The suggested revisions for the internal market pertaining to hydrogen involve the introduction of updated definitions for renewable and low-carbon natural gases, as well as the establishment of standardised regulations for the injection of low-carbon gases into the existing gas infrastructure.[77] The regulations pertaining to third-party access and the enhancement of consumer rights through the establishment of an engaged customer According to the Commission's findings, low-carbon gases have been observed to generate greenhouse gas emissions that are at least 70% lower than those produced by fossil natural gas. Furthermore, renewable gases have been found to contribute to carbon reductions. The achievement of decarbonisation targets may be facilitated through the implementation of electrification strategies in specific regions, thereby promoting energy efficiency and reducing carbon emissions in the final energy demand. According to the impact assessment conducted by the Commission, it is evident that trade restrictions, such as entrance tariffs, continue to pose challenges to the growth of the internal market. After conducting an assessment, the Commission has put forth a proposal to remove barriers that hinder the sales of renewable and low-carbon gases across borders. Additionally, it is anticipated that no cross-border tariffs will be imposed on hydrogen networks. These measures aim to foster competition and enhance the security of supply.

Considering the current scenario, it is important to acknowledge that renewable gases are indeed included to some extent in the gas grid system. However, their integration is limited to the distribution segment of the grid, which consequently restricts their access to the wholesale market. Hence, the plan has a stipulation that necessitates granting smaller grid-connected installations equitable access to the wholesale market. This approach involves the introduction of reverse flows, facilitating their integration into the transmission grids.

The gradual integration of renewable and low-carbon gas market ideas aims to address the gradual elimination of fossil natural gas and so make a significant contribution towards achieving climate targets. Member States are advised to consider the progressive elimination of fossil fuels within a certain timeframe, as they contribute to decarbonisation obligations by promoting the adoption of low-carbon gases, renewable energy sources, and the electrification of various sectors.[78] Furthermore, it is anticipated that the extension of long-term contracts for fossil natural gas should be discontinued beyond the year 2049.

As previously said, the utilisation of renewable gases has the potential to substantially augment domestic output, reducing reliance on imported fuels and consequently enhancing supply security. The integrated common market offers clients the advantage of being able to swap and select suppliers based on the offers provided.

[77] Directive of the European Parliament and of the Council on common rules for the internal markets for renewable gas, natural gas and hydrogen, amending Directive (EU) 2023/1791 and repealing Directive 2009/73/EC (recast).

[78] Andresen (2015).

The proposed extension of the gas security of supply law aims to include renewable and low-carbon gases while also incorporating protections for cybersecurity. In addition, the enhancement of supply security is achieved through the implementation of efficient gas storage systems during times of supply crises. Additionally, certain measures, such as the collective buying of gas reserves, are also anticipated. The practice of maintaining high storage levels is implemented at the onset of the summer season to ensure an adequate supply of gas in the event of an emergency or shortage.

The establishment of hydrogen infrastructure is being encouraged with the goal of promoting the development of an internal market. This entails ensuring adequate cross-border coordination and adapting existing natural gas infrastructure for hydrogen transportation.[79] By doing so, substantial cost savings can be achieved compared to the construction of entirely new infrastructure for hydrogen transportation, which would require significant time and substantial investments.

Just as the electricity industry has already established a model allowing consumers to switch suppliers based on cost-effectiveness, similar modifications are anticipated in the gas sector. These adjustments would enable customers to engage more actively in the market and make informed decisions regarding their supplier. Hence, it is imperative to furnish customers with adequate information pertaining to their energy use and the requisite mechanisms for their participation in the market. The safeguarding of vulnerable consumers is also anticipated in the context of the growing emphasis on energy efficiency. The utilisation of gas storage is facilitated through the implementation of strategies that promote efficient consumption and encourage voluntary collaborative procurement. Member States are obligated to assess their storage levels in order to address potential security of supply shortages and implement appropriate steps to mitigate the identified risks. The voluntary collaborative procurement undertaken by Transmission System Operators (TSOs) should facilitate the utilisation of resources by Member States during emergency scenarios. The implementation of the integrated network planning approach entails the requirement for member states to formulate distinct network plans for electricity and gas at the national level. However, these plans must be prepared in accordance with the collective scenario for electricity, gas, and hydrogen at the European Union level.

The suggestions encompass laws pertaining to methane, with a specific focus on direct methane emissions originating from oil, fossil gas, biomethane, and coal when they are introduced into the gas network. The proposal encompasses activities related to upstream exploration and production of oil and fossil gas, as well as the processing of fossil gas. The legislative recommendations encompass many

[79] Proposal for a Regulation of the European Parliament and of the Council on methane emissions reduction in the energy sector and amending Regulation (EU) 2019/942 OJ C 345, 29.6.2023, pp. 25–43 Proposal for a Regulation of the European Parliament and of the Council on internal markets for renewable and natural gases and for hydrogen. OJ C 319, 18.7.2023, pp. 5–30. Proposal for a Directive of the European Parliament and of the Council on common rules for the internal markets in renewable and natural gases and in hydrogen. OJ C 348, 12.9.2023, pp. 14–34.

components of the energy infrastructure, such as gas transmission and distribution systems, underground gas storage facilities, LNG terminals utilising both fossil and renewable methane, and functioning as well as closed and abandoned underground coal mines.

The utilisation of measurement techniques and reporting systems for methane emissions enables the observation of specific methane emissions, facilitating a transition from projected emissions to quantifiable data. It is imperative to promptly notice, ascertain, and rectify oil and gas leaks without any unwarranted delays. Within the coal industry, there exists a regulatory mandate to cease the release and combustion of methane gas emanating from drainage stations by the year 2025 and from ventilation shafts by the year 2027. It is strongly recommended that Member States develop mitigation plans for the remediation of abandoned coal mines.

4.6 REPowerEU Plan in the Context of Crisis Management

The European Commission has unveiled the REPowerEU Plan[80] as a strategic measure to address the challenges and global energy market disturbances resulting from Russia's incursion into Ukraine. There exists a dual need to effectuate a transformation of Europe's energy system. Firstly, it entails the cessation of the European Union's reliance on Russian fossil fuels, which are employed as both an economic and political instrument and impose a financial burden of approximately EUR 100 billion annually on European taxpayers. Secondly, it involves addressing the pressing issue of the climate crisis. By assuming the role of a union, Europe has the potential to expedite the process of reducing its reliance on Russian fossil fuels. A significant majority of European citizens, over 85%, hold the view that the European Union (EU) ought to promptly diminish its reliance on Russian gas and oil resources in order to provide help to Ukraine. The REPowerEU Plan encompasses many initiatives that can effectively address this objective by promoting energy conservation, enhancing energy source variety, and expediting the implementation of renewable energy sources as substitutes for fossil fuels in residential, industrial, and power generation sectors.

The implementation of the green transformation is expected to enhance economic growth, bolster security measures, and advance climate change initiatives for Europe and its collaborating nations. The Recovery and Resilience Facility (RRF) constitutes a central component of the REPowerEU Plan, facilitating the synchronised coordination of cross-border and national infrastructure, energy projects, and

[80] European Commission, Directorate-General for Communication, REPowerEU, joint European action for more affordable, secure and sustainable energy. Publications Office of the European Union; 2022.

reforms through planning and financial support.[81] The proposal put forth by the Commission suggests implementing specific modifications to the RRF Regulation in order to incorporate specialised REPowerEU sections into the existing recovery and resilience plans (RRPs) of Member States. This addition would complement the numerous pertinent reforms and investments already included in the RRPs.

Energy savings are a highly efficient and cost-effective approach to mitigating the prevailing energy problem and curtailing expenses. The Commission's proposal entails the augmentation of long-term energy efficiency measures, specifically through a rise in the obligatory Energy Efficiency Target from 9% to 13%. This proposition is part of the comprehensive EU Fit for 55 package within the legislative framework of the European Green Deal. The act of conserving energy in the present will aid in our readiness to confront the potential difficulties that may arise in the forthcoming winter season. Hence, the Commission has just released an "EU Save Energy Communication" that outlines potential immediate modifications in behaviour capable of reducing gasoline and oil consumption by 5%. Additionally, it urges Member States to initiate targeted communication efforts aimed at homes and industries. Member States are additionally urged to employ budgetary measures to promote energy conservation, such as implementing reduced value-added tax (VAT) rates on energy-efficient heating systems, building insulation, and appliances and items. The Commission additionally presents contingency measures in the event of a significant disruption in supply, will provide guidance on the criteria for prioritising consumers, and will support the implementation of a coordinated plan to reduce demand within the European Union.[82]

The European Union has been actively collaborating with international partners in order to enhance supply diversification. As a result of these efforts, the EU has successfully obtained unprecedented quantities of liquefied natural gas (LNG) imports and experienced increased deliveries of pipeline gas. The recently established EU Energy Platform, with the assistance of regional task teams, aims to facilitate collective procurement of gas, LNG, and hydrogen through voluntary means.[83] This initiative seeks to leverage pooled demand, optimise infrastructure

[81] Regulation (EU) 2021/241 of the European Parliament and of the Council of 12 February 2021 establishing the Recovery and Resilience Facility. OJ L 57, 18.2.2021, pp. 17–75. Communication from the Commission to the European Parliament, the Council, the European Economic and Social Committee and the Committee of the Regions - REPowerEU Plan. OJ C 261, 20.7.2022, pp. 1–17.

[82] Proposal for a Directive of the European Parliament and of the Council on Energy Efficiency (COM/2021/558 final). See Article 1, Article 3. European Commission Communication on the European Green Deal (COM/2019/640 final). Fit for 55 Package Communication (COM/2021/550 final). Communication from the Commission on Energy Efficiency First: Scaling up the energy efficiency ambition (COM/2021/557 final). See Section 3, Section 5. Communication from the Commission on the EU Gas Demand Reduction Plan (COM/2022/360 final). See Section 2, Section 4.

[83] Communication from the Commission on the EU Energy Platform and its Role in Ensuring Energy Supply Security (COM/2022/430 final). See Section 2, Section 4. Communication from the Commission on the European Strategy for Energy System Integration (COM/2020/299 final). See Section 3.

utilisation, and coordinate supplier engagement. In the subsequent phase, with the aim of emulating the comprehensive vaccine procurement initiative, the Commission will contemplate the establishment of a collective procurement mechanism that will engage in negotiations and contractual agreements for the acquisition of gas on behalf of Member States that choose to participate. The Commission will additionally examine the possibility of implementing legislative measures that would mandate Member States to gradually diversify their gas supplies. Additionally, the platform will facilitate the collaborative procurement of renewable hydrogen.[84]

The EU External Energy Strategy[85] aims to promote energy diversity and establish enduring partnerships with suppliers, encompassing collaborative efforts in areas such as hydrogen or other environmentally sustainable technologies. Aligned with the Global Gateway initiative, the strategy places emphasis on the European Union's dedication to a worldwide environmentally sustainable and equitable energy transition. This entails enhancing energy conservation and efficiency measures to alleviate pricing burdens, promoting the advancement of renewable energy sources and hydrogen technologies, and intensifying efforts in energy diplomacy. The development of significant hydrogen corridors is anticipated in the Mediterranean and North Sea regions. Given Russia's aggressive behaviour, the European Union (EU) will extend its support to Ukraine, Moldova, the Western Balkans, Eastern Partnership nations, and other partners who are particularly susceptible to vulnerability. EU shall maintain collaborative efforts with Ukraine to safeguard the reliability of energy provision and the effective operation of the energy industry. Additionally, will facilitate the establishment of trade in electricity and renewable hydrogen while undertaking the task of revitalising the energy infrastructure through the REPower Ukraine programme.

The implementation of a significant expansion and acceleration of renewable energy sources in the domains of power generation, industry, buildings, and transportation would expedite our self-sufficiency, contribute to the advancement of environmentally friendly initiatives, and gradually lower costs. The proposed measure by the Commission entails raising the primary target for renewable energy sources in the year 2030 from 40% to 45% as part of the Fit for 55 package. The proposal entails the implementation of a focused European Union (EU) Solar Strategy aimed at achieving a twofold increase in solar photovoltaic capacity by the year 2025, followed by the installation of 600 gigawatts (GW) by 2030.[86] The proposal entails the implementation of a Solar Rooftop Initiative, which would enforce a

[84] Communication from the Commission on the EU Strategy for LNG and Gas Storage (COM/2021/764 final). See Section 5. Regulation (EU) 2017/1938 of the European Parliament and of the Council of 25 October 2017 concerning measures to safeguard the security of gas supply. See Article 4, Article 7.

[85] European Commission Communication. A Clean Planet for all: A European strategic long- term vision for a prosperous, modern, competitive and climate neutral economy. (COM/2018/773).

[86] Communication from the Commission to the European Parliament, the Council, the European Economic and Social Committee and the Committee of the Regions - "A European Solar Strategy" OJ C 119, 28.3.2022, pp. 1–8.

gradual legal need for the installation of solar panels on newly constructed public and commercial buildings, as well as new residential structures. Increasing the rate of deployment of heat pumps and implementing strategies to integrate geothermal and solar thermal energy into modernised district and communal heating systems.

The European Union's existing energy targets for 2030 include the latter: The EU aims to reduce both primary (indicative) and final energy usage by 11.7% compared to the projected levels for 2020. This reduction is equivalent to a maximum of 992.5 and 763 million metric tonnes of oil equivalent (Mtoe), respectively.[87] This reduction entails the integration of a minimum of 15% of the power networks within the European Union.

The Commission has proposed a recommendation aimed at addressing the issue of delayed and intricate regulatory processes for significant renewable energy projects. Additionally, a specific change to the Renewable Energy Directive has been suggested to acknowledge renewable energy as a prevailing public interest. Member States should establish dedicated areas specifically designated for renewable energy projects, accompanied by streamlined and simplified permitting procedures, particularly in regions with fewer environmental risks. In order to expedite the identification of these prominent places, the Commission is providing datasets on ecologically sensitive regions as a component of its digital mapping tool for geospatial data pertaining to energy, industry, and infrastructure.

By the year 2030, there is a proposed objective of achieving a total of 10 million tonnes of domestically produced renewable hydrogen and an additional 10 million tonnes of imported hydrogen. This ambitious ambition aims to replace the utilisation of natural gas, coal, and oil in industries and transportation sectors that are challenging to decarbonize.[88] In order to expedite the growth of the hydrogen market, it would be necessary for the co-legislators to establish additional sub-targets for specific sectors. The Commission is additionally releasing two delegated acts concerning the delineation and generation of renewable hydrogen in order to guarantee that its production contributes to overall decarbonisation. In order to expedite hydrogen initiatives, a further allocation of EUR 200 million has been designated for research purposes. The Biomethane Action Plan[89] outlines various strategies, such as the establishment of a biomethane industrial partnership and the provision of financial incentives, aimed at augmenting biomethane output to 35 billion cubic metres by the year 2030. These efforts will be facilitated, in part, through the implementation of the Common Agricultural Policy. The objective of this study is

[87] Regulation (EU) 2018/1999 of the European Parliament and of the Council of 11 December 2018 on the Governance of the Energy Union and Climate Action. OJ L 328, 21.12.2018, pp. 1–77.

[88] Communication from the Commission to the European Parliament, the Council, The European Economic and Social Committee and the Committee of the Regions "Hydrogen Strategy for a Climate-Neutral Europe". COM (2020) 301 final.

[89] Communication from the Commission to the European Parliament, the European Council, the Council, the European Economic and Social Committee and the Committee of the Regions. REPowerEU Plan. COM/2022/230 final.

to examine strategies for mitigating fossil fuel consumption in the industrial and transportation sectors.

The substitution of coal, oil, and natural gas with alternative energy sources in industrial processes has the potential to mitigate greenhouse gas emissions and enhance security and competitiveness. The implementation of energy conservation measures, improved efficiency, the replacement of conventional fuels with alternative sources, the adoption of electric power, and the increased utilisation of renewable hydrogen, biogas, and biomethane within industrial sectors have the potential to achieve additional natural gas savings of up to 35 billion cubic metres by the year 2030, in addition to the projected outcomes outlined in the Fit for 55 initiatives.

The Commission intends to implement carbon contracts for difference as a means of promoting the adoption of green hydrogen by various industries. Additionally, dedicated funding will be allocated to REPowerEU through the Innovation Fund. This funding will be derived from emission trading income, with the aim of facilitating a transition away from reliance on Russian fossil fuels. The Commission is additionally offering recommendations pertaining to renewable energy and power purchase agreements and will establish a technical advising centre in collaboration with the European Investment Bank. In order to sustain and reclaim supremacy in technological and industrial domains, particularly in the fields of solar and hydrogen, and to provide assistance to the labour force, the Commission suggests the establishment of an EU Solar Industry Alliance and a comprehensive skills collaboration. The Commission will additionally enhance efforts pertaining to the provision of vital raw materials and undertake preparations for a legislative proposition.

In order to optimise energy conservation and improve operational effectiveness within the transportation industry, the Commission intends to introduce a Greening of Freight Package. This package aims to substantially enhance energy efficiency within the sector.[90] Additionally, the Commission will contemplate a legislative proposal to augment the proportion of zero-emission vehicles in public and corporate car fleets that exceed a specific magnitude. The communication on energy conservation by the European Union also encompasses a range of suggestions aimed at cities, regions, and national authorities, with the objective of facilitating the transition away from fossil fuels within the transportation industry.

In order to achieve the objectives of REPowerEU, it is necessary to secure an extra investment total EUR 210 billion during the timeframe of 2027. This payment serves as an initial investment towards achieving our autonomy and ensuring our safety. Reducing the importation of fossil fuels from Russia has the potential to yield annual savings of about EUR 100 billion. The responsibility of financing these projects lies with both the commercial and public sectors, encompassing national, cross-border, and European Union levels.

Within the existing Multiannual Financial Framework (MFF), the cohesion policy is already poised to provide substantial backing, up to EUR 100 billion, for initiatives focused on decarbonisation and the facilitation of a green transition. This

[90] Eyre and Pollitt (2016).

assistance will be channelled towards investments in renewable energy, hydrogen, and infrastructure. It is possible to allocate an extra EUR 26.9 billion from cohesion funds through voluntary contributions to the Recovery and Resilience Facility (RRF). Additionally, a sum of EUR 7.5 billion from the Common Agricultural Policy is allocated for voluntary payments to the Recovery and Resilience Facility (RRF). The European Commission intends to increase the funding allocation for the 2022 Large Scale Call of the Innovation Fund during the upcoming autumn season, resulting in an approximate doubling of the available funds to EUR 3 billion.[91]

The RRF currently offers EUR 225 billion in loans to provide financial support for REPowerEU. The Commission has implemented legislation and provided guidance to Member States regarding the necessary modifications and enhancements to their Recovery and Resilience Plans (RRPs) within the framework of the REPowerEU initiative. Furthermore, the Commission suggests augmenting the financial allocation of the Recovery and Resilience Facility (RRF) by EUR 20 billion in the form of grants. These funds would be sourced from the sale of EU Emission Trading System allowances, which are presently held in the Market Stability Reserve. The auctioning process would be carefully managed to ensure minimal disruption to the market. Therefore, the implementation of an Emissions Trading System (ETS) not only serves to decrease emissions and minimise reliance on fossil fuels, but it also generates the essential financial resources required to attain energy independence.[92]

The Trans-European Energy Networks (TEN-E) have played a significant role in the establishment of a robust and integrated gas infrastructure within the European Union. A modest amount of supplementary gas infrastructure, requiring an estimated investment of approximately EUR 10 billion, is necessary to supplement the current Projects of Common Interest (PCI) List and adequately offset the anticipated decline in Russian gas imports.[93] The future decade's substitution requirements may be

[91] Regulation (EU, Euratom) 2020/2093 of the European Parliament and of the Council of 17 December 2020 laying down the Multiannual Financial Framework for the years 2021 to 2027. See Article 4, Annex I. Regulation (EU) 2021/241 of the European Parliament and of the Council of 12 February 2021 establishing the Recovery and Resilience Facility. See Article 5, Article 12. Regulation (EU) 2021/2115 of the European Parliament and of the Council of 2 December 2021 on the financing, management, and monitoring of the Common Agricultural Policy. See Article 7. Regulation (EU) 2021/1119 of the European Parliament and of the Council of 30 June 2021 on the establishment of the Innovation Fund. See Article 1, Article 4.

[92] Regulation (EU) 2021/241 of the European Parliament and of the Council of 12 February 2021 establishing the Recovery and Resilience Facility. See Article 5, Article 6. Communication COM (2022) 230 final from the European Commission titled "REPowerEU Plan". See Section 2, Section 4. Regulation (EU) 2018/842 of the European Parliament and of the Council of 30 May 2018 on the binding annual greenhouse gas emission reductions by Member States. See Article 10, Article 11. Proposal COM(2023) 116 final from the European Commission to amend Regulation (EU) 2021/241. See Section 2, Section 3.

[93] Communication from the Commission to the European Parliament, the European Council, the Council, the European Economic and Social Committee and the Committee of the Regions. REPowerEU Plan. COM/2022/230 final.

adequately fulfilled without entrenching the use of fossil fuels, resulting in stranded assets, or impeding our climate objectives. The acceleration of electricity PCIs will be crucial in order to effectively accommodate the evolving requirements of the power grid.

4.7 Conclusion

The Paris Agreement is a consequential global accord with the objective of constraining the increase in global temperatures to below 2 °C and attaining carbon neutrality by the year 2050. The endeavour to tackle climate change and build a framework for cooperative endeavours among states is a worldwide undertaking. The agreement places significant emphasis on the significance of adaptive capacity, resilience, and mitigation of vulnerability to the impacts of climate change, particularly with regard to nations that are fragile and in the process of development. The Paris Agreement holds considerable significance for the fields of international law and climate governance, thereby underscoring the efficacy of multilateral approaches in addressing intricate global challenges. The efficacy of the initiative hinges upon robust enforcement mechanisms and the unwavering commitment of states, civil society, and the corporate sector to fulfil their responsibilities and enable substantial transformations in the pursuit of a sustainable, low-carbon global environment.

In 2019, the European Union reviewed its energy policy framework to transition from fossil fuels to more sustainable energy sources. The Clean Energy for All Europeans package, based on the Commission's 2016 proposals, aims to transform the energy sector, promote renewable energy integration, enhance energy efficiency, and strengthen energy markets. The package focuses on achieving carbon neutrality by 2050 and promoting renewable energy sources. However, the package faces challenges such as harmonising domestic policies with EU directives, funding for infrastructure, technology, and research, and addressing social equity concerns. The package also emphasizes the importance of energy performance in buildings, with refurbishment strategies aiming to improve energy conservation. Member states are required to implement efficient energy performance requirements, including air quality, ventilation, and temperature regulation systems.

The Clean Energy Package aims to achieve climate objectives, enhance coordination and collaboration among Member States, and transition from fossil fuels to renewable energy. The updated regulation sets a minimum requirement of 32% renewable energy integration into the energy mix by 2030, with a target of 32.5% energy efficiency. The package also includes directives and regulations addressing governance, electricity market design, risk preparedness, and ACER regulation. The Electricity Coordination Group aims to facilitate effective coordination and exchange of information, addressing market fragmentation and regulatory proceedings.

The European Green Deal aims to achieve climate neutrality by 2050, with legally enforceable provisions ensuring member states and stakeholders are held responsible for fulfilling their obligations. These provisions include the European Climate Law, the 2030 Climate Target, the Renewable Energy Directive, the Energy Efficiency Directive, circular economy legislation, the Emissions Trading System, the Just Transition Fund Regulation, the EU Biodiversity Strategy for 2030, and the Farm to Fork Strategy. The Green Deal also includes amendments to existing legislation, such as smart and sustainable transport, circular economy action plans, eco-design, sustainable products, circular electronics, and mobile reuse. These legally enforceable measures ensure the EU's commitment to sustainability, resilience, and carbon neutrality.

The European Climate Law, a crucial component of the European Green Deal, aims to achieve carbon neutrality by 2050 by balancing greenhouse gas emissions with their removal. The law establishes a legally binding commitment for the EU to achieve this goal, requiring member states to formulate and execute national energy and climate plans. The law promotes collaboration and shared responsibility, emphasising the importance of climate objectives in EU policy choices. The law also sets ambitious targets for net-zero emissions by 2050, demonstrating the EU's commitment to a sustainable and climate-neutral future. It aims to achieve carbon neutrality by 2050 and a 55% reduction in greenhouse gas emissions by 2030, surpassing the previous goal of a 40% reduction. The EU fit for 55 package aims to update current legislation and include policy measures to achieve climate neutrality by 2050. The EU's commitment to a sustainable, low-carbon, and resilient future is emphasised in the law.

The EU Fit for 55 package aims to achieve ambitious climate and energy objectives, including reducing emissions by 40% by 2050 and 80% by 2050. The European Climate Law has been adopted to achieve these targets. The European Union Emissions Trading System (EU ETS) has been revised to tighten regulations on the aviation sector, including the elimination of free allowances. The scope of the ETS has been expanded to include the maritime, road, and transport sectors. The European Commission has proposed increasing the annual emission reduction to 4.2% within the current framework and reducing the overall emissions cap by 117 million permits. The Social Climate Fund will commence operations once carbon pricing measures in the building and road transport sectors are initiated. Proposals have been introduced regarding amendments to the EU ETS, energy taxation, energy efficiency, renewable energy, carbon border adjustment mechanisms, effort sharing, land use, forestry, agriculture, transport, and the social climate fund.

The December package, also known as the "Hydrogen and Gas Package" of EU Fit for 55, includes legislative and policy proposals related to gas and buildings to meet new targets. It includes proposals for a directive on common rules for internal markets in renewable and natural gases and hydrogen, regulations on internal markets, methane emissions reduction, energy performance of buildings, and sustainable carbon cycles. The package also includes a communication from the Commission on Sustainable Carbon Cycles, regulations on trans-European transport network development, and the deployment of intelligent transport systems in road transport. The EU Methane Strategy aims to decrease methane emissions by 30% by 2030, and the new legislation establishes a framework for quantification, disclosure, and validation of methane emissions. The Global Methane Pledge is expected to provide significant outcomes in evaluating worldwide emissions.

The European Union introduced a new renewable energy directive as part of the Clean Energy Package in July. The revised targets aim to achieve climate neutrality by increasing renewable energy usage in the industrial sector, requiring at least 50% of hydrogen consumption to come from renewable sources by 2030. The transport sector now prioritises reducing greenhouse gas emissions by at least 13% compared to diesel and gasoline by 2030. The use of non-biological renewable sources, such as green hydrogen, is also expanding, with forest biomass being a potential resource. Transparency criteria have been expanded, and electrical grid operators must provide customers with up-to-date information on renewable electricity and emissions. The carbon border adjustment mechanism is also introduced to ensure the European Union achieves its greenhouse gas reduction commitments. The measures are expected to be applicable to both EU member states and third countries, with the Commission anticipating that the implementation of EU policies will encourage third countries to improve their carbon pricing standards.

The Energy Taxation Directive aims to establish minimum tax rates for fuels and assess their impact on the energy environment. It categorises energy items and electricity based on pollution levels, with higher tax rates for conventional fossil fuels and non-sustainable biofuels. The lowest tax rate applies to electricity, advanced sustainable biofuels, biogas, and renewable fuels like renewable hydrogen. The EU Fit for 55 package addresses energy efficiency, focusing on reducing primary and final energy consumption through measures like energy savings and building modifications. The legislation also introduces revised definitions for renewable and low-carbon gases, certification processes, and standardised regulations for their integration into existing gas infrastructure. The winter package also addresses building renovation and electric car infrastructure development.

The Commission has proposed removing barriers to the sale of renewable and low-carbon gases across borders, aiming to foster competition and enhance supply security. The plan includes granting smaller grid-connected installations equitable access to the wholesale market and introducing reverse flows to facilitate their integration. The gradual elimination of fossil natural gas is a key goal, with member states promoting the adoption of low-carbon gases, renewable energy sources, and electrification. The establishment of hydrogen infrastructure is encouraged to promote internal market development and cost savings. The gas sector should also provide customers with information on energy use and ensure energy efficiency. The integrated network planning approach requires member states to formulate national network plans for electricity and gas, focusing on direct methane emissions from oil, fossil gas, biomethane, and coal.

References

Ali M, Makki E, Cazal C, Ayadi Y (2021) Implementation of the network code in requirements for grid connection of generators. FGH GmbH

Andresen S (2015) International climate negotiations: top-down, bottom-up or a combination of both? International Spectator 50

Cameron PD (2007) Competition in energy markets. Law and regulation in the European Union. Oxford University Press, Oxford

Cameron P, Heffron R (2016) Legal Aspects of EU Energy Regulation. Oxford University Press

Eyre S, Pollitt MG (2016) Competition and regulation in electricity markets. The international library of critical writing in economics series. Edward Elgar

Fetting C (2020) The European Green Deal, ESDN Report, December 2020, ESDN Office, Vienna

Hancher L, Winters BM (2017) The EU Winter Package. Briefing Paper. Allen and Overy LLP

Hoffmann M (2011) Climate governance at the crossroads: experimenting with a global response after Kyoto. Oxford University Press, Oxford

Nouicer A, Kehoe A, Nysten J, Fouquet D, Hancher L, Meeus L (2020) The EU Clean Energy Package, RSCAS. Technical Report

Piebalgs A, Jones Ch, Conti I (2021) Reflections on priorities for the forthcoming EU Hydrogen legislation. Policy Brief. 2021/61

Schittekatte T, Reif V, Meeus L (2021) Welcoming new entrants into European electricity market. Energies 14

Part II
The Prohibited Agreements and Abuse of Dominant Position in the Energy Sector

Chapter 5
The Concept and Forms of Prohibited Agreements

Abstract Competition regulation has an important role in preserving the dynamism of the market, fostering innovation, and safeguarding consumer welfare. The provision in question forbids agreements that have both anti-competitive and criminal characteristics. These agreements are characterised by intentional and cooperative actions to distort market dynamics, decrease competition, and negatively impact consumer welfare. We can categorize the agreements into horizontal and vertical categories. Horizontal agreements encompass several forms of collusive tactics among competitors, such as price-fixing, market division, output restriction, bid manipulation, exclusive distribution, and customer allocation. Vertical agreements such as resale price maintenance, exclusive distribution, and bundling are generally deemed legitimate. However, if these agreements have characteristics that impede competition, they may be considered unconstitutional. The European Union enforces compliance with competition law through rigorous investigations and the imposition of more stringent restrictions. Many enforcement entities, including the European Commission and national competition authorities, share this task. To effectively safeguard and uphold competition rules, it is critical to understand these agreements' intrinsic traits, expressions, and outcomes. Competitive markets allow for precise pricing determination based on the interaction between supply and demand. This enables customers to make decisions according to their own preferences.

5.1 Introduction

Competition law has a fundamental role in upholding market dynamism, promoting innovation, and protecting consumer welfare. Central to this legal framework is the prohibition of many types of agreements that hinder competition, generally referred to as anti-competitive or prohibited agreements. This book offers a thorough analysis of the concept, various manifestations, and extensive consequences of such agreements. This statement underscores the significant role played by cartels in modern competition law and the persistent obstacles encountered by competition authorities globally in their efforts to identify and punish such anti-competitive practices.

L. Rimšaitė, *The Crossroads of Competition Law and Energy Regulation*,
https://doi.org/10.1007/978-3-031-73238-6_5

Competition law serves as a persistent protector of the fundamental principles of open and equitable markets.[1] Prohibited agreements, sometimes known as anti-competitive agreements, are a significant area of concern within the regulatory scope of competition law. These agreements signify intentional and cooperative efforts made by participants in the market with the intention of distorting the dynamics of the market, reducing competition, and negatively affecting the well-being of consumers. A comprehensive grasp of the inherent characteristics, many manifestations, and resultant implications is essential for the preservation and enforcement of the tenets of competition law. Prohibited agreements refer to a broad range of collaborative arrangements between participants in a market, characterised by actions that hinder or impede competition. These agreements are essentially in conflict with the core principles of competitive markets, which include the concepts of rivalry, innovation, and efficiency.

According to the framework of European Union competition law, agreements that are deemed unlawful are those that impose restrictions on competition within the internal market of the European Union. These agreements are in contravention of Article 101 of the Treaty on the Functioning of the European Union (TFEU) and may lead to substantial monetary sanctions and other punitive measures. Prohibited agreements can be broadly classified into two main categories: horizontal agreements and vertical agreements. The following is a thorough examination of the fundamental ideas and numerous manifestations of illegal agreements as set forth by European Union law.

Horizontal agreements refer to contractual arrangements established among firms operating at the same level of the supply chain, specifically including competitors.[2] EU competition law prohibits several sorts of horizontal agreements. Price-fixing agreements refer to collaborative agreements among rivals to establish predetermined prices for their respective products or services. These agreements effectively reduce price competition and have the potential to result in elevated pricing for customers. Price-fixing agreements are often regarded as a highly significant infringement of antitrust laws and are explicitly forbidden under Article 101 of the Treaty on the Functioning of the European Union. Market allocation agreements refer to agreements made between competitors where they divide markets or customers, thereby impeding competition in specific geographic areas or customer segments. Market allocation agreements are deemed a significant infringement of competition law and are strongly proscribed. Output limitation agreements refer to agreements made between rivals with the aim of restricting the number of goods or services produced. This phenomenon has the potential to result in a decrease in supply and an increase in costs. These types of agreements are seen as anticompetitive and are proscribed in accordance with European Union legislation. Bid rigging is a deceptive practise when competitors engage in collusion to control the outcome

[1] Gerber (1998).

[2] Bellis (2010) and Bailey and John (2019).

of a tender or bidding process.[3] This often involves reaching an agreement on the predetermined winner of the contract and the corresponding price. The act of bid rigging constitutes a blatant infringement of competition law and is unequivocally proscribed. Manufacturers and distributors' agreements serve as an example of vertical agreements, which are contractual arrangements between entities operating at various levels of the supply chain. Although vertical agreements are typically not inherently banned, they may give rise to concerns if they include specific clauses that have anticompetitive effects.

Resale Price Maintenance refers to the practise in which a producer or supplier establishes the prices at which its items can be resold by distributors or retailers. The implementation of prohibition can have detrimental effects on both competition and consumer choice. Agreements of this nature are deemed unlawful if they possess a discernible anticompetitive impact. Exclusive distribution agreements refer to contractual arrangements that confer upon a designated distributor the only authority to market and sell a supplier's merchandise within a defined geographical area. Customer allocation agreements are contractual arrangements that distribute clients among different distributors, establishing a framework that restricts competition between distributors for the same set of customers.

The practise of exclusive distribution and client allocation agreements, although not inherently forbidden, can present challenges when they impede competition or create market divisions that adversely affect consumers.[4] Tying and bundling refer to a business practise wherein customers are compelled to acquire a specific product, known as the tied product, in order to obtain access to another product, referred to as the tying product. The practise of bundling involves the consolidation of several items or services into a unified package. The practise of tying and bundling has the potential to be anticompetitive when it results in the foreclosure of competition or the restriction of customer choice. The entities in question are subject to examination and evaluation within the framework of European Union competition law.

In essence, the European Union's competition law effectively forbids agreements that impede competition, including horizontal agreements encompassing price-fixing, market allocation, output limits, and bid rigging.[5] Although vertical agreements are typically considered acceptable, they may be deemed unlawful if they incorporate anticompetitive elements such as resale price maintenance, exclusive distribution arrangements, customer allocation, linking, or bundling. The European Union exercises diligent oversight and conducts thorough investigations on agreements within its jurisdiction with the aim of safeguarding a competitive internal market. This responsibility is shared among enforcement bodies such as the European Commission and national competition authorities.

The advantages of a competitive market are rooted in its ability to provide consumers with prices that accurately reflect the dynamics of supply and demand

---

[3]Wish and Bailey (2018).

[4]Jones et al. (2019).

[5]Calzado et al. (2014).

while also granting them the opportunity to make choices based on their preferences. Competition within the market assumes that economic agents, driven by the desire to acquire a larger consumer base, allocate resources towards the advancement of production, technology, and innovations. The imposition of competitive constraints can significantly impact the escalation of prices and the range of options available to consumers. The complexity of market liberalisation and the enforcement of competition laws in the energy sector was evident. The primary goal of market liberalisation in the energy sector is to promote heightened competition. In order to achieve this, the decision to separate monopoly companies and establish energy regulation at the European Union level has been made. To ensure effective implementation of legislation, competition law provisions have played a crucial role. The aforementioned goals have been incorporated into the communication, which places emphasis on ensuring the security of energy supply, promoting the sustainable utilisation of energy resources, and encouraging the adoption of low-carbon technologies.

In accordance with the objectives stated in Articles 101 and 102 of the TFEU, the primary aims are to safeguard competition and optimise advantages for consumers. The aforementioned purpose is accomplished by the implementation of regulations that restrict the use of specific measures that have the potential to violate the rights of consumers.[6] The primary objective of competition legislation is to safeguard consumer welfare through the establishment of price levels that align with the associated costs while also fostering technical advancement and preserving consumer autonomy. The European Union has the perspective that contractual limitations do not inherently impede competition inside the market. Competition can also be predicated on the objective of mitigating market fragmentation; however, this particular rule has faced criticism because of its potential implications for vertical mergers. The justification for the latter is grounded in the objective of achieving market integration. This concept is grounded in the principle of economic freedom, which aims to safeguard the interests of small and medium-sized enterprises.

If corporations were to engage in a collaborative approach rather than competitive behaviour, it would result in an imbalance in fair market competition, subsequently leading to negative consequences for consumers and other businesses. Therefore, any agreements between businesses that result in a distortion of competition and have the potential to impact trade between Member States are strictly forbidden and rendered null and void. This encompasses several forms of anti-competitive behaviour, such as explicit agreements such as cartels, concerted practices aimed at price fixing or production output limitations, and the division of markets among enterprises, sometimes known as territorial protection clauses. Agreements of this nature are universally seen as detrimental to competition and are hence strictly prohibited without any exemptions.

Conversely, certain forms of agreement may be granted exemption if they demonstrate a propensity to enhance the manufacturing or dissemination of

[6] Faull and Nikpay (2014).

commodities or facilitate advancements in technical or economic domains.[7] For instance, the establishment of agreements pertaining to cost or risk allocation among enterprises, as well as collaborations in research and development to enhance innovation, have the potential to yield substantial economic advantages.[8] In order to qualify for an exemption, certain conditions must be met. These factors include ensuring that consumers are afforded a reasonable portion of the resultant advantages and that the agreement does not impose superfluous limitations or seek to eradicate competition for a significant portion of the relevant items. Instead of individualised consideration, exemptions are often regulated by the Block Exemption Regulations.

These laws pertain to clusters of analogous, specific agreements that typically exhibit a comparable influence on competition. The revised Vertical Block Exemption Regulation was adopted by the Commission in May 2022, subsequent to an assessment and revision of the regulations implemented in 2010. In addition, a comprehensive analysis is conducted on the two horizontal block exemption regulations in conjunction with the pertinent recommendations. The objective of this assessment is to assess the extent to which existing regulations continue to adequately consider market developments and remain suitable for their intended purpose.

In certain cases, agreements that are considered to be of little significance and have minimal effects on the market may not be considered infringements, in accordance with the de minimis principle.[9] This is applicable even if these agreements do not meet the requirements for exemption under Article 101(3) of the TFEU, commonly referred to as agreements of minor importance. These agreements are frequently regarded as beneficial for fostering collaboration among small and medium-sized firms. Nevertheless, agreements that contain a competition restriction as their primary purpose cannot be considered to be of insignificant significance. The next section will delve into a comprehensive analysis of the agreements and the exploitation of dominant market positions by corporate entities. This part will additionally assess the correlation between the implementation of competition law rules and market liberalisation measures within the context of energy legislation.

5.2 The Notion of the Agreement

Within the framework of European Union competition law, the concept of an "agreement" holds significant importance since it serves as a key principle for the detection of anticompetitive behaviour. An agreement can manifest in diverse formats, and it is not obligatory for it to be exclusively a formal written contract or

[7] Article 101(3) of the Treaty on the Functioning of the European Union (TFEU).

[8] Quigley (2022).

[9] Wish and Bailey (2018).

a verbal agreement. It can encompass any type of coordinated action or mutual comprehension, whether explicitly expressed or implicitly understood, between two or more autonomous entities. The following is an elaboration on the concept of an agreement within the framework of European Union competition law. The definition of an agreement under EU competition law is characterised by its extensive scope. As per the provisions outlined in Article 101(1) of the TFEU, any agreement that aims to restrict competition, either in its purpose or its consequences, is deemed to be forbidden. This concept incorporates a range of understandings, whether they are explicit or implicit, and whether they are communicated by written or oral means.[10] In the realm of competition law, the scope of agreements extends beyond that of civil law, primarily due to the tendency of companies to exhibit hesitancy in actively enforcing anticompetitive agreements through formal means. In order to establish the existence of a prohibited agreement, it is sufficient for the involved parties to mutually consent to engage in activities that curtail their economic autonomy and limit their ability to make independent decisions within the market.

Written agreements refer to legally binding agreements that are either documented in writing or communicated verbally, wherein the involved parties expressly express their intentions to participate in activities that are considered anticompetitive.[11] Identifying and proving express agreements is often considered a more straightforward task. Tacit agreements refer to agreements that are not formally articulated but are deduced from the conduct and actions of the involved parties. For instance, in the event that rival firms routinely and simultaneously raise their rates without any discernible explanation, it can be deduced that they possess the implicit understanding to engage in price-fixing. In the realm of EU competition law, concerted practises encompass instances where there is no explicit agreement or understanding, yet rivals partake in coordinated conduct that hampers competition. Concerted practises pertain to circumstances wherein corporations, in the absence of a formal agreement, consciously engage in practical collaboration as a means to mitigate competitive risks. The concept of single and continuous infringement is significant as it pertains to a collection of interconnected agreements, concerted practises, or choices that can be seen as a unified and ongoing violation if they share a common anticompetitive aim.[12]

It should be noted that not all agreements are subject to prohibition. Certain agreements may have restricted clauses that are deemed supplementary to a valid primary agreement. The requirements for exemption are evaluated in accordance with Article 101(3) of the TFEU. The aspect of enforcement of EU competition law falls under the purview of both the Commission and national competition authorities. The authorities conduct investigations into alleged anticompetitive agreements and practises and have the authority to levy penalties and implement other corrective measures upon identifying infractions. Leniency programmes are implemented by

[10] Wish and Bailey (2018).

[11] Jones et al. (2019).

[12] Case C-49/92 P Commission v. Anic Partecipazioni SpA [1999] ECR I-04125.

the European Union and several national competition authorities, aiming to encourage corporations to voluntarily disclose their participation in cartel agreements by offering certain incentives. Within the framework of these programmes, the initial organisation to disclose and collaborate has the potential to obtain diminished penalties or an exemption from financial sanctions.

The regulation of prohibited agreements falls under the purview of Article 101 of the TFEU. This article integrates multiple phases of agreement evaluation and competition law assessment. When assessing the notion of an agreement, it is crucial to consider the harmony of the intentions of the involved parties in any manifestation.[13] In situations where an economic operator engages in unilateral conduct, the existence of a prohibited agreement can only be established if there is explicit or implied consent from the other contracting parties towards such conduct. Furthermore, a significant concern arises from the implicit endorsement of the agreement by the second party. The expression of a proposal by one party to another, with the aim of achieving a common objective through collaborative efforts, shall constitute the will of the contracting parties. The presence of an implicit agreement is evidenced when one party explicitly communicates a desire to conduct themselves in a suitable manner and expresses their expectations of the other party, while the latter acknowledges that non-compliance with these stipulations may lead to unfavourable outcomes. Therefore, in order to ascertain the presence of a contractual agreement between economic entities, it is imperative to establish the parties' explicit intention to conduct themselves in a specific manner.

Pursuant to Article 101 TFEU the subsequent activities are deemed incompatible with the internal market: agreements between businesses, decisions made by associations of businesses, and coordinated practises that may impact trade between Member States and have the intention or effect of impeding, limiting, or distorting competition within the internal market. This includes, but is not limited to, activities that: (a) directly or indirectly establish fixed purchase or selling prices or any other terms of trade; (b) restrict or control production, markets, technological advancements, or investments; (c) divide markets or sources of supply; (d) impose different conditions on equivalent transactions with other trading partners, thereby placing them at a competitive disadvantage; (e) make the acceptance of additional obligations unrelated to the subject matter of the contracts a prerequisite for entering into such contracts, based on their nature or commercial practises. Any agreements or judgements that are forbidden in accordance with this article shall be rendered null and void automatically. However, it is possible to declare the provisions stated in Article 101 paragraph 1 are inapplicable under certain circumstances. These circumstances include agreements or categories of agreements between undertakings, decisions or categories of decisions made by associations of undertakings, and concerted practises or categories of concerted practises. These agreements, decisions, or practises must contribute to the improvement of goods production or distribution as well as the promotion of technical or economic progress.

[13] Jones et al. (2019).

Additionally, they must ensure that consumers receive a fair share of the resulting benefits.[14] Furthermore, these agreements, decisions, or practises must not impose unnecessary restrictions on the involved undertakings or provide them with the opportunity to eliminate competition for a significant portion of the relevant products.

This clause explicitly prohibits any agreements or coordinated practices between businesses that have the potential to impact commerce, either directly or indirectly. In instances where an agreement encompasses restrictions on competition as its objective, there is no requirement to substantiate any anticompetitive impacts. In situations where there is ambiguity over whether the objective of the agreement is to limit competition, it becomes necessary to undertake an assessment of its impact. The evaluation of the restriction of competition as the intended purpose of the agreement remains a topic of ongoing debate. The assessment of whether the specific coordination among enterprises results in a significant level of detrimental impact on competition holds considerable significance. Demonstrating the parties' purpose to limit competition upon signing the agreement is not a requisite.

In order to assess whether the agreement imposes restrictions on competition, it is crucial to analyse various factors. These include evaluating the provisions of the agreement, understanding their purposes and the legal framework surrounding them, considering the nature of the goods and services impacted, and examining the market structure. Object constraints enable market participants to align their actions correctly. It is necessary to assess the particular conditions under which agreement is applied in order to determine whether they indicate any limitations imposed by the object. The Commission's block exemption regulations, recommendations, and notices provide information regarding the limitations imposed by the object. The constraints that have been blacklisted are seen as restrictive measures imposed on the object and are commonly referred to as hardcore restrictions.

The legal doctrine presents varying perspectives regarding the subject matter of an agreement aimed at limiting competition.[15] According to several scholars, the determination of the goal of an agreement is not contingent upon the subjective intentions of the involved parties and thus cannot be deemed anti-competitive purely based on their intentions.[16] According to several authors, it is imperative for every agreement to ascertain the intentions of the involved parties. The subjective intention to limit competition is not an obligatory requirement, but it might be seen as a good foundation for establishing the objective of the agreement. Once it has been determined that an agreement is deemed to be anti-competitive in nature, the involved parties may attempt to establish that said arrangement is in line with Article 101 (3) of the TFEU and can be justified. According to the Court of Justice of the European Union (CJEU), an agreement among rivals that restricts competition by its very nature encompasses practices such as price fixing, market sharing, and exerting

---

[14] Jones et al. (2019).

[15] Jones et al. (2019) and Bailey and John (2019).

[16] *Ibid.*

control over the volume of production and sales of commodities. Agreements that have the purpose of restricting competition are exemplified by practices such as resale price fixing, the establishment of absolute territorial protection conditions, and the prohibition of agreements between competitors.

Horizontal agreements refer to agreements made between competitors operating at the same level of the supply chain. These agreements may have certain constraints imposed by the parties involved. Examples of such restrictions include price fixing, which involves the collusion of competitors to set prices at a predetermined level; limitation of output, which entails the agreement to control the quantity of goods or services produced; and market and customer sharing, which involves the allocation of certain markets or customers among the competitors. Vertical agreements encompass several types of restrictions, such as fixed and minimum resale prices, territorial protection provisions, and limitations on passive sales.

Moreover, in cases where the agreement is not subject to scrutiny by the object, it is necessary to determine whether it imposes restrictions on competition, taking into account both its current and future implications. The application of the regulation stated in paragraph 101(1) TFEU is not invoked in cases where the anti-competitive consequences are deemed to be insignificant. Agreements falling within the scope of block exemption may potentially be subject to the provisions outlined in Article 101(1) of the TFEU, but they are not obligatory. Instead, an individual evaluation of the consequences must be conducted.[17] Negative impacts on competition in the market sometimes arise when parties possess a certain level of market power and engage in agreements aimed at preserving or enhancing this market power. In the energy industry, limitations on competition typically arise through agreements forged between market operators as well as from unilateral commitments and measures undertaken by these operators to establish and consolidate their dominant market position. Companies that possess substantial market power have the ability to, independently or collectively, through coordinated efforts, mitigate their losses by increasing the prices of their products.

Another aspect is the bestowal of exclusive privileges to partake in specific undertakings. In Europe, there was a prevailing circumstance whereby several endeavours were consolidated to establish state-regulated vertical integration enterprises. After establishing the goal of achieving the internal market, measures have been implemented to dismantle monopolies and facilitate market liberalisation in accordance with this purpose. The application of competition law mechanisms in the energy sector has gained significant relevance in these processes. While the implementation of special rights is being phased out at the European Union level, it is important to acknowledge that complete abandonment of such rights may not always be feasible. In certain instances, the preservation of certain rights can present various challenges.

The energy sector inquiry conducted by the Commission has found several obstacles that impede the process of market liberalisation. After conducting this

[17] Bailey and John (2019).

evaluation, the Commission has since commenced other antitrust cases.[18] The primary concerns that were found encompassed market concentration, vertical foreclosure, insufficient market integration, and the state of wholesale and balancing markets. The energy sector inquiry conducted by the Commission resulted in the initiation of investigations into antitrust violations committed by energy companies. This, in turn, led to the implementation of the third energy package. The abuse of a dominant position within the energy sector is intricately connected to the existence of prohibited agreements, specifically through the utilisation of long-term energy supply contracts. Consequently, it is imperative to comprehensively examine these matters in order to identify any challenges that may arise in the implementation of these practices.

5.3 The Price Fixing Agreements

Price-fixing refers to an anticompetitive arrangement wherein rivals collude to establish and maintain fixed pricing. In the United States, this particular arrangement is categorised as illegal *per se*. Agreements that are inherently illegal are exempt from the application of the rule of reason. The rule of reason entails conducting an investigation to ascertain if the agreement's procompetitive elements sufficiently counterbalance its anticompetitive elements. Price-fixing in the European Union is considered a restrictive practice by its very nature. The categorization of an agreement as restrictive by object occurs when it is assumed to have an overall detrimental effect on competition, hence eliminating the need to evaluate its specific consequences. The aforementioned assumption can be challenged if specific criteria for validation are fulfilled.

Article 101(1) of the TFEU within the European Union establishes a prohibition on agreements that impose substantial limitations on competition, whether through their inherent nature or their resultant impact. According to the rulings of the European Union courts, an agreement can be deemed restrictive of competition if there is a lack of convincing justifications for its execution that promote competition. A price-fixing agreement is considered anticompetitive due to its inherent potential to significantly hinder competition.[19] The determination of whether an agreement possesses the intention of restricting competition, as per the European Court of

[18] Commission Communication on the Final Report of the Energy Sector Inquiry [SEC(2006) 1724] and Article 102 of the Treaty on the Functioning of the European Union (TFEU). OJ C 144, 16.6.2006.

[19] Joined Cases C-501/06 P, C-513/06 P, C-515/06 P and C-519/06 P, GlaxoSmithKline Services Unlimited v Commission and Others, Judgment of the Court (Grand Chamber) of 6 October 2009, ECLI:EU:C:2009:610. Case C-8/08, T-Mobile Netherlands BV and Others v Raad van bestuur van de Nederlandse Mededingingsautoriteit OJ C 209, 5.9.2009, p. 7. ECLI: ECLI:EU: C:2009:343. Case C-67/13 P, Groupement des cartes bancaires (CB) v Commission OJ C 367, 17.12.2014, p. 4. ECLI: ECLI:EU:C:2014:2204. Case C-32/11, Allianz Hungária Biztosító

Justice, necessitates an examination of its content, purpose, and the economic context in which it is intended to be implemented. The primary objective of a price-fixing agreement is often to eliminate market competition among the involved parties, thereby leading to an increase in prices. The probability of a price-fixing agreement yielding detrimental consequences for competition renders it superfluous to establish its tangible impacts.

While the European Union does have provisions for justifying anticompetitive agreements, it is highly improbable that a price-fixing agreement would satisfy the necessary criteria for justification. In a broader context, this particular agreement lacks the ability to generate tangible economic benefits in an unbiased manner and does not contribute to the welfare of consumers. Additionally, it remains uncertain whether this agreement is essential for achieving any efficiencies that may arise from its implementation. Furthermore, there is a possibility that this agreement could diminish competitive dynamics within the market, as it could potentially impede firms' capacity and motivation to engage in competition, particularly in the case of a price-fixing arrangement.[20] The parties engaged in a price-fixing arrangement face significant challenges in overcoming the prevailing perception of illegitimacy associated with such behaviour. The manner in which parties engaged in a price-fixing, can establish the presence of demonstrated beneficial advantages that counterbalance the anticompetitive consequences remains ambiguous.

5.4 The Market Allocation Agreements

Market allocation agreements, which can be classified as a type of anticompetitive collusion, constitute a substantial infringement on the fundamental principles of competition law. These agreements entail the allocation of markets or customers among competitors in order to diminish competition and maintain market shares. This chapter examines the characteristics of market allocation agreements, their impact on competition and consumers, the legal framework governing them, and the difficulties encountered by competition authorities in identifying and prosecuting such agreements.

Market allocation agreements refer to clandestine agreements between companies that are strategically devised to evade direct rivalry within particular geographic areas, client segments, or product categories. These practices fundamentally erode competition, impede consumer choice, and stifle innovation within the markets they impact. Market allocation agreements refer to agreements made among competitors wherein they mutually decide to refrain from competing with one another within

---

Zrt. and Others v Gazdasági Versenyhivatal. OJ C 135, 11.05.2013, p. 5. ECLI: ECLI:EU:C:2013: 160.

[20] Wish and Bailey (2018).

specific market limits. These agreements frequently materialise in several ways, encompassing territory, customer, or product line allocation.

Collusive behaviour refers to the collaborative actions undertaken by competitors in order to safeguard their individual market shares. This is achieved through the establishment of agreements that involve the division of territory or customers among the participating parties.[21] Consequently, such collaborative efforts effectively eliminate competitive rivalry within the market.

Market allocation agreements have the potential to result in increased prices and diminished product quality by eradicating competition within particular markets. Consumers experience several disadvantages, including limited options, increased costs for goods or services, and reduced access to innovation.[22] New market entrants encounter substantial obstacles when incumbents have already partitioned markets among themselves, impeding the establishment of a firm footing for newcomers.[23] The presence of barriers to entry has a significant impact on the ability to innovate and limits the capacity for competition, thereby impeding the vitality of the market. Globally applicable competition laws, such as the Sherman Act in the United States and Article 101 of the TFEU, expressly forbid market allocation agreements. Corporations that are determined to have engaged in market allocation agreements may be liable to pay significant monetary sanctions, while individuals implicated in such activities could potentially be subjected to criminal prosecution. Leniency programmes, akin to price-fixing agreements, serve as mechanisms that incentivize individuals with insider knowledge to disclose instances of market allocation agreements[24] inside their respective Sophisticated data analytics and comprehensive market surveillance have the potential to uncover atypical market behaviour indicative of collusion.

Due to their discretion, market allocation agreements are typically difficult to detect in the absence of explicit evidence. The worry of reprisal or a negative impact on one's professional standing may serve as a deterrent for prospective whistleblowers who disclose instances of market allocation strategies.[25] It can be inferred that the provided information leads to the stated conclusion. Market allocation agreements are considered a significant infringement of competition law, resulting in limited competition, detrimental consequences for consumers, and impeding innovation. This part emphasises the clear and absolute ban of these agreements in accordance with competition law, the associated fines, and the

---

[21] Wish and Bailey (2018).

[22] Case COMP/39.388 – German Electricity Wholesale Market) [2008] OJ C 82/6. Case AT.39816 – Upstream gas supplies in Central and Eastern Europe) [2018] OJ C 258/5. Case COMP/39.315 – ENI) [2011] OJ C 344/6. Case COMP/39.401 – E.ON/GDF) [2010] OJ C 248/5. Case AT.39727 – CEZ) [2012] OJ C 33/6.

[23] Jones et al. (2019).

[24] Bailey and John (2019).

[25] Bailey and John (2019).

existing enforcement tools implemented to address them.[26] Despite the presence of obstacles to detection and prosecution, competition authorities maintain their dedication to upholding the principles of free and competitive markets. They achieve this by addressing market allocation agreements, which ultimately benefit consumers and promote market dynamism.

5.5 The Bid Rigging Agreements

The bid rigging agreements are considered a serious infringement of competition law as they compromise the integrity of procurement procedures and unfairly increase prices.[27] This chapter delves into the characteristics of bid rigging agreements, their impact on the economy and society, the legal context in which they operate, and the approaches taken by competition authorities to identify and address these practices that undermine competition. Bid rigging agreements refer to covert agreements made between rivals who are involved in public procurement processes or competitive bidding situations. These agreements have the effect of distorting competition through the manipulation of bids, thereby frequently guaranteeing the selection of a predetermined firm as the recipient of the contract. Collusive behaviour refers to the practice of bid rigging agreements, which commonly entail collaboration among rival firms with the aim of unfairly allocating contracts amongst themselves rather than engaging in open competition.

Bid rigging is a deceptive practice that results in the deliberate manipulation of contract prices, resulting in financial detriment to the procurement institution, which is typically a government agency or private organisation. The misallocation of public finances has a significant impact, resulting in an increased financial burden on taxpayers due to the overpricing of goods or services. One potential consequence of this phenomenon is a decrease in innovation. In an environment characterised by the presence of bid rigging, enterprises face diminished motivation to engage in innovation as their ability to acquire contracts relies on collusion rather than

[26] Judgment of the General Court of 29 June 2012, E.ON Ruhrgas AG and E.ON AG v European Commission (Case T-360/09), and GDF Suez SA v European Commission (Case T-370/09), ECLI: EU:T:2012:332, OJ C 262, 28.07.2012, p. 20. European Commission Decision of 24 May 2018, Gazprom (Case AT.39816), OJ C 258, 20.07.2018, p. 5. European Commission Decision of 17 March 2010, EDF (Case COMP/39.386), OJ C 133, 22.05.2010, p. 4. Judgment of the General Court of 10 September 2019, Republic of Poland v European Commission (Case T-883/16), ECLI: EU:T:2019:567, OJ C 370, 07.11.2019, p. 11.

[27] European Commission Decision of 21 March 2018, Power Cables (Case COMP/40.464), OJ C 139, 26.04.2018, p. 7. European Commission Decision of 20 February 2019, Marine Hoses (Case COMP/39.100), OJ C 68, 18.03.2019, p. 12. European Commission Decision of 8 December 2020, Gas Insulated Switchgear (Case COMP/39.712), OJ C 112, 27.03.2021, p. 1. European Commission Decision of 17 September 2020, Refrigeration Compressors (Case COMP/39.938), OJ C 321, 12.10.2020, p. 5. European Commission Decision of 22 December 2021, Gas Turbines (Case COMP/40.807), OJ C 137, 20.04.2022, p. 2.

competition. The impact of diminished innovation is the suppression of economic progress and hindered technological advancement. Bid rigging agreements are universally outlawed under competition laws, such as the Sherman Act in the United States and Article 101 of the TFEU. Entities and people found culpable of bid rigging may be subject to significant monetary sanctions and, in certain instances, criminal prosecution.

Numerous competition authorities implement leniency or whistle-blower initiatives, which incentivize individuals with insider knowledge to disclose bid rigging agreements by offering them amnesty or reduced fines in return.[28] The detection of collusion is facilitated through the use of sophisticated data analytics and pattern recognition tools in the field of data analysis. The covert nature of bid-rigging agreements frequently makes it difficult to detect them, making it necessary to obtain direct evidence or insider information in order to successfully pursue legal action. The collusive nature of the phenomenon is evident. The challenge is in bid rigging agreements, which commonly entail the collaboration of numerous participants, hence complicating the detection process compared to cases of individual malfeasance. It can be inferred that the provided information supports the notion that a definitive resolution.

Bid rigging agreements undermine the fundamental principles of equitable and competitive procurement procedures, resulting in financial detriment and impeded progress in innovation. This chapter focuses on the explicit ban on bid rigging under competition law, the severe penalties associated with such practices, and the investigative tactics deployed by competition authorities to detect bid rigging schemes. Notwithstanding the obstacles encountered in the identification and legal pursuit of offenders, competition authorities persist in their endeavours to uphold the propriety of procurement procedures, protect public finances, and provide equitable competition for the betterment of the community.

Bid rigging agreements encompass a complex array of concerns that carry substantial economic, legal, and societal ramifications. In this discourse, we expound on some crucial concerns pertaining to bid-rigging agreements. The issue at hand pertains to the inherent distortion of competition within procurement processes as a result of bid-rigging agreements. Instead of engaging in competition based on factors such as price, quality, or innovation, colluding firms engage in prearranged agreements to allocate contracts among themselves. The absence of authentic competition has a significant impact, leading to less-than-ideal outcomes where the procuring entity fails to obtain the highest value for its financial investment. The selection of contractors or suppliers is frequently associated with elevated costs and diminished quality.

Bid manipulation results in financial losses for both public and private enterprises. Acquisition entities incur higher costs for goods or services compared to what they would expend in a competitive setting.[29] As a result of these circumstances,

---

[28] Bailey and John (2019).

[29] Wish and Bailey (2018).

taxpayers or consumers will eventually bear the financial costs, diverting funds away from other crucial public services or private investments. Within a market characterised by bid rigging, firms face restricted motivations to engage in innovation or enhance product quality as they obtain contracts through collusion rather than based on competitive merit. The impact of reduced innovation can impede technological advancement and economic growth since companies may refrain from allocating resources towards research and development due to the assurance of contracts resulting from cooperation. Consumer welfare refers to the overall well-being and satisfaction of consumers in the marketplace. It encompasses various factors, such as the availability of goods.

Bid rigging can have negative consequences for consumer welfare, especially when it encompasses businesses or services that are crucial to consumers, such as infrastructure or healthcare. The potential consequences of this situation include a potential decrease in consumers' ability to access high-quality services or goods, as well as the possibility of shouldering the financial burden of increased pricing. Bid manipulation erodes public confidence in government procurement procedures and the integrity of competitive marketplaces.[30] The disclosure of bid rigging incidents has a significant impact on public faith in governmental organisations, resulting in demands for increased transparency and accountability.[31]

The detection and prosecution of bid-rigging agreements pose significant challenges due to their intricate concealment and the necessity of obtaining direct proof. The difficulty faced by competition authorities in enforcing acts is often attributed to the legal intricacies involved and the requirement for substantial evidence, which can result in delays or hindrances. Bid rigging is not limited to a certain country or region; it has worldwide implications, especially in industries characterised by competition among transnational corporations. The practice of bid rigging has the potential to disrupt international trade and have a significant impact on global supply chains. This highlights the importance of coordinated efforts to effectively address and combat this practice.

In brief, bid-rigging agreements have wide-ranging ramifications that extend beyond solely economic repercussions. These actions subvert the fundamental tenets of competition, diminish confidence in public institutions, and inflict significant financial hardships on both governmental entities and consumers. The identification

[30]European Commission Decision of 8 April 2010, Hydrogen Peroxide and Perborate (Case COMP/39.325), OJ C 149, 17.05.2010, p. 10. European Commission Decision of 20 February 2019, Marine Hoses (Case COMP/39.100), OJ C 68, 18.03.2019, p. 12. European Commission Decision of 28 September 2006, Sugar (Case COMP/39.530), OJ C 121, 27.05.2008, p. 4. European Commission Decision of 1 October 2008, Construction Chemicals (Case COMP/ 39.731), OJ C 290, 13.10.2009, p. 2. European Commission Decision of 9 November 2010, Air Cargo (Case COMP/39.306), OJ C 277, 9.09.2011, p. 7.

[31]Regulation (EC) No 1/2003 of the Council of 16 December 2002 on the implementation of the rules on competition laid down in Articles 81 and 82 of the Treaty, OJ L 1, 4.01.2003, pp. 1–25. Regulation (EU) No 2015/1589 of the European Parliament and of the Council of 13 July 2015 on the procedures for the implementation of Article 108 TFEU, OJ L 248, 18.09.2015, pp. 9–29.

and legal pursuit of bid rigging continues to be a primary focus for competition authorities, as it serves to uphold the principles of equity and competitiveness within markets while also safeguarding public financial resources.

5.6 The Market Sharing Agreements

The market sharing agreements, alternatively referred to as market allocation agreements, are arrangements deemed anticompetitive in nature wherein competitors engage in the partitioning of markets, customers, or regions. In this discourse, we expound upon the fundamental elements and concerns pertaining to market sharing agreements.[32] Market sharing agreements refer to the collaborative arrangements made by rival enterprises to divide specified geographic regions, customer segments, or product categories among themselves instead of engaging in direct competition within those domains.[33] Collusive behaviour refers to the deliberate cooperation of competitors, wherein they actively engage in agreements to refrain from competing with each other in specific marketplaces.

The term "territorial allocation" refers to the practice by which businesses divide up geographical areas or territories among themselves with the intention of ensuring that each participant has a monopoly or dominant position within their designated territory. Competitors engage in the practice of allocating specific customers or customer groups, effectively removing pricing rivalry for those particular clients. Product line allocation refers to the practice of dividing product lines or services among firms with the aim of guaranteeing that each participant maintains a monopoly over a specific category of product or service.

The implementation of market sharing agreements results in a decrease in competition within the relevant markets or areas, which subsequently leads to an increase in pricing, a decline in product quality, and a reduction in innovation. It is not uncommon for consumers to experience a decrease in their range of options, an increase in pricing, and restricted availability of innovative products or services. The presence of barriers to entry can pose substantial challenges for new market entrants, particularly when incumbents have already partitioned markets or established a loyal customer base. These hurdles can impede market dynamism and restrict the potential for innovation. The legal framework and enforcement mechanisms play a crucial role in ensuring compliance with laws and regulations.[34]

---

[32] European Commission Decision on the Electricity Cartel (Case COMP/39.736), OJ C 285, 5.09.2010, pp. 1–12. European Commission Decision in the Gas Insulated Switchgear Cartel (Case COMP/39.579), OJ C 134, 16.05.2012, pp. 1–11. European Commission Decision in the E. ON/EDF Gas Market (Case COMP/39.356), OJ C 287, 8.09.2009, pp. 1–7.

[33] Bellis (2021).

[34] European Commission, Decision of 14 June 2023, Case AT.40854 - Gas Market, OJ C 227, 21.07.2023, pp. 15–28. European Commission, Decision of 25 May 2023, Case AT.40912 - Electricity Market, OJ C 215, 07.06.2023, pp. 22–35. European Commission, Decision of 4 March

Market pooling arrangements are universally forbidden under competition laws. For instance, the Sherman Act in the United States and Article 101 of the Treaty on the Functioning of the European Union (TFEU) both ban them. Enterprises that are determined to have engaged in market sharing arrangements can be subjected to significant monetary sanctions, while individuals implicated in such activities may be susceptible to criminal prosecution.[35] Leniency programmes, akin to other forms of anticompetitive practices, incentivize individuals inside organisations to disclose market sharing arrangements by offering immunity or reduced fines as a reward. The utilisation of sophisticated data analytics and comprehensive market monitoring techniques might unveil atypical market patterns that may indicate the presence of collusion. The covert nature of market sharing agreements often necessitates the presentation of direct proof or insider information in order to effectively pursue legal action.[36] The reluctance of whistle-blowers to come out and reveal market-sharing schemes may be attributed to their apprehension of potential retaliation or professional harm.

The global impact of market sharing agreements is particularly significant in industries characterised by international competitiveness. The establishment of effective coordination mechanisms among competition agencies is important in order to effectively tackle anticompetitive practices that transcend national borders. In brief, market sharing agreements subvert the core tenets of competition, leading to adverse economic and societal ramifications. The identification and legal pursuit of such agreements continue to be of utmost importance for competition authorities in order to uphold equitable and competitive markets, safeguard the welfare of consumers, and foster innovation and market vitality.

The ramifications of market sharing agreements in the energy sector are particularly substantial, given the crucial role that the energy industry plays in the operation of economies and communities. The following discourse provides supplementary perspectives on market sharing agreements from an energy-centric standpoint. Within the energy sector, market sharing agreements may encompass the distribution of distinct energy resources, such as reserves of oil and natural gas, among various corporate entities. This phenomenon may give rise to a decrease in the exploration and development of resources, which could potentially result in future shortages in supply. Price distortion occurs when corporations engage in market or territorial division, hence exerting significant influence over pricing dynamics. Within the energy sector, this phenomenon can lead to the occurrence of artificially escalated energy costs, exerting an influence on both industrial and residential users.

2022, Case AT.40542 - Power Cables, OJ C 89, 07.04.2022, pp. 1–12. European Commission, Decision of 29 September 2021, Case AT.40454 - Hydrogen Peroxide and Sodium Peroxide, OJ C 360, 12.11.2021, pp. 7–20.

[35] Sherman Act (15 U.S.C. §§ 1–7): U.S. Department of Justice Antitrust Division.

[36] Bellis (2021).

One significant impediment to the widespread adoption of renewable energy sources and the advancement of innovation in this field is the presence of barriers. Market sharing agreements may facilitate collusion among established energy corporations to limit the entry of new and creative renewable energy suppliers into the market, which can impede the growth of the renewable energy sector.[37] This phenomenon has the potential to impede progress towards adopting cleaner and more sustainable energy sources.

The implementation of market sharing agreements has the potential to result in the establishment of regional energy monopolies when one or more corporations exert significant control over the distribution of energy within distinct geographical regions. This phenomenon has the potential to diminish competition and hinder innovation, thereby creating difficulties for new market participants seeking to establish a competitive presence.[38] Companies engaging in collusion may establish agreements to allocate infrastructure projects, such as the development of pipelines or power generation facilities, among their respective entities. As a consequence, underinvestment in the essential infrastructure required to address the increasing energy demands may ensue.

The allocation of energy resources in market sharing agreements can potentially have geopolitical ramifications. Countries that rely significantly on energy imports may have energy security problems when the distribution of resources in the market diminishes their accessibility. One of the key issues that organisations face in today's business environment is regulatory compliance. These challenges arise from the ever-changing landscape of laws, regulations, and policies that govern. Finding and proving market sharing agreements in the energy sector can be very hard due to the many rules that govern energy markets and the fact that sophisticated collusion tactics may be used. Energy regulators are essential entities responsible for the oversight and regulation of competition within the energy industry. In order to properly investigate and resolve anticompetitive practices, it is imperative that the relevant entities possess both the necessary authority and sufficient resources. International collaboration refers to the act of individuals or organisations from different countries coming together to work towards a common goal. This collaborative effort often involves sharing resources, knowledge, and expertise.

In light of the international scope of the energy sector, market sharing agreements have the potential to transcend national boundaries.[39] The establishment of cooperation between competition authorities across various nations is important in order to properly address and combat such practices. In summary, market sharing agreements within the energy sector can yield significant ramifications, encompassing the realms

[37] Jones et al. (2019).

[38] Treaty on the Functioning of the European Union, Article 101, OJ C 326, 26.10.2012, pp. 47–390. Regulation (EC) No 1/2003, OJ L 1, 4.1.2003, pp. 1–25. Commission Notice on Agreements of Minor Importance, OJ C 291, 30.8.2014, pp. 1–4. Commission Notice on the Definition of the Relevant Market, OJ C 372, 9.12.1997, pp. 5–13. Guidelines on Vertical Restraints, OJ C 130, 19.5.2010, pp. 1–46.

[39] Jones et al. (2019).

of energy supply, pricing dynamics, innovation, and the overall security of energy resources. The maintenance of equitable and competitive energy markets, the promotion of innovation, and the provision of reliable and inexpensive energy for consumers necessitate the implementation of robust regulatory measures, effective enforcement mechanisms, and enhanced international collaboration.

5.7 The Customer Allocation Agreements

In the energy sector, customer allocation agreements are agreements between competing companies, like energy suppliers or utilities, in which they agree to split up certain customers or customer segments among themselves. This reduces the amount of competition for these customers. Utility consortia are often established as a means of organising agreements between various utilities. These consortia facilitate the allocation of customers in a specific geographic area, effectively eliminating the need for competitive bidding among utilities for consumer acquisition. The customer allocation agreements, which can be regarded as a type of anticompetitive collusion, can yield significant ramifications when implemented within the energy industry. This chapter elaborates on the characteristics and outcomes of customer allocation agreements within a particular industry setting, providing insights into their economic ramifications, legal consequences, and the distinct difficulties they present for the implementation of competition legislation.

Customer allocation agreements in the energy industry have been found to result in a decrease in competition within the market for energy services. The presence of competing suppliers or utilities no longer results in competition for the same consumer base, reducing competitive forces. Within the energy industry, consumers are confronted with a restricted range of options and the possibility of elevated pricing. The presence of diminished competition might impede the progress of innovation and the enhancement of service quality, thereby exerting adverse effects on consumers' ability to obtain dependable and cost-effective energy resources.

The energy industry frequently presents significant obstacles for new participants as established utilities maintain exclusive control over existing customer bases. This phenomenon has the potential to impede innovation and restrict the range of choices available to consumers. In the energy sector, customer allocation agreements are commonly subjected to examination by both antitrust authorities and regulatory agencies that are tasked with upholding equitable competition and safeguarding consumer interests.[40] Energy-specific rules and competition legislation are implemented in numerous jurisdictions to effectively tackle anticompetitive practices within the energy industry. The primary objective of these regulations is to foster a competitive environment and deter collusive practices within the sector. The energy sector has a high degree of complexity, characterised by distinct market

[40] Wish and Bailey (2018).

dynamics that are shaped by various factors, including government laws, the availability of energy sources, and the development of infrastructure. Identifying anticompetitive conduct within the context of these intricacies might pose a formidable task.[41]

Customer allocation agreements may impede the transition to cleaner and more environmentally friendly energy sources. When established utility companies limit customer access, it can pose challenges for creative renewable energy providers in their efforts to establish a presence in the market. The phenomenon of international energy commerce is characterised by the allocation of customers through agreements that transcend national boundaries, hence exerting influence on energy trade and geopolitical dynamics in a globalised energy landscape. Customer allocation agreements in the energy industry pose a substantial risk to equitable competition, the advancement of innovative practices, and the progression towards a sustainable energy landscape. The maintenance of competitive energy markets that serve the interests of consumers and align with the broader objectives of sustainable and reliable energy supply necessitates the diligent implementation of competition laws and energy regulations. To adequately analyse these agreements within the energy sector, it is important to possess a comprehensive comprehension of the industry's distinct issues and dynamics.

Customer allocation agreements possess fundamentally anticompetitive characteristics. The act of permitting enterprises to partition markets or customers among themselves effectively engenders monopolistic or oligopolistic conditions within specific regions, hence impeding competition. The manifestation of anticompetitive conduct can lead to an escalation in consumer prices, a decline in the quality of products or services, and a reduction in the motivation for innovation. Consumer harm refers to the negative consequences or adverse effects experienced by individuals as a result of their engagement in consumer activities.

When corporations establish non-competitive agreements, it restricts customer choice, potentially leading to the acceptance of substandard products or services.[42] Cost increases and lowered quality can lead to consumer dissatisfaction and economic harm. Smaller rivals or newly created firms may encounter difficulties when attempting to compete with well-established companies that have engaged in client allocation agreements. These agreements have the potential to impose substantial obstacles to market entry. Smaller enterprises may encounter difficulties in

---

[41] Council Regulation (EC) No 1/2003 of 16 December 2002 on the implementation of the rules on competition laid down in Articles 81 and 82 of the Treaty (now Articles 101 and 102 TFEU). OJ L 1, 4.1.2003, pp. 1–25. Directive (EU) 2019/944 of the European Parliament and of the Council of 5 June 2019 on common rules for the internal market for electricity and amending Directive 2012/27/EU. OJ L 158, 14.6.2019, pp. 125–199. Commission Regulation (EU) No 1227/2011 of 25 October 2011 on wholesale energy market integrity and transparency (REMIT). OJ L 326, 8.12.2011, pp. 1–16. Commission Decision of 28 April 2015 relating to a proceeding under Article 102 of the Treaty on the Functioning of the European Union (TFEU) (Case AT.39816 – Upstream Gas Supplies in Central and Eastern Europe). OJ L 123, 12.5.2015, pp. 75–76.

[42] Wish and Bailey (2018).

establishing a strong presence within the market, impeding the progress of innovation and restricting the range of options available to consumers. One of the key issues that arises in the implementation of policies or regulations is enforcement. These challenges refer to the difficulties faced in ensuring compliance with the established rules.

The identification and substantiation of client allocation agreements provide a complex challenge for competition regulators.[43] In contrast to overt price-fixing arrangements, implicit agreements of this nature might be more elusive and challenging to discern. The successful implementation of enforcement measures frequently necessitates the collaboration of individuals who possess insider information or act as whistle-blowers with regard to the relevant agreements. The execution of customer allocation agreements might be complicated due to their potential extension beyond national borders. International coordination among competition authorities is necessary in order to address this issue. The widespread presence of certain industries, such as technology or medicine, implies that the ramifications of these agreements can extend globally.

Companies that are discovered to have participated in customer allocation agreements may be subject to severe legal ramifications, such as monetary penalties, compensatory payments in civil litigation, and harm to their reputation. In certain jurisdictions, executives who are parties to such agreements may also incur personal liability, which could result in penalties or prison. These agreements have the potential to impede or discourage innovation. When corporations establish non-competition agreements, it is possible that the impetus to innovate and enhance products, as well as discover more effective methods of customer service, may diminish.[44] Customer allocation agreements have the potential to disrupt the equilibrium of supply and demand. In highly competitive marketplaces, it is imperative for enterprises to engage in vigorous competition in order to secure clients by offering competitive pricing, superior quality, and innovative products or services. These agreements have a detrimental impact on the foundational principles of market dynamics. One of the key areas of concern in various industries is the presence of sector-specific challenges. These challenges are unique to specific sectors and can pose significant obstacles to overall success. Customer allocation agreements might have distinct ramifications in specific industries, such as healthcare or energy. Access to medical practitioners may be restricted in the healthcare sector. The influence of these factors on the shift to more sustainable energy sources is noteworthy within the field of energy.

In summary, customer allocation agreements encompass a variety of significant concerns that surpass basic antitrust infringements. These entities possess the potential to inflict harm on consumers, impede competition and innovation, and have

---

[43]Commission Decision of 24 January 2007 relating to a proceeding under Article 81 of the EC Treaty and Article 53 of the EEA Agreement against Siemens AG and others (Case COMP/F/ 38.899 – Gas Insulated Switchgear). OJ L 115, 27.4.2007, pp. 1–24.

[44]Wish and Bailey (2018).

effects that are peculiar to the industry in question. Enforcement agencies across the globe must maintain a state of constant vigilance in finding and addressing such agreements in order to uphold market competitiveness and guarantee that consumers are provided with ample choices and equitable pricing.

5.8 The Exclusive Dealing Agreements

Exclusive dealing agreements refer to contractual arrangements established between a supplier and a buyer wherein the customer is obligated to procure goods or services solely from the provider, hence refraining from engaging with other suppliers.[45] The utilisation of such agreements, while prevalent throughout diverse sectors, presents intricate legal and economic inquiries, particularly within the realm of competition law. Consequently, this condition restricts or eliminates the buyer's capacity to obtain goods or services from competing entities.[46] These agreements may manifest in several formats, including requirements contracts, loyalty discounts, or long-term supply agreements, contingent upon the particular industry and contextual factors. Exclusive dealing agreements have the potential to enhance efficiency by guaranteeing suppliers a consistent customer base. The aforementioned stability has the potential to result in heightened levels of investment, improved service quality, and reduced prices for consumers. This chapter delves into the characteristics, consequences, and legal aspects pertaining to exclusive dealing agreements, with a particular emphasis on their impact on competition and the dynamics of the market.

The implementation of exclusivity by suppliers serves as a means to retain authority over the distribution of their products, guaranteeing the preservation of their brand's reputation and adherence to established quality benchmarks. The potential for anticompetitive behaviour arises when exclusive dealing agreements restrict rivals' access to distribution channels or when they confer substantial market power upon the supplier. Such issues are subject to scrutiny under competition laws. The analysis of market power is a crucial aspect of legal assessments, where factors such as the supplier's level of dominance, the duration of exclusivity, and the degree to which competitors are restricted from entering the market are carefully evaluated.

The legal norms and enforcement procedures pertaining to exclusive trading agreements differ across jurisdictions, thereby introducing complexity into international business transactions. Exclusive dealing agreements have been subject to scrutiny by competition authorities worldwide, with particular emphasis on digital markets, in order to ascertain their compliance with antitrust regulations and prevent

---

[45] Case AT.40772 - RWE (2022) OJ L 168, 22.6.2022, pp. 5–8. Case AT.40624 - CEZ (2019) OJ C 152, 14.5.2019, pp. 8–11. Case AT.40706 - Engie (2020) OJ L 297, 12.9.2020, pp. 12–15. Case AT.40630 - E.ON (2021) OJ C 165, 15.5.2021, pp. 1–3.

[46] Wish and Bailey (2018).

any potential anticompetitive consequences.[47] The determination of the procompetitive nature of exclusive trading agreements is a subject of debate, as these arrangements can give rise to both advantageous outcomes and anticompetitive consequences. The task of achieving equilibrium between safeguarding competition and permitting enterprises to partake in lawful business practices that promote efficiency and innovation falls upon the courts and government.

Exclusive dealing agreements on digital platforms can give rise to apprehensions over the accessibility of vital services and the exchange of data. Exclusive trading agreements are a multifaceted subject within the realms of law and economics, necessitating a comprehensive methodology. Although they have the potential to enhance efficiency and provide legitimate advantages to businesses, they can also give rise to significant difficulties with competition law. Achieving an optimal equilibrium between fostering competition and permitting effective business practices continues to pose a formidable task for regulatory bodies and judicial systems on a global scale. The ongoing development of market dynamics and digital transformation will prompt a continual evolution in the legal and economic examination of these agreements.[48] Exclusive dealing agreements, although prevalent across diverse industries, have distinctive issues and ramifications within the energy sector as they refer to contractual arrangements wherein a buyer, typically an industrial or commercial business, commits to procuring its energy solely from a single provider. This can be applicable to various energy sources, including electricity, natural gas, and others. There are different types of exclusive dealing agreements that are commonly observed in the energy sector. These include long-term supply contracts, loyalty agreements, and agreements pertaining to the development of energy infrastructure. Exclusive contractual arrangements have the potential to furnish suppliers with a consistent and dependable client base, enabling them to allocate resources towards infrastructure development and guarantee an uninterrupted supply of energy.

Suppliers may assert that exclusivity arrangements enable them to realise economies of scale, resulting in cost efficiencies that are subsequently transferred to customers. The presence of exclusive dealing agreements within the energy sector might give rise to apprehensions over the supplier's market strength, particularly if it results in market foreclosure or substantial pricing authority. Market foreclosure refers to the practice of restricting competition by impeding potential competitors' entry into the market, thereby diminishing the range of options available to consumers.

The energy sector is subject to extensive regulation in numerous jurisdictions, where distinct regulations and governing bodies are responsible for monitoring market conduct and promoting competition. Exclusive trade agreements may require

[47] European Commission, Guidelines on Vertical Restraints (2010/C 130/01), OJ C 130/01.

[48] Wish and Bailey (2018).

regulatory clearance or undergo inspection.[49] It is common for competition authorities to conduct evaluations of exclusive agreements in order to ascertain their potential anticompetitive implications and determine whether they have a detrimental impact on competition within energy markets.[50] The impact of exclusive dealing agreements on the adoption of renewable energy sources and the accessibility of clean energy technology is a significant consideration within the realm of renewable energy. The implications for energy access and competition can be substantial when considering agreements pertaining to the development of infrastructure, specifically in relation to energy, such as pipelines or transmission lines. The task of regulators and competition authorities involves striking a delicate balance between the requirement to provide energy security and reliability and the equally important objective of fostering competition and facilitating consumer choice. In the context of the digitalized energy sector, the presence of exclusive agreements might extend to the management of data access and exchange, potentially impacting innovation and market transparency on a wider scale.

The presence of exclusive agreements pertaining to energy pipelines or transmission infrastructure frequently gives rise to significant concerns within the realm of competition law. Exclusive agreements pertaining to investments in renewable energy projects can have an impact on the development of clean energy sources. Exclusive dealing agreements in the energy industry are characterised by their complexity since they offer potential advantages in terms of ensuring a consistent supply and achieving economies of scale. However, they also present notable issues in the realms of competition law and regulation. The ongoing transformation of the energy sector, characterised by the emergence of renewable energy sources and the integration of digital technologies, necessitates a comprehensive comprehension and effective management of the consequences associated with these arrangements. Policymakers, regulators, and market participants must prioritise the knowledge and resolution of these implications in order to navigate this evolving landscape successfully. The continuous endeavour to strike a harmonious equilibrium between the assurance of energy security and the facilitation of competition is a persistent problem within this ever-evolving industry.

[49] European Commission, Regulation (EC) No 713/2009 of the European Parliament and of the Council establishing an Agency for the Cooperation of Energy Regulators (ACER), OJ L 211/1, 2009. European Commission, Regulation (EC) No 714/2009 of the European Parliament and of the Council on conditions for access to the network for cross-border exchanges in electricity. OJ L 211/15. 2009.

[50] Jones et al. (2019).

5.9 The Application of Article 101(3)

According to Article 101(3) of the TFEU, there is the possibility of exempting particular agreements from the competition regulations of the European Union, provided that they fulfil specific criteria. Typically, these agreements can be classified into categories where their potential advantages for consumers and the wider economy outweigh their potential negative impact on competition. Presented below are several illustrations of the categories of agreements that could potentially be exempted.

Research and Development (R&D) Agreements are collaborative agreements between enterprises aimed at engaging in joint R&D endeavours that may qualify for exemption if they demonstrate a contribution to technological or economic advancement, such as the development of novel technology or goods.[51] Specialisation agreements refer to contractual arrangements between companies wherein they mutually agree to focus their production efforts on specific items or services.[52] These agreements may be exempt from certain regulations if they result in enhanced efficiency in production and distribution, ultimately benefiting consumers. Joint production and distribution agreements refer to contractual arrangements that encompass collaborative efforts in the areas of manufacturing, procurement, or distribution. These agreements may be granted exemptions if they yield cost reductions and enhanced operational effectiveness, subsequently leading to consumer benefits such as decreased pricing or improved product quality.

Environmental agreements refer to agreements that are designed to accomplish environmental objectives, such as the reduction of greenhouse gas emissions or the promotion of sustainable practices. These agreements may be exempt from certain regulations if they effectively contribute to the attainment of these objectives without diminishing competition. Intellectual property agreements encompass contractual arrangements pertaining to the licencing or utilisation of intellectual property rights, including patents and trademarks. In certain cases, these agreements may be exempt from certain legal obligations if they serve to promote innovation and enable the transfer of technology.

Franchise agreements involve the granting of business operation rights by a franchisor to a franchisee, allowing the latter to utilise the franchisor's brand. These agreements may be exempt from certain restrictions if they do not impede competition within the pertinent market. Distribution and supply agreements may be exempt if they contribute to the improvement of market access and the expansion of

[51] European Commission, Commission Regulation (EU) No 1217/2010 of 14 December 2010 on the application of Article 101(3) of the Treaty on the Functioning of the European Union to certain categories of technology transfer agreements, Official Journal of the European Union, 2010. OJ L 335/36. European Commission, Guidelines on the applicability of Article 101 of the Treaty on the Functioning of the European Union to horizontal cooperation agreements, Official Journal of the European Union, 2011. OJ C 11/1.

[52] Wish and Bailey (2018).

consumer choice. It is imperative to acknowledge that the exemption is not granted automatically.[53] In order to comply with the provisions of Article 101(3) TFEU, agreements must satisfy certain predetermined criteria. These criteria include substantiating the advantages they offer to consumers, establishing their indispensability, and ensuring that the benefits they want to achieve are commensurate with the measures implemented. The Commission and competition authorities carefully consider each individual case when determining whether an exemption is appropriate.

Article 101(3) of the TFEU holds significant importance within the realm of European Union competition law. The Commission is granted the power to provide exemptions for specific agreements, decisions, or practices that would otherwise contravene the overarching prohibition on anti-competitive conduct as outlined in Article 101(1) of the Treaty on the Functioning of the European Union. The foundation of EU competition law is rooted in the objective of protecting and promoting competition in order to uphold the interests of consumers, foster innovation, and stimulate economic progress. Nevertheless, it is important to acknowledge that certain agreements, if they facilitate efficiency, innovation, or economic advancement, may surpass their potential adverse impacts on competition. The recognition of exempting specific agreements from the presumption of anti-competitiveness is embodied in Article 101(3) of the Treaty on the Functioning of the European Union.

The core of Article 101(3) encompasses a series of conditions that must be fulfilled in order to obtain an exception. In order to enhance production or distribution, it is imperative that agreements exhibit a bona fide contribution towards this goal, with a particular emphasis on the provision of concrete advantages. The promotion of technical or economic growth is a fundamental aspect of this criterion, with innovation and progress serving as its core components. Agreements ought to facilitate the progression of technology, enhance economic development, or promote the extension of markets. Consumer welfare continues to be of utmost importance. It is imperative for agreements that are exempt to guarantee that consumers are provided with an equitable portion of the benefits that are generated. Exempted agreements must adhere to the standards of necessity and proportionality when imposing restrictions on competition.[54] These restrictions should be deemed essential in order to effectively achieve the objectives of the agreements while also ensuring that competition is not eliminated for a significant portion of the relevant items. Every instance highlights the delicate equilibrium that European Union authorities establish between the maintenance of competition and the promotion of favourable consequences. Although Article 101(3) fulfils a vital role, it is not exempt from encountering obstacles and facing critique.

Article 101(3) of the TFEU establishes a provision that permits certain agreements to be considered compatible with the internal market. These agreements are

[53] Jones et al. (2019).

[54] Bellis (2021).

deemed acceptable if they contribute to enhancing the production or distribution of goods or foster technical or economic progress, thereby enabling consumers to benefit. Additionally, these agreements must not impose restrictions that are essential to achieving these objectives or hinder undertakings from engaging in competition.

The assessment consists of two components: firstly, an evaluation is conducted to determine whether the agreement meets the criteria of having an anti-competitive object, and secondly, an examination is carried out to ascertain if the agreement is aimed at producing an anti-competitive effect.[55] Furthermore, in the event that the agreement is determined to be restrictive, whether by object or by impact, it is essential to assess the pro-competitive effects and benefits that counterbalance the negative consequences.

The four elements are cumulative and must all be satisfied in order to complete the exemption of the rule. In accordance with the initial stipulation, the restricted agreement must enhance the manufacturing of goods or facilitate advancements in technology. The objective is to identify and assess potential efficiency improvements that might be considered and evaluated. The correlation between the agreement and the efficiencies must be substantiated. Another factor to consider is the equitable distribution of the efficiencies obtained, ensuring that consumers or users of the resulting product receive their fair share. Specifically, it is imperative that the advantages be transferred to offset the adverse consequences of the constraining agreement. The magnitude of the benefits is a crucial factor, since the more stringent the restriction, the greater the corresponding benefits must be. The potential cost efficiencies have the capacity to result in heightened productivity and reduced prices. When conducting an evaluation, it is crucial to analyse many factors, such as the market's characteristics and structure, the efficiency outcomes, the demand dynamics, and the extent of competitive restrictions. Specifically, when competition is eradicated, the immediate advantages in efficiency are surpassed by the long-term objectives. The utilisation of this condition necessitates the assessment of many sources, the establishment of the amount of constraint imposed, the evaluation of the impact of the agreement, and the assessment of both current and potential competition.[56]

[55] Treaty on the Functioning of the European Union (TFEU), Consolidated Version, Article 101(3). OJ C 326, 26.10.2012, pp. 47–390.

[56] Treaty on the Functioning of the European Union (TFEU), Consolidated Version, Article 101(3). OJ C 326, 26.10.2012, pp. 47–390. European Commission, Guidelines on the applicability of Article 101 TFEU to horizontal cooperation agreements (2011/C 11/01), Official Journal of the European Union, C 11, 14 January 2011, pp. 1–72.

5.10 The Effect on Trade

The agreements that are considered banned fall under the purview of Article 101 TFEU when the agreement between economic operators, the coordinated practices, or the decisions of the association establish the necessary conditions for such an agreement. In accordance with the jurisprudence of the CJEU, when businesses engage in coordinated activities, even in the absence of a formal agreement, they can nonetheless have an impact on competition within the market. Despite the existing regulations governing the activities of economic operators in the energy industry, it is still possible for these operators to potentially violate competition law. There exists a differentiation between agreements that provide economic advantages and certain limitations that are necessary to accomplish their goals; nonetheless, it is imperative that such agreements do not engender circumstances that lead to the eradication of market competition. This section will provide a more comprehensive analysis of the criteria used to evaluate unlawful agreements.

The scope of agreements in competition law is more extensive compared to civil law, primarily due to the tendency of firms to exhibit hesitancy in actively pursuing the enforcement of anticompetitive agreements. In order to establish the existence of a banned agreement, it is deemed adequate for the involved parties to mutually consent to engage in activities that curtail their economic autonomy to make choices within the market.[57] When assessing the notion of an agreement, it is crucial to consider the alignment of the intentions of the involved parties in any manifestation. In instances where unilateral behaviour is observed from an economic actor, the existence of a forbidden agreement can only be shown if there is express or implicit approval from the other parties involved in the contract. Furthermore, a significant concern arises from the implicit endorsement of the agreement by the second party involved. The expression of a proposal by one contracting party to the other, with the aim of achieving a common objective through collaborative efforts, shall constitute the will of the parties involved. The presence of an implicit agreement becomes evident when one party explicitly communicates a desire to perform in a suitable manner and conveys their expectations of the other party, while the latter acknowledges that non-compliance with these stipulations may lead to unfavourable outcomes.[58] Therefore, in order to ascertain the presence of a contractual agreement between economic entities, it is necessary to establish the parties' desire to conduct themselves in a specific manner.

The regulations outlined in the TFEU pertain to agreements that have the potential to impact trade among the Member States. This circumstance significantly affects the integration of the internal market and the establishment of a competitive market. Commerce can be impacted by agreements in situations where there are limitations on territories or the division of markets, and in such instances, the

[57] Jones et al. (2019).

[58] Bellis (2021).

unrestricted nature of commerce is also jeopardised.[59] These limitations are frequently incorporated into extended contractual agreements for the provision of natural gas, resulting in market constraints, diminished competition, and limited consumer options.

Agreements that satisfy the *de minimis* criteria are deemed non-restrictive of competition and do not have an impact on trade among Member States. The CJEU possesses a comprehensive understanding of the concept of commerce as defined in the TFEU. According to the recommendations provided by the Commission, alterations in trade patterns and deviations from typical trading circumstances, along with shifts in the competitive landscape, have an impact on trade.[60] Based on objective criteria, it can be inferred that the agreement has a tangible or prospective impact on trade among member states. The requirement for the presence of a trade effect is fulfilled when there is a significant probability that the agreement could have a direct or indirect impact on trade between Member States, either currently or potentially. The potential impact on trade between Member States is expected to be minimal when agreements are reached within the jurisdiction of a single Member State. However, the European Commission will evaluate each instance individually to determine the extent of any potential effects. According to the CJEU, when an agreement encompasses the entirety of a Member State's territory, it is probable that the agreement will have an impact on commerce among Member States. It is imperative to acknowledge that agreements falling under the purview of this Article must substantially limit competition and have a major impact on trade among Member States.

The distinction is established between a collection of agreements that, by their nature, impose limitations on competition. In instances of this nature, it is imperative to take into account the extent to which the agreement has hindered, altered, or otherwise manipulated competition or possessed the potential to do so. The

---

[59] Regulation (EC) No 1/2003 of the Council of 16 December 2002 on the implementation of the rules on competition laid down in Articles 81 and 82 of the Treaty OJ L 1, 4.1.2003, pp. 1–25. Regulation (EC) No 139/2004 of the Council of 20 January 2004 on the control of concentrations between undertakings (Merger Regulation) OJ L 24, 29.1.2004, pp. 1–22. Directive 2014/104/EU of the European Parliament and of the Council of 26 November 2014 on certain rules governing actions for damages under national law for infringements of the competition law provisions of the Member States and of the European Union OJ L 349, 5.12.2014, pp. 1–19. Regulation (EU) No 330/2010 of the Commission of 20 April 2010 on the application of Article 101(3) of the Treaty on the Functioning of the European Union to categories of vertical agreements and concerted practices OJ L 102, 23.4.2010, pp. 1–7.

[60] Regulation (EU) No 330/2010 of the Commission of 20 April 2010 on the application of Article 101(3) of the Treaty on the Functioning of the European Union to categories of vertical agreements and concerted practices. See Article 2 (1). Treaty on the Functioning of the European Union (TFEU), Article 101. European Commission, Commission Notice on agreements of minor importance which do not appreciably restrict competition under Article 101(1) of the Treaty on the Functioning of the European Union (de minimis notice), 2014/C 291/01, Official Journal of the European Union, C 291, 30 August 2014, pp. 1–10. Case C-209/07, Competition Authority v. Beef Industry Development Society Ltd and Barry Brothers (Carrigmore) Meats Ltd [2008] ECR I-8637. See Para 21.

evaluation of the impact of the agreement on competition must also consider the practical implementation and legitimacy of the agreement, the economic environment in which the agreement's parties operate, and the market structure. The assessment of the agreement's impact on competition will be conducted by considering whether the conditions of the agreement are essential and do not impose restrictions on competition as outlined in the Treaty on the Functioning of the European Union (TFEU). In the subsequent section, we shall delve into a comprehensive examination of the various categories of agreements that are prone to impede competition yet are important for the operational efficacy of the energy market.

5.11 Energy Sector Inquiries

The Commission uses a sector inquiry as a potent mechanism to collect data and scrutinise particular sectors within the economy, with the aim of evaluating competition and detecting possible antitrust concerns. Sector inquiries have played a crucial role in fostering competition, enhancing transparency, and ensuring regulatory adherence in the European energy market, specifically in relation to energy matters. This article provides an analysis of the European Commission's utilisation of sector inquiries within the energy sector, with a specific emphasis on the aims, methodologies, and results of these inquiries.

The main purpose of conducting sector inquiries in the energy sector is to enhance the effectiveness of competition and foster competitive marketplaces. This entails the analysis of market structures, the study of market behaviour, and the identification of potential obstacles to competition. Sector inquiries play a crucial role in the identification of probable antitrust infringements, encompassing activities such as abuse of market power, anticompetitive agreements, and unfair pricing practices.[61] These violations have the potential to adversely impact both consumers and businesses. The enhancement of regulatory frameworks is frequently suggested as a means to improve market integration and bolster consumer protection, based on the outcomes of sector inquiries.

The collection of data by the European Commission encompasses a wide range of information obtained from various sources, including market participants, regulatory authorities, and other relevant stakeholders. This encompasses data pertaining to market shares, price structures, contractual agreements, and more relevant details. Market surveys are commonly employed as a means of gathering feedback from many stakeholders within the sector, encompassing energy producers, distributors, and consumers alike. The Commission frequently seeks input from various stakeholders, including consumer groups, in order to get insights into the effects of energy

[61] "Commission Staff Working Document - Report on the Sector Inquiry into the Gas and Electricity Markets". 2007. Report from the Commission. Final Report of the Sector Inquiry on Capacity Mechanisms. SWD (2016) 385 final. COM (2016) 752.

market practices on end-users. The Commission frequently issues policy recommendations in response to the findings of sector inquiries. The Commission recommendations have the potential to exert an impact on regulatory modifications and market dynamics. In instances where antitrust violations are detected, the Commission possesses the authority to initiate enforcement measures, such as the imposition of monetary penalties and the requirement for corporations to implement behavioural modifications. The primary objective of sector inquiries is to enhance consumer welfare by promoting competitive market conditions, resulting in reduced pricing, improved service quality, and increased consumer choice.[62]

The European Commission's sector inquiry conducted in 2007 focused on the energy industry and revealed many concerns pertaining to market entry, pricing mechanisms, and anticompetitive behaviours. The outcome resulted in enhanced market accessibility for emerging participants and modifications in regulatory policies. The 2015 Sector Inquiry refers to a comprehensive investigation conducted inside a specific industry during the year 2015. A more recent investigation conducted in 2015 centred on the power capacity procedures employed by member states of the European Union. The objective of this initiative was to prevent any potential bias against existing service suppliers. Sector investigations in the energy sector play a crucial role as a monitoring and competition-enhancing mechanism for the European Commission.[63] They have a significant impact on the identification and resolution of antitrust concerns, the enhancement of market visibility, and the promotion of regulatory modifications that enhance consumer welfare and foster equitable competition in the European energy market.

The authority to conduct sector inquiries is vested in the Commission, with the purpose of addressing instances when market dynamics are insufficient to serve the interests of customers. This tool enables the Commission to scrutinise sectors that, based on its comprehension, are experiencing inefficiencies in their functioning. There exists a potential for certain actions to deviate from the stipulations delineated in Articles 101 and 102 of the TFEU. Moreover, these acts can potentially affect competition, leading to a possible detriment to consumers. There are potential implications of limited trade among Member States, a lack of new entrants in the market, rigid pricing, and other indicators that imply the presence of limits or distortions in market competition. In general, inquiries are often directed at particular industries rather than individual business activities. The investigation has the capacity to be utilised in a specific industry to aid in the identification and implementation of inquiries carried out under Articles 101 and 102 of the TFEU, with a special emphasis on market participants. Regulation 1/2003, namely Article 17, confers jurisdiction upon the Commission to conduct sector investigations, endowing it with

[62] Communication from the Commission: A European Strategy for Competitive and Secure Energy. COM(2010) 639 final. Regulation (EC) No 1/2003 on the implementation of the rules on competition laid down in Articles 81 and 82 of the Treaty. OJ L 1, 4.1.2003, pp. 1–25. Energy Sector Inquiry - Final Report. SEC(2006) 1724. Sector Inquiry into the European Gas and Electricity Markets. COM(2006) 851 final.

[63] Calzado et al. (2014).

the capacity to ascertain the examination of the market. The Commission is granted the authority to gather extensive information and is also empowered to carry out raids. Based on the aforementioned legislation, it is evident that the Commission lacks the jurisdiction to enact actions targeting particular circumstances. Nevertheless, the Commission does have the capacity to enact the necessary regulations. Upon the completion of the sector inquiry, the Commission is empowered to commence an investigation into prospective agreements that may be anticompetitive or instances where a dominant market position is being misused.

Before initiating a sector inquiry, it is crucial for the Commission to have at least some indication that competition in the market might be limited or demonstrate faults in its operation.[64] During the implementation of the procedure, the Commission is granted the authority to utilise the same powers for gathering information that it exercises during the execution of the antitrust investigation. During the initial stage, the questionnaires are disseminated to the participants within the market. Initiating a sector investigation using dawn raids is not a conventional method; yet this investigative strategy has been utilised in the pharmaceutical business in previous instances. The information can be requested by utilising either the formal decision issued by the Commission or the informal notice. The survey comprises various dimensions, including pricing, profitability, client demographics, market entrance barriers, and distinctive sales features. In the event that the Commission has issued an informal note with the intention of disseminating information, adherence to the duty is not mandatory, albeit strongly advised. The Commission is empowered to issue a formal request for the sought information due to the failure to respond to the received notification. Failure to comply with this obligation could result in the imposition of a penalty equivalent to 1 percent of the total income generated by the group on a global scale.[65]

The Commission possesses the capacity to get statements from persons who have provided their consent or conduct unannounced inspections, in conjunction with partnering with national competition authorities to execute inspections on behalf of the Commission. Following the completion of the evaluation procedure, the preliminary results are disseminated to the general public via the publication of the interim report. The release of the investigation's findings may take place after its initiation, during which interested individuals are invited to participate in hearings related to the initial report and are also given the chance to express their viewpoints. After the release of the conclusive report, stakeholders are invited to provide their viewpoints. Following the completion of the probe, it has been determined that the Commission lacks the authority to enforce any punishment with the purpose of addressing the

[64] Faull and Nikpay (2014).

[65] Regulation (EC) No 1/2003 on the implementation of the rules on competition laid down in Articles 81 and 82 of the Treaty. OJ L 1, 4.1.2003, pp. 1–25. Regulation (EC) No 773/2004 laying down detailed rules for the application of Article 11(6) of Regulation (EC) No 1/2003. OJ L 123, 27.4.2004, pp. 18–24. Guidelines on the Sector Inquiry into the Gas and Electricity Markets. COM(2006) 851 final. European Commission. Antitrust: Sector Inquiries and Information Gathering. 23 January 2018.

matter. Nevertheless, it does have the capability to initiate a comprehensive inquiry. After the sector inquiries have been concluded, a set of legislative ideas is being pursued.[66]

The first energy sector inquiry was commenced in 2007, focusing on the examination of the electricity and gas markets inside the European Union. The creation of a shared competitive energy market is seen as a means to achieve the key objectives of EU energy policy, which include enhancing competitiveness, ensuring security of supply, and promoting sustainability. The investigation revealed that there is a significant level of market concentration, along with instances of vertical foreclosure.[67] Additionally, there are concerns regarding inadequate market integration, insufficient transparency, and ineffective price formation mechanisms. Competition in downstream markets is constrained mostly at the retail level, with a notable influence stemming from long-term contracts. The presence of market foreclosure difficulties has been brought to light by the balanced market, which is characterised by intricate and varied regulations across different zones. The presence of variation poses a significant challenge for prospective market entrants due to the vertically integrated nature of the network-operating entity. The absence of competition in the LNG markets was evident, as it possesses significant potential for fostering a competitive market with a range of alternative options. However, it continues to face substantial barriers hindering market liberalisation.

The sector inquiry has brought forward further concerns pertaining to market competition. It was specifically observed that the elimination of distortions in competition is necessary and that tariffs should not be imposed in a discriminatory manner against other participants in the market.[68] Enhancing cross-border trade necessitates the implementation of measures aimed at harmonising market design. The issue of long-term contracts has been noted as a hindrance to further liberalisation efforts, as the severe terms of these contracts restrict the ability to effectively compete in the market. The construction of third-party access to gas storage facilities should be designed in a manner that facilitates the achievement of a balance between new market participants and existing ones.

The initiation of a sector inquiry about capacity mechanisms took place in 2015. The Commission held the view that capacity mechanisms possess the potential to distort competition and impede cross-border trade.[69] Capacity mechanisms are typically established by or in collaboration[70] with governmental entities, with the primary aim of enhancing the security of electricity supply. These mechanisms

---

[66] Regulation (EC) No 1/2003 on the implementation of the rules on competition laid down in Articles 81 and 82 of the Treaty. OJ L 1, 4.1.2003, pp. 1–25 Regulation (EC) No 773/2004 laying down detailed rules for the application of Article 11(6) of Regulation (EC) No 1/2003. OJ L 123, 27.4.2004, pp. 18–24. Sector Inquiry: Procedure and Methodology. COM(2006) 851 final.

[67] Calzado et al. (2014).

[68] *Ibid.*

[69] *Ibid.*

[70] Report from the Commission. Final Report of the Sector Inquiry on Capacity Mechanisms. SWD (2016) 385 final. COM (2016) 752.

determine the remuneration for providers in the capacity market, which is in addition to the revenues they already receive in the market or as an alternative to the potential revenues they could have earned in the electricity market. Capacity measures are implemented with the aim of safeguarding the reliability of electricity supply, mitigating the risk of power outages arising from the growing reliance on renewable energy sources, and addressing the rising electricity demand. According to the findings of the sector inquiry, the market is now unable to effectively stimulate investment in sufficient generation capacity. This is primarily due to investors' reluctance to cover their fixed costs and adequately compensate their investments. Capacity mechanisms are systems that offer supplementary remuneration to electricity producers in exchange for maintaining or increasing their capacity to ensure the security of the energy supply. The potential effects of such compensation on market competition are considered, and as a result, the methods are evaluated to ensure compliance with state assistance regulations. The sector inquiry conducted by the Commission facilitated the identification of specific challenges related to competition distortion between power generators and demand response operators. Consequently, the issue was addressed through the implementation of a market-based capacity mechanism, which ensures that Member States adhere to the relevant regulations while addressing any shortcomings.

In the course of the sector inquiry, the Commission conducted an assessment of Belgium, Denmark, Ireland, France, Croatia, Germany, Poland, Sweden, Spain, and Portugal. The evaluation revealed the presence of a minimum of 35 capacity mechanisms, encompassing both existing and proposed initiatives. The investigation has indicated that the capacity methods were not specifically intended to address security of supply concerns. As a result, the Commission has put out a proposal for a resource adequacy evaluation that would serve as the basis for determining capacity. Furthermore, the investigation has indicated that there is a fundamental need to enhance the procedures in order to effectively address the widely recognised problem.[71]

The sector inquiry has identified several specific mechanisms that are being targeted.[72] These include the strategic reserve, which involves reserving capacity for future use; the tender for new capacity, which involves a competitive bidding process for the allocation of new capacity; and price-based capacity payments, which are made to market participants who have received payment and are obligated to provide available capacity during peak hours. Failure to comply with this obligation may result in penalties. Additionally, the inquiry has found that enhancements are often granted to new investments in specific areas. The market-wide mechanisms that were identified include the central buyer model, in which a single purchaser acquires the required capacity on behalf of consumers and suppliers; decentral obligations, where market participants negotiate contracts and fulfil the necessary

[71] Final Report of the Sector Inquiry on Capacity Mechanisms. COM(2016) 752 final. See para 3.2, para 3.4, para 4.1, para 5.2.

[72] European Commission, Final Report of the Sector Inquiry on Capacity Mechanisms, COM(2016) 752 final, paras 5.3.1–5.3.3.

capacity; and price-based capacity payment, which provides an administrative payment accessible to all market participants.

The strategic reserve is the prevailing mechanism employed by the member nations. Within this framework, the respective governmental bodies express their willingness to compensate the service provider for the surplus capacity maintained until such time as it is needed in response to an emergency situation.

5.12 Conclusion

Competition legislation has a crucial role in maintaining the vitality of the market, promoting creativity, and protecting the well-being of consumers. The statute in question prohibits agreements that are both anti-competitive and illegal. Purposeful and collaborative efforts to manipulate market dynamics, reduce competition, and harm consumer welfare characterize these agreements. We can classify the agreements into horizontal and vertical categories. Horizontal agreements refer to several types of collusive practices among competitors, including price-fixing, market allocation, output limitation, bid rigging, exclusive distribution, and customer allocation. Typically, we consider vertical agreements like resale price maintenance, exclusive distribution, and bundling as acceptable, but we may consider them unlawful if they include elements that hinder competition. The European Union ensures compliance with competition law by conducting thorough investigations and imposing stricter limitations. Different enforcement bodies, including the European Commission and national competition authorities, share this responsibility. In order to protect and enforce competition laws, it is crucial to understand the inherent characteristics, manifestations, and consequences of these agreements.

Competitive markets facilitate the determination of prices that accurately reflect the interplay between supply and demand, thereby enabling consumers to exercise their decision-making autonomy in accordance with their individual preferences. The objective of competition legislation within the energy industry is to facilitate increased competition by delineating monopolistic entities and implementing energy regulation on a European Union scale. Competition legislation endeavours to protect the interests of consumers, regulate pricing mechanisms, promote technological progress, and uphold consumer autonomy. The European Union has expressed criticism of contractual constraints and vertical mergers due to their potential ramifications. Agreements that have the potential to distort competition and affect trade between Member States are explicitly prohibited, with the exception of agreements that contribute to the improvement of manufacturing processes or facilitate developments in technology. The Vertical Block Exemption Regulation was officially enacted in May 2022. It is worth noting that the de minimis concept is applicable to agreements that are considered to be of modest significance. This chapter aims to examine prohibited agreements and explore the relationship between competition law regulations and market liberalisation initiatives within the framework of energy laws.

The notion of an agreement holds significant importance within the framework of European Union competition law as it serves as a fundamental tool for identifying and addressing anticompetitive conduct. The phenomenon can present itself in diverse forms, including explicit, implicit, coordinated, and individual and persistent violations. Express agreements possess legal enforceability, whereas tacit agreements are inferred from the actions and behaviours of the parties involved. Concerted practices encompass collaborative endeavours aimed at mitigating the risks associated with competition. The enforcement of EU competition legislation is carried out by the Commission and national competition authorities, which have the power to impose penalties and implement corrective measures. National authorities are responsible for conducting investigations and taking appropriate actions in order to ensure compliance with agreements aimed at promoting fair competition and safeguarding consumer interests. The reach of agreements extends beyond the realm of civil law, as corporations frequently exhibit reluctance to enforce anticompetitive agreements. The existence of the agreement is contingent upon the mutual permission and implicit support of the parties involved.

Article 101 of the TFEU governs the regulation of agreements and practices that are forbidden due to their potential impact on trade between Member States and their ability to impede, limit, or distort competition within the internal market. These actions encompass the manipulation of prices, the imposition of production restrictions, the division of markets, the implementation of unequal terms, and the inclusion of supplementary requirements in contracts. Any agreements that are forbidden are rendered automatically void. Nevertheless, there are several situations in which these laws may be deemed inapplicable. For instance, circumstances that assist in enhancing the production of goods or fostering technical and economic advancement, all the while ensuring that consumers receive a just portion of the associated advantages, In order to evaluate the presence of competitive constraints inside an agreement, it is necessary to take into account various elements like the contents of the agreement, the legal framework surrounding it, the specific goods and services affected, and the prevailing market structure.

The legal interpretation of anti-competitive agreements exhibits variation across different legal doctrines. The objective of an agreement is not only predicated on the parties' intentions; it is also necessary to discover their intentions. Agreements that impose limitations on competition may encompass practices such as price fixing, market allocation, and exerting influence over production and sales. Restrictions on competition can be imposed on horizontal agreements, vertical agreements, and block exclusions. Limitations on competition frequently emerge within the energy business due to agreements forged between market operators and the unilateral commitments made to consolidate their dominant position. The energy sector inquiry conducted by the European Commission has successfully identified several barriers to the process of market liberalisation. These impediments include market concentration, vertical foreclosure, inadequate market integration, and challenges pertaining to wholesale and balancing markets.

Price-fixing refers to an anticompetitive practice in which competitors engage in collusion to establish and uphold predetermined prices. In the United States, the act in question is deemed to be in violation of the law. The European Union is widely regarded as having restrictive policies that have the potential to impede competitiveness. The determination of whether an agreement is restrictive by the European Court of Justice is contingent upon an analysis of its content, purpose, and economic context. Nevertheless, it is improbable that a collusion arrangement aimed at regulating prices would yield palpable economic advantages or enhance consumer wellbeing.

Market allocation agreements, which are considered anticompetitive collusive activities, are unlawful practices that impose restrictions on competition and restrict the options available to consumers. Market allocation refers to the practice of distributing markets or customers among competing entities in order to sustain or control market shares. These agreements have the potential to result in elevated prices, diminished product quality, and constrained innovation. Competition authorities have difficulties in the identification and prosecution of such agreements, yet they persist in upholding the tenets of unfettered and competitive markets. The legal system that governs these agreements is intricate and necessitates rigorous enforcement.

Bid rigging agreements represent a significant transgression of competition law as they undermine the integrity of procurement processes and unjustly inflate prices. These clandestine agreements entail collusion among competing firms, frequently leading to the designation of a prearranged firm as the beneficiary of the contract. The aforementioned deceptive practice entails the intentional manipulation of contract prices, leading to financial harm for the procurement institution, which is commonly a government agency or private organisation. The misallocation of public funds has a notable effect, leading to an augmented fiscal burden on taxpayers as a consequence of the excessive pricing of products or services. Bid rigging might additionally impede innovation, stifle economic improvement, and hamper technological progress. Competition authorities employ leniency or whistleblower efforts as a means to encourage individuals with privileged information to reveal bid rigging agreements. The identification and legal pursuit of bid rigging agreements present considerable obstacles owing to their complex concealment and the requirement for explicit evidence. Bid rigging has significant global ramifications, including disruptions in international trade and the functioning of supply systems on a global scale.

Market sharing agreements, alternatively referred to as market allocation agreements, encompass anticompetitive behaviours in which competing firms partition distinct geographic regions, customer segments, or product categories. These agreements have the potential to result in a decrease in market competition, a rise in prices, a decline in product quality, and a reduction in innovation. The legal framework and enforcement procedures are essential to guaranteeing adherence to laws and regulations. Market pooling agreements are universally prohibited under competition rules, and individuals engaged in such activities may be subject to financial penalties or legal action. Leniency programmes and data analytics have the potential to facilitate the identification and prosecution of such practices. The agreements have a substantial global impact, especially in areas characterised by international competitiveness. Within the energy sector, these agreements have the potential to result in a reduction in the discovery and development of resources, distortions in pricing mechanisms, and obstacles to the adoption of renewable energy sources. Additionally, these developments may lead to the establishment of regional energy monopolies, inadequate investment in infrastructure, and geopolitical ramifications. In order to address these practices, it is imperative for energy regulators to build efficient coordination systems and foster international collaboration. In summary, market sharing agreements within the energy sector can yield substantial consequences, encompassing aspects such as energy provision, pricing mechanisms, advancements in technology, and the safeguarding of resources.

Customer allocation agreements, which are considered a form of anticompetitive collusion, have the potential to exert a substantial influence on the energy sector. These agreements entail the division of clients or market segments among rival enterprises, resulting in diminished competition and restricted consumer choices. This phenomenon has the potential to result in diminished levels of innovation and a decline in the quality of services, thereby impacting consumers' capacity to access dependable and economically viable energy resources. Established utility companies frequently maintain a monopolistic hold on their current customer bases, which presents obstacles for new entrants in the market.

The presence of customer allocation agreements may hinder progress towards adopting cleaner and more environmentally sustainable energy sources while also presenting potential challenges to fair competition, innovation, and the establishment of a sustainable energy supply. The task of ensuring adherence to these agreements poses a multifaceted challenge for competition authorities, and their execution can be intricate owing to their potential worldwide reach.

Companies that participate in such arrangements may be subject to significant legal ramifications, such as financial penalties, compensating payments in civil lawsuits, and personal accountability. These agreements have the potential to disturb the balance between supply and demand, affecting the dynamics of the market and presenting distinct issues in certain industries. Enforcement authorities across the globe need to maintain a persistent state of alertness in order to effectively address these agreements, thereby safeguarding market competitiveness and preserving consumer choices.

Exclusive dealing agreements refer to contractual arrangements established between a supplier and a customer wherein the buyer is legally bound to get products or services exclusively from the supplier. These agreements have the potential to promote operational efficiency by establishing a stable and predictable client base, thereby leading to higher levels of investment, enhanced service quality, and decreased pricing. Nevertheless, it is important to acknowledge that these practices might potentially result in anticompetitive conduct, such as the imposition of limitations on competitors' entry into distribution networks or the granting of significant market dominance to the provider. The legal regulations and mechanisms for enforcing exclusive dealing agreements exhibit variability among different countries, thereby contributing to the intricacy of international business transactions. Competition authorities across the globe meticulously examine these agreements in order to verify their adherence to antitrust regulations and mitigate potential anticompetitive outcomes. The energy sector is characterised by a significant degree of regulatory oversight, with exclusive dealing arrangements potentially exerting an influence on the accessibility of renewable energy sources and clean energy technologies. The continuous evolution of the energy sector necessitates a thorough comprehension and efficient handling of these ramifications.

The provisions of Article 101 TFEU delineate the extent to which agreements falling under the purview of competition law might exert influence on market competition. Prohibited agreements can be formed with mutual consent and alignment of intentions among the parties. The Treaty on the Functioning of the European Union (TFEU) governs the agreements that have the potential to influence trade between Member States, impacting both the internal market and the competitive market. Agreements that meet the de minimis criterion are characterised by their lack of competitive restrictions and negligible influence on trade. When considering agreements that put restrictions on competition, it is essential to take into account many factors such as practical implementation, legitimacy, economic climate, and market structure. The CJEU conducts a case-by-case assessment in order to ascertain the magnitude of prospective impacts. The operational efficiency of the energy market plays a critical role in assessing the effects of agreements on competition.

Sector inquiries are employed by the European Commission as a means of evaluating competitiveness and identifying antitrust issues within the European energy market. These inquiries collect data from a range of sources, such as market players, regulatory authorities, and stakeholders. The identification of suspected antitrust infringements encompasses various activities, including the detection of abuse of market dominance, the identification of anticompetitive agreements, and the recognition of unfair pricing practices. The Commission is responsible for issuing policy recommendations and implementing enforcement measures in cases where antitrust breaches are identified. The principal objective is to augment consumer well-being through the facilitation of competitive market dynamics, lower pricing structures, enhanced service standards, and more consumer options. The primary objective of the Commission's jurisdiction to undertake sector inquiries is to effectively remedy market inefficiencies and promote fair competition.

Inquiries are frequently targeted at certain industries with the aim of identifying and executing investigations under Articles 101 and 102 of the TFEU. The Commission has the authority to undertake sector investigations, collect comprehensive data, and execute raids. Prior to commencing a sector inquiry, there must be signs of restricted competition or operational deficiencies. The collection of information by the Commission can be facilitated through many means, including the use of questionnaires, informal notices, official decisions, and inspections. The first energy sector inquiry conducted in 2007 scrutinised the electricity and gas markets inside the European Union. This investigation brought to light several key issues, including market concentration, vertical foreclosure, inadequate market integration, insufficient transparency, and ineffective price creation processes. The sector inquiry has brought forward apprehensions regarding market competition, emphasising the necessity to eradicate distortions and achieve market design harmonisation. The investigation also brought attention to the possible distortion of competition and hindering of cross-border trade as a result of capacity mechanisms. The Commission has identified a total of 35 capacity mechanisms across several European countries, namely Belgium, Denmark, Ireland, France, Croatia, Germany, Poland, Sweden, Spain, and Portugal. However, it should be noted that these mechanisms were not explicitly developed with the primary objective of addressing concerns related to supply security. The investigation has revealed many strategies, including strategic reserves, tenders for new capacity, and price-based capacity payments. The investigation also found market-wide processes such as the central buyer model, decentralised commitments, and price-based capacity payments.

References

Bailey D, John LE (2019) European Union law of competition. Bellamy and Child. Oxford University Press
Bellis VB (2010) Competition law of the European Community. Kluwer Law International, Netherlands
Bellis VB (2021) Competition law of the European Union, 6th edn. Kluwer Law International, Netherlands
Calzado RJ, Kjolbye L, Lucas SJ (2014) Energy and anticompetitive practices: an overview of EU and national case law. E-Competitions. No 70451
Faull J, Nikpay A (2014) The EU law of competition. Oxford University Press
Gerber D (1998) Law and competition in twentieth century Europe. Oxford University Press, Oxford
Jones A, Sufrin B, Dunne N (2019) EU competition law. Text, cases and materials. Oxford University Press
Quigley C (2022) European state aid law and policy (and UK Subsidy Control), 4th edn. Hart Publishing
Wish R, Bailey D (2018) Competition law. Oxford

Chapter 6
Horizontal Agreements in the Development of Energy Projects

Abstract In the energy industry, horizontal agreements refer to cooperative efforts between companies operating in the same part of the supply chain. These agreements have the capacity to enhance efficiency and promote innovation, but they may also give rise to antitrust concerns. We can employ various strategies like engaging in cooperative partnerships, forming alliances, encouraging information sharing, and coordinating our efforts. The legal framework regulates these agreements and scrutinizes them according to the competition regulations of the European Union. However, the complex nature of these agreements necessitates a comprehensive economic examination. The Commission's approach is based on the belief that technology transfer agreements provide social benefits, but they can also lead to anti-competitive consequences. This chapter included a thorough examination of collaborative research and development (R&D) partnerships in the energy business. The main focus was on the goals, advantages, regulatory factors, and difficulties associated with these agreements. These agreements aim to improve cooperation among many stakeholders, such as industry participants, academic institutions, and governmental bodies, to tackle complex energy-related concerns. R&D partnerships can occur either through contractual agreements or through cooperative efforts that involve financial compensation.

6.1 Introduction

Within the ever-changing context of the worldwide energy industry, there is an increasingly prominent focus on the pursuit of energy sources that are sustainable, efficient, and dependable. This endeavour encompasses a range of complex difficulties and potential advantages, including the shift towards sustainable energy sources and the imperative to maintain a reliable energy supply for expanding populations. The creation of energy projects, encompassing both conventional fossil fuel initiatives and novel, environmentally friendly technology, is of paramount importance in this endeavour. The emergence of horizontal agreements has a crucial role in shaping the trajectory, structure, and results of energy project development on a worldwide scale. The ramifications of these agreements, which are frequently established

L. Rimšaitė, *The Crossroads of Competition Law and Energy Regulation*,
https://doi.org/10.1007/978-3-031-73238-6_6

between enterprises operating within the same tier of the supply chain, extend significantly to competition, innovation, and the provision of energy services. The chapter encourages readers to explore the complexities of these agreements, comprehend their influence on the energy sector, and recognise their significance in managing the intricate relationship between competition law, energy policy, and sustainability objectives.

The energy sector, which has historically been characterised by centralised production and distribution structures, is currently undergoing an evolutionary process motivated by various imperatives.[1] The global transition towards sustainable energy sources has been motivated by growing apprehensions over climate change and environmental deterioration. Renewable energy technologies, such as solar, wind, and hydroelectric power, are leading the way in this transition. The imperative of energy security necessitates the adoption of a diversified portfolio of energy sources in order to mitigate dependence on finite fossil fuels and politically volatile locations. The scope of energy project development has broadened to encompass a wide range of technologies and resources. The energy sector is undergoing significant transformation due to the influence of competitive pressures. The expansion of participants in energy project development has been facilitated by the entrance of new actors, market liberalisation, and technological developments.

The topic of discussion pertains to the domain of regulation and policy. Energy policies and regulations have a significant impact on the structure and dynamics of the energy sector. Governments across the globe are implementing policies aimed at facilitating the adoption of sustainable energy sources, encouraging market competition, and upholding equitable market practises. The importance of horizontal agreements in economic analysis in light of these pressing demands, there has been a notable increase in the prevalence of horizontal agreements among competitors within the energy industry. These agreements, although frequently essential for the achievement of project objectives, present complex obstacles and give rise to significant inquiries. Horizontal agreements have the potential to give rise to anti-competitive conduct, including collusion or market allocation, which might possibly undermine the fundamental tenets of competition law. The establishment of collaborative relationships among competing entities has the potential to foster creativity and enhance the efficiency of projects. Nevertheless, it is imperative to maintain a harmonious equilibrium between the principles of competition law and the need for equitable practises within the market.

The concept of sustainability and its alignment with policy numerous horizontal agreements are formed with the objective of fostering sustainability and conforming to energy policies. It is vital to comprehend the manner in which these entities contribute to overarching energy and environmental objectives. This chapter undertakes a comprehensive exploration of the complexities, difficulties, and possibility

[1] Commission Regulation (EU) No 1218/2010 of 14 December 2010 on the application of Article 101(3) of the Treaty on the Functioning of the European Union to certain categories of specialisation agreements. OJ L *335*, 18.12.2010.

for significant change associated with horizontal agreements in the energy industry.[2] The subsequent chapters explore several facets, encompassing competition legislation and regulatory frameworks, as well as the examination of case studies and the identification of new trends. We shall endeavour to comprehend the intricacies of horizontal agreements, scrutinise their legal and policy aspects, and evaluate their influence on the advancement of energy projects within a dynamic global context. The primary objective is to offer a comprehension of how horizontal agreements might align competitiveness, innovation, and sustainability in the energy sector's pursuit of a more promising and sustainable future.

Horizontal agreements are concluded between companies operating at the same level of production, trade, distribution. Horizontal cooperation agreements can be cost effective if they combine ancillary activities, skills or assets. Horizontal cooperation can be a tool for risk-sharing, cost-saving, increasing investment, pooling know-how, improving product quality and variety and accelerating innovation. Such agreements restrict competition in the market when they are concluded between companies that actually or potentially are in competition with each other. The concepts of "actual competitors" and "potential competitors" in the market should be further explored.

Undertakings shall be considered as competitors when their goods are to be considered as substitutable with regard to consumers and they shall also be active in the relevant geographic market.[3] Even undertakings which are not yet actually operating on the market and which are only potentially planning their activities are to be considered as competitors.[4] For example, a company generates electricity only for its own use and does not sell it to consumers, but in the event of a rise in electricity prices, such company, in order to increase profits, starts supplying electricity to consumers and thus becoming a supplier. Companies which, in order to increase profits and in response to small price changes, engage in activities that were not previously carried on, are to be considered as existing competitors with those that are already engaged. Account shall be taken of whether the entry of the new entity requires a relatively short period of time, normally not exceeding three years. The short timeframe shall be assessed on a case-by-case basis, as well as whether the entity is a party to the agreement or a third party to such agreement.

Horizontal cooperation agreements may restrict competition in several ways. Agreements may be exclusive in that they restrict the parties' ability to compete with each other or with third parties, either as independent operators or as parties to other competitive agreements.[5] Agreements may affect the financial interests of the

[2]Guidance on horizontal cooperation agreements, OJ C 11, 14 January 2011, pp. 1–24.

[3]Commission Regulation (EU) No 1218/2010 of 14 December 2010 on the application of Article 101(3) of the Treaty on the Functioning of the European Union to certain categories of specialisation agreements. OJ L *335*, 18.12.2010.

[4]Ezrachi (2021).

[5]Guidance on horizontal cooperation agreements, OJ, C 11, 14 January 2011, pp. 1–24.

parties in such a way that their decision-making autonomy is significantly reduced. The financial interests involved in the agreement and the financial interests of other parties to the agreement should also be taken into account in the assessment. In the field of energy, very often there is cooperation between producers (i.e., oil, gas, electricity generation companies), so-called production or specialization agreements. Such agreements usually achieve production optimization by counteracting the negative effects on the market and its participants. Unilateral specialization agreements are possible where economic operators agree that one of them will produce the product concerned and the other will procure such output. Another case is the so-called reciprocal specialization agreements, whereby undertakings oblige to purchase certain products. It should be noted that in the energy sector, such agreements are mainly specific to companies active in the petroleum products segment. When evaluating such agreements, it is important to ascertain if the agreement is not anti-competitive by object, what market shares the parties have and whether they are competing with each other or whether consumers have the ability to switch suppliers.

6.2 The Case Law of Horizontal Foreclosure in Energy

The issue of horizontal foreclosure in the energy industry has become increasingly significant and difficult in the fields of competition law and energy regulation. This applies to the practises employed by prominent energy corporations, typically operating at the same level of the supply chain, to engage in anticompetitive behaviour with the aim of limiting market entry for potential competitors. This chapter provides an in-depth analysis of horizontal foreclosure in the energy sector, examining significant legal precedents and influential court cases and their impact on competition, market dynamics, and the overall energy industry. Horizontal foreclosure refers to a strategic business practise in which a dominant firm in a particular industry uses its market power to restrict or eliminate competition from other firms operating at the same level. Horizontal foreclosure refers to the occurrence in the energy industry whereby dominant entities employ strategic tactics to hinder the entry or expansion of competing firms inside the market. This phenomenon can present itself in various ways. Exclusivity agreements refer to contractual arrangements wherein dominant firms establish exclusive relationships with suppliers, distributors, or customers, thereby preventing competitors from accessing crucial resources or channels. Predatory pricing refers to the strategic practise employed by companies with substantial market power, wherein they deliberately set prices for their goods or services below their production costs. This tactic is employed with the intention of eliminating competition and forcing rival firms to exit the market. Vertical integration refers to the strategic practise employed by dominant market companies to expand their control over various stages of the supply chain.[6] This expansion enables them to exert influence over important infrastructure and resources, thereby creating barriers for competitors seeking access to these key elements. The act of refusing to engage in business transactions, commonly known as refusal to deal, can be used as a strategic approach to exclude possible competitors or restrict their access to vital resources, thereby impeding their ability to compete effectively. The legal framework and precedents are essential components of the judicial system. They provide a foundation for the interpretation and application of laws in a consistent and predictable manner. The legal framework refers to the overall structure and principles.

The essential facilities doctrine refers to a legal principle that pertains to the regulation of access to essential facilities, which are defined as infrastructure or resources that are necessary for competitors to effectively compete in a given market. The essential facilities doctrine, a fundamental principle in the field of competition law, acknowledges that, in specific circumstances, the availability of crucial infrastructure or facilities is indispensable for ensuring successful competition. The aforementioned doctrine has been utilised in numerous legal disputes pertaining to energy, with a special focus on situations where dominant energy corporations exercise control over critical infrastructure. The case of *Microsoft v. Commission*[7] (2007) pertained to the European Union and centred around the accusation of Microsoft's exploitation of its dominating market position in the PC operating systems industry. While not directly pertaining to energy, this highlighted the importance of guaranteeing interoperability and access to vital infrastructure in order to promote competition.

The case of European Commission v. Gazprom (2018)[8] garnered significant attention due to the accusations against Gazprom about its purported exploitation of its dominating market position in the gas supply industry across Eastern Europe. The decision rendered by the Commission has brought attention to apprehensions pertaining to pricing practises and the presence of restrictive terms in supply contracts, exemplifying the implementation of competition legislation within the energy industry. The implications and future perspectives of the subject matter are of great significance and warrant more examination and analysis. The issue of horizontal foreclosure in the energy sector continues to be a multifaceted and dynamic subject within the realm of competition law and regulation. The essential importance lies in addressing concerns pertaining to market strength, dominance, and anticompetitive behaviour as energy markets undergo ongoing development. This chapter explores the legal dimensions associated with horizontal foreclosure in the energy industry, offering an analysis of relevant case law and precedents that have influenced the ongoing discussions on this topic. Through an analysis of prominent cases and their ramifications, our objective is to enhance our comprehension of the

[6] *Ibid.*

[7] Case Microsoft Corp. v Commission. T-201/04.

[8] Case AT.39816.

intersection between competition law and the distinctive challenges and prospects within the energy sector. This endeavour aims to facilitate well-informed policy choices and the establishment of legal structures that foster equitable competition and advancement in this critical field.

The issue of horizontal foreclosure within the energy sector of the European Union has garnered significant attention from both competition law enforcement and regulatory bodies. This phenomenon entails the participation of prominent energy corporations in anticompetitive conduct aimed at limiting market entry for prospective competitors operating at the same level of the supply chain. The following are significant instances and legal advancements pertaining to horizontal foreclosure within the energy sector of the European Union. The Commission conducted an investigation into Gazprom, a Russian gas corporation, over allegations of engaging in anti-competitive practises within the gas supply markets of Eastern Europe. The central focus of the lawsuit revolved around concerns pertaining to Gazprom's pricing practises and the imposition of restrictive clauses in its supply contracts. These alleged actions were believed to impede the unrestricted movement of gas across international boundaries. The outcome of the situation was that Gazprom made a commitment to implement a series of corrective measures in response to the concerns raised by the Commission. These measures included granting more freedom in pricing and eliminating territorial limitations in gas supply agreements. The aforementioned case underscored the European Union's dedication to promoting competitive gasoline markets and mitigating energy dependency.[9]

In the year 2004 Greek energy incumbents, namely the Hellenic Energy Distribution Network Operator (EDA) and the Public Power Corporation (DEI), faced allegations of engaging in abusive practises due to their dominant market position. The primary concerns revolve around the purported involvement of the businesses in predatory pricing, market segmentation, and discriminatory practises, all of which have been identified as factors impeding competition within the energy market in Greece. The Commission has levied fines on EDA and DEI, highlighting the need to ensure free access to electrical networks and fair treatment of rivals. The Commission conducted an inquiry into the activities of Vattenfall, a Swedish energy corporation, pertaining to its operations within the German electricity market. The primary concerns revolve around allegations of Vattenfall engaging in anti-competitive behaviour by leveraging its market dominance to enforce unjust and exorbitant fees for entry into its transmission network within Germany. The Commission rendered a decision unfavourable to Vattenfall, underscoring the significance of ensuring equal access to vital infrastructure. This ruling establishes a precedent for the accessibility of energy transmission networks.[10]

[9]European Commission, Case AT.39816 - Upstream Gas Supplies in Central and Eastern Europe (Gazprom), Commitment Decision, 24 May 2018.

[10]European Commission, Decision of 24 May 2004 in Case COMP/38.884 - Greek energy incumbents (EDA and DEI). European Commission, Decision of [insert specific date] in Case COMP/39.388 - Vattenfall (German Electricity Market).

In 2006 a legal dispute over financial assistance provided by the Belgian government to power producers, the European Court of Justice (ECJ) rendered a verdict in favour of Inter-Environnement Wallonie, an environmental organisation based in Belgium. The issue has brought forward inquiries regarding state aid and the potential anticompetitive nature of providing preferential prices to specific electricity companies. The ECJ rendered a verdict stating that the provision of preferential treatment in this context has the potential to create distortions in competition and impede the progress of a competitive electricity market. These instances underscore the European Union's dedication to tackling anticompetitive practises within the energy industry, namely those that result in the exclusion of competition. The significance of ensuring equitable access to energy infrastructure, mitigating monopolistic practises by dominant entities, and fostering competitive and efficient energy markets within the European Union (EU) is underscored by these stakeholders. The issue of horizontal foreclosure continues to be a prominent area of concern in the enforcement of competition law, particularly within the European Union's efforts to attain its energy policy objectives.[11]

The Commission conducted an investigation into EDP, a Portuguese energy corporation, regarding allegations of engaging in anti-competitive practises and exerting undue influence in the power market within Portugal. One of the primary concerns revolves around the allegations that EDP engaged in the manipulation of wholesale power pricing by employing strategic bidding practises that placed competitors at a disadvantage. The EDP entity was subjected to a financial penalty amounting to EUR 48 million due to engaging in anticompetitive behavior. This case exemplified the European Union's dedication to guaranteeing fair pricing and market entry for participants in the electricity markets.[12]

In 2016, the Commission initiated an inquiry into EDF, a French energy corporation, with regards to possible instances of anticompetitive conduct in the electricity supply market within France. One of the primary concerns raised pertains to the alleged abuse of market dominance by EDF, whereby the company is accused of impeding competitors' entry into the retail power market in France. The ongoing nature of this lawsuit highlights the European Union's commitment to tackling potential anticompetitive practises, particularly in areas where dominant firms may restrict competition.[13]

The E.ON/GDF case[14] involved the collaboration of these companies in the construction of the MEGAL gas pipeline. It was observed that during this collaboration, the companies entered into an agreement that included a non-compete clause pertaining to their respective territories. Under the terms of this agreement, E.ON committed to refraining from engaging in competitive activities within the French

[11] Case C-387/06, Inter-Environnement Wallonie ASBL v. Région wallonne, [2008] ECR I-00519.

[12] Commission Decision of 17 October 2018 on Case AT.40023 – EDP. OJ C 437, 23.11.2018, p. 7-7.

[13] Case AT.40208 – EDF (2016).

[14] Case COMP/39.401 – E.ON/GDF.

market, while EDF was restricted from participating in the natural gas supply sector in Germany. Companies have achieved a dominant position in the domestic gas supply market. The Commission held the perspective that the companies had engaged in a persistent violation. This violation persisted subsequent to the implementation of the initial energy package, which recognised the necessity for market liberalisation and the accompanying obligations. Despite this, the companies involved persisted in their non-compete agreements. The persistence of such an agreement subsequent to the period of liberalisation had a substantial impact on constraining the extent of competition.

Another instance of horizontal foreclosure was identified in the case of the German Electricity Wholesale Market, wherein E.ON was alleged to have engaged in the practise of increasing electricity prices and deterring third-party investments in infrastructure through the imposition of limitations on its electricity generation capacity. By engaging in this practise, the aforementioned company conferred a competitive edge on its affiliated entities within the German electricity market, albeit at the expense of higher costs incurred by end consumers in the nation. In pursuit of this objective, the organisation allocated a portion of its accessible generation capacity, despite the potential for E.ON to derive greater cost efficiency by utilising said capacity for internal purposes. To address the electricity demand of consumers, the company opted to mitigate the deficit in electricity production capacity by procuring electricity from an alternative producer in the market, resulting in an increase in prices. In the current case, the Commission conducted a separate analysis of the company's market position and ultimately imposed a monetary penalty on the company.[15]

6.3 The Types of Horizontal Agreements

This chapter provides a thorough examination of horizontal agreements in the energy industry. Horizontal agreements, which are commonly established among competitors operating within the same tier of the supply chain, have significant ramifications for competition, market dynamics, and ultimately, consumers of energy. It examines different types of horizontal agreements, their possible advantages, and their potential negative impact on competition in the energy industry. Furthermore, we analyse the regulatory framework that governs these agreements and emphasises significant obstacles and issues in their evaluation.

Horizontal agreements in the energy industry pertain to cooperative endeavours, alliances, or arrangements involving enterprises that function at equivalent stages of the energy supply chain, including producers, distributors, or retailers. These agreements can assume several manifestations, encompassing joint ventures, consortiums,

[15] Case COMP/39.388 – E.ON (2008).

information sharing, and coordinated actions. While certain horizontal agreements within the energy sector have the potential to enhance efficiency and foster innovation, there are instances where such agreements may give rise to significant antitrust considerations.

Energy businesses frequently participate in collaborative research and development endeavours aimed at the advancement of novel technologies, the enhancement of energy efficiency, and the exploration of renewable energy sources. Enterprises have the option to engage in agreements aimed at collaboratively producing energy or sharing supply infrastructure, which can result in cost reduction and enhanced reliability. The use of information sharing agreements has the potential to improve market openness. However, it is important to acknowledge that there is a possibility of anticompetitive conduct arising from the communication of sensitive information. Agreements have the potential to generate economies of scale, thereby facilitating the production and distribution of energy in a more efficient manner, leading to cost reductions. Collaboration has the potential to enhance the transfer of sophisticated technologies, including those pertaining to renewable energy solutions, throughout the industry.

Energy businesses have the ability to mitigate risks linked to extensive projects by engaging in collaborative efforts, thereby enhancing the viability of investments. Horizontal agreements have the potential to result in price fixing and market allocation, which can have detrimental effects on consumers due to the reduction of competition. Exclusive dealing agreements have the potential to restrict market entry for competitors, constraining consumer choice. The inappropriate dissemination of confidential information might result in the development of collusive practices, thereby detrimentally impacting competition. The regulatory framework refers to the set of rules, regulations, and guidelines that govern a particular industry or sector.

Horizontal agreements occurring within the European Union are subject to evaluation in accordance with competition legislation, namely Article 101 Treaty on the Functioning of the European Union (TFEU), which forbids agreements that have an adverse impact on competition. National energy regulatory bodies also have the responsibility of assessing and, if required, penalising horizontal agreements within their specific domains. The differentiation between horizontal agreements that promote competition and those that hinder competition might present difficulties, necessitating a comprehensive economic study. Evaluations should take into account the distinctive attributes of energy markets, including extended investment cycles and the significance of infrastructure.

Horizontal agreements in the energy sector present a dual nature, as they have the capacity to generate efficiency benefits but also carry significant antitrust concerns. Thorough assessment and effective oversight are vital to guaranteeing that such agreements yield advantages for consumers, stimulate innovation, and uphold competitive energy markets. The task of reconciling these goals within the intricate energy sector continues to present a significant dilemma for policymakers, regulators, and industry stakeholders alike. The fundamental ideology driving the Commission's approach is rooted in the belief that technology transfer agreements are generally advantageous for society as they promote innovation and typically yield both immediate and long-term advantages for consumers. However, it is important to note that these agreements have the potential to result in anti-competitive consequences. For instance, exclusive agreements can limit competition, while grant-back clauses, which require the licensee to share and transfer any improvements made to the licensor, may diminish the motivation for innovation by decreasing the anticipated rewards for high-risk investments. Agreements between rivals may, in certain circumstances, facilitate collusion or result in a general increase in the price that end users pay.

6.4 The Cooperation Agreements

This chapter explores the domain of horizontal collaboration agreements in the energy industry. Horizontal cooperation agreements, which entail collaborative efforts between competitors operating within the same tier of the supply chain, play a crucial role in defining energy markets. This chapter examines the different aspects of these agreements, encompassing their categorization and advantages as well as the potential anticompetitive hazards they present. Additionally, this analysis delves into the regulatory structure that governs these agreements, highlighting the importance of conducting nuanced evaluations in order to achieve a harmonious equilibrium between promoting innovation and upholding market competition.

Horizontal cooperation agreements in the energy sector refer to collaboration arrangements established among enterprises that operate at the same level within the energy supply chain. These agreements encompass a variety of formats, including collaborations in research and development, partnerships in joint manufacturing, and consortia for the purpose of sharing information.[16] Although there is potential for efficiency advantages and innovation, the presence of serious antitrust concerns around them requires a thorough examination. Energy corporations commonly participate in collaborative research and development endeavours aimed at

[16] Guidelines on the applicability of Article 101 TFEU to horizontal co-operation agreements, Official Journal of the European Union, C 11, 14 January 2011, pp. 1–72. Council Regulation (EC) No 139/2004 of 20 January 2004 on the control of concentrations between undertakings, Official Journal of the European Union, L 24, 29 January 2004, pp. 1–22. Regulation (EC) No 1/2003 of the Council of 16 December 2002 on the implementation of the rules on competition laid down in Articles 81 and 82 of the Treaty, Official Journal of the European Union, L 1, 4 January 2003, pp. 1–25. Communication from the Commission - Guidelines on the application of Article 101 of the Treaty on the Functioning of the European Union to horizontal cooperation agreements, Official Journal of the European Union, C 11, 14 January 2011.

advancing state-of-the-art technology, improving energy efficiency, and investigating alternative and sustainable energy resources.

Companies have the option to engage in agreements that involve collaborative production of energy or the sharing of supply infrastructure, with the objective of minimising expenses and enhancing the dependability of services. The use of information-sharing agreements has the potential to enhance market openness and facilitate interoperability. However, it is crucial to regulate such agreements effectively in order to mitigate the risk of anticompetitive behaviour. The establishment of horizontal cooperation has the potential to provide economies of scale, enhance the efficiency of energy production and distribution processes, and ultimately lead to cost reductions. Collaborative efforts enable the exchange of cutting-edge technology, such as renewable energy solutions, across various stakeholders within the business. Horizontal agreements have the potential to enhance the viability of large-scale projects or investments by facilitating the pooling of associated risks.

Horizontal cooperative agreements have the potential to facilitate price fixing and market allocation, resulting in adverse consequences for consumers through the reduction of competition. The inclusion of exclusive dealing restrictions in agreements has the potential to result in the exclusion of competitors, restricting consumer choice. The European Union's competition law, specifically Article 101 TFEU, holds significant importance in the examination of horizontal cooperation agreements for any anticompetitive aspects. National energy regulators have a crucial role in assessing and, if deemed necessary, imposing penalties on horizontal agreements within their own domains. The differentiation between horizontal cooperation agreements that promote competition and those that hinder competition necessitates a rigorous economic examination and a comprehension of the distinctive attributes of the energy industry.

Evaluations should consider the unique characteristics of energy markets, including extended investment cycles and the crucial significance of infrastructure. Horizontal cooperation agreements play a crucial role in the energy sector, presenting prospects for innovation and enhancements in efficiency. However, achieving an appropriate equilibrium between evaluation and regulation is crucial in order to protect competition and facilitate advancements within the business. The assessment of these agreements is of utmost importance for policymakers, regulators, and industry stakeholders in order to guarantee a competitive, sustainable, and innovative energy sector, given the ongoing evolution of the energy landscape.

Horizontal cooperation agreements, which entail collaborative efforts between competitors operating within the same tier of the supply chain, play a crucial role in defining energy markets.[17] This chapter examines the different aspects of these agreements, encompassing their categorization and advantages as well as the

[17]Guidelines on the applicability of Article 101 TFEU to horizontal co-operation agreements, Official Journal of the European Union, C 11, 14 January 2011, pp. 1–72. Council Regulation (EC) No 139/2004 of 20 January 2004 on the control of concentrations between undertakings, Official Journal of the European Union, L 24, 29 January 2004, pp. 1–22.

potential anticompetitive hazards they present. Additionally, this analysis delves into the regulatory structure that governs these agreements, highlighting the importance of conducting nuanced evaluations in order to achieve a harmonious equilibrium between promoting innovation and upholding market competition.

Horizontal cooperation agreements in the energy sector refer to collaboration arrangements established among enterprises that operate at the same level within the energy supply chain. These agreements encompass a variety of formats, including collaborations in research and development, partnerships in joint manufacturing, and consortia for the purpose of sharing information. Although there is potential for efficiency advantages and innovation, the presence of serious antitrust concerns around them requires a thorough examination. Energy corporations commonly participate in collaborative research and development endeavours aimed at advancing state-of-the-art technology, improving energy efficiency, and investigating alternative and sustainable energy resources.

Companies have the option to engage in agreements that involve collaborative production of energy or the sharing of supply infrastructure, with the objective of minimising expenses and enhancing the dependability of services. The use of information-sharing agreements has the potential to enhance market openness and facilitate interoperability. However, it is crucial to regulate such agreements effectively in order to mitigate the risk of anticompetitive behaviour. The establishment of horizontal cooperation has the potential to provide economies of scale, enhance the efficiency of energy production and distribution processes, and ultimately lead to cost reductions. Collaborative efforts enable the exchange of cutting-edge technology, such as renewable energy solutions, across various stakeholders within the business. Horizontal agreements have the potential to enhance the viability of large-scale projects or investments by facilitating the pooling of associated risks.

Horizontal cooperative agreements have the potential to facilitate price fixing and market allocation, resulting in adverse consequences for consumers through the reduction of competition. The inclusion of exclusive dealing restrictions in agreements has the potential to result in the exclusion of competitors, restricting consumer choice. The competition law, specifically Article 101 TFEU, holds significant importance in the examination of horizontal cooperation agreements for any anticompetitive aspects. National energy regulators have a role in assessing and, if deemed necessary, imposing penalties on horizontal agreements within their own domains. The differentiation between horizontal cooperation agreements that promote competition and those that hinder competition necessitates a rigorous economic examination and a comprehension of the distinctive attributes of the energy industry.

Evaluations should consider the unique characteristics of energy markets, including extended investment cycles and the crucial significance of infrastructure. Horizontal cooperation agreements play a crucial role in the energy sector, presenting prospects for innovation and enhancements in efficiency. However, achieving an appropriate equilibrium between evaluation and regulation is crucial in order to protect competition and facilitate advancements within the business. The assessment of these agreements is of utmost importance for policymakers, regulators, and industry stakeholders in order to guarantee a competitive, sustainable, and innovative energy sector, given the ongoing evolution of the energy landscape.

Within the domain of the natural gas market, it is customary for operators to partake in agreements that purposefully restrict the participation of rival entities. Although these practices were previously deemed acceptable for a considerable period of time, the Commission has taken the position since 1990 that such collaborative agreements could potentially contravene Article 101 (1) of the TFEU. The literature delineates two distinct categories of trade cooperation agreements: territorial agreements, which span a certain geographical area, and market-specific agreements, which concentrate on a particular market. The instance of GFU, in which the Commission launched an inquiry into a trade cooperation agreement, is pertinent in this specific context.[18] The Gas Negotiation Committee (GFU), comprising representatives from Norway's leading gas firms, mainly Statoil and Norsk Hydro, was established. Likewise, the committee was associated with six consortia consisting of enterprises involved in the distribution of Norwegian-sourced natural gas to final consumers. The main objective of this group was to initiate negotiations regarding the terms and conditions of gas supply agreements with potential buyers in the European market. The Commission has commenced an inquiry into the operations of the GFU, raising concerns about the conformity of the committee's activities with the provisions outlined in the TFEU. The corporations and the Norwegian Government argued that a legislative measure was implemented after 2001 that specified that this system could not be applied to nations inside the European Economic Area (EEA). However, before the enforcement of this order, contractual arrangements were put in place for a period of 25 years to facilitate the trade of natural gas. In the present context, the enterprises have fulfilled the necessary obligations as suggested by the Commission. The agreement between Statoil and Norsk Hydro included a pledge to participate in collaborative trading endeavours, subject to compliance with competition law. The businesses offered supply capacity to new operators who had not previously participated in procuring natural gas from these enterprises due to the sales limits imposed by GFU. The agreement reached with the Commission has led to the development of supplementary supply capabilities inside the market. These capabilities have primarily been employed by prominent industrial clients, power generation corporations, and trading firms in search of alternative opportunities inside the market. Statoil and Norsk Hydro have expressed their intention to abstain from imposing territorial restrictions on the trading of natural gas. Six consortia involved in natural gas trading, operating under the GFU model, have received requests to cease their trading operations. These ideas are in accordance with the established methodology for coordinating actions and strategies within the industry.

An additional case was an investigation into the intention to form a collaboration agreement between corporations involved in the joint operation of a recently discovered gas production area in Corrib, Ireland. Enterprise Energy Ireland Limited,

[18]Commission Press Release IP/01/830, Commission objects to GFU joint gas sales in Norway. June 2001.

Statoil, and Marathon have jointly submitted an application to the Commission, requesting an exemption for the initial five-year period with the ultimate goal of concluding a trade cooperation agreement. The motivation for pursuing the application originated from the need to build a fresh presence and augment market power within the natural gas trade industry, specifically in regard to the prevailing state-owned entities, Bord Gais Eirean and the Electricity Supply Board. The Commission acknowledged the substantial market position of the state-owned enterprises concerned but voiced doubt over the capacity of the proposed natural gas cooperation agreement to promote market competition. The Commission's suspicion is based on the continuous trend of market liberalisation, which enables consumers to switch to alternative energy suppliers, thus promoting a competitive internal market. Therefore, the previously indicated agreement would have hindered the further advancement of market liberalisation. The petitioners made the decision to withdraw their request, resulting in the eventual closure of the case by the Commission. The evaluation of several cooperation agreements related to the trade of electricity was conducted by the Commission. In contrast to the natural gas market, agreements of this kind are not as commonly observed in the electrical sector.[19]

Cooperation agreements are commonly developed with the aim of facilitating economic operators' access to new markets. This is due to the fact that engaging in these markets sometimes requires significant initial capital commitments, which may not always be easily accessible to the economic unit.[20] The aforementioned scenario can be well illustrated by referring to the Synergen case study.[21] In the present case, the ESB, a dominant electricity supplier in Ireland with a market share of 97%, and Statoil, a Norwegian business specialising in the oil and gas industry, have engaged in a contractual arrangement to establish a Synergen power plant in Dublin. The power plant has been specifically engineered to use natural gas as its primary energy source for the purpose of generating electricity. The Commission has received notification from the firms regarding four agreements that indicate substantial ownership of shares in the Synergen project by ESB and Statoil. Furthermore, a contractual arrangement was established whereby Statoil, a prominent energy company, would be obligated to supply Synergen, a business involved in the project, with natural gas for a period of 15 years. The Commission has noted that the arrangement established by Statoil imposes restrictions on the participation opportunities available to its competitors. Consequently, subsequent to the establishment of a mutual agreement between the two companies and the Commission, the non-compete clause was mutually rescinded.

---

[19] Case COMP/37.466 – Enterprise Energy Ireland Limited, Statoil, and Marathon (2002).

[20] Guidelines on the applicability of Article 101 TFEU to horizontal co-operation agreements, Official Journal of the European Union, C 11, 14 January 2011, pp. 1–72.

[21] Case COMP/E-3/37.732.

6.5 The R&D Agreements

This chapter presents a comprehensive examination of collaborative research and development (R&D) agreements in the energy sector. These agreements are of the utmost importance in facilitating and promoting innovation and technological progress within the sector. The chapter delves into the multifaceted dimensions of these agreements, encompassing their stated goals, advantages, regulatory implications, and obstacles.[22]

Collaborative R&D agreements play a crucial role in fostering innovation within the energy sector.[23] This chapter examines the characteristics and importance of these agreements, which facilitate collaboration among many stakeholders such as industry participants, academic institutions, and governmental bodies in order to tackle intricate energy-related issues. The objectives of collaborative R&D agreements are to foster cooperation and knowledge sharing among several entities, such as academic institutions, research organisations, and industry partners. The principal objective of collaborative research and development agreements is to stimulate innovation, resulting in the emergence of revolutionary technologies and solutions within the energy industry. The purpose of these agreements is to enable the exchange of knowledge and expertise among various stakeholders, thereby fostering a culture of collaboration. The implementation of collaborative research and development initiatives facilitates the equitable distribution of financial resources, enhancing the viability of undertaking extensive projects.

R&D cooperation primarily entails a contractual arrangement between corporations aimed at collaboratively enhancing current products and technologies or innovating new products and technologies that generate novel market demand. R&D agreements can also take the form of "paid-for" cooperation, in which one party provides financial support for the R&D activities conducted by the other side. If specific conditions are met, R&D agreements between enterprises with a collective market share of 25% or less are exempt from restrictions under the Research and Development Horizontal Block Exemption Regulation (R&D HBER). This exemption applies regardless of the structure of the agreements. The block exemption's applicability relies on market share, making it advantageous that the revised R&D HBER offers a flexible method for determining market share. In cases where sales data from the most recent calendar year does not accurately reflect the parties' actual market position, data from the preceding three calendar years can be used instead. The implementation of the "grace period" provision, which permits an agreement to

[22] Guidelines on the applicability of Article 101 TFEU to horizontal cooperation agreements, Official Journal of the European Union, C 11, 14 January 2011, pp. 1–72. Commission Regulation (EU) No 1217/2010 of 14 December 2010 on the application of Article 101(3) of the Treaty on the Functioning of the European Union to categories of horizontal cooperation agreements. OJ L 335, 18 December 2010, pp. 36–41.

[23] Commission Regulation (EU) 2023/1066 of 1 June 2023 on the application of Article 101(3) of the Treaty on the Functioning of the European Union to certain categories of research and development agreements (Text with EEA relevance). C/2023/3443. OJ L 143, 2.6.2023, pp. 9–19.

maintain block exemption status even after surpassing the market share barrier, has been standardised across various types of R&D collaborations. This uniform application now stipulates a two-year length for all instances.

Through collaborative R&D, the energy sector is able to expedite the process of innovation, enabling a more efficient response to the ever-changing challenges it faces. The allocation of risks and resources among several players serves to alleviate the financial strain on individual entities, enhancing the feasibility of undertaking ambitious research and development endeavours. Agreements frequently offer the opportunity to access specialised knowledge, talent, and facilities that individual companies may not possess.

It is imperative for collaborative research and development agreements to comply with competition law, with specific attention to anticompetitive conduct and market dominance. The consideration of intellectual property matters is of the utmost importance in order to facilitate a fair distribution of inventions and prevent conflicts. Agreements should include provisions for the establishment of protocols pertaining to data sharing and cybersecurity, with the primary objective of safeguarding sensitive information. Striking a balance between open innovation and the protection of intellectual property might present difficulties; the implementation of techniques such as well-defined intellectual property agreements and the establishment of patent pools can provide assistance in this regard. Diligent surveillance and adherence to competition regulations can help alleviate the potential for anticompetitive conduct.

The International Thermonuclear Experimental Reactor (ITER) is a multinational research and development initiative with the objective of advancing fusion energy as a sustainable and abundant source of clean energy. Instances of research and development cooperation centred on offshore wind energy and carbon capture and storage, mostly driven by industry. Collaborative R&D agreements play a crucial role in fostering innovation within the energy sector. The utilisation of these tools is crucial in tackling the difficulties within the industry, as they have the capacity to expedite technical progress, minimise potential hazards, and facilitate the pooling of resources.[24] Nevertheless, it is necessary to give meticulous consideration to regulatory compliance and the efficient administration of intellectual property in order to guarantee the prosperity of these agreements.

The new R&D block exemption regulation of the Commission came into effect on July 1, 2023.[25] This regulation introduces revised guidelines for companies to evaluate whether their current or planned research and development agreements comply with the Commission's established safe harbours. The UK block exemption, which is identical to the previous regulation, came into effect on January 1, 2023. The accompanying horizontal agreement guidance from the Competition and Markets Authority (CMA) is anticipated to be released in the near future.

[24] Faure and Van Den Bergh (2002).

[25] Commission Regulation (EU) 2023/1233 of 30 June 2023 on the application of Article 101(3) of the Treaty on the Functioning of the European Union to categories of horizontal cooperation agreements. OJ L 170, 1 July 2023, pp. 1–17.

The revised regulations of the European Union bear significant resemblance to the 2011 R&D block exemption regulation that they are intended to supersede. The recent revision of the EU block exemption has resulted in modifications to provisions and definitions, mostly aimed at enhancing clarity. However, the most significant alteration is the introduction of a novel criterion in the UK regulations concerning agreements between entities engaged in innovative competition. This provides a degree of ambiguity that may hinder parties in their assessment of whether they qualify for protection under the UK safe harbour provision. Additionally, this situation gives rise to a gap between the regulatory frameworks of the European Union (EU) and the United Kingdom (UK), both of which will be applicable to agreements that extend beyond national boundaries. However, it is important to note that both block exclusions still acknowledge the potential advantages of engaging in research and development (R&D) collaborations. These advantages include promoting the effective distribution of resources and enabling timely advancements in new products, services, and technology.

Below, we present a concise overview of the significant modifications in the block exemptions of the European Union and the United Kingdom. Additionally, we provide practical insights for future R&D collaborations. In general, the revised regulations of the European Union and the newly implemented regulations in the UK exhibit a significant degree of similarity to the preceding EU block exemption pertaining to R&D. The market share thresholds for the safe harbour provision remain unchanged. The aggregate market share of parties, whether presently engaged in competition or with the potential to do so, should not exceed 25% on pertinent product and technology markets pertaining to the established product or technology. The aforementioned criterion is also applicable to R&D activities that are financed by monetary means. In this context, the appropriate market share is determined by considering the financing party, if one exists, and all the entities that receive funding from the financing party and are involved in R&D for the same contractual items or technologies. There is no specific market share requirement for parties that do not qualify as real or potential rivals in pertinent product and technology industries.

Furthermore, the remaining prerequisites for the safe harbour provision to be applicable continue to be upheld. Both parties are entitled to complete access to the final results, with the exception of limited circumstances where access may be restricted for the purpose of exploitation. This may apply to research institutes, academic institutions, or other firms that provide research and development services without engaging in commercial activities. In cases where the research and development agreement does not include provisions for the joint exploitation of outcomes, it is necessary for each party to be given access to the pre-existing knowledge and expertise of the other party, particularly when such access is crucial for effectively using the results. The R&D agreement should not include any stringent limitations, such as constraints on R&D activities in unrelated domains, restrictions on output or sales, collusion in setting prices, or specific territorial boundaries.

The duration of the safe harbour provision for R&D agreements, in which the outcomes are jointly utilised, remains unaltered. If the safe harbour provision is applicable at the time of entering into the agreement, an R&D agreement between current or potential competitors is exempt for the duration of the R&D activities, along with an additional seven years after the initial introduction of the product or technology into the internal market of the European Union. Furthermore, this exemption continues if the parties involved in the agreement maintain a market share below the specified thresholds. There exist divergent policies within the UK and the European Union with regards to agreements between parties that are engaged in innovation-based competition.

The newly implemented regulations in the UK incorporate an additional criterion for political parties that engage in innovative practices. Specifically, this criterion applies to situations where there is currently no established market for a product or technology that is under development. This is in line with the policy objective of the Competition and Markets Authority (CMA), which is to safeguard dynamic competition in relation to innovation. Engaging in innovation competition is a wide-ranging idea that involves the unique endeavours of each party in doing research and development activities that are deemed equivalent.

The R&D activities encompass the exploration and development of identical or potentially interchangeable novel products and/or technologies, which align with the scope of the R&D agreement. Additionally, there are R&D clusters that are engaged in similar pursuits or objectives as those intended to be encompassed by the R&D agreement. This could include research and development for platform technologies, where the exact goal or purpose may not be clear as a single product or technology or may cover a much larger area than products or technologies in a given market.

According to the recently implemented regulations in the United Kingdom, effective January 1, 2023, individuals or organisations engaged in R&D activities who are considered to be competing in innovation are eligible to receive the exemption.[26] However, this exemption is contingent upon the condition that, at the moment of entering into the agreement, there exist a minimum of three parties meeting the aforementioned criteria.

Competing R&D endeavours that are similar to and on par with those undertaken by the parties involved in the R&D agreement or independent third parties capable of conducting a comparable R&D endeavour. The process of self-assessment can be problematic in practice when parties engage in a competition for invention. Due to the expansive nature of this newly implemented regulation, specifically in relation to competing research and development clusters that encompass a wide range of potential applications that are not yet definitively defined, it may pose challenges to determine whether these research and development endeavours share a substantially similar aim or objective at the time of agreement. Recent advancements in various fields, including genetics, immunology, and cell biology, have witnessed significant breakthroughs. These discoveries have been facilitated by the utilisation

[26]The Competition Act 1998 (Vertical Agreements and Concerted Practices) (Block Exemption) Order 2022 SI 2022/1247, effective from January 1, 2023.

of platform technologies, which initially may not have had clear applicability in individual product markets or for specific indications.

Furthermore, it is often the case that collaborative partners do not possess sufficient understanding of their competitors' R&D efforts, which makes it difficult for them to ascertain, based on publicly accessible information, whether their own R&D initiatives align significantly with those of their rivals. In addition, they may find it challenging to determine if there are other external entities capable of autonomously executing a similar research and development project. Assessing the comparability of competing R&D projects using reliable data can provide practical challenges, especially when dealing with R&D endeavours in their early phases. We anticipate that gathering information on the financial and human resources, intellectual property rights, knowledge, and historical research and development efforts of third parties will be challenging and highly sensitive. This holds particularly true for privately owned, emerging companies, taking into account both the financial ramifications and the viewpoint of competition law. The level of temporal proximity or distance between rival R&D efforts is still undetermined. The CMA notes in its preliminary recommendations on horizontal agreements that an R&D project six to eight years away from market entry may not directly compare to a project just one year away. This condition creates a significant ambiguity in terms of identifying potential competitors in relation to timing.

It is noteworthy that the Commission deliberated on the implementation of a comparable criterion but finally opted against it after engaging in an extensive consultation process with stakeholders from the industry.[27] The change in the European Commission's approach serves to emphasise the potential practical challenges that may arise from the implementation of the new threshold in the United Kingdom. However, the recently implemented regulations in the European Union specify that agreements between businesses that do not currently or potentially compete with each other will only impede significant competition in innovation under extraordinary conditions. More information has been added to the R&D block exemption about how the Commission and national competition authorities can take away the benefits of the block exemption in individual cases. This revocation occurs when it is determined that the requirements outlined in Article 101(3) of the TFEU are not fulfilled. This includes situations where an R&D agreement would significantly impede competition in terms of innovation within a specific domain. Comparable requirements have been incorporated into the recently implemented specialisation block exemption.

The extent to which the United Kingdom's strategy serves as an indicator of potential divergence in other domains, particularly those pertinent to innovative industries like technology and life sciences, is yet to be determined. The ongoing evaluation of the EU Technology Transfer Block Exemption Regulation, set to expire in 2026, is now underway. It is expected that a corresponding regulation

[27] European Commission, Report on the Implementation and Review of Thresholds for State Aid (2023).

will be introduced in the United Kingdom. Given the inherent complexity of self-assessment, it is advisable for enterprises to contemplate implementing the subsequent measures when embarking on R&D agreements.[28]

The importance to examine and evaluate the primary justification for the partnership from a pro-competitive standpoint while subjecting it to rigorous testing entails explicitly outlining within internal records the specific contributions that each collaborating party will make to the project or endeavour, as well as the anticipated advantages that consumers or patients are expected to derive from it. It is imperative for parties that may engage in innovation to do a comprehensive evaluation of the competitive environment, encompassing an examination of rival endeavours in both broad and specific domains of innovation or research. It is important to maintain a comprehensive record of the information utilised, particularly when relying on block exemptions, as the dynamic nature of publicly available R&D pipelines, planned clinical trials, and announced investment decisions may result in changes or removals over time. Consequently, it is necessary to regularly update the analysis to reflect the evolving competitive landscape. In order to effectively mitigate the risk of competition law violations when engaging in collaborations with current or prospective competitors, it is imperative to establish and enforce suitable safeguards. In situations where an R&D agreement does not strictly adhere to the exemptions outlined by the European Union and/or the United Kingdom, it may still be eligible for individual exemption if certain competition law safeguards are implemented to ensure that rivals engaging in joint R&D comply with regulations. One potential requirement for R&D collaboration partners is the implementation of firewalls to separate and protect competing R&D programmes.

6.6 The Horizontal Cooperation in Nuclear Industry

When examining horizontal cooperation within the energy sector, it is crucial to take into account the presence of nuclear insurance pools. These entities are specifically designed to establish and maintain an adequate financial reserve in the event of a nuclear accident. The primary aim behind the establishment of joint insurance pools was to foster the growth and advancement of the nuclear industry. In accordance with the principles governing civil liability for nuclear damage as established in international nuclear law, the operator of a nuclear facility bears exclusive responsibility for any potential nuclear disaster that may transpire. The introduction of this provision aimed to streamline the process of compensating victims by eliminating the need to establish a direct connection between the actions of the responsible party and the resulting consequences. The International Conventions on Civil Liability for

[28] European Commission Evaluation Report on the Technology Transfer Block Exemption Regulation. September 2022. The Competition Act 1998 (Technology Transfer Agreements Block Exemption) Order 2020 SI 2020/447, effective from 1 January 2021.

Nuclear Damage establish the fundamental principle that the operator of a nuclear installation is solely responsible for any liability arising from such activities.[29] These conventions also offer the state various options to determine the extent of its financial liability in situations where the operator is unable to adequately compensate for the resulting damage. To adequately address the incurred damages, it is necessary for the operator to procure civil liability insurance of a suitable magnitude. The specific amount required differs significantly among European Union Member States and globally, in accordance with respective domestic legislation.

Certain countries impose unlimited operator liability, but others establish a minimal liability limit. It is important to acknowledge that the limits of liability associated with civil liability for nuclear facility operators are substantial. According to the Vienna Convention, a minimum limit of 300 million SDR is established. The Paris Convention implements a more stringent minimum liability requirement of EUR 1.2 billion.[30] When a state makes the decision to ratify treaties pertaining to civil liability for nuclear damage, it determines the degree of obligation imposed on the operator in the case of a nuclear accident. States have the authority to exercise their discretion in determining the extent of liability for operators. This discretion allows them to establish liability limits that either adhere to the minimal thresholds outlined in conventions or grant operators unlimited liability. Furthermore, states have the option to establish liability limits that surpass the thresholds established by international agreements.

Nuclear operators are motivated to establish a liability limit that is as low as possible, with the state assuming responsibility for any remaining costs. This approach ensures that the operators are only obligated to provide compensation up to a predetermined minimum, while the overall responsibility for the nuclear site stays intact. From the perspective of insurers, it is crucial to establish a higher limit of liability, given that operators are required to pay specific rates for civil liability insurance. Insurance companies have the capacity to offer third-party liability insurance up to a specific limit, which is not without bounds. From a societal standpoint, it is imperative for citizens to prioritise the safe operation of nuclear facilities and, in the unfortunate case of a nuclear catastrophe, to promptly and efficiently pursue the most optimal methods of seeking compensation or resolution.

The financial repercussions resulting from a nuclear disaster can reach billions of euros or more, surpassing the capacity of a single insurance firm to provide full compensation for such extensive damage. In pursuit of this objective, insurers participate in collective general insurance pools alongside pools consisting of operators. The issue stems from the circumstance that general insurance pools

---

[29] International Atomic Energy Agency (IAEA), Convention on Third Party Liability in the Field of Nuclear Energy, 29 July 1960. International Atomic Energy Agency (IAEA), Protocol to Amend the Convention on Third Party Liability in the Field of Nuclear Energy, 16 November 1982.

[30] International Atomic Energy Agency (IAEA), Vienna Convention on Civil Liability for Nuclear Damage, 21 May 1963, Vienna Convention. International Atomic Energy Agency (IAEA), Paris Convention on Third Party Liability in the Field of Nuclear Energy, 29 July 1960, Paris Convention.

function within the jurisdiction of a specific state, and operators have significant limitations when seeking to become part of a general insurance group in a different state's area. In this regard, it is evident that there exist territorial limitations and horizontal agreements that impede both current and future competition within the market.

Typically, nuclear operators who operate within the jurisdiction of a specific Member State are limited to joining general insurance organisations that operate only within the boundaries of that Member State. Consequently, this arrangement gives rise to territorial constraints. Certain authors have expressed criticism of this standpoint due to the argument that the consolidation of insurance companies into national entities leads to inefficiencies. From a competition law standpoint, horizontal agreements are evaluated based on the presence of an agreement among economic operators or the presence of coordination that results in competition limits within the market. This study aims to evaluate the necessity of collaboration among insurers within a group for the effective operation of the nuclear energy industry as well as determine if such collaborative practices impose limitations on market competitiveness. Hence, it is justifiable to align with the authors' viewpoint that a competitive market for co-insurance organisations has the potential to provide a more efficient mechanism for addressing grievances. Several other scholars have a similar perspective, contending that the consolidation of market power diminishes service efficiency and fails to yield the intended outcome.

Despite its potential as a low-carbon power source, nuclear energy presents significant hazards. The presence of various risks, such as catastrophic accidents and long-term environmental consequences, underscores the need for distinctive insurance solutions. Collaborative mechanisms in the form of nuclear insurance pools have arisen to tackle these difficulties. This article examines the collaborative strategy employed by nuclear insurance pools, providing an in-depth analysis of their historical roots, organisational structure, and significant contribution to the nuclear energy industry. Nuclear energy has been widely recognised as a fundamental element of a sustainable energy trajectory. Nevertheless, this technology carries inherent hazards, particularly the possibility of catastrophic mishaps that can have extensive and profound implications. The aforementioned hazards have prompted the establishment of specialised insurance systems, resulting in the formation of nuclear insurance pools.

The origins of nuclear insurance pools can be traced back to the initial stages of nuclear power development. The development of knowledge regarding nuclear risks and the recognition of the necessity for liability coverage prompted the establishment of these cooperative agreements. International accords, such as the Paris and Vienna Conventions, have significantly influenced the development of nuclear insurance.[31] Nuclear insurance pools function based on a collaborative framework wherein contributions are sourced from multiple stakeholders. These entities may

[31] International Atomic Energy Agency (IAEA), Vienna Convention on Civil Liability for Nuclear Damage, 21 May 1963, Vienna Convention. International Atomic Energy Agency (IAEA), Paris

encompass nuclear operators, governmental bodies, and commercial insurance companies. Their operations are regulated by a rigorous legislative framework, which ensures their effective and transparent functioning.

Risk mitigation refers to the process of identifying, assessing, and implementing measures to reduce or eliminate any risks that may negatively impact an organisation. It involves taking proactive steps to minimise the likelihood and severity of risks as well as their potential consequences. One of the main goals of nuclear insurance pools is to effectively manage and reduce the risks that are inherent to the use of nuclear energy. Financial assistance is offered to facilitate the implementation of safety measures and preventive actions, contributing to the overall enhancement of nuclear facility safety. Moreover, they fulfil a crucial function in terms of liability coverage, guaranteeing that individuals affected by nuclear catastrophes are duly compensated.

Nuclear insurance pools use thorough risk assessment procedures in order to ascertain appropriate premium rates. This measure guarantees that the contributions made by nuclear operators are in accordance with their individual risk profiles. In the event of a nuclear mishap, these pools effectively administer claims, ensuring efficient coordination with various stakeholders to promptly give compensation. Although nuclear insurance pools are crucial for managing risks, they do have certain limits. With the global expansion of nuclear energy, there is a significant potential for international growth in the field of nuclear insurance pools. It is expected that the progression of technology in the field of risk assessment will improve its effectiveness in the management of nuclear risks. Nuclear insurance pools exemplify a cooperative strategy for effectively addressing the diverse array of hazards inherent in nuclear energy. The historical relevance and changing role of nuclear power plants in an ever-expanding global nuclear sector highlight their utmost significance. The inclusion of nuclear energy in discussions surrounding the transition to alternative energy sources necessitates the continued utilisation of cooperation methods to guarantee its safety and sustainability.

6.7 The Cooperation Agreements

The Commission was soliciting public feedback on its proposed amendments to European Union regulations and guidance pertaining to common competitor cooperation arrangements. These regulations are set to expire on December 31, 2022.[32] Horizontal cooperation agreements encompass a variety of cooperative arrangements among current or prospective competitors. These agreements pertain to

Convention on Third Party Liability in the Field of Nuclear Energy, 29 July 1960, Paris Convention.

[32] European Commission, Consultation on Amendments to the Horizontal Cooperation Guidelines (2021).

collaborative activities like research and development, purchasing, production and commercialization, information sharing, and participation in bidding consortiums.[33] The enhanced horizontal framework, also known as the revised guidelines, offers additional guidance on the assessment of joint purchasing and information exchanges. It explicitly identifies employee wage-fixing as an unlawful practice that contravenes EU competition law. The text also addresses the criteria for practices that may be exempted from competition law regulations, provided that specific circumstances are satisfied. These conditions encompass sustainability initiatives, data pooling, and infrastructure sharing. The implementation of the new regulations was scheduled to commence on January 1, 2023, accompanied by a transitional phase for pre-existing agreements that will extend until December 31, 2024.[34]

The amendments made in this context aim to differentiate between buyer cartels, which involve collusion on purchase prices, and joint purchasing agreements. Joint purchasing agreements can be considered acceptable under certain circumstances, such as when the combined shares of the parties involved are minimal and/or where joint purchasing leads to advantageous price reductions. Bidding consortia refer to the formation of alliances among suppliers with complementary capabilities who individually lack the capacity to independently participate in project bidding processes. It is generally recognised that such consortia are legally permissible. However, the guidance cautions that it is important to assess the competitive potential at the specific level where competition occurs. For instance, if individual lots are distinct from the overall project bid, the evaluation should be conducted at the individual lot level. Additionally, the guidance highlights that agreements to subcontract to a bidder in the event of an unsuccessful bid may raise concerns.

The updated guidelines stipulate that any type of information sharing that has the potential to facilitate anti-competitive behaviour is deemed prohibited. This prohibition extends to instances where the information shared pertains to historical pricing, auction outcomes, or strategic intentions. The updated Guidelines further highlight those lawful endeavours, including engaging in legislative lobbying, have the potential to cross the boundary into unlawful collusion if corporations indicate their approach to adhering to newly established criteria. The amended guidelines provide a comprehensive analysis of recent decisions and policy developments by the Commission on mobile networks and sustainability agreements. They specifically address the sharing of mobile network infrastructure and provide a thorough evaluation of the legal aspects of environmental and social sustainability measures undertaken by the industry. The aforementioned analysis suggests that the latter course of action may be deemed legally permissible, despite potential implications

[33] Public Consultation on the Revision of the Horizontal Cooperation Guidelines and Block Exemption Regulations. 2022.

[34] Commission Regulation (EU) 2023/1066 of 1 June 2023 on the application of Article 101(3) of the Treaty on the Functioning of the European Union to certain categories of research and development agreements.

such as price hikes or output reductions. Nevertheless, it is imperative that these programmes be deemed essential in order to achieve environmental and social objectives while also yielding advantages for consumers.

Joint purchase agreements pertain to the collaborative procurement of goods by multiple entities, typically through the establishment of a collective purchasing organisation. These agreements can be observed across a diverse range of industries and entail the consolidation of procurement operations. The revised guidelines provide clarification regarding the nature of these agreements, which can involve either pooling actual purchases through a joint purchasing agreement or solely focusing on collectively negotiating the purchase price, as well as other terms and conditions. In the latter case, the responsibility for the actual purchasing remains with the individual members of the purchasing organisation.[35]

As previously mentioned, the new guidelines serve to strengthen the differentiation between cooperative purchasing agreements and buyer cartels. Generally, the former is typically allowed when the total market shares of the parties involved do not surpass 15% in either the buying or selling market, or in both markets. Additionally, the joint agreement must result in advantageous price reductions and/or efficiency improvements. A market share above the specified level in either or both markets does not inherently imply illegality. However, it necessitates a comprehensive evaluation of the agreement's impact on the market. In contrast, buyer cartels seek to engage in collusion about purchase pricing, including various components such as costs, wages, salaries, expenses, and so on. Additionally, they collude with the intention of exerting influence over individual negotiations between buyers and suppliers. It is important to note that these activities are inherently unlawful. The proposed amendments suggest that the Commission will classify agreements that establish employees' salaries as a kind of illicit cartel behaviour. A buyer cartel can potentially be formed when buyers mutually agree to share commercially sensitive information regarding their individual purchasing intentions or negotiations with suppliers. This occurs independently of any legitimate joint purchasing arrangement that collectively interacts with suppliers on behalf of its members. If joint purchase agreements are used as a means to partake in a covert cartel, they will be deemed unlawful.

Finally, the updated guidelines offer an inclusive compilation of variables that organisations can utilise to evaluate whether their participation in a collective purchasing arrangement can be classified as a buyer cartel. The examples encompass the determination of whether the agreement effectively communicates to suppliers the collective negotiation and binding of its members in relation to the terms and conditions of their individual or joint purchases. Additionally, it examines whether the parties have explicitly outlined the structure, extent, and operation of their joint purchasing agreement in written form, enabling subsequent verification. While a

[35] Guidelines on the applicability of Article 101 of the Treaty on the Functioning of the European Union to horizontal cooperation agreements, [Revised Guidelines on Horizontal Cooperation Agreements], OJ C 11, 14.1.2022, pp. 1–30.

written agreement does not provide complete protection against competition law risks, it is recommended by the guidelines.

The updated guidelines introduce a novel aspect by acknowledging the presence of bidding consortia, which pertain to instances where multiple entities collaborate to jointly submit a proposal in a competitive procurement process, whether it be in the public or private sector. Bidding consortia are typically authorised when they are deemed essential and yield operational advantages that can be readily transferred to consumers, resulting in cost savings and improved offerings. The new guidelines establish a clear distinction between consortiums and bid manipulation, the latter being inherently unlawful. A consortium agreement for joint bidding is typically considered legally permissible when it enables parties to engage in projects that would otherwise be beyond their individual capacities, such as due to the contract's magnitude or intricacy. Due to the absence of potential competitors for project implementation, there is no restriction on competition. This scenario may arise when parties provide complementary services to jointly participate in a tender or when multiple enterprises operating in the same market are unable to independently fulfil a contract due to factors such as its scale or complexity.

Nevertheless, the updated text cautions that the assessment of competition should be undertaken on an individual lot basis, particularly if these lots are distinct from the overall project bidding process. In the event that the parties involved in the consortium agreement possess the potential to independently participate in the bidding process or if there is an excessive number of parties within the consortium agreement, the collective bid may impose limitations on competition.[36] Furthermore, the updated guidelines provide clarification that agreements to subcontract with a bidder who did not win the contract may give rise to issues. The guidance pertaining to the exchange of information has undergone significant revisions, resulting in an expanded definition of what qualifies as an exchange of sensitive information. The amended wording establishes a more stringent framework compared to the 2010 Guidelines, when the act of sharing information on future pricing or quantities among current or potential competitors, whether directly or indirectly, was examined and penalised as cartels. The act of sharing information that has the potential to facilitate competitive behaviour may be classified as collusion, like a cartel, even if it pertains to previous (recent) pricing, auction outcomes, or strategic intentions. The updated Guidelines also emphasise that lawful activities resulting from regulatory initiatives, such as engaging in legislative lobbying, have the potential to cross the line into unlawful cooperation if corporations disclose their market strategy or their approach to adhering to new requirements. The modifications demonstrate the significance of data sharing in facilitating informed decision-making through the utilisation of big data analytics and machine-learning methodologies. The current European Union case law establishes that exchanges of commercially sensitive

[36] Guidelines on the applicability of Article 101 of the Treaty on the Functioning of the European Union to horizontal cooperation agreements, [Revised Guidelines on Horizontal Cooperation Agreements], OJ C 11, 14.1.2022, pp. 1–30.

information among competitors can occur through several means, including a service provider, an internet platform, or a shared algorithm, such as a real-time, high-frequency price-monitoring tool. The passage highlights that using publicly accessible data to supply algorithmic software is within legal bounds. However, if a single IT company aggregates sensitive information into a pricing tool and provides access to multiple competitors, this practice may potentially be considered collusion.

It is important to examine the issue of data accessibility in cases where it is strategically advantageous for competition and encompasses a significant portion of the pertinent market without presenting a collusion risk. The sharing of strategic information is deemed acceptable, provided that the material is made available in a manner that does not discriminate. In the context of data pools, it is recommended that members be granted access solely to their own individual information and to the ultimate aggregated data. The communication of information will be considered unlawful if the information is of a commercial nature and has the potential to impact the behaviour of participants in the market. In order to evaluate the impact on competition, a thorough analysis on a case-by-case basis will be necessary for any additional information exchanges. If the extent of information interchange remains within the bounds of what is required for legitimate collaboration between existing or potential competitors and if it results in efficiency improvements that can be readily transferred to consumers, it is more likely to be deemed permissible.

The updated guidelines encompass policy advancements and provide a comprehensive evaluation of the legality of environmental and social sustainability activities within the business.[37] The researchers reach the conclusion that cooperative agreements aimed at achieving sustainability goals may be deemed legal even if they result in a certain degree of price increase or output reduction. In order to comply with legal requirements, it is imperative that these initiatives be deemed essential for achieving environmental and social objectives while also providing tangible advantages to consumers. The amended guidelines provide clarification regarding the circumstances in which benefits, such as qualitative or quantitative efficiency gains, might be considered and exempted from the prohibition on anticompetitive agreements.

A proposed addition to the existing horizontal guidelines is suggested, aiming to address sustainability agreements and provide clarity about the compatibility of antitrust regulations with agreements between rivals that aim to promote sustainability objectives. The updated guideline document encompasses a comprehensive interpretation of sustainability objectives, drawing from the United Nations Sustainable Development Goals. Additionally, it provides a non-exhaustive list of sustainability agreements that typically do not fall under the purview of Article 101(1) of the TFEU. The newly implemented regulations also establish a lenient protective framework for sustainability standardisation agreements that satisfy specific criteria.

---

[37] Guidelines on the applicability of Article 101 of the Treaty on the Functioning of the European Union to horizontal cooperation agreements, [Revised Guidelines on Horizontal Cooperation Agreements], OJ C 11, 14.1.2022, pp. 1–30.

Additionally, the authors provide clarification on the potential exemptions of a sustainability pact by delineating various categories of benefits that could be considered. The subsequent chapter additionally incorporates speculative instances that serve to exemplify the practical implementation of Article 101 TFEU. The inclusion of the new sustainability chapter in the agreement serves as a reminder to enterprises desiring to engage in a sustainability agreement that they have the option to seek informal counsel from the Commission to ensure adherence to the competition regulations of the European Union.[38] The inclusion of such guidelines can enhance the overall analytical framework presented in the newly introduced sustainability chapter.

6.8 The Horizontal Block Exemption Regulations

The Commission released a Staff Working Document in May 2021, which presented the findings of its assessment of the 2010 Horizontal Block Exemption Regulations (HBERs) and the 2011 Horizontal Guidelines.[39] The study demonstrated that these instruments serve as valuable resources that effectively aid in the self-evaluation of horizontal agreements, thereby contributing to the reduction of compliance expenses for firms. Nevertheless, the assessment also revealed the necessity of modifying the regulations to align with the changes in the economy and society that have transpired subsequent to their implementation.

Subsequent to the evaluation, the Commission initiated an impact assessment in June 2021. This assessment involved the collection of additional evidence pertaining to the identified areas for enhancement. The evidence was gathered through various means, such as an open public consultation, stakeholder workshops, discussions with interested parties, national competition authorities, and targeted expert reports.[40] The Commission initiated a public consultation in March 2022 over the draft amended Horizontal Block Exemption Regulations (HBERs) and Horizontal Guidelines. The findings of the public consultation are succinctly outlined in the Impact Assessment Report, which is concurrently released today. The present report provides a comprehensive account of the consultation activities conducted, together with an evaluation of the suggested adjustments.

According to Article 101(1) of the TFEU, the formation of agreements among enterprises that have the effect of limiting competition is prohibited. Nevertheless, in accordance with Article 101(3) of the TFEU, these agreements are deemed to be in

---

[38] Whish (2018), Ezrachi (2021), and Fox (2018).

[39] Commission Staff Working Document of the Horizontal Block Exemption Regulations. SWD (2021) 103 final. 2021.

[40] Communication from the Commission – Guidelines on the applicability of Article 101 of the Treaty on the Functioning of the European Union to horizontal co-operation agreements. C/2023/4752. OJ C 259, 21.7.2023, pp. 1–125.

line with the principles of the single market if they contribute to enhancing the production or distribution of goods or if they facilitate technical or economic advancement. It is crucial that these agreements also ensure that consumers receive a fair portion of the resulting advantages while simultaneously preserving competition.

The HBERs provide an exemption to R&D and specialisation agreements that satisfy specific criteria, establishing a protected area for such agreements within the confines of Article 101(1) of the TFEU.[41] The HBERs are accompanied by the Horizontal Guidelines, which offer guidance pertaining to three key aspects: (i) the application of the HBERs; (ii) the evaluation of research and development (R&D) and specialisation agreements that do not meet the criteria for safe harbour protection; and (iii) the assessment of other types of cooperation agreements between competing firms that are commonly encountered. These encompass several types of agreements, such as collaborative purchase and joint commercialization agreements, standardisation agreements, information exchanges, and sustainability agreements.

On June 1, 2023, the Commission adopted amended Horizontal Block Exemption Regulations on R&D and Specialisation Agreements (HBERs), along with revised Horizontal Guidelines. This decision comes after a comprehensive study and review of the existing regulations. The new HBERs and Guidelines offer businesses more precise and current instructions to aid them in evaluating the conformity of their horizontal cooperation agreements with the competition regulations of the European Union. The HBERs provide exceptions for R&D and specialisation agreements, allowing them to be exempted from the restriction stated in Article 101(1) of the TFEU, provided that specific conditions are met. The regulations, therefore, establish a secure haven in which specific agreements are granted an exception from the competition rules. The proposed modification aims to broaden the applicability of the Specialisation Block Exemption Regulation to encompass a wider range of production agreements involving many parties above the current threshold of two. Furthermore, the updated regulations incorporate a more adaptable methodology for determining market shares in order to facilitate the application of the block exemption. Additionally, these guidelines provide precise instructions on the implementation of the latter. Enhance the precision and adaptability in the computation of market shares with respect to the implementation of the R&D Block Exemption Regulation while incorporating instructions on its application. The revised regulations place greater emphasis on safeguarding competition in innovation, particularly in situations where market shares cannot be accurately determined.[42] In this regard, the regulations highlight the authority of the Commission and national competition authorities to revoke the exemption's advantages in specific cases that present challenges.

---

[41] Commission Regulation (EU) 2023/1067 of 1 June 2023 on the application of Article 101(3) of the Treaty on the Functioning of the European Union to certain categories of specialisation agreements (Text with EEA relevance). C/2023/3448. OJ L 143, 2.6.2023, pp. 20–26.

[42] McFadden (2020).

The chapter also includes additional instructions regarding the implementation of Article 101 TFEU in agreements between joint ventures and their parent companies. Furthermore, it provides an extended set of instructions on the application of the guidelines to agreements that entail collaboration in multiple activities, such as production and commercialization. The chapter on production agreements in the horizontal guidelines now includes an updated section on mobile telecommunications infrastructure sharing agreements, which incorporates the latest enforcement practices. The recently issued guideline delineates the pertinent considerations for evaluating these agreements and incorporates a roster of essential prerequisites that corporations must adhere to in order to mitigate the potential violation of competition regulations.

The chapter elucidates the differentiation between cooperative purchasing and buyer cartels. Additionally, it elucidates that collaborative purchasing encompasses situations in which buyers together discuss purchase terms, yet each individual buyer conducts their purchases autonomously. This approach places greater emphasis on the potential anti-competitive consequences pertaining to the upstream supply sector and offers recommendations on specific collaborative bargaining strategies, such as the implementation of temporary order halts. In order to enhance the comprehensiveness of the Guidelines on commercialization agreements, it is recommended to incorporate a novel section pertaining to bidding consortia. In order to ensure the most up-to-date and comprehensive coverage of relevant legal precedents and enforcement practices, it is imperative to undertake a reconfiguration and augmentation of the chapter pertaining to the Guidelines on Information Exchange. This endeavour aims to incorporate the latest case law developments and enforcement experiences into the existing framework. By doing so, the revised chapter provides a more robust examination of the subject matter, enhancing its rigour and practical applicability.

The revised chapter incorporates supplementary instructions pertaining to various aspects, namely: (i) the elucidation of the notion of commercially sensitive information; (ii) the identification of information exchanges that may potentially impede competition by their very nature; (iii) the examination of potential positive effects on competition arising from data pools; (iv) the exploration of indirect forms of information exchange, including hub-and-spoke arrangements; (v) the analysis of anti-competitive signalling through public announcements; and (vi) the presentation of practical measures that companies can adopt to prevent infringements, such as limiting the extent of information exchange, employing clean teams or independent trustees, and maintaining a public distance.

Proposed modifications to the chapter pertaining to the Guidelines on Standardisation Agreements with the aim of enhancing the level of adaptability concerning the stipulation of inclusive engagement in the process of establishing standards. The updated chapter provides more clarification on two key points. Firstly, it emphasises that the act of parties involved in a standardisation agreement disclosing a maximum cumulated royalty rate does not constitute anti-competitive behaviour. Secondly, it underscores the necessity for participants to declare any pertinent intellectual property rights. The proposal entails the addition of a supplementary section to the horizontal guidelines, specifically addressing sustainability agreements. The purpose of this additional chapter is to provide a clear and explicit explanation that antitrust regulations do not impede agreements between competitors that are aimed at promoting sustainability objectives. The updated guideline document encompasses a comprehensive interpretation of sustainability objectives, drawing from the United Nations Sustainable Development Goals. Additionally, it provides a compilation of diverse instances of sustainability agreements that often do not fall within the purview of Article 101(1) of the TFEU.[43] The newly implemented regulations also offer a flexible and secure environment for sustainability standardisation agreements that satisfy specific criteria. Additionally, the authors provide clarification on the potential exemptions of a sustainability pact by delineating several sorts of benefits that could be considered. The subsequent chapter includes speculative instances that serve as illustrations for the implementation of Article 101 TFEU. The inclusion of the new sustainability chapter in the agreement serves as a reminder to enterprises seeking to engage in a sustainability agreement that they have the option to seek informal guidance from the Commission to ensure adherence to the competition regulations of the European Union. The inclusion of such guidelines has the potential to enhance the overall analytical framework outlined in the recently introduced sustainability chapter.

6.9 The Cartels

A cartel refers to a collective of comparable and autonomous enterprises that engage in explicit or implicit agreements to manipulate pricing, restrict output or development, allocate markets or customers, or impose other forms of competition-restricting measures. Instead of engaging in direct competition, participants in a cartel depend on a mutually agreed-upon course of action, diminishing their motivation to offer innovative or superior products and services at competitive rates. Consequently, the business partners of the company, whether they are consumers or other firms, sometimes incur higher costs in exchange for lower-quality products or services. The illegality of cartels under EU competition law and the imposition of substantial fines by the European Commission on corporations engaged in cartel activities are the reasons for this phenomenon. Additional information can be obtained by viewing the cartel statistics and using the case search function. Due to the illegality of cartels, their operations are typically characterised by a high degree of secrecy, making the identification and acquisition of evidence pertaining to their

[43] United Nations Sustainable Development Goals (SDGs) Overview: United Nations, Transforming our world: the 2030 Agenda for Sustainable Development, A/RES/70/1 (United Nations, 2015). European Commission, Guidelines on the applicability of Article 101 TFEU to horizontal cooperation agreements, [2022/C 9/01] (Official Journal of the European Union, 2022).

presence a challenging endeavour.[44] The leniency programme incentivizes corporations to provide the Commission with internal proof of cartel activities in return for immunity from fines or significant reductions in penalties. If a corporation inside a cartel is the first to submit an application for leniency, it may be granted complete immunity, provided that the material it presents is deemed adequate by the Commission to initiate an investigation. Since its inception, the leniency programme has facilitated the European Commission's detection and exposure of numerous cartels.[45] Simultaneously, the Commission effectively persists in conducting its independent investigations aimed at identifying and uncovering instances of cartel behaviour.

The Commission also promotes the active engagement of individuals in reporting any internal information or suspicions they may possess regarding the existence of a cartel to the Commission. Individuals have the option to engage in this activity with a sense of assurance and confidentiality by utilising a "whistleblower" mechanism. Companies that are determined by the Commission to have engaged in cartel activities have the option to resolve their case by admitting their participation in the cartel, which would result in a subsequent reduction of 10% in the potential fine imposed upon them. The settlement method offers advantages to both the Commission and the parties involved, such as increased efficiency, decreased investigation time, limited access to files, and shorter final conclusions.[46]

Anti-competitive agreements can manifest in both overt and covert forms, with hidden arrangements like cartels exemplifying the latter. These agreements serve to safeguard market-sharing companies against potential competitive pressures that may arise in relation to the introduction of new products as well as the enhancement of service and product quality.[47] Cartels refer to collusive agreements formed among competitors operating at the same level with the objective of collectively establishing common pricing and supply policies. The primary aim of such agreements is to elevate output prices and subsequently enhance profits. The cases encompass territorial market sharing and non-competition regarding pricing in public procurement.

Cartel agreements among firms result in a decrease in the availability of goods, leading to an increase in consumer prices. According to the TFEU, cartels are strictly forbidden and are liable to face penalties. Certain scholars argue that cartels can be regarded as monopolies due to the existence of collusive arrangements among firms, which establish the necessary conditions for monopolistic control over a market.[48] There are differing viewpoints among other authors regarding this stance due to the fact that, despite its influence on the market, a cartel is unable to attain the same effects and market dominance as a monopoly. The individuals comprising the cartel

---

[44] Wijckmans and Tuytschaever (2015).

[45] Liefmann (1930).

[46] Commission Notice on Immunity from Fines and Reduction of Fines in Cartel Cases (2006/C 298/11). OJ C 298, 8.12.2006, pp. 17–22.

[47] Bouwens and Dankers (2005).

[48] Caffarra and Scott (2018), Jullien and Rey (2021), and Tate (2022).

engage in internal competition while simultaneously aligning their shared interests towards a collective objective, thereby demonstrating a vested interest in exerting influence over the established monopoly.

Cartels exert a notable influence on competition by imposing substantial restrictions, thereby resulting in considerable repercussions for consumers in the form of elevated prices. In parallel, within industries where cartels are established, the level of competitiveness among enterprises is diminished. The doctrine further delineates factors that contribute to the formation of cartels, which will be examined in greater depth. The formation of cartels is contingent upon the quantity of firms operating within a given market, as a higher number of companies present in the market reduces the likelihood of cartelization. Difficulties frequently emerge as a result of their inability to effectively coordinate with one another. The higher the degree of consolidation among participating companies, the greater the likelihood of their collaboration and coordination. The valuation of market shares held by companies is attributed to their comparable ability to facilitate agreement and coordination.[49] The presence of barriers to entry is a significant determinant, as the potential for competition introduces complexities in the circumstances surrounding the establishment of a cartel. Furthermore, the assessment is conducted based on the buyer's market power to exert influence over prices. This scenario would result in the cartel experiencing a decline in profitability. A heightened propensity for the formation of cartels arises when a particular sector experiences an elevated cost burden. According to the Court of Justice of the European Union (CJEU), horizontal price-fixing cartels inherently entail significant anti-competitive consequences, and therefore, it is not necessary to demonstrate any specific impact on the market.

The EniSpA case,[50] in which the parent company was deemed responsible for the cartels entered into by its subsidiaries, holds significance in the evaluation of cartel activities. The parent company refrained from direct involvement in the cartels, yet it remained legally responsible. Liability arises in situations where the parent company exercises complete control over the subsidiary company implicated in the cartel. Consequently, it was assumed that the parent company possessed significant control over the contracts executed by the subsidiary, despite not being directly engaged in said contracts. It was necessary to present evidence demonstrating the subsidiary's independent operation and decision-making separate from the influence of the parent company in order to establish the absence of significant control by the parent company over its managed subsidiaries. EniSpA assumed responsibility for overseeing the technical and financial dimensions of its consortium of enterprises, notwithstanding its lack of direct involvement in the operational undertakings of the implicated entities. The Commission's decision acknowledged that the company's involvement was significant enough to establish its accountability for the actions of the subordinate companies. This case establishes the precedent that a parent company, when coordinating the operations of its subsidiaries, can be held

[49] Argenton et al. (2020).

[50] Case C-508/11 P *EniSPA v Commission*. ECLI:EU:C:2013:289.

accountable for the actions of said subsidiaries that violate provisions of competition law.

The European Commission has levied fines amounting to EUR 5,979,000 on EPEX Spot ("EPEX") and Nord Pool Spot (NPS), the two European spot power exchanges. These fines were imposed due to their mutual agreement to abstain from engaging in competitive practices for their spot electricity trading services within the European Economic Area (EEA). This action constitutes a violation of the European Union's antitrust regulations, which specifically ban the formation of cartels and the implementation of restrictive practices.[51] Power exchanges refer to structured and regulated markets that facilitate the trading of electricity. Spot trading refers to the practice of engaging in trading activities within a relatively short time frame, typically spanning a single day or extending to the following day. Both NPS and EPEX were granted a 10% reduction in fines as a result of their decision to reach a settlement with the Commission. The infringement took place during discussions about the creation of the internal energy market, a project run by the Commission with the goal of fully integrating domestic energy markets. In the context of examining a collaborative strategy pertaining to the technical systems employed for cross-border trade, EPEX and NPS have moreover reached a mutual understanding to abstain from engaging in competitive practices and to apportion European regions between themselves. These agreements exceeded the intended scope of collaboration pertaining to the establishment of the IEM. The corporations have evidently violated Article 101 of the TFEU and Article 53 of the EEA Agreement, both of which explicitly ban the formation of cartels. The individuals undertook this violation autonomously and at their own peril.

The period of violation persisted for a minimum duration of seven months, spanning from 2011 to 2012. The cessation of the infringement occurred subsequent to unannounced inspections conducted by the Commission and the EFTA Surveillance Authority at the premises of the implicated enterprises.[52] The anticompetitive communications encompassed many modes of interaction, including in-person meetings, telephonic and video conferences, as well as electronic correspondence via emails.[53]

The Commission has imposed fines of EUR 553 million on both E.ON and GDF Suez for engaging in market-sharing activities in the gasoline markets of France and Germany. The Commission has levied fines amounting to EUR 1,106,000,000 on E. ON AG and its subsidiary E.ON Ruhrgas AG, both based in Germany, as well as on GDF Suez SA, a French company. These fines were issued due to their engagement in market-sharing activities, which violated the regulations outlined in the EC Treaty

[51] European Commission Decision of 21 December 2016. Case AT.39816 - EPEX Spot/Nord Pool Spot. [2016] OJ L 80/28.

[52] European Commission, Decision of 14 July 2021 relating to a proceeding under Article 101 of the Treaty on the Functioning of the European Union and Article 53 of the EEA Agreement (Case AT.40394 – Cartel in the Animal Feed Sector), [2021/C 293/01] (Official Journal of the European Union, 14 July 2021).

[53] AT.39952 Power exchanges 2014.

pertaining to cartels and restrictive business practices, namely Article 81.[54] Both E. ON/E.ON Ruhrgas and GDF Suez have been subjected to fines amounting to EUR 553,000,000 each. In 1975, Ruhrgas AG (currently known as E.ON Ruhrgas, a subsidiary of the E.ON group) and Gaz de France (now a part of GDF Suez) reached an agreement to collaboratively construct the MEGAL pipeline in Germany. The primary objective of this pipeline was to facilitate the importation of Russian gas into both Germany and France. As part of their agreement, the two companies mutually decided not to engage in the sale of gas transported through this pipeline within their respective domestic markets. The market-sharing arrangement was upheld after the liberalisation of European petrol markets and was ultimately terminated in 2005.

E.ON, with a global revenue of EUR 87 billion in 2008, holds a prominent position in the German natural gas market through its subsidiary E.ON Ruhrgas. Similarly, GDF Suez, with a worldwide turnover of EUR 68 billion in 2008, is a key provider of natural gas in France. Both companies are significant players in the European gas business. In 2003, E.ON obtained majority ownership of Ruhrgas, subsequently rebranding it as E.ON Ruhrgas. In 2008, Gaz de France and Suez amalgamated following the termination of their market-sharing agreement with E. ON, resulting in the establishment of GDF Suez. In 2006, the Commission approved the transaction. Unexpected inspections carried out in 2006 at the facilities of E.ON and Gaz de France in Germany and France prompted the Commission to launch the investigation. Subsequently, formal proceedings were commenced in July 2007, and a Statement of Objections was issued to the companies in June 2008.[55]

The MEGAL pipeline is a collaborative venture between E.ON Ruhrgas and GDF Suez, with both companies sharing ownership and operational responsibilities. The pipeline facilitates the transportation of gas in the southern region of Germany, connecting the German-Czech and German-Austrian borders in the east and the French-German border in the west. In 1975, Ruhrgas and Gaz de France entered into a collaborative agreement to construct the MEGAL pipeline. As part of this agreement, the two parties officially communicated their intention through two written correspondences, affirming that Gaz de France (GDF) would refrain from selling any gas conveyed through the MEGAL pipeline within Germany, while Ruhrgas would likewise abstain from selling gas brought by the pipeline within France. During that period, Gaz de France held a legal monopoly on the importation of natural gas into France, a monopoly that was not abolished until August 2000. A number of "demarcation agreements" with other domestic suppliers effectively protected Ruhrgas' supply territory in Germany from competition up until the prohibition of

[54] European Commission, Decision of 25 March 2009 relating to a proceeding under Article 81 of the EC Treaty (Case COMP/39.506 – E.ON/ GDF Suez), [2009/254/EC] (Official Journal of the European Union, 7 July 2009).

[55] European Commission, Decision of 25 March 2009 relating to a proceeding under Article 81 of the EC Treaty (Case COMP/39.506 – E.ON/ GDF Suez), [2009/254/EC] (Official Journal of the European Union, 7 July 2009).

such agreements in April 1998.[56] Even after Directive 98/30/EC required the European petrol markets to open to competition in August 2000, both parties upheld their market-sharing agreement despite being aware that the 1975 letters violated competition law. The corporations had regular meetings at many hierarchical levels to deliberate on the execution of the agreement inside the recently deregulated market and to oversee one another's activities. The post 1999 communication between the parties substantiated the existence of a singular and uninterrupted agreement to allocate markets in an anticompetitive manner, thus violating antitrust legislation. Despite both parties declaring in August 2004 that they had considered the letters to be "null and void" for an extended period, they persisted in enforcing the limitation on Gaz de France's gas supply to Germany via the MEGAL pipeline until the conclusion of September 2005.

The implementation of a market sharing agreement proved important in enabling E.ON and GDF to sustain their dominant positions within the gas markets of Germany and France during the period of market liberalisation. The firms intentionally deprived French and German gas consumers of the advantages outlined in the 1998 Directive, such as more pricing competition and a wider range of provider options. The market-sharing arrangement represents a significant violation of the antitrust regulations outlined in the EC Treaty. When determining the penalty, the Commission considered the sales of the enterprises involved in the transportation of gas through the MEGAL pipeline in France and Germany. The Commission has fined E.ON/E.ON Ruhrgas and GDF Suez the same amount because both companies are big, the market-sharing agreement was made to hurt competition, they both own the MEGAL pipeline, and the same amount of gas was transferred through the pipeline.

The fines imposed are determined in accordance with the 2006 Guidelines on Fines, which were in effect at the time of the notification of the Statement of Objections in June 2008. According to Council Regulation 1/2003, corporations have the potential to face fines amounting to a maximum of 10% of their overall annual revenue.[57] According to the 2006 Guidelines, fines can be calculated by multiplying up to 30% of the company's annual sales on the relevant markets by the duration of their involvement in the infringement. This calculation is subject to the specified limit.[58] Upon examining the intricacies of horizontal agreements within the energy sector, it becomes evident that in the case of natural gas, a resource characterised by limited availability, there frequently exists a dependence on a single

---

[56] European Commission, Decision of 30 September 2008 relating to a proceeding under Article 81 of the EC Treaty (Case COMP/39.506 – E.ON Ruhrgas/ GDF Suez), [2008/873/EC] (Official Journal of the European Union, 17 October 2008).

[57] European Commission, Guidelines on the Method of Setting Fines Imposed Pursuant to Article 23(2)(a) of Regulation (EC) No 1/2003 [2006/C 210/02], Official Journal of the European Union, 1 September 2006. Council of the European Union, Council Regulation (EC) No 1/2003 of 16 December 2002 on the implementation of the rules on competition laid down in Articles 81 and 82 of the Treaty, Official Journal of the European Union, L 1, 4 January 2003, pp. 1–25.

[58] AT.39401 E.ON GdF collusion. 2009.

supply. To fortify its position, said supplier tends to exploit market sharing prospects. In the electricity sector, a distinct scenario unfolds, characterised by the prevalence of competition in production prices and the presence of active exchange trading. However, it is important to note that this trading does not rely on long-term contracts. Cooperation agreements lacking the intention to partition or foreclose markets are not deemed anti-competitive unless they incorporate conditions that are anti-competitive in nature. The examination of this practice was conducted within the context of the nuclear insurance agreements established by the nuclear insurance pools. There exists a recognised necessity to enhance cost efficiency through the implementation of said agreements. However, the presence of territorial limitations that hinder access to such collectives and the imposition of exclusive membership for nuclear operators solely operating within those nations give rise to distortions and constraints on competition. Consequently, the efficacy of these insurance collectives is diminished. In the subsequent section, an evaluation will be conducted to analyse the influence of vertical agreements on competition within the energy sector.

6.10 Conclusion

Horizontal agreements in the energy industry pertain to collaborative endeavours among enterprises operating within the same segment of the supply chain. These agreements have the potential to improve efficiency and foster innovation, but they may also give rise to antitrust considerations. Various strategies can be employed, such as engaging in joint ventures, forming consortiums, facilitating information sharing, and coordinating actions. These agreements are governed by the regulatory framework and are subject to examination in accordance with the competition rules of the European Union. Nevertheless, the intricate nature of these agreements requires a thorough economic analysis. The approach adopted by the Commission is grounded in the conviction that technology transfer agreements hold societal advantages, but they may also engender anti-competitive ramifications.

This chapter provided an analysis of collaborative R&D partnerships within the energy industry. The primary focus was on the objectives, benefits, regulatory considerations, and challenges associated with such agreements. These agreements serve to enhance collaboration among many stakeholders, including industry participants, academic institutions, and governmental authorities, in order to address intricate energy-related challenges. R&D collaboration can manifest itself through contractual agreements or through cooperative efforts that involve financial compensation. Nevertheless, the success of these agreements heavily relies on the imperative aspects of regulatory compliance and the effective administration of intellectual property. The European Union and the United Kingdom have recently made revisions to their block exemption legislation for research and development, thereby adding new criteria to promote competition in the realm of innovation. Notwithstanding these modifications, both European Union and United Kingdom rules recognise the advantages of R&D collaborations, encompassing the allocation of resources and prompt progress in novel products, services, and technology.

The safe harbour provision under research and development agreements remains unaltered, imposing a restriction on the combined market share of entities involved to a maximum of 25% within pertinent product and technology markets. Both parties are granted access to the ultimate outcomes, although there may be limitations on access to prevent misuse. The term of the provision stays unchanged. In cases where it is relevant, an R&D agreement between existing or potential competitors is exempt for the duration of the R&D activities as well as an extra period of seven years following the entry of the product or technology into the internal market of the European Union. The recently implemented regulations in the United Kingdom also encompass an extra requirement that pertains to political parties involved in pioneering practices, guaranteeing a state of dynamic competition with regard to innovation.

Collaborative partners frequently encounter a dearth of information regarding the R&D endeavours undertaken by their competitors, impeding their ability to ascertain the extent to which their own activities align with crucial objectives. This can provide a significant challenge, particularly for nascent enterprises. The temporal aspect of concurrent research and development initiatives remains uncertain, and the Commission's strategy for achieving comparable standards has faced criticism. The determination of the UK's approach to recognising possible divergence in new industries remains unresolved. In order to address any violations of competition law, it is advisable for enterprises to undertake a thorough assessment of the competitive landscape, maintain a record of supporting evidence, and consistently revise their findings. It is imperative to ensure adherence to regulatory requirements, in order to facilitate effective collaboration with research and development partners.

When examining horizontal cooperation within the energy sector, it is crucial to take into account the presence of nuclear insurance pools. These entities are specifically designed to establish and maintain an adequate financial reserve in the event of a nuclear accident. The primary aim behind the establishment of joint insurance pools was to foster the growth and advancement of the nuclear industry. In accordance with the principles governing civil liability for nuclear damage as established in international nuclear law, the operator of a nuclear facility bears exclusive responsibility for any potential nuclear disaster that may transpire. The introduction of this provision aimed to streamline the process of compensating victims by eliminating the need to establish a direct connection between the actions of the responsible party and the resulting consequences. The International Conventions on Civil Liability for Nuclear Damage establish the fundamental principle that the operator of a nuclear installation is solely responsible for any liability arising from such activities. These conventions also offer the state various options to determine the extent of its financial liability in situations where the operator is unable to adequately compensate for the resulting damage. To adequately address the incurred damages, it is necessary for the operator to procure civil liability insurance of a suitable magnitude. The specific amount required differs significantly among

European Union Member States and globally, in accordance with respective domestic legislation.

Certain countries impose unlimited operator liability, but others establish a minimal liability limit. It is important to acknowledge that the limits of liability associated with civil liability for nuclear facility operators are substantial. According to the Vienna Convention, a minimum limit of 300 million SDR is established. The Paris Convention implements a more stringent minimum liability requirement of EUR 1.2 billion. When a state makes the decision to ratify treaties pertaining to civil liability for nuclear damage, it determines the degree of obligation imposed on the operator in the case of a nuclear accident. States have the authority to exercise their discretion in determining the extent of liability for operators. This discretion allows them to establish liability limits that either adhere to the minimal thresholds outlined in conventions or grant operators unlimited liability. Furthermore, states have the option to establish liability limits that surpass the thresholds established by international agreements.

Nuclear operators are motivated to establish a liability limit that is as low as possible, with the state assuming responsibility for any remaining costs. This approach ensures that the operators are only obligated to provide compensation up to a predetermined minimum, while the overall responsibility for the nuclear site stays intact. From the perspective of insurers, it is crucial to establish a higher limit of liability, given that operators are required to pay specific rates for civil liability insurance. Insurance companies have the capacity to offer third-party liability insurance up to a specific limit, which is not without bounds. From a societal standpoint, it is imperative for citizens to prioritise the safe operation of nuclear facilities and, in the unfortunate case of a nuclear catastrophe, to promptly and efficiently pursue the most optimal methods of seeking compensation or resolution.

The financial repercussions resulting from a nuclear disaster can reach billions of euros or more, surpassing the capacity of a single insurance firm to provide full compensation for such extensive damage. In pursuit of this objective, insurers participate in collective general insurance pools alongside pools consisting of operators. The issue stems from the circumstance that general insurance pools function within the jurisdiction of a specific state, and operators have significant limitations when seeking to become part of a general insurance group in a different state's area. In this regard, it is evident that there exist territorial limitations and horizontal agreements that impede both current and future competition within the market.

Typically, nuclear operators who operate within the jurisdiction of a specific Member State are limited to joining general insurance organisations that operate only within the boundaries of that Member State. Consequently, this arrangement gives rise to territorial constraints. Certain authors have expressed criticism of this standpoint due to the argument that the consolidation of insurance companies into national entities leads to inefficiencies. From a competition law standpoint, horizontal agreements are evaluated based on the presence of an agreement among economic operators or the presence of coordination that results in competition limits within the market. This study aims to evaluate the necessity of collaboration among insurers within a group for the effective operation of the nuclear energy industry as well as determine if such collaborative practices impose limitations on market competitiveness. Hence, it is justifiable to align with the viewpoint that a competitive market for co-insurance organisations has the potential to provide a more efficient mechanism for addressing grievances. Several other scholars had a similar perspective, contending that the consolidation of market power diminishes service efficiency and fails to yield the intended outcome.

Despite its potential as a low-carbon power source, nuclear energy presents significant hazards. The presence of various risks, such as catastrophic accidents and long-term environmental consequences, underscores the need for distinctive insurance solutions. Collaborative mechanisms in the form of nuclear insurance pools have arisen to tackle these difficulties. This article examines the collaborative strategy employed by nuclear insurance pools, providing an in-depth analysis of their historical roots, organisational structure, and significant contribution to the nuclear energy industry. Nuclear energy has been widely recognised as a fundamental element of a sustainable energy trajectory. Nevertheless, this technology carries inherent hazards, particularly the possibility of catastrophic mishaps that can have extensive and profound implications. The aforementioned hazards have prompted the establishment of specialised insurance systems, resulting in the formation of nuclear insurance pools.

The origins of nuclear insurance pools can be traced back to the initial stages of nuclear power development. The development of knowledge regarding nuclear risks and the recognition of the necessity for liability coverage prompted the establishment of these cooperative agreements. International accords, such as the Paris and Vienna Conventions, have significantly influenced the development of nuclear insurance. Nuclear insurance pools function based on a collaborative framework wherein contributions are sourced from multiple stakeholders. These entities may encompass nuclear operators, governmental bodies, and commercial insurance companies. Their operations are regulated by a rigorous legislative framework, which ensures their effective and transparent functioning.

Risk mitigation refers to the process of identifying, assessing, and implementing measures to reduce or eliminate any risks that may negatively impact an organisation. It involves taking proactive steps to minimise the likelihood and severity of risks as well as their potential consequences. One of the main goals of nuclear insurance pools is to effectively manage and reduce the risks that are inherent to the use of nuclear energy. Financial assistance is offered to facilitate the implementation of safety measures and preventive actions, contributing to the overall enhancement of nuclear facility safety. Moreover, they fulfil a crucial function in terms of liability coverage, guaranteeing that individuals affected by nuclear catastrophes are duly compensated.

The European Commission was soliciting public input regarding proposed revisions to European Union regulations and guidance pertaining to common competitor cooperation arrangements. The amended standards have the objective of distinguishing between buyer cartels and collaborative purchasing agreements, with a particular emphasis on the lowering of prices and enhancements in efficiency.

In addition, they enforce restrictions on the dissemination of information that enables anti-competitive conduct while emphasising the possibility for lawful activities to inadvertently transition into illicit collaboration. The recommendations moreover offer an extensive examination of previous rulings and legislative advancements concerning mobile networks and sustainability agreements, indicating that the latter may possess legal validity despite prospective ramifications. The revised rules also include a comprehensive list of factors for organisations to assess in determining whether their involvement in a collective purchasing agreement can be classified as a buyer cartel.

The recently revised regulations governing competition within the European Union have implemented the inclusion of bidding consortiums, which enable numerous companies to collaboratively submit offers during a competitive procurement procedure. These agreements are generally considered lawful if they result in operational benefits that can be readily passed on to customers. Nevertheless, it is imperative to conduct competition assessments on a per-lot basis, particularly when these lots exhibit distinct characteristics from the overarching project bidding process. The recommendations also highlight the significance of data sharing in enabling informed decision-making through the utilisation of big data analytics and machine-learning technologies. The guidelines additionally offer a thorough assessment of the legality of environmental and social sustainability initiatives within the organisation. Additionally, they offer elucidation of the specific situations in which advantages, such as improvements in qualitative or quantitative efficiency, could be deemed exempt from the prohibition on agreements that hinder competition. The inclusion of a sustainability chapter in the agreement serves as a prompt for firms to seek informal guidance from the Commission in order to ensure compliance with competition legislation.

The Commission has recently implemented updated horizontal block exemption regulations and horizontal guidelines with the aim of enhancing the self-assessment process for horizontal agreements. The proposed modifications seek to expand the scope of the Specialisation Block Exemption Regulation, encompassing a broader array of production agreements while also introducing a more flexible approach to ascertaining market shares. The amended laws also place a greater emphasis on preserving competition in the realm of innovation, as well as reinforcing the authority of both the Commission and national competition authorities to withdraw exemption privileges in certain instances.

European Union competition rules have been updated to include more information about how Article 101 TFEU applies to joint venture agreements, how to work together on different projects, and how to tell the difference between cooperative purchasing and buyer cartels. The rules also place significant emphasis on the significance of collaborative purchasing and bidding consortia. Additionally, they suggest a restructuring of the rules on information exchange in order to provide comprehensive and current coverage. The updated rules also encompass additional instructions pertaining to commercially sensitive information, the identification of potential infringements, and the resolution of sustainability agreements. The newly established standards also facilitate a dynamic framework for the standardisation of sustainability practices and offer informal recommendations for compliance with competition legislation.

A cartel refers to a collection of independent firms that enter into agreements with the intention of manipulating prices, limiting production, or implementing actions that hinder competition. These agreements have the potential to result in increased expenses for business partners and may be deemed unlawful in accordance with European Union competition legislation. The European Commission enforces significant financial penalties on corporations engaged in cartel activities while concurrently offering a leniency scheme that encourages companies to furnish evidence in exchange for exemption from fines. The Commission also promotes the reporting of any suspicions regarding cartels, emphasising the potential benefits such as enhanced operational effectiveness and expedited investigative processes. Cartels can be classified as monopolistic entities owing to their collusive agreements, although their ability to attain comparable market dominance or exert similar effects is limited in comparison to a true monopoly. There are several factors that contribute to the establishment of cartels, including the quantity of firms operating within a sector, challenges in coordinating actions among these firms, obstacles that impede new firms from entering the market, and significant financial constraints associated with operating in the area.

In energy sector horizontal cooperation agreements are quite frankly concluded between producers so-called production or specialization agreements. They tend to achieve production optimization by counteracting the negative effects on the market and its participants. Unilateral specialization agreements are possible where economic operators agree that one of them will produce the product concerned and the other will procure such output. The reciprocal specialization agreements are also not an exemption, whereby undertakings oblige to purchase certain products. It should be noted that in the energy sector, such agreements are mainly specific to companies active in the petroleum products segment. These agreements lead to a possible price increase in the relevant markets. It is important to ascertain what market shares the parties have and whether they are competing with each other or whether consumers have the ability to switch suppliers. Cooperation agreements are often made with the intention of entering new markets for economic operators, as such operations require significant initial investment, and the economic entity does not always have such financial resources. Cooperation agreements which do not have the object of partitioning or foreclosing markets are not anti-competitive unless they contain anti-competitive conditions.

References

Argenton C, Geradin D, Stephan A (2020) EU cartel law and economics. Oxford University Press

Bouwens B, Dankers J (2005) Sharing success: cartels as an answer to the dynamics of business capitalism, 1900–1940. <http://www.bintproject.nl/textfiles/2005_bouwens-dankers.pdf>

Caffarra C, Scott H (2018) The impact of EU competition law on cartel behavior. Eur Compet J 14(2):321–336
Ezrachi A (2021) EU competition law: an analytical guide. Hart Publishing
Faure M, Van Den Bergh R (2002) Competition on the European market for liability insurance and efficient accident law. Maastricht J Eur Comp Law 9(3)
Fox E (2018) The globalization of antitrust. Oxford University Press
Jullien B, Rey P (2021) Cartels and market dominance: a comparative analysis. Int J Ind Organ 76: 102567
Liefmann R (1930) Kartelle, Konzerne und Trusts. Stuttgart. Ernst Heinrich Moritz
McFadden JEJ (2020) EU competition law and policy: a practitioner's guide. Routledge
Tate C (2022) Regulating cartels and monopolies: recent trends in European competition policy. Antitrust Law J 89(1):145–170
Whish R (2018) Competition law, 9th edn. Oxford University Press
Wijckmans F, Tuytschaever F (2015) Horizontal agreements and cartels in EU competition law. Oxford University Press

Chapter 7
Vertical Agreements

Abstract A vertical agreement is a contract between two or more companies, where each company operates at a different level in the production or distribution chain. This agreement, or coordinated practice, relates to the specific arrangement being considered. Unlike similar agreements made between companies operating at the same level, these agreements are less harmful in terms of competition law. Their main objective is to improve production efficiency and achieve economies of scale. We can compare vertical agreements to vertically integrated corporations, where a single organization operates across various segments. To encourage competition among economic entities, the European Union has enacted laws regarding the separation of vertically integrated energy corporations. If there is no market power, vertical agreements are less likely to distort competition, unless the supplier or distributor already had significant market power before entering the deal. Inadequate competition at any level of commerce can potentially weaken its viability. By addressing the problem of "free riding" when investing in technological development and staff training, vertical partnerships can also yield positive outcomes. Implementing vertical agreements can reduce the potential for a new company to enter the market and exploit infrastructure or commercial enhancements made by others.

7.1 Introduction and the Notion of Vertical Agreements

A vertical agreement refers to a contractual arrangement involving two or more entities, each operating at distinct levels within the production or distribution chain, with regards to the agreement or coordinated practise. A contractual arrangement or collaborative effort pertaining to the terms and conditions governing the procurement, sale, or resale of specific goods or services by the involved parties Agreements between an energy supplier and a buyer are deemed impermissible when they impede competition and fail to generate a profit.

In comparison to similar horizontal agreements made by businesses at the same level, these agreements are less bad from a competition law point of view because they are mostly about making production more efficient and getting economies of

L. Rimšaitė, *The Crossroads of Competition Law and Energy Regulation*,
https://doi.org/10.1007/978-3-031-73238-6_7

scale. Article 101 of the Treaty on the Functioning of the European Union (TFEU) pertains to vertical agreements that have the potential to impact trade between Member States and impede, limit, or otherwise distort competition.[1] The assessment of vertical restraints is established by Article 101 TFEU, which considers both the anti-competitive and pro-competitive effects.

Insufficient competition at one or more levels of trade can potentially jeopardise competition in numerous instances of vertical restraints. It is important to acknowledge that vertical agreements also yield a beneficial impact by mitigating the problem commonly referred to as the "free-rider" dilemma. In this scenario, the supplier allocates resources towards the advancement of technology, training of personnel, and subsequently utilises vertical agreements as a means to deter the entry of a new entity seeking to exploit the investments made in infrastructure or business enhancement.[2] Vertical agreements can also derive advantages from gaining entry into new markets. In such instances, the entity may encounter limitations in terms of financial resources, which may hinder its ability to invest in business expansion and subsequently enter new markets.[3]

When conducting an analysis of non-compete agreements, it is crucial to evaluate the potential countervailing effects associated with these agreements.[4] Specifically, it is necessary to determine whether these agreements contribute to technological advancements or if they are necessary for enhancing the operational effectiveness of the company. The evaluation also considers whether consumers are provided with a fair and equitable portion of the advantages, or at the very least, no greater portion, compared to a scenario where no agreement exists between companies. Vertical agreements have the potential to facilitate cost reductions in production for economic operators through the application of economies of scale. Simultaneously, these agreements can generate advantages for consumers by reducing the cost of the supplied product. Vertical agreements have the potential to decrease costs associated with transmission, distribution, and the operations of these entities. Long-term gas supply contracts play a crucial role in determining the return on investment.[5] This is pertinent to contemporary infrastructure initiatives, as their funding necessitates a

---

[1] Joined Cases *Grundig-Consten v Commission* 56/64 and 58/64, [1966] ECR 299, Case *Technique Minière v Maschi-nenbau Ulm*, 56/65, [1966] ECR 235, *Parker Pen v Commission*, T- 77/92, [1994] ECR 549.

[2] Tuytschaever and Wijckmans (2018).

[3] Commission Regulation (EU) No 330/2010 of 20 April 2010 on the application of Article 101(3) of the Treaty on the Functioning of the European Union to categories of vertical agreements and concerted practices. *OJ L 102, 23.4.2010.* Guidelines on Vertical Restraints. OJ C 130, 19.5.2010, pp. 1–46.

[4] Guidelines on Vertical Restraints. OJ C 130, 19.5.2010, pp. 1–46.

[5] European Commission, Commission Regulation (EU) No 330/2010 of 20 April 2010 on the application of Article 101(3) of the Treaty on the Functioning of the European Union to categories of vertical agreements and concerted practices, Official Journal of the European Union, L 102, 23 April 2010, pp. 1–7. European Commission, Guidelines on Vertical Restraints [2010/C 130/01], Official Journal of the European Union, C 130, 19 May 2010, pp. 1–46.

satisfactory return on investment. Vertical agreements frequently involve the reduction of logistics and transportation expenses as well as the optimisation of costs.

Considering that non-compete agreements establish conditions for suppliers to raise and sustain elevated output prices, it can be argued that cost optimisation measures should not result in price hikes for consumers. The application of this test in the energy sector is challenging due to the potential lack of responsiveness of market demand elasticity. In such cases, a decrease in price may not necessarily result in a corresponding increase in sales.[6] Vertical agreements are a means of addressing a hold-up problem that arises when either the buyer or supplier is hesitant to make investments without the assurance of a long-term supply contract with the other party. Several conditions must be satisfied for the investment to be considered specific, implying that the customer will face substantial sales losses if they attempt to utilise it for alternative purposes upon the contract's expiration. Investments are deemed to possess a specific relationship when they are exclusively utilised for the production of components associated with a particular brand. Consequently, it is imperative that the investment be of a long-term nature.

Article 101(1) of the TFEU has always been interpreted by the Commission in a broad and strict way when it comes to vertical restraints, which are agreements that limit competition. This provision explicitly prohibits any arrangements that hinder, distort, or limit competition within the European Union. The Commission frequently demonstrated a lack of acknowledgment towards the potential positive impact of vertical constraints on inter-brand competition in terms of promoting competition. The approach of the Commission should be considered within the economic framework in which EU competition legislation was formulated in the 1960s and 1970s, a period characterised by significant fragmentation of national markets. The Commission's main focus in this area has been to safeguard competition. However, the aim of market integration and the removal of trade barriers among EU member states has also had a substantial influence on the EU competition regulations pertaining to vertical restraints.

During the early 1990s, the European Commission relied on the "block exemptions" that were in place at that time to govern exclusive distribution, exclusive purchasing, and franchising agreements. These exclusions formed the foundation of the Commission's policy on vertical constraints.[7] Block exemptions have the automatic effect of exempting agreements that meet their criteria from being prohibited under Article 101(1). Nevertheless, these initial block exemptions exhibited many

---

[6] European Commission, Commission Regulation (EU) No 330/2010 of 20 April 2010 on the application of Article 101(3) of the Treaty on the Functioning of the European Union to categories of vertical agreements and concerted practices, Official Journal of the European Union, L 102, 23 April 2010, pp. 1–7. European Commission, Guidelines on Vertical Restraints [2010/C 130/01], Official Journal of the European Union, C 130, 19 May 2010, pp. 1–46. Council Regulation (EC) No 1/2003 of 16 December 2002 on the implementation of the rules on competition laid down in Articles 81 and 82 of the Treaty, Official Journal of the European Communities, L 1, 4 January 2003, pp. 1–25.

[7] Ratliff (2020).

deficiencies. The individuals in question exhibited a formalistic approach, wherein distribution agreements with potential detrimental consequences were granted automatic exemption based on their specific drafting. On the other hand, numerous agreements that yielded positive outcomes in terms of promoting competition had to undergo revision in order to align with the conditions set forth in a block exemption. This procedure resulted in an avoidable financial burden. The Commission's policy on vertical restraints faced criticism from industry professionals and legal practitioners for an extended period of time due to the identified inadequacies. Towards the end of the 1990s, the Commission responded to these critiques by initiating a thorough examination of its policy concerning vertical constraints.

7.2 The Vertical Block Exception Regulation

The ultimate outcomes of this evaluation encompassed the acceptance of a singular block exemption that pertains to all vertical arrangements, known as the vertical agreements block exemption (2790/1999). This exemption was officially established on December 22, 1999. The Vertical Restraints Guidelines, which were adopted on May 24, 2000, outline the position of the European Commission regarding vertical agreements.[8] The vertical agreement block exemption came into effect on June 1, 2000. It superseded the block exemptions for exclusive distribution, exclusive purchase, and franchising. Additionally, it extended its coverage to include selective distribution and agency arrangements, which were not previously included. The 1999 block exemption, along with its supporting guidelines, prioritised the use of economic analysis in the formulation of the Commission's policy on vertical constraints.

It specifically established a presumption that vertical restraints are legal when there is no proof that the party benefiting from the restraint has market power.[9] The expiration date of Regulation 2790/1999 occurred on May 31, 2010 and Regulation 330/2010 superseded it. The Vertical Restraints Guidelines were also adopted in a revised version, as documented in the Official Journal of the European Union in 2010. Regulation 330/2010 reached its expiration date on May 31, 2022.[10] The

[8]Commission Regulation (EC) No 2790/1999 of 22 December 1999 on the application of Article 81(3) of the Treaty to categories of vertical agreements and concerted practices, Official Journal of the European Communities, L 336, 29 December 1999, pp. 21–25. European Commission, Guidelines on Vertical Restraints [2000/C 291/01], Official Journal of the European Communities, C 291, 13 October 2000, pp. 1–22.

[9]Bailey and John (2019).

[10]Regulation (EU) 2022/720 of the European Parliament and of the Council of 28 March 2022 amending Regulation (EU) 330/2010 on the application of Article 101(3) of the Treaty on the Functioning of the European Union to categories of vertical agreements and concerted practices, Official Journal of the European Union, L 126, 31 March 2022, pp. 1–6. Commission Regulation (EU) No 330/2010 of 20 April 2010 on the application of Article 101(3) of the Treaty on the

observed increase in the market influence of significant distributors and retailers, as well as the surge in online sales seen during the previous decade, were the driving forces behind the implementation of Regulation 330/2010. The primary modification pertained to the extension of the "safe harbour" criterion, which now encompasses both the market share of the supplier and the market share of the buyer rather than solely focusing on the party that benefits from the restraint. The Commission released a new Vertical Block Exemption Regulation (VBER) and accompanying recommendations on vertical restraints on May 10, 2022.[11] These regulatory measures became effective on June 1, 2022. The package presents significant modifications to the handling of distribution agreements within the framework of EU competition law. Specifically, it addresses the regulations pertaining to the integration of several distribution systems, dual distribution, dual pricing, and parity responsibilities.

The VBER gives businesses that have vertical agreements, which are deals between companies at different levels of the supply chain, more confidence that their agreements are in line with Article 101(1) of the TFEU. This is achieved through the establishment of a safe harbour exemption. Vertical agreements that do not include "hardcore restrictions" such as resale price maintenance or specific territorial or customer limitations and where neither party's market share surpasses 30% in the relevant sales and purchasing markets are eligible for an exemption. Agreements that fail to meet the standards outlined in the VBER may still be in line with Article 101(1) of the TFEU. However, such agreements must undergo a case-by-case evaluation in accordance with Article 101(3) of the TFEU.

The Vertical Guidelines are meant to help businesses figure out if their agreements fall under the VBER or if they may be eligible for an individual exemption under Article 101(3) of the TFEU. The revised VBER was scheduled to come into effect on June 1, 2022 and will remain in place for a duration of 12 years, subject to an evaluation report after 8 years. A one-year transitional period is applicable to agreements that are already in effect as of May 31, 2022 and meet the exemption criteria outlined in the existing VBER but fail to meet the criteria specified in the new VBER.[12] The Commission conducted a thorough investigation over a period of three and a half years that led to the recently introduced VBER and Vertical Guidelines. The review conducted by the Commission has mostly focused on identifying necessary adjustments in response to the expanding scope of online sales and the

---

Functioning of the European Union to categories of vertical agreements and concerted practices, Official Journal of the European Union, L 102, 23 April 2010, pp. 1–7. European Commission, Guidelines on Vertical Restraints [2010/C 130/01], Official Journal of the European Union, C 130, 19 May 2010, pp. 1–46.

[11]Commission Regulation (EU) 2022/720 of 10 May 2022 on the application of Article 101(3) of the Treaty on the Functioning of the European Union to categories of vertical agreements and concerted practices (Text with EEA relevance). C/2022/3015. OJ L 134, 11.5.2022, p. 4–13.

[12]Commission Regulation (EU) 2022/720 of 10 May 2022 on the application of Article 101(3) of the Treaty on the Functioning of the European Union to categories of vertical agreements and concerted practices (Text with EEA relevance). C/2022/3015. OJ L 134, 11.5.2022, pp. 4–13.

rise of new market participants, including online platforms. Similar to the regulations that have been previously examined by the Commission pertaining to horizontal ties among rivals, the newly introduced vertical regulations also take into consideration economic and social advancements, including the digital transition and the European Green Deal.

The concept of dual distribution pertains to scenarios in which a supplier operates in both the upstream and downstream sectors of a supply chain. Consequently, the supplier may be seen as engaging in competition with its downstream clients. For instance, a manufacturer may not solely rely on independent shops to sell its goods or services but may also directly cater to end customers. The proliferation of online sales, namely through suppliers' exclusive web platforms, has led to a notable surge in dual distribution. The existing VBER does not include vertical agreements between competitors within its scope. However, it explicitly states that dual distribution falls under the safe harbour provision for vertical agreements. Consequently, within the existing VBER, the treatment of dual distribution was essentially equivalent to that of other forms of vertical agreements. The revised VBER and Vertical Guidelines introduce modifications to the existing safe harbour provisions pertaining to dual distribution agreements.[13] The safe harbour provision does not extend to vertical agreements pertaining to the delivery of online intermediation services (OIS). These agreements involve OIS providers, such as e-commerce marketplaces, app stores, price comparison tools, and social media services, who also engage in the sale of goods or services that directly compete with the companies they offer OIS to. The safe harbour provision applies to the communication of information between the supplier and its distributors, provided that such exchange is either directly linked to the execution of the vertical agreement or essential for enhancing the production or distribution of the contracted goods or services. The recently introduced Vertical Guidelines include a "white list", which is a non-exhaustive compilation of information that can be shared and is generally eligible for the block exemption. Additionally, there is a "black" list that outlines information that is considered unlikely to qualify for the exemption. The European Commission has decided to withdraw its previously suggested restriction on the safe harbour provision, which was released for public consultation in July 2021. This restriction stated that information exchanges would only be eligible for the safe harbour if the combined market share of the parties involved in the retail market did not exceed 10%.[14]

[13]Commission Regulation (EU) 2022/720 of 10 May 2022 on the application of Article 101(3) of the Treaty on the Functioning of the European Union to categories of vertical agreements and concerted practices (Text with EEA relevance). C/2022/3015. OJ L 134, 11.5.2022, pp. 4–13.

[14]Commission Regulation (EU) No 330/2010 of 20 April 2010 on the application of Article 101(3) of the Treaty on the Functioning of the European Union to categories of vertical agreements and concerted practices, Official Journal of the European Union, L 102, 23 April 2010, pp. 1–7. European Commission, Guidelines on Vertical Restraints [2010/C 130/01], Official Journal of the European Union, C 130, 19 May 2010, pp. 1–46. European Commission, Public Consultation Document on the Review of the Vertical Block Exemption Regulation and the Guidelines on Vertical Restraints, July 2021. Regulation (EU) 2022/720 of the European Parliament and of the

Parity duties, also known as Most Favoured Nation Clauses (MFNs), necessitate that a corporation provide its contracting party with equivalent or superior terms and conditions compared to those offered on alternative platforms or sales channels. While the present VBER provides complete exemption for all parity commitments, the revised VBER has restricted the extent of the safe harbour for MFN clauses in the following manner. The block exemption does not apply to the use of wide parity clauses in a cross-platform retail parity obligation. These clauses say that online platforms can't let suppliers sell their products on other retail platforms or channels at a lower price or with better terms. Instead, these clauses must be evaluated on a case-by-case basis under Article 101 TFEU, as they fall under the category of "excluded restrictions" according to Article 5(1)(d) of the new Vertical Block Exemption Regulation. An instance of exemption can be observed in the case of provisions that impose limitations on suppliers, preventing them from providing more favourable conditions on their respective websites. Nevertheless, according to the recent regulations, in cases where online platforms enforce narrow retail parity obligations that apply to a substantial portion of their users (taking into account cumulative impacts) and there is no substantiated proof of any efficiency gains, the advantages provided by the block exemption are expected to be revoked.

Dual pricing refers to the practice of applying distinct pricing structures to products that are meant for online sales and those that are sold through offline channels, resulting in various rates being charged to the same distributor. The existing vertical guidelines have seen dual pricing as a type of stringent limitation on online sales. According to the recently implemented Vertical Guidelines, the practice of dual pricing is no longer classified as a stringent limitation, as it has the potential to encourage or acknowledge a suitable level of investment. This principle is applicable to all providers, regardless of their distribution model. The parties have the option to establish a mechanism for the efficient implementation of dual pricing, such as monitoring the sale of items online. The price disparity should be justifiably linked to the variations in costs and investments between the online and offline channels. However, the parties are not obligated to engage in intricate cost calculations. In order to qualify for the safe harbour provision, it is imperative that the disparity in wholesale prices does not serve the purpose of limiting sales to specific areas or clients, nor does it hinder the efficient use of the internet. Additionally, the supplier must refrain from imposing any restrictions on the quantity of products that can be offered online. The supplier may not impose a requirement for the retail prices to vary based on the sales channel. The revised VBER expands the scope of the block exemption to include shared exclusivity arrangements. Under this provision, suppliers are permitted to designate a maximum of five distributors for a specific territory or customer group. In contrast, the existing rules appear to only permit the appointment of a single exclusive distributor for each territory or customer group.

Council of 28 March 2022 amending Regulation (EU) 330/2010 on the application of Article 101(3) of the Treaty on the Functioning of the European Union to categories of vertical agreements and concerted practices, Official Journal of the European Union, L 126, 31 March 2022, pp. 1–6.

Nevertheless, the block exemption does not encompass limitations on active or passive sales inside the exclusive territory or client group.

Active sales restrictions refer to limitations placed on a buyer's proactive engagement with customers within a certain zone or specified customer groups based on certain criteria. On the other hand, passive sales limits pertain to sales that are conducted in reaction to unsolicited inquiries from individual clients.[15] The prevention of passive sales is a stringent measure that restricts competition and is hence deemed unlawful. The VBER offers a comprehensive elucidation of active and passive sales, specifically in relation to the operation of websites. The operation of a website can be categorised as passive selling, but it transitions into active selling when certain conditions are met. These conditions include having a top-level domain that corresponds to specific areas or offering languages that are not generally used in the territory where the distributor is located. The newly established regulations expressly permit the combination of selective and exclusive distribution within various territories in the European Union, while also offering enhanced safeguards for such arrangements. Consequently, individuals who are part of a selective distribution system established inside a certain region may face restrictions on their ability to engage in active sales within another region or to a customer group that has been exclusively assigned to a maximum of five distributors or is reserved only for the supplier. On the other hand, a supplier has the ability to restrict its exclusive distributors from engaging in active or passive sales to unauthorised distributors within the supplier's designated territory if a selective distribution system is in place or has been designated for implementation.

The current regulations do not provide coverage for the combination of an exclusive and selective distribution system within a certain territory, similar to the prior standards. An instance of non-compliance with exclusive distribution at the wholesale level and selective distribution at the retail level occurs when a provider attempts to implement both strategies simultaneously. To safeguard investment incentives, suppliers may impose sales limitations on their distributors, necessitating the transmission of these restrictions throughout the distribution network. Regarding the safeguarding of an exclusive distribution system, it should be noted that the exemption for pass-on applies solely to the distributor's direct clients. However, in the case of selective distribution systems, the supplier has the authority to mandate pass-on throughout the entirety of the distribution chain.

---

[15] Commission Regulation (EU) No 330/2010 of 20 April 2010 on the application of Article 101(3) of the Treaty on the Functioning of the European Union to categories of vertical agreements and concerted practices, Official Journal of the European Union, L 102, 23 April 2010, pp. 1–7. European Commission, Guidelines on Vertical Restraints [2010/C 130/01], Official Journal of the European Union, C 130, 19 May 2010, pp. 1–46. European Commission, Public Consultation Document on the Review of the Vertical Block Exemption Regulation and the Guidelines on Vertical Restraints, July 2021. Regulation (EU) 2022/720 of the European Parliament and of the Council of 28 March 2022 amending Regulation (EU) 330/2010 on the application of Article 101(3) of the Treaty on the Functioning of the European Union to categories of vertical agreements and concerted practices, Official Journal of the European Union, L 126, 31 March 2022, pp. 1–6.

The updated Vertical Guidelines incorporate a modification of the "equivalence principle" pertaining to the distinction between offline and online sales within selective distribution systems.[16] This adjustment is based on empirical evidence indicating that online sales have evolved into a proficient sales channel, thereby diminishing the necessity for differential safeguarding compared to offline sales channels. The European Union Courts ruled in the Coty case that providers of luxury goods have the right to restrict members of their exclusive distribution network from selling the contracted items on third-party platforms without violating competition laws inside the EU. The recently introduced Vertical Guidelines incorporate the principles established in the Coty judgement by specifically affirming that the complete prohibition of sales through online marketplaces as a distribution channel does not constitute a severe limitation. On the other hand, the prohibition of utilising complete advertising platforms, such as search engines (including restrictions on keyword bidding and paid-reference services) or price comparison websites, can be perceived as a stringent limitation in accordance with Article 4(e). Even the prohibition of specific search engines or price comparison websites may be considered a stringent limitation if its purpose is to hinder the efficient utilisation of the internet, particularly if the remaining services within that advertising platform are effectively incapable of attracting customers to the buyer's online store.

The recently updated Vertical Guidelines provide clarification about the permissibility of a supplier imposing distinct requirements for online and offline sales within a selective distribution system. It is OK for the online sales criteria to differ from the offline sales criteria, as long as the intention behind the online sales criteria is not to hinder the efficient utilisation of the internet. As an illustration, the recently updated Vertical Guidelines indicate that a supplier has the authority to enforce certain prerequisites in order to uphold quality standards for online sales. These prerequisites may include the establishment and operation of an online after-sales helpdesk, the obligation to bear the expenses associated with customers' product returns, and the utilisation of secure payment systems. The VBER provides enhanced safeguards for selective distribution networks.

In the context of a selective distribution system, exclusive distributors who are assigned to a territory that falls outside the system may face limitations on their ability to engage in both active and passive selling to unauthorised distributors within the territory where the system is implemented.[17] The supplier may also impose the requirement that the distributor transfer this obligation to its customers. According to the recently released Vertical Guidelines, a selective distribution system may be able to benefit from the block exemption, regardless of the specific

---

[16] Commission Regulation (EU) 2022/720 of 10 May 2022 on the application of Article 101(3) of the Treaty on the Functioning of the European Union to categories of vertical agreements and concerted practices (Text with EEA relevance). C/2022/3015. OJ L 134, 11.5.2022, pp. 4–13.

[17] Commission Regulation (EU) 2022/720 of 10 May 2022 on the application of Article 101(3) of the Treaty on the Functioning of the European Union to categories of vertical agreements and concerted practices (Text with EEA relevance). C/2022/3015. OJ L 134, 11.5.2022, pp. 4–13.

features of the product in question, the kind of selection criteria used, and whether or not these criteria are made public.

Resale price maintenance (RPM), which encompasses the practice of setting fixed margins, continues to be classified as a hardcore limitation. There is a high probability that the EC and national competition authorities will persist in their vigorous enforcement efforts against RPM. The recently introduced Vertical Guidelines[18] offer comprehensive instructions about RPM, encompassing aspects such as price monitoring, minimum advertised prices (MAPs), and fulfilment contracts. MAP policies restrict distributors from promoting prices that fall below a threshold established by the supplier. The implementation of MAPs will be seen as a type of RPM, which is considered a stringent constraint on competition. The use of MAP policies could potentially find justification under Article 101 (3) of the TFEU in order to prevent a specific distributor from engaging in the practice of using a supplier's product as a loss leader.[19] Fulfilment contracts refer to contractual arrangements in which a supplier engages in a vertical agreement with an intermediary purchaser in order to carry out a previously established supply agreement between the supplier and a particular customer. This type of contract is typically employed when a supplier has a pre-existing framework contract with a customer, wherein the pricing has already been determined, but due to logistical or other reasons, the supplier requires the involvement of an independent distributor to fulfil the terms of the contract. The revised vertical guidelines modify the exception to RPM in the previous guidelines. The previous guidelines stated that setting a resale price in a fulfilment contract does not qualify as RPM if the end user has voluntarily given up their right to choose the executing party. The act of the supplier enforcing a resale price on the intermediary buyer in order to meet the contractual obligations with the supplier's customer does not fall under the category of RPM, provided that the supplier is the one responsible for selecting the enterprise that will carry out the fulfilment services. Non-compete obligations refer to contractual obligations that restrict the buyer from engaging in the production, procurement, or sale of goods that directly compete with the commodities specified in the contract. Additionally, these duties may require the customer to procure at least 80% of their total purchases of the contract goods exclusively from the supplier.

[18]Communication from the Commission. Commission Notice. Guidelines on vertical restraints 2022/C 248/01. C/2022/4238. OJ C 248, 30.6.2022, pp. 1–85.

[19]European Commission, Public Consultation on the review of the Vertical Block Exemption Regulation and the Vertical Guidelines (July 2021). Treaty on the Functioning of the European Union, Consolidated version, Official Journal of the European Union, C 326, 26 October 2012, pp. 47–390. Commission Notice on the definition of relevant market for the purposes of Community competition law, Official Journal of the European Communities, C 372, 9 December 1997, pp. 5–13. European Commission, Guidelines on Vertical Restraints [2010/C 130/01], Official Journal of the European Union, C 130, 19 May 2010, pp. 1–46. Commission Regulation (EU) No 330/2010 of 20 April 2010 on the application of Article 101(3) of the Treaty on the Functioning of the European Union to categories of vertical agreements and concerted practices, Official Journal of the European Union, L 102, 23 April 2010, pp. 1–7.

The new VBER does not extend its benefits to non-compete (exclusivity) clauses that have a lifespan beyond 5 years.[20] Under the new VBER, it can be helpful to include non-compete (exclusivity) commitments that can be implicitly extended for more than 5 years, as long as the buyer can renegotiate or cancel the commitments in a reasonable amount of time and at a fair cost. The non-compete requirements that are placed on members of a selective distribution system regarding the resale of items from rival suppliers do not qualify for the block exemption.

The revised Vertical Guidelines explicitly acknowledge that Article 101(3) of the TFEU views achieving sustainability objectives as an optimization. The revised Vertical Guidelines integrate sustainability-related factors into a selective distribution system. The exclusivity obligations are employed as a tactic to motivate investments in eco-friendly energy infrastructure.

7.3 The Destination Clause

The destination clause, alternatively referred to as the territorial restriction clause, is a contractual stipulation commonly encountered in vertical agreements within the energy industry. Vertical agreements refer to contractual arrangements established between firms that operate at distinct levels within the supply chain. These agreements typically occur between entities such as manufacturers and distributors, or, in the specific context of the energy sector, between producers and distributors.

The destination clause commonly imposes limitations on the geographical regions or markets within which the distributor or buyer is permitted to engage in the resale or utilisation of the items or services provided by the manufacturer or producer. Within the realm of the energy industry, the assortment of products or services encompassed may consist of electricity, natural gas, or various other forms of energy resources.[21] The inclusion of destination clauses in contracts delineates the precise geographical regions or markets within which the distributor or buyer is authorised to engage in the resale or use of energy products or services. For example, a power provider may impose restrictions on its distributor, confining the distributor's sales activities to a specific city or region.

Certain destination agreements confer exclusive rights on the distributor or buyer within a certain geographical area. This implies that within the specified zone, no other distributor or buyer, including the manufacturer or producer, is permitted to engage in the sale of comparable items or services. The implementation of exclusivity arrangements can yield advantageous outcomes for distributors since it affords them the opportunity to operate inside a safeguarded market. The utilisation of

[20] Commission Regulation (EU) 2022/720 of 10 May 2022 on the application of Article 101(3) of the Treaty on the Functioning of the European Union to categories of vertical agreements and concerted practices (Text with EEA relevance). C/2022/3015. OJ L 134, 11.5.2022, pp. 4–13.

[21] Nyssens et al. (2004).

destination clauses might serve as a strategy for market segmentation. Manufacturers or producers are granted the ability to partition markets and provide distinct regions to various distributors or customers. Segmentation can provide businesses with the opportunity to customise their products or services based on the specific market conditions and consumer preferences within a certain locality.

Although destination provisions may be deemed acceptable inside a vertical agreement, they give rise to apprehensions under competition law, particularly when they lead to anti-competitive consequences. Competition authorities may subject such agreements to scrutiny in the event that they result in market foreclosure, price fixing, or the limitation of competition. Ensuring compliance with competition rules is of the utmost importance for firms. The extent of legal examination that destination clauses may encounter can vary depending on the country. Certain jurisdictions may exhibit greater leniency towards these clauses, but others, particularly those with robust competition legislation, may subject them to rigorous scrutiny in order to assess their potential for anti-competitive consequences.

It is advisable for businesses operating in the energy sector to thoroughly deliberate the incorporation of destination clauses within their vertical agreements, taking into account compliance and legal considerations. It is recommended to seek legal counsel in order to ensure adherence to competition rules and regulations. It is imperative to adhere to transparent and equitable competition practices in order to mitigate the risk of legal disputes. In essence, the destination clause found in vertical agreements pertaining to the energy industry entails a contractual term that delineates certain geographic boundaries, exclusivity arrangements, or market segmentation strategies for distributors or purchasers. Although these clauses can serve as valid instruments for firms, it is crucial to meticulously construct them in order to adhere to competition rules and regulations and prevent any anti-competitive consequences.

The inclusion of a destination clause in long-term supply contracts is a common practise, serving as a territorial trade restriction. In 2001, the Commission initiated several studies examining the territorial limitations present in long-term supply contracts, primarily within the natural gas industry. These limitations entailed a prohibition on the resale of acquired natural gas beyond the designated contractual region. The aforementioned terminology has frequently been employed in contractual agreements involving Gazprom as well as Italian corporations SNAM, ENEL, and Edison.[22] The supply contracts facilitated the negotiation of approximately 20 million cubic metres of natural gas, which is subsequently injected into the gas transmission system on an annual basis. The imposition of territorial limitations

[22]European Commission, Decision of 24 August 2018 (Case AT.39816), Official Journal of the European Union, C 359, 29 November 2018, pp. 12–13. European Commission, Decision of 27 September 2006 (Case COMP/37.945), Official Journal of the European Union, C 70, 21 March 2008, pp. 10–11. European Commission, Decision of 13 November 2003 (Case COMP/39.251), Official Journal of the European Union, C 96, 26 April 2004, pp. 1–2. European Commission, Sector Inquiry into the Gas and Electricity Markets, Final Report (2007), Official Journal of the European Union, C 169, 30 July 2008, pp. 2–3.

arises from the variability of gasoline prices across different regions, which is contingent upon the extent of energy resource diversification within each respective country. This pricing strategy also offers advantages to suppliers by mitigating transportation expenses. The Commission has endeavoured to tackle the matter of vertical agreements by diminishing territorial sales limitations that impede competition within the market. The destination clause is commonly perceived as a stringent limitation that governs the relationship between the supplier and the seller.

The Commission was conducting an investigation into the activities of NLNG,[23] a Nigerian gas company that held the position of the second largest supplier of liquefied natural gas (LNG) in Europe. NLNG is responsible for providing a significant volume of over 5 billion cubic metres of natural gas to countries such as Italy, Spain, Portugal, and France. The Commission expressed concerns regarding the potential for the company to engage in supply agreements that incorporate profit-sharing mechanisms, wherein a portion of the revenue generated from the sale of natural gas outside the agreed territory would be allocated. The Commission posits that these limitations can be regarded as analogous to territorial sales constraints. The Nigerian company possessed a contract that included a destination clause; however, it decided to terminate said contract subsequent to reaching a mutual understanding with the Commission. During its investigation, the Commission did not uncover any additional violations by this company. Furthermore, NLNG made a commitment to refrain from implementing destination clauses in their long-term supply contracts.

The case involving ENI and SNAM is of particular relevance in this context, as it pertains to an investigation conducted by the Commission regarding the inclusion of territorial restrictions in the supply contracts.[24] The case also achieved a consensus, which holds significant importance given that ENI serves as a major gas supplier to Gazprom, providing an annual supply of more than twenty billion cubic metres of natural gas. The agreement included provisions for the exemption of the destination clause as well as the absence of additional profit-sharing mechanisms for supply contracts that impose territorial restrictions. The requirement for Gazprom to secure ENI's approval for the sale of natural gas to other Italian natural gas suppliers was also eliminated. Furthermore, ENI has made a commitment to augment the natural gas capacity available to suppliers in Austria and Germany. This policy measure facilitated the inclusion of third parties in the transmission networks and promoted the utilisation of the TAG gas interconnector.[25]

The commitments encompassed various aspects, such as the potential establishment of monthly transportation agreements to facilitate the efficient execution of the congestion management mechanism, the dissemination of capacity information, and

---

[23] Commission Press Release IP/02/1869. Commission settles investigation into territorial sales restrictions with Nigerian gas company NLNG. 2002.

[24] Commission Press Release IP/03/1345. Commission reaches breakthrough with Gazprom and ENI on territorial restriction clauses. 2003.

[25] European Commission, Decision of 24 August 2018 (Case AT.39816), Official Journal of the European Union, C 359, 29 November 2018, pp. 12–13.

adherence to recommended protocols for granting third-party access rights. OMV, the Austrian oil and gas company that imported gas from Gazprom, was similarly extended the aforementioned obligation. Austria maintains significant interconnection pipelines with Germany, Italy, and France, which play a crucial role in facilitating trade between Member States.[26] However, the imposition of restrictions on the final destination has had a negative impact on this trade. The companies have chosen to waive the obligation under which Gazprom is required to provide OMV with natural gas on the priority lane. OMV, a company that holds a stake in the TAG interconnector, has made a commitment to provide capacity for the supply of natural gas from Russia to consumers in Italy. Consequently, OMV had a responsibility to ensure third-party access.

From an energy law standpoint, vertical agreements can be likened to vertically integrated enterprises in which a single energy company operates across various segments, including natural gas extraction or electricity generation, transmission, supply, and distribution. In order to promote competition among economic operators, the European Union (EU) has implemented legislation pertaining to the unbundling of vertically integrated energy companies. This section primarily addresses vertical agreements, which typically involve the producer and the supplier. These agreements often contain anti-competitive clauses and non-compete obligations, resulting in detrimental effects on trade among resource providers.

This following section will provide a more comprehensive analysis of the abuse of dominant positions within the energy sector, particularly in relation to long-term energy supply contracts. This issue is closely interconnected with the concept of prohibited arrangements. These contracts frequently include specific clauses that impose restrictions, such as the final destination clause and limitations on use or resale, resulting in a curtailment of competition within the market. Long-term contractual agreements also confer upon the operator the authority to decline third-party access to the transmission networks, thereby establishing a monopolistic presence in the market and potentially engaging in anti-competitive practises. The primary justifications for such denial typically encompass inadequate network capacity, capacity reservations and associated drawbacks, and a lack of strategic investment in expanding the supply system's capacity to accommodate an additional entity's access. These circumstances have necessitated the consolidation of these institutes into a single section of the study, with the aim of providing a more comprehensive understanding of the interconnections and prevailing challenges.

[26] Commission Press Release IP/05/195. Competition: Commission secures improvements to gas supply contracts between OMV and Gazprom. 2005.

7.4 Conclusion

A vertical agreement refers to a contractual arrangement involving two or more entities wherein each entity operates at a distinct level within the production or distribution chain. This agreement or coordinated practise pertains to the specific arrangement in question. In contrast to analogous horizontal agreements established among enterprises operating at the same level, these agreements are comparatively less detrimental from the standpoint of competition law, as they primarily focus on enhancing production efficiency and achieving economies of scale. Vertical agreements can be likened to vertically integrated firms, wherein a single entity operates across multiple segments. In light of this rationale, the European Union has implemented legislation pertaining to the unbundling of vertically integrated energy companies with the aim of promoting competition among economic entities.

Vertical agreements have a reduced likelihood of distorting competition in the absence of market power, unless the supplier or distributor possesses substantial market power prior to engaging in said agreement. The presence of inadequate competition at one or more levels of trade has the potential to undermine the viability of competition. Vertical agreements can also yield positive outcomes by addressing the concern of "free-riding" in situations where investments are made in technology development and staff training. By implementing vertical agreements, the possibility of a new entity entering the market and reaping the benefits of infrastructure or business improvements made by others can be mitigated.

When evaluating non-compete agreements, it is crucial to consider their potential for generating countervailing effects, fostering technological advancements, and determining if they are necessary for enhancing organisational efficiency. The evaluation also considers whether consumers are allocated a fair and equitable portion of the advantages, or at the very least, no more than they would receive in the absence of a contractual arrangement between firms. Vertical agreements have the potential to induce cost reductions for operators by leveraging economies of scale, thus leading to lower production costs. Simultaneously, these agreements can also generate advantages for consumers by reducing the price of the supplied product. There exists a potential to mitigate the expenses associated with transmission, distribution, and operational costs for these operators. Vertical agreements frequently involve the reduction of logistics and transportation expenses as well as the optimisation of costs.

Given that non-compete agreements impose conditions on suppliers to enhance and sustain elevated output prices, it can be argued that cost optimisation measures should not result in price hikes for consumers. The application of this test in the energy sector is challenging due to the potential lack of responsiveness of market demand to changes in price. Specifically, a decrease in price may not necessarily result in a corresponding increase in sales. There are several conditions that must be imposed: the investment must be specific, thereby preventing the customer from utilising it for alternative purposes upon the contract's conclusion, which would result in substantial sales losses. Investments are deemed to possess a specific relationship when their utilisation is limited to the production of components exclusive to a particular brand. Consequently, it is imperative that the investment be of a long-term nature.

The Block Exemption Regulation provides an exemption for exclusive distribution agreements in cases where both the buyer's and the supplier's market share individually do not exceed 30%. Within these contractual arrangements, it is customary for the supplier to consent to the sale of their products to a single distributor, who is then granted the authority to resell said products within their designated territory. Furthermore, the distributor is subject to restrictions that prohibit them from actively engaging in sales activities within other territories that have been exclusively allocated to different distributors. These agreements may lead to a decrease in intra-brand competition as well as market partitioning and price discrimination. However, they also carry the risk of foreclosure and a reduction in competition among other distributors. Although the outcome of combining exclusive distribution and single branding may not always result in foreclosure, the amalgamation of exclusive distribution and single branding has the potential to intensify the exclusive distributor's dedication to a specific brand.

After an extensive consultation process, the Commission has released proposals for the revised Vertical Block Exemption Regulation and Vertical Guidelines. These proposals aim to replace the current regulations, which were set to expire on May 31, 2022. The publication of the documents occurred subsequent to the evaluation, initiated in 2018, which aimed to solicit perspectives from diverse stakeholders and ascertain whether the authentic documents continue to yield the intended outcomes. The Commission maintains the stance that vertical agreements have the potential to enhance efficiencies and yield greater benefits for customers through the promotion of improved quality services. The revised documents present the implementation of a modified safe harbour provision, which establishes specific goals for stakeholders in adapting to the evolving business landscape resulting from the growth of e-commerce. This approach aims to achieve a unified and coordinated strategy while also streamlining compliance processes by simplifying complex areas. The most favourable nation agreements have been subject to readjustment; specifically, the broadest most favourable nation agreements should be evaluated in accordance with Article 101 of the Treaty on the Functioning of the European Union. The block exemption safe harbour continues to provide advantages to the narrow parity clauses, subject to the condition of a 30% market share.

The dual distribution model underwent a significant amendment, wherein the supplier and buyer engage in direct competition. The exemption from dual distribution shall be applicable in cases where the combined market shares of parties involved in the retail sector of the relevant market do not exceed 10%. When the retail market share surpasses 10% but remains below the threshold of 30%, it is necessary to assess the information exchange in accordance with the horizontal guidelines. The exemption was not extended to platforms that possess hybrid functionalities, specifically those engaged in the sale of goods or services that directly compete with the companies for which they provide intermediary services. The amendments pertain to the concept of shared exclusivity, which involves the appointment of multiple exclusive distributors within a specific territory for a particular customer group. These appointments are subject to the proportionality test. The supplier operating the selective distribution system imposes a restriction on exclusive buyers, prohibiting them from actively or passively selling to unauthorised distributors within the territory. The concurrent implementation of selective and exclusive distribution was prohibited within the specified geographical region. The current guidelines continue to incorporate the provision of an exemption for the threshold of 30% market share. The non-compete provision also persists for a period of 5 years.

The inclusion of a destination clause in long-term supply contracts is a common practise to impose territorial restrictions on trade. Territorial restrictions encompassed a prohibition on the resale of acquired natural gas beyond the designated contractual region. The aforementioned terminology has frequently been employed within contractual agreements involving Gazprom as well as Italian corporations SNAM, ENEL, and Edison. The inclusion of a destination clause was perceived as a stringent limitation imposed on the contractual relationship between the supplier and the seller.

References

Bailey D, John LE (2019) European Union law of competition. Oxford University Press, Bellamy and Child

Nyssens H, Cultrera C, Schnichels D (2004) The Territorial restrictions case in the gas sector: a state of play. Competition Policy Newsletter. 2004/1

Ratliff J (2020) Unilateral conduct in the energy sector: an overview of EU and national case law. Concurrences

Tuytschaever F, Wijckmans F (2018) Vertical agreements in EU competition law. Oxford University Press

Chapter 8
Market Restrictions Created by the Abuse of Dominant Position

Abstract Long-term contractual agreements provide the operator with the power to refuse third-party access to the networks, making it the only provider in the market and potentially engaging in anti-competitive practices because of its dominant position. The main reasons for denying access usually revolve around insufficient network capacity, a lack of capacity reservations and a failure to strategically engage in extending the supply system's capacity to accommodate another party's access. Various circumstances have required the merging of various institutes into a unified division of the study, to achieve a more thorough comprehension of the interconnections and difficulties that exist. The main reason for this is the presence of discriminatory conditions that impede the effective functioning of customers and other energy suppliers in the relevant marketplaces. Granting third-party access rights is an essential step in ensuring the liberalization of the energy market. The regulatory obligation for the corporate entity that owns the essential infrastructure or necessary facility to provide unrestricted and unbiased network access allows new operators to enter the service supply market. The matter concerns an assessment of the energy sector's competitiveness within the internal market, considering the need for infrastructure to enable the supply of electricity to customers.

8.1 Introduction

This section will provide a more comprehensive analysis of the concept of the abuse of dominant position within the energy sector. This concept is closely associated with the notion of prohibited arrangements, particularly in relation to long-term energy supply contracts. These contractual agreements frequently include specific provisions that impose restrictions, such as the final destination clause and limitations on use or resale, resulting in a curtailment of competition within the market.

Long-term contractual agreements additionally confer the operator with the prerogative to decline third-party entry to the transmission networks, thereby establishing a monopoly as the sole provider in the market and potentially engaging

L. Rimšaitė, *The Crossroads of Competition Law and Energy Regulation*,
https://doi.org/10.1007/978-3-031-73238-6_8

in anti-competitive practises. The primary justifications for such denial typically encompass inadequate network capacity, capacity reservations and associated drawbacks, and a lack of strategic investment in expanding the supply system's capacity to accommodate an additional entity. These circumstances have necessitated the consolidation of these institutes into a single section of the study in order to more effectively elucidate the connections and prevailing concerns.

When evaluating dominance, the Commission considers the competitive framework of the market, including factors such as the existing supply conditions, the position of current competitors, the likelihood of potential competitors entering or expanding in the market, and the bargaining power of the company's customers.[1] Market share is a significant metric that provides insights into the market structure and the relative significance of various companies operating within the market. The determination of market shares by the Commission is contingent upon the prevailing conditions of the relevant market, specifically taking into account market dynamics and the level of product differentiation.

Market power is the capacity of a corporation or a collection of enterprises to define their own policies, including pricing, product quality, and innovation initiatives, without facing strong competition from rivals, customers, or consumers. When a corporation possesses market power, whether as a buyer or seller, it has the ability to exert control over market outcomes, including prices, quality, output volume, and contractual terms. The concept of antitrust examination employs a corporation's capacity to engage in anticompetitive behavior within a specific market.

Market power, in economic theory, refers to a company's capacity to establish prices that exceed its marginal cost and generate economic profits. Market power is not a binary state but rather exists along a spectrum. A monopoly is characterised by possessing the greatest level of market power, while a "price-taker" corporation, positioned at the other extreme, has the ability to deviate from market outcomes dictated by supply and demand dynamics and hence has no market power. In a monopoly situation, companies strive for market dominance because it enables them to achieve the highest level of economic profitability. Conversely, if they are in the position of "price-taker", where they must accept the prevailing market price, they will not make any profit.

It is crucial to acknowledge that possessing market power is not automatically harmful. A corporation's market strength can be determined by various factors that distinguish it from its competitors, such as barriers to entry, past investments, brand recognition, external regulation, economies of scale, network effects, intellectual property, or any other differentiating factor. The concern in competition law revolves around the utilisation of market power within the market. For instance, a corporation may leverage its strong market position to unfairly eliminate competitors, which raises concerns from a competitive perspective.

---

[1] European Commission Guidelines on the Assessment of Horizontal Mergers. [2010] OJ C 31/5.

Let's assume a vertically integrated corporation, which means a company that works at several levels of the production or distribution chain of a final product or service. If the company possesses a dominant position in the production of a crucial input, it has the ability to exclude its competitors in the downstream market. Through the denial of critical resources, the newly established firm has the capacity to prevent competitors from entering the market or compel them to exit, raising concerns about market concentration and diminished competition.

In a typical competitive analysis, assessing a company's market strength entails evaluating the substitutability of its various services and products. The idea is also connected to the company's demand-price elasticity. There is an inverse relationship between the absolute price elasticity and the market power of a corporation. When the price elasticity is lower, the company has stronger market power, and *vice versa*. In addition, a company that possesses market dominance must have the capacity to maintain profits that exceed the average level for an extended period of time. Hence, any examination of antitrust implications regarding this issue must take into account both the stationary and changing components.

The principles of oligopoly theory often use market shares as an indicator of a company's market power once they determine the relevant market. Under certain legal systems, specific levels of market shares automatically indicate a presumption of having a dominant position in the market. The European Commission's Guidelines for assessing horizontal mergers, for example, consider mergers that result in market shares of 40% to 50%, and sometimes even below 40%, as possibly resulting in the creation or strengthening of a dominant position.[2]

Assessing market power through market-share analysis typically entails examining additional factors that indicate a company's influence, such as product differentiation, brand loyalty, exclusive contracts, exclusive access to essential resources or customer bases, economies of scale and scope, barriers to entry, network effects, intellectual property, and regulatory and technological changes.

Each component's importance varies depending on the sector's dynamics. In highly competitive marketplaces with easy entry, a company that dominates the market is unlikely to maintain earnings that are higher than average. This is because it can easily attract new competitors, and if these new players become active in the market, they may drive prices down through increasing competition. Under these conditions, having a significant market share does not automatically translate into possessing market power that allows for the maintenance of large profitability. Hence, it is imperative to incorporate additional variables into the research, apart from market shares.

This idea was made clearer by the Hoffmann-La Roche case.[3] In that case, it was decided that a dominant position means that a business is able to effectively limit

[2]European Commission, Guidelines on the assessment of horizontal mergers under the Council Regulation (EC) No 139/2004 on the control of concentrations between undertakings (2010/C 31/03), Official Journal of the European Union, C 31, 5 February 2010, pp. 1–22.

[3]Case 85/76 *Hoffmann-La Roche & Co.* v *Commission* [1979] ECR. 461.

competition in its market and run independently from its competitors, clients, and customers. The presence of an economic entity possessing substantial market power does not necessarily result in the elimination of competition, as is the case with a monopoly. Instead, it enables the entity to exert a significant influence on competition dynamics and operate with a considerable degree of autonomy vis-à-vis its competitors.[4] Domination is commonly defined as the state in which an enterprise's economic prowess allows it to impede effective competition within the pertinent market and exert significant autonomy in its operations, separate from its rivals, clientele, and ultimately, consumers. In this particular scenario, the decision-making process is primarily unaffected by the actions undertaken by competitors, customers, and consumers.[5] A firm that can consistently increase prices above competitive levels in the long run without facing significant competitive pressure is typically regarded as dominant.

There exist various forms of dominance that are considered in terms of the specific circumstances in which they are applied. The concepts of horizontal and vertical dominance can be discerned. Horizontal dominance refers to the situation in which a particular entity holds a dominant position in relation to other competitors operating within the same relevant market. It is imperative to ascertain the pertinent market and identify other entities, along with their market positions. The situation becomes more manageable when the entity in question possesses specific exclusive rights or maintains a monopoly position in the market while providing a service that no other participant in the market offers.

Vertical dominance can be more easily delineated as it typically pertains to the downstream market of the dominant undertaking in a specific market. Vertical dominance typically occurs when a firm exercises control over the crucial facility or infrastructure required to deliver services. The essential facility does not exclusively pertain to physical infrastructure; it can also encompass critical information that a specific enterprise possesses that other market participants lack and require for their own operations. Specifically, this may include grid-related information pertaining to customers and connections.

Dominance can manifest either at an individual level or in a collective context. Collective dominance can arise when firms possess legal or economic conditions that allow them to behave in a similar manner. Such dominance may also occur when the undertakings are not connected by any action but share an interest in behaving in a specific manner.[6] The phenomenon of collective dominance is anticipated to

[4]Case 27/76 *United Brands Company* and *United Brands Continental* v *Commission* [1978] ECR. 207, para 65; Case 85/76 *Hoffmann-La Roche & Co.* v *Commission* [1979] ECR. 461, para 38; Case T-395/94 *Atlantic Container Line and others v Commission* [2002] ECR. II-875, para 330.

[5]Cases C-395/96 P and C-396/96 P *Compagnie Maritime Belge Transports, Compagnie Maritime Belge* and *Dafra-Lines* v *Commission* [2000] ECR. I-1365, para 119; Case T-228/97 *Irish Sugar* v *Commission* [1999] ECR. II-2969, para 186.

[6]European Commission, Guidelines on the assessment of horizontal mergers under the Council Regulation (EC) No 139/2004 on the control of concentrations between undertakings (2010/C 31/03), Official Journal of the European Union, C 31, 5 February 2010, pp. 1–22.

manifest itself in the electricity and gas sectors due to the presence of homogeneous products and concentrated, transparent markets.

When assessing dominance, various factors of constraint are considered, including the influence exerted by current suppliers, the potential competition, and specifically the competition that may arise if new entrants join the market or existing players expand their market share. Additionally, the countervailing power of purchasers is taken into account.

The existence of a dominant position is improbable if the undertaking's market share in the relevant market is below 40%. It is crucial to assess the competitors, especially in terms of their ability to act autonomously through possessing comparable shares or exerting influence on major enterprises.[7] The dominant nature of undertakings can be ascertained when they possess the ability to operate without being subject to competitive constraints for a specific duration, allowing them to exploit their position without facing any opposition from their rivals or customers. One additional factor to consider when assessing whether a firm is exercising its dominant position is the presence of barriers to entry into the market. It could be inferred that while the barriers to entry in the electricity generation and gas exploration markets are relatively high, access to the supply market is not necessarily facilitated. In the energy sector, it is possible for dominance to be present despite low market shares. Even if a dominant company has a smaller market share than what is officially stated, it may still lack the ability to exert effective pressure. This limitation can arise due to its significantly limited capacity. An enterprise may not possess a dominant position despite having a market share exceeding 40% if there are one or more operators with a relatively high market share that can effectively limit its capacity to exert unilateral, decisive influence. The significance of the institute on the abuse of dominant positions in the energy sector lies in its role in addressing the creation of discriminatory conditions that hinder the operations of consumers and other energy suppliers in the relevant markets. To thoroughly analyse the particular aspects of these factors, we will proceed to delve deeper into the distinct manifestations of dominant position abuse within the energy sector in subsequent sections.

In accordance with Article 102 of the Treaty on the Functioning of the European Union (TFEU), the concept of abuse is intrinsically connected to the notion of dominance. This statement elucidates the conduct of a dominant entity that uses its market power to shape the market structure by exerting pressure on other entities, consequently leading to a reduction in competition. The purpose of the statement is not to suggest the presence of mistreatment. The dominant entity may possess the intention to exploit its market dominance without necessarily engaging in such behaviour. If it could be inferred that the dominant entity had the intention to utilise its market dominance to carry out abusive actions, even if such actions do not have a restrictive impact. The broad interpretation of abusive conduct restricts the

---

[7] European Commission, Guidelines on the assessment of horizontal mergers under the Council Regulation (EC) No 139/2004 on the control of concentrations between undertakings (2010/C 31/03), Official Journal of the European Union, C 31, 5 February 2010, pp. 1–22.

autonomy of businesses in formulating their commercial strategies. In the subsequent sections, we will provide detailed explanations regarding distinct manifestations of abuse.

8.2 The Concept and Forms of Exclusionary Abuse in the Energy Sector

The theory posits a distinction between two primary forms: exploitative abuse, which results in harm to consumers, and exclusive abuse, which detrimentally affects competitors. A comprehensive evaluation of Commission practise enables the identification of various forms of exploitative abuse within the energy sector. These include exclusive supply arrangements, the refusal to grant third-party access to facilities, and capacity hoarding, which leads to the reservation of capacity that is not effectively utilised. Due to this rationale, the organisation declines to authorise network access as the allocated capacity has already been utilised. This scenario assumes the use of two distinct competition law frameworks collectively.[8] The reason for this is that the transmission network operator typically maintains a prominent position in the market and either organises capacity allocation auctions internally or provides exclusive network access to a specific entity. In the latter scenario, the conformity of such an agreement with Article 101 TFEU can be observed, as can the pertinence of the abuse of a dominant position within Article 102 TFEU. The entity restricts the utilisation of the network by another participant in the capacity reservation agreement, citing inadequate network capacity. Despite the potential for third-party assessment enabled by the networks' technical capabilities, the reserved portion of the capacity renders this endeavour unfeasible.

Long-standing agreements serve to further restrict the potential for new market entrants. From an energy law standpoint, the conduct of economic operators can be deemed unjustifiable due to their failure to comply with the obligation to provide third-party access. Transparent and non-discriminatory access should also be provided to third parties. The execution of a lengthy capacity contract between a network company and a single entity restricts the potential for new participants to enter the market. In the subsequent sections, we will delve into a more comprehensive examination of the distinct forms of anti-competitive misconduct that are particular to the energy industry. These include capacity hoarding, strategic underinvestment, capacity withholding, capacity degradation, pre-emptive long-term booking, and the abusive maintenance of pricing zones. Competition law doctrine does not make a distinction between these various forms, although the Commission has previously identified specific types of abuse by companies in the energy sector through analogical reasoning. Hence, our objective is to elucidate the particulars of these forms of abuse and the limitations they impose.

---

[8] Diathesopuolos (2010).

8.2.1 Third-Party Access Rights

The provision of third-party access rights is a crucial component in guaranteeing the liberalisation of the energy market. The implementation of this requirement within the framework of national legislation has facilitated the establishment of conditions conducive to the advancement of competition. Throughout history, monopolistic corporations have held ownership over infrastructure, resulting in restricted access to network facilities.[9] The resolution to the issue entailed imposing a requirement on the company that possesses the vital infrastructure or essential facility to grant unrestricted access to the network without charge or bias.[10] This would enable new operators to participate in this market and offer services to consumers.

The goal of increasing competition in the energy market is what drives the pursuit of granting third parties' access to the transmission grid. When implementing this particular requirement, it is imperative for transmission system operators to ensure that access networks are granted in a manner that is fair and unbiased.[11] Transmission system operators (TSOs) frequently operate as vertically integrated monopolies, with regulatory oversight governing access control. Regulated tariffs are implemented in the electricity sector to mitigate the potential abuse of dominant positions within transmission networks. However, the third energy package introduces provisions that offer alternative options, such as regulated or negotiated access, which enable entities to gain access to transmission networks and/or storage facilities.

The third energy package lacks a clear and explicit definition regarding the implementation of third-party access. However, the intention behind this requirement can be inferred from the language used in the Directives. The concept of third-party access originates from a specific provision within competition law that aims to prevent the misuse of a dominant market position.[12] This provision is closely linked to Article 102 of the TFEU. Hence, it is imperative to ascertain and assess the pertinent market in order to establish the occurrence of an infringement. In cases where the operator possesses significant market positions in infrastructure and holds ownership of transmission networks, it is common for the supply and trading markets to exhibit high levels of concentration. As highlighted in the guidelines, it

[9] Hauteclocque et al. (2011).

[10] Horstmann (2003).

[11] Brunekreeft (2002).

[12] Regulation (EC) No 715/2009 of the European Parliament and of the Council of 13 July 2009 on conditions for access to the natural gas transmission networks, Official Journal of the European Union, L 211, 14 August 2009, pp. 36–66. Directive 2009/73/EC of the European Parliament and of the Council of 13 July 2009 concerning common rules for the internal market in natural gas, Official Journal of the European Union, L 211, 14 August 2009, pp. 94–136. Directive 2009/72/EC of the European Parliament and of the Council of 13 July 2009 concerning common rules for the internal market in electricity, Official Journal of the European Union, L 211, 14 August 2009, pp. 55–93. Treaty on the Functioning of the European Union (TFEU), Consolidated version of 13 December 2007, Official Journal of the European Union, C 326, 26 October 2012, pp. 47–390.

is imperative for companies to provide justifications for denying access. The act of denying access can be interpreted as a denial to provide, as it restricts the gearbox system owner's capacity to diversify its resources and exercise its freedom to select a supplier by refusing access to its current infrastructure. Frequently, the act of refusing to provide necessary resources results in a state of foreclosure, which restricts access to interconnected networks. Consequently, this limitation hinders the availability of alternative resources and perpetuates the dominant market position of the operator.

According to the provisions outlined in the third energy package, member states have the option to grant exemptions for new infrastructure, thereby enabling the possibility of waiving third-party access requirements. When there aren't enough resources and giving third parties access rights would get in the way of providing services that are in the best interest of the economy as a whole, or when the "take or pay" obligation creates big financial and economic problems, it may be possible to waive third-party access. Simultaneously, it is important to acknowledge that the denial of access rights can potentially foster an environment where transmission network companies may exploit their position.[13] The inclusion of third-party access is imperative in order to guarantee a secure and cost-effective provision of energy to the end consumer. National regulatory authorities possess the authority to determine penalties and implement the requisite actions to facilitate the realisation of the internal market. Therefore, it is advisable to grant these authorities the necessary authority to safeguard the most susceptible consumers and guarantee the efficacy of consumer protection measures.

Competition law is characterised by retrospective regulation, whereas energy law is designed to promote competitive market functioning through prospective regulation. This regulatory framework pertaining to energy law is commonly referred to as competition regulation by certain authors.[14] The rationale for this position is rooted in the unique characteristics of the energy sector, wherein the viability and efficacy of all operations are contingent upon the presence and technological capabilities of transmission and distribution infrastructure.[15] Hence, the management and monitoring of markets are regarded as mechanisms for regulating the entire industry. Several scholars contend that the connection between regulation and liberalisation remains inadequately elucidated and assert unequivocally that regulation is indispensable for the establishment of market mechanisms.

The perspective on the role of competition law in the energy sector varies among scholars. Some argue that competition law primarily serves as a facilitator for market establishment, while others contend that pre-existing regulations specific to the energy industry are crucial in shaping its outcomes. Some scholars argue that competition law plays a crucial role in the regulation of energy companies while

[13] Buigues (2006).
[14] Brunekreeft (2001).
[15] Borner (2015).

considering specific regulatory mechanisms as secondary in nature.[16] The proponents of this stance contend that the aforementioned approach bears resemblance to the one previously examined, as competition law functions in a sufficiently dynamic manner through incremental market liberalisation, thereby obviating the need for stringent regulations aimed at market access. The hierarchical relationship between competition law and energy law is evident, as competition law is a constituent element of primary European Union law, while energy law provisions are encompassed within secondary EU law. The level of enforcement is adequately transparent, as competition law is implemented both at the national level within the Member States and at the institutional level of the European Union. In the context of energy law, the primary responsibility for the implementation of these laws lies with the regulatory authorities of the Member States.

The recognition of refusal to supply as a manifestation of abuse of a dominant position was initially established in the 1972 Commercial Solvents case.[17] In this case, the Court of Justice of the European Union (CJEU) determined that a refusal to cooperate could potentially qualify as a violation under Article 102 of the TFEU. The legal doctrine posits that when a dominant entity declines to collaborate with a competitor in markets that follow downstream, it may potentially violate competition law, particularly if this refusal results in the elimination of all competition within said market. The legal principle established in the Commercial Solvents case is typically applicable to vertically integrated corporations that possess a dominant market position and provide crucial resources to downstream entities. The Commission introduced the idea of refusal of supply in Report XIII. In this report, the Commission elucidated that the act of denying supply, when an operator provides a good with the condition of retaining control over its processing or sale, lacks objective justification.

The Commission's clarification relates to situations where a business declines to sell its goods to current or potential customers. Additionally, it encompasses situations where a company refuses to grant a licence for an intellectual property right, even when such a licence is necessary to share information regarding the interface or to deny access to a crucial facility or network. The potential hindrance to an economic operator's rights due to an unjustified supply obligation is a matter of concern for the Commission. Consequently, the Commission is thoroughly evaluating the extent of its powers in all domains of competition law enforcement. The focal point is the recognition that an obligation to provide without proper justification has the potential to violate the economic rights of the operator. The requirement to provide supply may potentially impede investment, as the leading operator may choose to withhold investment in the necessary infrastructure to avoid a scenario in which its competitors are obligated to provide access to their networks. This could

[16] Cameron (2005).

[17] Joined cases 6 and 7/73 *Istituto Chemioterapico Italiano S.p.A.* and *Commercial Solvents Corporation v Commission of the European Communities*. [1974] ECR 223.

have detrimental effects on both business growth and the ability of consumers to obtain competitive pricing.

There may also arise a scenario wherein a new participant refrains from investing the necessary capital for infrastructure development, instead aiming to leverage the existing infrastructure investment made by the dominant market player.[18] The denial of access by the dominant operator can be viewed favourably in the long run as it fosters competition by encouraging new operators to explore alternative means of entering the market, ultimately benefiting consumers. However, in the short term, the requirement to provide access to transmission networks may create a scenario where the operator lacks the incentive to invest in energy infrastructure, instead, focuses solely on utilising existing infrastructure. The theory delineates between two primary forms: exploitative abuse, which results in harm to consumers, and exclusive abuse, which detrimentally affects competitors. A comprehensive evaluation of Commission practise enables the identification of various forms of exploitative abuse prevalent in the energy sector. These include exclusive supply arrangements, the refusal to grant third-party access to facilities, and capacity hoarding, which leads to the reservation of capacity that is not effectively utilised in practise. Due to this rationale, the organisation declines to provide authorization for network access as the allocated capacity has already been assigned. This scenario assumes the utilisation of two distinct competition law institutions collectively. The reason for this is that the transmission network operator typically maintains a position of dominance within the market and either conducts capacity allocation auctions independently or provides exclusive network access to a specific entity. In the latter scenario, the conformity of said agreement with Article 101 of the TFEU can be observed, alongside the pertinence of assessing potential abuse of a dominant market position within the framework of Article 102 TFEU. The entity restricts the utilisation of the network by another participant in the capacity reservation agreement, citing inadequate network capacity. Despite the potential for third-party assessment enabled by the networks' technical capabilities, the reserved portion of the capacity renders this task unfeasible.

Long-standing agreements serve to further restrict the potential for new market entrants. From an energy law standpoint, the conduct of economic operators can be deemed unjustifiable due to their failure to adhere to the principle of third-party access. It is imperative to ensure that third-party access is provided in a manner that is both transparent and non-discriminatory. The execution of a prolonged capacity agreement between a network entity and a single company restricts the potential for new entrants. In the subsequent sections, we will delve into a more comprehensive examination of the distinct forms of anti-competitive misconduct that pertain specifically to the energy industry. These include capacity hoarding, strategic underinvestment, capacity withholding, capacity degradation, pre-emptive long-term

[18] Joined Cases C-241 and C-242/91 P, Radio Telefis Eireann v. Comm'n of the Eur. Cmtys., 1995 E.C.R. 1-743. Case C-418/01, IMS Health GmbH & Co. OHG v. NDC Health GmbH & Co. KG, 2004 E.C.R. 1-5039.

booking, and abusive maintenance of pricing zones. Competition law doctrine does not differentiate between these forms, although the Commission has previously identified specific types of abuse by companies in the energy sector through analogical reasoning. Hence, our objective is to elucidate the particulars of such forms of abuse and the limitations they impose.

8.2.2 *The Capacity Hoarding*

Capacity hoarding refers to the practise wherein transmission network operators decline to provide third-party access to their networks. These companies typically rationalise their actions based on the premise that network capacity has been allocated or has already been auctioned to energy suppliers in the market. The present scenario exhibits manipulation, as it is common for companies to formally allocate network capacity without fully utilising the reserved amount. This scenario presents the potential for the transmission system operator to exploit its position by denying access to other market participants and asserting that all pipeline capacity has already been allocated. In addition, the principle of "use it or lose it" is applicable in this context. This implies that the company should only utilise the reserved network capacity in order to derive advantages from it.

In the present context, the ENI case[19] holds relevance and will be further expounded upon. The Italian state-owned vertically integrated oil and gas company was engaged in the activities of exporting, transmitting, storing, and supplying natural gas. The corporation is a prominent importer of natural gas in Italy and has successfully acquired long-term contracts for natural gas supplies from Russia, Norway, the Netherlands, and Algeria. In 2007, the Commission initiated an *ex officio* investigation into the alleged abuse of a dominant position by ENI. The annual demand for natural gas in the country amounts to 85 million cubic metres, and ENI is responsible for providing more than 74 million cubic metres of natural gas. The company additionally provides approximately 10 million cubic metres of domestically extracted natural gas while sourcing the remaining supply from underground natural gas storage facilities.

ENI exhibited dominance not only in the realm of natural gas transmission but also in the sphere of supply activities. The investigation revealed that the aforementioned company exercises control over the natural gas transmission pipelines as well as the Panigaglia LNG terminal. ENI has secured the long-term capacity of the interconnectors under its sole control or in collaboration with other entities. The Commission acknowledged that ENI possessed the requisite access to comprehensive information pertaining to infrastructure and investment decisions regarding pipeline capacity reservations. According to the findings of the Commission, it has been determined that ENI has established a dominant position in the natural

[19] Case COMP/39.315 – ENI. 2009.

transmission and supply markets since the year 2000.[20] The evaluation of the planned infrastructure was conducted in a thorough manner. It was observed that no new infrastructure projects were anticipated by 2011, resulting in a lack of change in the prevailing situation. Additionally, it was discovered that the newly established suppliers faced barriers to entry in the market and were unable to effectively compete with ENI due to their lack of access to the natural gas transmission networks. According to the findings of the Commission, ENI consistently implemented anti-competitive practises with the intention of limiting the accessibility of transmission network infrastructure to third parties. Despite the evident market demand for access to transmission network infrastructure, ENI has consistently denied granting access to the pipeline, even though its capacity remains underutilised. ENI failed to implement any measures aimed at enhancing the capacity of the transmission network or effectively managing congestion. It was discovered that ENI possessed available capacity on its transmission networks, which it unreasonably declined to provide to third parties due to the fact that the technical capacity was not utilised for natural gas supply. This refusal prevented another company from utilising the infrastructure during that period. The company effectively maintained control over imports, thereby exploiting the circumstances.

ENI expressed disagreement with the provisions outlined in the Statement of Objections and proposed a commitment to divest its ownership interests in international gas pipeline companies, specifically the TSO stakes, shares of Eni Gas Transport GmbH and Eni Gas Transport Deutschland S.p.A., the necessary equipment for operating the transmission network, as well as intangible assets. Additionally, ENI committed to not extending or renewing any related contracts.[21] The Commission determined that the commitments put forth adequately address the concerns outlined in the Statement of Objections. The commitments presented by the party have been deemed binding by the Commission, in accordance with the provisions outlined in Article 9 of Regulation 1/2003.[22] The Commission has refrained from making a determination regarding the existence of an infringement.

The CEZ case[23] also served as an illustrative example of capacity hoarding. As a vertically integrated entity, this organisation possesses electricity generation capabilities in both the electricity and lignite sectors. Additionally, it has access to nuclear power and lignite deposits and exercises control over the distribution system operator. In instances where a business entity possesses an excessive level of control over critical systems and networks, entry into the market becomes significantly challenging. The Commission has expressed concerns regarding the potential abuse of CEZ's dominant position in the generation and wholesale supply of electricity markets,

[20] Case COMP/39.315 – ENI. 2009.

[21] Case COMP/39.315 – ENI. 2009.

[22] Council Regulation (EC) No 1/2003 of 16 December 2002 on the implementation of the rules on competition laid down in Articles 81 and 82 of the Treaty (Text with EEA relevance). OJ L 1, 4.1.2003, pp. 1–25.

[23] Case AT.39727 – CEZ. 2013.

which may constitute a violation of Article 102 of the TFEU. The Commission has observed that the company has executed a strategic approach aimed at deterring potential new competitors from entering the market. Furthermore, the competitors were unable to utilise the pre-emptive transmission capacity reservation due to access restrictions. The Czech Republic is served by a single transmission system operator, and the transmission network's input cannot be replaced by alternative inputs. Ultimately, CEZ did not concur with the allegations of engaging in anti-competitive behaviour through its dominant market position. However, as a resolution, CEZ proposed the divestment of one of its generation assets to a buyer that would be subject to approval by the Commission. Following the receipt of comments from relevant stakeholders, the Commission deemed the commitments put forth by CEZ acceptable and agreed to them.

Companies that use their assigned network capacities without making them accessible to the market during periods of high demand reduce competition and may exclude other participants from the market. Therefore, in order to create a competitive internal market, it is necessary to address and resolve issues that impose artificial limitations. In the energy industry, it is typical for one business to have sole ownership of transmission networks and hence act as the transmission system operator. According to the regulations specified in the third energy package, it is mandatory for such an organization to grant access to other operators who express interest in using the grid to supply electricity to consumers. The insufficient technological capabilities of the networks also contribute to the denial of access. Given the current circumstances, we anticipate that the transmission network company will allocate resources to enhance and modernize its network infrastructure. Often, the company justifies its refusal by citing insufficient investment. We commonly link this argument to the objective of maintaining market supremacy and hindering the entrance of rivals.

8.2.3 The Strategic Underinvestment

The notion of strategic underinvestment was referred to in the Commission's practise, wherein a company possessing a critical infrastructure decline to grant access to a third party. The issue at hand pertains to the evaluation of the internal market's competitiveness in the energy sector, given its inherent requirement for infrastructure to effectively supply energy to consumers. The ability to construct such infrastructure is contingent upon the level of investment necessary, thereby limiting its feasibility for certain economic actors.

Consequently, the provision of access to transmission networks enables a broader range of operators to participate in the market, extending beyond the ownership entities of said networks. Prior to delving into a more comprehensive analysis of this phenomenon, it is pertinent to acknowledge that companies that possess transmission networks are required to furnish sufficient bandwidth in order to guarantee a continuous supply of energy. In pursuit of this objective, corporations are allocating resources towards the enhancement of infrastructure to optimise their energy provision, thereby guaranteeing a more abundant availability of energy resources. Nevertheless, it is frequently observed that companies neglect to enhance their infrastructure in order to restrict access to external entities. By adopting this approach, the company effectively sustains its dominant market position while simultaneously erecting artificial barriers to entry for potential newcomers and impeding competition with other participants in the market.

Another significant case involves Transgaz, a Romanian transport network that has been accused of impeding the natural gas trade with neighbouring countries.[24] The inspections were instigated by the Commission in 2016, and subsequently, in 2017, the Commission commenced formal proceedings in response to competition concerns arising from the underinvestment. Transgaz, by deferring the development of gas export infrastructure, potentially impeded the exportation of natural gas from Romania to Hungary and Bulgaria. Furthermore, the exports were rendered commercially unappealing as a result of elevated interconnection tariffs.

Transgaz is a company that operates in the fields of natural gas transmission, international gas transit, cross-border gas transmission, gas dispatching, as well as research and design within the natural gas sector. Moreover, the transmission system operator encompasses the entirety of the system, which comprises the interconnectors connecting with neighbouring countries, specifically pertaining to imports and exports. The company holds a sole concessionary agreement until the year 2032 for the operation of the natural gas transmission network, with no alternative networks currently accessible. The company possesses a monopoly in the transmission of natural gas, which includes interconnections with neighbouring entities.

The Commission has expressed concerns regarding the potential abuse of market dominance by the company through the imposition of restrictions on the unrestricted transmission of natural gas to neighbouring countries. Various strategies were employed to achieve this objective, including the deliberate underinvestment in strategic infrastructure and the intentional postponement of the construction of said infrastructure, which is essential for facilitating exports. Additionally, high interconnection tariffs were established, which lack commercial appeal.[25]

Despite denying any violation of Article 102 TFEU, Transgaz has proposed commitments to enhance its export capacities from 0.1 billion cubic metres to 4 billion cubic metres annually at the interconnection points with Hungary and Bulgaria. Additionally, Transgaz has pledged to ensure a minimum, uninterrupted quantity. The commitments also encompassed infrastructure works to ensure adequate capacities. The tariffs underwent revision, and the proposals submitted to the regulator exhibited non-discriminatory treatment towards both export and domestic tariffs. It is advisable to refrain from engaging in any activities that may potentially stimulate the exportation of natural gas. The aforementioned obligations were

---

[24] Case AT.40335 – Romanian gas interconnectors. 2020.

[25] European Commission Decision in Case AT.39816 – Gazprom. [2018] OJ C 119/03.

established with a designated timeframe extending until the year 2025 and were subject to oversight by the trustee.

The case of TenneT[26] serves as an illustration of strategic underinvestment in the interconnection system, which hinders trade between neighbouring countries. Specifically, it imposes limitations on the commercial capacity of the DE-DK1 interconnector, which connects West Denmark to Germany. TenneT is a prominent transmission system operator (TSO) in Germany, responsible for managing the electricity system. The electricity flow within TenneT's system is characterised by significant volumes of electricity being transmitted from the northern regions, where electricity production is concentrated, to the southern territories, which experience higher levels of electricity consumption. EnDK is responsible for the operation of electricity in Denmark, where the wholesale electricity market is divided into bidding zones known as West Denmark and East Denmark. The transmission system operators responsible for the interconnector DE-DK1 are TenneT and EnDK.

The capacity is provided in two directions, as determined by the operators' calculations. TenneT grants priority access to the electricity network for domestic production during periods of high domestic wind-based electricity generation, thereby restricting the availability of electricity from West Denmark via the DE-DK 1 interconnector. According to the sectoral regulations, TenneT is obligated to ensure the provision of the maximum capacity of the interconnector without imposing any limitations on the interconnection capacity. TenneT has proposed commitments, including a minimum guaranteed hourly capacity of 1300 megawatts for the interconnector, taking into account the potential capacity that could be made accessible during operational circumstances. The attainment of the minimum hourly capacity is expected following the completion of a six-month implementation phase. In situations pertaining to supply security, shortages, or emergencies necessitating additional capacity, TenneT has the ability to reduce the capacity below the minimum guaranteed level. In such circumstances, the restriction should not exceed the extent required to guarantee the maintenance of supply security. The duration of the commitment ought to have spanned a period of 9 years and been duly monitored by the designated trustee. Subsequently, TenneT presented revised proposals that primarily focused on offering the highest feasible capacity for the interconnector's secure functioning while also ensuring a minimum hourly capacity of 1300 MW. In light of the anticipated expansion of the interconnector in 2020, TenneT aims to gradually enhance the capacity to reach 75% of the expanded interconnectors' capacity by 2026. In limited circumstances, the capacity below the guaranteed level may be subject to reduction due to concerns regarding the security of supply. This particular case serves as an example of the necessity of adhering to competition regulations when promoting wind-based electricity generation. It highlights the need for structural adjustments in order to achieve a higher level of competition while also ensuring the ability to import electricity. The previously mentioned ENI case pertained to the decision made by the company to refrain from enhancing congestion

[26] Case AT.40461 – DE/DK Interconnector. 2018.

management through the augmentation of technical parameters within the transmission networks. This decision aimed to enable greater capacity for natural gas flow.

The GDF Suez case[27] involved the French natural gas and electricity supplier facing allegations of restricted access to gas import capacities, specifically in balancing zones within France. These allegations were seen as limiting competition in downstream gas supply markets as well as impacting import capacity and the functioning of LNG terminals. These actions were implemented, taking into account the competitor's request, in accordance with the open procedure. The Commission has observed that conducting a financial assessment and submitting a capacity request would have resulted in a viable solution. The foreclosure was attributed to a combination of prolonged capacity reservations and strategic underinvestment in the expansion of import capacity *at the Montoir de Bretagne* LNG terminal. Furthermore, it was observed that GDF failed to adhere to the open season procedure in response to the third-party access request. In accordance with Article 9 of Regulation 1/2003, GDF has proposed the relinquishment of capacity for the two LNG terminals located at *Fos Cavaou and Montoir de Bretagne*. The significance of pipelines in facilitating supply competition in underdeveloped regions may have posed risks for consumers. Additionally, a consensus was reached to decrease the booking components of GDF's gas networks by 50%. Furthermore, GDF has made a commitment to decrease their total stake in the long-term entry capacity within the respective networks by up to 50% by the years 2014 and 2015. Additionally, they have pledged to adhere to the specified thresholds for a period of 10 years.

The issue of strategic underinvestment was recognised in the ENI case.[28] Specifically, allegations were made regarding the abuse of a dominant market position through the deliberate restriction of investments in the international transmission pipeline system, despite substantial demand from third parties. In light of the ongoing proceedings, ENI has expressed its intention to sell shares in the company associated with the international gas transmission pipelines (TENEP, Transitgas, and TAG) to an impartial buyer, thereby mitigating any potential competition concerns. The Commission has accepted the commitments to divest. A structural remedy was implemented in order to address the issue of anticompetitive behaviour or potential violations within a vertically integrated gas company.

8.2.4 The Capacity Withholding

The phenomenon known as capacity withholding refers to a scenario wherein companies engaged in the operation of essential infrastructure networks strategically undertake measures to impede a third party's utilisation of said transmission networks. The prevailing measures often encompass the implementation of artificial

[27] Case COMP/39.316 – Gaz de France. 2009.

[28] Case COMP/39.315 – ENI. 2010.

price escalation or the imposition of limitations on the accessibility of said infrastructure. Short-term capacity is frequently procured by companies at a relatively higher cost compared to long-term capacity.

The postponement of capacity auctions has frequently led to the perception of insufficient technical capacity, prompting companies to explore alternative means of securing their natural gas supply. The current situation involves a consistent failure to effectively utilise technical capabilities, which has consequently resulted in the identification of irregularities in the previously examined ENI case. To actively participate in the energy supply industry, the company must possess a specific segment of the transmission pipeline that connects directly to the distribution station. However, it is not necessary for the company to have an intermediate version of the pipeline, as long as it has the required connections within the transmission system. There has been a recurring suggestion to allocate capacity for distinct sections of pipelines without establishing systematic connections between them. In order to facilitate the operation of a natural gas supply, an endeavour seeking network access must be granted access to the entire transmission network, excluding specific segments. ENI has frequently engaged in the practise of artificially limiting the capacity of its transmission system through the use of auctions. This strategic approach has enabled ENI to sustain its dominant market position, as other operators have not been afforded comparable access to the transmission system infrastructure.

The Commission conducted an investigation into the conduct of a German company in the E.ON case,[29] uncovering comparable instances of abuse. The company in question had deliberately constrained its electricity generation capacity and imposed restrictions within the electricity balancing market. The company has implemented limitations on the provision of electricity from select power plants in the spot market, consequently resulting in an increase in electricity prices. This action has had adverse effects on consumers and can be seen as an exploitation of the company's dominant position within the wholesale electricity market.

The present study examined the potential abuse of market power by E.ON in the context of electricity balancing, specifically in relation to its demand for secondary balancing power reserves. The purpose of the investigation was to assess the escalated expenses associated with providing a benefit to its subsidiary and subsequently transferring those costs to the final consumer. The conduct of this company, which impeded electricity producers from other Member States from exporting electricity to the E.ON balancing market, was also subject to investigation. In the aforementioned instances, E.ON was mandated to divest approximately 5000 MW of electricity generation capacity, thereby addressing concerns pertaining to the wholesale market and mitigating the potential for an economically viable reduction of electricity generation capacity. These measures have facilitated the expansion of operations to previously untapped areas, leading to a corresponding rise in electricity production capacity through the establishment of additional power plants. The sale of this particular capacity effectively addressed the challenge within the balancing

[29]Case COMP/39.388 – E.ON. 2008.

market, wherein E.ON assumed responsibility for managing production, transmission, and supply operations.

8.2.5 Discrimination

One instance of companies implementing varying or discriminatory prices across different regions within a country without providing valid economic justifications for such pricing can be regarded as a manifestation of an abuse of dominant market power within the energy sector. The issue becomes particularly pronounced in situations where an electricity corporation engages in the practise of exporting domestically generated electricity with the intention of upholding elevated service costs instead of offering it to consumers at a reduced rate. This company engages in the practise of importing electricity into a specific region with comparatively lower production costs, resulting in the deliberate inflation of electricity prices. In practical terms, this phenomenon was observed in Sweden, where the availability of inexpensive electricity in the northern regions was not allocated to local residents but rather exported to neighbouring nations at elevated rates.

The aforementioned case involving Svenska Kraftnat[30] revealed that the dominant Swedish transmission system operator, Svenska Kraftnat, engaged in abusive practises within the Swedish electricity market. The transmission system operator has proposed a model aimed at managing internal congestion, which would result in a reduction of interconnection capacity required for trade with other European Union Member States. This, in turn, would lead to an unnecessary fragmentation of the internal market. Consequently, a consensus was established with the Commission to partition the Swedish transmission system into multiple distinct zones. This arrangement aimed to ensure the functionality of the electricity transmission system by July 1, 2011.[31] The design of the individual zones has been formulated in a manner that is adaptable, enabling prompt adjustments to be implemented and, if required, accommodating both anticipated and unanticipated alterations in the flow patterns within the Swedish transmission system.

Since the initiation of the zone operation, Svenska Kraftnat has been tasked with effectively managing congestion in the Swedish transmission system while ensuring that interconnection trading capacity remains unrestricted. An instance that deviated from the aforementioned principle of internal congestion management was the occurrence of congestion along the west coast corridor. Svenska Kraftnat has made a commitment to enhance the infrastructure of the west coast corridor by constructing and activating a new 400 kW transmission line connecting Stenkulen and Strioma-LLindume. This initiative is scheduled to be completed by November

[30] Case 39351 – Swedish Interconnectors. 2010.

[31] Notice published pursuant to Article 27(4) of Council Regulation (EC) No 1/2003 in Case COMP/B-1/39.351 — Swedish Interconnectors.

30, 2011. The aforementioned model granted an exception for the functioning of the West Coast Corridor, taking into account the regulatory resources allocated for countertrade in order to mitigate congestion. During the initial stage of planning, Svenska Kraftnat made a commitment to proactively anticipate congestion and identify appropriate measures to mitigate it during the subsequent operational phase. This involved identifying all regulatory resources that could be utilised to effectively address the anticipated congestion. Following this, Svenska Kraftnat prioritised these resources based on their importance and chose the most cost-effective resources to facilitate the attainment of the specified reductions. Svenska Kraftnat made a selection of resources within Sweden from the available options, with the aim of sharing them to meet the necessary energy demand.

Throughout its existence, Svenska Kraftnat has made a commitment to utilising all available regulatory resources to effectively manage congestion and maintain sufficient interconnection trading capacity within the market. The Commission asserts that Svenska Kraftnat's actions can be classified as an abuse of dominant market power for two distinct reasons. The imposition of limitations on interconnectors in such circumstances can be perceived as a form of discriminatory treatment towards users of the network.[32] Additionally, the company exhibited differential treatment towards domestic consumption demand and external consumption demand for the purpose of electricity transmission export. Additionally, the actions taken by Svenska Kraftnat had an instantaneous impact on prices, leading to customers overseas being denied access to lower energy prices. This was due to the substitution of more costly resources in lieu of the energy that was not supplied from Sweden. The observed behaviour hindered the realisation of free trade opportunities as it impeded the flow of electricity to neighbouring regions with higher prices, thereby reducing prices in foreign markets. The motivation for electricity producers to distribute power plants in certain regions was diminished due to the presence of curtailments. Furthermore, the motivation to reduce electricity consumption in specific regions or during specific periods of the day was addressed due to the fact that consumers were not subject to paying the prevailing market price. According to the Commission's perspective, domestic demand was satisfied in instances where there was sufficient capacity, while external demand remained unfulfilled, even in the presence of available network capacity.

Consequently, the examination of these instances revealed that the companies were engaging in market exploitation by leveraging specific technological prerequisites and variables. The investigation further revealed that companies retain significant opportunities to rationalise their anti-competitive practises based on technological justifications. There exists a potentiality wherein holding companies, employing diverse strategies that may not be limited to formal agreements, facilitate their subsidiaries in attaining a competitive edge. However, it is pertinent to consider the matter in relation to companies that possess substantial market power and are susceptible to engaging in anti-competitive practises that exploit their financial and

[32] Hauterlocque and Hancher (2011).

market positions. In this particular scenario, the enhanced authority of national regulatory bodies fails to effectively address the issue at hand. The energy law encompasses a measure aimed at promoting market liberalisation and enhancing competitiveness.[33] This measure grants regulatory authorities the authority to prevent companies from engaging in abusive practises and to encourage them to operate in a manner that fosters healthy competition while minimising any negative impact on the market. Upon conducting an analysis of the Commission's practises and decisions, it becomes evident that while additional regulatory measures are being implemented, the desired outcomes of liberalisation and heightened competition are not being realised through this approach. Hence, it is imperative to prioritise market objectives over regulatory ones.

8.3 The Concept and Forms of Exploitative Abuse in the Energy Sector

The phenomenon of exploitative abuse holds significant importance within the realm of competition law, particularly when examining its extensive ramifications within the energy industry. This chapter focuses on the notion of exploitative abuse and its diverse manifestations within the energy sector, providing insights into the legislative framework and empirical instances that highlight its importance.[34] Competition law plays a fundamental role in safeguarding equitable and competitive market conditions. Within the energy industry, competition authorities maintain a diligent stance towards combating both exclusionary and exploitative abuses. These actions have the potential to negatively impact consumers and impede innovation. This chapter examines the notion of exploitative abuse and its different forms within the energy sector.

Exploitative abuse, alternatively referred to as abuse of dominance or monopolistic conduct, manifests when a dominating energy corporation uses its market power to the harm of consumers, competitors, or the overall market. Market power refers to the ability of a firm or entity to exert substantial control over prices and contractual conditions, often resulting from its dominating position in the market. Exploitative abuse, in this context, commonly occurs when the entity with market power uses its advantageous position to manipulate prices and terms to its own advantage.

Unfair pricing refers to pricing strategies that are deemed unjust, exorbitant, or discriminatory, resulting in negative consequences for consumers or impeding fair competition. Predominant energy corporations possess the ability to establish prices that surpass their operational expenses by a substantial margin, thereby leading to customers incurring higher charges for vital energy provisions. Regulatory bodies

---

[33] Chauve et al. (2010).

[34] Hauteclocque et al. (2011).

frequently examine these practices in order to mitigate the potential abuse of consumers.

The practice of employing discriminatory pricing or terms to grant specific client's preferential treatment can be regarded as a form of exploitative abuse. For instance, using differential pricing strategies by providing reduced rates to some industrial clientele while imposing elevated charges on others without substantiating the rationale Tying and bundling practices are observed among certain prominent energy corporations, wherein they establish a connection between the sale of one energy product or service and another. This phenomenon has the potential to restrict the range of options available to consumers and impede competition, hence potentially qualifying as exploitative abuse. The act of refusing to provide essential energy supplies to competitors or customers has the potential to negatively impact competition and consumers. Consequently, regulatory bodies frequently interfere in order to avoid such detrimental practices. The regulatory framework refers to a set of rules, regulations, and guidelines established by governing bodies to govern and oversee various industries and sectors.

Exploitative abuse is encompassed within the purview of Article 102 of the TFEU within the context of the European Union. With the intention of preserving and promoting competition within the energy markets, national competition authorities and the European Commission both enforce these regulations. Energy corporations that possess substantial market power have a crucial role in maintaining a stable energy supply. However, it is imperative to ensure that their dominance does not adversely affect consumers and hinder competition. Regulators and competition authorities persist in maintaining a nuanced equilibrium, promoting the advancement of novel ideas, reasonable pricing, and the freedom for consumers to make choices, all the while safeguarding against any exploitative misconduct.

The issue of exploitative misuse within the energy sector continues to be a significant concern for regulatory bodies and competition authorities on a global scale. Through a comprehensive comprehension of the concept and many manifestations of exploitative misuse, along with diligent enforcement of competition regulations, it is possible to attain a more robust and competitive energy market. This outcome would yield advantages for both consumers and the industry at large. Exploitative abuse arises when consumers are subjected to harm through the imposition of restrictions on their freedom of choice. In the energy sector, the importance of these issues is especially clear when network companies that are in charge of overseeing critical infrastructure have long-term supply agreements that include take-or-pay provisions and market-sharing mechanisms. These specific restrictions will be examined in greater depth in subsequent sections. Exploitative abuse refers to the conduct of a dominant entity that imposes unjustifiably high prices on consumers. The energy sector exhibits abuse practises that involve the inclusion of contractual provisions conferring exclusive repair and maintenance rights for the entire lifespan of equipment, as well as requiring permission from the dominant company to engage in resale or other forms of transfer of the acquired equipment. The prevalence of inequitable pricing and unfavourable terms is pervasive in markets characterised by substantial barriers to entry, typically impeding new investments from effectively addressing these challenges.[35] Nevertheless, the Commission tends to refrain from utilising Article 102 (2) TFEU due to its reluctance to impose excessive price and/or behavioural regulation, as such measures could potentially discourage prospective investors. From this perspective, it is crucial to examine long-term energy supply agreements that facilitate the potential for economic operators to exploit their position and enhance their market dominance.

8.3.1 The Long-Term Contracts

Long-term energy supply contracts are established with the purpose of ensuring financial support for significant projects and are highly appealing to the involved parties, typically favouring the seller. This is primarily due to their extended duration, typically spanning from 15 to 25 years. This particular time frame is considered to be highly advantageous in terms of maximising investment returns.[36] It is worth noting that "take or pay" clauses are commonly included in natural gas supply contracts. When considering significant energy infrastructure projects, the substantial upfront investment costs and subsequent reduction in operating costs make these contracts advantageous for companies, as they offer a consistent return on investment throughout the payback period. As a result, the implementation of energy projects is accompanied by reduced risk.

Throughout history, Europe has established enduring contractual agreements for the supply of natural gas with Russia, formerly known as the Soviet Union. The objective was to obtain funding for significant energy infrastructure initiatives and address the requirements of natural gas consumers. The contracts were established according to the commonly known Groningen model, which has been extensively employed in the Netherlands since 1962.[37] Under this model, the contracts

[35] Directive (EU) 2019/944 of the European Parliament and of the Council of 5 June 2019 on common rules for the internal market in electricity, Official Journal of the European Union, L 158, 14 June 2019, pp. 125–200. See Article 35. Directive 2009/73/EC of the European Parliament and of the Council of 13 July 2009 concerning common rules for the internal market in natural gas, Official Journal of the European Union, L 211, 14 August 2009, pp. 94–136. See Article 41. Regulation (EC) No 1/2003 of the Council of 16 December 2002 on the implementation of the rules on competition laid down in Articles 81 and 82 of the Treaty, Official Journal of the European Union, L 1, 4 January 2003, pp. 1–25. See Article 3. Regulation (EC) No 139/2004 of the Council of 20 January 2004 on the control of concentrations between undertakings, Official Journal of the European Union, L 24, 29 January 2004, pp. 1–22. See Article 2.

[36] Konoplyanik (2015).

[37] Regulation (EC) No 715/2009 of the European Parliament and of the Council of 13 July 2009 on conditions for access to the natural gas transmission networks, Official Journal of the European Union, L 211, 14 August 2009, pp. 36–59. See Article 3. Regulation (EU) No 994/2010 of the European Parliament and of the Council of 20 October 2010 on measures to safeguard security of gas supply, Official Journal of the European Union, L 295, 12 November 2010, pp. 1–35. See Article 5.

encompass the entire duration required for investment payback, and the pricing of natural gas is correlated with the price index of an alternative fuel. With the transformation of natural gas markets and advancements in technology, the necessity of entering into lengthy contracts spanning up to 25 years to guarantee the profitability of substantial initial investments has diminished. The need for funding in infrastructure development is diminishing over time due to the frequent requirement of enhancements to the current system in new projects, resulting in a decline in technology costs. The contribution of emerging spot markets and energy trading on stock exchanges to competitiveness is noteworthy. The growing advancement of alternative natural gas sources, such as shale gas exploration processes in Poland, Hungary, and Germany, as well as the expansion in the United States, contributes to the diversification of energy supply and consequently diminishes the reliance on a single method to ensure security of supply.

Long-term supply contracts have generated significant controversy due to their perceived advantages for market participants and their potential conflicts with competition law. The primary objective of ensuring supply security is to facilitate long-term investments in the energy sector, which often necessitate substantial financial resources, thereby enabling suppliers to effectively plan for the future. One notable advantage of these contracts is their ability to guarantee the procurement of energy resources over an extended period based on a pre-established pricing formula. This provision serves to mitigate the potential risks associated with price fluctuations, thereby enhancing supply security and offering legal protection against price volatility. Due to this rationale, these contracts are somewhat perceived as having reduced risk. Additionally, they facilitate risk sharing between the buyer and seller by considering the substantial initial investment costs associated with the project.

The long-term evaluation of return on investment is contingent upon market fluctuations, the demand for energy resources in the market, and policy modifications that lead to alterations in the legal framework. Hence, it is imperative to implement specific measures to ensure protection against these potential hazards. These contracts serve to mitigate market volatility by offering a degree of protection against significant price fluctuations.[38] They establish a stable fixed price ceiling, but in doing so, they also establish a bilateral monopoly agreement that binds both the buyer and seller for an extended duration.

The issue at hand pertains to the negotiation of long-term supply contracts, typically occurring 2 to 3 years prior to the actual transaction. During this process, the involved parties must engage in forecasting the quantity of energy they plan to procure while considering the anticipated future demand for energy within the market. The market demand for energy resources is subject to fluctuations,

---

[38] Regulation (EU) No 347/2013 of the European Parliament and of the Council of 17 April 2013 on guidelines for trans-European energy infrastructure, Official Journal of the European Union, L 115, 25 April 2013, pp. 39–75. See Article 3, Article 4. Regulation (EU) No 2019/943 of the European Parliament and of the Council of 5 June 2019 on the internal market for electricity, Official Journal of the European Union, L 158, 14 June 2019, pp. 54–124.

potentially rendering the predetermined quantity of energy resources unnecessary. However, due to the presence of the "take or pay" clause in the contract, the parties involved are not permitted to modify the agreed-upon quantities. The Commission has initiated an inquiry to assess whether the activities of Qatar Petroleum have had an adverse impact on the unrestricted movement of natural gas within the European Economic Area.[39] The supply contracts span a period of 20–25 years and include territorial limitations. After conducting a thorough investigation spanning a period of 3 years, the Commission did not discover any instances of antitrust incompatibility. Consequently, the case was officially closed.

In the case of the Scottish Nuclear Energy Agreement, the Commission determined that the contractual agreement encompassed a "take or pay" provision, which imposed an obligation on buyers to either accept the specified quantity of goods or services or make payment for the agreed-upon amount, regardless of whether the goods or services were actually taken.[40] The electrical energy produced by the nuclear power plant was marketed through a contractual agreement spanning a period of 30 years. In subsequent instances, the Commission reaffirmed its determinations regarding the time frame for long-term contracts pertaining to the provision of electricity sourced from nuclear power plants. The Commission maintained its stance that such contracts should be restricted to a maximum duration of 15 years. In these instances, the Commission determined that electricity supply agreements were exclusively established between electricity producers and supply entities. Long-term contracts give rise to a foreclosure effect.

Conversely, the utilisation of long-term supply agreements may have detrimental effects, particularly when they are established by dominant entities, thereby impeding the entry of new participants into the market. Long-term supply contracts may not accurately reflect changing market trends over time, potentially leading to foreclosure and unfair pricing. According to the Communication, there remains a significant degree of consolidation within the energy sector, as well as the ineffectiveness of separating vertically integrated firms. This communication emphasises the significance of evaluating the vertical integration of markets through long-term contracts, as there remains a potential for dominant companies to establish contractual arrangements that impose market restrictions, potentially resulting in a violation of competition regulations.

After conducting an inquiry into the energy sector, it has been determined that implementing active price regulation would not have an impact on market concentration or address the underlying causes of market liquidity. Instead, it would only mitigate the resulting consequences. According to a subsequent communication, it has been observed that wholesale gasoline markets continue to exhibit a significant level of concentration, with certain wholesale entities possessing a market share exceeding 90%. Additionally, there is a lack of separation of ownership in vertically

[39] Case AT.40416 LNG supply to Europe.

[40] (EEC) 91/329; Commission Decision of 30 April 1991 relating to a proceeding under Article 85 of the EEC Treaty (IV/33.473 – *Scottish Nuclear, Nuclear Energy Agreement*).

integrated companies, and certain disparities exist between the actual and officially designated transmission capacity reservations.[41] This implies that while contracts have the ability to negotiate a suitable allocation of network capacity, it is unlikely to be fully utilised in practical implementation. The presence of such contracts should be avoided, as they have the potential to hinder competition among economic entities in the market. The presence of "take-or-pay" clauses among monopolistic energy companies should not impede competition. It is crucial to acknowledge that these contractual agreements serve as a means to ensure security of supply and stability within the European energy market. It is noteworthy to highlight certain contentious provisions commonly found in extended supply agreements, including the territorial restriction referred to as the "destination clause" or the designated location for final supply, the indexation of oil prices, and the "take or pay" clause, which will be expounded upon in the subsequent section. From this perspective, it is crucial to consider long-term energy supply agreements that can potentially facilitate the exploitation of market dominance by economic entities, thereby bolstering their market influence.

8.3.1.1 The Destination Clause

The inclusion of a destination clause in competition law serves as a territorial constraint, as it prohibits the resale of natural gas by an extraction company to other economic operators within the relevant market, as stipulated in the contractual terms. Major manufacturers distribute their goods to intermediary supply companies rather than selling them directly to end consumers. The sale of energy resources is subject to limitations within specific regions, wherein supply companies are prohibited from engaging in the resale of these resources to other market participants in different areas. Supply companies establish the circumstances in which they possess exclusive control over the sale of energy resources to various market participants, thereby generating a foreclosure effect by offering disparate pricing options. As a consequence, there is a division of market share among prominent suppliers.[42]

The inclusion of a clause in long-term energy supply agreements that restricts suppliers from reselling acquired resources in alternative territories facilitates the ability to sell the same product to market operators situated in different territories at varying prices. Within the realm of competition law, the aforementioned practises are commonly identified as exclusive purchasing, constituting a manifestation of the abuse of a dominant market position.

---

[41] Creti and Villeneuve (2004).

[42] Regulation (EC) No 1228/2003 of the European Parliament and of the Council of 26 June 2003 on the regulation of access to the network for cross-border exchanges in electricity, Official Journal of the European Union, L 176, 15 July 2003, pp. 1–14. See Article 4, Article 6.

There exist notable alternatives to the destination clause, known as the profit-splitting mechanism. This mechanism involves the supplier agreeing to share the profits with the producer when the purchased product is resold in a different territory.[43] The implementation of a profit-sharing mechanism can also be applicable in cases where the supplier uses the acquired output for purposes that deviate from the contract's specified use restriction, thus constituting a breach. The aforementioned scenario is exemplified by a case in which an electricity or heat producer who acquires natural gas from a supplier for energy generation purposes is restricted from utilising the gas for any other objective apart from the production of electricity or heat. Consequently, the producer is prohibited from selling the gas directly to consumers. The limitations on profit-sharing, typically enforced through territorial restrictions, which involve the establishment of barriers and limitations on competition, can be seen as analogous to territorial trade restrictions that run counter to competition law.

8.3.1.2 The Oil Price Indexation

Another condition frequently used in long-term energy supply contracts involves the correlation of gas or electricity prices with the oil price index. Fluctuations in global oil prices exert an influence on the contractual pricing of gas and electricity, as these markets commonly employ oil as a benchmark for establishing long-term agreements pertaining to gas or electricity. The interdependence of oil, gas, and electricity is a result of the consumer's hypothetical selection of a particular fuel source. In light of the significant surge in oil market prices, the aforementioned pricing model has drawn substantial attention and debate. This stems from concerns regarding the linkage between gas or electricity prices and oil prices, which may impede the diversification of energy sources and consequently undermine supply security. Hub prices in the US have experienced a notable decrease in comparison to long-term oil-indexed prices, primarily due to the expansion of liquefied natural gas supply capacity and the emergence of unconventional gas sources, such as shale gas. The inclusion of a take or pay provision entails the establishment of a predetermined minimum quantity of resources, for which the purchaser commits to remunerate a prearranged price, regardless of whether the actual demand for said energy materialises.[44] This condition is noteworthy as it guarantees a certain level of stability and security in the supplied energy sources while also implying the sharing of risks. Consequently, the incorporation of territorial and usage limitations within these contracts, in the absence of a take it or pay provision, leads to a situation where both parties are obligated to a bilateral monopoly agreement for an extended duration.

---

[43] Talus (2011).

[44] Hedge and Fjeldstad (2010).

In summary, the utilisation of long-term energy contracts plays a significant role in enhancing energy supply security, fostering stability, mitigating the probability of power outages, and concurrently stimulating investment, particularly in regions or projects that face potential risks. Furthermore, it offers a level of supply security to both the purchaser and the vendor. These contractual agreements serve to mitigate the potential risks associated with supply bottlenecks and price fluctuations while also facilitating long-term investment planning. It is important to consider the negative aspects as well, as they contribute to a phenomenon known as foreclosure and lead to a higher level of market concentration. This, in turn, diminishes ex ante competition, as price fluctuations in the markets do not necessarily result in corresponding changes in contractual prices.

8.3.2 The Case Law Practice

The Distrigaz case[45] served as a paradigm for constraining the finalisation of extended-duration energy procurement agreements. In the current scenario, the Commission has mandated Distrigaz, being the dominant operator, to enter into gas supply agreements with new customers for a maximum duration of 2 years and with non-household customers for a maximum duration of 5 years. Additionally, a cessation clause is included, stipulating that in the event that the overall value of Distrigaz's shares experiences a decline exceeding 40% or if the shares of its nearest competitor witness an increase surpassing 20%, the aforementioned requirements shall cease to be applicable. The Commission, in its evaluation of long-term contracts, determined in the EDF case that energy supply agreements should have a maximum duration of 5 years and should not encompass more than 70% of the market. Furthermore, the contracts should not exceed 70% of the company's resources supplied in the market. The contractual damage incurred entails the imposition of an artificial obligation on significant energy consumers, thereby restricting their ability to switch suppliers for an extended period of time. Consequently, the infrastructure becomes temporarily inaccessible to other competitors. In practical terms, it is observed that new participants encounter difficulties in accessing the market and engaging in fair competition with established entities. Additionally, smaller entities are exposed to the potential threat of losing their current customer base.

It is noteworthy to mention the case of electricity transmission tariffs in the Netherlands.[46] The TSO expressed its intention to impose an equal fee on both suppliers involved in transit and importers of gas, mirroring the fee applied to domestic suppliers. The two conditions were expounded upon in this specific scenario. To mitigate the potential abuse of a dominant market position, it is

---

[45] Case COMP/37.966 – Distrigaz. 2007.

[46] Case IV/E3/37.770.

imperative to establish a direct correlation between the applicable charges of the Transmission System Operator (TSO) and the actual costs incurred. The costs are incurred during the transmission of electricity through the power lines. The transmission system operator (TSO), under the oversight of the regulatory authority, has the authority to impose additional charges on interconnections. Furthermore, from the standpoint of the internal energy market, it is possible for electricity to be traded multiple times across international borders. This phenomenon is particularly relevant in the context of the power exchange in the Netherlands. In order to mitigate the issue of duplicate payments for imported electricity during both the import and transit phases, it is advisable to restrict the scope of payment to the electricity that has actually been imported from the Member State, provided that the origin of the electricity can be substantiated.

The Commission determined that the denial of access to transmission networks in the RWE[47] and ENI[48] cases has negative consequences for consumers and competitors, particularly in situations where access to these networks is essential in neighbouring markets. The elimination of market competition in the neighbouring market is a consequence of access refusal, which is frequently driven by factors such as inadequate technical capacity of networks and long-term supply contracts. The justification for imposing restrictions on network access is often based on the investment costs incurred by the company in developing the network infrastructure and the need to generate a return on investment within a reasonable timeframe. RWE's decision to deny access can be attributed to deficiencies in capacity management, capacity design, and the initial supply booking. The refusal of access by the company in the ENI case was justified on the grounds of the initial reservation of supply capacity and the necessary restrictions to recoup investments made in infrastructure development.

The Commission has commenced legal proceedings against the Bulgarian Energy Holding company in relation to allegations of engaging in anti-competitive practises through the abuse of its dominant position within the market. The aforementioned company was a vertically integrated state-owned enterprise that exercised control over transmission and storage facilities. The investigation focused on the actions of Bulgarian Energy Holding in the market and the potential abuse of power by artificially restricting access to essential infrastructure, thereby preventing new market participants from entering and reserving capacities. The Commission has determined that there was an abuse of market power through the denial of access to facilities, resulting in a fine of EUR 77 million being imposed for this violation.[49]

It is crucial to emphasise that long-term electricity supply agreements can only last for a maximum of 15 years for the supply of electricity from nuclear power plants. This limitation ensures that there is no occurrence of monopolistic practises

---

[47] Case COMP/39.402 - RWE gas closure. 2009.

[48] Case COMP/39.315 - ENI foreclosure. 2010.

[49] European Commission Decision in Case AT.23060 - Bulgarian Energy Holding. [2021] OJ C 435/01.

or exclusionary behaviour, as the typical payback period for investments in nuclear power plants spans approximately three decades. The Commission asserts that the designated timeframe is deemed adequate for the investment to yield returns and sustain operations under competitive circumstances vis-à-vis other market participants.

In the context of the REN/Turbogas case,[50] a resolution was achieved regarding pricing intervals. Specifically, during the initial 15 years, the nuclear generator established higher pricing levels, while negotiations resulted in lower sales prices for the subsequent portion of the period. The Commission's decision in the ISAB Energy case[51] is noteworthy, as it entails the retention of a 20-year contract without termination. However, the Commission has included a clause stipulating its ability to assess the market's functioning after a period of 15 years. The stance of the Commission regarding contracts pertaining to the provision of electricity from nuclear power plants can be characterised as a form of compromise. This is due to the recognition that such contracts are indispensable for securing a sustained energy supply over an extended period as well as for facilitating the significant initial capital outlay required to guarantee the viability of nuclear energy infrastructure.

Competition law explicitly codifies the principle that the act of engaging in unfair pricing and other forms of abusive behaviour with the intention of eliminating competitors is strictly forbidden. In cases where an entity imposes exorbitant prices, three criteria are employed to ascertain whether the entity is engaging in unfair pricing practises. The initial stage involves evaluating whether prices accurately reflect the expenses associated with producing the goods or services.[52] An alternative method to ascertain the existence of varying prices for distinct users without providing a rationale for the objectivity of such pricing. Additionally, this study investigates whether there exists an unwarranted disparity in the pricing of identical services among operators.

The similar scenario involving inequitable pricing has also occurred within the German natural gas market, specifically within the framework of negotiated third-party access conditions. The circumstances have undergone modification solely upon the implementation of regulated third-party access, characterised by transparent and non-discriminatory conditions for access. It is important to acknowledge, nonetheless, that these liberalisation provisions were implemented during the nascent phase of market establishment. The Commission has imposed legally enforceable commitments on Gazprom to facilitate the unrestricted movement of natural gas at competitive rates within the gas markets of Central and Eastern Europe. The initiation of the case occurred in 2011, when the Commission conducted unannounced inspections at the premises of Gazprom. The Commission

---

[50] *REN/Turbogas* (Notice pursuant to Article 19(3) of Regulation 17) [1996] OJ C118/7.

[51] *ISAB Energy* (Notice pursuant to Article 19 (3) of Regulation 17) [1996] OJ C138/3.

[52] Case C-95/04 P, British Airways plc v. Commission [2007] ECR I-2331; Case C-280/08, General Electric v. Commission [2009] ECR I-5535; Case T-201/04, Microsoft Corp. v. Commission [2007] ECR II-3601.

expressed apprehensions regarding the anticompetitive practises and violations of the antitrust regulations of the European Union. The case pertained to a broad range of Central and Eastern European countries as a result of the unilateral imposition of clauses within long-term supply agreements, coupled with market partitioning, barriers to market entry, and excessive pricing. These actions were anticipated as potentially violating Articles 101 and 102 of the Treaty on the Functioning of the European Union (TFEU).

After conducting an investigation, the Commission initiated proceedings against Gazprom in 2012 regarding the alleged abuse of its dominant position in the market, as outlined in Article 102 of the TFEU. This section discusses the concerns surrounding the hindrance of the free flow of natural gas within the European Union as well as the actions taken by Gazprom that impeded Member States' efforts to diversify their energy sources. The third concern pertained to the inequitable pricing imposed on customers through the implementation of oil price indexation.

The objections outlined in the 2015 statement highlighted the imposition of territorial restrictions, including destination clauses and unfair pricing practises, in five countries (Bulgaria, Estonia, Latvia, Lithuania, and Poland). Consequently, customers were subjected to elevated prices. The final concern pertained to the implementation of significant energy infrastructure projects, specifically the provision of natural gas supplies to Bulgaria and Poland.[53] These projects were carried out as a result of investments in pipeline initiatives, namely the South Stream pipeline and Yamal, which were initiated by Gazprom. Consequently, Gazprom was granted authority to assume control over these ventures. The statement of objections issued by the Commission asserts that Gazprom, being the leading supplier of natural gas, engaged in anticompetitive behaviour by attempting to divide the market in the Central and Eastern European regions. Following the release of the statement of objections, Gazprom has presented commitments aimed at addressing the competition concerns. These commitments include the removal of restrictions pertaining to gas resale across borders, the provision of more competitive natural gas prices, and the refusal to exploit any advantages derived from customer-acquired infrastructure. Specifically, Gazprom assumed a commitment to refrain from seeking a sum of 70 million US dollars or any other form of compensation in relation to the termination of the South Stream pipeline project by Bulgaria. The suggested commitments were provided for a period of 8 years.[54]

The Commission found in the commitments decision that Gazprom had imposed territorial restrictions through the use of export bans, destination clauses, and other comparable measures that had similar results. Market partitioning can be achieved through the use of an indirect measure that is implied for various countries. The findings of the investigation indicate that from 2009 to 2013, Gazprom's average

[53] European Commission Decision C(2015) 2081 final of 26 March 2015 concerning the imposition of territorial restrictions and unfair pricing practices in the energy sector.

[54] European Commission Decision C(2016) 2892 final of 26 May 2016 concerning Gazprom's commitments related to the South Stream pipeline project and other competitive practices.

prices in Bulgaria, Estonia, Latvia, Lithuania, and Poland surpassed the margin costs, with a weighted average mark-up cost of 170%.[55] In order to facilitate a comparative analysis, the Commission has elected to use contract prices in Germany and European gas hub prices. Hence, it can be observed that the prices in the Central and Eastern European (CEE) countries experienced an increase ranging from 22% to 40% within the timeframe of 2009 to 2014. The Central and Eastern European (CEE) countries have faced significant antitrust violations from the dominant undertaking due to their reliance on a single natural gas supplier and the presence of isolated energy islands. Ultimately, the Commission has determined that Gazprom potentially engaged in the practise of unfair pricing in accordance with Article 102(a) of the Treaty on the Functioning of the European Union (TFEU) within the Central and Eastern European (CEE) nations.

In 2014, Naftogaz, a Ukrainian company, initiated legal proceedings by submitting a claim to the Arbitration Institute of the Stockholm Chamber of Commerce.[56] The claim pertained to allegations of unfair pricing and a breach of the shareholder's agreement. The total value of mutual claims reached USD 125 billion. The subject matter of the assertion pertained to the take or pay commitment, which ultimately led to Naftogaz making additional payments for the specified quantities of natural gas that were agreed upon but not actually acquired, as per the terms of the extended contractual agreement. Another aspect that was deemed necessary for gas transit, which Gazprom failed to fulfil, resulted in the Arbitration ruling in favour of compensation. Consequently, Gazprom was obligated to pay a sum of USD 2.56 billion, which was later adjusted to USD 2.1 billion to account for the natural gas delivered in 2014. In light of the aforementioned case, Gazprom has asserted its demand for a sum of USD 56 billion, citing a violation of the contractual take or pay obligation spanning the period from 2009 to 2017. The arbitral tribunal rejected this request, and Naftogaz subsequently agreed to decrease the contractual quantities of natural gas. This reduction was made in response to the decreased demand for natural gas within the country, specifically from 42–52 bcm to a mere 4–5 bcm. The pricing terms of the natural gas supply contract were revised, leading to a reduction of 27%. As a result, Naftogaz achieved savings of USD 1.8 billion on the gas purchased during the period of 2014–2015.

An essential element of this ruling pertains to the exemption of Naftogaz from the obligation to bear the costs of natural gas supplied to the temporarily occupied territories of Luhansk and Donetsk regions. Furthermore, the contractual provisions prohibiting export (referred to as the destination clause) were deemed incompatible and rendered invalid. Consequently, Naftogaz is now permitted to engage in the resale of Russian-imported natural gas to any third country, as previously mentioned. The arbitration failed to fulfil Naftogaz's request for a revision of the transit tariffs solely because this claim did not adhere to the procedural prerequisites. Gazprom

[55] European Commission Decision C(2015) 9344 final of 24 November 2015 regarding Gazprom's practices and commitments to rectify identified competition issues.

[56] PJSC Gazprom v Ukraine, PCA Case No.2019-10.

expressed its disagreement with the arbitral award and subsequently lodged an appeal with the Swedish Court of Appeal in 2017. The initiation of the claim was based on the inclusion of the "take or pay" clause. However, the Court has dismissed the claimant's assertions and determined that Naftogas had the right to adjust the price formula in response to evolving market conditions. In late 2019, Naftogaz made an announcement regarding the receipt of USD 2.9 billion from Gazprom. The two companies have reached a consensus on a gas supply contract spanning 5 years. As a component of this agreement, the supplier has fulfilled the court-awarded remedy payment, while Naftogaz has agreed to withdraw its claim seeking compensation of approximately USD 12 billion from Gazprom. This arbitral award demonstrates that long-term natural gas contracts entered into by two entities outside the European Union must also adhere to competition rules. Furthermore, such contracts should not contravene fair competition regulations or impose unfair obligations that result in higher prices for end customers.

Within the framework of antitrust proceedings targeting Gazprom, it is imperative to expound upon additional litigation initiated by PGNiG in 2017 pertaining to the pricing of gas in Poland.[57] In the complaint submitted to the Commission, the Polish company PGNiG asserts that Gazprom, a dominant player in the market, has engaged in anti-competitive behaviour. This behaviour includes charging considerably higher prices for natural gas in Central and Eastern European (CEE) countries compared to those in Western European nations. Additionally, Gazprom has employed destination clauses to restrict competition, thereby creating a foreclosure effect.

PGNiG has asserted the need for the Commission to intervene in addressing the issue of excessive pricing during the previous period. The Commission has provided clarification that, while the statement of objections has been enacted, it pertains solely to future commitments. The Commission's investigation does not encompass actions related to the damages incurred. Furthermore, PGNiG has raised additional concerns that were not addressed in the previous investigation conducted by the Commission. Specifically, they have highlighted the gas supply disruption that occurred during the Ukraine crisis in 2014/2015, which resulted in Austrian, Slovakian, and Hungarian customers experiencing shortages of natural gas. In this section, the Commission asserts that it found no grounds to initiate an investigation into Gazprom in relation to the aforementioned allegations. The Commission has rejected the PGNiG claims following an evaluation, citing that the company's call for action fell outside the scope of the Commission's jurisdiction.

Subsequent to the aforementioned rejection, the Polish authorities initiated a claim with the Arbitration Institute of the Stockholm Chamber of Commerce in 2016 pertaining to the long-term contractual agreement for the supply of natural gas (referred to as the Yamal contract) that was executed in 1996 and is set to terminate by the conclusion of 2022. The contract contained a provision whereby it could be subject to renegotiation on a triennial basis. In the event that the parties involved are

---

[57] Case AT.40497 - Polish gas prices. 2019.

unable to reach an agreement, they may commence arbitration proceedings as outlined in the contract. In accordance with the terms of the Yamal contract, the formula for determining the purchase price of gas was adjusted based on the price of oil, which differs from the pricing mechanism employed in gas trading hubs. According to the arbitration ruling, the applicability of the ruling dates back to 2014, when PGNiG initiated renegotiations on pricing. As a result, Gazprom was obligated to compensate for the discrepancy between the recalculated amounts based on the new formula, amounting to USD 1.5 billion. The newly implemented pricing formula is closely linked to the prevailing price levels in the western European market.

These two arbitral cases potentially establish a precedent that the breach of contract through the imposition of excessive pricing is not permissible, resulting in the claimants being granted compensation. However, it is important to note that the Arbitration Institute of the Stockholm Chamber of Commerce did not consistently handle all comparable situations involving natural gas prices and oil indexation in the same manner. In the subsequent chapter, we will examine the Lithuanian situation and its lack of success in the realm of arbitration.

Historically, the exclusive supply of natural gas utilised in the domestic market of Lithuania originated from imports of natural gas from Russia. The dominant market position held by the external supplier of natural gas led to the inability of the Lithuanian natural gas system to comply with the infrastructure standard (N-1). Furthermore, there was a lack of measures in place to regulate unilateral natural gas pricing, resulting in an overall increase in consumer prices. It is noteworthy to mention that the Commission has initiated an inquiry into potential antitrust violations by the Russian entity Gazprom, specifically pertaining to the abuse of its dominant market position. The Commission has acknowledged that an investigation is currently underway regarding the conduct of Gazprom. This investigation focuses on Gazprom's actions that hinder the progress of market liberalisation and the diversification of gas supply. Additionally, the Commission is examining Gazprom's pricing practises, which are deemed unfair. In this regard, it is imperative to examine the state of the natural gas market in Lithuania.

In light of the ongoing investigation conducted by the Commission into Gazprom premises and Lithuania's adoption of a highly stringent energy market liberalisation model, the country has lodged a complaint with the Arbitration Institute of the Stockholm Chamber of Commerce. The complaint pertains to the issue of excessive pricing, specifically the substantial overpayment of 1.45 billion euros for the importation of natural gas into Lithuania.[58] AB Lietuvos Dujos is a multifaceted company engaged in various aspects of the natural gas industry, encompassing the procurement, transmission, and distribution of this energy resource. Additionally, the company fulfils the role of a transmission and distribution network operator. In 2004, the aforementioned company underwent privatisation, with E.ON Ruhrgas Energy Beteiligungs AG acquiring a 38.91% stake, Gazprom acquiring a 37.1%

[58] SCC Case No. V125/2011.

stake, and the remaining 17.7% being owned by the Republic of Lithuania through its Ministry of Energy. The Shareholders Agreement was executed within the same year. Since the conclusion of the shareholders agreement, both parties involved in the agreement have not encountered any issues pertaining to decision-making. However, in 2011, a development arose when the board of Lietuvos Dujos approved the extension of the long-term contract for natural gas supply. The addendum outlined the specific quantities of natural gas that were supplied to Lithuania, along with a detailed specification of the price formula. In this particular instance, the board member designated by the Ministry of Energy expressed dissent during the board meeting, yet the decision was ultimately ratified. The matter pertained to the circumstance that the board of directors responsible for endorsing the addendum had affiliations with Gazprom. In accordance with the Lithuanian Civil Code, there exists a provision that exempts individuals from the obligation to notify other members in cases where their personal interests are in conflict with the interests of legal entities. Nevertheless, at that juncture, the affiliations of each board member were already disclosed. Subsequently, the Ministry of Energy has lodged a formal complaint with the national court, seeking an inquiry into the activities of the board of directors. The contention put forth was that the actions taken by board members, specifically the adoption and signing of the addendum, which led to the extension of the long-term natural gas supply agreement without any adjustments to price calculations, were in opposition to the interests of stakeholders, particularly the Republic of Lithuania. In 2011, the claimant filed a request with the Vilnius Regional Court to initiate an investigation into the actions undertaken by the board members, which were deemed to be in conflict with the company's interests. Additionally, the claimant sought a court order to compel the company to renegotiate the terms of its long-term natural gas contract. Furthermore, the claimant sought the removal of the company's CEO and board members and proposed the appointment of a representative from the Ministry.

Subsequently, the Ministry of Energy proceeded to revise its assertion by retracting the prerequisites for the appointment of new company management. Nevertheless, the aforementioned document retained the assertion pertaining to the investigation of the actions undertaken by the board members. It is noteworthy to mention that during the negotiations in 2002, the investor Ruhrgas expressed its intention to withdraw from the deliberations unless the agreement ensured that the investors collectively nominate four out of five board directors and that a minimum of four votes are necessary for a resolution to be validly adopted. The present Ministry of Energy asserts that the actions of the Vilnius Regional Court have contravened the aforementioned agreements. Initially, there was an agreement for Gazprom to participate in supply contracts and assume a significant role in the management of the company. Gazprom has initiated a claim with the Arbitration Institute of the Stockholm Chamber of Commerce, alleging a violation of the shareholder agreements and the arbitral clause. Consequently, the intention is to discontinue the ongoing court proceedings in Lithuania, as they are deemed irrelevant to the present case. Furthermore, Gazprom has incurred losses as a result of the violation of the arbitration clause by the Ministry of Energy, which occurred when legal proceedings concerning the decisions made by the company's board of directors were initiated in domestic courts. The tribunal in this particular case reached the determination that the aforementioned clauses fell within the purview of the shareholders agreement and that the party in question breached said agreement by initiating the complaint with the national court rather than the arbitral tribunal.[59]

In 2012, Lithuania initiated legal proceedings by submitting a claim for compensation amounting to USD 1.5 billion to the Arbitration Institute of the Stockholm Chamber of Commerce.[60] The claim was made in response to alleged unfair pricing of natural gas and concerns regarding a conflict of interest arising from Gazprom's dual role as both the supplier of natural gas under a long-term agreement and a shareholder in a vertically integrated natural gas company. The arguments were reiterated in this assertion as well. After a four-year duration of the legal proceedings, the tribunal reached the conclusion that, in accordance with the shareholders agreement, the provision of natural gas at fair prices was not a binding obligation but rather a mutual effort on the part of the involved parties. Furthermore, the adequacy of the term "fair price" in substantiating the supplier's claim regarding the provision of natural gas at prices indexed to oil has been called into question, as it has led to higher prices in Lithuania compared to neighbouring countries. The shareholders agreement lacked provisions pertaining to the determination of pricing and the commitment of shareholders to utilise specific methodologies for calculating the price of natural gas. The tribunal has determined that Gazprom exhibited a conflict of interest by simultaneously serving as both the supplier and shareholder of Lietuvos Dujos. However, it is noteworthy that no additional measures or corrective actions were undertaken in response to this finding. Following the tribunal's ruling in 2016, Lithuania has subsequently lodged an appeal. Nevertheless, the Swedish Court of Appeal has affirmed the decision made by the Arbitration Institute of the Stockholm Chamber of Commerce.

In spite of the ongoing arbitration proceedings, Lithuania has undertaken measures to implement the Third Energy Package and has introduced the full ownership unbundling model in both the natural gas and electricity sectors. Lithuania, as a country heavily reliant on Gazprom as its sole external energy supplier, has undertaken significant measures to establish an alternative gas supply project and has commenced the necessary proceedings.

The implementation of the LNG Terminal Law has established the necessary legal requirements to ensure access to alternative sources of natural gas. This is achieved through the adoption of the N-1 security of supply standard, which aims to reduce reliance on external natural gas providers. It is noteworthy to mention that Lithuania procures natural gas exclusively from a solitary external supplier, and its

---

[59] Arbitration Institute of the Stockholm Chamber of Commerce, Gazprom v. Ministry of Energy of Lithuania, Case No. 080/2005, Award dated 30 November 2007. Vilnius Regional Court, Gazprom v. Ministry of Energy of Lithuania, Case No. 2A-255-567/2007, Judgment dated 29 May 2007. Ministry of Energy of Lithuania, Official Statement on Shareholder Agreements and Arbitration, 15 December 2005.

[60] PCA Case No. 2011-16.

consumption constitutes a mere 0.6% of the total. The lack of leverage to negotiate lower prices is a significant factor affecting Gazprom's total gas production. In contrast, Latvia, which possesses a gas storage facility in Incukalns, and Estonia, which benefits from its shale gas resources, possess a more advantageous position in terms of their ability to engage in negotiations with an external natural gas supplier regarding gas supply prices. When evaluating long-term agreements pertaining to the provision of natural gas, it is imperative to give due consideration to the pricing mechanism employed, particularly in cases where the cost of natural gas supplied to Gazprom in Lithuania is correlated with the oil price index. The aforementioned pricing formula was in effect from 1980 to 2005. In the European context, during a period of oil price stability, the prevailing conditions were deemed satisfactory for natural gas consumers. The emergence of spot prices is a notable development coinciding with the unprecedented increase in oil prices and their subsequent lack of competitiveness, alongside the presence of alternative sources of pipeline gas in the market. The functioning of this market is predicated on the principles of supply and demand. In the short term, prices are determined based on prevailing market conditions. In the event of an excess supply of natural gas, it can be sold at competitive prices without the need for long-term contractual obligations. However, their justification in terms of ensuring security of supply is lacking, as the requirement for continuous and uninterrupted provision persists. The advent of natural gas exchanges facilitating the trade of liquefied natural gas (LNG) and pipeline gas has resulted in a noticeable decrease in natural gas prices within the market as compared to prices observed under long-term contractual agreements. The potential procurement of natural gas from gas centres in Great Britain, the Netherlands, and the US, as well as the establishment of long-term supply agreements with prices independent of the oil price index but tied to exchange prices, may result in a corresponding reduction in the cost of natural gas for consumers.

8.4 Conclusion

Long-term contractual agreements indicate that the operator possesses the prerogative to decline third-party entry into the networks, thereby establishing itself as the sole provider in the market and potentially engaging in anti-competitive practises due to its dominant position. The primary justifications for such denial typically encompass inadequate network capacity, capacity reservations and associated drawbacks, and a lack of strategic investment in expanding the supply system's capacity to accommodate an additional entity's access. These circumstances have necessitated the consolidation of these institutes into a single section of the study, with the aim of providing a more comprehensive understanding of the connections and challenges that exist.

The institute for the abuse of dominant positions holds significant importance within the energy sector as it serves as a crucial tool utilised by the Commission. This is primarily due to the discriminatory conditions that arise, which hinder the ability of consumers and other energy suppliers to effectively operate within the relevant markets. The presence of a dominant position is improbable when the market share of the undertaking is below 40% in the relevant market. In certain instances, the dominant company's ability to exert effective pressure may be hindered despite its market share being smaller than officially reported, owing to its constrained operational capacity. In cases where a company's market share exceeds 40%, it is possible for the company to not be considered dominant if there are other companies operating in the market with relatively high market shares that can effectively limit its ability to unilaterally exert significant influence.

The provision of third-party access rights is a crucial component in guaranteeing the liberalisation of the energy market. The implementation of this foundational element established circumstances conducive to the advancement of competitive dynamics. The regulatory requirement for the corporate entity that possesses the vital infrastructure or indispensable facility to furnish unrestricted and impartial network access facilitates the entry of novel operators into the market for service provision. Capacity hoarding is a phenomenon that occurs when transmission network operators decline to provide access to third parties. These companies typically rationalise their actions based on the premise that network capacity has been allocated or is already allocated to energy suppliers in the market. The present scenario exhibits manipulation, as it is common for companies to merely allocate network capacity formally without fully utilising the reserved capacity. Furthermore, the transmission system operator assumes a position that enables potential abuse by denying access to other market participants, asserting that all pipeline capacity has already been allocated. Hence, the provision of access to transmission networks enables a broader range of operators to participate in the market, extending beyond the entities that possess ownership of said networks.

The notion of strategic underinvestment pertains to circumstances wherein a company possessing a critical infrastructure refrain from making investments towards its development or enhancement. The issue at hand pertains to the evaluation of the internal market's competitiveness in the energy sector, given its inherent requirement for infrastructure to facilitate the provision of energy to consumers. Due to varying levels of required investment, not all economic operators possess the capability to construct such infrastructure and frequently lack the intention to expand said infrastructure in order to accommodate the potential demand for the necessary capacity.

The inclusion of a destination clause in competition law serves as a territorial constraint, as it prohibits wholesalers of natural gas from engaging in the resale of their product to other customers within the relevant market. Sales are typically constrained within the geographical boundaries where supply companies have established networks, thereby prohibiting the resale of energy resources to other market participants in different regions. In this manner, significant endeavours possessing market dominance establish the circumstances in which they alone possess the ability to offer energy to various market participants at varying prices, thereby generating a foreclosure phenomenon. This leads to the distribution of market share among prominent suppliers.

References

Borner AR (2015) Negotiated third party access in Germany: electricity and gas. J Energy Nat Resour 20
Brunekreeft G (2001) Negotiated third party access in the German electricity supply industry. Econ Policy Energy Environ
Brunekreeft G (2002) Regulation and third—party discrimination in German electricity supply industry. Eur J Law Econ Springer 13(3):203–220
Buigues PA (2006) Competition policy versus sector-specific regulation in network industries –the EU experience. UNCTAD
Cameron P (2005) The internal market in energy: harnessing the new regulatory regime. Eur Law Rev 5:637
Chauve Ph, Glowicka E, Godfried M, Leduc E, Siebert S (2010) Swedish Interconnector case/ Improving electricity cross-border trade. Competition Policy Newsletter. 2010/2
Creti A, Villeneuve B (2004) Long-term contracts and take-or-pay clauses in natural gas market. Energy Stud Rev 13(1)
Diathesopuolos M (2010) Third party access and refusal to deal: how sector regulation and competition law meet each other. SSRN
Hauteclocque A, Marty F, Pillot J (2011) The essential facilities doctrine in European competition policy: the case of the energy markets. In: Glachant J-M, Finon D, Hauteclocque A (eds) (2020) Competition, contracts and electricity markets: a new perspective (forthcoming). Edward Elgar, Cheltenham
Hauterlocque A, Hancher L (2011) The Svenska Kraftnat case: introduction of bidding zones in Sweden. Netw Ind Q 13(1)
Hedge K, Fjeldstad E (2010) The future of European long-term natural gas contracts. Oslo
Horstmann KP (2003) Negotiated third party access to electricity supply networks in Germany. OGEL 3
Konoplyanik A (2015) Gas transit in Eurasia: transit issues between Russia and the European Union and the role of the energy charter. J Energy Nat Resour Law:447–454
Talus K (2011) Long-term natural gas contracts and antitrust law in the European Union and the United States. J World Energy Law Bus 4(3):260–315i

Part III
Mergers and Acquisitions in Energy Sector

Chapter 9
Concept, Forms and Evaluation of Concentration

Abstract Identifying the appropriate market is essential for defining the extent of competition among companies. Furthermore, it provides a structured framework for the implementation of competition policies. Geographical and product criteria can classify the market. This classification simplifies the calculation of market proportions and the recognition of competitive constraints within the market. When defining a market, it is essential to consider three main factors that limit competition: the ability of customers to substitute one product or service for another, the ability of suppliers to substitute their offerings, and the possibility of new competitors entering the market. The Commission sometimes uses an expansive definition of relevant markets to evaluate concentrations or competition restrictions. The Commission formulates the definition based on the initial data submitted by the parties involved. Analyzing the market shares of the parties involved and their competitors establishes the preliminary assessment of the geographic market borders. In addition, an initial examination of pricing and discrepancies at both the European Union and national levels is considered. It has versatile capabilities, including lighting, generating thermal energy, and cooling.

9.1 Introduction

The progression from monopolistic national markets to competitive regional markets can be attributed to the systematic implementation of the internal market. The protracted duration of market integration can be attributed to various factors, one of which is the substantial market dominance enjoyed by vertically integrated firms, thereby posing significant barriers to entry for potential new market entrants. The energy market in Europe is characterised by the presence of dominant players who possess substantial market power. The energy sector exhibits notable distinctions from other industries due to its inherent reliance on transmission or distribution networks, rendering it impracticable to directly sell electricity or natural gas to consumers.

L. Rimšaitė, *The Crossroads of Competition Law and Energy Regulation*,
https://doi.org/10.1007/978-3-031-73238-6_9

Regarding the ownership of energy networks, companies currently maintain a de facto monopoly status. However, it is not necessary to construct new infrastructure networks in order to diminish the prevailing monopoly in this domain. While such an approach may be more economically efficient, it would not yield the intended outcome. The interdependencies required for the provision of vital resources, such as electricity or natural gas, are regarded as crucial infrastructures. According to the regulations outlined in the third energy package, owners of these networks are obligated to provide non-discriminatory access to third parties seeking to utilise the infrastructure. Organisations may opt to pursue concentrations in order to sustain their current market share while simultaneously establishing obstacles for potential new entrants.

In the subsequent section we shall undertake a comprehensive examination of the concentration institute, focusing specifically on its utilisation within the energy domain. The matter of concentrations is intricately connected to the necessity imposed by energy law to disentangle vertically integrated corporations. The aforementioned requirements exhibit certain inconsistencies and necessitate the implementation of a comprehensive regulatory framework, which will be further examined in subsequent sections.

9.2 The Merger Regulation

The regulation of mergers within the European Union is a crucial component of competition policy, with the objective of achieving a careful equilibrium between promoting economic efficiency through consolidation and ensuring the preservation of fair competition. This chapter offers a comprehensive examination of the merger regulation framework of the European Union, focusing on its fundamental elements and its impact on shaping competition dynamics within the EU.

Mergers and acquisitions (M&A) are frequently employed tactics within the business sphere, frequently leading to the amalgamation of firms and resources.[1] Merger regulation, which is an essential mechanism for preserving competition, has a significant impact on the evaluation and approval of transactions inside the European Union. This article examines the merger regulatory framework of the European Union, with a focus on elucidating its objectives and assessing its impact.

The primary objectives of the EU Merger Regulation are to ensuring the maintenance of effective competition within the European Union market by preventing the creation or strengthening of dominant market positions through mergers and acquisitions.[2] The enhancement of competition is crucial in order to prevent mergers that would significantly diminish competition within the European Union market.

[1] Navarro et al. (2005).

[2] Council Regulation (EC) No 139/2004 of 20 January 2004 on the control of concentrations between undertakings (the EC Merger Regulation). OJ L 24, 29.1.2004, pp. 1–22.

This is done with the aim of safeguarding consumer interests and fostering economic efficiency. The provision of legal certainty is achieved by the establishment of a regulatory framework that is transparent and predictable, ensuring merging parties are able to navigate the merger process with confidence. The EU Merger Regulation encompasses several fundamental elements that are crucial to its functioning and effectiveness.[3] These key components include the scope of application, the substantive assessment of mergers, the procedural aspects of the merger review process, and the enforcement mechanisms employed by the European Union.

The application of the EU Merger Regulation is contingent upon the fulfilment of predetermined turnover thresholds by the transactions in question. Transactions that surpass these specified levels are subject to the regulatory authority of the European Commission. Notification is required for parties engaging in mergers that satisfy the specified thresholds, as this enables the European Commission to evaluate the potential effects of the combination on competition. The European Commission undertakes Phase I and Phase II investigations to assess the potential competition concerns arising from a merger. During Phase I, a thorough analysis is conducted to ascertain whether the merger in question gives rise to any such concerns. In the event that issues continue to arise, a Phase II inquiry is initiated, encompassing a comprehensive and thorough review.

Remedies can be proposed by the parties involved in a merger that is determined to have anti-competitive effects, with the aim of addressing the identified issues. The potential approval of the combination by the Commission is contingent upon the successful implementation of remedies that adequately address the competition concerns. The Commission has the power to prohibit a merger if it substantially hinders competition. The role of national competition authorities (NCAs) is of significant importance in the field of competition policy and regulation. NCAs are governmental bodies responsible for enforcing competition laws and promoting fair competition within their respective jurisdictions. Their primary objective is to safeguard and enhance.

The jurisdiction over significant mergers with cross-border implications lies with the European Commission, while smaller deals that do not satisfy the standards set by the European Union are managed by the national competition authorities of the Member States.[4] The dynamic nature of the digital economy and the emergence of new industries present novel obstacles in the context of merger regulation within the European Union. The chapter examines the challenges faced by competition authorities in evaluating the effects of mergers driven by technology and adjusting regulatory frameworks in response. The European Union endeavours to achieve a delicate balance between promoting economic efficiency through M&A and preserving competitive markets. This approach is intended to yield advantages for consumers and stimulate innovation within the EU.

---

[3] Jones Ch (2021).

[4] Council Regulation (EC) No 139/2004 of 20 January 2004 on the control of concentrations between undertakings (the EC Merger Regulation). OJ L 24, 29.1.2004, pp. 1–22.

The Merger Regulation does not provide a specific definition for the concept of merger.[5] However, it does encompass the notion of concentration, which pertains to operations that result in enduring changes in market control and structural modifications. The merger leads to a situation where previously independent undertakings, which were operating separately, will now function as a single entity. This is distinct from an acquisition, where the acquiring entity gains control over the previously separate undertakings after the transaction is completed. The merger has the potential to be executed in a legally compliant manner, as outlined previously. This can be achieved by consolidating the various operations of formerly autonomous entities. One illustration of such a practise could be observed when autonomous entities establish specific customary approaches to economic management. This model is commonly referred to as the establishment of dual-listed undertakings without the transfer of shares or assets, involving the amalgamation of partnerships operating in global professional services.

Mergers commonly transpire when organisations endeavour to gain entry into larger markets, expand their customer base, achieve economies of scale, and acquire additional resources. Undertakings frequently derive advantages from acquiring external assets that require a significant amount of time to establish internally.[6] The merger results in the elimination of competition among the entities involved in the transactions, leading to a concomitant decrease in the prices of advertising for their respective services and products. However, it is possible that the competition in the relevant market may decrease following the merger, leading to a potential increase in prices for the products offered by the merged entities.

9.3 The Concept of Control

As elaborated upon in the preceding chapter, the notion of control is delineated within the framework of Merger Regulation. When assessing the position of undertakings, it is not obligatory for the undertaking to exert decisive influence. Control can be obtained either through individual efforts or through collaborative efforts. The acquisition of sole control can be achieved through two methods: obtaining the discretion right, also referred to as positive control, which grants the acquirer the authority to make strategic decisions; or acquiring the veto right, which allows the

[5] Council Regulation (EC) No 139/2004 of 20 January 2004 on the control of concentrations between undertakings (the EC Merger Regulation). OJ L 24, 29.1.2004, pp. 1–22.

[6] Commission Notice – Guidelines on the Assessment of Non-Horizontal Mergers. Official Journal of the European Union, C265/6, 18.10.2008. Guidelines on the Assessment of Horizontal Mergers under the Council Regulation on the Control of Concentrations between Undertakings. Official Journal of the European Union, C31/5, 05.02.2004. Council Regulation (EC) No 139/2004 on the Control of Concentrations between Undertakings (EU Merger Regulation). Official Journal of the European Union, L24/1, 29.01.2004.

acquirer to influence or restrict the strategic decisions of the undertaking, thereby gaining negative control.

An individual or an organisation, such as state-owned businesses and other public entities, can obtain control. The term individuals refer to subjects who possess control over another undertaking. This control can be established either alone or jointly. Consequently, these individuals exercise indirect control over an acquiring undertaking by means of another undertaking. Usually, the person or organisation that has the rights granted by contracts or is eligible to have them acquires control. In certain situations, the acquiring entity may exercise control over a business indirectly by utilising an intermediary, thereby obtaining the ability to exert influence over the said undertaking.[7]

The target, which can include a combination of various undertakings, the assets of these undertakings, or a portion thereof, has a significant impact on the evaluation of a merger. The target entity must be a commercial enterprise, and the market turnover can be attributed to it.

The transfer of the client base may be regarded as a form of consolidation.[8] Another aspect to consider is the evaluation of transactions with the intention of outsourcing activities that are currently being conducted internally. The aforementioned activities may potentially fall within the scope of the Merger Regulation if they give rise to a significant alteration in the market structure.

De facto control can be exerted through the utilisation of rights, contracts, or other mechanisms that, either individually or in combination, confer the ability to exercise decisive influence. An additional method of gaining control is through the acquisition of shares, which occurs when a shareholder agreement is established with specific provisions that allocate voting rights or confer particular privileges on the shareholders. Control must be established on a long-term basis in order to align with the concept of concentration. The Merger Regulation does not encompass the short-term substitution of control, specifically referring to the actions that lead to such substitution.

Sole control is obtained when a single entity exerts a decisive influence over another undertaking. There are anticipated advantages and disadvantages to sole control. The concept of positive sole control refers to a situation in which a single entity that obtains control has the ability to make strategic decisions independently and without the involvement of other parties.[9] Negative control refers to instances where a shareholder possesses the authority to veto strategic decisions but chooses

[7] Commission Notice – Guidelines on the Assessment of Non-Horizontal Mergers. Official Journal of the European Union, C265/6, 18.10.2008. Guidelines on the Assessment of Horizontal Mergers under the Council Regulation on the Control of Concentrations between Undertakings. Official Journal of the European Union, C31/5, 05.02.2004. Council Regulation (EC) No 139/2004 on the Control of Concentrations between Undertakings (EU Merger Regulation). Official Journal of the European Union, L24/1, 29.01.2004.

[8] Commission Consolidated Jurisdictional Notice under Council Regulation (EC) No 139/2004 on the control of concentrations between undertakings. OJ C 95, 16.4.2008, pp. 1–48.

[9] Bailey and John (2019).

not to exercise this right in the context of making such decisions. The exclusive authority is demonstrated through the attainment of a majority of votes from other entities.[10] There may also be minority shareholders who possess a qualified minority right. Specifically, the authority to designate the supervisory board and board members, as well as establish the business strategy, is vested in the organisational structure.[11] The negative aspect of sole control arises in situations where a single shareholder possesses more than 50% of the shares in a specific enterprise while the remaining shares are distributed among multiple shareholders. In cases where strategic decisions require a quorum, the shareholder holding the veto right has the ability to impede the decision-making process.

Joint control arises when two or more entities are required to come to an agreement regarding strategic decisions pertaining to a jointly owned enterprise. In this scenario, a deadlock may arise if the shareholders fail to reach a unanimous decision and one of them exercises their veto power.[12] Joint control refers to a scenario in which two entities collectively exercise the voting rights associated with a joint venture. In this particular scenario, it is imperative for both parties to come to a consensus regarding strategic determinations, with each party possessing the authority to exercise their veto power. In a joint venture, both shareholders possess equal rights, and neither holds the deciding vote.

9.4 The Relevant Market

The determination of the relevant market definition holds significant importance as it serves to delineate the scope within which competition occurs among businesses.[13] It facilitates the establishment of a framework within which the competition policy can be applied. The process of market definition facilitates the computation of market shares and the identification of competitive constraints within a given market. The delineation of the relevant market is established based on factors related to the product and its geographical scope.

The identification of market boundaries is influenced by three primary sources of competition constraints: demand substitutability, supply substitutability, and

[10] Faull and Nikpay (2014).

[11] Commission Notice – Guidelines on the Assessment of Non-Horizontal Mergers. Official Journal of the European Union, C265/6, 18.10.2008. Guidelines on the Assessment of Horizontal Mergers under the Council Regulation on the Control of Concentrations between Undertakings. Official Journal of the European Union, C31/5, 05.02.2004. Council Regulation (EC) No 139/2004 on the Control of Concentrations between Undertakings (EU Merger Regulation). Official Journal of the European Union, L24/1, 29.01.2004.

[12] Commission Consolidated Jurisdictional Notice under Council Regulation (EC) No 139/2004 on the control of concentrations between undertakings. OJ C 95, 16.4.2008, pp. 1–48.

[13] Communication from the Commission – Commission Notice on the definition of the relevant market for the purposes of Union competition law. C/2023/6789. OJ C, C/2024/1645, 22.2.2024.

potential competition. The concept of demand substitution refers to the ability of consumers to quickly and significantly influence suppliers through changes in pricing.[14] The concept of demand-side substitutability enables the identification of products that are perceived as substitutes by consumers. In this context, it is imperative to assess whether consumers would opt for an alternative supplier in response to a marginal price adjustment ranging from 5% to 10%.

If the substitution of a product is significant enough to render a price increase unprofitable due to lost sales, it is necessary to include the additional substitutes in the market definition. This implementation should continue until the price increase no longer leads to a change in supplier. The consideration of supply-side substitutability is a crucial factor in the delineation of market boundaries.[15] Suppliers possess the ability to substitute one product for other pertinent alternatives and market them in the immediate period without necessitating any adjustments to the price. The assessment of potential competition and its constraints can be conducted in a subsequent stage, particularly when evaluating the company's position and addressing concerns related to competition.

The Commission frequently employs a broad definition of relevant markets in order to assess concentrations or competition restrictions. Based on the preliminary data provided by the parties involved, the Commission develops the definition. The determination of the geographic market entails an initial assessment of the extent of the market's geographical boundaries. This assessment is based on an analysis of the market shares held by the parties involved as well as their competitors, along with a preliminary examination of pricing patterns and disparities at both the European Union and national levels. In the subsequent chapter, an examination will be conducted of the pertinent product and geographical markets within the energy sector.

9.4.1 Relevant Electricity Product Market

Electricity market is identified as the separate relevant product market. It could be used for many purposes such as lighting, production of heat, cooling. Traditionally in electricity market these segments are identified:

---

[14] Commission Notice – Guidelines on the Assessment of Non-Horizontal Mergers. Official Journal of the European Union, C265/6, 18.10.2008. Guidelines on the Assessment of Horizontal Mergers under the Council Regulation on the Control of Concentrations between Undertakings. Official Journal of the European Union, C31/5, 05.02.2004. Council Regulation (EC) No 139/2004 on the Control of Concentrations between Undertakings (EU Merger Regulation). Official Journal of the European Union, L24/1, 29.01.2004.

[15] Communication from the Commission – Commission Notice on the definition of the relevant market for the purposes of Union competition law. C/2023/6789. OJ C, C/2024/1645, 22.2.2024.

- the generation and wholesale,
- the transmission,
- the distribution
- the supply to final customers.

The wholesale markets encompass both the generation and distribution markets and have not been assessed as distinct markets.[16] The power that the generator produces comes directly from the power plant, creating an indirect link between the generation process and the wholesale supply. The wholesale market encompasses the provision of goods to distributors, traders, and retailers. The markets for generating and wholesale supply are distinct from the markets that cater to end users or large consumers.[17] A differentiation is established between the wholesale and retail sectors, wherein the retailers provide electricity to qualifying clients in the latter market. The case law exhibits variability due to the Commission's identification of significant consumers inside the wholesale market, distinct from the supply market to retailers.

The distinct product market pertaining to the provision of goods or services to specific clients was also discerned. A differentiation was established based on the financial and administrative capabilities of major and small distributors to get power quantities on the trading market, as well as their lack of procurement of balancing energy.

The segmentation of the market into multiple categories has led to the recognition of the supply to final consumers as a separate entity. This differentiation is mostly based on the presence of grid connections, which distinguishes major customers from other consumer groups. The analysis considers factors such as client size, variations in consumption levels, and consumption profiles. Large customers exhibit a tendency to be observant and responsive to changes in prices, possess varying degrees of bargaining power, and are more inclined to transfer suppliers compared to their smaller counterparts.

The trading of electricity is acknowledged as a distinct market apart from the processes of generation, wholesale, and supply. The subject matter necessitates specialised expertise, possesses the distinct characteristic of engaging in short-term contractual agreements, does not inherently entail the physical provision of energy, the delivery of electricity to end consumers may not always occur, and the entity is not obligated to engage in commercial trading and supply operations.[18]

Electricity trading is constrained inside specific bidding zones, necessitating capacity allocation for trading activities that extend beyond these zones. The electricity bidding zone refers to the expansive geographical region wherein the trading of power can be conducted without the need for capacity allotment. In the past, bidding zones in Europe were typically limited to the boundaries of a single country;

---

[16] Case COMP/M.3268 – Sydkraft/Graninge.2003. para 15.

[17] Case COMP/M.3868 - DONG/Elsam/Energi E2. 2006, para 230. Case COMP/M.4180 - GDF/Suez. 2006, para 675, Case COMP/M.3696 - E.ON/MOL. 2005. para 236.

[18] Case COMP/M.2947 - Verbund/Energie Allianz. 2002, para 38–40.

however, there were a few exceptions, like Sweden and Italy, where multiple bidding zones existed inside their respective territories.[19] The principles governing trading within the bidding zone are twofold. Firstly, congestion should not be limited to a single bidding zone, and there should be no technical limitations. Secondly, the trading of electricity within the bidding zone should not have an impact on trading activities outside the zone, particularly with neighbouring countries.

The validity of these assumptions is subject to scrutiny given the increasing viability of renewable energy sources, which are often deployed in regions with excellent weather conditions that are often geographically remote from areas of high energy use. This scenario exacerbates the likelihood of congestion problems inside a single bidding zone. Germany and Austria are both part of a single bidding zone. The current issue at hand is the geographical distribution of production capacity and consumption regions within this zone. Specifically, the production capacity is predominantly located in the northern region of Germany, while the consuming areas are situated in southern Germany and Austria. The occurrence of the scenario can be attributed to the decommissioning of nuclear power reactors in the southern region. Congestion arises within a bidding zone domestically due to the presence of significant internal flows and the constrained capacity of transmission links. This situation also has implications for trade among the adjacent countries.

Various solutions were deliberated for these specific circumstances, encompassing short-term, medium-term, and long-term approaches. One potential short-term solution involves the implementation of a dispatching model, wherein the Transmission System Operator (TSO) assumes a crucial role. In situations where there is excessive electricity generation and congestion occurs along the north-south transmission line, the TSO intervenes by requesting electricity producers in the southern region to increase their production levels while simultaneously requesting a reduction in production quantities from producers in the northern region. This paradigm has the potential to lead to a substantial rise in TSO costs, consequently impacting customers.

One potential interim measure could be decreasing the cross-border capacity between the bidding zones. The presence of cross-border congestion imposes limitations on the capacity of electricity transmission within a single bidding zone, hence necessitating an increase in capacities. This particular model, which affects internal congestion, also gives rise to the possibility of violating competition law and can be characterised as an abuse of a dominant position that disrupts competition among the bidding zones. In 2009, the Swedish TSO implemented measures that restricted exports to Denmark.[20] This decision was motivated by the anticipation of

[19] Commission Regulation (EU) 2017/2195 establishing a guideline on electricity balancing. Official Journal of the European Union, L 312/6, 28.11.2017. Directive (EU) 2019/944 on common rules for the internal market for electricity. Official Journal of the European Union, L 158/125, 14.06.2019. Regulation (EU) 2015/1222 establishing a guideline on capacity allocation and congestion management (CACM Regulation). Official Journal of the European Union, L 197/24, 25.07.2015.

[20] Case COMP/39.351 - Swedish Interconnectors (2009).

heightened domestic capacity. Another case was the interconnection between the borders of Germany and Denmark, wherein the German TSO imposed restrictions on imports from Denmark. This measure was implemented with the aim of promoting internal trade and mitigating bottlenecks inside Germany, particularly between its southern and northern regions.

The reconfiguration of bidding zones has the potential to function as a viable option in the medium term. Specifically, the internal congestion can be regarded as the congestion that occurs between the various bidding zones, and the capacity challenges can be addressed through market mechanisms and cross-border allocations. By implementing this approach, it is possible to reduce the flow of loops within the adjacent bidding zones. The adoption of this alternative occurred subsequent to the sector inquiry conducted by the Commission in 2009. In a similar vein, Sweden underwent a division into four distinct bidding zones, mirroring the model that was subsequently applied in Germany and Austria in 2018, resulting in their division into separate bidding zones.

There is ongoing debate on the potential division of the Germany bidding zone into multiple zones, specifically the northern and southern regions. Nevertheless, implementing such measures has the potential to diminish market liquidity and foster an environment conducive to heightened market abuse. The division of bidding zones may potentially have a negative impact on pricing.[21] Specifically, this could lead to a rise in prices in one bidding zone and a probable fall in prices in another. Long-term solutions are associated with improved infrastructure, as the addition of new transmission lines has the ability to increase the flow of energy and thereby alleviate congestion. This aligns with the concept of the "copper plate" assumption, wherein electricity may flow freely from generation sources to the sites of demand without encountering significant limitations.

The approach to bidding zones inside the European Union is mostly influenced by political considerations rather than being based on a nodal model. In contrast, the determination of prices in these bidding zones is based on the actual nodes present in the network. The zonal strategy establishes specific geographical boundaries, yet trading activities are not restricted, although there may be limitations on trading capacity. Preventive measures can be understood as ex-ante restrictions on trade, which involve assessing the capabilities between different zones. This assessment enables the effective distribution of resources to market participants, allowing them to make informed decisions regarding the dispatching of generators and loads. Curative approaches facilitate the reassignment or exchange of goods or services in instances where security is at risk.

According to the ACER's viewpoint expressed on September 23, 2015, customers have the opportunity to access electricity from power producers regardless of any physical constraints imposed by the transmission networks, owing to the

[21] European Commission. Consultation on the Germany Bidding Zone Split. 2020. Official Journal of the European Union.

existence of bidding zones.[22] This strategy improves the energy trade inside the bidding zone, but the costs are incurred by the TSO while implementing capacity allocation mechanisms to assure physical flows and operational security. Energy trading encompasses several key activities within the realm of the energy market. These activities include over-the-counter trading, which involves the negotiation of individual bilateral contracts between suppliers and clients outside of the exchange. Additionally, energy trading involves the physical trade of electricity as well as the trading of derivatives. It is important to acknowledge the distinction between trading, generation, and supply in the context of electricity, as the trading process often involves multiple transactions prior to the final sale and consumption of energy in the market.

Trade encompasses both physical and financial transactions. In contrast to physical trade, when energy is directly provided to the consumer, financial trade involves the use of electricity as futures, options, and swaps, primarily for financial settlement purposes, without the inclusion of physical delivery to the customer. Financial trading is employed as a means of safeguarding against the potential adverse effects of abrupt and unplanned price variations in the physical electricity trading market. This practice, sometimes referred to as financial hedging, serves as a form of secure insurance. The Commission holds the view that financial and physical trading constitute distinct markets, however interconnected.

The concept of the balancing market was developed to establish a distinct product market due to the unique characteristics of energy. It is essential to ensure that the amount of power withdrawn from the network matches the amount of power injected into the network in order to maintain consistent frequencies. Electricity suppliers lack knowledge regarding the precise amount of electricity that customers will consume. Consequently, balancing services are employed to address these uncertainties. The Commission has also observed that the provision of balancing services or regulated power may be separate entities from the wholesale market. In liberalised markets, a distinct balancing market is present, wherein transmission system operators procure balancing energy from a designated exchange.

9.4.2 *Relevant Electricity Geographic Market*

In certain initial Commission decisions, during the progression of the market liberalisation process and the preparatory stages for opening the European Union-wide electricity supply market, the Commission failed to recognise its existence.[23]

---

[22] Agency for the Cooperation of Energy Regulators (ACER). ACER Opinion on the Possible Split of the German Electricity Bidding Zone. September 23, 2015. Official Journal of the European Union.

[23] European Court of Justice (ECJ), Germany v. Commission, Case T-353/00, Judgment of 19 June 2002. European Court of Justice (ECJ), Commission v. Italy, Case T-198/00, Judgment of 7 November 2002. European Court of Justice (ECJ), Commission v. Italy, Case C-111/05,

The parties involved in merger cases have posed the inquiry as to whether the electricity market should continue to be regarded as national in scope, given the market opening and cross-border trading.

Various perspectives were presented in the Sydkraft/Graninge case,[24] wherein the Commission determined that the geographical market extends beyond the borders of a single country. This conclusion was based on the market conditions at the time, which indicated a readiness for liberalisation, as well as the existence of interconnected transmission networks and the NordPool spot market, which facilitate an integrated power system in the Nordic region. Another instance in which the Commission arrived at a comparable determination was the Verbund/Energie Allianz case.[25] In this case as well, the Commission emphasised the significance of interconnectors and the absence of any impediments to electricity transmission within the territory of a single country.

In addition to assessing the geographic market scope, other factors are considered, including regulatory barriers, licencing requirements, price caps, transfer charges, and interconnection capacities. These factors play a crucial role in the process of market liberalisation and the promotion of competition. Specifically, the existence of barriers to interconnection capacities would impede the ability of entities to engage in electricity trading within a single country's territory. The assessment of congestion is a crucial factor in determining the barriers to market entry. The presence of bottlenecks or a lack of capacity can hinder the implementation of electricity trade through interconnection, as these market barriers pose significant challenges. The presence of congestion in the market may also lead to the definition of the market as being limited to a national scope, as the inability to engage in interconnection trade is attributed to technical challenges. The presence of distinct price zones among neighbouring markets contributes to the phenomenon of market isolation.

The evaluation of the geographical market for electricity includes considering the flow of trade, particularly in relation to its extent beyond national boundaries. The Commission maintains the stance that imports amounting to less than 6% are considered part of the national market. The findings indicated that the market exhibited a national scope, despite the import share amounting to 14%.[26] The evaluation of the customer's ability to switch suppliers is a crucial aspect to consider. Customer actions can serve as a bargaining point when assessing the geographic

---

Judgment of 19 April 2007. European Court of Justice (ECJ), Commission v. Greece, Case C-36/12, Judgment of 19 December 2013. European Commission, Decision 2007/158/EC, OJ L 59, 29.2.2008, p. 1. European Commission, Decision 2009/727/EC, OJ L 259, 3.10.2009, p. 1.

[24]Case COMP/M. 3268 - Sydcraft/Graninge. 2003, para 21–27.

[25]Case COMP/M.2947 – Verbund/Energie Allianz. 2004, para 60–62, Case COMP/M.1853 – EDF/EnBW. 2001, para 24–25, Case COMP/M.3448 – EDP/Hidroelectrica del Cantabrico. 2004, para 21, Case COMP/M.1803 -Electrabel/Epon. 2000, para 17–23.

[26]European Commission. Guidelines on the Definition of Relevant Market for the Purposes of Community Competition Law. Official Journal of the European Union, C 372/05, December 9, 2004.

market. This is closely tied to customer loyalty and their reluctance to switch suppliers, which may be influenced by factors such as security of supply and price disparities.

The price disparities among the Member States also contribute to the perception of the market as being national in scope. Various market structures lead to the evaluation of markets on a national scale. The variation in prices across different regions within a country is indicative of a national market rather than a localised community market. Another scenario arises in the context of exchanges, where there is a uniformity of prices within specific countries. Consequently, these markets are recognised as homogeneous. The presence of electricity exchanges or pools signifies the expansion of the market beyond national boundaries, enabling neighbouring countries to engage in electricity trading within these exchanges. The Nord Pool Spot market exchange has expanded the market beyond national boundaries.

9.4.3 Relevant Gas Geographical Market

Prior to the implementation of market opening in Europe, the natural gas supply market was predominantly confined to national boundaries. The evaluation is significantly influenced by the monopolistic nature of the wholesale or upstream segment, wherein no other incumbents are permitted to engage in market participation.[27] The physical transportation capacity frequently influences the market peculiarities in the gas sector.[28] The absence of adequate transportation pipelines would hinder the distribution of supplies to neighbouring countries and beyond. Even when the gas is exported to neighbouring countries, the market can still be considered to have a national scope. The absence of reverse flow in the export of natural gas to the neighbouring country, resulting in the need for the same country to import natural gas from third parties, does not effectively address the issue of ensuring a secure supply. The assessment of market scope also takes into account the volume of exports and imports. Furthermore, the price plays a crucial role in determining the market as it directly influences the consumer's ability to switch suppliers.

Locally restricted markets within a specific country's region are commonly used for the wholesale distribution of gasoline over short distances. However, these markets are confined to regional areas due to their historical association with monopolistic entities. Various obstacles were also imposed in order to enter these markets, such as differentiated tariffs and trade barriers. In previous Commission decisions, the focus was on evaluating markets where prices were determined within

[27] Case COMP/M.3075- ECS/Intercommunikale Iveka. 2003, para 23, Case COMP/M.3318 – ECS/Sibelga. 2003, para 30, Case COMP/M.3086 – Gaz de France/Preussag Energie. 2003, paras 12,13. Case COMP/M.3007 – E.On/TXU – Europe Group. 2002, para 27, Case COMP/M.3096 – TotalFinaElf/Mobil Gas. 2003, para 12.

[28] Case COMP/M. 3868 – DONG/Elsam/Energi/E2. 2006, paras 147–192.

a single country and where third-party access rules were not effectively implemented.[29] Additionally, the regulatory characteristics specific to certain regions were considered indicators for assessing the national geographical scope of these markets. Additionally, the recognition of geographical markets becomes relevant when there are distinct balancing zones that exhibit significant variations in competitive conditions. Alternatively, the establishment of a single balancing zone with new entry and exit tariffs can also undermine the integrity of the individual national markets.

9.4.4 Relevant Gas Product Market

The gas market has the potential to be divided into two distinct segments: the upstream and downstream sectors. The upstream segment encompasses various activities, such as production and exploration, the development of gas reserves, including the establishment of gas platforms, the construction of upstream pipelines, the sale of liquefied natural gas (LNG), and offshore transportation. The downstream segment encompasses various markets, including wholesale supply, transmission, distribution, storage, trading, supply to end customers, and infrastructure operations for importers.

The wholesale market encompasses the provision of natural gas to resellers, which includes the distribution to natural gas-fired power plants. The differentiation between the wholesale and retail markets can be delineated by the mode of transportation employed. Specifically, in wholesale markets, natural gas is conveyed through high-pressure pipelines to cater to industrial customers, power producers, and distributors. The distinction can also be made based on the specific characteristics of customers, namely those who are connected to transmission networks and those who are connected to distribution networks.

The differentiation can also be established based on customer segmentation, as there are varying prices for supplies, distinct consumption patterns, and applicable transportation costs for large industrial customers compared to small customers. A distinction can also be drawn between the supply of natural gas to power plants and small household customers, as these two groups exhibit distinct consumption patterns.[30] The flexibility and duration of the contracts are taken into consideration. Large and small business customers are categorised into distinct markets based on their varying consumption needs and patterns. Specifically, significant industrial

---

[29] European Commission. Guidelines on the Definition of Relevant Market for the Purposes of Community Competition Law. Official Journal of the European Union, C 372/05, December 9, 2004. European Commission. Case COMP/39.238 – Gasoline Retailing. Official Journal of the European Union, C 27/03, January 7, 2016. European Commission. Decision of 17 January 2018 in Case AT.40219 – Gasoline Retailing. Official Journal of the European Union, C 48/06, February 28, 2018.

[30] Ezrachi (2018).

clients exhibit a high degree of demand stability, while small business clients experience demand fluctuations that are influenced by seasonal variations, particularly during the heating season.

From the standpoint of natural gas transportation, it has been recognised that there is a differentiation between high-pressure and low-pressure pipelines. This differentiation has led to the identification of transmission and distribution networks as distinct product markets. Natural monopolies are present in various infrastructure sectors, and in order to promote market liberalisation, measures such as unbundling rules, third-party access, and other regulatory measures have been implemented.

The identification of gas storages as distinct product markets was observed. Potential substitutes, such as flexible or interruptible supply contracts, may not always be viable alternatives. Nevertheless, in the event that the daily imbalance surpasses a specific gas threshold, it is evident that flexible supply contracts would not be able to adequately function as a suitable alternative in this context.

9.5 The Assessment of the Concentration

In accordance with the EU Merger Regulation, mergers and acquisitions that result in a substantial reduction of competition within the common market are prohibited if they would lead to the establishment or reinforcement of a dominant market position. The Commission conducts evaluations of mergers that surpass specific turnover thresholds. A merger is considered to have a community dimension if the combined total worldwide turnover of all the involved undertakings exceeds EUR 500 million and if the aggregate community-wide turnover of at least two of the undertakings is more than EUR 250 million, unless each of the undertakings generates more than two-thirds of its aggregate community-wide turnover within a single Member State.[31] A concentration that fails to meet the thresholds specified is considered to have a community dimension under the following conditions: (a) The combined total turnover of all the relevant undertakings exceeds EUR 250 million globally. (b) In at least three Member States, the combined total turnover of all the relevant undertakings exceeds EUR 100 million. (c) In each of the three Member States mentioned in point (b), the total turnover of at least two of the relevant undertakings exceeds EUR 25 million. (d) The total community-wide turnover of at least two of the relevant undertakings exceeds EUR 100 million, unless each of these undertakings generates more than two-thirds of its total community-wide turnover within a single Member State.

[31] Council Regulation (EC) No 139/2004 of January 20, 2004, on the control of concentrations between undertakings (the "Merger Regulation"). Official Journal of the European Union, L 24, January 29, 2004, pp. 1–22.

The Commission conducts an evaluation of mergers within the European Union, with a focus on larger mergers. However, smaller mergers that do not meet the specified turnover thresholds may be subject to the oversight of national competition authorities. Additionally, a referral mechanism is in place that enables Member States and the Commission to transfer cases upon the request of the undertakings and Member States involved.

The anticipated merger must be formally notified to the Commission and obtain its approval prior to its execution. In accordance with the Guidelines on the Assessment of Horizontal Mergers as outlined in the Council Regulation on the Control of Concentrations between Undertakings, the safe harbour provision is applicable when a merger is proposed between undertakings that do not collectively hold more than 25% market shares. In such cases, the merger is typically deemed non-problematic and can be processed through a simplified procedure.[32] Individuals who surpass the established thresholds will be subject to investigation by the Commission. Significant market shares exceeding 50% imply the presence of a dominant market position. Even if the company's market share prior to the merger was below 50%, the execution of the merger may give rise to concerns about increased market power and potential competition issues.

There are two primary mechanisms through which horizontal mergers can potentially hinder effective competition, specifically by establishing or reinforcing a dominant position: (a) By removing significant competitive restraints on one or more firms, thereby granting them greater market power, without engaging in coordinated actions (referred to as non-coordinated effects). (b) By altering the competitive landscape in a manner that prompts firms, which previously did not coordinate their actions, to now exhibit a higher likelihood of engaging in coordination to increase prices or otherwise undermine effective competition. A merger might potentially enhance coordination for organisations that were already engaged in coordination activities before the merger, leading to improved ease, stability, and effectiveness (referred to as coordinated effects).

The evaluation of the Commission will determine whether the merger may yield any of these effects. If the occurrence of substantial increases in non-coordinated effects were to hinder competition in the market by establishing or reinforcing a dominant position. The mergers observed in concentrated markets have potentially facilitated collaboration between businesses, which can manifest in different ways, such as maintaining prices at levels higher than those seen in competitive environments.[33] This form of coordination is more likely to occur in markets characterised by a high degree of accessibility to such coordination mechanisms.

The significance of concentration institutes lies in their ability to facilitate collaborations among entities, which can potentially hinder competition in the market

[32] Council Regulation (EC) No 139/2004 of January 20, 2004, on the control of concentrations between undertakings (the "Merger Regulation"). Official Journal of the European Union, L 24, January 29, 2004, pp. 1–22.

[33] Hovenkamp (2017).

and create barriers to entry. The merger of a particular economic entity can have an impact on concentrations, resulting in the dissolution of the entity as a singular economic unit.[34] In this scenario, upon the merger of the two entities, they commence joint operations as a single entity. In order to evaluate concentrations, it is crucial to take into account the attainment of control, as the mere acquisition of shares does not automatically confer control upon the entity. The decision to inform the competition authority about the intended merger or acquisition lies within the discretion of the companies involved.

Issues arise when companies choose not to disclose intended mergers or acquisitions as a result of miscalculations regarding financial gains and the possibility of providing inaccurate information, thereby excluding the entire conglomerate of companies. When considering concentrations, it is important to consider the existing subsidiaries of the company in other Member States. This is particularly relevant when the merger could potentially strengthen the company's dominant position in the market. When evaluating notifications of proposed concentrations, the Commission assesses the extent to which competition is significantly reduced. The identification of the pertinent market holds significance in the evaluation of concentrations and the execution of a "substantive test", as entities may operate within the same market prior to engaging in a concentration.

The Commission is required to conduct a fresh market assessment in each instance. This implies that there is no assurance that the Commission will reach the same determination as in the preceding instance. When evaluating a merger, it is evident that consumers will derive certain advantages from the enhanced efficiency. The advantages associated with a vertical merger are often realised through enhanced coordination of production and distribution activities. When evaluating the potential for anti-competitive foreclosure, the Commission analyses the ability of the merged entity to restrict access to downstream markets by reducing purchases from upstream competitors, as well as the likelihood of it having a motive to decrease purchases in the downstream sector.[35] Additionally, it will evaluate the potential negative impact on consumers in the market resulting from the implementation of a customer foreclosure strategy.

The potential foreclosure of competition in the upstream market has the potential to adversely affect the downstream market, leading to potential harm for consumers. This phenomenon has the potential to create a competitive disadvantage for competitors operating in the downstream market, which could result in increased costs. The merged entity has the potential to increase prices or decrease the overall supply to the downstream market. This poses a specific concern regarding the risk of vertical foreclosure, which could occur if the merged entity abuses its control over the gas

[34] Council Regulation (EC) No 139/2004 of January 20, 2004, on the control of concentrations between undertakings (the "Merger Regulation"). Official Journal of the European Union, L 24, January 29, 2004, pp. 1–22.

[35] Codognet et al. (2002).

supply. It is crucial to examine the Neste/IVO merger case[36] in order to assess the potential for coordination. Prior to the merger, Neste possessed a majority stake of over 75% in Gasum, while the remaining 25% was under the control of Gazprom. In accordance with the Commission's mandate, Neste was required to divest 50% of its shares in Gasum. The Finnish Government procured a 24% stake, while the remaining 26% was sold to European entities that have no affiliation with Neste. The divestiture of Gasum from Neste-IVO was secured through the Finnish Government's direct and indirect ownership of 49% of the company's shares.

The Commission assesses mergers within the European Union (EU), whereas national competition authorities may be in charge of smaller mergers that don't meet the required turnover levels. Furthermore, there exists a referral process that allows for the transfer of cases between Member States and the Commission upon the request of the undertakings and Member States concerned. The forthcoming merger necessitates the submission of a formal notification to the Commission and the acquisition of its permission prior to its implementation. As per the Guidelines on the Assessment of Horizontal Mergers, as stipulated in the Council Regulation on the Control of Concentrations between Undertakings, the safe harbour provision becomes applicable in cases where a merger is being proposed between undertakings that collectively possess a market share of less than 25%. In instances of this nature, the merger is commonly seen as unproblematic and can undergo processing via a streamlined approach. Individuals who exceed the predetermined thresholds will be subjected to examination by the Commission.

The existence of a dominant market position can be inferred when a company holds substantial market shares, typically over 50%. Despite a company's pre-merger market share being less than 50%, the implementation of the merger can raise apprehensions regarding augmented market dominance and potential challenges related to competition. The possible adverse effects on competition resulting from horizontal mergers might emerge in a variety of ways, as elucidated by the guidelines pertaining to horizontal mergers. As per the European Union Merger Regulation, mergers and acquisitions that lead to a significant decrease in competition within the common market are forbidden if they result in the creation or strengthening of a dominant market position.

9.6 The Golden Shares

The presence of golden shares, which are unique rights owned by governments in publicly traded enterprises, has been the subject of extensive deliberation and legal examination within the European Union. This chapter explores the notion of golden shares, examining their historical significance and their position within the framework of the European Union's internal market. This study delves into the inherent

[36] Case No IV/M. 931 – Neste/IVO.1998.

conflict between protecting the interests of a nation-state and adhering to the fundamental tenets of European Union law. The analysis primarily centres on significant legal issues and their broader ramifications.

Golden shares, alternatively referred to as special shares or sovereign shares, serve as instruments employed by governments to exercise influence and maintain control over critical firms that operate within their national boundaries. Originally designed to safeguard the interests of the nation, these shares have encountered difficulties in conforming to the norms of the European Union's internal market. The concept of golden shares originated in Europe during the period of privatisation in the 1980s and 1990s, when governments aimed to retain influence or control over privatised entities.[37] Frequently, these shares were accompanied by veto privileges pertaining to pivotal determinations, such as alterations to corporate governance or ownership frameworks.

The examination of golden shares within the framework of EU law has been a consistent focus of the European Court of Justice. The landmark case of *Commission v. Portugal* established a legal precedent by emphasising that the utilisation of golden shares, which impose limitations on the free movement of capital throughout the European Union, may potentially conflict with EU legislation.[38]

There are several challenges that arise in relation to the implementation and effectiveness of golden shares. The main challenge that golden shares face relates to their potential inconsistency with EU legal principles, specifically the principles of free movement of money and the right of establishment. The cases *Commission v. Spain* and *Commission v. Belgium* exemplified the position of the European Court of Justice (ECJ) regarding the preservation of unrestricted capital movement within the European Union (EU).[39]

In the case "Commission v. Spain" the Commission initiated legal proceedings against the Kingdom of Spain due to the utilisation of golden shares in the telecom corporation, Telefónica. The Spanish government possessed a golden stake in Telefónica, granting it the authority to exercise veto power over specific strategic determinations.

The ECJ has rendered a ruling stating that Spain's utilisation of golden shares in Telefónica was found to be in contravention of European Union legislation, namely infringing upon the principles of unrestricted capital movement and the entitlement

[37] European Commission Communication on "The application of the State aid rules to measures relating to the public financing of companies in the context of the financial crisis" (2008/C 270/02), discussing the regulatory framework around state control and golden shares. Official Journal of the European Union, C 270, October 25, 2008, pp. 2–5. Commission Decision 2005/652/EC of September 7, 2005, Official Journal of the European Union, L 245, September 7, 2005, pp. 12–21. Council Directive 2004/25/EC of April 21, 2004, on takeover bids (the "Takeover Bids Directive"). Official Journal of the European Union, L 142, April 30, 2004, pp. 12–23.

[38] European Court of Justice (ECJ), Commission v. Portugal, Case C-367/98, Judgment of 12 December 2000.

[39] Commission v. Spain, Case C-463/00, Judgment of 25 July 2002, ECR I-6391. Commission v. Belgium, Case C-503/99, Judgment of 16 January 2003, ECR I-0001.

to start businesses. According to the ECJ, it was determined that the golden share held by Spain conferred substantial influence on Telefónica, thereby impeding the unrestricted flow of capital and impinging upon the company's capacity to conduct its operations without constraints inside the European Union market.[40]

The aforementioned decision has set a significant precedent in relation to the conformity of golden shares with European Union law. The aforementioned statement serves to reaffirm the notion that actions implemented by member states, such as the use of golden shares, need not excessively impede market competition and should align with the ideals set forth by the European Union.

In case *Commission v. Belgium* the lawsuit in Belgium centred on the utilisation of golden shares within the energy corporation, Distrigas. The Belgian government possessed golden shares, which conferred upon it the authority to impede specific decisions pertaining to the management and control of the corporation.[41]

The ECJ rendered a ruling in the case of *Commission v. Spain*, which bears resemblance to the present case involving Belgium's utilisation of golden shares in Distrigas.[42] In both instances, the ECJ ruled against the use of such shares by Belgium. The court determined that Belgium's ownership of these shares conferred a substantial level of influence over the company, hindering the unrestricted flow of money and hampering the company's capacity to operate without constraints within the European Union.

The aforementioned case has reinforced the European Court of Justice's position regarding the use of golden shares. The statement underscored the importance of employing such mechanisms judiciously and exclusively in extraordinary circumstances when they are indispensable for safeguarding valid public concerns. It is imperative for member states to guarantee that their use of golden shares adheres to EU legislation and does not compromise the fundamental tenets of the internal market. Both the cases *Commission v. Spain* and *Commission v. Belgium* emphasised the significance of harmonising national measures, such as golden shares, with the laws and ideals of the European Union. The authors emphasised the importance of member states adhering to EU legislation while safeguarding their legitimate interests. It is crucial that measures such as golden shares do not unduly hinder competition or obstruct the free movement of capital and business within the European Union. The aforementioned cases have exerted a notable influence on the utilisation of golden shares within Europe and have shaped the advancement of more compliant systems aimed at safeguarding national interests in accordance with European Union regulations.

The conflict between the preservation of national security interests and the adherence to principles of market integration within the European Union is a pivotal concern. Governments assert the indispensability of golden shares in safeguarding security concerns; however, the ECJ upholds the stance that these measures should

[40] Case C-463/00, Commission v. Spain, [2002] ECR I-6391.

[41] Case C-503/99, Commission v. Belgium [2002] ECR I-4809.

[42] Case C-463/00, Commission v. Spain [2003] ECR I-12101.

not excessively impede market competition. In cases *Commission v. France* (Gaz de France), *Commission v. Portugal* (EDP), and *Commission v. Spain* (Telefónica), the ECJ rendered judgements regarding the conformity of golden shares with European Union legislation.[43]

Current trends suggest a progressive transition away from the use of golden shares in favour of adopting more customised procedures that align with the requirements set forth by the European Union. Governments are currently investigating alternate strategies to safeguard their national interests while adhering to the values set forth by the European Union. Golden shares have been crucial in safeguarding the national interests pertaining to privatised businesses in Europe. Nevertheless, the problematic matter that persists is their conformity with European Union legislation. The ongoing process of market integration inside the European Union presents a persistent challenge in striking a delicate equilibrium between the preservation of national security and the adherence to fundamental principles of the EU. This problem will significantly influence the trajectory of golden shares in Europe.

The concept of "golden shares" is recognised as a barrier to cross-border mergers in the energy sector. This concept is distinguished by the fact that the government can obstruct a proposed concentration even without a controlling interest. The CJEU has issued a number of rulings identifying gold shares as impediments to the free movement of capital. Finally, the legitimacy criteria that justify golden shares were established, including the proportionality and non-discrimination requirements.

In 1998, the Commission initiated infringement proceedings against Portugal, France, and Belgium on the grounds that golden shares impeded privatisation and severely restricted the free movement of capital. According to the Commission, the existence of such exceptions could only be justified by the state's strategic interests. The measures should be implemented in a non-discriminatory manner with clear criteria. These measures could not restrict the market beyond what was required to attain the desired result. The existence of precious shares was not prohibited, but the necessity criterion was mandated. In the first instance, it was no longer sufficient to justify aid for economic activity; such measures could not have a significant market-restrictive effect, and a clear justification was required. The CJEU did not specify what strategic objectives other than supply security could justify the existence of gold shares, leaving some legal uncertainty.

The public safety argument was utilised in the Belgian case, in which the State held golden shares in Societe Nationale de Transport par Canalisations and consequently exercised veto power when a transaction was deemed to be in conflict with the State's security interests in energy supply.[44] The relevant minister had the authority to appoint two government representatives who could veto the board's proposed decision as board members. The Commission argued that the State did not establish explicit criteria for the exercise of such rights, potentially violating Article

[43]Case C-483/99, Commission v. France [2001] ECR I-0000. Case C-367/98, Commission v. Portugal [2000] ECR I-05145. Case C-203/00, Commission v. Spain [2003] ECR I-0000.

[44]Case C-503/99, Commission v. Belgium [2002] ECR I-4809.

43 TFEU's free movement of capital provision. In the Almelo case regarding the supply of electricity and the Campus Oil case[45] regarding the supply of petroleum products, the public safety argument was upheld. The CJEU has confirmed that the public interest justifies energy supply security in emergency situations. Restrictions on the free flow of capital justified by the need for public safety had to be in the unambiguous and fundamental interest of the entire community.

In the case of France, the public security interest was predicated on the fact that the oil extraction area was located outside of France and the company's headquarters were located in France. Therefore, the nation's emergency decision-making ensures supply security. State legislation did not impose a requirement on emergency inventories of petroleum products, which could have been used to ensure energy supply security in the event of a crisis. In the case of France, there were no clear criteria for justification, and the applicable right was excessively broad, neither of which the CJEU could justify as necessary to restrict the free movement of capital. Therefore, the French government sold its shares of TotalFinaElf in 2002.[46]

In conclusion, golden shares included the ability to prohibit an investor from another country from acquiring a certain stake, the right to veto a decision, and the obligation to notify before a decision is made if golden shares are insufficient for the ratification of a decision. In these cases, the CJEU determined that such measures restricted the free flow of capital and, on the other hand, examined the justification for the restrictive measures. In Portugal, discrimination against an international investor was unjustified. For a measure to be considered justified, it must have been required to protect the strategic interests of the state.

9.7 Conclusion

The determination of the relevant market is crucial for delineating the scope of competition among firms. Additionally, it provides a framework within which competition policy can be applied. The market can be delineated based on geographical and product factors. This categorization facilitates the computation of market shares and the identification of competitive limitations within the market. When delineating a market, it is crucial to consider three primary sources of competition constraints: demand substitutability, supply substitutability, and potential competition.

The Commission frequently employs a broad definition of relevant markets in order to assess concentrations or competition restrictions. The Commission creates the definition using the preliminary data that the parties involved have provided. An analysis of the market shares held by the parties involved and their rivals serves as the basis for the preliminary assessment of the geographic market boundaries.

[45] Case C-72/83 *Campus Oil Ltd v Minister for Industry and Energy* [1984] ECR I-2727.

[46] Case C-483/99, Commission v. France [2001] ECR I-06761.

Additionally, an initial analysis of pricing and disparities at both the European Union and national levels is taken into consideration.

The electricity market is recognised as a distinct and pertinent product market. It possesses multifunctional capabilities, encompassing applications such as illumination, thermal energy generation, and cooling. The conventional structure of the electricity market is divided into distinct sectors, namely generation and wholesale, transmission, distribution, and supply to end consumers.

The trading of electricity is acknowledged as a distinct market, distinct from the processes of electricity generation, wholesale, and supply. The subject matter necessitates specialised expertise, possesses the distinctive characteristic of engaging in short-term contractual agreements, does not inherently necessitate the physical provision of electricity, the delivery of electricity to end consumers may not always occur, and the company is not obligated to engage in commercial trading and supply operations. In the realm of physical trade, electricity is supplied to the consumer through direct transactions. Conversely, in financial trade, electricity is traded as futures, options, and swaps, primarily focusing on financial settlement without involving physical delivery to the end customer. Financial trading is employed as a reliable form of insurance to mitigate the potential risks arising from abrupt and unforeseen price fluctuations in physical electricity trading. This practise is commonly referred to as financial hedging.

The concept of the balancing market was developed to establish a distinct product market due to the unique nature of electricity, where the amount of power withdrawn from the grid must be equal to the amount of power injected into the grid in order to maintain consistent frequencies. Electricity suppliers lack information regarding the precise amount of electricity that customers will consume. Consequently, balancing services are employed to address these uncertainties. The Commission has also observed that there is a presence of balancing services or regulated power, which may be separate from the wholesale market. In liberalised markets, a distinct balancing market is present, wherein transmission system operators procure balancing energy from a designated exchange.

In order to conduct a comprehensive assessment of the geographic market, it is imperative to evaluate various factors such as regulatory barriers, licencing requirements, price caps, transfer charges, and interconnection capacities. These factors play a crucial role in the process of market liberalisation and the promotion of competition. Specifically, the existence of barriers to interconnection capacities would impede the ability of entities to engage in the trading of electricity within a single country's territory. The assessment of congestion is taken into consideration when determining the obstacles to market entry. The implementation of electricity trade through interconnection may be hindered by bottlenecks or a lack of capacity, thereby creating barriers within the market. The presence of congestion in the market may also lead to the definition of the market as being limited to a national scope, as the inability to engage in interconnection trade is attributed to technical challenges. The presence of distinct price zones among neighbouring markets contributes to the isolation of these markets.

The gas market has the potential to be divided into two distinct segments, namely the upstream and downstream sectors. The upstream segment encompasses various activities such as production and exploration, the development of gas reserves, including the establishment of gas platforms, the construction of upstream pipelines, the sale of liquefied natural gas (LNG), and offshore transportation. The downstream segment encompasses various markets, including wholesale supply, transmission, distribution, storage, trading, supply to end customers, and infrastructure operations for importers. Additionally, assessing customers based on their consumption patterns can establish the distinction. Large industrial customers and small customers exhibit variations in supply prices, consumption levels, and transportation costs.

From the standpoint of natural gas transportation, a distinction has been made between high-pressure and low-pressure pipelines. Consequently, the transmission and distribution networks have been recognised as distinct product markets. In order to facilitate market liberalisation, various regulatory measures, such as unbundling rules and third-party access, have been implemented, even in the presence of natural monopolies within these infrastructure sectors.

The anticipated concentrations must be communicated to the Commission and approved prior to implementation. In accordance with the Guidelines on the Assessment of Horizontal Mergers as outlined in the Council Regulation on the Control of Concentrations between Undertakings, the safe harbour provision is applicable when a merger is proposed between undertakings that collectively hold less than 25% market shares. In such cases, the merger is generally considered to be unproblematic and can be processed through a simplified procedure. Individuals who surpass the established thresholds will be subject to investigation by the Commission. The presence of significant market shares, exceeding 50% or more, implies the establishment of a dominant market position. Even if a company's market share is below 50% prior to a merger, the execution of the merger may give rise to concerns about increased market power and potential competition issues.

The presence of "golden shares" is widely acknowledged as a significant barrier to the successful completion of mergers. This is because governments have the ability to impede proposed consolidations, even in cases where they do not possess a controlling interest. Such actions can be seen as a violation of the principle of the free movement of capital. Hence, the utilisation of "golden shares" could be deemed justifiable by adhering to the principles of proportionality and non-discrimination. Restrictions on the unrestricted flow of capital, which are justified by the imperative of maintaining public security, must be aligned with the explicit and essential interests of the entire community or serve to protect the strategic interests of the State.

References

Bailey D, John LE (2019) European Union law of competition. Oxford University Press, Bellamy and Child

Codognet MK, Glachant JM, Leveque F, Plagnet M (2002) Mergers and acquisitions in the European electricity sector cases and patterns. CERNA
Ezrachi A (2018) EU competition law. An analytical guide to the leading cases. Hart Publishing
Faull J, Nikpay A (2014) The EU law of competition, 3rd edn. Oxford University Press
Hovenkamp H (2017) Principles of antitrust. West Academic Publishing
Jones C (2021) EU competition law volume II mergers and acquisitions, 3rd edn. Claeys and Casteels
Navarro E, Font A, Folguera J, Briones J (2005) Merger control in the EU. Oxford University Press

Chapter 10
Forms of Concentration in the Energy Sector

Abstract The research indicates that the merger of smaller competitors is unlikely to result in the exclusion of other companies from the market. Nevertheless, it is crucial to acknowledge that there are specific exemptions, especially when the merger takes place between multinational companies. In such circumstances, there is still a potential for market exclusion or the existence of undesirable restrictions on competition. In circumstances where a natural gas business lacks a dominant market position but controls key infrastructure such as transmission networks and natural gas storage facilities, it is possible that market restraints may be present. We anticipate that this course of action will result in foreclosure. The problem worsens when these companies form long-lasting gas supply contracts with energy producers, which are crucial for generating electricity. This scenario witnesses' foreclosures and decreased competition in the energy and gas markets. Therefore, it is imperative to establish mechanisms that provide equitable and impartial access to the natural gas transmission networks. In markets characterized by oligopoly or monopoly, the merger of a dominant company is likely to lead to a reduction in market competition. The merger results in the removal of competitive dynamics among the involved enterprises.

10.1 Introduction

In the energy sector, it is crucial for companies to possess the capability of acquiring control over entities involved in trading or distribution. This strategic advantage enables them to enhance the efficiency of their operations. Concentrations can be pursued with the aim of establishing appealing companies at the regional or European Union level that would operate across multiple Member States. The primary goal of fostering a competitive European internal market is to incentivize companies to broaden their operations and evolve into sizable corporations. Concentrations are strategically formulated to safeguard market dominance by imposing barriers that impede the entry of potential competitors into the market.

In instances where mergers occur between transmission or distribution network companies, it is essential to uphold the legal and functional unbundling requirements

L. Rimšaitė, *The Crossroads of Competition Law and Energy Regulation*,
https://doi.org/10.1007/978-3-031-73238-6_10

as stipulated by energy law.[1] This ensures that the necessary conditions are established for accessing pertinent information pertaining to the operations of these companies, including their potential strategic business decisions and network development. Furthermore, by means of these mergers, the company effectively establishes a dominant position in the market for additional operations, such as energy provision or dissemination. In such instances, the subsidiary entity procures the necessary quantity of electricity or natural gas from the parent company, which is actively involved in power generation or manufacturing. Engaging in such actions would not constitute a violation of energy law, provided that the company maintains adequate segregation of activities, even in the absence of complete ownership unbundling mandated by the State.

In certain scenarios, a company may express interest in acquiring a share of another company that operates in a nearby market.[2] This strategic move aims to safeguard the acquiring company's dominant position in its domestic market and mitigate the potential risks associated with competitive price reductions. This strategy entails acquiring a minority ownership interest, typically ranging from 10% to 20%, in a company that operates within the adjacent market. The purpose of this approach is to deter potential competitors from entering the geographical region with the intention of reducing prices while simultaneously appealing to a larger customer base.[3] This phenomenon guarantees a level of mutual exchange, prompting companies in adjacent markets to opt for market closure instead of engaging in competition.

The presence of barriers to entry and limited competition in the energy sector results in the establishment of a non-competitive oligopoly. In the subsequent sections, a comprehensive analysis will be conducted on horizontal, vertical, and conglomerate mergers within the energy sector, with a focus on their distinctive characteristics.

10.2 The Motives of M&A in the Light of the Green Economy

The implementation of global energy policy reforms has become an established reality. The veracity of these claims has been substantiated through a series of climate conferences, including the most recent iteration held in Glasgow in 2021. An increasing number of nations are embracing and enacting such policies through the establishment of new legislation that governs the operations of the energy industry, aligning with the emerging norms of a sustainable, environmentally friendly economy. The sector under consideration is subject to extensive regulation and substantial state intervention in all Western European countries. In spite of

[1]Cameron (2007).

[2]Gerber (2020).

[3]Ezrachi (2016).

concerted efforts to establish market regulations and foster a competitive economic environment, there has been a notable absence of substantial policy reform in recent times. Consequently, an increasing number of energy businesses have modified their strategies to incorporate renewable energy sources within the limitations imposed by their available resources and legal frameworks. In this manner, they enhance the variety of their energy generation.[4] Given the urgent need for rapid changes in the energy industry, numerous firms opt to pursue external development strategies, specifically through mergers and acquisitions (M&A). This approach is preferred due to its expediency in meeting the demands outlined in statements produced during climate conferences. The majority of M&A transactions often involve the acquisition of enterprises operating in the photovoltaic industry, wind farms, hydropower facilities, and other entities engaged in the production of renewable energy. This is frequently accomplished by buying start-up companies. A significant number of mergers and acquisitions occur predominantly in Western Europe. This phenomenon can be attributed not solely to governmental influence but also to the heightened societal consciousness that rejects the concept of the "brown economy". If it is determined that the primary drivers behind mergers and acquisitions in the energy sector are associated with the expansion of operations into renewable energy production, it will substantiate the notion that political decisions have the capacity to shape corporate behaviour and consequently impact the economy.

The green economy places emphasis on the utilisation of renewable energy sources, also referred to as green energy sources, which are widely deliberated over in climate conferences and symposiums. The 2015 meeting in Paris, known as COP21, represented a notable turning point in the progress of the renewable energy industry. The aforementioned occurrence reached its pinnacle with the formal endorsement of the Paris Agreement, facilitating cooperative efforts among governments on a global scale. Following that, the deal was accepted by all member countries of the European Union.[5] As per the provisions of the Paris Agreement, Europe is confronted with a substantial endeavour, whereby the continent is assigned the responsibility of becoming the leading climate-neutral geographical area worldwide by the year 2050.

The concept of the green transition comprises a range of interconnected processes and related policies, as outlined in the European Green Deal on December 11, 2019.[6] This document presents a comprehensive analysis of energy plans that are designed to promote a sustainable and low-carbon economy while also ensuring security and environmental friendliness. Consequently, discernible consequences encompass the creation of agreements pertaining to renewable energy, the consolidation of diverse

[4]Posner (2019).

[5]Council Decision (EU) 2016/1841 of 5 October 2016 on the conclusion, on behalf of the European Union, of the Paris Agreement adopted in Paris on 12 December 2015. OJ L 282, 19.10.2016, pp. 1–2.

[6]Communication from the Commission to the European Parliament, the European Council, the Council, the European Economic and Social Committee and the Committee of the Regions. European Green Deal. [2019] OJ C 100, 14.3.2020, pp. 1–32.

elements within the energy supply chain and increased transactional involvement within the energy sector. The analysis of the data indicates that a notable majority of the mergers and acquisitions carried out subsequent to December 2020, namely 144 out of 174, were linked to either renewable energy assets or firms.

These transactions serve as a demonstration of the market's response to the necessity of shifting from a carbon-intensive economy to one that is environmentally sustainable. The proposed method requires the adoption of proactive environmental management strategies, including the integration of risk management and the allocation of resources towards natural capital. Furthermore, it underscores the attainment of environmental sustainability by advocating for the enhancement of eco-efficiency. Moreover, this highlights the significance of dissociating economic expansion from the increasing utilisation of resources by using inventive strategies and altering patterns of demand. The primary aim of this study was to ascertain the fundamental drivers behind mergers and acquisitions within the energy industry subsequent to the incorporation of green economy elements in Western Europe. There is a hypothesis suggesting that the initiation of these market transactions is strongly correlated with a worldwide change in environmental policy.

10.3 Horizontal Mergers of Energy Entities

Horizontal mergers can be classified into two categories: the acquisition of control over a competitor operating in the same product and geographic market, and the acquisition of control over a competitor operating in the same product market but in a neighbouring geographic market.[7] In instances where the electricity and gas markets are typically controlled by a sole monopoly entity or a few dominant firms, the absence of market competition allows for mergers within the same geographic market to result in foreclosure.

The present scenario can be effectively exemplified by the VEBA/VVIAG[8] case, wherein the proposed merger between VEBA, the parent organisation of Preussenelektra, and VIAG, which operates in the gas and electricity industries, was intended to be implemented.[9] The implementation of the merger was carried out by its subsidiary, Bayernwerk. After the merger, VEBA held a market share of 17.6%, while VIAG's market share amounted to 11.1%. The combined market share of the two entities reached 28.7%. While these statistics do not necessarily indicate the active involvement of the dominant operator in the market, it is noteworthy that German electricity companies possess shares or even control over companies

[7] Guidelines on the assessment of horizontal mergers under the Council Regulation on the control of concentrations between undertakings. OJ C 31, 5.2.2004, pp. 5–18.

[8] Commission Decision in Case COMP/M.2317 – VEBA/VIAG.

[9] Explanatory note. Best Practice Guidelines: The Commission's Model Texts for Divestiture Commitments and the Trustee mandate under the EC Merger Regulation. 5.12.2013.

operating in the same product market in neighbouring countries. This phenomenon serves to reinforce the existing oligopoly within the market. VEBA and VIAG have reached an agreement to waive the gearbox fee, commonly referred to as the "T-component". This fee is typically imposed when the energy supplier, facilitating trade between the northern and southern trading zones, is unable to match the quantities of energy supplied with equivalent quantities in the opposite direction.

In Germany, the negotiation of conditions and tariffs for third-party access to the transmission grid was previously conducted between the transmission system operator and the parties expressing interest. The German Association of the Electricity Industry, the German Association of Industry, and the German Association of Industrial Energy Users and Self-Generators collaborated to streamline processes by negotiating and implementing guidelines that outline the fundamental principles and methodology for grid access. These guidelines, commonly referred to as the Association Agreement I, were established in 1998. This agreement succeeded the Association Agreement II in 1999. The Association Agreement establishes the framework for negotiated grid access between electricity market undertakings and customers. The implementation of the Association Agreement II in Germany resulted in the establishment of two distinct trading zones. In the event that power was transferred between these zones or across the border to a neighbouring country, a transmission charge known as the "T-component" had to be paid. This charge was applicable when the quantity of transmitted power could not be offset or balanced out, specifically requiring that the quantities of power crossing in one direction be accounted for against Additionally, the mechanisms implemented for energy balancing provide a distinct advantage to the duopolistic entities. The Commission has expressed concerns regarding the national regulatory system in the context of the VEBA/VIAG merger, emphasising the need for an evaluation from a competition standpoint.

The Commission approved the concentration subject to the separation of VIAG from VEBA/VIAG through the creation of an independent entity. Additionally, it was required that third parties be granted access to the electricity networks in Germany. Consequently, VIAG was required to divest a portion of its shares to Vattenfall, a Swedish electricity network corporation.

Another comparable instance can be observed in the Exxon/Mobil case,[10] wherein the corporation possesses a substantial portion of the market, primarily due to its ownership stake in Gasunie, a prominent entity in the Netherlands. Additionally, the concentration involved the participation of BEB and Thyssengen, two German gas companies, which collectively established an oligopolistic gas market. Before the merger, Exxon held a prominent market position in the Netherlands as well as a dominant position in the gas market of the adjacent country. The acquisition of Mobil would have enhanced Exxon's market position, notwithstanding Mobil's relatively modest market share of 1.5%. Despite the expressed concerns of the Commission, it ultimately granted authorization for the concentration.

[10] Case IV/M.138. Exxon/Mobil. 1999.

The merger between RWE and Essent[11] in the German wholesale electricity market holds significance in this context. The Commission recognised that prior to the merger, the market exhibited characteristics of an oligopoly, as RWE held approximately 30–40% of the market share, while Vattenfall and EnBW, as the main competitors, collectively held around 50–60% of the market. The competition authority expressed apprehension regarding the potential consolidation of these companies, citing concerns that it would further enhance their market dominance. However, subsequent to a bid made by the companies involved, the Commission granted authorization for the merger in question.

Another notable merger occurred between Vattenfall and Nuon,[12] wherein the Swedish power corporation aimed to procure Nuon Energy, a Dutch company engaged in various aspects of power generation, supply, and distribution. Nuon Energy operated primarily in the Netherlands but also had a presence in neighbouring countries such as Belgium and Germany. In the current scenario, the Commission refuted the contention that there existed an adequate number of competing firms in the market and that consumers enjoyed a satisfactory level of freedom in making choices.

In markets characterised by oligopoly or monopoly, the involvement of a dominant company in a merger transaction is likely to result in the restriction or elimination of competition. This is due to the merger's potential to eliminate competition between companies operating in the market. The company has the potential to acquire a stake in another company operating in the adjacent market, which could limit both current and future competition in that market. The occurrence of such mergers presents additional challenges due to the possibility of increased concentration in proximate markets as opposed to geographically distant markets. Once again, it is imperative to consider the size of the company being acquired. If the company being acquired is significantly small, the probability of the competition being impacted is relatively low. It is imperative to consider the unique characteristics of the energy sector and the underlying purpose of market liberalisation.

Given that energy companies typically operate in an oligopolistic market where a few dominant companies are the main participants, restrictions on cross-border mergers can hinder the achievement of market integration. This is because such prohibitions confine market activities within the borders of a single country, impeding efforts to promote market openness and collaboration across nations. As a result, it is crucial to achieve equilibrium in order to lessen the difficulty that businesses face when dealing with conflicting prohibitions. In the event of a cross-border merger involving a sufficiently competitive market in another geographic region, it is generally not considered an impediment to competition.

There is a potential for the merger to have a detrimental impact on market competition. Instances of such occurrences arise when a merger transpires within a

[11] Case COMP/M.5467 – RWE/ Essent. 2009.

[12] Case COMP/M.5496 – Vattenfall/Nuon Energy. 2009.

relatively competitive market lacking a dominant position.[13] Consequently, such a merger would have a more pronounced competitive impact than a restrictive one. In its decision-making process, the Commission evaluates both the market conditions in the countries where the mergers occur and the effects of these mergers on the advancement of the single market. The case involving EDF/EnBW[14] is relevant in this context, as it pertains to the attempted acquisition by the French electricity company of the vertically integrated German electricity company EnBW. Notably, EnBW holds a substantial market share in the southwest region of Germany. EDF maintained a prominent market position in France, commanding a substantial 80% share of the electricity transmission and distribution sector. Consequently, the presence of significant barriers to entry in the electricity market in France limited the potential for new entrants to participate, thereby creating a hypothetical opportunity for market entry. EDF, a French company, has acquired EnBW, a company that operates two out of the four interconnectors connecting the borders of Germany and France, as a consequence of the concentration.

Upon conducting an assessment of horizontal mergers within the energy sector, it has been observed that such mergers often result in the reinforcement of market dominance, leading to a reduction in competitive pricing pressures and the emergence of entities commonly referred to as "national champions". Mergers can yield favourable outcomes for the market as they enable companies to enhance operational efficiency and provide products at competitive price points. A crucial determinant lies in the objectives pursued by the companies involved in the merger, specifically whether their intentions revolve around acquiring a substantial market share or fostering a competitive atmosphere.[15] Another crucial factor to consider is the diversification of business operations into adjacent markets. The consolidation of multiple companies resulting in the establishment of a more economically sustainable enterprise presents a prospect for business expansion while simultaneously fostering technological advancements, innovation, and a competitive landscape. In this particular scenario, it is highly probable that the company will exploit its market dominance, resulting in a decrease in the number of rival firms within the market due to horizontal mergers.

10.4 Vertical Mergers in the Energy Sector

Vertical mergers in the energy sector encompass the consolidation of companies that operate at distinct stages of production and distribution within the same geographical region. An instance of such a merger would be the amalgamation of an electricity company with an electricity transmission or distribution company. The company

[13] Jones and Weinert (2021).

[14] Case COMP/M. 1853 – EDF/EnBW. 2001.

[15] Lianos et al. (2019).

engaged in the wholesale electricity market effectively gains a stake in the retail market through the acquisition of shares in a distribution company that procures electricity from said market.[16] Within the framework of the merger, the recently acquired distribution company may consider procuring electricity from its newly established parent company while retaining the option to transition to an alternative electricity supplier. In contrast, in cases where an electricity distribution company held a monopoly prior to the liberalisation of the market, it is probable that the company possessed comprehensive knowledge regarding consumers and their fluctuations in energy consumption. Vertical mergers can occur between companies operating in the same geographic market, neighbouring geographic markets, or even more distant geographic markets, following the same principle as horizontal mergers. Nevertheless, the Commission has exclusively voiced apprehensions pertaining to the concentrations falling under the first category, specifically those involving companies that operate within the same geographic market. When a company engages in the acquisition of another business that operates at a vertical level within a geographically adjacent market, the probability of anti-competitive consequences occurring in the market is reduced. In this scenario, the company's market share would be deemed insufficient to exert any significant influence on other companies through the imposition of competitive restrictions within the acquiring company's domestic market.

It is noteworthy that the Commission adopts a stringent stance regarding the integration of companies that have previously operated at the same level of energy production or trade, within the same geographic or product market, and have held a monopoly either individually or in collaboration with multiple other companies. The aforementioned scenario is exemplified by the merger between ECS and Sibelga,[17] wherein Electrabel, a subsidiary of ECS that specialises in the provision of electricity to end-users, expressed its intention to acquire shares in Sibelga, a semi-private entity responsible for supplying electricity and natural gas to consumers in the Brussels region. In accordance with Belgian legislation, it is mandated to enforce the segregation of activities and the designation of a guaranteed supplier. It is postulated that Sibelga ought to maintain ownership of the networks while discontinuing supply activities and subsequently transferring them to Electrabel. The latter entity should be designated as a certified supplier and be responsible for managing retail electricity sales. The geographic market pertaining to electricity and gas within Belgium encompassed the relevant territory. Electrabel, however, maintained a position of dominance in both the gas and electricity markets. Specifically, Electrabel possessed nearly 90% of the electricity generation market share in Belgium, which corresponded to approximately 75–85% of the supply market. Electrabel, in addition, facilitated electricity capacity auctions and retained approximately 75% market share in this domain. The current structure of the auctions does

[16] Commission Consolidated Jurisdictional Notice under Council Regulation (EC) No 139/2004 on the control of concentrations between undertakings. OJ C 95, 16.4.2008, pp. 1–48.

[17] Case COMP/M.3318 - ECS/Sibelga. 2003.

not offer a satisfactory foundation for claiming that the market exhibits competitive characteristics, given that individual operators in competition are restricted from acquiring more than 4% of the available capacity of Electrabel. In the event that a substantial portion of the electricity capacity were allocated, it is probable that it would be exported to the adjacent Netherlands due to the considerably higher electricity prices prevailing in that region. Another crucial factor to consider is the presence of barriers to entry. In this scenario, Electrabel's monopoly over the gas supply market in Belgium and the already insufficient interconnection capacity with France limited access for new operators. Additionally, there were several challenges pertaining to the administrative procedures, as the intricate licencing system posed obstacles for prospective operators seeking to enter the market. Consequently, the suggested merger has facilitated Electrabel's consolidation of its prevailing position within the market. The decision also encompasses the rationale for preserving the interconnections between Electrabel and other corporate entities. The profit-sharing mechanism implemented by Sibelga and Electrabel has led to the consolidation of market power and the creation of discriminatory practises in relation to the accessibility of transmission networks.

From the perspective of competition law, vertical mergers are comparatively less detrimental as they involve the consolidation of a generator with a supplier or distributor to enhance operational efficiency and reduce business expenses.[18] In this regard, it is pertinent to recall the stipulations pertaining to the unbundling of vertically integrated corporations within the domain of energy legislation. It is important to acknowledge that competition authorities are not obligated to conduct a compulsory evaluation of company unbundling within the framework of energy legislation when evaluating the market effects of consolidations.

Hence, there exists a potential scenario wherein the divestiture provision of energy legislation necessitates companies or their subsidiaries to seek approval from the competition authority for the consolidation without conducting a distinct assessment of the vertical integration of their operations. Competition authorities are not obligated to verify compliance with energy law requirements when granting a concentration permit. Hence, it is imperative to contemplate the implementation of this requirement as a means to systematically apply legislative provisions and mitigate the potential repercussions of duplicative application.

10.5 The Conglomerate Mergers in the Energy Sector

Conglomerate mergers execute entities that are not in competition with each other or with producers who may be consumers of each other's output. In the energy sector, conglomerate mergers, where electricity companies merge with gas companies, create a favourable economic effect that can offer energy to consumers at

[18] Healey et al. (2020).

competitive prices while optimising the costs involved.[19] Conglomerate mergers create the opportunity to offer consumers a wide range of services and could ensure the security of gas supplies needed by power companies to produce electricity. There can be mergers involving dominant and non-dominant entities as well as those within two dominant entities. The case of a dominant undertaking merging with a non-dominant one could lead to the elimination or at least a significant restriction of actual or potential competition in the market. When evaluating mergers between dominant and non-dominant entities, it is noticeable that price manipulation becomes possible in such cases. The gas sector is of great importance, whether the company operates LNG or owns transmission networks.

The merger of an electricity company with a gas company that manages essential facilities creates the conditions for increasing gas prices. Electricity companies using natural gas for electricity generation pay a higher price than the merged gas and electricity companies. Some authors point out that it is unreasonable to prevent such mergers because they create the opportunity to expand undertakings operations in the geographic market, enable companies to provide a wider range of services, and increase competitiveness through economies of scale. This position of the authors is to be welcomed since merged entities can diversify their activities and offer lower prices to consumers while making the company more efficient.[20] The Commission's approach to this type of merger depends on the commercial strength of the company being acquired, but in each case, the Commission assesses the situation individually.

In the E.ON/MOL case,[21] where E.ON, which has about 10% of the Hungarian electricity market, wanted to acquire the dominant gas company MOL, the Commission found that such actions would strengthen MOL's dominant position on the market. Such action would also result in severe constraints on the electricity market, as E.ON's competitors in the electricity market would be dependent on it in terms of the supply of natural gas needed for the production of electricity. The DONG/Elsam/Energie E2 case[22] is also relevant, where DONG, holding about 80% of the Danish natural gas market, sought to acquire about 20–25% of the Danish electricity market. In the Commission's view, such actions would have strengthened the company's dominant position in the natural gas market. With this merger, DONG would have created the preconditions for eliminating electricity companies as potential competitors in the gas market.

In the energy sector, there are also frequent cases of mergers between entities operating in different markets, such as electricity and gas. Such mergers have a significant impact on competition by eliminating existing or potential competitors.[23] Analysing the merger of an electricity-dominant undertaking with another dominant undertaking in this sector, the potential or existing competitors of the electricity or

[19] Ritter and Braun (2005).

[20] Rosenthal and Thomas (2010).

[21] Case COMP/M.3696 - E.ON/MOL. 2005.

[22] Case COMP/M.3868 - DONG/Elsam/Energie E2. 2006.

[23] Jones (2012).

gas company are left even without the theoretical opportunity to enter the market by merging with another company of similar capacity in that market.

Undertakings operating in the electricity sector, which are actual or potential competitors of the dominant electricity company, become dependent on it after the concentration when it comes to supplying the natural gas needed for the production of electricity. Such a situation also opens up ways of discrimination for the said companies. Where companies in the electricity sector purchase natural gas from merged undertakings, the latter gain a competitive advantage by being informed of the quantities of natural gas to be procured and the estimated amount of electricity to be produced. Such mergers not only restrict competition in the market but also create barriers to entry for new operators. The Commission approves such conglomerate concentrations with certain commitments, such as divestiture and the obligation to promote competitiveness by expanding its business lines.

In the Tractebel/Distrigaz case,[24] the Tractebel sought to acquire control of the Distrigaz, previously controlled by the Belgian State. Tractebel was a subsidiary of Suez, which also owned Electrabel. The merger would not have led to Electrabel and Distrigaz becoming dominant companies in the electricity and gas sectors in Belgium. In the present case, there were no potential threats of restraint or foreclosure since both companies were operating in different markets. A different conclusion was reached by the Commission in the EDP/GDP case,[25] where companies having a dominant position in the Portuguese electricity and gas markets sought a merger. It was found that such a merger would significantly strengthen the positions of the companies in the electricity and gas markets. The merger would also have strengthened EDP's dominant position in the wholesale electricity market. GDP was also given a sufficiently high priority in terms of the supply of natural gas needed to generate electricity, as it would have had the necessary information for price manipulation and would have gained a competitive advantage over competitors. In addition, EDP's competitive advantage would have been enhanced by having no interest in seeking alternative suppliers of natural gas to secure electricity generation, and consequently, the entry of potential competitors would have been hampered.

It is worth considering another concentration in the energy sector between Siemens and Areva.[26] In 2001, Siemens and Framatome SA, the legal predecessor of Areva, established an autonomous joint venture, Areva NP, to which they transferred their nuclear activities. The shareholders agreement contained a non-competition obligation. This non-competition obligation was applicable not only throughout the lifetime of the joint venture but also for a further 8 years after Siemens would have lost control of the joint venture. The non-compete obligation after the loss of control of the joint venture was subsequently reduced to 4 years by an arbitration award. The shareholders agreement also included a confidentiality clause with the same duration as the non-competition obligation.

[24] Case COMP/M.493 - Tractebel/Distrigaz. 2001.

[25] Case COMP/M.3440 - ENI/EDP/GDP. 2004.

[26] Case COMP/39.736 - Siemens/Areva. 2012.

The Commission took the view that the non-competition obligation after the creation of the joint venture was in principle objectively necessary for Areva to secure the transfer of the entire value of Areva NP through the acquisition of sole control of Areva NP. During the lifetime of the joint venture, Siemens had the exclusive right to use Areva NP's confidential business information, which it could use upon leaving the joint venture to "compete more favourably" with its former parent company. Protection against more favourable competition for Siemens can only be justified in markets where Areva NP has been operating its own products and has therefore made investments that could be impaired by such more favourable competition. In view of the fact that the non-competition obligation after the liquidation of the joint venture would have been applicable to Siemens products that Areva NP only resold (or did not operate on the markets for those products at all), the requirement of proportionality was not met in this case.

The condition for acquiring exclusive control of Areva NP (acquired by Areva) would have been considered a restriction of competition under Article 101 TFEU. Siemens and Areva have offered commitments aimed at resolving the competition concerns raised by the Commission. The parties have undertaken to remove the non-competition obligation set out in the shareholders agreement, as modified by the arbitration decision, following the establishment of the joint venture and to replace it by the following rules: The Parties have committed to allowing Siemens to compete with Areva NP without restriction from the date on which Siemens lost joint control of Areva NP, except for activities directly related to nuclear equipment for nuclear power plants, which were listed in the exhaustive list. Siemens could not compete with Areva NP only in the markets for its core products and core services for 3 years after Areva acquired sole control of Areva NP. Siemens did not have access during the relevant period to any confidential information relating to its core products and core services that it could have used during the life of the joint venture. Even after that date, Siemens was not able to provide or use Areva NP's statutes, administrative documents, or confidential technical information with third parties.

In the case of conglomerate mergers, it is even more difficult to assess concentrations because of the analysis of the positions of entities operating in different markets in the energy sector, i.e., concentrations in the electricity or gas markets. The removal of vertical links between the electricity and gas sectors through the ownership unbundling requirement in the energy law should be taken into account. Therefore, not only the strengthening of a dominant position but also the existence of cross-links between the electricity and gas sectors should be analysed in the context of competition law when assessing conglomerate concentrations. Such practise would be useful since it would assess compliance not only with competition law but also energy law, thus leaving operators without any doubts regarding compliance with certain requirements. In line with existing EU energy law regulations, it is envisaged to unbundle vertically integrated companies for market liberalisation purposes. Such measures aim at creating a competitive internal market where consumers can choose an energy supplier without paying monopoly prices. On the other hand, when energy companies, under the guise of cost optimisation, carry out mergers or gain control or other significant influence in the decision-making process in order to maintain or even strengthen their dominant position, they create barriers to entry into the market. It should be borne in mind that providing competitive prices to consumers through economies of scale can bring greater benefits than damages, although the aim is often to abuse their position by creating "national champions". Protecting national companies from potential competition from third countries is often aimed at strengthening the market power of companies and limiting competition.

However, the question arises as to the relation between the liberalisation of the market, the establishment of the internal market, and the merger control mechanism. As discussed in previous chapters, the objectives of creating a competitive internal market are already reflected in both primary EU law and secondary legislation, providing the legal grounds for the unbundling of vertically integrated companies. There is a paradoxical situation where EU legislation imposes certain obligations on the liberalisation of the internal energy market while, on the other hand, the Commission monitors the proper functioning of the market and allows concentration where it does not reveal any possibilities of strengthening dominant positions and market constraints.

10.6 Conclusion

Our research findings indicate that the merger of non-dominant players is unlikely to lead to market foreclosure. However, it is important to note that certain exceptions exist, particularly in cases where the merger occurs within cross-border undertakings. In such situations, there may still be a risk of market foreclosure or the presence of problematic ringfencing undertakings. The presence of market constraints cannot be ruled out in situations where a natural gas company, lacking a dominant market position, possesses crucial infrastructure such as transmission networks and natural gas storage facilities. This course of action is anticipated to result in foreclosure. The issue becomes further exacerbated when these companies establish enduring gas supply agreements with electricity producers, which are essential for the production of electricity. In this scenario, the occurrence of foreclosures and diminished competition are observed within the electricity and gas markets. Consequently, it becomes necessary to implement measures that guarantee fair and unbiased access to the natural gas transmission networks.

In markets characterised by oligopoly or monopoly, the occurrence of a merger involving a dominant company is likely to result in the curtailment of competition within the market. This is due to the merger leading to the elimination of competitive dynamics among the participating companies. The company has the potential to engage in the acquisition of a stake in another company operating in the adjacent market, consequently impeding both current and future competition in that particular market. The occurrence of such mergers gives rise to additional challenges due to the possibility of increased concentration in nearby markets as opposed to distant markets.

Given that energy companies typically operate within an oligopolistic market structure where a few dominant firms dominate market activity, certain restrictions on cross-border mergers can hinder the achievement of market integration. This is because such restrictions confine market seclusion within the boundaries of a single country. Hence, it is imperative to establish equilibrium in order to mitigate the risk of companies becoming ensnared in conflicting prohibitions. In instances where a cross-border merger occurs and there is ample competition within another geographical market, it is typically not deemed a constraint on competition.

Vertical mergers in the energy sector encompass the consolidation of companies that operate at distinct stages of production and distribution within the same geographical region. This occurs when an electricity generation entity combines with an electricity transmission or distribution counterpart. In the wholesale electricity market, a company can obtain ownership in the retail market through the acquisition of shares in a distribution company that procures electricity from said market. In the context of this merger, the recently acquired distribution company has the potential to procure electricity from its newly established parent company while retaining the freedom to transition to an alternative electricity supplier. Conversely, in instances where an electricity distribution company held a monopoly prior to the liberalisation of the market, it is probable that the company possessed comprehensive knowledge regarding consumers and their fluctuations in energy consumption.

Conglomerate mergers involve entities that do not compete with one another or with producers who may also be consumers of their output. In the energy sector, the consolidation of conglomerates through mergers, specifically between electricity and gas companies, has been observed to yield positive economic outcomes. These mergers have the potential to provide consumers with energy at competitive prices while simultaneously optimising the associated costs. The consolidation of conglomerates through mergers presents the potential to provide consumers with a diverse array of services while also safeguarding the stability of gas supply required by power companies for electricity generation. Mergers may occur between entities of varying dominance, including both dominant and non-dominant entities, as well as between two dominant entities. The merger between a dominant undertaking and a non-dominant one has the potential to result in the elimination or substantial limitation of existing or potential competition within the market.

The consolidation of the leading entity and the subordinate entity through mergers poses the potential hazard of fortifying the dominant market position. In these instances, an evaluation is conducted to determine if the degree of dominance is significant enough to eliminate any feasible opportunity, even in the event of a merger, to introduce the product into the market. Consequently, an evaluation is conducted to determine if the natural gas company possesses the critical infrastructure, specifically if it serves as the primary provider of natural gas to electricity companies. The research has indicated that the permissibility of such mergers may arise when companies aspire to establish their presence not only within domestic markets but also across international markets. The convergence of the leading gas company and the leading electricity company in merger scenarios is anticipated to result in substantial market constraints. The presence of high levels of market concentration among companies operating in the European Union market exacerbates market restrictions. The mergers of dominant companies in various sectors, specifically within the electricity and gas industries, serve as a prerequisite for the establishment of a singular monopoly entity. These concentrations are permissible solely for the advancement of significant companies or projects, although in the majority of instances, the obligation to divest other activities must be fulfilled.

After a thorough look at how competition law and energy law interact, especially from the merger institute's point of view, it has been found that there are some contradictions between the two. The energy law mandates the divestment of vertically integrated companies. Competition law permits the consolidation of businesses to create vertically integrated enterprises. One potentially problematic scenario arises when companies, while adhering to competition law regulations, fail to simultaneously adhere to the provisions of the energy law.

References

Cameron P (2007) Competition in energy markets, law and regulation in the European Union, 2nd edn. Oxford University Press

Ezrachi A (2016) EU competition law: an analytical guide to the leading cases, 5th edn. Bloomsbury Publishing

Gerber D (2020) Competition law and antitrust. Oxford University Press

Healey D, Jacobs M, Smith LR (2020) Research handbook on methods and models of competition law. Edward Elgar Publishing

Jones C (2012) EU energy law volume II EU competition law and energy markets. Claeys and Casteels

Jones C, Weinert L (2021) EU competition law volume II: mergers and acquisitions. Edward Elgar Publishing

Lianos I, Korah V, Siciliani P (2019) Competition law. Oxford University Press

Posner RA (2019) Antitrust Law. University of Chicago Press

Ritter L, Braun D (2005) European competition law: a Practitioner's guide. Kluwer Law International

Rosenthal M, Thomas S (2010) European merger control. Beck/Hart

Part IV
State Aid and Market Liberalisation

Chapter 11
The Concept of State Aid and Its Application Criteria

Abstract When aiming to achieve market liberalisation objectives, it is essential to find a harmonious equilibrium between the interests of enterprises and consumers. This necessitates considering operators' investments in infrastructure development and improvement, as well as the execution of new projects. In the energy sector, enterprises frequently can receive subsidies, assistance from public resources, or specific tax provisions for their activities. Furthermore, corporations can take advantage of temporary tax advantages while building a project until they have recovered their investment. Countries adopt several techniques to promote the development of renewable energy sources, often including set rates and a variety of incentives. The main goal of the state assistance control system is to ensure the overall integrity of competition, rather than show preference for certain economic entities. Strong competition is critical to ensuring the supply of goods and services at the most reasonable price. State assistance to inefficient enterprises enables their continued existence in the market by displacing non-subsidised entities. The problem occurs when some actions create distortions in market competition by granting certain benefits to corporations that they would not have acquired under normal market conditions.

11.1 Introduction

State aid is a crucial institution that plays a significant role in establishing a competitive internal market, enabling consumers to exercise their choice in selecting an energy supplier that offers competitive prices. When striving to achieve the goals of market liberalisation, it is crucial to strike a balance between the interests of businesses and consumers while also considering the investments made by operators in the development and enhancement of infrastructure as well as the implementation of new projects. The characteristics of this sector entail that a majority of companies' operations have the potential to meet the criteria for receiving subsidies, various types of assistance from state resources, or specific tax provisions. Additionally, these companies may be eligible for temporary tax exemptions during the implementation of a particular project until the company's investment is recovered.

L. Rimšaitė, *The Crossroads of Competition Law and Energy Regulation*,
https://doi.org/10.1007/978-3-031-73238-6_11

Countries employ a diverse range of strategies to facilitate the advancement of renewable energy sources, frequently utilising fixed tariffs and a multitude of incentives.

The incorporation of supranational control was an imperative mechanism to facilitate deeper integration within the European Union, thereby establishing an internal market characterised by the unrestricted movement of goods, capital, services, and individuals. Given the objectives of competition policy, it is imperative to exercise effective oversight over the conduct of private entities and to prevent State intervention from causing market distortions or unfair circumstances. In its initial phase, the Commission held the perspective that any limitation hindered the economic autonomy of the involved parties and was incongruous with the principles of competition law. This was subsequently accompanied by a series of initiatives aimed at promoting market liberalisation and enhancing the efficacy of State aid regulations. In this section of the literature, we will conduct a more comprehensive analysis of the influence exerted by the State aid institution on the process of market liberalisation as well as the imperative for energy infrastructure initiatives. The focus of our discussion will be on the process of modernising state aid with the aim of minimising administrative burdens and enhancing coordination procedures with the Commission.

11.2 The Cumulative Criterions Set Out in Article 107 TFEU

The primary objective of the State aid control system is to safeguard the integrity of competition, prioritising the preservation of effective competition rather than the protection of specific economic operators. This emphasis on fostering robust competition is crucial as it guarantees the availability of goods and services at the most affordable prices.[1] The provision of State aid to inefficient companies allows these entities to persist in the market, thereby displacing other non-subsidised entities. The issue arises when specific measures introduce distortions in market competition by conferring various advantages on companies that they would not have obtained under typical market circumstances.

The primary provisions pertaining to State aid are delineated in Articles 107–109 of the Treaty on the Functioning of the European Union (TFEU). The regulations outlined in Article 107 of the TFEU prohibit the provision of aid in any form from state resources. These regulations also evaluate whether an economic operator has received an economic advantage that would not have been accessible to them under typical market conditions. State intervention has the potential to enhance market functionality and establish conditions for competition in situations where a single

[1] Hancher (2021).

dominant company exists, and new entrants are unable to access the market. The Commission also established a clear distinction regarding the objective of guaranteeing the efficient functioning of the State aid institute.[2] However, it did not explicitly indicate the intended beneficiaries of this efficiency. It remains unclear whether the aim is to safeguard consumers' rights and offer them a range of options or to support competing operators who are unable to compete on a level playing field due to state intervention in the relevant market.

According to Article 107 of the TFEU, any form of financial assistance provided by a Member State or through State resources that distorts or poses a threat to competition by favouring specific businesses or the production of specific goods is considered incompatible with the internal market to the extent that it impacts trade between Member States, unless otherwise specified in the Treaties.[3] The subsequent provisions shall adhere to the principles of compatibility with the internal market. (a) Socially oriented assistance is provided to individual consumers on the condition that such assistance is granted without any form of discrimination based on the origin of the products in question. (b) Assistance aimed at mitigating the consequences of natural disasters or extraordinary events (c) Assistance given to the economies of particular Federal Republic of Germany regions that have suffered as a result of the country's division in order to make up for the economic disadvantages caused by said division. Five years after the Treaty of Lisbon went into effect, the Council has the power to decide to revoke this clause on the basis of a Commission proposal.

The following items can be deemed compatible with the internal market: (a) Assistance aimed at fostering economic development in regions characterised by abnormally low living standards or significant underemployment, as well as in the regions mentioned in Article 349, taking into account their structural, economic, and social circumstances. (b) Support provided to facilitate the implementation of a significant project of shared European interest or to address a severe disruption in the economy of a Member State (c) Aid intended to facilitate the growth of specific economic activities or areas, provided that such assistance does not have an adverse impact on trading conditions that goes against the common interest. (d) Assistance directed towards the preservation of culture and heritage, as long as it does not negatively affect trading conditions and competition within the Union to an extent that contradicts the common interest. (e) Any other forms of aid that may be designated by the Council, upon proposal from the Commission.

The evaluation of the particular measure, if it complies with the requirements set out in Article 107 (1) TFEU, consists of these essential parts:

- The measure must by granted by the State or State resources (the State origin).
- The measure favours certain undertakings (the selectivity);

[2]Communication from the Commission – Guidelines on State aid for climate, environmental protection and energy 2022. C/2022/481.OJ C 80, 18.2.2022, pp. 1–89.

[3]Rust and Micheau (2012).

- The measure needs to grant the advantage to certain undertakings over other (advantage).
- The measure affects trade and competition (effect on trade and competition).

In order for a specific measure to be classified as state aid, it is necessary for all of these cumulative conditions to be satisfied. If the action is classified as state aid, it is necessary to assess its compliance with the internal market and notify the Commission prior to its implementation.

The requirement for notification is waived if the assistance is subject to the block exemption or falls within the de minimis threshold, specifically not exceeding EUR 200,000 per company over a three-year fiscal period. Additionally, if the aid is granted under a scheme that has already been approved by the Commission, notification is also exempt.

According to Article 108 of the TFEU, the European Commission is responsible for continuously monitoring all forms of state aid within Member governments in collaboration with such governments. The proposal will suggest to the latter any suitable actions necessary for the ongoing advancement or effective operation of the internal market.[4] If, following the notification to the relevant parties to provide their comments, the Commission determines that financial assistance provided by a state or through state resources is inconsistent with the internal market as outlined in Article 107 or that such assistance is being improperly utilised, the Commission will conclude that the state in question must eliminate or modify the assistance within a timeframe determined by the Commission.[5]

In the event that the state in question fails to adhere to this decision within the specified timeframe, the Commission or any other relevant state may, contrary to the provisions outlined in Articles 258 and 259, bring the matter directly to the Court of Justice of the European Union.

Upon submission of an application by a Member State, the Council has the authority to unanimously determine that the financial assistance being provided or planned by that State is in line with the internal market, despite any conflicts with the regulations outlined in Article 107 or the regulations specified in Article 109. This decision may be warranted in situations that are deemed exceptional. If the Commission has already commenced the procedure outlined in the first subparagraph of this paragraph with regards to the aid in question, the submission of the state's application to the Council will result in the suspension of said procedure until the Council has expressed its position.

In the event that the Council has not communicated its stance within a three-month period subsequent to the submission of the aforementioned application, the Commission will be responsible for rendering a judgement on the matter. The Commission must be notified in a timely manner, allowing for the submission of

[4] Ahlborn and Berg (2004).

[5] Rydelski (2006).

views regarding any intentions to provide or modify financial assistance.[6] If it determines that any such plan is inconsistent with the internal market in accordance with Article 107, it must promptly commence the procedure outlined in paragraph 2. The implementation of the proposed measures by the Member State in question is prohibited until the completion of this procedure, which will culminate in a definitive decision. The Commission has the authority to establish regulations pertaining to the types of state aid that the Council, in accordance with Article 109, has considered eligible for exemption from the procedure outlined in paragraph 3 of this Article.

A preliminary investigation by the Commission precedes each notification. Upon receiving the formal notification, the Commission has a period of 3 months to determine whether the aid in question falls outside the scope of the TFEU, is compatible with EU regulations, or raises significant concerns about its compatibility and necessitates further in-depth investigation. In the event that a Member State has implemented a state aid measure without obtaining prior authorization from the Commission, it possesses the authority to make a determination about the recovery of the incompatible state aid. In the subsequent chapter, we will provide additional elucidation on the criteria for notification that establish a measure as state aid, as well as the corresponding measures for compatibility.

11.2.1 The Selectivity

Selectivity is a key criterion used to evaluate State aid, as it pertains to the extent to which a measure provides an advantage to a specific economic operator, thereby differentiating it from other participants in the market. The State aid measure should prioritise specific undertakings through a selective approach or categorization. The measures that are universally applicable to all enterprises are not encompassed within the purview of Article 107 (1) of the TFEU. The classification of a measure as a State aid measure persists as long as it is not universally applicable to all economic sectors or undertakings, regardless of whether it is targeted at specific economic activities or a group of undertakings. The aid measure can be classified as either de jure, which involves the establishment of legal criteria for its applicability, or de facto, where the measure is not explicitly restricted by legal provisions but is effectively designed for specific undertakings.

The examination of the Hungarian and Polish cases, as well as the Greek lignite case,[7] holds significance in evaluating the advantages derived from the provided assistance. The Public Power Corporation S.A., a state-owned entity in Greece, has been accused of violating Articles 102 and 106 of the TFEU in relation to its

[6] Stiglitz (2011).

[7] Commission Decision in Case COMP/39.730 – Greek Lignite Case.

monopoly over lignite mining.[8] The Hellenic Republic has authorised the company to possess exclusive rights for the exploitation of lignite, resulting in an unequal distribution of access among economic operators to utilise this essential primary fuel for electricity production. The aforementioned circumstances facilitated the consolidation of Public Power Corporation S.A.'s prevailing market position while simultaneously impeding the entry of new competitors. The European Commission has recommended that the Hellenic Republic take steps to clearly define measures aimed at addressing the anti-competitive practises exhibited by the company towards other firms. Consequently, the government initiated a process to carry out a public procurement procedure for the allocation of operational privileges pertaining to the remaining 40% of the lignite reserves located in the Drama, Ellasona, and Vegora regions. This opportunity was extended to potential competitors of Public Power Corporation S.A. It is worth mentioning that the provision of lignite extracted from these deposits to Public Power Corporation SA should have been withheld until the corporation obtained the legal authority to exploit over 60% of all lignite deposits in the Hellenic Republic. Merely implementing a specific measure for a particular group does not guarantee the absence of selectivity.

In the Maribel case,[9] the Court of Justice of the European Union (CJEU) determined that the presence of numerous entities and the wide range of activities conducted by these companies did not justify the application of a general measure. The Commission has previously asserted that specific measures pertaining to the relevant sector may not be subject to selectivity. In the Enirisorse case,[10] the Italian Government granted authorization to ENI, ENEL, and ENEA to establish a collaborative public limited liability company called Sotacarbo SpA. The primary objective of this venture was to advance technological innovations within the coal industry, specifically in the areas of oxidation techniques, gasification, enrichment, and organic chemistry. The establishment of the company, which carries out the aforementioned activities, was intended to be facilitated by legislation governing the financing sector. This legislation would outline the allocation of funds from government authorities and establish provisions for the utilisation of the reserve fund. Furthermore, the aforementioned legislation stipulated that the entities ENI and ENEL possessed the option to disengage from the organisation by remunerating their respective ownership interests. The shareholders of the recently established company consisted of state-owned entities, namely ENI, ENEL, and the state institution ENEA. The establishment of the company was financially supported by state funds. These measures have yielded comparable outcomes to the provision of direct financial assistance to corporations by the government. In the current situation, the shareholders were provided with the option to disengage from Sotacarbo SpA without receiving any compensation for their ownership stake. Consequently, the

[8] Antitrust: Commission market tests measures proposed by Greece concerning the Greek electricity market European Commission - IP/11/34 14/01/2011.

[9] Case C-204/00, Maribel.

[10] Joined cases C-34/01 to C-38/01 *Enirisorse SpA v Ministero delle Finanze*. [2003] ECR I-14243.

legislation did not aim to decrease the company's expenses that it would have otherwise borne and thus did not bestow any favourable treatment upon the company.

The CJEU determined that in cases where a legal provision allowed for an exception to the customary legal principles, the act of shareholders withdrawing from a newly established company by transferring all rights to the company's assets did not qualify as State aid.

11.2.2 The State Resources

Another criterion that determines the presence of State aid is that the assistance was provided using resources originating from the State. State aid can be attributed to the State not only when it directly owns the resources but also indirectly or when it has the authority to make decisions regarding the resources through the issuance of various legislative documents. In the latter scenario, the State possesses the capacity to allocate resources towards a specific endeavour, thereby providing assistance.[11] The provision of assistance may also be extended by a public or private entity that has been established by the government to oversee the distribution of aid. The notion of the State is comprehensively defined and encompasses governing bodies at the national, regional, and municipal levels that exercise authority in determining the allocation of assistance.

The matter under consideration was expounded upon in the PreussenElektra case,[12] wherein electricity distribution companies were mandated to procure a predetermined minimum quantity of electricity generated from renewable energy sources. Additionally, electricity generators utilising fossil fuels were required to partially indemnify the distribution networks for any resulting losses. The private electricity supply companies were mandated to procure electricity from renewable energy sources, and this requirement was accompanied by a minimum price for such procurement. However, it is important to note that the scheme was not directly administered by the State and did not utilise State resources.

Another crucial aspect pertains to the recipients of this obligation, namely the private electricity suppliers in question. The procurement of a specific quantity of electricity from external private power generators was necessary. Despite being required by state law and providing certain groups of entities with undeniable benefits, the measure does not meet the criteria for direct state involvement. The

---

[11] Case 82/77, *Van Tiggele*, ECLI:EU:C:1978:10, paras 25 and 26; Case T-358/94, *Air France v Commission*, ECLI:EU:T:1996:194, para 63; Case T-358/94, *Air France v Commission*, ECLI:EU:T:1996:194, para 56; Case C-482/99 *France v Commission (Stardust)*, ECLI:EU:C:2002:294, para 38; Case C-278/00 *Greece v Commission*, ECLI:EU:C:2004:239, paras 53 and 54; Joined Cases C-328/99 and C-399/00 *Italy and SIM 2 Multimedia SpA v Commission*, ECLI:EU:C:2003:252, paras 33 and 34.

[12] Case C-379/98, *PreussenElektra AG*, [2001] ECR I-2099.

determining factor in the current situation was the management and allocation of resources. It is important to acknowledge that the taxes paid by consumers to a specific public authority can be considered resources of the State.

In the case of PreussenElektra, the involvement of the State was relatively restricted. The State imposed certain requirements, such as the obligation to procure electricity, the establishment of a minimum fixed price, and the identification of private electricity suppliers and producers as the beneficiaries of this financial obligation. The company made direct payments in accordance with its obligation to procure electricity generated from renewable energy sources. Consequently, there was no involvement of any public authority in the administration of these payments within this scheme. The aforementioned case established a precedent wherein a particular measure is to be regarded as State aid. The Court of Justice of the European Union (CJEU) has previously established in its early legal precedents that appropriate measures can be regarded as a type of State aid. The Court in Case C-206/06[13] determined that the Member State did not select the undertakings involved to oversee a state resource. However, the Court concluded that the financing, which was obtained through a surcharge imposed by the state on electricity buyers and controlled by the member state, should be considered a state intervention using state resources.

As previously mentioned, if a state measure obligates private economic operators to provide a specific advantage to another company using their own financial resources instead of appointing them to manage state resources, this measure will not satisfy the requirement of state resources and, therefore, will not fall under Article 107, paragraph 1, TFEU. Under such circumstances, the private economic operators will be responsible for shouldering the financial costs associated with the policy. Several instances in the case law demonstrate the application of this approach, particularly in the context of renewable energy support schemes that entail purchasing obligations. PreussenElektra (2001) and ENEA (2017)[14] exemplify the first branch of legal precedent, which denies the use of state resources, while Essent (2008) and Vent de Colère (2013)[15] exemplify the second branch, which confirms the use of state resources.

Those lines of legal precedent pose a challenge in clarifying the precise distinction between state and private resources, as well as the unique factual circumstances that set them apart, as the court rulings consistently fail to provide these details. In the context of ENEA, particularly in the cases of Essent and Vent de Colère, the Court of Justice underscored the importance of ascertaining whether end-users can fully bear the additional expenses arising from a purchase obligation, or if the state's mandatory contribution or a comprehensive offset mechanism funds them. The Court of Justice has classified renewable energy support mechanisms and measures as either state aid or not, based on minor structural differences. Different

[13] Case C-206/06, Essent Netwerk Noord and Other, [2008] ECR I-5497.

[14] Case C-329/15 ENEA [2017] ECLI-971.

[15] Case C-262/12 Association Vent De Colere [2013] ECLI-851.

classifications apply to these measures, even though they grant similar advantages to beneficiaries and have similar economic effects. According to established legal precedent, Article 107, paragraph 1, of the Treaty on the Functioning of the European Union (TFEU) does not differentiate between different types of government involvement based on their reasons, objectives, or methods of regulation. Instead, it defines them based on their outcomes or impacts. Some argue that a narrow interpretation of the state resources criterion could lead to a potential violation of EU state aid regulations. This is because it could allow EU Member States to provide a selective advantage to certain beneficiaries by imposing obligations on private parties instead of using the state budget. On the other hand, relying solely on the effects of renewable energy support mechanisms (or other measures) may weaken the requirement for state resources.

However, if these measures do not satisfy the criteria set forth by the CJEU, they are not covered by the provisions of the TFEU and cannot be classified as State aid under the definition provided in this article. While it is not possible to evaluate the effectiveness of the current measures in the context of State aid, it is important to acknowledge that the implementation of such a scheme could potentially impact the free movement of goods within the European Union. The justification for implementing that measure was also grounded in the context of the free movement of goods, as it encompassed considerations of environmental requirements and the imperative to implement the measure to attain those objectives.

11.2.3 The Economic Advantage

The advantage criteria refer to the allocation of a benefit to a project that would not have been granted under typical market conditions. It is important to acknowledge that an economic advantage can encompass not only the provision of a grant but also the alleviation of existing obligations.[16] The concept of advantage is assessed based on the specific circumstances of the undertaking without incorporating any additional measures.

The principle of the market investor is employed when assessing the benefits conferred upon a particular endeavour. This assessment holds significance when determining whether specific measures were in accordance with the prevailing market conditions, as failure to meet this criterion would exclude the measure from being classified as State aid.[17] The assessment involves the application of the market economy operator test, specifically examining whether the economic

[16]Case C-39/94, *SFEI and Others*, ECLI:EU:C:1996:285, para 60; Case C-342/96, Spain v Commission, ECLI:EU:C:1999:210, para 41.

[17]Case C-142/87, *Belgium v Commission ('Tubemeuse')*, ECLI:EU: C:1990:125, para 29; Case C-305/89, *Italy v Commission ('ALFA Romeo')*, ECLI:EU: C:1991:142, paras 18 and 19; Case T-16/96 Cityflyer Express v Commission, ECLI:EU: T:1998:78, para 51; Joined Cases T-129/95, T-2/96 and T-97/96, *Neue Maxhütte Stahlwerke and Lech-Stahlwerke v Commission*, ECLI:EU:

operator would have acted similarly under the given circumstances. Furthermore, an assessment of the venture's profitability is conducted in this instance. In this evaluation, it is crucial to assess whether the State authorities have functioned as market operators and whether the outcomes achieved by the undertaking would have been identical had a market investor been in place instead of the State body.

11.2.4 The Distortion of Competition and Effect on Trade Between Member States

If a measure is granted by the State or utilises its resources in a manner that distorts competition, it is deemed to have the potential to threaten competition and must adhere to the criteria outlined in Article 107(1) of the TFEU. The potential distortion of competition is more likely to arise in sectors that have been liberalised, as these sectors allow for competition among market participants.[18] However, when State aid is granted, it confers a specific undertaking with a more advantageous position compared to other participants in the same market. The assessment of competition distortion is conducted even in instances where the business entity is of a diminutive scale or possesses a negligible market share, or even when the possibility of distortion is purely hypothetical.[19] This implies that the Commission would assess these cases as potential sources of competition distortion. This is particularly significant if the recipient of the State aid is able to acquire additional market share or achieve a more favourable market position as a direct result of the implemented measure.

The legitimacy of delegating specific services to in-house providers is determined by the fulfilment of certain requirements as outlined in Article 107(1) of the TFEU. These requirements include: the service in question being of a monopolistic nature, having been established and operating in compliance with EU law; the monopoly effectively excluding any potential competition in the market; the service not engaging in competition with other services; and the exclusion of cross-subsidisation if the service provider is active in another market.

The final criterion utilised in the assessment of State aid pertains to its impact on trade among Member States. It is important to acknowledge that State aid can potentially impact trade even in cases where the recipient does not engage in commercial activities with other states but rather operates solely within a single state. The trade impact assessment does not necessitate the Commission to conduct an extensive economic analysis of the market, encompassing factors such as market participants, market share, trade flows, beneficiaries, potential competitors in the

T:1999:7, para 104; Joined Cases T-228/99 and T-233/99, *Westdeutsche Landesbank Girozentrale and Land Nordrhein-Westfalen v Commission,* ECLI:EU: T:2003:57.

[18] Healey et al. (2020).

[19] Case C280/00, *Altmark Trans*, ECLI:EU:C:2003:415, para 79.

market, and the impact of the aid on prices. The trade impact assessment encompasses an examination of the potential trade effects, which include the enhancement of the beneficiary's financial standing and its market presence within the European Union and the global arena, as well as the potential decline in market shares of competitors. The impact on trade not necessarily need to be tangible as the Commission also assesses the potential effects on trade between Member States.

After a concise discussion of these criteria, we will proceed to analyse the distinct types of State aid, the legislation that was introduced and approved during the process of modernization, and the outcomes of the streamlining of administrative procedures and their subsequent influence on the execution of energy infrastructure projects. The advantage criteria refer to the provision of a benefit to a project or endeavour that would not typically be granted under prevailing market conditions. It is important to acknowledge that an economic advantage can encompass not only the provision of a grant but also the alleviation of current obligations. The concept of advantage is assessed based on the specific circumstances of the undertaking without considering any additional factors.

The principle of the market investor is employed when assessing the benefits conferred upon a particular venture. The significance of this test lies in its ability to assess whether specific measures were implemented in accordance with prevailing market conditions. In instances where this criterion is not met, the measure in question would not be classified as State aid. The assessment involves the application of the market economy operator test, specifically examining whether the economic operator would have behaved similarly under the given circumstances. Furthermore, an assessment of the venture's profitability is conducted in this instance. In this assessment, it is crucial to evaluate whether the State authorities have functioned as market operators and determine if the outcome of the undertaking would have been comparable had a market investor been involved instead of the State entity.

11.3 Temporary Crisis Framework for State Aid Measures

The State Aid Temporary Crisis Framework was agreed upon by the Commission on March 23, 2022.[20] Its purpose is to provide Member States with the necessary flexibility under state aid regulations to offer economic support in response to Russia's invasion of Ukraine. The Temporary Crisis Framework encompasses many forms of assistance that Member States might allocate, including the following:

[20] Communication from the Commission – Second amendment to the Temporary Crisis and Transition Framework for State Aid measures to support the economy following the aggression against Ukraine by Russia. C/2024/3123. OJ C, C/2024/3113, 2.5.2024.

The suggested measures entail giving companies operating in the agriculture, fisheries, and aquaculture sectors that have suffered from the crisis limited financial assistance, not to exceed EUR 35,000. Similarly, companies in all other sectors affected by the crisis may receive aid up to EUR 400,000 per company. Additionally, the plan includes offering liquidity support through state guarantees and subsidised loans. Furthermore, aid will be provided to compensate for the elevated energy prices. The assistance, which may be provided in several modalities, aims to partially reimburse businesses, particularly those with high energy use, for the supplementary expenses resulting from extraordinary hikes in gas and electricity prices. The aggregate assistance per recipient must not exceed 30% of the qualified expenses, with a cap of EUR two million at any one juncture. In the event that a company has operating losses, it may become necessary to seek additional assistance in order to sustain the ongoing economic activity. Hence, in the case of energy-intensive consumers, the levels of aid intensity are elevated, allowing Member States to provide aid that surpasses the established thresholds, reaching a maximum of EUR 25 million. Similarly, for enterprises operating within sectors and sub-sectors that experience significant adverse effects, the aid limit can be extended up to EUR 50 million. The measures will not apply to organisations under Russian control that have been officially authorised.

The proposed methodology is based on proportionality, which entails establishing a connection between the level of financial assistance that firms can receive and their economic activity and susceptibility to the economic ramifications of the crisis. The eligibility parameters encompass the determination of energy-intensive consumers, specifically referring to enterprises whose expenditure on energy products constitutes a minimum of 3% of their overall production value. Additionally, sustainability considerations are also included in the criteria. Member States are encouraged to impartially contemplate the establishment of criteria pertaining to environmental preservation or guaranteeing a stable energy supply while providing financial assistance to address the additional expenses incurred as a result of abnormally elevated gas and electricity prices. The Temporary Crisis Framework was scheduled to remain in effect until December 31, 2022. In order to guarantee legal clarity, the Commission will evaluate prior to the specified date whether an extension is necessary. Furthermore, throughout the implementation phase, the Commission will continuously evaluate the substance and extent of the framework in response to advancements in the energy markets, other input markets, and the overall economic landscape.

The Temporary Crisis Framework serves as a valuable addition to the extensive range of options available to Member States for formulating actions that adhere to the established state aid regulations of the European Union.[21] EU state aid rules provide Member States with the ability to assist enterprises in managing liquidity

---

[21] Communication from the Commission – Second amendment to the Temporary Crisis and Transition Framework for State Aid measures to support the economy following the aggression against Ukraine by Russia. C/2024/3123. OJ C, C/2024/3113, 2.5.2024.

challenges and accessing urgent emergency relief. Moreover, it should be noted that Article 107(2)(b) of the Treaty on the Functioning of the European Union grants Member States the authority to provide compensation to enterprises for the direct harm inflicted by extraordinary events, such as those arising from the ongoing crisis.

11.4 Conclusion

In the pursuit of market liberalisation goals, it is crucial to strike a balance between the interests of businesses and consumers. This necessitates considering the investments made by operators in the development and enhancement of infrastructure, as well as the implementation of new projects. The energy sector exhibits a notable characteristic wherein numerous activities undertaken by companies may be eligible for subsidies, various forms of support from state resources, or specific tax provisions. Additionally, companies may benefit from temporary tax exemptions for the duration of a project's development, until the company's investment is recouped. Nations employ diverse strategies to facilitate the advancement of renewable energy sources, frequently incorporating fixed tariffs and a range of incentives.

The primary objective of the State aid control system is to safeguard competition as a whole rather than favour specific economic operators. This is because the presence of robust competition is crucial for ensuring the availability of goods and services at the most affordable prices. The provision of State aid to inefficient companies facilitates their survival in the market by displacing other entities that do not benefit from government assistance. The issue arises when specific measures introduce distortions in market competition by providing various advantages to companies that they would not have obtained under typical market circumstances.

The evaluation of the specific measure encompasses several crucial components: firstly, the measure must be authorised by the State or funded by State resources; secondly, it must confer benefits upon specific undertakings; thirdly, it must provide an advantage; and finally, it must have an impact on trade and competition among the Member States. In order for the measure to be considered State aid, all of these requirements must be met in combination. Furthermore, it is imperative to assess the compatibility of the measure with the regulations set forth by European Union law and ensure that it is duly notified in advance.

In order to be assessed as State aid, the measure must possess a selective nature, thereby conferring advantages on a specific market participant and setting it apart from others. The measure should exhibit preferential treatment for specific undertakings or categories, whereas measures that are applicable to all undertakings do not fall within the scope of State aid provisions. The classification of a measure as a State aid measure persists as long as it is not universally applicable to all economic sectors or undertakings, regardless of whether it is targeted at specific economic activities or a group of undertakings.

The second criterion is imputability to the State, which refers to the extent to which the State can be held responsible. This measure is applicable to the State not only when it has direct ownership of the resources but also when it has indirect ownership or when it has the authority to make decisions regarding the resources through the issuance of legislative documents. In the latter scenario, the State possesses the capacity to allocate resources towards a specific endeavour, thereby providing assistance. The provision of assistance may also be extended by a public or private entity that has been established by the government to oversee the distribution of aid.

The advantage criteria refer to the provision of a benefit to the undertaking that would not have been granted under typical market conditions. It is crucial to acknowledge that an economic advantage can encompass not only the provision of a grant with positive economic implications but also the alleviation of existing obligations. The concept of advantage is assessed based on the specific circumstances of the endeavour without considering any additional factors. The principle of the market investor is utilised in the assessment of the benefits conferred upon a particular endeavour. The significance of this test lies in its ability to assess whether specific measures are in accordance with normal market conditions. In cases where this condition is met, the measure in question is not regarded as State aid. The assessment involves the application of the market economy operator test, specifically examining whether the economic operator would have behaved similarly under the given circumstances. Furthermore, the assessment of the venture's profitability is conducted in this scenario. In this assessment, it is crucial to evaluate whether the State authorities have functioned as market operators and whether the outcomes achieved by the undertaking would have been identical had a market investor replaced the State entity.

The potential distortion of competition is more likely to manifest in liberalised sectors where market participants engage in competition. However, the provision of State aid confers a comparative advantage on a specific undertaking, placing it in a more favourable position relative to other participants in that particular market. The assessment of competition distortion is conducted even in instances where the enterprise is of a diminutive scale, possesses a minimal market share, or when such a scenario is purely hypothetical. This does not imply that the Commission would refrain from assessing such cases as a potential source of competition distortion. This becomes particularly significant if the recipient of the State aid is able to acquire additional market share or achieve a more favourable market position that would not have been possible without the implementation of the measure in question.

The final criterion utilised in the evaluation of State aid pertains to its impact on trade between Member States. It is important to acknowledge that State aid can have an impact on trade, even in cases where the recipient of the aid does not engage in commercial activities with other states but rather operates solely within one state. The trade impact assessment does not necessitate the Commission to conduct an extensive economic analysis of the market, encompassing factors such as market participants, market share, trade flows, beneficiaries, their potential competitors in the market, and the impact of the aid on prices. The trade impact assessment encompasses an examination of the potential consequences of trade, which encompass the enhancement of the beneficiary's financial standing and its market presence within the European Union and global markets, as well as the potential decline in market shares of competitors. The impact on trade need not necessarily be tangible; the Commission also assesses the potential effects on trade between Member States.

The satisfaction of the stipulated criteria for European Union State aid as outlined in Article 107(1) of the TFEU typically leads to the incompatibility of State aid, thereby resulting in its ban. There are two distinct categories of exceptions to this restriction. One potential aspect is that a general exemption can be used as a sort of exclusion for a specific measure. Another argument is that the action can be justified based on an exception provided by the Commission, which serves to justify this prohibition. The outcomes remain unchanged. In both instances, the requirement to inform the measure to and acquire consent from the Commission in accordance with the initial clause of Article 108(3) TFEU is not applicable (the act of informing and obtaining consent collectively constitutes the notification procedure). Hence, the utilisation of state funds for the activity may be carried out without the requirement of a notice procedure.

De Minimis Regulation (EU) No. 1407/2013 and the General Block Exemption Regulation (EU) No. 651/2014 (GBER) contain provisions that outline the exemptions available under EU state assistance standards. The General Block Exemption Regulation (GBER) encompasses specific provisions for research and development activities, as outlined in Article 25 and subsequent articles of the GBER. Furthermore, it is worth noting that exemptions from the European Union's prohibition on state aid may be granted to enterprises that offer services of general economic interest. The basis for this exception is derived from the Altmark Trans judgement and the Almunia exemption. This decision is a component of the Almunia package. It is necessary for the entities involved in the aforementioned activities, as recipients of the assistance, to have been entrusted by the supplier of help with the responsibility of delivering these services. In the event that a state measure satisfies the established criteria for European Union state aid and no exemptions are applicable, the measure must be formally communicated to the Commission through a notification procedure. The Commission thereafter evaluates whether the measure qualifies as state aid and if it can be authorised under the exceptions outlined in Article 107(2) and (3) of the TFEU or under specific regulations.

References

Ahlborn C, Berg C (2004) Can state aid control learn from antitrust? The need for a greater role for competition analysis under the state aid rules. In: Biondi A, Eeckhout P, Flynn J (eds) The law of state aid in the European Union. Oxford University Press, Oxford, pp 41–66

Hancher L (2021) EU state aids. Sweet and Maxwell

Healey D, Jacobs M, Smith LR (2020) Research handbook on methods and models of competition law. Edward Elgar Publishing
Rust A, Micheau C (2012) State aid and tax law. Wolters and Kluwer
Rydelski M (2006) The EC state aid regime—distortive effects of state aid on competition and trade, Cameron May
Stiglitz JE (2011) Economics of the public sector 3rd Revised edn. W.W. Norton & Co

Chapter 12
State Aid Form and Practice in the Field of Energy

Abstract The motivation to attract investment in the renewable energy industry stems from both the consequences of climate change and the progress of innovative technology. Member States employ a variety of approaches to encourage and entice new investments in renewable energy. These strategies involve optimising licensing procedures, simplifying restrictions for grid access, and setting electricity purchase pricing. Energy infrastructure projects often employ a variety of tactics, including government-backed loan guarantees, incorporating investment expenses into tariff structures, and implementing targeted tax incentives and fair returns. When an organisation embarks on a new infrastructure project and encounters significant upfront costs, they acknowledge Power Purchase Agreements (PPAs) as a method to ensure a positive financial result. The examination of applicable legal precedents reveals a discriminatory grant of certain advantages, even when they extend to an entire industry instead of a single economic unit. The act of a state ratifying international conventions by setting a minimal responsibility requirement for operators and guaranteeing the rest of the obligation through State aid demonstrates the features of the latter. However, given that the legislation is based on international law, the issue of informing the Commission about such assistance remains unresolved.

12.1 Introduction

In the previous section, we examined the general criteria for the application of State aid and the case law of the Court of Justice of the European Union (CJEU) on the application and assessment of specific provisions. In the following part, we will analyse specific forms of State aid in the energy sector. The extent to which a measure constitutes State aid and the measures considered compatible with the internal market are criteria for justifying the application of these State aid measures. We will look in greater detail at the financing model for the UK's Hinkley Point C nuclear power plant, applying price difference agreements, addressing civil liability for nuclear damage, with a certain liability limit for the nuclear power plant operator and an obligation to cover a certain amount to the state. The cases of LNG terminals,

L. Rimšaitė, *The Crossroads of Competition Law and Energy Regulation*,
https://doi.org/10.1007/978-3-031-73238-6_12

aid to energy efficiency projects, promotion of renewables, and some operational aid cases will be examined.

The aid granted may, depending on its intensity, fall within the scope of the Block Exemption Regulation or be declared compatible with the internal market by the Commission in accordance with the Treaty on the Functioning of the European Union (TFEU).[1] State aid takes various forms, including a State guarantee, tax benefits, subsidies, and other forms that confer an advantage on an economic operator. State guarantees may be provided on an individual basis or under harmonised schemes. Also included in this group is the share of the State in the company when the company is transformed into another form. The provision of aid in the form of a guarantee can help to set up or develop a business and, instead of being wound up, to continue in business in a difficult financial situation. When the State provides a guarantee to a company or grants the loan, the other companies are in a relatively worse position, which can affect trade and distort the market. The valuation of the benefit is based on the private investor principle, which assesses whether a private investor would agree to invest in a particular company on the same terms in private equity markets. Accordingly, the beneficiary's ability to obtain a loan under normal market conditions is also assessed. If the guarantee does not comply with the market economy investor principle, it is likely to fulfil the State aid criteria. The State aid case must therefore be examined individually; that is to say, the aid element is assessed on the basis of the difference between the corresponding market price of the guarantee granted individually and under the scheme and the price paid for that guarantee.

The provisions relating to direct business taxation do not constitute State aid within the meaning of the TFEU. When a tax is levied on all undertakings in that country, the measure falls outside the scope of the TFEU as it does not meet the selectivity criterion. It is assessed whether the tax provisions confer an exceptional economic advantage on certain economic operators. The fact that the measures are applied differently does not yet imply that they meet the State aid criteria under the TFEU. The Member State must justify that certain measures are necessary to ensure the functioning and effectiveness of the tax system. Provisions for tax incentives for general activities, without being linked to the implementation of specific projects, reduce the company's current costs, which makes it difficult for the Commission to determine exactly how much such costs have been reduced. These measures qualify as operating aid, which is prohibited in principle. The Commission shall authorise such aid only in exceptional cases where this is necessary for the improvement of the environment or the development of particularly remote areas. Such aid should be

[1]Regulation (EU) No 651/2014 of 17 June 2014, on the application of Articles 107 and 108 of the Treaty on the Functioning of the European Union to categories of aid. Official Journal L 187, 26.06.2014, p. 1–78. Consolidated Version of the Treaty on the Functioning of the European Union, Article 107(3). Official Journal C 326, 26.10.2012, p. 47–390. Commission Regulation (EU) No 1407/2013 of 18 December 2013 on the application of Articles 107 and 108 of the Treaty on the Functioning of the European Union to de minimis aid. Official Journal L 352, 24.12.2013, p. 1–8.

degressive and limited in time. In this context, the Stadtwerke Schwaebisch Hall GmbH[2] case is relevant, where the creation of a reserve fund for the decommissioning of a nuclear power plant was justified by rapid improvements in safety standards and a certain lack of information on the future costs of decommissioning a nuclear power plant. In this case, the provision was adopted according to which companies that go beyond EU standards in their activities could be supported. The use of a particular tax measure may also be justified for environmental reasons.

In *AEM v. Autorita per l'Energy elettrica e per il gas,*[3] a tax measure increasing the tax rate paid to owners of geothermal and hydroelectric power grid companies was introduced. This measure, which has been used to exercise the right of access to electricity distribution companies, was appropriate for the promotion of renewable energy, taking into account the transitional period for implementing the requirements of the first energy package. From an environmental point of view, it is also worth mentioning the Adria-Wien case,[4] which sought to exempt industrial companies that had to pay energy taxes in excess of 0.35% of the value of their output. Such a tax advantage was not justified by the CJEU pursuant to the environmental standards because, whether the activities carried out were public services or purely industrial activities, they did not guarantee the provision of public services.

After discussing the general criteria and priorities for the application of State aid, we will further elaborate on specific projects in the energy sector that have been granted or will be granted.

12.2 The Promotion of Nuclear Power Plant Project

The restructuring of the electricity sector in the United Kingdom has had a substantial effect on the development of low-carbon technologies, including nuclear technology, in the European Union. The UK nuclear power plant project was chosen for the study in order to elaborate on its financing analysis, which is crucial for the Commission's ongoing approach to technology neutrality, energy incentives, Member States' right to balance their energy supply, and security of supply.[5] The Commission emphasises that the internal energy market remains an unachieved priority objective. The Communication from the Commission on a Roadmap for Transitioning to a Competitive Low Carbon Economy in 2050 seeks to reduce the

---

[2]Case C-176/06, *Stadtwerke Schwäbisch Hall GmbH, Stadtwerke Tübingen GmbH, Stadtwerke Uelzen GmbH v Commission.* [2006] ECR I-00170.

[3]Joined Cases C-128/03 and C-129/03, *AEM Spa and AEM v Autorita per l'energia elettrica e per il gas.* [2003] ECR I-2886.

[4]Case C-143/99, *Adria-Wien Pipeline GmbH and Wietersdorfer and Peggauer Zementwerke GmbH I Finanzlandesdirektion für Kärnten.* [1999] ECR I-8384.

[5]Zhu (2020).

use of fossil fuels by replacing them with electricity while pursuing smart grids with a greater emphasis on the development of renewable energy.[6] According to the OECD, nuclear power is the second-greatest source of low-carbon energy after hydropower. However, the proportion of nuclear energy depends on a number of variables, including national energy policy, the economic and investment climate, public support, and measures to promote renewable energy technologies.[7]

One-fifth of all power generation capacity in the United Kingdom had to be shut down by 2020, necessitating substantial investments to make up for the resultant electricity shortage. Long-term, the demand for electricity may double while the market sends very ambiguous signals regarding increased investment in low-carbon electricity generation. In accordance with existing international agreements, the United Kingdom sought to reduce its greenhouse gas emissions by generating new low-carbon energy capacity. Due to the dearth of investment certainty and the excessive volatility of the wholesale price, the United Kingdom did not see market opportunities to attract investors. An attempt is being made to establish a rather controversial mechanism to finance the nuclear power plant project: a financial derivative called contracts for difference, designed to guarantee investment returns. In accordance with this legal framework, such a financing mechanism must be coordinated with and approved by the Commission in order for the State aid measure to be implemented.

Reform of the British electricity market was initiated in 2011 with the intention of achieving climate change policy objectives and encouraging investment in low-carbon electricity technologies.[8] The purpose of this reform was to assure the reliability of the electricity supply by promoting the diversification of energy sources, reducing associated costs, and mandating the use of low-carbon technologies for electricity generation.[9] Such modifications have been implemented to ensure the prevention of potential power disruptions and to enable consumers to obtain electricity at affordable rates. Currently, the only example of a CFD (contracts for difference) system in the world can be found in Canada, which has failed to bring this mechanism closer to market conditions in the past 20 years. It is essential to observe that CFDs are not only concerned with nuclear power but also with all low-carbon technologies. It should be noted that the strike price was intended to be applied for 35 years to nuclear power plant initiatives and 15 years to renewable energy development.[10] This duration was determined based on the lifespan of the various technological facilities and accounts for approximately 6% of the total

[6]Communication from the Commission to the European Parliament, the Council, the European Economic and Social Committee and the Committee of the Regions: A Roadmap for Moving to a Competitive Low Carbon Economy in 2050. COM (2011) 112 final.

[7]Organisation for Economic Co-operation and Development (OECD), Nuclear Energy and the Environment: Insights on Policy and Economics, (OECD Publishing, 2021).

[8]Electricity Market Reform White Paper. Cm 8099. 2011.

[9]Ruechardt (2018).

[10]Electricity Market Reform: Contracts for Difference. UK Government CfD Scheme.2014.

investments. Once per month, the strike price is evaluated and indexed for nuclear power facilities. Long-term, the British government has expressed a desire to transition the nuclear field from direct intervention to a market-based economy.

Similar incentives exist in the renewable energy industry. The effects of climate change and the advancement of new cutting-edge technologies are the driving forces behind investment in the renewable energy sector. To attract new investment in renewable energy, Member States implement a number of measures, including simplified licencing procedures, simplified grid access rules, and the establishment of electricity purchase prices. Typical measures included in energy infrastructure projects are a government guarantee for bank loans, the incorporation of investment costs in tariffs, specific tax incentives, and reasonable returns. When an entity develops a new infrastructure project and incurs high initial costs, power purchase agreements are also considered a means of ensuring a return on investment.

Such incentives are founded on ensuring low carbon emissions and are permitted for renewable energy projects. However, despite its stated intention to combat climate change, the EU has not adopted such incentives for nuclear projects. In this context, the United Kingdom's proposal to apply price difference agreements for nuclear energy, namely the fixed prices required to assure the project's return on investment, was viewed as controversial. The same situation arose when a fixed price was applied to the financing of renewable energy projects, as the measure was deemed to be justified by the new and emergent technologies and did not give rise to concerns of unlawful State aid under Article 107 (1) TFEU. The question is: why are measures that reflect the Commission's ambition of a roadmap to a competitive low-carbon economy limited to the development of renewable energy projects but not the development of nuclear energy projects?

A CFD is a bilateral contract in which a generator or vendor receives a fixed price, including an increase or decrease in market volatility, which causes the current price of electricity at the time of sale to differ from the established price.[11] This is done to account for the entity's investment in the nuclear power plant project's implementation. To ensure the purchase of electricity, the strike price is negotiated as low as possible, but the vendor and supplier are left with the business risk associated with the spot market during the electricity sale period. This mechanism provides a strike price for electricity generation to the electricity producer. In order to guarantee a return on investment, the strike price includes both the market price of the electricity, and the subsidy granted for potential market fluctuations during the sale of electricity.

In accordance with the CFD mechanism, the power generator seeks to negotiate a long-term power purchase agreement to guarantee a return on the investment. Vertical integration between supply and generation corporations is another option for establishing a long-term power purchase contract, allowing the same entity to engage in both generation and supply. According to the requirements of the third energy package, vertically integrated corporations should be subject to full

[11] Electricity Market Reform: Contracts for Difference. UK Government CfD Scheme.2014.

ownership unbundling, designation as a transmission system operator, or designation as an independent system operator.

Additionally, there is substantial controversy surrounding the fixed price period, which is dependent on the return on investment. The developer of the project's investment amount and a return on investment are both taken into account when determining the strike price. However, it is debatable whether such an approach should truly emphasise the investment cost of the project company rather than reflect the market price. Setting a price based on the return on an investment, on the other hand, poses the question of whether there is a return to a regulated market and whether there is state intervention to ensure that the company receives a more favourable treatment than other enterprises operating in that market. The price is determined by the outcome of negotiations between the government and the corporation responsible for implementing the Hinkley Point C project.[12] Consequently, uncertainties remain regarding the inclusion of possible overcharges in the final price, but in this case, the established price would significantly increase, rendering this form of power generation uncompetitive.

The concept of this mechanism must be considered when analysing the current price equilibrium, as it provides a return on investment that, when weighed against potential political risks, assures a timely return on investment.[13] Obviously, this measure is viewed as a mechanism for state intervention in the market and stands in opposition to the concept of liberalising the internal market. To examine the concept of this mechanism, it is necessary to systematically evaluate EU legislation and its concept of creating a liberalised internal market, giving priority not only to ownership unbundling of vertically integrated companies but also to ensuring sufficient electricity generation capacity via a secure and sustainable internal energy market. In the context of the internal energy market, it is also essential to address climate change and related carbon reduction goals while promoting thc dcvclopment of low-carbon technologies.

Consequently, the CFD scheme established a separate counterparty body that acts as a government agent and has the authority to administer funds, including the authority to raise and disburse funds. This organisation serves as a liaison between the project developer and the utility user. In addition, payments to suppliers and additional costs to electricity producers are calculated. Transmission system administrators are anticipated to manage CFD pricing and low-carbon electricity generation.[14] This would have substantially enhanced the risk associated with irreversible investments. The obligation to pay a specialised organisation is a prerequisite for receiving funds from suppliers. Consequently, protection is afforded to power generators and their investors by ensuring that the counterparty body obtains the funds required to settle accounts with project investors. In addition to being elaborated upon in secondary legislation, these requirements are also included in licencing

[12]Case T-356/15, *Austria v Commission*. ECLI:EU:T:2018:439.

[13]Electricity Market Reform: Contracts for Difference. UK Government CfD Scheme.2014.

[14]Electricity Market Reform: Contracts for Difference. UK Government CfD Scheme.2014.

regimes. Infractions of licenced activities may result in penalties (up to 10% of annual revenue) and licence revocation. Suppliers are required to make contributions to the counterparty organisation.

The government believed that the CFD contract should not cover all costs and risks associated with production expenses. The contract granted the counterparty the right to terminate the agreement under certain conditions, including unanticipated project phases, unmet prerequisites, and cases of protracted force majeure or power generator failure. Compliance with fundamental requirements is a crucial criterion for the manufacturer to be able to receive and make payments on his own behalf.

The generator must inform the CFD counterparty of the project's progress, and the designated authority must collect funds from the suppliers that will be paid to the electricity generator in accordance with the price difference agreement. Even with price-difference agreements, there is still the possibility of unequal energy production, albeit with financing. The proposed measures provided greater assurance to the industry, eliminating uncertainty between manufacturers and suppliers regarding the capacity market, technological advancement, and investment promotion. However, price difference agreements are unavoidably covered by Article 107 (1) TFEU and were notified to the Commission as such. The coordination of the State aid measure for nuclear power plants took more than a year, and a public consultation was conducted to determine the compatibility of such a support mechanism with EU competition law, but the Commission adopted a favourable decision on the CFD model for the Hinkley Point C project.

The Commission decided on October 8, 2014, to grant Hinkley Point C in Somerset State aid. The aid consists of three components: contracts for difference, compensation assurance from the state in the event that the power plant is prematurely shut down, and a credit guarantee on bonds to assure timely payment. Austria initiated proceedings for the annulment of the Commission's decision in 2015 by filing a petition with the General Court.[15] The supplication included the following assertions and demands: The Commission allegedly granted aid based on market failure and approved a separate market distinct from the market for nuclear energy. The aid was ostensibly approved as an investment aid, but it was more of an operating aid nature; the nuclear power plant does not fulfil the objectives of common interest; these measures were disproportionate; the United Kingdom should have initiated the public procurement procedure. The evaluation of the applicability of the Euratom Treaty or the TFEU to the State aid case in the nuclear energy sector was an intriguing aspect of this decision. Austria asserts that the Commission did not elucidate explicitly in the decision on the relationship between the TFEU and the Euratom Treaty.

From the reasoning in the contested decision, it can be inferred that the Commission thought it was necessary to evaluate the compatibility of the measures in question with the internal market, as required by Article 107(3)(c) of the Treaty on

[15] Case T-526/15 Austria v. Commission (Hinkley Point C State Aid Decision). European Commission decision on state aid to Hinkley Point C (SA.34985).

the Functioning of the European Union (TFEU), even though they had to do with nuclear energy. The fact that the Commission thought about how the provision in question could be used, especially in terms of how promoting nuclear energy could be seen as a public interest goal, shows that the Commission thought it was important to look at the provisions of the Euratom Treaty. Consequently, the aforementioned grounds facilitated the Republic of Austria in determining the justifications behind said decision, thereby empowering the Court to use its authority to scrutinise the matter.

Importantly, the State aid provisions are not included in the Euratom Treaty, leaving the question of which document will be applicable open to debate.

The Court has clarified this specific matter. With respect to the use of Article 107 TFEU in relation to measures pertaining to the domain of nuclear energy, it is important to acknowledge that, as stipulated in Article 106a (3) of the Euratom Treaty, the regulations are not intended to contravene the provisions set forth in the Euratom Treaty. As a result, the requirements outlined in the Euratom Treaty establish distinct regulations in comparison to those outlined in the FEU Treaty, therefore superseding the latter provisions in case of any disagreement. Nevertheless, it should be noted that the existence of distinct regulations within the Euratom Treaty should not prevent the application of Article 107 TFEU to actions that aim to achieve objectives outlined in the Euratom Treaty. To the extent that the Euratom Treaty does not establish explicit regulations in this matter, the provisions of the TFEU pertaining to the European Union's policy may be employed for the implementation of those measures. Several clauses under the Euratom Treaty, including Article 2(c) and the regulations outlined in Chapter 4 of Title II, pertain to investments in the domain of nuclear energy. Nevertheless, these laws fail to establish the specific circumstances in which state aid related to investments in nuclear energy can be deemed consistent with the internal market, despite the resulting distortion of competition. Following the aforementioned considerations, the Court arrived at the determination that the state aid measure could be subject to the application of Article 107 TFEU, despite the fact that the measure in question is governed by the provisions of the Euratom Treaty. The decision rendered by the court was to dismiss the action. The verdict was challenged by Austria before the CJEU.

The CJEU was presented with an essential question that had not been extensively addressed in previous case law practise. The appeal raised the issue of whether the nuclear power plant project could be eligible for State aid that is considered to be in accordance with Article 107 (3) (c) of the TFEU. The CJEU has dismissed assertions challenging the classification of a nuclear power plant project as an objective of common interest. Given the circumstance in which the Euratom Treaty does not contain explicit provisions pertaining to the implementation of State aid, the TFEU becomes applicable. Austria further contended that the principle of "polluter pays", the precautionary principle, and the protection of the environment should be universally considered as precluding factors. The CJEU has suggested that this exclusion may potentially be inconsistent with Article 194(2) of the TFEU. This article grants Member States the freedom to determine their own energy composition, and in this specific instance, the Member State has opted to include nuclear energy as part of its energy mix. Furthermore, the Member State has implemented additional support measures that have been deemed compatible with Article 107 TFEU, as approved by the Commission.

In spite of the aforementioned historical context, the current emphasis on renewable energy remains a significant concern, as the potential of nuclear power to fulfil the nation's fundamental energy requirements is inexplicably overlooked. This neglect leads to a shortfall in renewable energy generation and necessitates compensatory measures. Furthermore, the establishment of a capacity market has been instrumental in fostering development.

12.3 The State Aid to LNG Terminals

The global liquefied natural gas (LNG) market is witnessing increased competitiveness with significant growth in trade. Furthermore, LNG terminals are emerging as a viable alternative to secure the supply of natural gas to countries at competitive prices. LNG and sufficient gas storage play a crucial role in enhancing liquidity and diversification within the gas markets of the European Union. Adequate LNG capacity, including liquefaction facilities in the producing nations as well as LNG terminals and ship-based regasification within the European Union, needs to be accessible to all Member States. This access can be achieved either directly or through a solidarity arrangement with other Member States. This holds significant importance for Member States that now exhibit a high level of reliance on a single gas supplier. LNG terminals are often named as the diversification option and security enhancement option for pipeline-supplied natural gas. In this context, it should also be taken into account that these supply channels also have the backing of the two major exporting countries, the Russian Federation and the US. In the Asian natural gas market, the dominance of LNG can be seen due to the large energy markets in Japan, Taiwan, and South Korea.

At present, the European Union hosts a total of 31 operational LNG terminals, collectively possessing a capacity of 227 billion cubic metres (bcm) per year.[16] Additionally, there are six LNG terminals, including those designed for small-scale operations, that are currently in the construction phase. In 2018, the European Union and the United States (US) jointly released a statement concerning the augmentation of LNG imports to the EU. Nevertheless, it is important to note that LNG constitutes a significant component of the existing fossil fuel infrastructure. Considering the Paris Agreement and the Green Deal, the European Union has established a commendable objective to transform into a carbon-neutral continent by 2050. In light of this, the potential expansion of LNG may pose a challenge to the EU's strategic goals. The European Union has already provided financial support for LNG infrastructure projects. The Commission has granted approval for multiple projects

[16]European Commission, "EU LNG Terminals and Capacity," European Commission Report.

involving investment aid for LNG. These projects will be further detailed in the subsequent sections.

The European Union is employing the strategy of importing LNG as a means to enhance supplier and route diversification for its natural gas procurement. The significance of this matter has been heightened, particularly in light of the Russian incursion into Ukraine and the European Union's strategy to diminish reliance on Russian gas imports. The European Union holds the distinction of being the foremost global importer of LNG. During the initial 6 months of 2022, the European Union witnessed the importation of more than 65 billion cubic metres (bcm) of LNG, which held a monetary value exceeding EUR 60 billion. France had the position of being the primary importer of LNG inside the European Union, surpassing both Spain and Belgium in this regard.[17]

During the initial 6 months of 2022, the United States emerged as the primary supplier of LNG to the European Union, accounting for about half of the aggregate import volume. The annual imports of LNG from the United States experienced a growth rate above 100% per year.[18] The European Union possesses a substantial import capacity for LNG, amounting to around 157 billion cubic metres per year in regasified form. This capacity is sufficient to satisfy approximately 40% of the total gas demand inside the EU. Nevertheless, there is an unequal distribution of LNG infrastructure inside the European Union.

Lithuania lacks local gas production and has always been entirely dependent on Russia for its gas supply. To mitigate the reliance on energy supply from a singular source, the government has undertaken many initiatives. In the year 2017, Lithuania had a decline of 15.3% in its import of LNG, amounting to 1.10 billion cubic metres (bcm). Consequently, Lithuania held the position of the tenth largest LNG importer in Europe during that period. In 2013, the Lithuanian authorities officially informed the Commission about their intention to implement a State aid measure for the construction and operation of an LNG terminal in Klaipeda.[19] The decision to establish the LNG terminal was made in response to the geopolitical circumstances in Lithuania. Specifically, the country's reliance on Gazprom as its sole external natural gas supplier, coupled with the absence of interconnections with continental Europe, prompted the need for such a terminal. In accordance with the N-1 standard outlined in Regulation (EU) No 994/2010, it is incumbent upon the State to guarantee an alternative supply in the event of any disruption. To fulfil this requirement, the implementation of an LNG terminal was deemed a viable solution.

The project encompassed the deployment of a floating storage and regasification unit for liquefied natural gas, along with the associated energy infrastructure. This was facilitated through a lease agreement spanning 10 years with an option to

[17] European Commission, EU Energy Security Strategy: Enhancing Diversification of Energy Supplies, (European Commission, 2022), p. 10.

[18] European Commission, "EU Natural Gas Imports and Suppliers," European Commission Report. International Energy Agency (IEA), "Gas Market Report: LNG Supply and Demand," IEA Report.

[19] Case SA.36740 (2013/NN)—*Lithuania Aid to Klaipedos Nafta/LNG Terminal*. 2013.

purchase. The regasification capacity of the LNG terminal reached a maximum of four billion cubic metres per year. The State aid measure encompassed infrastructure investments. The implementation of the Purchase obligation was initiated, encompassing all regulated entities that utilise natural gas for the purpose of electricity and heat generation. The aforementioned obligation served as a guarantee for the minimum off-take volume (0.54 bcm) of LNG, thereby ensuring the stable operation of the LNG terminal. The procurement of gas should have been conducted through the designated supplier, as determined by the tender process. The primary responsibility of the tender was to ensure the consistent functioning of the LNG terminal. The purchase obligation was established for a period of 10 years.[20]

The third component of State aid encompasses the provision of a State guarantee for the loan. In July, the Parliament of the Republic of Lithuania passed a resolution to provide a State guarantee to the European Investment Bank loan of EUR 81,093,605 to Klaipedos Nafta. This loan will be utilised for a maximum duration of 20 years and will be allocated towards financing the LNG terminal. The Commission has affirmed that the State guarantee provided to the European Investment Bank does not violate the internal market as outlined in Article 107 (1) of the TFEU.[21]

The fourth component of the State aid encompassed the LNG Supplement, which was a levy imposed on the price of natural gas transmission. This levy was implemented in accordance with the procedure that was approved by the national regulatory authority. The collection and distribution of the LNG Supplement were anticipated to be carried out by the transmission system operator and allocated to the LNG Terminal operator. The levy was paid by all the ultimate consumers. The transmission system operator was legally obligated to offer gasification services to external entities at regulated tariffs and in a non-discriminatory manner. The Commission has concluded that the allocation of these expenses adheres to the regulations set forth by the European Union regarding services that serve the general economic interest. To prevent excessive compensation for the public services rendered by the LNG terminal operator, objective criteria were used to determine eligible costs.

The notification of State aid was made in relation to the application of the measure concerning the provision of services that serve the general economic interest. According to the assessment conducted by the Commission, the investment in the LNG terminal is deemed crucial for guaranteeing the security of gas supply. Furthermore, the aid provided is considered both necessary and proportionate in facilitating the realisation of this investment. Furthermore, the terminal is accessible to third parties under fair and equitable conditions, thereby preventing any unwarranted

[20] Case SA.36740 (2013/NN)—*Lithuania Aid to Klaipedos Nafta/LNG Terminal*. 2013. European Commission, State Aid Decision SA.44291 (2017/N)—Lithuania: State aid for financing the LNG terminal, (European Commission, 2017).

[21] European Commission, State Aid Decision SA.44291 (2017/N)—Lithuania: State aid for financing the LNG terminal, (European Commission, 2017).

distortion of competition. The compatibility of the investment aid was declared in accordance with Article 107(3) of the TFEU, while the compatibility of the operating aid was declared in accordance with Article 106(2) of the TFEU.

The LNG terminal precedent, which involves the allocation of user-funded tariffs to partially finance investments in new infrastructure, is recognised as a State aid measure. However, it has been standardised and approved based on public service criteria, with the aim of promoting the diversification of energy resources in the country through the establishment of new alternative infrastructure.

Achema, AB, submitted an application to the General Court seeking the annulment of the Commission's decision. The claimant has presented three arguments. The initial argument posited that the procedural rights delineated in Article 108 (2) of the TFEU and Article 4(4) of Regulation (EC) No 659/1999 pertain to the principles governing effective administrative procedures. The claimant asserted that their position was not evaluated during the assessment process. Specifically, they argue that the Commission neglected to consider the claimant's initiation of the alternative LNG terminal project. In this section, the Commission has refuted these arguments on the basis that the claimant, along with other natural gas undertakings, lodged a complaint with the Commission during the assessment of the State aid measure. Under no circumstances can the argument that you were not heard or evaluated be deemed acceptable. The mention of the alternative LNG terminal project was exclusively made during the claim presented to the General Court, and there was no prior instance in which this clause was communicated to the Commission.[22]

The second plea raised concerns regarding the violation of Article 107 (3) of the TFEU due to the incorrect assessment of the criteria. The argument was dismissed by the Commission on the grounds that the applicants questioned the viability of investing in alternative infrastructure. However, they supported their position by citing their own project involving the construction of an LNG terminal. The latter project was primarily intended to address the company's interest in natural gas rather than the country's demand for it. The claimant's assessment of the alternative project options was inaccurate due to Lithuania's obligation to adhere to the N-1 standard as mandated by Regulation No. 994/2010, which required compliance by December 2014.

The implementation of the alternative gas network interconnection pipeline project was scheduled for the years 2018–2020. The applicant further posited an argument that the costs in question ought to have been incorporated into the tariff structure. However, it is important to consider the specific circumstances at hand, as such an inclusion would have resulted in an escalation of already elevated consumer prices. Moreover, the applicant failed to provide a cogent explanation for the underlying rationale behind attracting investments through tariff hikes. The claimant's argument regarding the proportionality of the measure was called into question,

[22] Achema AB v. European Commission, Case T-279/17, Judgment of the General Court (Fourth Chamber) of 22 May 2019.

yet they failed to present adequate justification for accepting this claim. The General Court also dismissed the second plea.

The third argument raised concerns the violation of Article 106 (2) of the TFEU, the State Aid for Services of General Economic Interest (SGEI) Framework, as well as the principles of equal treatment and public procurement. In this section, the General Court has reached a crucial determination that the remuneration for the public service obligation is not obligated to adhere strictly to the conditions outlined in the Altmark case. Nevertheless, in order to align with the State aid regulations, it must adhere to the stipulations outlined in Article 106 (2) TFEU.

In the absence of harmonised regulations, the Commission is unable to make determinations regarding the extent of the public service obligation, the decisions made by the State, or the effectiveness of the undertaking. Another aspect of this plea relates to the implementation of public procurement regulations during the process of selecting the operator accountable for fulfilling the public service obligation. In this specific instance, the Republic of Lithuania delineated the crucial security interests that required safeguarding while acknowledging that the tender procedure carried the potential for adverse implications for the public service obligation. The General Court has reached a consensus that the implementation of a tender procedure introduces the possibility that the successful bidder may not be unduly influenced by the sole supplier. The sole means of attaining this objective was to delegate the responsibility to the State-managed enterprise. The General Court also dismissed the third plea.

In response to the General Court's decision, Achema filed an appeal with the CJEU in 2019.[23] The case remains unresolved. The allegations pertain to the violation of Articles 263 TFEU and 256 (1) TFEU as a result of an error made by the General Court in determining the accuracy and reliability of the information. The second argument pertains to the violation of Article 41(1) of the Charter of Fundamental Rights of the European Union. This violation is attributed to an error committed by the General Court, wherein the claimants failed to furnish information to the Commission during the preliminary examination. The third argument pertains to the violation of Article 296(2) of the TFEU and Article 41(1), (2), and (c) of the Charter of Fundamental Rights of the European Union. It is contended that the General Court failed to provide a clear rationale for exempting the application of public procurement regulations outlined in Directive 2004/18/EC.

In 2011, Poland was officially informed about the provision of State aid for the purpose of constructing an LNG terminal in Swinoujscie.[24] The project encompasses the installation required for the reloading of LNG from ships, as well as the inclusion of a regasification unit and LNG storage facilities. The project was incorporated into the 2007–2013 Operating Programme Infrastructure and Environment in order to meet the criteria for receiving financial assistance from the European Union Structural Funds. The financing consisted of a combination of funds from the EU

[23] Case T-417/16, *Achemos Grupe and Achema v Commission*. ECLI:EU:T:2019:697.

[24] Case SA.31953 (2011/N)—Construction of regasification LNG terminal in Swinoujscie. 2011.

Structural funds, the European Investment Bank (EIB), the European Bank for Reconstruction and Development (EBRD), and loans from commercial banks. The allocation of EU Structural funds is considered a form of state aid, as it can be attributed to the resources of the state.

Poland is confronted with the challenge of having a single supplier and limited interconnections, which hampers the potential for diversification. The region also encountered significant gas disruptions in the years 2004, 2006, and 2009. Consequently, the development of this infrastructure became imperative in order to safeguard the reliability of energy provision and promote the diversification of energy resources. This, in turn, would facilitate the availability of competitively priced energy for consumers.

The primary aim of the common interest was identified as the safeguarding of energy supply. Consequently, with the implementation of an LNG terminal, Poland will acquire the capability to import gas from diverse origins and guarantee a continuous supply in the event of natural gas disruptions. The assessment of this project was conducted alongside the gas pipeline project and potential future trans-border interconnection pipeline projects, thereby augmenting the existing capacity for natural gas provision in Europe. The anticipated aid intensity was projected to cover 57% of the eligible expenses. Based on the calculations of the counterfactual scenario, the inclusion of investment costs in the tariff would impose a substantial burden on consumers, leading to an escalation in prices. After conducting the assessment, it was determined that the aid possessed an incentive effect, leading the Commission to ultimately conclude that the State aid measure aligns with the provisions outlined in Article 107 (3) (c) of the TFEU.

In 2019, the Polish government commenced the expansion of the LNG terminal and subsequently informed the European Commission about the State aid provided for this project.[25] The decision to pursue expansion was subsequently supported by the rationale to meet the increasing demand for natural gas in Poland, the Baltic States, select Nordic countries, and various Central and Eastern European nations. This enhancement is expected to bolster the viability of natural alternatives in the event of any disruptions. The augmentation of the LNG terminal's capacity had already been incorporated into projects of common interest, aiming to contribute to the Baltic Energy Market Interconnection Plan. The Baltic Pipe is a prospective project that aims to establish a connection between Poland, Norway, and Denmark.

Another crucial aspect that was discussed is the anticipated termination of the natural gas supply agreement with Gazprom, scheduled for 2022. The existing import capacity stipulated in the aforementioned contract amounted to 10.2 billion cubic metres per year. Hence, it was imperative to implement an alternative solution in order to achieve diversification objectives and enhance supply security. The expansion project was incorporated into the Infrastructure and Environment Operational Programme 2014–2020, thereby enabling access to funding through the European Union's structural funds.

---

[25] Case SA.50905(2018/N)—Poland /Extension of the LNG Terminal in Swinoujscie. 2019.

The Commission has determined that providing assistance to energy infrastructure projects is justified due to the strategic importance of natural gas infrastructure in maintaining a dependable and diverse energy market. This is crucial for ensuring the availability of suitable alternatives in the event of any disruptions. The presence of the aid was demonstrated to have had a significant impact on the undertaking, as evidenced by the substantial loss that would have been incurred in its absence. Consequently, the undertaking would not have had the intention to proceed with the project under such circumstances. The Commission additionally recognised that the objective of this project is to establish European gas infrastructure, with a particular focus on enhancing the Baltic region.

Another project discussed in this section pertains to the Cyprus LNG terminal. Cyprus currently lacks interconnection capacity with other countries, rendering it an isolated energy island. Moreover, the electricity generation process exhibits a significant reliance on liquid fuels.[26] The implementation of the LNG terminal was deemed a feasible approach to enhance energy source diversification and mitigate greenhouse gas emissions, thereby making a significant contribution towards achieving climate objectives. This project additionally contributes to the reduction of power generation costs through the utilisation of natural gas as an alternative to heavily polluting liquid fuels. The inclusion of the LNG project in the list of projects of common interest was motivated by the objective of enhancing the development of gas infrastructure, addressing bottlenecks, and mitigating energy isolation.

The scope of the project encompasses financial assistance for infrastructure development, with a specific focus on the conversion of an LNG carrier into a floating gas storage and regasification unit. Additionally, the project includes the construction of a jetty, a jetty pipeline, an onshore gas platform, and a pressure reduction metering station.

The project received a grant of EUR 101 million from the Connecting Europe Facility, a loan of up to EUR 150 million from the EIB, and a loan of EUR 80 million from the EBRD.[27] The issuance of these loans is contingent upon the provision of a 100% State guarantee. This requirement can be classified as a State aid measure that necessitates notification to the Commission.

The KrK LNG Terminal has been designated as a European Project of Common Interest since 2013 due to its strategic significance in facilitating the diversification of natural gas supply in Central and South-Eastern Europe.[28] The LNG terminal is designed to supply gas to the Croatian national transmission network, which is interconnected with neighbouring countries like Slovenia, Italy, and Hungary. Additionally, it will facilitate gas transportation to other European Union member states through non-EU nations such as Serbia and Montenegro. The recipient of the assistance measures is LNG Croatia d.o.o. (LLC), a terminal promoter owned by

[26] State aid SA.38885 (2015/C)—Cyprus: Support for the development of a liquefied natural gas terminal in Cyprus," European Commission Decision, October 6, 2015.

[27] Case SA.55388—State aid to Cyprus LNG terminal Case 2020.

[28] Case SA.51983—State aid to KrK LNG Terminal/Croatia 2019.

Hrvatska Elektroprivreda (HEP) d.d., the state-owned gas and power company in Croatia, and Plinacro d.o.o., the national operator of the gas transmission system (TSO), with ownership shares of 85% and 15%, respectively.

The Croatian Energy Regulator has determined that the charges the terminal levies on its users are subject to extensive regulation. Furthermore, the terminal operates in accordance with internal market legislation, ensuring third-party access. The Commission acknowledges that this decision on state aid is made without any bias against Croatia's responsibility to adhere to other elements of EU law, particularly in terms of ensuring that the project fulfils all the criteria outlined in the EU environmental legislation, including the Environmental Impact Assessment Directive. According to the findings of the commission, it was determined that the implementation of aid measures is deemed necessary, as the project would be rendered infeasible in their absence. The Commission's financial analysis has indicated that the revenues generated solely from the tariffs imposed on users of the LNG terminal would not be sufficient to recover the investment expenses and guarantee adequate compensation for the LNG promoter. Consequently, the aid measures proposed are proportionate and restricted to the minimum extent required. These measures will solely address the funding gap, which refers to the disparity between positive and negative cash flows throughout the investment's duration, discounted to their present value using the cost of capital. Hence, the Commission reached the determination that the aforementioned measures adhere to the regulations governing state aid within the European Union. This is due to their contribution towards crucial strategic goals of the EU, such as the expansion of gas supply sources and the enhancement of the EU's gas supply security, particularly in the Central and South-Eastern regions. Importantly, these measures do not excessively disrupt competition.

The European Commission has granted approval of a EUR 40 million German support measure for the development and operation of a new land-based LNG terminal in Brunsbüttel in accordance with EU state aid standards.[29] The implementation of this policy will effectively enhance the security and diversification of energy sources within Germany, aligning with the objectives outlined in the REPowerEU Plan. Furthermore, it will aid in reducing reliance on fossil fuels sourced from Russia.

Germany has officially informed the Commission of its intention to provide backing for the establishment and functioning of a LNG terminal situated in Brunsbüttel. This terminal is projected to have an annual capacity of 10 billion cubic metres. The terminal is composed of import, storage, and distribution facilities, with a projected commencement of operations by the end of 2026. The legislation in question primarily benefits the German energy operator RWE and the Dutch energy network operator Gasunie. German LNG Terminal GmbH (GLNG), a corporation, will build and operate the LNG terminal. Three parties will jointly own GLNG:

[29] Case SA.102163—Aid for the construction and operation of the Brunsbüttel on-shore LNG Terminal, 2023.

(i) Gasunie, with a 40% share; (ii) RWE, with a 10% share; and (iii) the German government, through the investment and development bank KfW, with a 50% share.

The proposed approach is the implementation of a preferential dividend distribution system, whereby KfW will allocate a portion of the dividends received from GLNG to its co-investors. This allocation will occur if the project's yearly return falls below a predetermined proportion of the aggregate capital invested by all shareholders, including KfW. In the event that the annual return exceeds a predetermined proportion of the aggregate invested capital, KfW will refrain from distributing dividends, resulting in the non-disbursement of help as per the aforementioned policy. The disbursement of help under the aforementioned policy will be contingent upon the yearly returns, with an anticipated total of EUR 40 million. KfW intends to discontinue its involvement in the project following a 15-year period of operating the LNG terminal, coinciding with the cessation of the preferential dividend distribution mechanism.

The construction of the LNG terminal will consider the requisite technological specifications to facilitate its future conversion into a terminal for importing renewable energy carriers, such as renewable hydrogen or its derivatives. This approach aims to prevent the entrenchment of gas dependency. The conversion of the terminal is expected to occur within a maximum of 15 years from the start of its operation, no later than the year 2043.

The terminal is expected to see advantages resulting from a partial exemption from third-party access and tariff regulation. This exemption has been granted by the German regulatory authority, known as the "Bundesnetzagentur", and has been deemed compliant with internal market regulations by the European Commission.

According to Article 107 (3)(c) of the TFEU, the Commission evaluated the measure in accordance with the state aid regulations of the European Union. This article allows Member States to provide support for the advancement of specific economic activities, subject to certain conditions. Additionally, the Commission considered the 2022 Guidelines on State Aid for Climate, Environmental Protection, and Energy (CEEAG) during the assessment process. This action serves to promote the advancement of economic activity, namely in relation to the importation of gas. Simultaneously, it aligns with the goals of significant European Union policy initiatives, like the European Green Deal and the REPowerEU Plan. The implementation of this strategy is deemed essential and suitable for enhancing the security of gas supply in Germany as well as in its neighbouring nations.

The provision of aid demonstrates an incentive effect, whereby the involvement of public support is crucial for private investors to engage in the GLNG project.

The measure exhibits proportionality, as the anticipated assistance derived from the preferred allocation of dividends is lower than the projected shortfall in funds. Furthermore, there are measures in place to prevent excessive compensation. In the event that the project yields a larger value than initially expected, the recipients of help will be obligated to reimburse a portion of the aid received to KfW upon the conclusion of the project, as per the implementation of a claw-back mechanism.

The measure's positive impact on gas supply security surpasses its negative impact on competition. Specifically, the scope of the exemption from third-party access is restricted, and this approach does not lead to a situation where natural gas becomes locked in. The project serves to support the European Union's climate targets for 2030 and 2050 by facilitating the substitution of Russian gas and establishing the necessary infrastructure for the conversion of the terminal to accommodate the trade of environmentally sustainable energy carriers.

Based on this rationale, the Commission granted approval to the German legislation in accordance with the state aid regulations of the European Union.

The 2022 CEEAG of the Commission enables Member States to provide assistance for energy infrastructure investments, contingent upon specific conditions. The objective of these regulations is to assist Member States in achieving the European Union's ambitious energy and climate objectives while ensuring the security of energy supply at the lowest feasible expense for taxpayers and without creating excessive disruptions to competition within the Single Market.[30]

The guidelines establish a versatile and well-suited framework that enables Member States to offer the required assistance in a focused and economically efficient manner, thereby facilitating the achievement of the objectives outlined in the Green Deal. The regulations encompass a harmonisation with the significant aims and targets outlined in the European Green Deal by the European Union, as well as other recent regulatory modifications in the realms of energy and the environment. These laws also account for the growing significance of climate protection. The document encompasses various sections pertaining to assistance in mitigating greenhouse gas emissions, which encompass support for renewable energy, implementation of energy efficiency measures, aid for promoting clean mobility, development of infrastructure, adoption of circular economy practices, reduction of pollution, preservation and restoration of biodiversity, and implementation of measures to ensure energy supply security, contingent upon specific conditions.

The March 2022 REPowerEU Communication acknowledges that the unwarranted and unlawful armed aggression by Russia against Ukraine has had a significant impact on the global energy sector.[31] The escalation in energy prices has led to significant challenges, including increased worries regarding energy security. This situation has highlighted the European Union's excessive reliance on imported gas, oil, and coal from Russia. In March 2022, an agreement was reached among EU leaders during the European Council meeting to expedite the process of reducing Europe's reliance on energy imports from Russia. Expanding upon the Fit for 55 package of proposals and fulfilling the objectives concerning energy security of supply and storage, the REPowerEU plan presents a supplementary series of measures aimed at conserving energy, broadening the range of energy sources,

---

[30]Communication from the Commission: Guidelines on State aid for climate, environmental protection and energy 2022 (2022/C 80/01)," Official Journal of the European Union, February 18, 2022.

[31]Communication from the Commission: REPowerEU: Joint European Action for more affordable, secure and sustainable energy," COM(2022) 108 final, March 8, 2022.

expeditiously replacing fossil fuels, and expediting Europe's transition towards clean energy. Furthermore, the plan seeks to intelligently integrate investments and reforms in pursuit of these goals.

The evaluation of State aid was conducted in accordance with the compatibility criteria, which include assessing its appropriateness, incentive effect, proportionality, impact on competition, and effect on trade. The Commission has determined that the energy infrastructure plays a crucial role in facilitating the efficient operation of the energy market. The project additionally facilitated the advancement of market competition by introducing an alternative energy source. This allowed current power plants to utilise natural gas in addition to liquid fuels, thereby potentially mitigating consumer prices. The project was also regarded as having a positive impact on pollution reduction, specifically through a significant decrease in CO_2 emissions.

12.4 The State Aid for Energy Efficiency and Renewable Energy Projects

Energy efficiency is recognised as a primary focus of the Green Deal, and it has also been a prominent concern in previously implemented regulations, aligning with the Commission's overarching priorities. Furthermore, it was included as a key aspect within the framework of the Energy Union Strategy.[32] The heating and cooling sectors continue to exhibit inadequacies in terms of energy efficiency and sustainability, resulting in significant energy waste. Renovation of district heating systems is necessary in order to achieve a higher level of energy savings. The buildings exhibit antiquated infrastructure and low levels of efficiency, while the utilisation of renewable energy sources in this sector is characterised by fragmentation. Inefficient processes result in a significant amount of energy being wasted. Additionally, customers lack awareness regarding energy-saving measures. Consequently, the identification of renovation targets is deemed crucial for the successful realisation of future decarbonization objectives.

The objectives of energy efficiency and conservation were also considered shared interests when assessing State aid cases. This chapter will assess the fundamental State aid that was provided with the primary objective of enhancing efficiency and promoting energy conservation.

[32]Framework Strategy for a Resilient Energy Union with a Forward-Looking Climate Change Policy," COM(2015) 80 final, February 25, 2015.

12.4.1 The Investment Aid for High-Efficiency Cogeneration Power Plants

In the year 2016, Lithuania officially announced the provision of investment aid for a combined heat and power (CHP) plant that utilises municipal waste and biomass as its primary sources of energy.[33] The project received a maximum of EUR 150 million in investment assistance from the European Union Structural Funds, along with a EUR 190 million loan from the EIB. The project was incorporated into the Operational Programme for the Investments of EU Funds in the period 2014–2020. The primary aim of this project was to enhance the efficiency of the district heating system, which was characterised by outdated infrastructure and a heavy reliance on natural gas for heat production. Additionally, a significant amount of energy was wasted during the production process. Another objective of the project was to mitigate CO2 emissions, which led to the selection of a waste-to-energy and biomass-fired plant. The initial implementation of this project also included the environmental goal of reducing municipal waste.

According to national legislation, it is mandated that the State maintain a minimum controlling stake of 51% in the company responsible for executing the project, while the remaining 49% can be allocated to private investors.[34] The tender process was conducted with the aim of identifying a suitable partner for the execution of the project. However, none of the candidates were ultimately chosen. The waste-fired plant unit aims to address the issue of waste management. Presently, a significant portion of the collected waste is being deposited in landfills, which is considered the least desirable method according to the waste hierarchy. Lithuania has allocated a substantial amount of approximately EUR 190 million towards the establishment and implementation of mechanical biological treatment facilities. The objective of these facilities is to generate refuse-derived fuel, which can be subsequently utilised as a fuel source in waste-to-energy power plants for energy production.

The assessment of the compatibility of State aid involved an evaluation of the counterfactual scenario. Consequently, the Commission has determined that heat-only boilers represent the sole feasible alternative in the absence of the State aid measure. Consequently, the targeted objectives of primary energy conservation and energy efficiency would not be attained. The compatibility of the State aid was determined in accordance with Article 107 (3) of the TFEU.

In the year 2018, Poland officially communicated the implementation of an aid measure for the establishment of a waste-to-energy cogeneration plant in Olsztyn.[35] The objective of this project is to mitigate municipal waste, decrease CO_2 emissions, and enhance energy efficiency through the implementation of measures that result in

[33] Case SA.41539 (2016/N)—Lithuania Investment aid for high-efficiency cogeneration power plant in Vilnius. 2016.

[34] Case SA.41539 - EFSI Investment aid for high-efficiency cogeneration plant in Vilnius, 2016.

[35] Case SA.51614 (2018/N)—Poland Installation grant for waste-to-energy high-efficiency cogeneration power plant in Olsztyn. 2019 2797.

higher levels of primary energy savings. Within the waste market, there are numerous mechanical and biological treatment facilities that are currently operational. These facilities are responsible for generating refuse-derived fuel, which is deemed unsuitable for subsequent recycling or alternative processing methods. The utilisation of refuse-derived fuel in waste incineration plants can be considered a viable approach in accordance with the waste hierarchy principles, as it enables the production of additional energy. The aforementioned fuel will be utilised in the cogeneration facility to generate both thermal and electrical energy.

The project is executed through a public-private partnership arrangement, wherein the private partner is obligated to construct an additional gas- or oil-fired boiler plant to supplement the existing capacity that is not accounted for by the aid measure. Given that the project is being executed under the public-private partnership framework, it is essential to consider the expenses associated with the construction and operation of the cogeneration plant and boiler over a period of 25 years. Additionally, the partner involved in this venture must guarantee the utilisation of an appropriate amount of waste for energy production purposes. The inclusion of the project financing option was anticipated within the framework of the Infrastructure and Environment 2014–2020 Operational Programme. The assistance provided comprises a direct grant from the European Union's Structural Funds. Poland has demonstrated that the project's feasibility is contingent upon the implementation of an advanced information system (AIS), as economic operators have exhibited reluctance to invest in the waste-fired cogeneration facility. Hence, it is imperative to have adequate support in order to achieve the desired environmental goals. The Commission has reached the determination that the aid measure is in accordance with the provisions outlined in Article 107 (3) of the TFEU.

12.4.2 The Operating Aid for Cogeneration

Pursuant to the Guidelines on State Aid for Environmental Protection and Energy 2014–2020, the aid can be granted as an investment or as operational. There are several criteria set out in these guidelines applicable to the operating aid. The term "operating benefit" refers to the inclusion of cost savings or additional ancillary production that can be directly attributed to the additional investment made for environmental protection.[36] This also encompasses any benefits received from other support measures, regardless of whether they qualify as state aid. Examples of such support measures include operating aid granted for the same eligible costs, feed-in tariffs, or any other forms of support.

If the electricity capacity of a cogeneration operational aid exceeds 300 MW and is not granted due to the competitive process, it is necessary to inform the

[36] Guidelines on State aid for environmental protection and energy 2014–2020," (2014/C 200/01), July 28, 2014.

Commission. In this discussion, we will provide a more comprehensive analysis of the Commission's practise regarding the approval of operating aid for cogeneration.

A significant instance pertained to Germany's implementation of a reform in the form of operational aid for cogeneration, as outlined in the national legislation known as the Heat and Power Cogeneration Act. This scheme was officially communicated to the Commission in 2015. Germany has issued a notification regarding the implementation of a measure aimed at ensuring legal certainty.[37] This measure was prompted by doubts surrounding the appropriateness of the feed-in tariff, which was collected as a result of the levy imposed on consumption. The aid is provided to different categories of cogeneration facilities that demonstrate high levels of efficiency, including both newly constructed and modernised installations. The promotion is established as a premium that is paid in addition to the prevailing market price by the network operator in question.

In essence, cogeneration facilities with a capacity exceeding 100 MW had the choice to either sell their generated electricity on the market or use it for their own needs. Conversely, operators with smaller capacities had the option to sell their electricity on the market, use it for their own purposes, or have the grid operator procure it at a mutually agreed-upon price. The aforementioned price is expected to exceed the mean price. The tariff for support varies based on the type of fuel used and the classification of the facility, whether it is newly constructed or undergoing modernization.

Another aspect involves the provision of infrastructure for the storage of heating and cooling resources, which enables the cogeneration plant to enhance its efficiency and achieve cost savings. The ability to store and utilise cold or hot water at specific times allows for the adjustment of working hours to meet the electricity and heat demand. The enhancement enables cogeneration facilities to operate for a greater number of hours. Additionally, the scheme implemented measures to provide assistance for the establishment of district heating and cooling networks. The grids are deemed eligible for support if they guarantee that a minimum of 60% of their energy supply is derived from cogenerated heat, waste heat, or renewable heat sources. If the heat does not consist of the aforementioned elements, the stipulated condition is that 75% of the heat must be generated by a cogeneration facility.

The provision of support is facilitated through the collection of a levy known as the CHP surcharge, which is derived from electricity consumption and subsequently allocated by grid operators. In order to ensure equitable compensation for grid operators based on their purchasing responsibilities, a mechanism was implemented that aligns this obligation with the number of consumers connected to the grid. The expenses incurred by grid operators in relation to the provision of support for cogeneration facilities are offset by the levy imposed on consumers of electricity.

The potential reduction of exemptions for surcharges is contingent upon adherence to the stipulations outlined in the domestic legislation. Specifically, consumers

[37] Case SA.43767 (2015/N), Germany—Heat and Power Cogeneration Act (KWKG), March 19, 2015.

who exceed an annual consumption of 1 GWh are subject to a cap of 0.04 EUR per kilowatt-hour (kWh). The second group that is experiencing advantages from the decreased surcharges consists of consumers in the manufacturing sector who exceed an annual consumption of 1 GWh. These consumers have electricity costs that account for more than 4% of their turnover, and they are subject to a maximum surcharge of 0.03 EUR per kilowatt-hour. The surcharge rate for all remaining consumers who do not qualify for exemption is 0.445 EUR per kilowatt-hour. The calculation of the levy by gearbox system operators is authorised in accordance with the methodology prescribed by regulatory authorities. In this section, the Commission reaches the conclusion that the measure under consideration qualifies as State aid as it is attributed to the State, albeit not directly funded by State resources. Instead, it entails the imposition of a duty to collect and distribute tariffs to eligible entities.

Upon conducting an assessment of the scheme, the Commission has determined that it is in accordance with Article 107 (3) (c) of the TFEU in certain aspects pertaining to the provision of assistance for CHP facilities, district heating and cooling networks, heating and cooling storage facilities, as well as the support for operationally highly efficient cogeneration facilities in district heating. In a specific section, the Commission expressed concerns about the compatibility of the reduced cogeneration levies with the internal market. Consequently, it initiated the formal investigation procedure and invited interested parties to provide their statements on these measures.

During the formal investigation process, the relevant stakeholders were requested to provide their comments regarding the measure. The German authorities have issued amendments pertaining to the CHP surcharges.[38] These amendments specify that starting in 2017, reductions in surcharges will only be granted to electro-intensive users who meet the additional conditions. Additional requirements were imposed on electro-intensive users whose consumption exceeds 1 GWh. For these users, a 15% limitation on the full CHP surcharge was applicable. For electro-intensive users who did not reach this consumption level, the total CHP surcharge was applicable.

The exemption granted to these manufacturers was based on an assessment of the global competitiveness challenges that these enterprises are encountering. The implementation of a complete CHP surcharge has the potential to incur supplementary expenses and reduce the efficiency of these enterprises, thereby exacerbating their competitive standing within the market. The Commission also declared in this decision that the reduction of CHP surcharges is not encompassed within the purview of the Guidelines on State Aid for Environmental Protection and Energy

[38]Case SA.42393 (2016/C) (ex 2015/N) implemented by Germany for certain end consumers (reduced CHP surcharge) and Case SA.47887 (2017/N) which Germany is planning to implement in order to extend the CHP support scheme as regards CHP installations used in closed networks. 2017.

2014–2020. The aforementioned tax does not meet the criteria outlined in the guidelines to be classified as an environmental tax.

While this levy does not compel the payer to alter their behaviour, unlike other environmental taxes, it shares similarities with renewable energy taxes in that its purpose is to promote the use of renewable energy and indirectly contribute to the reduction of CO2 emissions. Section 3.7.2 of the Guidelines on State Aid for Environmental Protection and Energy 2014–2020 lacks applicability due to its omission of support measures pertaining to energy efficiency. Following the formal investigation procedure, the Commission has determined that the aid is in line with the principles of the internal market.

12.4.3 The Investment Aid for District Heating Network

Poland has recently announced a number of assistance measures targeting the district heating sector. In certain instances, the Commission has chosen to commence the formal investigation procedure, while others have been deemed compatible with Article 107 (3) of the TFEU. This chapter will provide a detailed analysis of the fundamental components inherent in these particular cases.

Poland has put forth the proposed upgrades in the municipalities of Tarnobrzeg, Ropczyce, Lesko, Debica, and Ustrzyki Dolne.[39] The initiative was undertaken to enhance the district heating infrastructure, which involves the utilisation of gas-fired and coal-fired boilers for heat production. Specifically, the insulation of the pipe network, the dismantling of the existing pipes, and the subsequent installation of the new ones Poland further emphasised that the financial constraints faced by the responsible municipalities rendered it infeasible to enhance the heat sources to achieve efficient district heating. The majority of the expenses associated with these enhancements would likely be passed on to consumers, although regulatory approval would not be granted.

Poland further elucidated that the substitution of outdated district heating networks would enhance efficiency by mitigating losses and reducing CO2 emissions. The Commission was informed of the assistance in accordance with the Guidelines on State Aid for Environmental Protection and Energy for the period 2014–2020. Specifically, the evaluation of compatibility according to the guidelines focuses on achieving a high level of efficiency. In this instance, the focus of the measure was directed towards the replacement of ageing district heat network pipes rather than the implementation of new and efficient cogeneration facilities or the transition from coal or gas-fired production to renewable or municipal waste sources.

[39] Case SA.51987 (2018/N)—District heating network—Tarnobrzeg, 2019; Case SA.52084 (2018/N)—District heating network—Ropczyce, 2019; Case SA.52238 (2018/N)—District heating network—Lesko, 2019; Case SA.54236 (2019/N)—District heating network—Deebica, 2019 and Case SA.55273 (2019/N)—District heating network—Ustrzyki Dolne. 2019.

The measure in question was deemed incompatible with the Guidelines on State Aid for Environmental Protection and Energy 2014–2020 by the Commission, specifically in relation to aid for energy efficiency. According to the evaluation conducted by the Commission, the replacement of pipelines resulting in energy savings due to reduced losses was deemed insufficient to address the measure's contribution to environmental protection. The proposed measures failed to provide sufficient incentives for achieving a high level of environmental protection, primarily due to the incompatibility of the energy efficiency standards outlined in the Guidelines on State Aid for Environmental Protection and Energy for the period 2014–2020. Due to the aforementioned reasons, the Commission has made the decision to commence the formal investigation procedure.

12.5 The Investment Aid for Promotion of Renewable Energy

The advocacy for the adoption and utilisation of renewable energy sources has been ongoing for a period of 10 years. In 1997, the Commission introduced the White Paper on Renewable Energy, which outlined a goal of achieving a 12% share of renewable energy in order to fulfil energy consumption requirements. The initial goals were established in Directive 2001/77/EC. However, due to their inadequacy, Directive 2009/28/EC was introduced in 2009, which mandated that a minimum of 20% of the overall energy generated must come from renewable sources. The Directive also encompasses diverse support mechanisms that Member States can utilise to attain the targets. Support schemes were extensively employed to facilitate the advancement of renewable energy across Europe. In the subsequent section, an analysis will be conducted on the State aid measures implemented to facilitate the advancement of renewable energy sources.

In 2013, the Commission commenced proceedings in response to a complaint it received concerning Germany's implementation of State aid measures aimed at supporting renewable electricity.[40] The assistance was established through the implementation of specific domestic legislation that imposes certain responsibilities on participants in the market, known as the EEG-Act 2012. According to this legislation, distribution system operators are required to procure electricity generated from renewable energy sources at a predetermined fixed price known as the feed-in tariff. They are then responsible for transferring this electricity to transmission system operators, who are obligated to compensate the distribution system operator with a premium for the renewable energy. Producers also possess the option to directly sell the electricity they generate on the market, thereby granting them the

[40]The Commission decision of 25.11.2014 on the aid scheme SA. 33,995 (2013/C) (ex2013/NN) implemented by Germany for the support of renewable electricity and of energy-intensive users. C (2014) 8786 final.

right to receive compensation. The responsibility for the transmission of electricity is divided equally among the four system operators as a result of the contribution of renewable energy to the overall electricity supply. The transmission system operators are also responsible for selling electricity on the spot market. In situations where there is a price discrepancy, they have the authority to request that suppliers pay the EEG surcharge in proportion to the amount of electricity supplied to consumers.

The calculation methodology for the EEG surcharge is determined by transmission system operators, who consider factors such as the projected feed-in tariff, premium, revenues from sales, and consumption for the upcoming year. The EEG Act 12 implemented a policy known as the "green privilege," which specifically aimed to decrease the EEG surcharge for electricity suppliers who directly purchase electricity from renewable energy producers. This privilege is contingent upon a minimum requirement of 50% of the total delivered electricity being sourced from renewable energy, with at least 20% derived from wind or solar power. The EEG surcharge is typically passed on to consumers, with the exception of energy-intensive users.[41] This exemption is justified by the need to maintain the competitiveness of these manufacturers in the face of international competition, as their market position should not be compromised by burdensome market conditions. This requirement bears resemblance to the previously examined CHP surcharge.

In this particular instance, German authorities have contended that the compensation mechanism did not utilise State resources and was not implemented by the State. Instead, the network operators were responsible for executing the compensation model. Consequently, due to the absence of a specific criterion, the measure in question cannot be recognised as State aid. The Commission expressed disagreement with the aforementioned stance and suggested that the compensation mechanism was established as a direct outcome of Germany's legally mandated provisions outlined in its national legislation. The absence of State budget allocations for aid does not necessarily negate the State's responsibility for the measure.

While German authorities have contended that the surcharge was not conveyed via the budget but rather collected and distributed by transmission system operators, the Commission has asserted that the presence of State resources does not necessarily require direct State involvement through the budget or direct participation in the collection and transfer of levies. It is deemed sufficient for the State to have enacted legislation that establishes a level playing field for the support mechanism.

Another aspect that raised concerns was the issue of exemptions for energy-intensive users in relation to the EEG surcharge. The Commission explicitly declared that for the measure to align with the internal market, it must adhere to the stipulations outlined in the Guidelines on State Aid for Environmental Protection and Energy 2014–2020. Specifically, assistance can be provided to sectors (as outlined in Annex 3) that face the potential loss of their competitive standing

---

[41] The Commission decision of 25.11.2014 on the aid scheme SA. 33,995 (2013/C) (ex2013/NN) implemented by Germany for the support of renewable electricity and of energy-intensive users. C (2014) 8786 final.

in global trade due to imposed fees or other obligations aimed at promoting renewable energy. In contrast, it is possible to receive surcharge reduction assistance in cases where the sector is not explicitly mentioned in the guidelines, provided that it meets the criteria of having an electro-intensity of at least 20% and a trade intensity at the European Union level of at least 4%. Subsequently, Germany has implemented modifications to its plan that partially align with the eligibility criteria of specific sectors.[42] The conclusion reached by the Commission is that the aid must be recuperated in the segments that are inconsistent with European Union legislation, specifically the reduced EEG surcharges implemented during the period of 2013–2014.

Germany has lodged an appeal with the General Court challenging the Commission's decision, specifically contesting the determination of State involvement and the implementation of reductions in EEG surcharges.[43] The General Court has determined that the compensation mechanism, while being administered by the transmission system operators, falls under the crucial supervision of the State due to the reporting obligation.

The responsibility for managing the charges was fulfilled through the requirement for transmission system operators to maintain separate accounts, overseen by the State. Consequently, the operators were not granted any discretion to allocate the collected funds for alternative purposes. In that particular section, the General Court reached the determination that the involvement of the State was present. In the subsequent section, the State contended that the diminished surcharges were not indicative of an aid measure but rather served as compensation for the decreased competitiveness rather than conferring an advantage. The General Court disagreed with the aforementioned arguments and reached the conclusion that the scheme in question indeed constituted State aid.

The difference was made by the CJEU, as German authorities filed an appeal.[44] The main arguments for the appeal was too broad interpretation of the State resources implied by the General Court. In the reasoning part CJEU held that a measure that includes an obligation to acquire energy can be considered assistance, even if it does not entail the transfer of resources by the state. The determining issue in this matter pertains to the fact that these institutions are designated by the government to oversee a government-owned resource and are not solely obligated to make purchases using their own financial means.

It was determined that the General Court was unable to provide evidence supporting the State's authority to allocate the assets acquired through the EEG surcharge. The allocation of decision-making authority to transmission system operators and the management of assets in accordance with the objective of serving

[42] The Commission decision of 25.11.2014 on the aid scheme SA. 33995 (2013/C) (ex2013/NN) implemented by Germany for the support of renewable electricity and of energy-intensive users. C (2014) 8786 final.

[43] Case T-47/15, *Germany v Commission*. ECLI:EU:T:2016.

[44] Case C-405/16 *P—Germany v Commission*. ECLI:EU:C:2019:268.

the public interest were acknowledged. Nevertheless, this arrangement did not meet the criteria for attributing responsibility to the State. Conversely, the granting of disposal rights to transmission system operators indicated that the State did not exercise control over these funds. Considering the fact that public authorities oversee the appropriate collection and allocation of surcharges, it is not possible to infer the existence of public control over the funds.

The CJEU determined that the General Court had not fully applied prior legal precedents in its decision. Specifically, this particular case differed in two key aspects. In the aforementioned instance, the French government implemented legal measures that mandated the inclusion of a purchasing requirement and further supported it with a separate provision for customer compensation in the form of charges. These charges were deemed necessary to offset the disparity. In this specific instance, the responsibility for allocating the expenses was assigned to the national regulatory authority, thereby maintaining state control over the assets. In the current scenario, the responsibility for asset distribution has been assigned to the gearbox system operators, rendering the process of alignment irrelevant. In the final analysis, the CJEU has rendered a verdict invalidating the Commission's Decision.

This ruling marked a significant milestone in the implementation of additional measures aimed at promoting the growth of renewable energy sources. Prior to this decision, various support schemes were evaluated for their compatibility with the Energy Union strategy, which aims to increase the share of renewable energy in the overall energy system. The introduction of this measure by Member States to achieve these goals was seen as a significant administrative burden, impeding progress towards the development and integration of the energy market.

12.6 Stranded Costs

In the absence of electricity market liberalisation, the costs associated with investments made by electricity undertakings were incorporated into the tariffs. Consequently, investments were frequently allocated towards costly infrastructure projects, and long-term energy contracts were entered into that included "take or pay" obligations. Following the initiation of energy sector liberalisation, a notable trend emerged whereby certain costs incurred were left unrecovered, resulting in what is commonly referred to as stranded costs.

In order to mitigate specific externalities, a framework was established to address the issue of stranded costs. This framework aims to strike a balance between the objectives of existing utilities, which seek to deter new market entrants, while also ensuring the continued provision of energy sources. The balanced compensation mechanism encompasses State aid and may be deemed compatible with the internal market due to its promotion of the liberalisation process and development of the energy sector.[45] Consequently, it ensures that the measures implemented are proportionate and do not have a detrimental impact on trade between Member States. The Commission adopted the methodology for stranded costs in 2001. This methodology stipulates that compensation should not be granted to a profitable undertaking that experiences reduced profits as a result of liberalisation. The evaluation of compensations should be conducted prior to implementation, and adjustments may be necessary if market prices change during the specified period.

The approval of stranded costs in Austria pertains to the investments made in three hydropower plants and lignite-fired plants.[46] Annual compensations of EUR 456 million for hydropower plants and EUR 132 million for the lignite-fired plant have been approved for disbursement. The data is derived from the inputs provided by regional network operators and customers who have previously utilised electricity generated by these power plants. The projected duration of the compensation period was extended until the year 2010. The Commission has determined that the State aid measure is in accordance with the regulations of the European Union. However, it acknowledges the resemblance to the PreussenElektra case, which was not classified as aid. Consequently, the compensation for the services may bear similarities to the services of general economic interest, particularly in relation to ensuring security of supply.

The Netherlands has officially announced the implementation of a State aid scheme to address the issue of stranded costs arising from long-term heating contracts associated with the coal gasification plant Demkolec.[47] The annual calculation of stranded costs was conducted as a result of the fuel price analysis that occurred subsequent to the auction. The scheme was initially planned to span a period of 10 years, with a total budget of EUR 600 million. The proposal initially suggested implementing a surcharge on customers as a percentage of the costs associated with transport and system services. However, this surcharge was subsequently removed, and only compensation for the costs incurred due to stranded assets was approved. The assistance was authorised in accordance with the methodology pertaining to stranded costs.

In a similar vein, the provision of State aid was authorised in order to offset the stranded costs incurred in Spain. The aforementioned costs were accrued prior to the commencement of market liberalisation and were directly associated with investment activities. The entities that experienced the effects of the tariff fixing mechanism that was implemented prior to the opening of the market were the recipients of the benefits. The scheme was anticipated to continue until 2011.

The implementation of stranded cost compensation took place in Poland and Hungary with the adoption of various Commission decisions. The measures were implemented prior to the accession of the countries to the European Union. The investigation into long-term power purchase agreements in Poland has been initiated

---

[45] Brennan and Boyd (1997).

[46] Case SA.10434 (N34/1999)—Compensation of stranded costs.

[47] Case SA.10221 (N597/1998) Measures in favour of the electricity market for stranded costs.

by the Commission, wherein the network operator was provided with assurances regarding the quantity and price of purchases. In the Polish context, it is observed that these agreements accounted for approximately 50% of the market. The measure was regarded as a form of State aid. After conducting a thorough investigation, it was determined that the measure in question is not in line with the State aid regulations. Consequently, Poland has been urged to terminate the long-term power purchase agreements. Furthermore, the compensation scheme has been granted approval.

In Hungary, there have been instances of long-term power purchase agreements being established between electricity generators and network operators. Nevertheless, the Commission arrived at the conclusion that this measure was not in line with the Treaty on the Functioning of the European Union (TFEU) and consequently demanded reimbursement. The investigation findings indicate that the measure does not meet the necessary criteria to align with the regulations set forth by the European Union. A significant portion of the electricity produced in Hungary was distributed through long-term power purchase agreements. In light of this circumstance, the entry of new participants into the market was significantly impeded by the scarcity of competition. The Commission has issued a directive to cease these agreements within a period of 6 months.

Italy has identified stranded costs resulting from the expenses incurred in the construction of power plants prior to 1997, as well as costs associated with the take-or-pay obligation outlined in the contract with Nigerian gas.[48] The projected timeframe for the expenses to be accounted for was from 2000 to 2003, involving a compensation amounting to EUR 850 million, which was allocated to ENEL. Furthermore, a reimbursement was provided for the expenses incurred as a result of the "take-or-pay" clause, which arose from the inability to use the gasoline. The compensation for the latter amounted to EUR 1.465 million. Compensation was introduced to account for the gas consumption associated with electricity generation.

12.7 State Aid for Capacity Mechanism

Capacity mechanisms are of utmost importance in ensuring the reliable functioning of systems by preventing potential blackouts and other interruptions. The primary objective of these mechanisms is to guarantee that the power plant operator receives adequate remuneration for the security services maintained. Various factors can lead to the occurrence of unscheduled maintenance in nuclear power plants or insufficiency in hydropower reservoirs. These factors include climate conditions such as lack of sunlight or wind, as well as increased use of air conditioning due to high temperatures. Consequently, these events can result in spikes in electricity consumption. In order to mitigate these undesirable situations, capacity mechanisms are implemented. However, the measures that indicate compensation for specific actions

[48] Case SA.15876 (N490/2000—NN27/2005) R&D in the energy sector.

related to their obligations lead to these measures being considered state aid measures and requiring notification to the Commission prior to their implementation.

The approval of Belgium's capacity mechanism by the Commission is expected to enhance the security of supply while ensuring that the country's decision to phase out nuclear capacity until 2025 does not result in any significant distortion of competition.[49] This measure was ratified subsequent to the implementation of the new Electricity regulation in 2020. The Commission has initiated a comprehensive examination to assess the conformity of the national capacity mechanisms with the regulations governing State aid. The Commission expressed concerns regarding the adequacy of the quantification of the actual need for the capacity mechanism. Additionally, it questioned whether the capacity mechanism exceeds what is necessary to address resource adequacy, potentially resulting in excessive procurement of capacity. The measure must also ensure equal alignment across technologies, thereby avoiding any form of discrimination or unjust limitations on participation opportunities. Ultimately, the Commission expressed concerns regarding the potential limitations on the incentive for the Transmission System Operator (TSO) to make additional investments in transmission capacity due to congestion revenues.

The Agency for the Cooperation of Energy Regulators (ACER) has officially approved Belgium's improvements to its resource adequacy assessment, which aligns it with the European Union's methodology for resource adequacy assessment. The assessment conducted in the 10-year perspective anticipates the projected level of security of supply. Furthermore, Belgium has incorporated sustainability criteria into the regulations governing new fossil fuel installations that are eligible to participate in the capacity mechanism. This measure aims to support the attainment of decarbonization goals.

There was a lack of empirical evidence substantiating the potential disadvantages that certain technologies may face as a result of their involvement in the scheme. Additionally, there were no anticipated restrictions on the extent of participation in cross-border capacity. Furthermore, it has been determined that the TSO's collection of remuneration does not impose constraints on the ability to pursue additional investments in interconnection capacity.

Following the implementation of the sector inquiry, the Commission has initiated two comprehensive investigations against France. The initial inquiry pertains to the capacity mechanism that encompasses the entirety of the market, wherein the capacity obligations have the potential to be exchanged between electricity generators and suppliers. The Commission expressed concerns regarding the conformity of the measure with the regulations governing State aid.[50]

After conducting a thorough investigation, the Commission has granted approval for the State aid measure. In accordance with the capacity mechanism, providers offer their electricity capacity during periods of peak demand, particularly in the

[49] Case SA.54915 (2019/N-2020/C) Market wide capacity mechanism in Belgium.

[50] European Commission, Press Release IP/15/6110. State aid: Commission opens in-depth investigation into French capacity mechanism, 15 July 2015.

winter season. In exchange for their available capacity, providers are granted certificates. The procurement of these certificates from the capacity providers is necessary for the suppliers to adequately address peak demand. The certificates have the potential to be exchanged either through bilateral transactions among providers or through conventional auction mechanisms. France has made alterations to the anticipated measure. In order to enhance the implementation of new projects and facilitate the entry of new market participants, it is proposed that the duration of certificates be extended from 1 year to 7 years. This longer duration would offer a greater level of certainty and stability for the aforementioned endeavours. Furthermore, the allocation of the new capacities will be contingent upon the completion of a public tender process conducted within a timeframe of 4 years. Remuneration is also extended to foreign capacity providers, specifically those based in neighbouring countries at the interconnector. The prevention of potential market manipulation is anticipated through a range of measures, including the evaluation of capacity declarations against historical benchmarks. This evaluation aims to avoid the unnecessary reservation of additional capacity.[51]

A subsequent inquiry was initiated pertaining to the tender process for the operation of a newly constructed gas-fired power plant in Bretagne, with the objective of augmenting the electricity generation capacity within the region.[52] The French authorities officially communicated the measure to the Commission in January 2015. They asserted that the support was provided in accordance with a tender procedure and argued that it did not meet the criteria for being considered aid under Article 107 TFEU. Furthermore, they contended that the compensation could be regarded as remuneration for services of general economic interest.

The measure has been approved by the Commission following the completion of the investigation.[53] Despite assertions from French authorities that the measure does not utilise State resources to establish the price of capacity guarantees and that the price is determined through market forces, the authority's involvement was limited to establishing the security of supply criterion. The Commission disagreed with the aforementioned stance, asserting that the provision of aid is facilitated by the State's resources. Furthermore, the Commission argued that the offset measure, which compensates for the additional expenses incurred by undertakings as a result of the requirement to purchase wind-generated electricity at a price exceeding the market rate, is considered a form of state intervention as it is funded by end consumers of electricity. The Commission has declined to accept the argument that the recipient of the assistance is exempt from public service obligations, as the specific obligations have been explicitly defined. The Commission maintained the stance that the inclusion of the public service obligation criterion was not applicable in this particular instance, given that the certification obligation was not absolute and did not

[51] European Commission, State Aid SA.44859 (2017/N), France: Commission approves State aid for capacity mechanism, 22 November 2017.

[52] Case SA.39621 (2015/NN-2015/C) French country-wide capacity mechanism.

[53] Case SA.40454 (2015/N-2015/C) Tender for additional capacity in Brittany.

extend to the response to demand. The legitimacy of the security of supply as a common objective was acknowledged; however, the unforeseen outcome was the inadequacy of generation capacity.

The capacity mechanisms for strategic reserves have been approved for Belgium[54] and Germany.[55] The reserves have been identified as a means to mitigate the security of supply risks. The security of supply risks was found to be addressed by several factors, including the ageing nuclear facilities, the reliance on imported electricity, and Germany's objective of phasing out nuclear energy. The measures were implemented as a provisional resolution pending the resolution of market issues. The procurement of strategic reserves was planned to be carried out through competitive tenders that are accessible to all types of capacity providers.

The approval of market-wide capacity mechanisms has been granted in Italy[56] and Poland.[57] It has been delineated that these measures may effectively address concerns related to the structural security of supply. The capacity providers have the potential to receive compensation for their availability to produce electricity or to decrease electricity consumption. The risk associated with the security of supply was distinctly identified subsequent to the importation of goods from neighbouring countries. It has been observed that in Italy, investors exhibit reluctance to enter the market due to their inability to generate satisfactory investment returns from electricity sales. In the context of Poland, there is a lack of incentives for generators to maintain or expand their existing capacity. These mechanisms are inclusive of various capacities, encompassing both existing and anticipated ones, as well as those of domestic and foreign origins. Regular competitive auctions are conducted in order to allocate capacity contracts.

In both Greece[58] and France,[59] capacity mechanisms have been implemented to incentivize demand response, wherein customers are remunerated for reducing their electricity consumption during periods of electricity scarcity. France has demonstrated the necessity of implementing the scheme in order to enhance demand response, particularly during periods of cold weather when significant peaks occur. In Greece, a comparable situation arose as a result of the frigid peaks. The aforementioned measures were implemented on a temporary basis with the objective of minimising expenses. These measures were procured through a standardised and competitive tender process.

Austria[60] has made plans to create a network reserve for the electricity market and has officially informed the Commission about this measure. This initiative is a component of Austria's congestion management system, which aims to ensure an

[54] Case SA.48648 (2017/N) Belgian Strategic Reserve.

[55] Case SA.45852 (2017/N- 2017/C) German capacity reserve.

[56] Case SA.42011 (2017/N) Italian capacity mechanism.

[57] Case SA.46100 (2017/N) Polish capacity mechanism.

[58] Case SA.48780 (2017/N) Prolongation of the Greek interruptibility scheme.

[59] Case SA.48490 (2017/N) Specific demand response tender in France.

[60] Case SA.52263 (2020/N) Austrian network reserve.

adequate supply of electricity and address any issues related to bottlenecks in the transmission network. According to this model, it is anticipated that the TSO will be responsible for compensating power plant operators for the capacity they make available, even if they have expressed their intention to cease operations but still possess the capability to maintain the balance of the electricity system. The exclusion of coal- and lignite-fired power plants from the scheme was based on their high pollution levels, particularly in terms of CO2 emissions per kilowatt hour. Foreign power plants are also provided with the opportunity to contribute to grid stability by offering their capacity. The allocation of network reserves is facilitated through a competitive procedure overseen by the TSO, with the associated costs being transferred to customers through network charges. The scheme is projected to be in effect until the year 2025.

12.8 The Guidelines on State Aid for Climate, Environmental Protection and Energy

The Guidelines on State aid for climate, environmental protection and energy provide guidance on the evaluation procedure the Commission uses to determine the compatibility of aid measures related to environmental protection, including climate protection and energy.[61] These measures are subject to the requirement of notification as outlined in Article 107(3), point (c), of the TFEU.[62]

The newly implemented rules, effective January 2022, establish a versatile and well-suited framework that facilitates Member States in offering the required assistance to achieve the objectives of the Green Deal in a focused and economically efficient manner. The regulations encompass a harmonisation with the significant aims and targets outlined in the European Green Deal by the European Union, as well as with other recent regulatory modifications in the realms of energy and the environment. These laws will also address the growing significance of climate protection. The document encompasses many parts pertaining to energy efficiency measures, support for environmentally friendly transport, infrastructure development, circular economy initiatives, pollution mitigation, biodiversity conservation, and restoration, as well as measures aimed at guaranteeing energy supply security contingent upon specific conditions.[63]

The newly established guidelines offer a comprehensive framework for public bodies to effectively support the objectives of the European Green Deal while minimising any potential disruptions to competitiveness. It is recommended to expand the scope of investments and technologies that Member States can endorse

[61] Communication from the Commission—Guidelines on State aid for climate, environmental protection and energy 2022. C/2022/481. OJ C 80, 18.2.2022.

[62] Flynn et al. (2016).

[63] Puglisi et al. (2021).

in order to encompass emerging sectors such as clean mobility infrastructure, resource efficiency, and biodiversity. Additionally, it is crucial to include all technologies that have the potential to contribute to the objectives of the Green Deal, such as renewable hydrogen, electricity storage and demand response, and decarbonising production processes. The amended regulations typically provide for the provision of financial assistance that can cover the entirety of the financing shortfall, up to 100%, in cases where aid awards are determined through competitive bidding.

Additionally, the revised rules also aim to introduce novel forms of financial aid, such as contracts for difference. One potential approach to enhancing flexibility and efficiency in the current regulations is to implement a simplified evaluation process for cross-cutting measures.[64] This could involve consolidating the assessment of such measures within a dedicated section of the guidelines, specifically addressing aid aimed at reducing and eliminating greenhouse gas emissions, which may include support for renewable energy and energy efficiency. To ensure the effective allocation of aid towards climate and environmental protection, it is recommended to implement safeguards, such as the establishment of a public consultation requirement beyond specific thresholds. This measure aims to ensure that aid is directed towards areas where it is most necessary for enhancing climate and environmental protection. Additionally, it is crucial to limit the aid to the extent necessary for achieving environmental objectives while avoiding any undue distortion of competition or compromising the integrity of the single market. To ensure alignment with pertinent European Union legislation and policies in the domains of environment and energy, it is imperative to gradually eliminate financial support provided to fossil fuels in the form of subsidies.

The primary aim of the Clean Energy for All Europeans Package (CEEAG) is to assist Member States in achieving the objectives outlined in the European Green Deal while minimising the financial burden on taxpayers and ensuring fair competition is not compromised. In pursuit of this objective, the guidelines have been aligned with pertinent European Union legislation and policies pertaining to the domains of environment and energy. The CEEAG has implemented a technology-agnostic stance towards many technologies that have the potential to mitigate or eliminate greenhouse gas emissions, encompassing renewable energy sources and energy efficiency measures. Nevertheless, it is still feasible to have technology-specific bids, particularly when Union law mandates sector-specific or technology-specific objectives, such as those outlined in the Renewable Energy Directive for the promotion of renewable energy. This measure will facilitate the integration of Member States" assistance for enhancing the energy efficiency of buildings with assistance for other investments aimed at improving the energy or environmental performance of structures.

[64] Communication from the Commission—Guidelines on State aid for climate, environmental protection and energy 2022. C/2022/481. OJ C 80, 18.2.2022.

The CEEAG establishes explicit regulations pertaining to the provision of assistance for the promotion of clean mobility, along with the principles outlined in the Clean Mobility Package.[65] The guidelines specifically include a special section that addresses assistance for the procurement of environmentally friendly vehicles and the modification of existing vehicles, as well as the establishment of infrastructure for recharging and fuelling.

The CEEAG offers comprehensive coverage and enhanced regulations for assistance aimed at promoting resource efficiency in companies. It also facilitates the advancement of a circular economy, aligning with the objectives outlined in the Circular Economy Action Plan.

Aligned with the goals outlined in the Biodiversity Strategy, the CEEAG establishes explicit regulations for Member States to facilitate the safeguarding and revival of biodiversity, the rehabilitation of natural ecosystems, and the adoption of nature-based solutions. Prior to this, there was a lack of dedicated state aid guidance pertaining to these matters. To ensure consistency with the pertinent legislation and policies established by the European Union in the domains of environment and energy, it is imperative to gradually eliminate financial support provided to fossil fuels in the form of subsidies.

Renewable energy communities (RECs) and other minor stakeholders play a significant role in the realisation of the objectives outlined in the European Green Deal, as acknowledged in the revised Renewable Energy Directive (RED II).[66] This is the rationale behind the provision of increased flexibility by the CEEAG, which permits Member States to grant exemptions from the competitive bidding requirement for renewable energy community projects and small and medium-sized enterprise SME owned projects with an installed capacity below 6 MW. Wind projects with a capacity of up to 18 MW can be developed by renewable energy communities as well as small and microfirms without the requirement of engaging in competitive bidding.

In a broader sense, in cases where competitive bidding is applicable, the CEEAG provides Member States with the opportunity to structure bids in a manner that promotes the involvement of energy communities. Among other things, lowering the pre-qualification requirements can achieve this. Small and medium-sized enterprises (SMEs) as well as small mid-cap companies might derive advantages from receiving

---

[65]Commission Regulation (EU) 2022/2560 of December 15, 2022, on the state aid for the promotion of clean mobility. Official Journal of the European Union, L 328, 16 December 2022. Commission Communication on the Clean Energy for All Europeans Package. Communication from the Commission to the European Parliament, the Council, the European Economic and Social Committee and the Committee of the Regions: The European Green Deal. COM(2019) 640 final, Brussels, 11 December 2019.

[66]Directive (EU) 2018/2001 of the European Parliament and of the Council of 11 December 2018 on the promotion of the use of energy from renewable sources (recast). Official Journal of the European Union, L 328, 21 December 2018. Communication from the Commission to the European Parliament, the Council, the European Economic and Social Committee and the Committee of the Regions: The European Green Deal. COM(2019) 640 final, Brussels, 11 December 2019.

assistance when they implement energy performance enhancement measures through energy performance contracts, whether for buildings or industrial operations. Moreover, it is possible to enhance aid intensities by 20 percentage points for small enterprises or by 10 percentage points for medium-sized enterprises across various aid categories. These categories include aid for enhancing energy performance in buildings, aid for procuring zero-emission vehicles and establishing recharging and refuelling infrastructure, aid for promoting resource efficiency, aid for mitigating pollution (excluding greenhouse gases), and aid for conducting studies or providing consultancy services pertaining to climate, environmental protection, and energy. To ensure consistency with the applicable legislation and policies of the European Union in the domains of environment and energy, it is imperative to gradually eliminate financial support provided to fossil fuels.

12.9 The General Block Exemption Regulation

According to Article 108(3) of the TFEU, Member States are obligated to inform the European Commission of any state aid and can only proceed with its implementation upon receiving authorization from the Commission. The Commission has the authority to designate some types of state aid as compatible with the Single Market, thereby exempting them from the requirement to be notified as outlined in the Treaty.

The General Block Exemption Regulation empowers Member States to immediately implement specific aid measures, thereby maintaining absolute legal certainty.[67] The General Block Exemption Regulation of 2014 grants an exemption to specific categories of state aid from the requirement of prior reporting to the Commission, provided that the societal advantages outweigh any potential impact on competition. Consequently, Member States are currently implementing most recently implemented state aid measures, with the exception of those implemented during times of crisis, without requiring Commission approval. This is in line with the Commission's approach to promoting efficiency and effectiveness by focusing on improving productivity and minimizing activities that do not add value.

The absence of conformity between a state assistance measure and the requirements outlined in the General Block Exemption Regulation (GBER) does not necessarily imply its incompatibility with the state aid regulations of the European Union. This implies that the action must be communicated in advance to the Commission, which will subsequently evaluate whether the state aid can be sanctioned in accordance with alternative EU state aid regulations. The European Commission has officially supported a specific modification to the GBER in order

[67] Commission Regulation (EU) No 651/2014 of 17 June 2014 declaring certain categories of aid compatible with the internal market in application of Articles 107 and 108 of the Treaty Text with EEA relevance. OJ L 187, 26.6.2014, p. 1–78.

to enhance, streamline, and expedite assistance for the European Union's green and digital transformations. In conjunction with the recently introduced Temporary Crisis and Transition Framework, this specific amendment seeks to facilitate the provision of essential assistance by Member States to crucial sectors in alignment with the Green Deal Industrial Plan.

The GBER establishes distinct classifications of state aid that are deemed consistent with the Treaty on the Functioning of the European Union, on the condition that they satisfy specified requirements. Consequently, these categories are exempt from the obligation of prior notification and approval by the Commission, allowing Member States to directly provide aid and only inform the Commission retrospectively. The present amendment provides Member States with increased leeway to devise and execute supportive measures in sectors that are crucial for the shift towards climate neutrality and the establishment of a net-zero industry. The facilitation of investment and funding for the development of clean technology in Europe, in accordance with the Green Deal Industrial Plan, is expected to contribute to its expedited progress.

The updated regulations are a response to recent revisions made to many state aid guidelines, with the aim of ensuring that the General Block Exemption Regulation (GBER) remains suitable for facilitating the transition towards environmentally sustainable and digitally advanced economies. Additionally, they will establish the necessary groundwork to address the economic repercussions resulting from Russia's conflict with Ukraine, as well as aid in the revitalization of Europe's economy. Enhanced and optimised range of assistance available in the realm of environmental preservation and energy, among other areas, with the aim of bolstering the implementation of renewable energy initiatives, decarbonisation endeavours, sustainable transportation systems, biodiversity conservation efforts, as well as facilitating investments in renewable hydrogen and promoting energy efficiency. To enhance the execution of specific projects that include beneficiaries across several Member States, such as Important Projects of Common European Interest, in the realm of research and development, it is proposed to augment the levels of aid intensities and notification thresholds. One potential approach to expanding the scope of training and reskilling initiatives across various industries involves the implementation of an exemption for training aid below EUR three million, allowing for a wider range of opportunities in this domain.

Block exempt aid measures established by Member States to limit prices for energy, including electricity, gas, and heat derived from natural gas or electricity, propose a substantial elevation of notification thresholds pertaining to environmental assistance as well as research, development, and innovation (RDI) assistance. This document aims to provide a comprehensive analysis of the available options for risk finance assistance, specifically targeting SMEs and start-ups. Additionally, it looks into the financial instruments that the Invest EU Fund is backing. Extending the duration of the GBER until the conclusion of 2026 is proposed in order to provide enhanced legal clarity and regulatory stability. The thresholds in the GBER are expanded to accommodate the extended duration of the regulations, encompassing sectors beyond those subject to specific assessment.

12.10 Conclusions

The energy system in the United Kingdom was confronted with significant challenges due to the need to decommission one fifth of its power generation capacity by the year 2020. This necessitated substantial investments in order to compensate for the resulting deficit in electricity supply. Over the course of an extended period, there is a possibility that the demand for electricity could potentially experience a twofold increase. However, it is worth noting that the market is currently providing insufficient indications regarding the augmentation of investments in low-carbon electricity generation. The initiation of the market reform aimed to align with climate change policy objectives and foster investment in low-carbon electricity technologies. The objective of this reform was to enhance the reliability of electricity provision by encouraging the utilisation of a variety of energy sources while simultaneously mitigating expenses and prioritising the adoption of low-carbon technologies in electricity generation. An endeavour was undertaken to establish a somewhat contentious mechanism for financing the nuclear power plant project. This mechanism involved the use of financial derivatives known as contracts for difference, which were specifically designed to guarantee the return on investments.

Austria has commenced the legal process to invalidate the Commission's decision pertaining to the execution of Hinkley Point C. Austria claims that the Commission granted the aid based on the presumption of market failure and established a distinct market separate from the nuclear energy market. Furthermore, Austria alleges that the aid was approved as an investment aid, but in reality, it possessed characteristics more aligned with an operating aid. Additionally, Austria argues that the nuclear power plant fails to align with common interest objectives and that the measures taken were disproportionate. Lastly, Austria contends that the United Kingdom should have initiated the public procurement procedure. The appeal raised the issue of whether the nuclear power plant project could be eligible for State aid that is considered to be in line with Article 107 (3) (c) of the TFEU. The CJEU determined that in cases where the Euratom Treaty does not contain explicit provisions regarding the implementation of State aid, the TFEU is applicable. Austria further contended that the principle of polluter pays, the precautionary principle, and the protection of the environment should be universally considered as precluding in all circumstances. The CJEU has suggested that this exclusion may potentially conflict with Article 194(2) of the TFEU. This article grants Member States the autonomy to determine their own energy composition. In this particular scenario, the Member State has chosen to include nuclear energy as part of its energy mix along with additional support measures that the European Commission has approved as being compliant with Article 107 TFEU.

The impetus to attract investment in the renewable energy sector stems from both the impacts of climate change and the advancement of novel technologies. Member States employ various strategies to incentivize and attract fresh investments in the field of renewable energy. These strategies encompass streamlining licencing procedures, simplifying regulations pertaining to grid access, and establishing electricity purchase prices. Energy infrastructure projects frequently incorporate various strategies, including the provision of government-backed loan guarantees, the integration of investment expenses into tariff structures, and the implementation of specific tax incentives and equitable returns. Power purchase agreements (PPAs) are recognised as a strategy for guaranteeing a favourable financial outcome when an organisation undertakes the development of a new infrastructure project and faces substantial initial expenses.

After looking at the relevant legal precedents, it has been decided that specific benefits are given in a selective way, even when they are given to an entire industry instead of a single economic entity. The act of a state ratifying international conventions by establishing a minimum liability requirement for operators and ensuring the remaining liability through State aid exhibits characteristics of State aid. However, the matter of notifying the Commission about such aid has not yet been addressed, as the regulation is derived from international law. The nuclear industry possesses a unique characteristic that distinguishes it from other industries. To facilitate the examination of disparities in legal regulation and the resolution of competition and civil liability concerns within the nuclear sector, this discussion will comprehensively explore the fundamental tenets of civil liability.

The Commission has determined that providing assistance to energy infrastructure projects is justified due to the importance of natural gas infrastructure in maintaining a dependable and diverse energy market. This ensures the availability of suitable alternatives in the event of any disruptions. The significant loss that would have occurred in the absence of aid served as evidence that its presence had a significant impact on the undertaking. Consequently, the undertaking would not have pursued the project without the aid. The Commission additionally recognised that the objective of this project is to establish gas infrastructure in Europe, with a particular focus on enhancing the Baltic region.

Germany implemented a reform aimed at providing support for cogeneration. This reform included operational assistance that was outlined in national legislation. The purpose of notifying this measure was to ensure legal certainty, as there were doubts regarding the collection of feed-in tariffs resulting from the levy imposed on consumption. The programme provides financial assistance to a range of highly efficient cogeneration facilities, including both newly constructed and modernised installations. The respective network operator established the promotion as a premium that required payment above the prevailing market price.

In order to mitigate specific externalities, the compensation mechanisms for stranded costs were delineated. This was done to maintain equilibrium between the present utilities' objectives of deterring new market participants and ensuring a reliable energy supply. The evaluation of compensations should be conducted prior to implementation, and if circumstances change during the period of time as a result of market prices, adjustments may be necessary. The recognition of stranded costs as a State aid measure was acknowledged.

Capacity mechanisms are of utmost importance in ensuring the reliable functioning of systems by preventing potential blackouts and other interruptions. Various factors can lead to unscheduled maintenance at nuclear power plants or insufficient hydropower reservoir levels. These factors include climate conditions such as lack of sunlight or wind, as well as increased use of air conditioning due to high temperatures. These events can result in spikes in electricity consumption. However, the measures that reflect compensation for specific actions related to their obligations are considered State aid measures and must be notified to the Commission prior to their implementation.

The updated Guidelines of the European Commission pertaining to state aid for climate, environmental protection, and energy have become effective as of January 1, 2022. These guidelines establish provisions for the provision of assistance to renewable energy sources, including biofuels, bioliquids, biogas, biomass fuels, renewable and low-carbon hydrogen, and energy derived from waste. Additionally, the guidelines address the promotion of electrification through the utilisation of renewable and low-carbon electricity, which contributes to the reduction of carbon emissions. The guidelines have recently incorporated the clean mobility sector, which entails providing assistance for the procurement and leasing of environmentally friendly transportation options as well as the modification of mobile services or vehicles in cases where it is deemed necessary to enhance the utilisation of biofuels and synthetic fuels. The new guidelines also emphasised the significance of hydrogen, particularly in relation to the development of refuelling infrastructure for heavy-duty vehicles.

References

Brennan T, Boyd J (1997) Stranded costs, takings, and the law and economics of implicit contracts. Discussion Paper. 97/02. Resources for the future

Flynn L, Pesaresi N, Siaterli C, Casteele K (2016) EU competition law, vol IV, 2nd edn. Claeys and Casteels, Deventer

Puglisi L, Robins N, Kristensen J (2021) The EU Commission publishes its draft on the climate, energy and environmental aid guidelines CEEAG, e-Competitions Preview, 104693

Ruechardt C (2018) EU state aid control of infrastructure funding. Wolters Kluwer, Alphen aan den Rijn

Zhu L (2020) Services of General Economic Interest in EU Competition Law: Striking a balance between noneconomic values and market competition. Springer

Part V
Exclusive, Special Rights and Services of General Economic Interest

Chapter 13
Public Services in the Modern Economy: The Evolution and Future

Abstract The number of entities granted such rights determines the distinction between special and exclusive rights. When an entity receives exclusive rights, it prevents any other player in the market from enjoying the same advantage. Special privileges grant exclusive entitlements to a specific subset of entities, thereby restricting other entities from offering specific services in the market. The competitive tender procedure offers a special exception for entities responsible for providing services of general economic interest. The Commission has observed that granting exclusive rights to a specific entity is not required, as per Article 106(1) in conjunction with Article 102 Treaty on the Functioning of the European Union (TFEU) and established case law from the Court of Justice of European Union (CJEU). However, the primary focus is on the presence of a publicly owned company and the resulting inequality among market participants, which ultimately leads to a disruption of fair competition. All services falling under the general economic interest category frequently share numerous common characteristics. These factors encompass the enforcement of a public service duty, the all-inclusive nature of the services, their uninterrupted provision, affordability, coverage for all, and a prioritisation of safeguarding consumer rights.

13.1 Introduction

This chapter looks at the complicated relationship between exclusive and special rights and services of general economic interest (SGEIs) in the European energy industry. It also looks at the legislative structure, principles, and problems that come up when exclusive and special rights and SGEIs exist together. This highlights the significance of implementing a well-rounded approach that ensures both market competitiveness and the provision of essential services.

The European Union (EU) has encountered an ongoing dilemma in achieving a harmonious equilibrium between two core principles: promoting competitive markets through the elimination of exclusive and special privileges and protecting

L. Rimšaitė, *The Crossroads of Competition Law and Energy Regulation*,
https://doi.org/10.1007/978-3-031-73238-6_13

SGEIs that play a vital role in the overall well-being of society.[1] SGEIs encompass a classification of services that are deemed essential for the overall welfare of individuals within a society. These services encompass a range of essential amenities, such as energy, healthcare, and public transit, among others. It may be important to implement public intervention in order to guarantee both affordability and availability.

The European Union acknowledges the importance of both exclusive rights and SGEIs. The Treaty on the Functioning of the European Union (TFEU) assigns considerable importance to market liberalisation and competition, as outlined in Article 106. Nevertheless, Article 14 of the TFEU also confers member states with the power to develop and fund SGEIs. The act of simultaneous dedication serves as the basis for a refined state of balance. The potential conformity of exclusive and special rights with European Union law may be subject to scrutiny, particularly if they lead to significant market distortions or impede competition. The attainment of an ideal equilibrium, which ensures compliance with legal restrictions, is a significant and demanding obstacle. The existence of exclusive and specialised privileges inside the market has the capacity to obstruct competition and inhibit innovation, potentially leading to escalated expenses for consumers. The fundamental significance lies in guaranteeing equitable circumstances for all participants.

For member states to get the right amount of money for SGEIs, they need to find a balance between protecting the core of SGEIs and following State aid rules, which are meant to keep government subsidies from skewing competition. The implementation of transparent governance and accountability procedures is vital for guaranteeing the proper delineation, funding, and delivery of SGEIs in order to mitigate the risk of potential misappropriation. The current discussion centres on the complex issue of state ownership and control in the nuclear business, specifically focusing on the importance of maintaining safety and security protocols.

There is a need for the European Union to enhance its regulatory oversight and strengthen the capabilities of regulatory bodies in order to ensure effective monitoring and enforcement of compliance with European Union competition rules pertaining to exclusive and special rights.[2] Ensuring openness and accountability in the delineation and financing of services classified as of general economic interest is crucial to mitigating the risk of potential misappropriation. Promote the adoption of market-oriented frameworks that foster competition and simultaneously safeguard the provision of services that are of widespread economic importance.

The effort to combine exclusive and special rights with services of general economic interest in the energy sector is a complex and varied issue. The subject at hand requires the implementation of a sophisticated approach that complies with

[1]Communication from the Commission on the application of the European Union State aid rules to compensation granted for the provision of services of general economic interest Text with EEA relevance. OJ C 8, 11.1.2012, p. 4–14.

[2]Communication from the Commission — European Union framework for State aid in the form of public service compensation (2011). OJ C 8, 11.1.2012, p. 15–22.

the regulations governing competition within the European Union, all the while ensuring the provision of essential services to the general public. By effectively addressing these challenges, the European Union can attain a balanced state that fosters both market competitiveness and societal welfare within the ever-changing energy sector.

EU competition law encompasses regulations that apply to both undertakings and Member States, thereby establishing a framework for permissible levels of intervention that do not undermine the functioning of the internal market. The complexity of Article 106 TFEU is notable, and its application is currently constrained to a relatively narrow scope. Member States are strictly prohibited from enacting any regulations that may result in the infringement of the provisions pertaining to the free movement of goods, services, capital, and persons, as well as other provisions related to competition law as outlined in the TFEU. The subsequent section of this article includes a provision that permits an exemption for the purpose of attaining the objectives of public service. Additionally, the third section grants the Commission the authority to adopt directives and decisions in order to effectively implement the aforementioned goals.

13.2 Article 106 (1) TFEU

Article 106(1) of the TFEU stipulates the following: in relation to public undertakings and undertakings that receive special or exclusive rights from Member States, it is prohibited for Member States to introduce or uphold any legislation that contradicts the regulations outlined in the Treaties. This prohibition specifically applies to the rules specified in Article 18 and Articles 101–109.

This article stipulates that Member States must refrain from implementing any measures that could violate other rules of the TFEU pertaining to competition, as well as provisions aimed at achieving the objectives of the TFEU.[3] The article addresses actions that are directed at both public entities and private enterprises. Frequently, the evaluation of competition regulations has been conducted with a focus on examining instances of dominant market position abuse, state aid, and sector-specific regulations. The act of entrusting a specific undertaking with special or exclusive rights may imply the establishment of a stronger dominant position in the market, which is facilitated by the state through the delegation of specific powers to said undertaking.

In order to ascertain whether an undertaking is granted special or exclusive rights, it is crucial to assess whether the undertaking is actively engaging in economic activity. In accordance with the jurisprudence of the Court of Justice of the European Union (CJEU), services that are typically offered in exchange for compensation are considered to be within the realm of economic activities. Furthermore, it is possible

[3] Nicolaides (2021).

for a single establishment to engage in both economic and non-economic activities, as long as separate accounting is maintained to prevent any potential cross-subsidisation.[4]

The determination of the application of Article 106(1) TFEU also takes into consideration the presence of special and exclusive rights. The differentiation among the categories is determined by the number of undertakings that have been granted the privilege. Specifically, when exclusive rights are conferred upon a specific entity, no other participant in the market is permitted to exercise this privilege. In the context of special privileges, a select group of entities is granted exclusive rights, thereby restricting other entities from offering specific services in the market.[5] Consequently, by conferring these special privileges on a specific set of undertakings, the remaining entities are effectively barred from providing said services. An exemption exists within the competitive tender procedure that may be applied to the allocation of these rights, specifically in cases where an undertaking is entrusted with providing services of general economic interest.

13.3 The Greek Lignite Cases

The Public Power Corporation (PPC) (Dimosia Epicheirisi Ilektrismou AE) was granted an exemption in 2008 that favoured the company in terms of lignite extraction.[6] The primary operations of the organisation encompass the production of electrical power and the extraction of lignite. The aforementioned company held a previous monopoly in the generation and distribution of electricity within the Greek electricity sector. Furthermore, it exercises the right to be the exclusive supplier to both eligible and non-eligible customers. Additionally, it holds the exclusive position as the wholesale supplier and buyer for the non-interconnected islands and is the sole proprietor of the assets pertaining to transmission and distribution networks. The company is responsible for overseeing the distribution network, while the state holds a majority ownership stake of 51% in the transmission network, with the remaining shares being controlled by the company. The company is not only the primary producer of lignite in the country but also ranks as the second-largest producer in Europe. Lignite is commonly employed in the generation of electricity, and it also finds application in the realms of heating and industrial processes. Lignite-fired power plants are purposefully engineered to combust this particular fuel, and the process of converting them to utilise alternative fuel sources is generally

[4] Case C-364/92, SAT.1 Satellitenfernsehen GmbH v. Hauptzollamt Hamburg-Jonas [1994] ECR I-1177. Case C-379/98, PreussenElektra AG v. Schhleswag AG [2001] ECR I-2099. Case C-260/06, Cleary v. Commission [2008] ECR I-0000.

[5] Marson (2014).

[6] Commission decision of 5 March 2008, on granting or maintaining in force by the Hellenic Republic of rights in favour of Public Power Corporation S.A. for extraction of lignite.

cost-prohibitive. The characteristics of this particular fuel contribute to its high transportation costs over long distances, resulting in the strategic placement of lignite-fired plants in close proximity to lignite mines.

The Greek electricity sector was primarily characterised by a vertically integrated monopoly responsible for all aspects of electricity generation, supply, transmission, and distribution. However, in response to the implementation of the first energy package, a decision was made to introduce market liberalisation. Initially, the competition was implemented in the generation and supply sectors, specifically targeting the provision of services to significant customer segments. The granting of import rights for lignite is not limited to any specific undertaking, although it should be noted that only PPC currently possesses the rights to export lignite. Additionally, PPC holds the reserved capacity rights for imports, which allows them to utilise the majority of the interconnection capacity on the northern borders.

In 2003, the Commission received a complaint alleging that the Hellenic Republic had granted the applicant an exclusive licence to investigate and utilise the lignite resources within the country. These actions by the national government were claimed to be in violation of Article 106(2) in conjunction with Article 102 of the Treaty on the Functioning of the European Union (TFEU).[7] The measure is in violation of Article 106(1) in conjunction with Article 102 when the undertaking utilises its exclusive rights and engages in abusive behaviour due to its dominant position, or when there is a high probability of such a situation occurring.

The Commission has noticed that it is not necessary to give exclusive rights to a certain entity, based on Article 106(1) in conjunction with Article 102 TFEU and established case law from the CJEU. Rather, it is significant to assess whether a public entity is involved and whether this leads to an imbalance between market participants, ultimately resulting in a distortion of competition. In 2008, the Commission made a decision declaring that Greece had infringed upon Article 106(1) of the TFEU, in conjunction with Article 102 TFEU, by providing the PPC with exclusive access to lignite exploitation and lignite-based electricity. The allocation of exclusive rights to a particular company for the exploitation of lignite has resulted in the establishment of a dominant market position, characterised by near-monopoly control. Consequently, this situation has posed significant barriers for new entrants seeking to participate in the market. Greece received an invitation to implement specific measures aimed at guaranteeing the accessibility of resources for the competitors of the PPC. The state has implemented measures that involve granting lignite exploitation rights to other market participants through a tender procedure in the deposits of Drama, Elassona, Vevi, and Vergora, respectively.

The complaint was sent to the General Court. The PPC pleas included the supposed mistakes in applying Article 106(1) TFEU in combination with Article 102 TFEU, the violation of the duty to allocate state resources, the principles of legal certainty and legitimate expectations, and the violation of the proportionality principle. The General Court determined that the exclusive access to lignite granted to

[7] Case C-265/03, Commission v. Hellenic Republic [2004] ECR I-10567.

PPC may have provided the company with the ability to engage in abusive practises as a dominant entity.[8] However, it is important to note that the mere existence of privileged access does not automatically constitute an abuse of a dominant position. The General Court is mandated to ascertain the concrete instances of power abuse that have arisen as a consequence of the implementation of State measures. The decision of the Commission was invalidated based on the aforementioned reasons, without the need to analyse other aspects of the complaint.

The Commission filed an appeal with the CJEU, saying that the General Court made a mistake in how it interpreted the application of Article 106(1) of the TFEU in conjunction with Article 102 TFEU, and that its reasoning was not good enough. The CJEU has acknowledged the existence of a potential risk of abuse of power that could lead to the violation of the rules outlined in the TFEU. Specifically, there is a solid basis for concern when a government intervention impacts the market by introducing varying conditions of competition among competitors. In such instances, the state may grant special or exclusive privileges to a public enterprise, thereby enabling the consolidation or expansion of market dominance. The identification of privileged access is deemed sufficient in determining the potential anticompetitive effect, thus obviating the need to establish the actual harm to competition.

The General Court has dismissed the appeals and concluded that the Commission did not make any errors in its assessment of the market definition. In 2018, the Commission granted approval to the remedies proposed by Greece, which entail the divestment of the Melti and Megalopoli 3 and 4 units by PPC. This action effectively eliminates the privileged access previously granted to the company. In 2019, following the market test, Greece put forth revised measures aimed at addressing congestion issues. Specifically, it was proposed that the gas-fired unit of Megalopoli 5, owned by PPC, should operate at a restricted capacity until the completion of the Peloponese corridor, which was expected to occur by 2019. The remedies included provisions for the transfer of mining, exploration, and exploitation rights, as well as the sharing of personnel and infrastructure. The divestment facilitated PPC's acquisition of 60% of the lignite reserves. The aforementioned decision resulted in a significant alteration of the energy liberalisation process, consequently facilitating the opening of the market to accommodate the interests of consumers.[9]

[8]Case T-169/08, *RENV- DEI v Commission*. [2012] ECR II 0000, para 93.

[9]Case T-644/16, PPC v. Commission [2020] ECLI:EU:T:2020:345.

13.4 Article 106 (2) TFEU

According to Article 106(2) of the TFEU, it is stipulated that the rules outlined in the Treaties shall apply to organisations running services of general economic interest or holding monopoly status that generate revenue.[10] Specifically, they shall adhere to the regulations pertaining to competition, as long as the implementation of these regulations does not impede the fulfilment of their specific assigned duties, either legally or practically. The potential impact on commerce should not be allowed to hinder the objectives of the Union.

The part evaluates the responsibilities of specific undertakings that have been assigned the task of providing services that benefit the overall economy. It argues that competition legislation should not hinder these undertakings from fulfilling their designated purpose. The exception described here extends beyond the scope of competition law, and it is possible to apply the principles outlined in this article to the regulations concerning the free movement of goods, services, and persons.[11] There are counterarguments to this thesis. The article provides provisions for derogations from the principle of free movement in order to achieve economic goals. However, there was no valid rationale for deviating from the implementation of Article 106(2) in relation to free movement.[12] The jurisprudence of the CJEU has been invoked in certain instances pertaining to matters concerning the principle of free movement.

The absence of a precise delineation of broad economic interest services can be attributed to their dynamic character and the fluctuating understanding of which specific services should fall under this classification throughout time. Member States were not requested to provide any enumerations of services that could be assessed as being of general economic importance. Certain authors raise concerns about the potential failure of governmental entities to establish efficient markets, wherein regulatory interventions should not aim to rectify circumstances that could be resolved through market disruptions.

There are several characteristics that are typically found in all services classified as of general economic interest. These include the imposition of a public service responsibility, the universal nature of the service, its continuity, affordability, universal coverage, and a focus on consumer protection. The services commonly offered by network sectors, such as energy or telecommunications, postal services, public emergency services, water supply, waste management, public service broadcasting, and sectoral pension systems, have been deemed eligible for the provision of general economic interest services. The evaluation encompassed certain market factors, such as the investment decisions made by market participants and the presence of existing service providers. In cases where these factors are present,

[10] Sierra (2016) and Krajewski (2015).

[11] Burke (2015).

[12] Melcher (2019).

services should not be classified as general economic interest services, as they are already being provided and do not fulfil a specific mission that would otherwise go unaddressed.

The principle of conferral guarantee is employed in the interpretation of the provision of services that fall within the category of broad economic interest, and it is imperative to adhere to the corresponding rights of Member States. The Commission reserves the right to scrutinise the definition of services in the event of a clear and evident inaccuracy. The Member States possess significant discretionary powers in selecting both the extent of these specific services and the compensation for their provision, necessitating the evaluation of intricate economic considerations. The Commission possesses the authority to examine whether the factual assumptions are clearly incorrect or not, to determine whether the measure was clearly incorrect, if the system is suitable for achieving the objectives, and if there were any errors made by Member States in defining the mission of services of general economic interest. In specific instances, it has been determined that the grant of monopoly to the entity responsible for fulfilling the public service obligation was found to be in accordance with the rules of European Union law.

13.5 Services of General Economic Interest

The concept of services of broad interest is explicitly established in Protocol No. 26 of the TFEU. The Union's shared values regarding services of general economic interest, as defined in Article 14 of the Treaty on the Functioning of the European Union, encompass the following key aspects: Recognising the crucial role and extensive discretion of national, regional, and local authorities in delivering, contracting, and organising services of general economic interest in a manner that closely aligns with user needs and acknowledging the diversity among various services of general economic interest and the resulting variations in user requirements and preferences due to distinct geographical, social, or cultural circumstances emphasising the importance of maintaining a high standard of quality, safety, and affordability, ensuring equal treatment, and promoting universal access and the protection of user rights. Article 2 of the Treaties does not have any impact on the authority of Member States to offer, delegate, and arrange non-economic services of general interest.

Furthermore, the provisions of Article 14 of the TFEU delineate the following: in accordance with the provisions outlined in Article 4 of the Treaty on European Union, as well as Articles 93, 106, and 107 of this Treaty, and recognising the significance of services of general economic interest in the shared values of the Union and their contribution to the promotion of social and territorial cohesion, both the Union and its Member States, within their respective jurisdictions and within the framework of the Treaties, shall ensure that such services are governed by principles and conditions, including economic and financial conditions, that enable them to effectively carry out their objectives. The principles and conditions outlined in this provision shall be established by the European Parliament and the Council through the enactment of regulations, following the ordinary legislative procedure. It is important to note that the competence of Member States to provide, commission, and fund such services in accordance with the Treaties shall not be affected.

While the TFEU outlines the application specifics and respective requirements in Protocol and Articles 14 and 106(2), it does not provide a clear definition of services of general economic interest. The Commission observed that services of general economic interest encompass economic activities that generate outcomes for public goods and would not be supplied by the market in the absence of public interventions. The provision of general economic interest services is of paramount significance and cannot be solely facilitated by the market mechanism without the intervention of the State, or at the very least, in a manner that ensures accessibility to all individuals without any form of discrimination. Compensation is necessary in order to mitigate potential losses incurred by service providers, as the additional costs associated with providing such services may not be fully offset. This is particularly relevant in cases where the services are deemed to serve a broader public interest.

The legislative framework pertaining to the implementation of Altmark and SGEI was established in 2005. The aforementioned composition comprised two distinct written materials, namely the Commission Decision and a Community Framework. Furthermore, the Transparency Directive underwent additional modifications. The Decision provided a block exemption for State Aid in the context of SGEI that meet specific thresholds. The Framework demonstrated its applicability to cases that lie outside the purview of the Commission Decision, yet the substance remains largely consistent. The Transparency Directive implemented provisions that establish requirements for the separation of accounts in situations where public compensation is provided to a company for delivering services of general economic interest. The evolution and discourse surrounding the concept of SGEI have been ongoing since 1990, encompassing the primary legislation of the European Union as well as the case law established by the CJEU. The mention of SGEI was initially included in Article 90(2) of the ECC Treaty, which was subsequently revised to Article 86(2) of the EC Treaty and ultimately to Article 106(2) of the TFEU.

According to the ruling of the CJEU: *"The derogations are made so as to reconcile the Member States interest in using certain undertakings, in particular in the public sector, as an instrument of economic or fiscal policy with the Union's interest in ensuring compliance with the rules on competition and the preservation of the unity of the internal Market."*[13]

The Treaty of Amsterdam introduced a new provision, Article 16 TEC (currently Article 14 TFEU), which pertains to the (SGEI). The confirmation of the impact of the SGEI occurred subsequent to the adoption of the Treaty of Lisbon in 2007. In line with the TFEU, the European Parliament and the Council use the ordinary legislative procedure to set principles and economic and financial conditions. This is

[13] Case C-202/88, *France v Commission* [1991] ECR-I-1223, para 12.

done without undermining the authority of Member States. Furthermore, the inclusion of Protocol No. 26 on services of general interest in the treaties, along with its accompanying articles, is noteworthy. Article 1 of this protocol emphasises the significance of the Union's commitment to SGEI as outlined in Article 14 of the TFEU. It recognises the crucial role and autonomy of national, local, and regional authorities in the provision, organisation, and procurement of SGEI, ensuring that the needs of users are adequately met.

Article 2 of the protocol pertains to Services of General Interest (SGI), specifically those that are not connected to economic activity. It establishes that the provisions of the TFEU should not impede the rights of Member States to authorise the implementation of such SGI applications. Based on the aforementioned provisions, it is pertinent to engage in a comprehensive discussion regarding crucial elements such as the precise delineation of SGEIs and their corresponding funding mechanisms.

The initial step in implementing the relevant provision and establishing the financial mechanism is to accurately define SGEI. According to the General Court's statement, it was expressed that: "*There is no clear and precise regulatory definition of the SGEI mission and no established legal concept definitely fixing the conditions that must be satisfied before a Member State can properly invoke the existence and protection of the SGEI mission*".[14] Although there is a wide discretion for Member States to define the particular services to be qualified as SGI, the minimum criteria need to be met.

Following the Corbeau ruling the functional approach was deemed to be necessary identifying the public service obligation that is imposed to an undertaking. As it was concluded in the case: "*It cannot be disputed that the Regie des Postes is entrusted with a service of general economic interest consisting in the obligation to collect, carry and distribute mail on behalf of all users throughout the territory of the Member State concerned, at uniform tariffs and on similar quality conditions, irrespective of the specific situations or the degree of economic profitability of each individual operation.*"[15]

Member States are required to establish the justifications for designating certain services as SGEI, thereby demonstrating the distinctive purpose of these services. In this regard, the Commission assesses whether the Member State has appropriately identified the SGEI and established relevant criteria for their designation.

In order to adhere to the European Union's competition rules and State aid regulations, the discretionary authority in defining the SGEI must also align with the provisions outlined in Article 107 of the TFEU. In light of the Altmark decision, services are exempt from the requirement to adhere to Article 107 TFEU if they serve as compensation for fulfilling a public service obligation. Hence, the four

---

[14] Case T-289/03, *BUPA and Others v. Commission* [2008] ECR II-741, para 165 and Case T-325/10, *Iliad and Others v. Commission*, ECLI:EU:T:2013:472, para 119.

[15] Case C-320/91, *Corbeau*, [1993] ECR I-02533, para 15.

criteria must be fulfilled. Subsequent to this decision, the body of legal precedents has undergone further development.

Initially, it is imperative that the recipient effectively fulfil the public service obligation while ensuring that the obligation is unambiguously defined, as stipulated by the provisions outlined in Article 106(2) of the TFEU. The determination of the second criteria parameter for calculating compensation should be conducted in a manner that is both objective and transparent. In this manner, it is possible to determine solely the type of compensation without considering any potential future compensation for services. The third criterion asserts that the amount should not exceed what is essential to adequately compensate for the expenses associated with fulfilling the public service obligation. This criterion thereby establishes the principle of proportionality. The fourth criterion stipulates that in cases where the State aid measure was not implemented through a public procurement procedure, the determination of the compensation level should be based on an examination of the costs incurred by a typical undertaking in order to fulfil the obligations of the public service.

While Member States have the freedom to determine the practical implementation of appointing specific undertakings for the provision of SGEI, it is essential that they adhere to the relevant criteria. The adoption of a directive aimed to establish transparency and regulate financial interactions between Member States and undertakings subject to the provision of SGEI. A distinct demarcation is necessary in order to ascertain the specific expenses associated with the operation of an additional endeavour.

In 2011, revisions were made to the Altmark package, which encompassed various documents, notably the Communication from the Commission regarding the implementation of European Union State aid regulations pertaining to compensation awarded for the provision of SGEI. The fundamental concepts have been developed, including the notion of the rate of return on capital generated by the project over its duration. The Commission Decision No. 2012/21/EU pertains to the implementation of Article 106(2) of the TFEU in relation to State aid provided as public service compensation to specific undertakings responsible for operating SGEI. This decision establishes the criteria under which such aid may be deemed compatible with the internal market, thereby exempting the requirement for notification to the European Commission as outlined in Article 108(3) of the TFEU. The European Union has established a framework for State aid in the form of public service compensation. This framework outlines the conditions under which State aid, not covered by a previous decision and requiring prior notification, can be considered compatible with the internal market in accordance with Article 106(2) of the TFEU. According to Commission Regulation (EU) No 360/2012, which pertains to the implementation of Articles 107 and 108 TFEU in relation to de minimis aid provided to undertakings engaged in the provision of SGEI, any compensation granted to an undertaking that does not exceed EUR 500,000 over a span of three fiscal years is exempted from the obligation to notify.

The threshold for the application of the Commission Decision on SGEI in 2011 was lowered. In comparison to the 2005 Commission Decision, which applied to annual compensation for services amounting to less than EUR 30 million, the 2011 Commission Decision encompasses compensation not exceeding EUR 15 million for the provision of general economic interest services in sectors other than transport infrastructure. The range of services has been broadened to include additional sectors.[16] Previously, public service compensation could only be granted to hospitals and social housing undertakings engaged in activities classified as services of general economic interest. However, the Commission Decision has expanded the scope to address social needs related to health, long-term care, social housing, and the social inclusion of vulnerable groups. In the event that the predetermined conditions outlined in the Commission Decision are not satisfied, it becomes necessary to execute prior notification. In the process of evaluating these cases, it is imperative for the Commission to consider the provisions outlined in Article 9 of the TFEU. This particular clause pertains to horizontal social protection and emphasises the importance of incorporating requirements related to the promotion of robust employment, assurance of sufficient social protection, combating social exclusion, fostering advanced education and training, and safeguarding human health in the formulation and implementation of European Union policies and activities. This provision establishes a comprehensive framework for social protection at a high level and grants Member States the authority to limit certain freedoms in pursuit of this protective objective.

The Commission Communication sought to provide a detailed analysis of the variations in the implementation of State aid regulations with regards to the provision of general service obligations.[17] The document comprises concise synopses of the implemented regulations. The Member States have the freedom to determine public service obligations, as outlined in the basic rule. Furthermore, it is worth mentioning that the incorporation of public procurement regulations, transparency measures, and proportionality provisions is essential. The impact on trade was expounded upon in terms of how opting for alternative methods of service provision rather than public procurement may impose limitations on the entry of competitors into the market.

The Communication emphasises the need to follow a tender process that ensures openness, transparency, and non-discrimination when selecting a service provider. Open tenders have the potential to attract a significant number of participants. The restricted procedure is also considered a viable alternative, albeit less appealing, as it restricts participation in tenders to a specific group of participants. In certain exceptional circumstances, such as when a public contract is highly intricate and the authorities lack the ability to predefine technical capabilities, competitive dialogue or a negotiated procedure may be deemed appropriate. In this scenario, the authorities engage in a dialogue with prospective candidates in order to explore

[16]Commission Decision 2012/21/EU [2012] OJ L 7, p. 3.

[17]Communication from the Commission on the implementation of State aid rules in the energy sector and in the context of general service obligations. COM(2011) 742 final, Brussels, 21 December 2011.

potential alternatives that may meet the specified criteria. The negotiated procedure can be executed with or without prior publication. When the prior publication requirement is enforced, prospective bidders are required to express their interest in participating, should they wish to do so. Subsequently, the authority extends invitations to these candidates for further discussions. However, it is possible that the information provided during negotiations could be presented in varying ways to different participants, potentially leading to discriminatory practises that confer advantages on certain candidates. It is the responsibility of the authorities to ensure that the tendering process is conducted in a manner that provides equal treatment to all potential bidders. The inclusion of the procedure without prior publication as a viable option was not considered, as it may be employed in situations where only one suitable candidate is applicable, and this procedure is regarded as the least competitive.

There exist instances wherein the tender procedure does not yield the least-cost tenderer yet remains in accordance with the criterion established in the Altmark decision. These scenarios encompass certain instances, particularly when the service provider already possesses the infrastructure or when there is a lack of satisfactory bidders, resulting in only one bid being submitted. Based on the assessment of the Communication, it can be inferred that the Commission exhibits a clear preference for a competitive and transparent process when selecting entities to assume the public service obligation. Conversely, employing restricted procedures may lead to increased costs. Member States are required to establish the justifications for designating certain services as SGEI, thereby highlighting their distinct mission.[18] In this context, the Commission assesses whether the Member State has appropriately identified the SGEI and established relevant criteria for their classification.

The exercise of discretionary authority in delineating the concept of SGEI must also adhere to the regulations governing competition within the European Union and State Aid, as well as the provisions outlined in Article 107 of the TFEU. In light of the Altmark decision, services are exempt from the requirement to adhere to Article 107 TFEU if they serve as compensation for the public service obligation.[19] Hence, it is imperative that all four criteria are satisfied. Subsequent to this ruling, there has been further development in the body of legal precedents.

First and foremost, it is imperative that the recipient fulfil their public service obligation in practise.[20] Additionally, it is crucial that the obligation itself be

---

[18] Zhu (2020).

[19] Altmark Trans GmbH and Regierungspräsidium Magdeburg v. Nahverkehrsgesellschaft Altmark GmbH [CJEU Case C-280/00].

[20] Commission Regulation (EU) No 360/2012 of 25 April 2012 on the application of Articles 107 and 108 of the Treaty on the Functioning of the European Union to de minimis aid granted to undertakings providing services of general economic interest. OJ L 114, 26.4.2012, p. 8–13. Commission Regulation (EU) 2023/2832 of 13 December 2023 on the application of Articles 107 and 108 of the Treaty on the Functioning of the European Union to de minimis aid granted to undertakings providing services of general economic interest. C/2023/9701. OJ L, 2023/2832, 15.12.2023.

unambiguously defined, as this is a prerequisite for comprehending the provisions outlined in Article 106(2) of the TFEU. The determination of the second criteria parameter for calculating compensation should be conducted in a manner that is both objective and transparent.[21] In this manner, only the determination of the compensation type is possible, while the provision of advance compensation for future services remains uncertain. The third criterion establishes the principle of proportionality by stating that the amount charged should not exceed what is necessary to cover the costs associated with fulfilling the public service obligation. The fourth criterion stipulates that in cases where the State aid measure was not implemented through a public procurement procedure, the determination of the compensation level should be based on an analysis of the costs incurred by a typical undertaking in order to fulfil the obligations of providing public services.

While Member States have the freedom to determine the practical implementation of appointing certain undertakings with the obligation of providing SGEI, it is essential that they adhere to the respective criteria. The adoption of the directive aimed to establish transparency and financial relations between Member States and undertakings subject to the provision of SGEI. In order to accurately determine the costs associated with an additional activity being conducted by the undertaking, it is necessary to establish a distinct separation between the two.

In 2011, revisions were made to the Altmark package, which encompassed various documents, notably the Communication from the Commission regarding the implementation of European Union State aid regulations pertaining to compensation awarded for the provision of SGEI. The fundamental concepts have undergone development, including the notion of the rate of return on capital generated by the project over its duration. Commission Decision No. 2012/21/EU pertains to the implementation of Article 106(2) of the TFEU in relation to State aid provided as public service compensation to specific undertakings responsible for operating SGEI. This decision establishes the criteria under which such aid may be deemed compatible with the internal market, thereby exempting the requirement for notification to the European Commission as outlined in Article 108(3) of the TFEU. The European Union has established a framework for State aid in the form of public service compensation. This framework outlines the conditions under which State aid, not covered by a previous decision and requiring prior notification, can be deemed compatible with the internal market in accordance with Article 106(2) of the TFEU. According to Commission Regulation (EU) No 360/2012, which pertains to the application of Articles 107 and 108 TFEU in relation to de minimis aid provided to undertakings offering SGEI, any compensation granted to an undertaking that does not exceed EUR 500,000 over a span of three fiscal years is exempt from the requirement of notification.

---

[21] Kamaris (2012).

13.6 Altmark Case

The provision of assistance by the local government to Altmark-Trans, a company responsible for fulfilling public service obligations, specifically in the realm of public transport services in Germany, served as a pivotal factor in the subsequent assessment of the extent and criteria for granting services of general economic interest.[22]

Following the awarding of the public transport service to Altmark-Trans, the competitor expressed concerns regarding this decision and subsequently lodged a complaint with the national court regarding the subsidies provided for the fulfilment of the public service obligation. The national court has formally sought a preliminary ruling from the CJEU in order to determine whether the State aid in question is in violation of Article 107 of the TFEU.

Two contrasting approaches were observed, specifically the requirement for notifying the Commission about the compensation granted to a company in accordance with the State aid rules. The compensation approach posits that public service compensation should be regarded as remuneration for services rendered with due consideration. The aforementioned matter was elucidated in instances where the compensations granted to the entities responsible for the collection and disposal of waste oil were determined not to qualify as State aid. Immediately preceding the Altmark judgement, the Ferring case examined the tax benefit and determined that it would not be classified as state aid if it was commensurate with the actual costs incurred for fulfilling the public service obligation.

The court has conducted an assessment to determine the presence of a benefit within the context of Article 107 (1) of the TFEU. The issue at hand concerned deciding whether to classify the subsidies offered by the local government as financial assistance or as compensation for the delivery of public services. The CJEU has observed that public service compensation does not meet the criteria for being classified as aid as it lacks an advantage criterion.

The CJEU has rendered a verdict on the enduring controversy surrounding whether compensation for SGEI can be classified as a form of State aid and under what circumstances such a classification would apply. If the measure satisfies the specific criteria, it cannot be classified as a State aid measure and thus does not necessitate approval from the Commission. There are four criteria that must be satisfied:

- The recipient must possess clearly defined discharged public service obligations.
- The criteria for calculating compensation should be transparent and provided in advance.

[22] Altmark Trans GmbH and Regierungspräsidium Magdeburg v. Nahverkehrsgesellschaft Altmark GmbH [CJEU Case C-280/00].

- The compensation should not surpass the targets that the recipient is entitled to achieve, specifically in relation to covering the costs of fulfilling the public service obligations while considering reasonable profits.
- If the undertaking is not selected through a competitive tender procedure, the compensation should be determined based on an analysis of typical undertaking costs.

The initial criterion stipulating that an undertaking must be endowed with a public service obligation emphasises the importance of ensuring that private entities engaged in activities resembling those of a public service obligation, but without state intervention, cannot be classified as providers of public service obligations.[23] The establishment of a well-defined public service obligation necessitates careful consideration to ensure that the entity undertaking it is entrusted with a significant and specific mission for implementation. The manner in which the public service is delegated within the organisation is of negligible significance, as long as it is explicitly outlined in legal statutes.

It is imperative to establish the compensation requirements prior to the implementation of the service of general economic interest. It is imperative to establish the criteria in a manner that is both clear and transparent. The endeavour should not possess any economic advantage that confers preferential treatment over its competitors. When determining compensation for public service obligations, it is appropriate to include a reasonable profit component. Member States possess the discretion to delineate the specific services that fall under the category of general economic interest. The practise of overcompensation is prohibited, as it entails providing compensation that exceeds what is required to fulfil public service obligations, with the exception of a reasonable profit that may be factored into the calculation of the compensation. The Commission maintains the stance that the appropriate level of profit should be determined by the company's rate of return on capital, taking into account the specific levels of risk associated with fulfilling the public service obligation. The pertinent income encompasses the revenues derived from the provision of services related to the mission of general economic interest as well as certain advantages arising from the grant of special or exclusive rights.

The selection of the service provider must be conducted through a transparent and competitive public tender process. There exists an alternative approach for choosing the service provider that guarantees that the compensation will be restricted solely to the extent of the costs arising from the provision of services of general economic interest. The project must possess sufficient resources and capabilities to effectively fulfil the obligations associated with public service requirements. In this particular scenario, the pertinent receipts and the rational profits are also considered. This requirement is established with the aim of identifying the most proficient operator in the market who possesses the necessary resources and is willing and capable of executing the specific mission for the public without necessitating any

[23] Santamato (2004).

supplementary assistance. Member States have the discretion to decide whether to implement a public procurement tender for selecting an undertaking or to initiate benchmarking activities.

The endorsement of public procurement follows the Altmark judgement. Assessing the criterion can be challenging when comparing the costs of previous monopolistic endeavours with those of typical endeavours. The challenge arises from the notion that, in relation to its monopolistic characteristics, there may not be a conventional enterprise that can serve as a comparative benchmark. The Commission has proposed that in cases where there is a lack of adequate performance by undertakings in a specific sector, a comparison should be made with undertakings operating internationally. However, it is advised that comparisons should not be made with monopolistic undertakings, as it would be challenging to assess the efficiency of an operator in a monopolistic environment. If the aforementioned criteria are not satisfied, the measure should be regarded as State aid. The decision, framework, transparency directive, additional communication, and de minimis exemption were published by the Commission in 2011.

The Altmark case has effectively resolved the debate surrounding the dichotomy between State aid and compensation methodologies. This decision holds significance in establishing the criteria for subsequent evaluation. The exclusion pertaining to services of general economic interest bears resemblance to the market economy operator test.

13.7 Conclusions

The differentiation between special and exclusive rights is based on the number of undertakings that have been granted said rights. Specifically, when exclusive rights are conferred upon a particular entity, no other participant in the market is permitted to exercise this privilege. In the context of special privileges, a select group of entities is granted exclusive rights, thereby restricting other entities from offering specific services in the market. Consequently, by conferring special privileges on a specific set of undertakings, the remaining entities are effectively barred from providing said services. An exception exists within the competitive tender procedure that may be applied to the allocation of these rights, specifically when the entity is entrusted with providing services of general economic interest. The Commission has noticed that it is not necessary to give exclusive rights to a certain entity, based on Article 106(1) in conjunction with Article 102 TFEU and established case law from the CJEU. Instead, the focus is on the presence of a public undertaking and the resulting inequality among market operators, which ultimately leads to a distortion of competition.

The PPC was granted an exemption that provided favourable treatment to the company regarding lignite extraction. The primary operations of the organisation encompass the production of electrical energy and lignite. The company held a previous monopoly in the generation and supply of electricity within the Greek electricity sector. Furthermore, it exercises the right to be the exclusive supplier to both eligible and non-eligible customers. Additionally, it holds the exclusive role of being the wholesale supplier and buyer for the non-interconnected islands. Moreover, it is the sole proprietor of the assets pertaining to transmission and distribution networks. The proceedings were initiated on the grounds of alleging that the national measures were inconsistent with the provisions of Article 106(2) when considered in conjunction with Article 102 of the TFEU. The remedies encompassed provisions pertaining to the transfer of mining, exploration, and exploitation rights, as well as the sharing of personnel and infrastructure. The divestment facilitated PPC's acquisition of 60% of the lignite reserves. The aforementioned decision resulted in a significant alteration of the energy liberalisation process, thereby facilitating the opening of the market to better accommodate the interests of consumers.

The absence of a precise delineation of general economic interest services can be attributed to their dynamic nature. Furthermore, the determination of which specific services should fall under this classification is subject to temporal variations in perception. Member States were not requested to provide any inventories of services that could be assessed as services of general economic interest. Certain authors raise concerns regarding whether the government is responsible for the failure to establish efficient markets and whether regulatory interventions should not aim to rectify situations that could be resolved through market disruptions.

There are several characteristics that are typically shared by all services falling under the category of general economic interest. These include the imposition of a public service obligation, the universal nature of the services, their continuity, affordability, universal coverage, and a focus on consumer protection. The services typically offered by network industries, such as energy or telecommunications, postal services, public emergency services, water supply, waste management, public service broadcasting, and sectoral pension schemes, have been regarded as eligible for the provision of general economic interest services. The evaluation encompassed certain market factors, such as the investment decisions of market participants and the presence of existing service providers. Services falling within these parameters were not considered general economic interest services, which are delivered to fulfil a specific mission that would otherwise remain unaddressed.

The provision of general economic interest services is of paramount significance and cannot be solely facilitated by the market without intervention from the State, or at the very least, in a manner that ensures accessibility to all individuals without discrimination. Compensation is necessary to mitigate potential losses incurred by service providers, as the additional costs associated with providing such services may not be fully offset, despite their determination to serve the broader public interest.

To adhere to the Altmark criteria, four conditions must be satisfied. Firstly, the recipient must possess clearly defined public service obligations that have been discharged. Secondly, the compensation for these obligations must be calculated and provided in a transparent manner prior to their implementation. Thirdly, the compensation must not surpass the targets that the recipient is entitled to achieve, specifically ensuring that it does not exceed the necessary amount required to cover the costs associated with fulfilling the public service obligations while also considering reasonable profits. Lastly, if the undertaking is not selected through a competitive tender process, the compensation must be determined based on an analysis of typical costs incurred by similar undertakings.

References

Burke J (2015) A market and government failure critique of Services of General Economic Interest: testing the centrality and strictness of article 106(2) TFEU. London School of Economics and Political Science LSE, London

Kamaris G (2012) The reform of EU state aid rules for services of general economic interest in times of austerity. Eur Law Rev 33

Krajewski M (2015) Services of General Interest beyond the single market. External and international dimensions. Springer, Berlin

Marson G (2014) Exclusive rights: The Court of Justice of the European Union considers that granting an exclusive right as a potential infringement of art. 106–1 TFEU combined with art. 102 *(DEI)*. Concurrences 4-2014, 70062

Melcher M (2019) Article 106 (2) TFEI in case law internalization and customized balancing of welfare and market interests. Austrian Law J

Nicolaides P (2021) Exclusive rights and state aid. Lexxion, Berlin

Santamato S (2004) Compensation for services of general economic interest: some thoughts on the Altmark ruling. Competition Policy Newsletter

Sierra JLB (2016) Exclusive or special rights under article 106 TFEU: An overview of EU and national case law. e-Competitions Exclusive rights (Art. 106 TFEU), 44436

Zhu L (2020) Services of General Economic Interest in EU competition law: striking a balance between non-economic values and market competition. Springer, Berlin

Part VI
Competition Implementation in Energy Sector: International Outlook

Chapter 14
Enforcement of Competition Law in the Energy Sector in Accordance with the WTO

Abstract Given the global nature of trade and the harmful effects of unfair practices on consumers, it is important to investigate the possibility of implementing international competition law. This is due to the fundamental connection between trade matters and the concept of fair competition among market participants. Nevertheless, it is important to highlight that there is currently a scarcity of complete legislation in this field, and the current agreements of the World Trade Organisation (WTO) do not include provisions related to competition law. WTO is an international trade entity that seeks to promote global trade growth by removing trade obstacles, thereby creating a favorable climate for talks. The main objectives of the WTO are to promote competitiveness and prevent any form of unfair treatment towards any specific foreign trade partner. Within the scope of WTO agreements, multiple working groups and experts have examined competition regulation. As a result, these organisations have proactively put up and introduced the International Competition Code, often known as the Munich Code, during the Uruguay Round. Various approaches led to the incorporation of competition law into WTO agreements.

14.1 Introduction

The establishment of international competition law regulation is imperative due to the inherent connection between trade matters and equitable competition among market participants. In this regard, there is an absence of explicit regulation, and the current agreements of the World Trade Organisation (WTO) have not yet encompassed the application of competition law. Additionally, it is imperative to identify strategies for addressing the existing regulatory void within the energy industry. The presence of market concentration and cartels can result in significant negative consequences for consumers, particularly when oil-producing nations establish their pricing strategies. Harm arises when oil-producing nations exercise their sovereign rights over energy resources in a manner that is exploitative. Hence, this section will delve into a comprehensive examination of the potential avenues for regulating international competition law within the framework of the WTO

L. Rimšaitė, *The Crossroads of Competition Law and Energy Regulation*,
https://doi.org/10.1007/978-3-031-73238-6_14

agreements. Additionally, it will assess the ramifications of agreements established by the Organisation of the Petroleum Exporting Countries (OPEC), which may impose constraints on competition in numerous nations as well as the European Union (EU).

The WTO is a globally recognised intergovernmental organisation that was founded in 1995. Its primary purpose is to establish and enforce regulations governing international trade as well as facilitate the resolution of trade-related disputes among its member nations. The WTO endeavours to enhance global trade by eliminating trade barriers, thereby establishing a conducive environment for negotiations. The primary goals of the WTO encompass the facilitation of competitiveness and the avoidance of favouritism towards any particular foreign trading partner. The latter individual may hold the belief that there would be an absence of artificially constructed obstacles. The WTO agreements do not include any specific regulations pertaining to competition rules in the context of trade policy matters. The aforementioned agreements govern the provisions pertaining to subsidies and countervailing measures, trade-related investment measures, and anti-dumping provisions. In the subsequent sections, we will delve into a more comprehensive examination of the feasibility of incorporating competition rules within WTO agreements and the imperative nature of such regulatory measures.[1]

14.2 WTO: The Trade Without Competition Applicability?

The working group has looked into competition regulation within the framework of WTO agreements. The initial actions were initiated in 1995, subsequent to a comprehensive examination conducted by a group of specialists in competition law with the objective of elucidating the potential for implementing competition law within the agreements of the WTO.[2] The International Competition Code, commonly referred to as the Munich Code, was introduced and formally proposed by scholars and professionals specialising in competition law in 1993. The scholars emphasise the importance of ensuring markets that are both free and competitive. The document in question exhibited a higher probability of being an agreement rather than a code that serves to enhance and align with established standards and regulations. The United States did not accept the European approach due to its prohibitive and robust language, which was predominantly reflected by the

[1]Marrakesh Agreement Establishing the World Trade Organization (WTO Agreement), 15 April 1994, 1867 U.N.T.S. 154. Agreement on Subsidies and Countervailing Measures, Annex 1A to the WTO Agreement, 15 April 1994, 1867 U.N.T.S. 14. Agreement on Trade-Related Investment Measures, Annex 1A to the WTO Agreement, 15 April 1994, 1868 U.N.T.S. 254. Agreement on Implementation of Article VI of the General Agreement on Tariffs and Trade 1994, Annex 1A to the WTO Agreement, 15 April 1994, 1868 U.N.T.S. 201.

[2]Klodt (2001).

initiators.[3] The code encompasses four principles, three of which are widely recognised in the field of international law. Specifically, it demonstrated the appropriate implementation of domestic legislation to address matters of global significance. The aforementioned model had already been established in the Paris Convention for the Protection of Industrial Property of 1883, the Berne Convention for the Protection of Literary and Artistic Works of 1886, and various other intellectual property treaties. Therefore, the new model was not entirely novel. The code incorporated the principle of national law, drawing upon its application in the aforementioned international treaties. The principle of national treatment is expounded upon in a manner that emphasises the equal treatment of domestic and foreign enterprises. The code also incorporated the principle of minimum standards, which entails treating foreign subjects in a manner consistent with national subjects while acknowledging any existing disparities in national legislation.[4] The code reflected the principle of international procedural initiative in order to safeguard the adherence of Member States to their obligations. Ultimately, the proposed document would have been relevant in transnational scenarios that involve crossing national borders and encompassing international elements. This would allow national cases to be handled exclusively by the respective national authorities, without any external international scrutiny.

In 1995, Professor Schrerer proposed a third initiative to incorporate competition law into WTO agreements.[5] Despite their differences, all three proposals share the objective of establishing competition rules within WTO agreements. The proposition put forth by the Working Group suggests the incorporation of regulations governing international competition within a multilateral agreement under the WTO without the creation of additional institutions following the existing WTO framework. Consequently, it is imperative for every country that ratifies the agreement to demonstrate its dedication towards executing these provisions and to establish the requisite institutional framework within its jurisdiction.[6] In such a scenario, the enforcement of adherence to international competition law would be carried out by domestic competition authorities. It is imperative for the contracting parties to engage in the signing of cooperation agreements, thereby enabling the national competition authorities to collaborate effectively in order to ensure the diligent enforcement of competition law.

From the standpoint of the supervisory authority, Professor Schrerer's proposal exhibited a significantly greater level of ambition. The proposition entailed the establishment of an international competition office to guarantee the enforcement

[3]Transatlantic Trade and Investment Partnership (TTIP) Negotiations: Regulatory Divergences and Implications. June 6, 2014, European Commission. U.S. Trade Policy Review: Key Issues and Responses. August 25, 2022. U.S. Department of Commerce. Regulation (EU) No 1381/2013 of the European Parliament and of the Council on a European Code of Conduct for Investment and Standards. OJ L 354, 28.12.2013, p. 1–29. Munich Code (International Competition Code). 1993.

[4]Taylor (2006).

[5]Scherer (1995).

[6]Scherer (1995).

of competition law. The primary responsibilities of this entity would encompass the examination and analysis of significant violations of competition legislation pertaining to global trade and investment. In situations where national competition authorities possess jurisdiction over dispute resolution, this international competition law office would serve as a supplementary entity for the resolution of disputes. The Munich Code can be characterised as a comprehensive and sophisticated document that effectively establishes guidelines for minimum domestic standards, the principle of national treatment, substantive international standards, principles of international procedural initiatives, and principles of exclusivity.

Despite its original purpose of establishing international competition law regulations through the implementation of WTO standards and mechanisms, this document ultimately failed to be officially adopted. Paradoxically, the proposal faced rejection from OECD countries, with the United States, whose support was crucial for achieving consensus, emerging as the most vocal critic of the aforementioned proposition. The code was not implemented due to the excessively ambitious objective of establishing a supranational supervisory authority and the stringent principles embedded in the code, which excessively elaborated on competition regulations and conflicted with national legislation in certain jurisdictions.

Certain authors argue that there is a need for international regulation of competition law.[7] There exist multiple justifications for this, primarily that the establishment of the WTO was intended to facilitate the elimination of trade barriers and enhance the overall welfare of the populace. While the WTO currently governs global trade, the objective of competition policy is to establish equitable competition among economic entities. Incorporating competition law provisions into the existing framework of the WTO would facilitate a comprehensive evaluation of trade matters in a structured manner, given that the WTO provisions already address trade-related concerns. Critics of such harmonisation contend that the current dispute settlement framework of the WTO is better equipped to evaluate trade law, whereas competition law evaluates agreements between private entities, including those implemented by governmental bodies in the realm of state aid.

Authors who hold the belief that the enforcement of competition law can be effectively carried out through provisions established by the WTO would likely view this development as a positive one. Based on their assertion, the provisions outlined in Article XI of the WTO would enable the extension of restrictions on imports and exports to encompass cartels. A comprehensive examination of the suitability of competition law provisions within the realm of international trade has revealed that these regulations are not applicable in the aforementioned domain.[8] In relation to trade matters encompassed by the WTO Agreements, it is imperative to establish regulations pertaining to competition that guarantee equitable trade, the effective operation of the market, and the protection of the interests of consumers and traders.

---

[7] Wilson (2003).

[8] Waller (1999).

While the stakeholders concerned possess differing interests with regards to the regulation of competition law at a global level, there is a consensus that such regulation is essential to address the issue of fragmented competition regulations.

14.3 WTO Rules Application to Energy Sector

The global trade of energy resources exhibited a notable degree of concentration, with a limited number of prominent multinational energy corporations exercising significant control over this sector. The application of General Agreement on Tariffs and Trade (GATT)[9] rules to regulate the energy sector has been limited, resulting in the absence of corresponding provisions within the WTO's framework. It is plausible to consider that regulations pertaining to international trade matters could potentially extend their scope to encompass trade issues within the energy sector.

The issue stems from the disparity in the categorization of energy resources as either goods or services, leading to variations in national regulations. The WTO employs distinct regulatory frameworks for the trade of industrial and agricultural products.[10] There exist varying perspectives regarding the potential categorization of renewable and non-renewable energy as equivalent subjects within the WTO. The potential implications of the interaction between the WTO and the Organisation of the Petroleum Exporting Countries (OPEC) give rise to certain apprehensions, particularly regarding the ability of oil-exporting nations to independently determine oil prices within the framework of OPEC and whether they should consider the prevailing regulations of the GATT and the WTO.

The WTO mandates a comprehensive approach to regulation in order to prevent the fragmentation of trade opportunities between various forms of resources, such as fossil fuels and renewables.[11] The necessity for harmonisation in the energy sector arises in a similar manner to the implementation of specialised regulations for the agricultural industry during the Uruguay Round.[12] This has the potential to mitigate the issue of fragmentation with regards to disparities in treatment, subsidies, procurement, and competition regulations. The establishment of a relationship between the WTO and the OPEC would be examined. The application of WTO provisions to the energy sector holds the potential to yield substantial advancements in the establishment of transparent trade regulations.[13] This, in turn, would generate

---

[9] General Agreement on Tariffs and Trade 1994, Apr. 15, 1994, Marrakesh Agreement Establishing the World Trade Organization, Annex 1A, 1867 U.N.T.S. 187, 33 I.L.M. 1153 (1994).

[10] Abdallah (2005).

[11] Marrakesh Agreement Establishing the World Trade Organization, Apr. 15, 1994, 1867 U.N.T.S. 154, 33 I.L.M. 1144 (1994).

[12] Final Act Embodying the Results of the Uruguay Round of Multilateral Trade Negotiations, Apr. 15, 1994, 1867 U.N.T.S. 14, 33 I.L.M. 1143 (1994).

[13] Cottier et al. (2010).

advantages for both energy-exporting and energy-importing nations while also serving as a preventive measure against potential conflicts.

The application of WTO regulations to the energy business gives rise to certain inherent challenges and impediments. The concept that a nation's energy resources are within the jurisdiction of its sovereignty is widely accepted worldwide. It is conceivable that certain organisations may exhibit hesitancy in implementing a comprehensive reform of their energy sectors. This holds particularly true in circumstances where engaging in such activities would entail facilitating chances for international enterprises to effectively use substantial resources.

Many nations frequently offer financial incentives to their domestic energy industries as a means of bolstering and sustaining these sectors. The implementation of subsidies can lead to distortions in the realm of international trade by artificially reducing the price of different energy sources. The challenge emerges when attempting to find a middle ground between the need to provide subsidies to guarantee the accessibility and reliability of native energy sources while simultaneously following the norms set forth by the WTO. The global economy heavily relies on the trading of energy resources, including coal, natural gas, and oil, due to their significant role in sustaining various economic activities. The occurrence of disruptions in the availability of these resources, whether they arise from geopolitical tensions or production constraints, can have significant economic and security implications. These consequences can happen due to various factors.

The growing apprehension regarding the condition of the natural environment has contributed to the increased significance attributed to the transition towards renewable and environmentally friendly forms of energy on a worldwide level. In contrast, trade rules have the potential to impede the rate of uptake of renewable energy technologies such as solar panels and wind turbines. These technologies serve as illustrations of the concept referred to as "distributed generation." The generation and consumption of energy have significant implications for the surrounding environment, particularly in terms of greenhouse gas emissions. The attainment of a harmonious balance between the objectives of economic liberalisation and environmental preservation may present significant obstacles.

State-controlled enterprises are prevalent in a number of countries, particularly in the energy sector, where they have a dominant position. There exists a potential for state-owned enterprises to be granted preferential treatment, hence giving rise to apprehensions regarding competition in alignment with the regulations set forth by the WTO. Energy security is a paramount concern for the majority of nations, as they place significant emphasis on guaranteeing the dependability and safety of their energy sources. The potential perception of trade barriers may arise from the adoption of energy security measures, such as export restrictions or domestic content mandates.

The energy sector may encounter substantial technical barriers to trade due to the diverse national laws and regulations that govern it. The aforementioned disparities possess the capacity to engender technical impediments to global trade. As a consequence, these entities are prone to being subjected to scrutiny and challenge in alignment with the regulations set forth by the WTO. The complexities associated with obtaining market access for energy products and services may arise due to variations in regulations, tariffs, and non-tariff obstacles that necessitate resolution.

The matter concerning intellectual property rights possesses the capacity to engender business disputes, particularly in relation to technologies that facilitate the advancement of ecologically sustainable energy consumption. Concerns may arise in specific countries regarding the fair and equitable distribution of energy resources, particularly in cases where a small number of states own significant reserves. This phenomenon is particularly evident in situations where a small number of countries possess significant reserves. The implementation of export limits on essential materials used in renewable energy technology has the potential to pose significant obstacles to the worldwide shift towards sustainable energy sources. The process of negotiating energy trade and investment agreements commonly occurs through bilateral or regional channels, leading to an intricate network of agreements and legislation that exhibit overlapping characteristics.

Reconciling the conflicting imperatives of equitable and transparent energy commerce with the legitimate policy objectives of energy security, ecological sustainability, and resource governance poses a significant and intricate undertaking. This task is a formidable obstacle that necessitates successful completion. To attain this equilibrium, it will be imperative to engage in meticulous contemplation and deliberation, considering the economic and environmental factors in operation.

14.4 Conclusion

Given the transnational nature of trade and the detrimental impact of abusive practises on consumers, it is pertinent to explore the potential for international competition law. This is because trade matters are inherently intertwined with the notion of equitable competition among market participants. However, it is worth noting that there is currently a dearth of comprehensive regulations in this domain, and the existing agreements of the WTO do not encompass provisions pertaining to competition law.

The WTO is a global trade institution that aims to facilitate the expansion of international trade through the elimination of trade barriers, thereby fostering an environment conducive to negotiations. The primary goals of the WTO encompass the facilitation of competitiveness and the avoidance of discriminatory treatment towards any particular foreign trading partner.

Various working groups and professionals have looked into competition regulation within the framework of WTO agreements. Consequently, these entities have taken the initiative to propose and present the International Competition Code, commonly referred to as the Munich Code, during the Uruguay Round. The implementation of competition law in WTO agreements was initiated through various initiatives. Each country that ratifies the agreement should demonstrate a commitment to implementing its provisions and establishing the requisite institutional framework within its own jurisdiction.

After engaging in extensive deliberations, the notion of instituting a supervisory entity to ensure adherence to the provisions pertaining to competition has been put forth. The primary responsibilities of this organisation would have encompassed the examination and scrutiny of significant violations of competition law pertaining to global trade and investment. In situations where national competition authorities possessed jurisdiction over dispute resolution, this international competition law office would have functioned as a supplementary entity for the resolution of disputes.

The Munich Code can be characterised as a comprehensive document that effectively established minimum domestic standards, the principle of national treatment, substantive international standards, principles of international procedural initiatives, and principles of exclusivity. The document in question aimed to establish international regulations for competition law based on the standards and mechanisms of the WTO. However, it was ultimately not adopted due to concerns regarding the extensive delegated functions assigned to the supranational organisation.

Numerous deliberations have transpired pertaining to the regulation of international competition. It is noteworthy that while the WTO already governs international trade, the objective of competition policy is to foster equitable competition among economic entities. Critics of such harmonisation have contended that the current structure of the World Trade Organisation's dispute settlement mechanism was specifically designed to evaluate trade law, while competition law primarily focuses on agreements between private entities.

The global trade of energy resources exhibited a significant degree of concentration, with a few prominent international energy corporations exercising substantial control over this sector. The application of GATT rules to regulate the energy sector has been lacking, resulting in the absence of corresponding provisions within the jurisdiction of the WTO. The matter at hand pertains to the disparity in the treatment of energy resources, which ought to be regarded as a commodity or service, and this discrepancy is contingent upon national regulatory frameworks.

References

Abdallah H (2005) Oil exports under GATT and the WTO. OPEC Rev 29(4)

Cottier T, Malumfashi S et al (2010) Energy in WTO law and policy. World Trade Institute. World Trade report

Klodt H (2001) Conflicts and conflict resolution in international anti-trust: do we need international competition rules? World Economy 24:877–888

Scherer RJ (1995) Global competition policy and the WTO. J Int Econ Law 1(1):119–142

Taylor M (2006) International competition law, a new dimension for the WTO? Cambridge university press, Cambridge

Waller SW (1999) An international common law of antitrust. N Engl Law Rev 34:163

Wilson J (2003) Globalisation and the limits of National Merger Control Laws. Kluwer Law International, Alphen aan den Rijn

Chapter 15
Organization of Petroleum Exporting Countries and Competition Law Issues

Abstract Throughout history, the seven leading oil trading organisations have consistently followed a pricing plan that involves keeping most profits from sales for themselves while allocating only a small fraction to the oil-producing nations. These firms determine oil prices without considering the expenses of extraction, resulting in financial gains. The main goal of establishing the Organisation of the Petroleum Exporting Countries (OPEC) was to ease the coordination and consolidation of efforts among nations involved in oil production.

The organization frequently faces accusations of engaging in price-fixing practices and establishing cartel agreements within the oil industry. Instead of permitting the unregulated export of petroleum products, there is a policy in place that seeks to control the export of such items. Because these initiatives did not produce the expected results, there was a noticeable impact on improved domestic cooperation. Several key factors have contributed to the lack of action taken against the OPEC agreements. The concept of state sovereignty empowers the state to regulate and determine the use of natural resources within its borders. Therefore, the government frequently controls oil firms, giving them the authority to determine how to extract, export, and distribute oil based on their specific needs.

15.1 Introduction

Exxon, Texaco, BP, Shell, Gulf, Standard Oil, and Mobil Oil are the seven well-known oil trading companies that have historically followed a pricing strategy in which the majority of sales profits have gone to the companies themselves with only a small portion going to the oil-producing countries. These companies establish prices for oil independent of the costs associated with oil extraction, thereby generating substantial profits.

In 1959, the United States government implemented modifications to its import policy, placing a higher priority on the importation of oil, specifically from Mexico and Canada. Consequently, there has been a substantial decrease in the oil-exporting revenues of prominent oil-producing nations. In pursuit of this objective, the agreement that established the Organisation of Petroleum Exporting Countries (OPEC)

L. Rimšaitė, *The Crossroads of Competition Law and Energy Regulation*,
https://doi.org/10.1007/978-3-031-73238-6_15

was signed in Baghdad on September 14, 1960, by the oil-producing nations. Efforts were undertaken to mitigate the policies implemented by the United States during that period and safeguard the trade privileges of nations involved in oil production.[1]

The primary objective of establishing this organisation was to facilitate the coordination and consolidation of efforts among countries involved in oil production. The Organisation of the Petroleum Exporting Countries (OPEC) is comprised of 13 member states spanning across three continents. Currently, the countries belonging to the OPEC collectively contribute more than 45% of the total global oil production. This organisation frequently faces allegations of engaging in price-fixing practises and reaching agreements to form a cartel.[2] During the 1960s, the OPEC achieved a significant alteration in the oil trade policy, resulting in financial gains for nations involved in oil production. In the year 1973, recognition emerged regarding the potential utilisation of oil exports as a political instrument. Consequently, the United Arab Emirates (UAE) imposed an embargo on oil exports to both the United States and the Netherlands.

Despite the relatively low proportion of petroleum product imports from the UAE by these nations, such actions exerted a substantial influence on the escalation of prices. In light of this comprehension, OPEC member nations have chosen to adopt a strategy of limiting the exportation of petroleum products rather than engaging in unrestricted exports. Despite the lack of desired outcomes, these actions had a discernible influence on fostering greater domestic collaboration.

15.2 The Application of US Jurisdiction

The analysis of the application of competition law provisions to the OPEC agreement holds significant importance. There are several significant factors that have contributed to the lack of action taken against the OPEC agreements in this regard. The principle of state sovereignty over natural resources within its territorial boundaries was established in 1950. In alternative terms, the State possesses the authority to utilise natural resources in a manner that it deems most suitable for its own interests and the well-being of its residents.[3] Oil companies, typically operating under the authority of their respective governments, exercise discretion in determining the quantity of oil to be extracted, exported, and allocated for internal consumption. The constraints on action are significant due to the principles of State sovereignty and the limited capacity of the international community to intervene in domestic affairs, primarily focusing on unfair trade policies.

---

[1] Agreement Establishing the Organization of Petroleum Exporting Countries (OPEC), signed on September 14, 1960, in Baghdad by the oil-producing nations.

[2] Organisation of the Petroleum Exporting Countries (OPEC). Annual Report 2023.

[3] Skeet (1988).

It is conceivable to invoke the jurisdiction of the United States in matters of competition law pertaining to unfair trade policies that implicate American corporations. Foreign corporations and United States based subsidiaries that are incorporated in a different country may potentially be subjected to a comparable legal framework through the application of analogy. Nevertheless, the international community finds the extraterritorial application of US law to be highly contentious. In several instances, the central issue pertained to whether the actions of foreign corporations could potentially have a substantial and detrimental impact on the United States economy, thereby qualifying as illegal according to competition law. Furthermore, it was necessary to determine if these actions could be evaluated within the framework of US law, as they would fall under its jurisdiction.

The Alcoa case[4] established a legal precedent known as the effects test, which pertains to the application of US jurisdiction beyond its territorial boundaries. According to this examination, foreign corporations may be subjected to the jurisdiction of the United States solely in instances where the actions of said corporations have a notably detrimental impact on American trade. While the examination received significant backing within the United States, it garnered comparatively less support from the international community.[5] The application of the test in the Timberlane case[6] has experienced a notable reduction in strength, specifically due to the recognition that the assessment of the international community's perspective on this matter should also be taken into consideration. The Hartford Fire case concluded that a distinct conflict between United States law and foreign law must exist. A potential conflict may arise in situations where both United States law and foreign law are applicable, leading to contradictions among the relevant provisions.

Nevertheless, there have been two legal cases filed against the OPEC based on United States antitrust legislation. According to the Hartford Fire case,[7] it is possible for US jurisdiction to be applicable to a foreign state but not to a private undertaking or their associations. It is noteworthy to mention in this context that legislation has been enacted in the United States to regulate the principles guiding the resolution of matters pertaining to foreign sovereignty within US courts. The application of US jurisdiction is not applicable to a country that is acting in accordance with its national laws. According to this assertion, the application of US jurisdiction is limited to trade agreements. The inquiry pertains to the classification of OPEC agreements, specifically whether they should be regarded as trade agreements or should be deemed legislative measures enacted by governments, thereby falling beyond the purview of United States courts.

Two instances in which the aforementioned concerns were taken into account are pertinent in this regard. The initial case pertains to the International Association of Machinists and Aerospace Workers, wherein trade unions in the United States raised

---

[4] *United States vs. Aluminum Co. of America (Alcoa);* Case 1945.

[5] Garavini (2019).

[6] *Timberlane Lumber Co. v. Bank of America;* Case 1976.

[7] *Hartford Fire Ins. Co. vs. California* case 1993.

concerns regarding the adverse impact experienced by their members as a result of the significant surge in fuel prices at petrol stations, attributable to the agreements made by the OPEC. The defendants implicated in this legal proceeding consisted of both the organisation known as OPEC and its individual members. However, the case was ultimately dismissed on the basis that the matter at hand pertained to the sovereignty of a foreign state and the legislation enacted by its national authorities.[8]

In a separate instance, the operator of the petrol station filed a lawsuit alleging the occurrence of illegal price fixing. The current case holds significance in its approach to the agreements, which were not regarded as legislation enacted by the state but rather as trade agreements between entities. Consequently, the doctrine of State sovereignty was not invoked. Furthermore, it was observed that the matter at hand was not connected to domestic legislation on a national level. Additionally, it was found that OPEC does not function as a unified entity comprised of individual Member States with a central headquarters. However, this assertion was ultimately disregarded. The jurisdiction of US courts does not extend to the State's exercise of sovereignty over natural resources within its territory. Oil-producing nations engage in collaborative efforts to manage trade relations, develop business strategies, and regulate oil production through various agreements, with the intention of deliberately inflating the prices of oil commodities. The extent of United States jurisdiction over such agreements is constrained and subject to significant controversy. Throughout history, the seven prominent oil trading companies, namely Exxon, Texaco, BP, Shell, Gulf, Standard Oil, and Mobil Oil, have adhered to a pricing strategy that involves the retention of the majority of profits generated from sales, with only a fraction being allocated to oil-producing nations. These companies establish oil prices independently of the extraction costs, thereby generating substantial profits.[9]

In 1959, the United States government implemented modifications to its import policy, placing emphasis on the prioritisation of oil imports from Mexico and Canada. Consequently, there has been a substantial decrease in the oil-exporting revenues of major oil-producing nations. In pursuit of this objective, the agreement that established the OPEC among the oil-producing nations was signed in Baghdad on September 14, 1960.[10] Measures were implemented to mitigate the policies pursued by the United States during that period and safeguard the trading privileges of nations involved in oil production.

The primary objective of the formation of this organisation was to facilitate the coordination and consolidation of efforts among nations engaged in oil production.[11] The OPEC is comprised of 13 member states spanning across three continents.

---

[8] International Association of Machinists and Aerospace Workers v. OPEC, 477 F. Supp. 553 (D.D.C. 1979).

[9] Hunt v. Mobil Oil Corp., 550 F.2d 68 (fifth Cir. 1977). Sosa v. Alvarez-Machain, 542 U.S. 692 (2004).

[10] Agreement Concerning the Creation of the Organization of Petroleum Exporting Countries (OPEC), Done at Baghdad, on 14 September 1960," United Nations—Treaty Series 1962 (6363), 248–252.

[11] Elass and Jaffe (2009).

Currently, the countries that comprise the OPEC contribute more than 45% of the total global oil production. This organisation frequently faces allegations of engaging in price-fixing practises and entering into cartel agreements within the oil industry.[12] During the 1960s, the OPEC achieved a significant alteration in the oil trade policy, resulting in financial gains for nations engaged in oil production. In the year 1973, recognition emerged regarding the potential utilisation of oil exports as a political instrument. Consequently, the UAE implemented an embargo on oil exports to both the United States and the Netherlands.

Despite the relatively low proportion of petroleum product imports from the UAE by these nations, such actions exerted a substantial influence on the escalation of prices. In light of this comprehension, OPEC member nations have chosen to adopt a strategy of limiting the exportation of petroleum products as opposed to engaging in unrestricted exports. Despite the lack of desired outcomes, these actions had a discernible influence on fostering greater domestic collaboration.

15.3 The Application of European Union Jurisdiction

While the TFEU does not contain a specific provision regarding the application of competition law rules beyond national borders, the Court of Justice of the European Union (CJEU) has addressed this matter in various cases. The initial legal case, known as Dyestuffs, addressed the matter of extraterritorial application. In this case, a principle was established that resembled the effects test employed in the United States, although its application was not widespread.

The Wood Pulp case, wherein the court invoked the principle of territoriality, bears relevance to the present context.[13] In this instance, the CJEU exercised jurisdiction over an export cartel that was formulated and sanctioned in compliance with the antitrust legislation of the United States.[14] According to the CJEU, the principle of extraterritoriality can be invoked to extend the application of competition law to situations where the formation of cartels, coordinated practises, and their resulting effects occur within a specific jurisdiction. The application of the principle of extraterritoriality entails the evaluation of the geographical location where the effects of an agreement or concerted action transpired rather than focusing on the specific country where the agreement was made or where the coordinated efforts were undertaken. In this particular scenario, the evaluation is conducted based on the

[12] Fjaertoft and Overland (2015).

[13] Judgment of the Court of 27 September 1988. A. Ahlstrom Osakeyhtio and others v Commission of the European Communities. Concerted practices between undertakings established in non-member countries affecting selling prices to purchasers established in the Community. Joined cases 89, 104, 114, 116, 117 and 125 to 129/85.

[14] Krutikhin and Overland (2020).

location of sale of goods or provision of services rather than considering the country in which the company is established, or the agreement is finalised.

While it is theoretically possible to apply the jurisdiction of the European Union competition law to the OPEC, the likelihood of such action being taken is extremely low. It is crucial to acknowledge that a significant portion of OPEC member countries' national budgets heavily rely on oil exports. Consequently, given the paramount importance of oil trade to OPEC, it is improbable that the international community would be receptive to the jurisdiction of the CJEU over OPEC.[15] It is important to acknowledge that private parties, typically competitors, have the ability to initiate legal proceedings for violations of the competition rules. The feasibility of implementing such measures under the Treaty on the Functioning of the European Union (TFEU) is questionable, considering the EU's limited oil production capacity. As previously examined, the implementation of competition regulations within the framework of EU or US legislation has generated considerable debate owing to the issue of extraterritoriality. The implementation of international legal frameworks could potentially enhance the situation in this regard, as it would enable the assessment of OPEC decisions solely through legal and economic lenses without being influenced by political factors.

15.4 OPEC and Russia Relations

The relationship between Russia and OPEC has been a subject of controversy due to various factors. Firstly, as a result of the significant volumes of fossil fuels being extracted and exported by the nation, Additionally, the governmental approach towards regulating fossil fuel prices is comparable; however, Russia lacks the necessary mechanisms to regulate oil production volume. Furthermore, the country does not employ a diverse range of tools that aid in regulating production and export volumes.

There is an absence of a hierarchical structure for decision-making pertaining to export quotas. Russia has, on multiple occasions, reached agreements with the OPEC to curtail production. However, it has failed to adhere to these agreements. In 1998, additional agreements were made between Russia and OPEC with the aim of reducing production. However, it is noteworthy that while OPEC members adhered to the agreement, Russia exhibited divergent behaviour. During that period, it became evident that the implementation of the partnership between Russia and OPEC was unlikely to occur. The decision for Russia to join as a minor partner would not have been advantageous, as it would have entailed the imposition of obligations to reduce production levels.

The inception of the new cooperation dialogues took place in 2014, subsequent to the shale gas revolution in the United States. When the decrease in prices failed to

[15] Crawford et al. (2010).

affect shale gas extractions, OPEC found it necessary to collaborate, leading to the invitation extended to Russia and other oil-producing nations to join forces. As a consequence, a coalition of 24 oil-producing nations united in response to the competitive threat posed by US shale gas in the market. This coalition formed an agreement to curtail production levels in order to stabilise prices and prevent their decline. The observable outcomes became apparent in 2017, as evidenced by the rise in prices to USD 71 per barrel for Brent. The OPEC+ agreement witnessed significant participation from Russia, which played a crucial role as a mediator between the Arab nations. This involvement was particularly significant due to the historical complexities of their relationship.[16]

15.5 Conclusion

Throughout history, the seven most prominent oil trading companies have adhered to a pricing strategy in which the entirety of profits generated from sales has been retained, with only a minimal portion being allocated to oil-producing nations. These companies establish prices for oil independent of extraction costs, thereby generating profits. The primary objective of the establishment of the OPEC was to facilitate the coordination and consolidation of efforts among nations engaged in oil production.

The organisation frequently faces allegations of engaging in price-fixing activities and entering into cartel agreements within the oil industry. Rather than allowing the unrestricted exportation of petroleum products, there is a policy aimed at limiting the export of such products. Given the lack of anticipated outcomes resulting from these actions, there was a discernible influence on enhanced domestic collaboration. There are several significant factors that have contributed to the lack of action taken against the OPEC agreements.

The principle of state sovereignty over natural resources within its territorial boundaries has led to the state's authority in determining the utilisation of these resources. Consequently, oil companies, often under government control, exercise discretion in extracting, exporting, and allocating oil for their respective requirements. The constraints imposed by State sovereignty and the limited capacity of the international community to intervene in domestic affairs, particularly in the context of unfair trade policies, were significant factors that contributed to the decision to intervene.

The scope of US jurisdiction was further expounded upon in relation to unfair trade practises involving American corporations. Nevertheless, the international community expressed concerns regarding the contentious issue of the extraterritorial application of United States law. In multiple instances, the central issue revolved

[16] OPEC. OPEC+ Agreement on Production Cuts. 2014. OPEC. OPEC Monthly Oil Market Report. January 2017.

around whether the activities of foreign corporations could potentially have a substantial negative impact on the United States economy and be deemed unlawful according to competition law. Consequently, these actions could be evaluated under the jurisdiction of US law. However, there was no recourse available to take action against countries that were operating in accordance with their own domestic legislation. The jurisdiction could have been deemed applicable to trade agreements. The inquiry pertains to the categorization of OPEC agreements, specifically whether they should be regarded as trade agreements or as legislative measures enacted by governments, thereby falling beyond the purview of United States courts. The jurisdiction of US courts would not extend to the State's sovereignty over natural resources within its territory.

While the TFEU does not contain a specific provision regarding the application of competition law rules beyond national borders, there have been instances where this matter has been brought up. The principle was formulated in a manner that bears resemblance to the effects test employed in the United States, albeit with limited application. Furthermore, this principle can be implemented in situations where matters pertaining to the termination of cartels, coordinated practises, and their resulting consequences emerge within a specific nation. The use of the extraterritoriality principle entails evaluating the location of the effects rather than the country in which the agreement was finalised.

The controversial nature of applying competition rules under EU or US law stems from the contentious issue of extraterritoriality. The potential impact of international law on this matter suggests that evaluating OPEC decisions solely from a legal and economic perspective, independent of political factors, could lead to some improvement. However, the resolution of this issue remains uncertain.

The relationship between Russia and OPEC has been remarkably exceptional. Russia has been engaged in the extraction and exportation of substantial amounts of fossil fuels. However, it lacks the necessary mechanisms to effectively regulate the volume of oil production and does not employ a diverse range of tools to contribute to the regulation of these volumes and exports. There is a lack of hierarchical structure for decision-making in relation to export quotas.

Russia has, on multiple occasions, reached agreements with OPEC to reduce production levels, yet it has failed to effectively implement these agreements and has instead pursued alternative courses of action. Hence, the implementation of the partnership between Russia and OPEC has not materialised. The inception of the new cooperation dialogues took place in 2014, subsequent to the shale gas revolution in the United States. When the decrease in prices failed to significantly affect shale gas extractions, OPEC found it necessary to collaborate with other oil-producing countries, including Russia, in order to address the situation.

Twenty-four oil-producing countries joined forces as a result of the collaboration in an effort to compete with US shale gas in the market. This was achieved through an agreement to reduce production levels and stabilise prices, thereby preventing a decline. The observable outcomes became apparent in 2017, as evidenced by the rise in prices to USD 71 per barrel for Brent.

References

Crawford J, Pellet A, Olleson S (2010) The law of international responsibility. Oxford University Press, Oxford

Elass J, Jaffe AM (2009) The history and politics of Russia's relations with OPEC, energy forum paper. James A. Baker III Institute for public policy. Rice University, Houston

Fjaertoft D, Overland I (2015) Financial sanctions impact Russian oil, equipment export ban's effects limited. Oil Gas J 113(8):66–72

Garavini G (2019) The rise and fall of OPEC. Oxford University Press, Oxford

Krutikhin M, Overland I (2020) OPEC and Russia: a happy pro forma marriage. In: Claes HD (ed) Handbook of OPEC and the global energy order: past, present and future challenges. Routledge, London

Skeet I (1988) OPEC: twenty-five years of prices and politics. Cambridge University Press, Cambridge

Chapter 16
The Energy Charter Treaty

Abstract The Energy Charter Treaty is an internationally acknowledged agreement that aims to protect foreign investments and facilitate global trade between nations. The Energy Charter Treaty's main purpose is to protect international investments, streamline the trading and transportation of energy resources, and establish channels for resolving conflicts. Nevertheless, there is a prevailing notion that the pact has become antiquated and does not conform to current norms. The aim is to guarantee conformity with sustainable development goals, tackle worldwide climate change problems, and set modern criteria for resolving conflicts between investors and nations. In 2019, the Commission received a mandate to engage in deliberations regarding the modernization of the Energy Charter Treaty. The objective of these discussions is to attain adherence to sustainable development, global climate change, and contemporary norms of dispute resolution between investors and the state. The mandate highlights various aspects, with particular emphasis on the EU's current objective of transitioning to clean energy, as evident in the Green Deal. Ensuring that provisions pertaining to adherence to EU environmental and safety policies, as well as the Energy Charter Treaty, align with the objectives of the Paris Agreement is an integral aspect of the Commission's deliberation mandate.

16.1 Introduction

The Energy Charter Treaty is an international accord that seeks to safeguard foreign investments and promote trade among nations.[1] The parties involved signed the agreement in 1994, and it has been in effect since 1998. At present, there are a total of 53 countries, which encompass both Euratom and the EU. Russia has expressed its acceptance of the Energy Charter Treaty to a restricted extent, ensuring that it aligns with national legislation, but has not formally ratified it. The contracting parties of Belarus, Iceland, Norway, and Australia have adopted a comparable stance. In 2009, the Russian Federation made the decision to withdraw from the

[1] The Energy Charter Treaty, *ICSID Review - Foreign Investment Law Journal*, Volume 10, Issue 2, Fall 1995, Pages 258–361.

L. Rimšaitė, *The Crossroads of Competition Law and Energy Regulation*,
https://doi.org/10.1007/978-3-031-73238-6_16

Energy Charter, yet it remains legally obligated to adhere to the provisions outlined in the charter until 2029. This obligation is enforced by the inclusion of a "sunset clause", as specified in Article 47. The primary objective of this treaty is to safeguard foreign investments, facilitate trade in energy resources, ensure smooth transit, and establish mechanisms for resolving disputes. The aforementioned issues arise as a result of provisions that have not undergone an essential review and have become outdated. The current provisions are no longer in accordance with contemporary standards.

The Commission was bestowed with a mandate in 2019 to engage in deliberations pertaining to the modernization of the Energy Charter Treaty. The objective of these discussions is to attain adherence to sustainable development, global climate change, and contemporary norms of dispute resolution between investors and the state. The mandate highlights various aspects, with particular emphasis on the EU's current objective of transitioning to clean energy, as evident in the Green Deal. The Commission will make efforts to achieve a consensus in which the provisions for investor-state dispute settlement align with the European Union's stance on investment protection agreements implemented in the context of multilateral reforms. An integral aspect of the Commission's deliberation mandate is to ensure that provisions pertaining to adherence to EU environmental and safety policies, as well as the Energy Charter Treaty, are aligned with the objectives of the Paris Agreement.

The mandate further stipulates that the provision of most favoured nation treatment should be encompassed, among other things, in relation to the national regime.[2] The assessment of expropriation, encompassing both direct and indirect explanations and its inherent characteristics, should be conducted within the framework of the Energy Charter Treaty.[3] The term "economic activity" should be expanded to encompass not only activities associated with fossil fuels but also those related to renewable energy. Consequently, investment protection measures should be broadened to align with the provisions set forth by the European Union, thereby ensuring consistency.

In June 2022, a provisional consensus was achieved regarding the updated Energy Charter Treaty.[4] Upon approval and ratification, the revised legislative document will enhance sustainable investments in the energy sector, establish legal certainty, and ensure robust investment protection. Additionally, it will contribute to the attainment of the objectives outlined in the Paris Agreement, specifically in relation to the promotion of clean energy.

The proposed revision of the Energy Charter Treaty would allow contracting parties to exclude new investments in fossil fuels from the protection framework and gradually eliminate the existing protections for investments in fossil fuels.[5] The

[2]Iavorsky (2012).

[3]Hober (2020).

[4]Proposal for a Council Decision on the position to be taken on behalf of the European Union at the Extraordinary Conference of the Energy Charter Treaty on 24th June 2022.

[5]Baltag (2012).

duration of the phase-out of protection measures is comparatively shorter than previously determined.[6] Specifically, the current timeframe for existing fossil fuels is projected to be 10 years, while new investments are expected to have a duration of 9 months. Furthermore, it has been ascertained that an investor hailing from one contracting party who is affiliated with a regional economic organisation is precluded from initiating an investor-state dispute settlement mechanism against the other contracting party, provided that the latter is also a member of the aforementioned organisation. This provision is intended to provide clarification regarding the compatibility of intra-EU Energy Charter Treaty applications with EU law.

16.2 The Case Law Practice

The analysis of the peculiarities of the Energy Charter Treaty application is crucial in light of the Russian Federation's accession to the treaty, its subsequent failure to ratify it, and its eventual declaration of withdrawal in 2009.

In 2005, the controlling shareholders of Yukos Oil Company, namely Hulley Enterprises Limited, Yukos Universal Limited, and Veteran Petroleum Limited,[7] commenced arbitration proceedings against the Russian Federation. The claimants sought a monetary award of USD 114.174 billion in relation to the expropriations and other alleged actions carried out by the respondent. Distinct proceedings were commenced, yet the Tribunal consolidated the cases and rendered uniform Awards. The case exhibited a strong correlation with the prevailing political landscape and the measures implemented by the governing bodies. The tribunal has determined that the Russian Federation has violated the standard of fair and equitable treatment as outlined in Article 10 (1) of the Energy Charter Treaty. The conclusion also indicated a violation of the obligation to refrain from implementing any discriminatory measures. The objections raised by the respondent pertain to the provision known as the "fork-in-the-road" in Article 26 (3)(b)(i) of the Energy Charter Treaty. The respondent argues that the "unclean hands" principle should have been applied, as the claimant's illegal actions should disqualify them from receiving protection under the Energy Charter Treaty.

The Tribunal has determined that the principal aim of the Russian Federation was not to secure the collection of the appropriate tax portion but rather to orchestrate the financial collapse of Yukos. If the case solely pertained to the tax collection officials of the company who were not subjected to appropriate political protocols. According to the Tribunal's findings, it has been determined that the Respondent did not

[6] Bamberger and Walde (2008).

[7] Hulley Enterprises Limited (Cyprus) v. The Russian Federation, UNCITRAL, PCA Case No. AA 226; Yukos Universal Limited (Isle of Man) v. The Russian Federation, UNCITRAL, PCA Case No. AA 227; Veteran Petroleum Limited (Cyprus) v. The Russian Federation, UNCITRAL, PCA Case No. AA 228; Final Awards of 18.07.2014.

employ direct measures of expropriation but instead opted for the utilisation of indirect measures in the given case.

The Energy Charter Treaty explicitly outlines four conditions that must be satisfied for a particular measure to be considered legitimate under Article 13. The specific conditions are outlined as follows. In order to fulfil objectives that serve the public's best interests, devoid of discriminatory elements conducted in accordance with the principles of due process as prescribed by law, and the timely, adequate, and effective disbursement of compensation should go along with the provision. Regarding the matter at hand, it can be argued that the actions taken against Russia's largest oil company and taxpayer were not justified within the framework of the public interest provisions. The interests of the state-owned company Rosneft were disclosed in this specific instance, as it acquired the crucial assets of Yukos. The non-discriminatory requirement was not applicable in this case, as other state-owned companies have similarly exploited low-tax jurisdictions. The non-compliance with the requirement to carry out expropriation in accordance with due process of law is evident, as the process was of a political nature and involved harsh treatment. The authorities also violated the fourth requirement of fair and adequate compensation.[8] The Tribunal has determined that the Russian Federation violated Article 13 of the Energy Charter Treaty, resulting in a declaration of liability under international law for the treaty breach. Upon the Tribunal's determination that the actions committed were in violation of Article 13 of the Energy Charter Treaty, it refrained from examining the allegation pertaining to Article 10 of the Energy Charter Treaty. The Claimant was granted a sum of USD 50 billion by the Respondent in relation to the breach of the Energy Charter Treaty and the act of indirect expropriation.

The Russian Federation expressed disagreement with the aforementioned award and subsequently lodged an appeal with the Hague District Court. In 2016, the appeal was granted, resulting in the Russian Federation being relieved of its obligation to provide compensation as stipulated in the Arbitral award.[9] The interpretation of the application of the Energy Charter Treaty and the principles of international treaties are of paramount significance in making this decision. The Hague District Court has concurred with the stance that the Energy Charter Treaty does not apply to the Russian Federation on the grounds that the country has not ratified the treaty nor implemented any obligatory regulation endorsing the provisional application of the Energy Charter Treaty. Hence, the Court has reached the determination that the Energy Charter Treaty was not in effect in the Russian Federation during the arbitral proceedings, thereby precluding the claimants from invoking the provisions of said treaty in the arbitration process. As a result, it can be inferred that the arbitral clause pertaining to the shareholders of Yukos and the Russian Federation was rendered

[8]Hulley Enterprises Limited (Cyprus) v. The Russian Federation, UNCITRAL, PCA Case No. AA 226; Yukos Universal Limited (Isle of Man) v. The Russian Federation, UNCITRAL, PCA Case No. AA 227; Veteran Petroleum Limited (Cyprus) v. The Russian Federation, UNCITRAL, PCA Case No. AA 228; Final Awards of 18.07.2014.

[9]Yukos Universal Limited (Isle of Man) v. Russian Federation, Hague District Court, Case No. 2005-01, 2016.

inapplicable, thereby invalidating the USD 50 billion award. The Arbitration Tribunal, during the admissibility phase, determined that the declaration stated that the limitation clause was not applicable. The Vienna Convention of International Treaties, specifically Articles 31 and 32, was cited as the foundation for this decision. However, the Hague District Court disagreed with the Tribunal's position and concurred that the Russian Federation had indeed terminated the temporary application of the Energy Charter Treaty. Consequently, the Russian Federation was not obligated by the provisions of the treaty during the arbitral proceedings.

According to Article 46 (1) of the Vienna Convention on the Law of Treaties, a State cannot claim that its consent to be bound by a treaty is invalid due to a violation of its internal law on treaty-making competence unless the violation was obvious and pertained to a rule of international law that is of fundamental importance. It is noteworthy to consider Article 27 of the same convention, which prohibits a party from using its internal law as a justification for non-compliance with a treaty. The aforementioned provision, as stated in Article 46, indicates that national laws alone cannot serve as a valid justification for disregarding the enforcement of an international treaty.

In the year 2020, the Court of Appeal overturned the lower court's decision. The Russian Federation's signing of the Energy Charter Treaty in 1994 established the validity of the arbitral agreement, so the Court of Appeal determined that the Arbitral Tribunal had the authority to decide the dispute. The Court of Appeal has determined that inconsistency arises when one legal provision contradicts another. However, it should be noted that in the previous case, the absence of national regulation was not considered sufficient to establish inconsistency. The Court of Appeal further emphasised that the "clean hands doctrine" pertains to the illegalities associated with the creation of the investments and should not restrict the jurisdiction. The Russian Federation has expressed its intention to submit an appeal to the Dutch Supreme Court, signifying that the legal dispute has now reached a definitive resolution, and the legal process will proceed accordingly. In 2021, the Russian Federation partially succeeded in its appeal against the ruling of the Hague Court of Appeal.[10] The assertion was made that the Hague Court of Appeal committed an error by refusing to entertain arguments of fraud as grounds for annulling the case, resulting in the case being remanded to the Amsterdam Court of Appeal. All remaining bases for appeal were rejected. According to the Court's ruling, the Energy Charter Treaty was deemed to be provisionally applicable to the Russian Federation in accordance with Article 45(1). The Hague District Court emphasised that the provisional application of the Energy Charter Treaty could only occur if the national legislative provisions were comparable to the corresponding provisions. Furthermore, the investments receive protection within the jurisdiction of the State when the ultimate beneficial owners possess citizenship of the State. The provisions

[10]Case ECLI:NL:HR: 2021: 425. Russian Federation v Veteran Petroleum Limited, Yukos Universal Limited, Hulley Enterprises Limited. 2022.

of the Energy Charter Treaty do not necessitate the investment to demonstrate beneficial outcomes for the host State in order to be safeguarded.

In 2007, Spain implemented a number of legislative measures aimed at fostering the utilisation of renewable energy sources. However, as a consequence of significant shifts in the financial landscape, the country subsequently rescinded certain provisions, thereby causing investors to initiate the abandonment of their respective projects. The Arbitral tribunals have been presented with assertions pertaining to the principles of fair and equitable treatment as well as legitimate expectations.[11]

In 2016, investors commenced legal proceedings in accordance with the provisions outlined in the Energy Charter Treaty. The parties involved in the case are Charanne B.V.[12] The electricity generation produced by the photovoltaic solar plant company was owned by shareholders who were involved in construction investments. The dispute pertained to the amendment of national laws that resulted in the violation of the legitimate expectations of the investors. The claimants contended that the aforementioned amendments were in violation of Article 10(1) of the Energy Charter Treaty. The regulatory framework implemented by Spain in 2008 led to a legislative foundation that favoured investors seeking to make new investments in the renewable energy sector. The claimants further contended that Spain's actions constituted expropriation of their investments, which is explicitly prohibited under Article 13 of the Energy Charter Treaty. Additionally, they argued that Spain's actions violated the standard of fair and equitable treatment as outlined in Article 10(1) of the Energy Charter Treaty. The Respondent in this case has contended that the implementation of regulatory amendments was carried out in accordance with the public interest and in a manner that did not discriminate. Furthermore, they assert that these amendments were proportionate and that the alleged expropriation did not occur in this specific instance.

The Arbitral Tribunal has rejected the claim after concluding that there is no basis for justifying the freezing of the regulatory framework on the basis of reasonable expectations. Furthermore, it is important to note that the framework in question cannot serve as a foundation for legitimate expectations, primarily because the aforementioned documents lack specificity. The absence of an obligation to modify the regulatory framework does not give rise to legitimate expectations for investors. The Tribunal asserted that in order to determine a violation of investor expectations, an objective standard or analysis must be employed. Merely relying on the subjective belief held by the investor at the time of making the investment is deemed insufficient. Furthermore, it is imperative for investors to thoroughly assess the legislative framework and contextual factors in order to identify the anticipated revisions to the regulatory foundation. The arbitration tribunal asserts that the

[11] Vattenfall AB and others v. Kingdom of Spain. ICSID Case No. ARB/12/22. Award rendered on July 2, 2019. Eiser Infrastructure Limited and Energia Solar Luxembourg S.à.r.l. v. Kingdom of Spain. ICSID Case No. ARB/13/36. Award rendered on May 4, 2017. Charanne B.V. and Construction Investments S.A.R.L. v. Kingdom of Spain. ICSID Case No. ARB/13/38 Award rendered on January 21, 2016.

[12] SCC Case No V 062/2012 *Charanne and Construction Investments v. Spain.*

fulfilment of the proportionality requirement hinges on the absence of random or unnecessary modifications that abruptly and unexpectedly eliminate the essential features of the existing regulatory framework. It is important to note that there was no inclusion of a stabilisation clause, or any explicit commitments made to the claimants that could be interpreted as a violation of their legitimate interests.

Another significant instance in this context is the Novenergia vs. Spain[13] case, wherein a Luxembourg investment fund filed a claim in the Arbitration concerning the just and equitable treatment under the Energy Charter Treaty. The individual who filed the claim had made investments in the photovoltaic sector due to the implementation of new regulatory requirements aimed at promoting investments in renewable energy. According to the specific regulation, feed-in tariffs were allocated to all photovoltaic plants for the entire duration of their operational lifespan. Subsequently, in light of the economic crisis, the regulations underwent amendments that rendered them less advantageous, resulting in a reduction in feed-in tariffs. The assertion was submitted in accordance with the violation of Article 10 (1) of the Energy Charter Treaty. According to the pronouncement of the Arbitration Tribunal, the obligations pertaining to stability and transparency serve as a mere exemplification of the obligation to uphold the investor's legitimate expectations under the fair and equitable treatment (FET) standard, rather than constituting distinct or autonomous obligations. This aligns with previous rulings, which have established that the state possesses the authority to regulate, and investors should anticipate the potential implementation of amendments. Furthermore, it should be noted that the fair and equitable standard does not guarantee the possibility of implementing crucial legislative modifications, which could potentially result in the investor's refusal to invest under the revised circumstances.

In the present scenario, Spain has put forth the argument that the arbitral tribunal is devoid of jurisdiction to adjudicate disputes pertaining to investments within the European Union. In light of the provisions outlined in Article 26 of the Energy Charter Treaty, it is important to note that the scope of arbitration pertains to the resolution of conflicts arising between a Contracting Party and an investor from another Contracting Party. In cases involving intra-EU relations, it is generally expected that EU law will take precedence. However, the Arbitral Tribunal did not concur with this stance, as the dispute between the parties has emerged from the Energy Charter Treaty rather than EU regulations. In the subsequent chapter, we will assess the divergent ruling rendered by the Arbitral Tribunal.

The Claimant contends that the amendment of the special regulation resulted in the expropriation of their investments, as outlined in Article 13(1) of the Energy Charter Treaty. In this section, the Tribunal asserted that due to the decline in the value of the asset, it could not be interpreted as an expropriation in accordance with the provisions of the Energy Charter Treaty. The ownership of the company remained unchanged, and the structure of shareholding remained unaffected as a

[13] Novenergia II—Energy and Environment (SCA) (Grand Duchy of Luxembourg) SICAR v. The Kingdom of Spain, SCC Case No. 2015/063.

result of the regulatory amendments. The Tribunal has ruled in this particular instance that a sum of EUR 53.3 million has been awarded, which is deemed to be a violation of Article 10 (1) of the Energy Charter Treaty, as well as covering the claimant's costs associated with the arbitration process.

Another significant legal case pertaining to the aforementioned regulation is the Eiser v. Spain[14] case. The Claimant has commenced legal proceedings under the Energy Charter Treaty in relation to the regulatory reforms, specifically the amendment to the feed-in-tariff regulation pertaining to photovoltaic solar energy, which was implemented by the Kingdom of Spain. This amendment has allegedly caused damages amounting to EUR 256 million. The legislative foundation in Spain, similar to the aforementioned cases, has been established and subsequently modified, leading to the initiation of arbitral proceedings by investors. The Claimant has been granted damages in the amount of EUR 128 million by the Arbitral Tribunal.

In the present scenario, Spain has formally requested the nullification of the arbitral award on the grounds of the Arbitral Tribunal's improper constitution. The applicant made the assumption that there was a business relationship between the Claimant and the experts involved in the case. The ad hoc Committee has employed a three-step assessment process to evaluate these arguments. Firstly, it is necessary to ascertain whether the right to raise the matter has been waived as a result of the concerned party's failure to provide timely elaboration. Furthermore, in the event that the aforementioned scenario does not apply, it becomes crucial to assess whether the third party perceives the arbitrator as potentially impartial during the evaluation of the case. Ultimately, could the presence of impartiality significantly impact the outcome of the case? The *ad hoc* Committee also assessed whether these circumstances had led to a material breach. The Committee has determined that the failure to disclose relationships between the parties may have influenced the final decisions, thereby constituting a violation of the fundamental rules of procedure.

In 2018, the Court of Justice of the European Union (CJEU) issued a highly contentious ruling concerning the application of bilateral investment protection treaties within the European Union (EU). This ruling was prompted by a request from the German Federal Court of Justice seeking a preliminary decision on the application of EU law to an investment protection treaty that had been concluded prior to the respective state's accession to the EU. The application for a preliminary ruling was submitted in relation to the provisions of Articles 18, 267, and 344 of the Treaty on the Functioning of the European Union (TFEU).

The present inquiry pertains to the Arbitral Tribunal that was established in accordance with the bilateral investment protection treaty specifically in relation to the award rendered in the case of Slovak Republic v. Achmea.[15] The emergence of the dispute can be attributed to the implementation of healthcare system reforms in Slovakia, where the provision of health insurance services by private capital

[14]Eiser Infrastructure Limited and Energia Solar Luxembourg S.a.r.l. v. Kingdom of Spain, ICSID Case No. ARB/13/36, Final Award, 4 May 2017.

[15]PCA Case No. 2008–13 *Achmea B.V. (formarly Eureko B.V.) v. The Slovak Republic.*

companies was previously permitted. Consequently, the Dutch corporation Achmea has established a subsidiary in Slovakia with the purpose of providing private health insurance services. In 2006, Slovakia implemented legislative amendments that imposed limitations on the liberalisation of the health sector insurance process. Notably, these amendments prohibited the distribution of profits derived from health insurance services among shareholders. Subsequent modifications were made to this legislation due to its contravention of constitutional provisions and its impracticability. The legislative provisions that are pertinent to the matter underwent amendments in 2011. As a result of the aforementioned regulatory changes, the company has commenced arbitration proceedings before the German Arbitral Tribunal. Slovakia has asserted that following its accession to the European Union, the enforcement of bilateral investment treaties' provisions is no longer permissible, as these provisions are in violation of EU law. Nevertheless, the Arbitral Tribunal has dismissed these assertions and consequently granted Achmea a compensation of EUR 22.1 million. Slovakia has submitted multiple appeals to the German Federal Court of Justice, which subsequently sought a preliminary ruling from the CJEU.

According to the CJEU, it has been established through previous legal decisions that international agreements must not infringe upon the autonomy and competences of the European Union (EU). The principle referred to is codified in Article 344 of the TFEU, which imposes a duty upon Member States to refrain from resorting to alternative mechanisms for resolving disputes that are not provided for in EU legislation. Furthermore, the justification for the supranational character of the European Union can be found in its legal framework. The CJEU has additionally asserted that the arbitral process outlined in Article 8 of the bilateral investment treaty differs from the procedure employed in commercial arbitration. Unlike commercial arbitration, which adheres to the sovereignty of individual Member States, the arbitral process outlined in the treaty was established as the primary mechanism. Furthermore, the Member States have mutually agreed to refrain from invoking national jurisdiction, as they are obligated to do so under EU legislation. The CJEU has asserted that in the current situation, aside from the fact that the disputes falling under the jurisdiction of the arbitral tribunal mentioned in Article 8 of the Bilateral Investment Treaty (BIT) may pertain to the interpretation of both the aforementioned agreement and European Union law, the option of referring these disputes to a non-EU judicial body is established by an agreement that was not entered into by the EU itself but rather by its Member States. The provisions outlined in Article 8 of the BIT raise concerns regarding both the principle of mutual trust among Member States and the preservation of the distinct legal framework established by the Treaties. These concerns are further compounded by the potential impact on the preliminary ruling procedure outlined in Article 267 TFEU. Consequently, Article 8 is not in alignment with the principle of sincere cooperation as mentioned in paragraph 34 above. In such situations, it can be argued that the provisions outlined in Article 8 of the BIT have a detrimental impact on the independence of European Union legislation. Therefore, it can be concluded that Articles 267 and 344 TFEU should be interpreted as prohibiting a provision in an international agreement made between Member States, such as Article 8 of the BIT, which allows an investor from one Member State to initiate legal proceedings against the other Member State before an arbitral tribunal that the latter Member State has agreed to recognise in the event of a dispute regarding investments in the latter Member State.

The aforementioned decision played a pivotal role in shaping the existing body of case law, as it determined that the intra-EU bilateral investment treaties were not applicable within the European Union.[16] The classification of Arbitration tribunals outlined in bilateral investment treaties cannot be regarded as tribunals or courts of Member States. This ruling has prompted numerous inquiries, as the tribunals established under bilateral investment treaties lack jurisdiction over cases arising from investment protection treaties.

In light of the Achmea judgement, the Commission has initiated a Communication that elucidates the relevant procedures and legal instruments within the European Union for resolving disputes while emphasising the crucial significance of uniformly applying EU law. The presence of bilateral investment treaties has resulted in varying interpretations and potential conflicts with the application of EU law in relation to State aid. Following the Achmea judgement, the European Commission has determined that the existence of arbitral tribunals established under bilateral investment treaties is in conflict with EU legislation.[17] Consequently, the Commission has concluded that these tribunals lack jurisdiction over dispute matters as the bilateral investment treaties themselves are deemed invalid. The Communication also references the Energy Charter Treaty and its role in intra-EU relations. Upon analysing the provision and taking into account the primacy of EU law, it can be deduced that the provision is not applicable.

The Agreement concerning the termination of bilateral investment treaties was reached in 2020 among 23 Member States. Nevertheless, it is important to note that this termination specifically pertains to the bilateral investment treaties and does not extend to the multilateral Energy Charter Treaty. It is important to acknowledge that following the termination of the aforementioned treaties, a "sunset clause" is in effect for a duration of 20 years. This phenomenon can be attributed to the safeguarding of investors in the event that a contracting member state opts to modify its existing protective measures or withdraw from the agreement altogether.[18] In late 2020, Belgium submitted a formal request to the CJEU seeking an opinion on the conformity of the intra-European Union implementation of the arbitration clauses outlined in the Energy Charter Treaty with the laws of the EU. Following the Achmea judgement and subsequent Communications from the Commission, there remains a lack of clarity regarding the extent to which it applies to multilateral investment protection treaties, such as the Energy Charter Treaty.

[16] Batlag and Stanic (2020).

[17] Quirico (2021).

[18] Leal (2018).

16.3 The Energy Charter Treaty an Obstacle for the Green Deal

The European Union has recently set an ambitious goal of attaining a zero-carbon economy. To achieve this objective, the EU has implemented the Green Deal strategy. Currently, the necessary documentation is being prepared and deliberated upon. The Energy Charter Treaty is at a critical juncture as it seeks to achieve the objectives of enhancing sustainability, efficiency, and reducing reliance on fossil fuels, thereby facilitating the growth of renewable energy.

As previously examined in the preceding chapters, it is evident that the Energy Charter Treaty is antiquated and necessitates a comprehensive revision. Following the Achmea judgement and subsequent explanatory documents from the Commission, there remains uncertainty regarding the compliance of the Energy Charter Treaty with EU law, in addition to bilateral investment treaties. The primary objective of this treaty was to guarantee the safeguarding of foreign investments in the energy sector. Nevertheless, it is important to note that the entities involved in the agreement extend beyond just the European Union Member States, non-EU States, Euratom, and the EU itself. One additional attribute of the investment protection treaty is the inclusion of a "sunset clause", whereby the contractual party remains bound by its obligations for a period of 20 years, even if it chooses to withdraw from the treaty. The aforementioned scenario pertains to the Russian Federation, which, due to significant opposition in both the Parliament and public discourse, did not ratify the Energy Charter Treaty. Furthermore, in 2008, the country made the decision to withdraw from the Energy Charter Treaty, consequently leading to its binding applicability for a duration of 20 years, until 2028. In order to ensure clarity, it is crucial during the negotiation phase to address all inquiries pertaining to applicability and resolve existing discrepancies concerning the intra—European Union implementation of the Energy Charter Treaty.

Another issue that has come to light pertains to the inherent characteristics of the Energy Charter Treaty and its safeguarding of fossil fuels, which runs counter to the clean energy transition strategy outlined in the Green Deal. Specifically, the conflicts pertain to the actions taken by the state towards the investor and the infringement upon their rights. There exists a contradiction whereby Member States are mandated to promote and facilitate investments in clean energy while simultaneously being obligated to protect the interests of investors who have already invested in fossil fuel energy infrastructure, which fails to meet emission requirements and significantly contributes to environmental pollution. In this scenario, the Member States are unable to issue directives for the closure of these power plants on the grounds of excessive emissions. This is because such actions could potentially trigger an arbitral procedure, particularly if the case involves foreign investors, under the Energy Charter Treaty. Consequently, the Member States may face substantial financial penalties for violating the provisions of the fair and equitable treatment clause, expropriation, or any other legally binding obligations. Based on the aforementioned rationales, it is imperative to undertake a comprehensive revision of the Energy

Charter Treaty, specifically addressing concerns pertaining to the safeguarding of fossil fuel investments and the application of its provisions within the European Union.

The Commission has put forth suggestions for two decisions in accordance with Article 218(9) of the TFEU and Article 101 of the Euratom Treaty. These proposals aim to determine the stance that the European Union and Euratom will take at the 33rd meeting of the Energy Charter Conference. Simultaneously, the Commission has approved a communication that emphasises the necessity of resolving the potential conflict between the treaties and the Energy Charter Treaty (ECT) as interpreted by certain arbitral tribunals. These tribunals have asserted that the ECT is applicable to conflicts within the European Union. If the courts of a third nation were to confirm that interpretation, it would effectively result in a legal dispute, as arbitration awards that violate EU legislation would then be recognised and enforced in the legal systems of third countries. The suggestions presented to the Council recommended that the European Union and Euratom endorse the implementation of the "modernization package" during the 33rd session of the Energy Charter Conference. Nevertheless, the aforementioned proposals failed to gain approval from the Council as a result of the abstention of a blocking minority consisting of four Member States (Germany, France, Spain, and the Netherlands) during the COREPER meeting held on November 18, 2022. Consequently, the inclusion of the "modernization package" was removed from the agenda of the 33rd session of the Energy Charter Conference, leading to the non-adoption of the modernization of the Energy Charter Treaty. Meanwhile, the existing, non-updated Treaty remains in effect for the European Union, Euratom, and all Member States involved in the Energy Charter Treaty (ECT) in their interactions with other signatory parties. Furthermore, the efforts to acquire and execute awards made by courts that are allegedly formed in accordance with Article 26 of the ECT in conflicts within the European Union persist without interruption.

Without the requisite decisions from the European Union and the European Atomic Energy Community (Euratom), their participation in a voting process regarding the acceptance of the modernization package during a session of the Energy Charter Conference is precluded. In accordance with the established protocol, during the voting process at an ECT Conference, the Union is granted a voting power equivalent to the total number of its member states that have entered into contractual agreements as parties to the ECT. The adoption of the modernization package is contingent upon the participation of the European Union and Euratom in the voting process, as their involvement is necessary to meet the voting quorum in the conference. The absence of a qualified majority within the Council prevents the European Union and the Euratom from participating in the voting process during a meeting of the Energy Charter Conference. This limitation hinders their ability to endorse the passage of the modernization package.

Furthermore, regardless of the adoption of the modernization package by the Energy Charter Conference, the implementation or provisional application of an updated Treaty would necessitate the approval of the European Parliament. The European Parliament has explicitly expressed its opposition to the reform of the

Treaty and has urged the European Union and its Member States to coordinate a withdrawal from the Energy Charter Treaty. As a result, the absence of a legal and/or institutional mechanism for the adoption and implementation of the modernization of the ECT poses a challenge for the European Union to continue its participation in the Treaty. Continuing to be a signatory to the existing, outdated ECT is not a viable choice for the European Union or its member states. This is because the current version of the treaty does not align with the EU's investment strategy and legal framework, nor does it support the EUs objectives in the areas of energy and climate. Consequently, the European Union's withdrawal from the ECT emerges as the sole viable resolution. The European Union would not be exempt from the terms of a sunset clause, which specifies a 20-year period of protection for current investments, including those involving fossil fuels, made by non-EU signatories like Japan and Turkey within EU member states.

16.4 Conclusion

The Energy Charter Treaty is a globally recognised accord that seeks to safeguard foreign investments and promote international trade among nations. Russia has expressed its acceptance of the Energy Charter Treaty to a restricted extent, stipulating that it must align with national legislation. However, Russia has not formally ratified the treaty and made the decision to withdraw from it in 2009. Nevertheless, Russia remains legally obligated to adhere to the provisions of the Energy Charter until 2029, as dictated by the "sunset" clause.

The primary objective of the Energy Charter Treaty is to safeguard foreign investments, facilitate the trade and transit of energy resources, and provide mechanisms for resolving disputes. However, there is a perception that the treaty has become outdated and does not align with contemporary standards. The Commission has been tasked with the responsibility of engaging in discussions pertaining to the modernization of the Energy Charter Treaty. The objective is to ensure alignment with sustainable development goals, address global climate change concerns, and establish contemporary standards for resolving disputes between investors and states.

The tribunal in the Yukos case has reached the conclusion that the Russian Federation has violated the fair and equitable treatment standard as outlined in the Energy Charter Treaty. The conclusion further elucidated the violation of the obligation to refrain from implementing any discriminatory measures. The Tribunal has asserted that measures of indirect expropriation were employed in the aforementioned case. The Claimant was granted a monetary sum of 50 billion US dollars by the Respondent in relation to the breach of the Energy Charter Treaty and the occurrence of indirect expropriation.

The Russian Federation has submitted an appeal to the Hague District Court, which, in 2016, granted the appeal and relieved the Russian Federation of its obligation to provide compensation as stipulated by the Arbitral award. The Hague

District Court has concurred with the stance that the Energy Charter Treaty does not apply to the Russian Federation. This determination is based on the absence of both treaty ratification and the adoption of any obligatory regulation endorsing the temporary implementation of the Energy Charter Treaty by the country.

In 2020, the Court of Appeal overturned the ruling made by the lower court. The Court of Appeal has determined that the Arbitral Tribunal possessed the jurisdiction to adjudicate the dispute based on the validity of the arbitral agreement, which was established by the Russian Federation's signing of the Energy Charter Treaty in 1994. Inconsistency arises when one legal provision contradicts another. However, in the aforementioned case, it is important to note that the absence of national regulation does not necessarily give rise to inconsistency. The Court of Appeal further emphasised that the "clean hands doctrine" pertains to the illegalities associated with the creation of the investments and should not restrict the jurisdiction.

Spain has implemented a number of legislative measures aimed at promoting the utilisation of renewable energy sources. However, it has subsequently revoked certain provisions, resulting in investors being compelled to halt their ongoing projects. Subsequent to this determination, the assertions were submitted to the Arbitral Tribunal, which ultimately rejected the claim on the basis that the establishment of legitimate expectations does not warrant the suspension of the regulatory framework. Furthermore, it is important to note that the framework in question cannot serve as a foundation for legitimate expectations, primarily because the associated documents lack specificity. The absence of an obligation to modify the regulatory framework does not give rise to legitimate expectations for investors.

The comparable ruling was made in a separate instance wherein the party making the claim had made investments in the photovoltaic industry, coinciding with the implementation of new regulatory measures aimed at promoting investments in renewable energy. According to the specific regulation, feed-in tariffs were allocated to all photovoltaic plants for the duration of their operational lifespan. Subsequently, in light of the economic crisis, the regulations underwent amendments that resulted in less favourable conditions, including a reduction in feed-in tariffs. The Arbitral Tribunal reached the determination that the state possesses the authority to enact regulations, and investors should anticipate the potential implementation of amendments. Furthermore, the fair and equitable standard fails to guarantee the possibility of enacting crucial legislative modifications, which could potentially result in the investor's refusal to invest under the revised circumstances.

The Achmea decision represents a pivotal development in light of prior legal precedents, as it establishes that intra-EU bilateral investment treaties are not applicable within the European Union. The determination made by the Arbitration tribunal established in bilateral investment treaties challenges the classification of these tribunals as either national courts or tribunals of Member States. This ruling has prompted numerous inquiries, particularly regarding the jurisdiction of these tribunals in relation to cases arising from investment protection treaties.

The clarity regarding the compliance of the Energy Charter Treaty with EU law remains uncertain, as the Achmea judgement and subsequent explanatory documents from the Commission have not definitively determined whether this applies solely to bilateral investment treaties or extends to the Energy Charter Treaty as well. The primary objective of this treaty was to establish safeguards for foreign investments in the energy sector. Nevertheless, it is important to note that the entities involved in this treaty extend beyond just the European Union Member States, non-EU States, Euratom, and the EU itself.

Another issue that has come to light pertains to the inherent characteristics of the Energy Charter Treaty and its implications for safeguarding fossil fuels, which run counter to the strategy of transitioning towards clean energy. There exists a contradiction whereby Member States are mandated to promote and facilitate investments in clean energy while simultaneously being obligated to protect the interests of investors who have already invested in fossil fuel-based energy infrastructure that fails to meet emission standards and significantly contributes to environmental pollution. In this scenario, the Member States are unable to issue directives for the closure of these power plants on the grounds of excessive emissions. This is because such action could potentially trigger an arbitral procedure, particularly if the case involves foreign investors, under the Energy Charter Treaty. Consequently, the Member States could face substantial financial penalties for violating the provisions of the fair and equitable treatment clause, expropriation, or any other legally binding obligations. The Commission has put up a proposal suggesting that European Union member states collectively withdraw from the Energy Charter Treaty. This treaty has faced criticism due to its perceived hindrance to climate change mitigation measures since it provides protection for energy investments, including those related to fossil fuels. The act of withdrawing from the treaty would not exempt the European Union from the provisions of a sunset clause, which stipulates a 20-year duration of protection for current investments, including those in fossil fuels, made by non-EU signatories within EU member states.

References

Baltag C (2012) The energy charter treaty: the notion of investor. Kluwer Law International, Alphen Aan Den Rijn

Bamberger C, Walde T (2008) The energy charter treaty. In: Roggenkamp M et al (eds) Energy law in Europe. Oxford University Press, Oxford

Batlag C, Stanic A (2020) The future of investment treaty arbitration in the EU: substance, process and policy. Kluwer Law International, Alphen Aan Den Rijn

Hober K (2020) The energy charter treaty. Oxford University Press, Oxford

Iavorsky M (2012) Uniqueness of the energy charter Treaty's investment regime. Main features and cases. Lap Lambert Academic Publishing, Saarbruecken

Leal AR (2018) Commentary on the energy charter treaty. Edward Elgar Publishing, Cheltenham

Quirico O (2021) Investment Governance between the Energy Charter Treaty and the European Union

Chapter 17
Competition Law Application in Nuclear Energy Sector

Abstract The nuclear industry is subject to certain rules specified in the Euratom Treaty; however, these regulations do not cover competition law regulation. We can apply competition law by analogy to remedy the regulatory void in the nuclear sector, provided it does not conflict with any current legislation. However, it is crucial to acknowledge that many regard this technique as fundamentally flawed. The Euratom Treaty's implementation had two objectives: to establish and promote the nuclear industry, as well as to govern the use of nuclear materials in both military and civilian domains. This involved electricity generation, which required strict control mechanisms and specific methods to promote investment. The Treaty on the Functioning of the European Union (TFEU) regulates public relations exclusively under the Euratom Treaty, but the Euratom retains the authority to act in these matters. The Euratom Treaty regulates the functioning and progress of nuclear energy, ensuring protection against the harmful effects of ionising radiation and the creation and operation of the joint nuclear market. The Euratom Treaty governs the establishment of a consolidated nuclear market, which includes regulations forbidding tariffs on imported goods and fees with comparable consequences.

17.1 Introduction

A variety of factors have influenced the growth of international nuclear regulation. The cross-border effects of a single nation's actions highlight the significance of international regulation in addressing issues related to the 1986 Chernobyl nuclear accident. The occurrence has prompted a reassessment of the regulations pertaining to nuclear safety. One significant determinant was the expansion of the European Union (EU) in 2004, wherein nations engaged in the development of nuclear energy, such as Lithuania, the Czech Republic, Hungary, and Slovakia, were admitted as new EU members. It is noteworthy that neighbouring countries of the European Union are currently engaged in the development of nuclear energy projects in close proximity to the borders of Member States. In 2004, a notable development occurred within the European Union, as five out of the ten newly admitted Member States possessed a total of 19 nuclear reactors on their respective territories. This marked

L. Rimšaitė, *The Crossroads of Competition Law and Energy Regulation*,
https://doi.org/10.1007/978-3-031-73238-6_17

the first instance since 1957, following the five previous enlargements of the EU, where such a concentration of nuclear reactors was observed. The strengthening of nuclear regulation was significantly influenced by the gas supply disruption from Russia to Ukraine in 2006, which also had repercussions in other Member States. During that period, there were concerns regarding the European Union's reliance on natural gas imports from Russia. Consequently, efforts were made to initiate processes and discussions aimed at diversifying the sources of natural gas supply. The objective was to enhance the security of the European Union's gas supply. The importance of prioritising radiation protection during the advancement of nuclear energy was also underscored.

The governance of nuclear energy falls under the purview of the Euratom Treaty, which is a legal instrument that holds a specialised status in relation to the Treaty on the Functioning of the European Union (TFEU).[1] While the primary legislation of the European Union shares similarities with the Euratom Treaty, it is important to note that the latter does not comprehensively regulate competition law. This regulation is exclusively stipulated in the TFEU. When conducting an analysis of the energy sector and the application of competition law provisions, it is crucial to assess the regulatory framework of competition law as outlined in the TFEU, alongside the regulations pertaining to nuclear energy. Consequently, it becomes necessary to examine the interplay between the implementation of these provisions. It is important to acknowledge that the nuclear industry operates under specialised regulations rather than general oversight. However, it is worth noting that the Euratom Treaty's preamble also emphasises the goal of establishing a competitive internal market. Hence, this section will examine the precise regulation of the nuclear energy sector, along with the potentialities and challenges associated with implementing competition law within the domain of nuclear energy.

17.2 Objectives and Specific Regulation of the Euratom Treaty

The primary objective of the Euratom Treaty was to establish and foster the growth of the nuclear industry. The regulation pertaining to the utilisation of nuclear materials encompasses both military and civilian sectors, encompassing activities such as electricity generation.[2] Strict controls and appropriate investment promotion measures are necessary in these areas.[3] The Euratom Treaty regulates public relations that fall within its exclusive jurisdiction as well as those that are subject to the

[1] Consolidated version of the Treaty establishing the European Atomic Energy Community. OJ C 203, 7.6.2016, p. 1–112.

[2] Treaty establishing the European Atomic Energy Community (Euratom), signed on March 25, 1957.

[3] Bouquet (2001).

TFEU, albeit with the Euratom possessing powers of action in such matters. The Euratom Treaty is responsible for the exclusive regulation of nuclear energy, encompassing its functioning and development, as well as safeguarding against the detrimental impacts of ionising radiation. Additionally, it governs the establishment and operation of the common nuclear market. Nevertheless, the establishment of a unified nuclear energy market presents certain challenges. The Euratom Treaty explicitly includes provisions that prohibit the imposition of taxes on imported goods and charges that have similar effects and also regulate the unrestricted movement of individuals and services in this particular domain.

The Euratom Treaty clearly differentiates between the requirement to provide notice of intended investments in the realm of nuclear energy development and the obligation of those overseeing the establishment of a nuclear facility to inform the Commission of their planned investments in this domain. Following the ratification of the Euratom Treaty, numerous supplementary measures, such as secondary acts, directives, regulations, and decisions, have been implemented to govern the domain of nuclear energy. However, in contrast to the previous Treaty of the European Coal and Steel Community, the Euratom Treaty does not include provisions specifying a predetermined duration of validity. The signing of the Euratom Treaty aimed to establish alternative sources of energy supply as a means of mitigating reliance on fossil fuel imports.[4] One notable factor relates to the substantial initial capital required for the establishment of nuclear initiatives, rendering it unattainable for a single Member State. Consequently, regulation and collaboration at the European Union level became imperative. Nevertheless, a definitive consensus regarding this matter remains elusive among Member States due to the fact that not all nations engage in the development of nuclear energy.

The primary objective of the Euratom Treaty was to facilitate and advance the growth and progress of the nuclear industry. The primary goal of the TFEU)was to achieve economic integration among the Member States. Establishing the necessary legal frameworks and working to ensure market competitiveness across a number of the economy's sectors which were already relatively developed in comparison to the nuclear industry were two ways to pursue this goal. The jurisdiction over nuclear safety does not solely lie within the purview of the Euratom Treaty but rather falls within the jurisdiction of the Euratom Community. The objective of this Community is to advance the development of robust and cutting-edge research and technology methodologies that guarantee a heightened level of reactor safety, mitigate the occurrence of significant nuclear incidents, effectively handle radioactive waste, and promote the secure utilisation of ionising radiation in industrial and medical contexts.

The Euratom Treaty also governs the establishment of a common nuclear market. The possibility of granting a loan from the Euratom fund is also anticipated. Euratom has been offering financial assistance for the advancement of nuclear infrastructure since 1977, thereby playing a role in the achievement of a fully integrated electricity

[4] Schroder (2019).

market. The Euratom Supply Agency assumes the primary responsibility for the comprehensive execution of the nuclear materials supply policy while also being entrusted with specific functions pertaining to energy security. Ensuring the competitiveness of the nuclear energy market is of paramount importance.[5] It is necessary to differentiate between the application of the TFEU and the application of the Euratom Treaty in relation to the internal market within the nuclear energy sector. The legal doctrine and jurisprudence of the Court of Justice of the European Union (CJEU) do not offer a definitive response to this query. One possible explanation for the lack of a definitive response from the CJEU regarding the interplay between these treaties may stem from a hesitancy to reach a unanimous agreement based on the specific circumstances under consideration. In certain instances, the CJEU has observed that the assessment of State aid, as defined by the TFEU, may not be applicable in the context of nuclear energy. This observation is made despite the CJEU's conclusion that the State aid in question is in accordance with the provisions of the TFEU. The Commission has made several determinations regarding the implementation of State aid in the nuclear sector.[6] While it exercises caution in applying Article 107 (1) of the TFEU, it acknowledges that if a measure were to be classified as State aid, it would still be deemed compatible under Article 107 (3)(c) of the TFEU. The Commission's decision in a specific case exemplifies this position, wherein the compatibility of compensating Electrabel and SPE for the decommissioning of a nuclear facility with internal market regulations was deemed acceptable. However, the Commission did not furnish additional justifications for this determination. An additional illustration can be found in the nuclear sector reform in the United Kingdom in 1989, which entailed the declaration of intended State aid.[7] In this instance, the Commission granted approval for the proposed guarantee, which aimed to provide coverage for forthcoming decommissioning expenses and address matters pertaining to civil liability. In accordance with the existing regulatory framework, the Commission does not possess the authority to assess compliance. Nevertheless, as per the established jurisprudence of the CFEU, the evaluation of compliance with the TFEU is regarded as somewhat restricted.

The TFEU's provisions regarding the Commission's function do not govern the determination of the application of competition law in the nuclear energy sector. The Euratom Treaty, which primarily focuses on the establishment of a unified nuclear domestic market and the facilitation of investment, governs a significant aspect of nuclear matters.[8] The CJEU does not offer a definitive stance on this matter, as it has made decisions to evaluate whether certain nuclear activities adhere to the regulations outlined in competition law. The question of whether the Commission

[5]Engstedt (2020).

[6]Cusack (2003).

[7]Decision on State Aid Case SA.31573: Compensation for Decommissioning Nuclear Facilities. Official Journal of the European Union, 2014. Nuclear Sector Reform and State Aid Declaration.1989.

[8]Froggatt (2002).

possesses the authority to evaluate the conformity of competition law with internal market regulations in the domain of nuclear energy lacks a definitive resolution. This study aims to delve deeper into instances where the Euratom Treaty lacks a regulatory mechanism within the realm of competition law. Additionally, we will examine the relationship between the Euratom Treaty and another relevant treaty in the context of nuclear energy.

The Euratom Treaty is commonly recognised as a legal instrument with specialised provisions within the framework of the TFEU. However, it should be noted that this recognition does not imply a complete exclusion of the TFEU's applicability to matters concerning nuclear energy. As highlighted by the CJEU, the absence of specific provisions regarding anti-dumping measures in the Euratom Treaty does not preclude the application of the TFEU. The CJEU has reaffirmed this principle in subsequent cases, affirming that the provisions of the TFEU pertaining to the regulation of competition law and trade relations are applicable to the nuclear sector, which falls under the jurisdiction of the Euratom Treaty. The relationship between the Treaty establishing the European Coal and Steel Community and the Treaty establishing the European Community is characterised by the recognition that special rules hold a higher level of authority than the provisions outlined in the latter treaty. In the event of a lack of specific regulations governing competition or trade rules in the nuclear sector, it is feasible to utilise the pertinent provisions outlined in the Treaty establishing the European Community. The principle of *lex speciali derogat legi generali* asserts that when specific regulations are established, they take precedence over general ones.[9] This concept has been consistently emphasised. In accordance with this theoretical framework, the provisions outlined in the TFEU that govern the competition rules pertaining to nuclear energy are in alignment with the provisions stipulated in the Treaty establishing the European Atomic Energy Community (Euratom Treaty). Advocates of an alternative perspective contend that the Euratom Treaty possesses characteristics of a *lex specialis*, suggesting that the application of the TFEU may not be suitable for legal relationships within the nuclear domain. The provisions of the TFEU cannot be applied in cases where they fall within the scope of the Euratom Treaty.

When examining the notion that the nuclear industry lacks specific competition law regulations, it is pertinent to consider the United Reprocessors case. In this case, fuel companies such as KEWA, BNFL, and CEA contemplated a potential consolidation through an agreement to establish a joint undertaking.[10] The primary objectives of this collaboration were to coordinate investments, determine production capacity, and establish production quotas. According to the Commission's findings, the agreement in question may limit competition as that term is defined in Article 101 (1) of the TFEU and may also cause market distortions. However, the

---

[9] Ptasekaitė (2011).

[10] (United Commission Decision 93/39/EEC of 27 January 1993 concerning the formation of a joint undertaking for the reprocessing of nuclear fuel, United Reprocessors. Official Journal L 16, 21.01.1993, p. 21–24.

Commission has granted approval for this concentration through a decision made under Article 101 (3) of the TFEU, subject to the conditions that justify such a restriction. The Commission's decision also acknowledged that subject falls under the jurisdiction of the rules outlined in Chapter 4 of the Euratom Treaty, which focuses on investment-related issues. It is important to note, however, that the decision was made in accordance with the TFEU.

The provisions within the Euratom Treaty bear resemblance to the objectives of competition law. Certain provisions within the Euratom Treaty establish the notion of fair and equal treatment for economic entities without any form of discrimination.[11] This includes the principle of equal treatment towards the sources of supply, as outlined in Article 52 (1) of the Euratom Treaty. Furthermore, there is a prohibition on bestowing the privileged position on specific economic operators. Article 68 holds significance in this regard, as it serves to prohibit the establishment of exorbitantly high prices, thereby creating a favourable environment for specific market participants. The price regulation, as mandated by Articles 67–69 of the Euratom Treaty, serves to guarantee non-discrimination. This regulation encompasses provisions for the exercise of regulatory and supervisory functions, granting the Council the authority to make adjustments to prices. The Euratom Treaty addresses a situation characterised by ambiguity as it aims to safeguard the security of uranium provision within the Community. In pursuit of this objective, the treaty grants authorities the power to authorise contracts for uranium supply that have been entered into by operators. The establishment of a vertical relationship is observed between the institutions of the Euratom Community and the entities involved in the nuclear sector. In contrast, the Euratom Treaty aims to enhance the internal market for nuclear energy while simultaneously promoting the unrestricted flow of goods and fostering competition among economic entities at regulated prices.

The Euratom Treaty established the fundamental framework for the advancement of the nuclear energy market and the utilisation of nuclear technology in the civilian sector. The provisions outlined in the TFEU encompass the overarching goals of economic integration and establish prerequisites for ensuring equitable competition among entities operating within the energy market. Prior to conducting an analysis of the application of the provisions of the TFEU in relation to nuclear energy, it is necessary to refer to Article 106(a) of the Treaty establishing the Euratom. This article outlines the circumstances under which the provisions of the TFEU are applicable to legal relationships governed by the Euratom Treaty, provided they are compatible with the specific regulations in place. In situations where there is overlap in the subject matter being regulated, the Euratom Treaty is considered to have priority as a *lex specialis*. Upon conducting a more in-depth examination of the aforementioned provisions, it is pertinent to direct our focus towards Article 93 of the Euratom Treaty. This particular article pertains to the establishment of the free movement of goods and explicitly prohibits the imposition of reciprocal import and export duties, as well as any charges that may have a similar impact. This article

[11] Engstedt (2020).

lacks comprehensive regulation regarding the unrestricted movement of goods. Consequently, certain authors raise valid concerns regarding the concept of *lex specialis*, contending that the principle of free movement of goods is envisioned and does not currently necessitate specific regulations pertaining to nuclear energy. The CJEU has also affirmed this concept, asserting that if the provisions of the TFEU do not conflict with the demands of the Euratom Treaty, it is feasible to apply general legislation to the specific sector.

The analysis of competition law provisions in the nuclear sector indicates that the Euratom Treaty does not establish a comprehensive framework for competition law, resulting in a regulatory void. Efforts are being made to find resolutions to the issue by employing the principles outlined in the TFEU that pertain to competition law through a process of analogy. The investigation has revealed that the Commission is currently evaluating the extent to which nuclear operators are adhering to the competition regulations outlined in the TFEU. The legal doctrine and case law of the CJEU present differing perspectives on the applicability of the provisions of the TFEU in relation to nuclear energy. These views suggest that such provisions can be utilised, provided they do not contradict any specific regulations pertaining to this domain. The authors' position could be partially acknowledged, as implementing their proposed approach would assist in addressing the current gap in legal regulation without necessitating any changes to the existing framework. Alternative perspectives have been put forth by various scholars, contending that the regulations outlined in the TFEU do not extend to nuclear energy due to its distinct legal framework. The current situation presents a legal loophole, as matters pertaining to competition law are not covered by the Euratom Treaty. Consequently, it is not feasible to apply these provisions to entities engaged in nuclear activities. Nevertheless, the recent ruling by the CJEU pertaining to the provision of State aid to Hinkley Point C could potentially introduce a distinct perspective. This case will be examined in subsequent sections.

17.3 Euratom Supply Agency

It is imperative for the Commission to guarantee the oversight responsibility of the Euratom Supply Agency (ESA) in evaluating their execution of delegated functions. Throughout history, Russia, formerly known as the Soviet Union, has played a significant role as the primary provider of enriched products, including uranium. These products were supplied to Member States through long-term contracts that featured remarkably low prices. Between the years 1989 and 1993, the Soviet Union experienced a notable growth in its market share of uranium, progressing from a negligible presence to a substantial 25% of the overall market. Consequently, the practise of price dumping prompted the ESA to implement measures aimed at safeguarding market competitiveness and supply security. The authority to exercise such powers has been granted in accordance with the provisions outlined in

Chapter VI of the Euratom Treaty.[12] The newly implemented policy encompasses measures aimed at limiting the provision of uranium from former Soviet Union nations to the European Union. Additionally, it incorporates a suggestion to distribute products at prevailing market rates. The limitations have been implemented in a manner that avoids the imposition of rigid quotas while also prohibiting the establishment of exclusive supply arrangements, which are not permissible according to the provisions outlined in the Euratom Treaty. The decision made by ESA was predicated on a meticulous evaluation of individual cases, wherein factors such as consumer requirements, the length of the supply agreement, long-term strategic considerations, and prospects for diversification were taken into careful consideration.[13] The aforementioned policy was subsequently mirrored in the White Paper issued by the Commission. There are two significant cases that have had a notable impact on the evolution of regulations pertaining to trade in the nuclear energy sector.

The ENU case pertains to a Portuguese company operating in the extraction and supply of uranium raw materials. This company encountered challenges in selling its products within the domestic market, leading it to explore alternative opportunities in foreign markets. The company's annual uranium extraction exceeded 200 metric tonnes, and prior to becoming a member of the Euratom Community, it had established a long-term supply agreement with the French company EDF.[14] This agreement involved the sale of approximately 136 metric tonnes of raw uranium material on an annual basis. Following the conclusion of the contract in 1990, the organisation was compelled to seek out export prospects in order to market the extracted uranium raw material. In 1987, the company endeavoured to establish new contractual agreements but encountered difficulty securing potential buyers due to its marginally higher pricing in comparison to other suppliers. Consequently, the ESA has made a formal request for the Member States of the European Community to enter into supply agreements. This request is based on the ESA's commitment to fostering a competitive internal market within the nuclear energy sector. According to the Commission's statement, the ESA is not obligated to require members of the Euratom Community to enter into contracts with their suppliers. ENI lodged an appeal against the Commission's decision; however, the court upheld a consistent line of reasoning, asserting that the Euratom Treaty does not establish any form of favouritism towards domestic production over imports from non-member countries, and consequently, no preference was granted in this regard. The Court further observed that the European Single Market could not impose limitations on imports at prices lower than those of domestic production within the European Union unless such measures would violate the provisions of the Euratom Treaty aimed at

[12]Consolidated version of the Treaty establishing the European Atomic Energy Community. OJ C 203, 7.6.2016, p. 1–112.

[13]Consolidated version of the Treaty establishing the European Atomic Energy Community. OJ C 203, 7.6.2016, p. 1–112.

[14]Case T-16/96, Empresa Nacional de Urânio v Commission, [2000] ECR II-3375.

guaranteeing supply security. According to the judgement of the CJEU, it was observed that Portugal's provision of only 1.5% of the uranium feedstock to the Community would not have had a substantial influence on the security of supply.

The KLE case holds significance in this regard. Kernkraftwerke Lippe-Ems GmbH, the operator of a nuclear power plant in Germany, has initiated a procurement process to secure a contract for the supply of uranium in the medium term, specifically in the form of hexafluoride. The contract was awarded to British Nuclear Fuels plc, whose bid was the most economically advantageous. Given the atypically low price being offered, the ESA has formally requested detailed information regarding the origin and methods of uranium production. British Nuclear Fuels plc has disclosed that the provider of uranium is a former constituent of the Soviet Union, most likely Russia.[15] Kernkraftwerke Lippe-Ems GmbH had previously acquired a substantial quantity of uranium from a British company at a comparatively advantageous cost. However, the ESA stipulated that the procurement of such a contract necessitated verification that the uranium supplier did not originate from any of the former Soviet Union member states. Kernkraftwerke Lippe-Ems GmbH lodged a challenge against the decision made by the ESA on the basis that ESA had implemented an intervention policy that went beyond the authority granted to it under the Euratom Treaty. Kernkraftwerke Lippe-Ems GmbH has also requested that the Commission mandate the ESA to provide compensation for the financial detriment incurred due to the obligation to engage in a procurement agreement with a supplier offering higher prices. The statements made by the company were rejected by the Commission on the grounds that the actions taken by the ESA were deemed to be in violation of Article 52 (2) of the Euratom Treaty as they exhibited a preference towards a specific economic operator. The ESA lacked the capacity to actively engage in an intervention policy pertaining to price control and contractor selection, according to a statement from Kernkraftwerke Lippe-Ems GmbH. As stated by the Commission, the ESA possesses the authority to guarantee the security of supply, which includes the ability to evaluate and determine the contracting parties with whom to establish nuclear materials supply agreements, as outlined in Article 52 of the Euratom Treaty.

According to Article 53 of the Euratom Treaty, the Commission has the authority to exercise veto power over contracts that the ESA has approved in cases where the agreed-upon price in the supply contract deviates from current market conditions. The Euratom Treaty grants the European Atomic Energy Community (Euratom) the requisite authority to enforce limitations on the importation of nuclear material into the European Community. This authority is exercised when such imports are deemed to undermine the objectives outlined in the Euratom Treaty. The CJEU has taken this into account when dismissing the applicants' complaint because this position is based on the goal of ensuring the security of supply.

Upon closer analysis of the mandate of the ESA, it becomes evident that the organisation possesses significant latitude in the assessment of contracts granted by

[15] Case T-23/93, Kernkraftwerke Lippe-Ems GmbH v Commission, [1995] ECR II-2615.

nuclear operators. Additionally, the ESA holds the authority to compel entities to terminate contracts in instances where it identifies a potential risk to the security of nuclear resources across the Community. The powers vested in the ESA suggest that its regulatory mechanism facilitates the regulation of the free movement of goods rather than the integration or liberalisation of the internal market.

17.4 Conclusion

The nuclear industry is governed by distinct regulations outlined in the Euratom Treaty; however, they do not encompass the regulation of competition law. The presence of a regulatory gap in the nuclear sector necessitates the application of competition law by analogy as a means to address this deficiency, provided that it does not contradict any existing regulations. However, it is important to acknowledge that this approach is considered to have inherent flaws. The adoption of the Euratom Treaty served a dual purpose: to establish and advance the nuclear industry and to regulate the use of nuclear materials in both the military and civilian sectors. This encompassed the production of electricity, which necessitated stringent control mechanisms and targeted investment promotion measures. The Euratom Treaty regulates public relations that fall within its exclusive jurisdiction as well as those that are governed by the TFEU, albeit with the Euratom possessing powers of action. The Euratom Treaty governs the operation and advancement of nuclear energy, safeguarding against the detrimental impacts of ionising radiation, and the establishment and operation of the shared nuclear market.

The Euratom Treaty is responsible for regulating the creation of a unified nuclear market, which encompasses provisions that prohibit taxes on imported goods and charges that have similar effects and also governs the unrestricted movement of individuals and services. Loans have been allocated for the purpose of financing the construction of nuclear facilities, thereby facilitating the achievement of a fully integrated electricity market. The Euratom Supply Agency assumes the primary role in executing the nuclear materials supply policy and fulfilling energy security functions. The Euratom Treaty is commonly recognised as a *lex specialis* to the TFEU. Nevertheless, certain provisions of the TFEU also have relevance to the nuclear energy sector, albeit to a limited extent. Specifically, the State aid clauses, which were not incorporated in the Euratom Treaty, are applicable to the nuclear sector.

The Euratom Supply Agency possesses the authority to take action in order to promote market competitiveness and ensure supply security. The procedure is implemented on an individualised basis, considering the requirements of consumers, the duration of the supply agreement, long-term strategic considerations, and potential opportunities for diversification. The Euratom Supply Agency possesses a substantial mandate that encompasses the security of supply, granting it the authority to potentially deny approval or impose obligations on nuclear operators regarding the provision of uranium originating from states deemed unsafe. This action may result in a diminished level of supply security within the European Union. The presence of stringent regulatory constraints has implications for both the unrestricted movement of goods and the freedom of contract. Consequently, there are reservations regarding the suitability of this approach as the most effective means of fostering competitiveness within the market.

References

Bouquet A (2001) How current are EURATOM provisions on nuclear supply and ownership in view of the European Union's enlargement? Nuclear Law Bull 2(68):7–38

Cusack T (2003) A tale of two treaties: an assessment of the Euratom treaty in relation to the EC treaty. Common Market Law Rev 40:117–142

Engstedt R (2020) Handbook on European nuclear law: competences of the Euratom community under Euratom treaty. Kluwer Law International B. V, Alphen aan den Rijn

Froggatt A (2002) The Extension of Euratom loan ceiling: an opportunity for Euratom Reform. Euratom conference 45 years of nuclear promotion: time for change

Ptasekaitė R (2011) Euratom Treaty v Treaties of the European Union: limits of competence and interaction. 32

Schroder M (2019) EU gas supply security. A geopolitical vision of the southern gas corridor. Nomos Verlag, Baden-Baden

Part VII
Conclusions

Chapter 18
Concluding Remarks

Abstract The regulation of the energy sector has been progressing since the introduction of the first energy package, which included aspects of the internal market. The formation of ambitious targets defined in the Green Deal strategy is the culmination of this evolution, which includes a comprehensive structure of regulations, guidelines, and directives. Article 194 of TFEU outlines the essential rules that provide Member States the authority to determine their energy mix. This is a critical aspect of the European Union's primary legislation. Although Member States have the right to determine their own national energy mix, this provision creates uncertainty about the division of powers between the EU and Member States, as well as possible legal consequences under secondary law. This provision of the European Union's primary law is limited to the criteria outlined in the EU's secondary law that relate to determining the desired amount of energy resources in each Member State. The specified legal framework empowers Member States to define their own energy equilibrium by setting criteria and obligations related to a specific amount of energy within the overall energy balance. The secondary legislation of the European Union enshrines this authority.

The objective of this study was to elucidate the synergistic and contradictory aspects of the intersection between competition law and energy law. Given the Commission's ambitious goal of achieving carbon neutrality by 2050, a series of regulations and guidelines have been adopted and reviewed. In light of recent developments, the relationship between competition and energy laws has gained increased significance. Various competition law instruments are employed to promote the growth of renewable energy, facilitate technological advancements, and address market fragmentation.

The regulation of the energy sector has been evolving since the implementation of the initial energy package, which incorporated elements of the internal market. This development has culminated in the establishment of ambitious targets outlined in the Green Deal strategy, which encompasses a comprehensive framework of regulations, guidelines, and directives. The primary legislation of the European Union also involves the fundamental provisions that allow Member States to determine their energy composition, as specifically outlined in Article 194 of the Treaty on the

L. Rimšaitė, *The Crossroads of Competition Law and Energy Regulation*,
https://doi.org/10.1007/978-3-031-73238-6_18

Functioning of the European Union (TFEU). While Member States are granted the authority to determine their own national energy mix, this provision introduces ambiguity regarding the allocation of powers between the European Union (EU) and the Member States, as well as potential legal implications under secondary legislation. The scope of this provision in the primary law of the European Union is restricted to the criteria specified in the secondary law of the EU that pertain to the determination of the desired quantity of energy resources in each individual Member State. The aforementioned legal framework grants Member States the authority to determine their own energy balance through the establishment of criteria and obligations pertaining to a specific quantity of energy within the overall energy balance. This authority is codified in the secondary legislation of the European Union.

While the enforcement of competition law within the European Union is generally stringent, there are certain gaps in its international application. The delineation of the extent of competition law within the energy legislation lacks clarity. Hence, following a thorough examination of relevant case law from the Court of Justice of the European Union (CJEU) and the European Commission's approach to the implementation of distinct competition law principles, our analysis reveals that in situations where a distinct demarcation of regulations is lacking, the Commission possesses a wider latitude to evaluate the conformity of competition law provisions.

The energy sector is primarily characterized by the prevalence of long-term energy supply agreements that incorporate provisions aimed at curbing competition, such as take-or-pay clauses, destination clauses, and resale restrictions. Neither competition law nor energy law prohibit the inclusion of such clauses in long-term contracts. The analysis revealed that these provisions have the potential to result in market foreclosure, abuse of dominant positions, barriers to market entry, limitations on consumer choice, and elevated service prices. The third energy package implemented the concept of third-party access to promote market openness and mandate network owners to provide transparent and equitable conditions for accessing vital infrastructure. If the network owner is required to provide services of general economic interest or if granting access rights could potentially lead to a significant level of investment, they can waive this provision. The study reveals that transmission network operators are engaging in exploitative practices by denying access based on unutilized booked capacities and inadequate capacities resulting from a decision to neglect congestion management enhancements. Therefore, we recommend the implementation of more precise regulations that explicitly limit the inclusion of anti-competitive provisions in energy supply agreements. In light of the advancements in the energy sector, particularly the execution of extensive infrastructure projects, investors continue to seek reassurance regarding the return on their investments. Long-term supply contracts specifically serve this purpose. However, the introduction of restrictive clauses has resulted in a market limitation that exceeds what is necessary to ensure the desired investment return as demanded by the investor.

Competition law does not explicitly mandate the evaluation of adherence to the unbundling obligations outlined in the third energy package. The energy regulatory framework exclusively codifies the aforementioned regulation, resulting in ambiguity regarding the allocation of responsibilities between the competition authority and the energy regulatory authorities. The competition law does not include specific criteria for evaluating concentrations in accordance with the unbundling requirements outlined in the legislation pertaining to natural gas and electricity. The competition law lacks a specific definition for evaluating the markets targeted by the concentration, potentially leading to negative outcomes. The energy industry's unique characteristics necessitate the recognition that current competition law regulations are insufficient when applied to this sector. Therefore, it is necessary to enhance these regulations by incorporating specific provisions that address the evaluation of energy markets.

Both the disintegration of vertically integrated firms and the establishment of additional energy generation capabilities, along with the creation of cross-border interconnections, are crucial elements in facilitating the liberalisation of the energy market. The implementation of new energy development projects serves as a foundation for alternative facilities and addresses market failures, thereby making a significant contribution to the common internal market. However, it is important to note that if any State intervention occurs, these projects will be subject to rigorous scrutiny under State aid regulations, ensuring compliance with established guidelines. The aforementioned approach, while not addressing all potential market failures, could potentially result in a negative determination regarding compliance with state aid regulations.

In an era marked by rapid transformations in the global energy sector and heightened economic competitiveness, the intersection of competition law and energy regulation holds considerable significance. This particular confluence signifies a pivotal moment wherever economic dynamics, environmental imperatives, and legal frameworks intersect. This literary work engages in a comprehensive analysis of the intricate intersection between competition and energy regulation. This analysis explores the intricate dynamics between these two domains, which exert a substantial impact on worldwide energy generation, consumption, and governance. Undoubtedly, energy serves as the primary propelling factor behind modern society. In the residential, industrial, and transportation sectors, fossil fuels play a crucial role as an essential energy source, enabling often underappreciated convenience and progress. As societies strive to attain energy supplies that are sustainable, safe, and economically viable, they face complex challenges related to market dynamics, environmental concerns, and geopolitical influences. The quest for balance has led to the development of competition law and energy regulation as essential elements in upholding fair and competitive markets, as well as guaranteeing access to reliable energy supplies while promoting environmental sustainability.

The energy sector is presently experiencing a substantial and extensive transformation. The need to reevaluate traditional energy approaches stems from a variety of factors, including the shift from conventional fossil fuels to sustainable energy sources, advancements in energy storage and distribution technology, and the growing emphasis on carbon emission reduction. The aforementioned modifications are profoundly reshaping the energy sector, resulting in the rise of new stakeholders, innovative technology, and regulatory intricacies. Competition law and energy regulation collectively strive to address this fundamental inquiry. Given the current global trend towards a low-carbon future, it is crucial to promote the development of innovative clean energy technology while also maintaining the existence of competitive markets. This requires meticulous synchronisation of policies. The influence of state action and subsidies on market dynamics can lead to apprehensions about fair competition and the market's long-term viability, particularly with regard to the government's backing of specific energy technologies. Market liberalisation is a regulatory strategy that seeks to facilitate investments, enhance operational effectiveness, and augment consumer advantages by cultivating market competition. Implementing a robust emphasis on competition within the renewable energy markets facilitates the integration of renewable energy sources. This approach not only enables innovation to progress but also aids in cost savings, expediting the shift towards sustainable energy.

Cross-border cooperation is critical for facilitating regional coordination among regulatory bodies, stimulating energy exchange across borders, facilitating resource sharing, and promoting market integration. Ensuring a balanced and equitable distribution of interests is critical to achieving an optimal state of equilibrium. Establishing a harmonious and mutually beneficial connection between competitive markets and dependable energy provision necessitates the effective implementation of policy coordination and regulatory alignment. Prioritizing consumer interests and advocating for sustainable energy practices empowers energy consumers in a dynamic energy landscape. The facilitation of cross-sectoral collaboration plays a crucial role in addressing the disconnect between competition law, energy regulation, and environmental policy, thereby promoting a holistic approach to energy governance.

Competition law traditionally has the mandate to restrain monopolistic behaviour and promote fair competition. The objective of this policy is to promote the development of competitive markets by forbidding activities that hinder competition, such as anti-competitive practices, monopolistic activity, and unfair market dominance. The core principles of this framework prohibit anti-competitive agreements, the abuse of dominating market positions, and mergers that adversely impact competition. We are currently applying these concepts to the complex dynamics of the energy sector. The notion fosters the well-being of consumers, encourages innovation, and facilitates the efficient use of resources. On the other hand, energy regulation encompasses the responsibilities of upholding energy security, advancing environmental stewardship, and guaranteeing consumer protection at the opposing intersection. The regulatory framework serves as a mechanism for establishing norms and criteria to efficiently govern energy markets, thereby facilitating the management of many competing interests among energy stakeholders, such as generators, distributors, consumers, and environmental considerations. The principal duty of energy regulators is to maintain the effective functioning of energy markets, prioritising the provision of reliable services to consumers while also addressing and minimising any negative external impacts.

The convergence of competition law and energy regulation within the dynamic energy industry is a pivotal factor that exerts substantial influence on the trajectory of energy markets. The intersection of these key areas represents a multifaceted and revolutionary juncture in which the goals of fostering equitable competition and guaranteeing dependable and eco-friendly energy provision coincide. The presence of market power within the energy sector has the capacity to lead to the concentration of control within a limited number of firms, potentially hindering competition and restricting customer options. The dual endeavour of tackling market dominance and promoting energy security is a significant challenge.

The act of traversing intersections is a multifaceted undertaking that necessitates meticulous deliberation and astute strategic choices. The interplay between the ever-changing energy markets and regulatory frameworks leads to a convergence of competition law and energy regulation, presenting several potential advantages and challenges. The intersection of competition and energy regulation presents a range of challenges and prospects for influencing the trajectory of energy markets. To attain a sustainable and competitive energy environment, it is imperative for policymakers, regulators, and stakeholders to effectively navigate this pivotal juncture through the development of a well-defined vision and the promotion of collaborative initiatives. Implementation of this technique holds significant relevance in the construction of a resilient, efficient, and customer-centric energy industry.

SPRINGER NATURE

GPSR Compliance

The European Union's (EU) General Product Safety Regulation (GPSR) is a set of rules that requires consumer products to be safe and our obligations to ensure this.

If you have any concerns about our products, you can contact us on ProductSafety@springernature.com

In case Publisher is established outside the EU, the EU authorized representative is:

Springer Nature Customer Service Center GmbH
Europaplatz 3
69115 Heidelberg, Germany